Tonight, On A Very Special Episode

WHEN TV SITCOMS SOMETIMES GOT SERIOUS
Volume 1

By Lee Gambin
AND A BUNCH OF VERY SPECIAL WRITERS

BearManor Media

2020

TONIGHT, ON A VERY SPECIAL EPISODE
WHEN TV SITCOMS SOMETIMES GOT SERIOUS
Volume 1
By Lee Gambin
All rights reserved.

No portion of this publication may be reproduced, stored, and/or copied electronically (except for academic use as a source), nor transmitted in any form or by any means without the prior written permission of the publisher and/or author.

Published in the United States of America by:

BearManor Media
4700 Millenia Blvd.
Suite 175 PMB 90497
Orlando, FL 32839

bearmanormedia.com
Printed in the United States.

Paperback ISBN 978-1-62933-635-0
Hardback ISBN 978-1-62933-636-7
Cover design by Darren Cotzabuyucas, @dc80
Text layout by Robbie Adkins, www.adkinsconsult.com

Dedicated to anyone who found solace in the warm glow of the television sitcom…

may this take you back to those treasured moments shared with the likes of the Bunkers, Maude, the Jeffersons, the Cunninghams and their beloved Fonzie, Punky, ALF, the girls of Eastland and beyond…

TONIGHT, ON A VERY SPECIAL EPISODE

Table of Contents

An Overview of the Very Special Episode 1
By Lee Gambin

Here's The Story: Early Examples of the Very Special Episode 11
1956 – 1969

Didn't Need No Welfare State, Everybody Pulled His Weight 36
1970 - 1973

Not Gettin' Hassled, Not Gettin' Hustled 111
1974 – 1977

You Take The Good, You Take The Bad 229
1978 - 1981

Everybody's Got A Special Kind Of Story 365
1982 – 1985

Contributing writers (my Very Special team) 515

Acknowledgements 526

About the Author 526

TONIGHT, ON A VERY SPECIAL EPISODE

Volume One:
1956 — 1985

TONIGHT, ON A VERY SPECIAL EPISODE

An Overview of the Very Special Episode
By Lee Gambin

What is a Very Special Episode?
In my research and in working on this book – which has been as rewarding and comforting as the classic American sitcoms that I grew up watching and continue to revisit and wholeheartedly embrace – I have come to the conclusion that there are in fact four variants of what constitutes a Very Special Episode (VSE) in a television situation comedy.

Number one is the most popular and the class of VSE that is most thoroughly examined: that is, an episode that addresses a social issue that counters the standard comedic lightheartedness of the series. These episodes are a one off example of exploring "serious" subject matter. These issues could involve drug addiction, rape, abortion, molestation, domestic violence, prostitution, homelessness, racism, coming out, disability and so forth.

The second example is an episode where a regular character's life is jeopardized or cut short – i.e. they are in an accident, diagnosed with a terminal illness or killed off. So these are not necessarily taking on social issues, but instead putting characters we have come to love in peril.

The third, and possibly the most ambiguous one, is where an event or happening occurs that would be classified as a social issue or social concern, but it's something that carries with it a history of dramatic influence throughout the entire series. In other words, topics and socially conscious subject matter will pop up throughout the sitcom's run. A perfect example of this are the varied episodes from say *The Mary Tyler Moore Show* (1970–1977) – a sitcom which continually addressed themes of sexism, women in the workplace, the plight of the decidedly single woman, contraception and more. These are commonly found in the advent of the dramedy fad which would rise to prominence in the late eighties and into the nineties with sitcoms such as *Roseanne* (1988–2018) being a clear example.

And the final example of a VSE are episodes that are landmarks – i.e. final episodes that leave a major impression, weddings, when characters leave or when characters who will become massive pop-culture icons are first introduced and so forth. "Goodbye, Farewell and Amen" from *M*A*S*H* (1972–1983) would actually be a feature TV film rather than a regular episode, making it an extra special VSE in a sense, and would boast one of the highest ratings in television history.

To get to where the Very Special Episode firmly established itself as a pop-cultural phenomenon, you have to look at the history of TV comedy. The fifties was the true starting point for what we now know as the traditional American situation comedy – and during this period, most of the shows were built around a star's appeal – be they from movies or theatre such as *The Donna Reed Show* (1958–1966), *The Phil Silvers Show* (1955–1959), *The Danny Thomas Show* (1953–1965), *The Bob Cummings Show* (1955–1959) and so forth. However, concept television was becoming incredibly popular and steady plot-driven situational comedy was winning the hearts of audiences spearheaded by shows such as *I Love Lucy* (1951–1957), *Leave it to Beaver* (1957–1963), *Father Knows Best* (1954–1960) and others. These provided halcyon ideals about America and domesticity. When the sixties hit, TV sitcoms were massively popular and were varied in theme and content, however, there was a definite running theme as to how they were conceived and constructed and their tone was almost in perfect synch with one another – something I like to call the "comfort zone" period of television, where everything was warm, inviting and fun.

Sixties sitcoms were very genre specific; for example *The Munsters* (1964–1966) used the classic Universal monsters as a launch pad, and some shows would be based on high concept ideas or loosely based on films that came before them, such as *Mister Ed* (1958–1966) which would be inspired by Universal's popular 1950s *Francis the Talking Mule* movies and a lot were fantastical and way out, such as *My Mother the Car* (1965–1966). These sitcoms were bright and completely developed to be escapist fare – absolutely fun and sweet, but not really reflecting the times they aired.

So along comes the seventies and TV "grows up". A landmark moment in television will come in the form of *All in the Family* (1971–1979) which would ultimately be the starting point in this trend of TV that went hard and hit home and delved into serious subject matters within a comedic format. *All in the Family* also came into popularity during a period in television called the rural purge, where shows with country settings were gradually disappearing off air and urban shows began to surface. *Green Acres* (1965–1971) and *Petticoat Junction* (1963–1970) would disappear, as audiences were welcomed to the gritty world of "real life" cities like New York.

The forerunner in this kind of television, would be writer/producer/show runner Norman Lear who would introduce direct and overt social commentary to his situation comedies, changing television forever. These TV shows and the descendants of the Norman Lear universe would be extensions of two major artistic influences from primarily the fifties – the social message film and the dawn of the PSA (the public service announcement).

I feel that the Very Special Episode is practically an off-shoot of these two distinctly American institutions – one being message movies that were tapping into social taboos during the final years of the Motion Picture Production Code (films that defied the censors and discussed sex, teen angst, drug warfare, race issues, adultery, abortion) and the PSA which came in varied forms such as white coat films or propaganda shorts which taught you about varied things such as STDs or how to spot communists among other "essentials".

Lear would create shows such as *Maude* (1972–1978), with a lead who was militantly feminist and leftist in her leanings, and *Good Times* (1974–1979), which would feature a black family struggling in the ghetto. Lear would also create revisionist television with *Mary Hartman, Mary Hartman* (1976–1977), an unconventional, almost eerie deconstruction of soap operas and the incredibly popular sitcom *The Jeffersons* (1975–1985) which ran for a long time and featured an affluent black family, something never before seen on TV.

All in the Family would originally air with a PSA, a disclaimer, warning audiences about what they were going to see. The series shocked audiences and ruffled a lot of feathers from both conservatives and liberals. The characters included Archie, a bigoted, sexist, racist, homophobic buffoon, who was also loveable and not without tenderness. His wife Edith, whose character came from a question which was "What would Jesus do?" simply because she was so sweet, loving, selfless and giving. (As an aside, I strongly feel that if the world were made up of Ediths, it would be a perfect place). Their daughter Gloria and husband Mike "Meathead" Stivic, two progressive pro-equality liberals, who are sexually liberated and atheists (the first overt atheists to appear in a TV sitcom). These differences of character in this poor working class household of course would make for great confrontation, and a lot of it comes from Archie's prejudices. There are many Very Special Episodes that ran through *All in the Family* –- shows dealing with counterculture, poverty, drugs, menopause, intellectual disabilities and so forth.

A lot of these would come from Archie dealing with issues that would fire him up – his conservative politics and bigotry getting in the way of "understanding". However, Archie would show some kindness here and there, and also learn and grow as a man. For instance, his compassionate side is on display in a very tender moment between him and his daughter Gloria in "Gloria Has A Belly Full", which was an early episode where Gloria falls pregnant, causing Archie grief, however as the episode moves forward the old cantankerous cigar chomper comes around and gets excited about the promise of a grandchild, only to find out that she has miscarried, which leads to a heartbreaking and touching scene that allowed to showcase some of Archie's sympathetic tenderness. Even though he can't say the words "I love you" to Gloria, she knows full well he does.

Edith would get her fair share of the Very Special Episode treatment as seen in "Edith's Christmas Story" where she finds a lump in her breast. This episode helped women across America learn about their own health and wellbeing and lead to an increase of women getting their breasts scanned. "Edith's Crisis of Faith" where Edith sparks a beautiful friendship with a gay drag performer Beverly LaSalle, a recurring character in a couple of episodes. In this episode Beverly is killed in a gay bashing and the heartbroken Christian Edith starts to question her faith in God. Atheist Mike ends up being the character who helps Edith come back to her faith. This show put a spotlight on homophobia and violence against gay people. And the groundbreaking "Edith's 50th Birthday", a landmark double episode where Edith is sexually assaulted, which was harrowing and shook audiences. However, the writing is so wonderful that the follow up episode leaves more of an impact. Gloria was also a victim of sexual assault in an earlier episode called "Gloria the Victim" and it's up to her to snap her mother out of her trauma in order to get her to a place of growth and freedom. There is a powerful sequence which renders the men in the background and voiceless, with the scene being all about the women finding their power. Also, this episode refers to a previous episode, which would make it one of the first sitcoms to acknowledge a set in place ongoing narrative arc. And also, when Edith fights off the rapist, it sparked one of the biggest studio audience cheers ever. Norman Lear consulted with the founder and director of the Rape Treatment Center at Santa Monica Hospital, and hosted advance screenings for police and hospitals across the country and the New York Police Department showed this episode to convey the woman's side of rape. It was also shown at rape crisis centers. The show would be so powerful that actor David Dukes who played Edith's would-be rapist, received persistent death threats from some viewers for years for his character – they couldn't separate the actor from the guy who tried to rape their beloved Edith. TV sitcoms would have this kind of power.

A perfect example of how shows would have such power and even influence votes and legislation would have to do with the Briggs Initiative where conservative state legislator John Briggs teamed up with Christian evangelist Anita Bryant to ban openly gay teachers from teaching. Along comes the groundbreaking *All in the Family* episode "Cousin Liz" and the power of visibility goes toe to toe with Briggs and Bryant. In this episode, Edith discovers that her cousin Liz, a school teacher, has passed away and that she had a long term lover Veronica, a fellow teacher. This show gave a face and voice to gay people and influenced voters who got to see the humanity and understand the love shared between Liz and Veronica. The show helped influence America to vote no on the Briggs Initiative. Edith comes to represent the collective compassion people's votes reflected and here she even stands up to Archie, something that will develop as the show moved forward.

And then there's Maude…

The excellent *Maude*, a spin-off from *All in the Family*, would be a groundbreaking sitcom that challenged people's political beliefs and one of the most controversial and influential episodes was "Maude's Dilemma" which had the mature aged Maude fall pregnant and consider an abortion. This double episode brought the issue of abortion to a public sphere with co-star Adrienne Barbeau as Maude's single mother daughter Carol championing a woman's right to choose. The show's star Bea Arthur received death threats for doing the episode, some states refused to air it and the United States

Catholic conference campaigned against it with over 17,000 letters of protest from conservatives and varied Christian groups.

Norman Lear considers *Maude* the favorite of his shows. Maude is a loud, brash, opinionated liberal. She is the antithesis of Archie Bunker and is so pro-everything that it drives everyone around her crazy. *Maude* dealt with multiple serious topics including manic depression and bipolar disorder, censorship, face lifts in response to ageing, race relations and more. Alcoholism in "Walter's Problem" had the issue of every day drinking taken for granted. When Maude's husband Walter develops a drinking problem there is voice for concern and there is a very dark moment where he slaps her. Suicide in "Walter's Crisis" where Walter tries to kill himself after his business falls apart and therapy is explored in the magnificent "Maude Bares her Soul" where Bea Arthur is given the opportunity to do so much in her performance. The thing about these VSEs, is that actors most commonly regarded for their comedic work, can do dramatic stuff. "Maude Bares Her Soul" was ultimately a one woman show, and there is some true gut-wrenching stuff where she talks about her father.

"Maude Bares Her Soul" would influence the incredible double episode "A, My Name Is Alex" from *Family Ties* (1982–1989). This aired outside its regular time slot and free from commercials. It dealt with Alex P. Keaton coping with the death of his friend and was set up like a theatrical piece, reminiscent of the American classic play *Our Town*. Michael J. Fox wowed critics with his poignant performance and this would garner multiple awards and proved to cynics that sitcoms most certainly could offer powerful examples of dramatic work. An eighties sitcom like *Family Ties* would deliver a lot of Very Special Episodes – a personal favorite being "Read it and Weep" about censorship in schools and a popular one would be "Speed Trap" where Alex gets hooked to diet pills so he can stay up and study for exams. Amphetamines would become the go-to drug of the eighties VSE.

Drug culture would infiltrate both the ghetto and urban landscapes which would provide the background for shows like *Welcome Back, Kotter* (1975–1979) and it would also find its way into suburban middle class homes presented in *Mr. Belvedere* (1985–1990) and one of the most successful shows to deliver the hard message of drug addiction would be found in *Good Times* in "J.J.'s *Fiancée*" where heroin addiction was given the sitcom treatment. Another Norman Lear show, and spin off from *Maude*, the excellent *Good Times* would showcase a vast number of VSEs ranging from child abuse, racial profiling, the effects of poverty and of course drugs.

Poor kids like Punky Brewster would face the dangers of drugs as well as kids adopted by rich parents as seen in *Diff'rent Strokes* (1978–1986). *Punky Brewster* (1984–1988) tapped into the latchkey kid market; kids who were pretty much babysat by their TVs and it was paired with a campaign that had been firmly established in American TV called "Do You Know Where Your Children Are?" which ran from the early sixties and wrapped by the late eighties. *Punky Brewster* also attempted to empower kids who were from broken homes and the series was established as one that would tackle social issues from the get go, one being the massive "Just Say No" campaign, where child actress Soleil Moon Frye went across America campaigning for this anti-drug initiative.

Nancy Reagan stood alongside child actor Gary Coleman during her appearance on an episode of *Diff'rent Strokes* and the new morality of Reagan-era America started to buy into network television and use it as an "in" to get some of their messages across. Conservatives who once despised situation comedies for their liberal ideals now used some shows to push their anti-drug agenda.

The wonderful *Diff'rent Strokes* and its spin-off *The Facts of Life* (1979–1988) would provide amazing celebratory reflections of togetherness and inclusion and would become record holders in the number of VSEs delivered throughout the late seventies and all the way through the eighties. Interestingly enough, *The Facts of Life* started life with a VSE with the pilot entitled "Rough Housing" being an episode that had tomboy Cindy question her sexuality making the sitcom a series that went straight into tackling complex subject matter. "Breaking Point" dealt with teen suicide, "Runaway" looked at teen prostitution and the much loved episode "Cousin Geri" gave voice to people living with cerebral palsy. The young actress and comedienne Geri Jewell who starred in the episode was bullied as a child for having cerebral palsy and her escape was TV, she would find solace in the characters she'd watch. When she got on *The Facts of Life* as a regular character she felt loved and accepted – and she would have a wonderful lifelong friendship with co-star Lisa Whelchel, who played Blair. The episode featured a powerful line that would become a war cry for people living with disabilities, which was: "Questions don't hurt, ignorance does". The episode "Fear Strikes Back" would tap into rape trauma and sexual assault issues and what it does is go into a second act where the girls start up self-defense. This episode would generate mass interest in girls across America to join karate classes and would prove influential in the nineties subculture Riot Grrrl off shoot of "Free to Fight" which encouraged girls to take classes to protect themselves from predators.

Diff'rent Strokes would feature a long list of VSEs from steroid use to epilepsy to the importance of vaccinating your dogs, but possibly the most famous or infamous of VSEs would be "The Bicycle Man", which left a huge impact on audiences and children growing up in the eighties. The episode opened with a special PSA announcement from actor Conrad Bain which was something some of these VSEs would feature, which would set the tone for the unsettling nature of the episode in question.

Mr. Belvedere also dealt with child molestation. The episode "The Counselor" featured a PSA as its coda with actors Brice Beckham who played Wesley Owens and Christopher Hewett as the housekeeper Mr. Belvedere addressing the audience as themselves and breaking the fourth wall. This series was another major contributor to the VSE. The character of young Wesley was very popular for kids – a new generation's Dennis the Menace. *Mr. Belvedere* presents child molestation very differently to *Diff'rent Strokes* in how it depicts the pedophile. Instead of a creepy lascivious older man, here the predator is young, athletic and good looking and earns Wesley's trust only to exploit it.

Just a quick personal note – I recall being a kid and not liking it when some of my favorite characters were hurt in any way. I wanted to jump in the TV and rescue them from revolting abusive people. It would be a case of "Don't do that to Wesley!" or "Don't do that to my Mallory!"

"Give Your Uncle Arthur a Kiss" from *Family Ties*, where the lovely Mallory as played by Justine Bateman is assaulted by a friend of her parents is another unsettling VSE. Mallory was a wonderfully conceived character who resonated with me at an early age because there was an episode where she gets upset at her family because none of them respect or care about the stuff she loves and is passionate about. For some reason I related. I guess sitcoms hit home for me and people like me – devotees of the format and genre, plus they would also possibly be the first word on major events that the world was trying to get its head around, such as a global crisis like HIV.

Come the eighties, the AIDS crisis became a major focal point in news reports and scared millions – television did its best to address the disease with made-for-TV films such as *An Early Frost* (1985) and *Our Sons* (1991) and sitcoms took on the issue as well, but generally shied away from the gay male aspect, and keeping the focus on transfusions and children with the disease. "Wesley's Friend" from *Mr. Belvedere* dealt with juvenile AIDS, and in an interview Ilene Graff, who played Marsha Owens, the mom of the family, explained that it combatted prejudices against children living with AIDS. The episode was based on the producer's manager's own children: one who passed away from AIDS and the other who didn't have it but for her entire childhood faced prejudice for being a twin of one who did.

Not shying away from gay male AIDS, the excellent *Designing Women* (1986–1993) delivers one of the most controversial episodes in sitcom history. "Killing All the Right People" infuriated conservatives and at the time, the Reagan administration wanted it pulled. The show's creator Linda Bloodworth-Thomason was not only a show runner, producer and writer but an activist. She was inspired to create this episode when she was in hospital visiting her mother who was dying of AIDS after a transfusion and overheard two orderlies say that they thought the disease was "Killing all the right people" – an insight into their bigotry primarily aimed at gay men, intravenous drug users and sex workers. The empowering speech from Julia Sugarbaker became yet another war cry for people living with the disease in the face of a government who rejected them and refused to treat them.

From one legendary woman to another, writer, producer and show runner Susan Harris would create some of the most influential shows in TV history. She transformed TV with her groundbreaking *Soap* (1977–1981), which was a revolutionary series that would satirize soap operas of the day, and developed her own universe with spin-offs such as *Benson* (1979–1986). *Empty Nest* (1988–1995) would also stem from another of her creations, the most successful and much loved series, *The Golden Girls* (1985 1992).

Empowering older ladies everywhere, Susan Harris singlehandedly gave a voice to elderly women with her hit series and rather than painting a picture of doting grandmothers with one dimensional niceties and eccentricities, she conceived an entire situation comedy that allowed her senior women to be intelligent as well as empty headed, sexual as well as conflicted, vulnerable, independent, headstrong and also delicate but ultimately very human. The show would feature many VSEs including "Dorothy's New Friend" which tackled anti-Semitism and the curse of the elitist country club, "Old Friends" where Sophia came to terms with a pal developing Alzheimer's Disease, an episode taking on suicide amongst the elderly in the heartbreaking "Not Another Monday" and the revolutionary "Sick and Tired" which brought chronic fatigue syndrome into the public consciousness. Susan Harris herself had this condition and modelled Dorothy on her own experiences. She addressed issues concerning malpractice, women not being listened to and the fact that the elderly are neglected and ignored. Dorothy's angry speech to her negligent doctor has since become a campaign for people living with fatigue and conditions such as fibromyalgia.

Earlier examples of the Very Special Episode before the advent of Norman Lear's works, included an episode of *Bewitched* (1964–1972) that got super topical with the heart-warming episode "Sisters at Heart", which opened with a special message from the show's star Elizabeth Montgomery. The episode was conceived by twenty seven mostly illiterate students from a public high school who all loved *Bewitched* and saw Samantha Stephens as an icon. Montgomery paid for them to visit the set and was so moved by hearing stories from their teacher on how these kids related to the whole concept of a witch being married to a mortal and how she has to repress her true powers in order to fit in, that Montgomery convinced the network to have the children write an episode about race relations and the vital importance of black pride. With the help of *Bewitched* writer Barbara Avedon, the children worked on a show where Tabitha and her best friend Lisa teach everyone about the magical powers of friendship that doesn't see color – in turn, this episode helped bridge gaps between black and white and was a critically revered moment in American TV history.

Early examples of VSEs come from shows such as *The Brady Bunch* (1969–1974) and *The Partridge Family* (1970–1974), but for the most part, the phenomenon would be a seventies and eighties invention. It would even find its place among fantasy escapist TV sitcoms during the eighties such as *Small Wonder* (1985–1989), which would feature an episode all about missing children which would spark a lot of heated debate among networks. But for the most part in the late eighties and early nineties, comedy would stay grounded in realism and the advent of dramedy would make its mark. These would be sitcoms that would have overriding arcs dealing with social issues such as addiction, domestic violence, racism, homophobia and other social concerns that would be ongoing incidents that carried over throughout the narrative, rather than treated as a one-off special, as seen in shows such as *Cheers* (1982–1993).

One of the last nineties sitcoms to continue the traditional VSE trend would be *Blossom* (1990–1995), which would really push the VSE and even have a catch phrase unto itself "Tonight, on a very special BLOSSOM". The show that marked the end of the VSE would be *Seinfeld* (1989–1998), which boasted that it would be a show most definitely without all the "feels" and no lessons learned.

Personally, as brilliant as *Seinfeld* is, its characters are completely unlikeable, whereas as saccharine as *Blossom* may be perceived, there was plenty of heart and tenderness, which I personally respond to more wholeheartedly. Television would start to lose its sweetness and warmth with cynical shows emerging, mostly spearheaded by seemingly edgy stand-up comedians.

So, as I wrap up this introduction and welcome you into this mammoth look at various VSEs as examined by myself and a host of incredibly gifted writers, I just want you all to remember how important these TV sitcoms are. There is a beauty and magic in the writing, the performances, the catchiness of each theme song, a magic in each character's plight, their hopes, their dreams, their alienation, their struggles. All this can be seen in examples such as the mournful episode of *Laverne & Shirley* (1976–1983) entitled "Why Did The Fireman…" which has Laverne finally think she has met the man of her dreams only to lose him in a devastating accident and the episode spends time with her, coping with loss and grief. While the wonderful late great Penny Marshall makes us laugh with her brilliant comic timing and ace hand at physical comedy, she can also break our hearts as we cry for this working class gal who wants a chance at love – and that is the power of the Very Special Episode.

Henry Fonda once hosted a special that showcased the best of *All in the Family* and he asked us: "What is bigger – the laughter or the lump in your throat?" And that is a perfect summation of the phenomena.

So, let's celebrate these great moments from some special episodes that have touched us in a special way, and remember how important these messages, these images, these characters and these stories were and always will be.

Moments such as the backdoor pilot for *The Jeffersons* where long-time friends Edith Bunker and Louise Jefferson have to say goodbye. Here, Louise is off to live the life of wealth and luxury, while Edith remains working class in a poor neighborhood. It is a heartbreaking farewell and a TV friendship akin to that of Wilma and Betty of *The Flintstones* (1960–1966) or Mary and Rhoda of *The Mary Tyler Moore Show* (1970–1977).

The darkness of child abuse in *Major Dad* (1989–1993) as seen in the episode "Conduct Unbecoming", or when ALF befriends a lonely blind woman on *ALF* (1986–1990), here a wise cracking alien makes an isolated woman feel good about herself. There was also that time where Zack learnt about his Native American heritage on *Saved by the Bell* (1989–1993) in "Running Zack" giving him a newfound respect for the eternal struggles of indigenous people or in "Baby of the Family" from *Gimme a Break!* (1981–1987) which dealt with racism. Drink driving on *Growing Pains* (1985–1992) in the episode "Second Chance" was made notable for Tracey Gold's heartbreaking performance and a title card PSA at the end explaining that people have died in drink driving accidents during the time we've spent watching that particular episode. Whether it's when Chachi finds out he has diabetes on *Happy Days* (1974–1984), or D.J. develops an eating disorder on *Full House* (1987–1995), or the dangers of cults on both *Charles in Charge* (1984–1990) and *Boy Meets World* (1993–2000), or the heartbreaking finale from *The Mary Tyler Moore Show* where our girl Mary tearfully thanks her colleagues for being her family. These are all important and wonderful moments of television, that are not only part of popular culture, but in many ways a reflection of the reality they spawn from. In an episode called "Mork in Wonderland" from *Mork & Mindy* (1978–1982), Mork disappears into a parallel universe where laugher and joy are not allowed. Mindy dies in this universe which breaks Mork, but when he returns to the real world to find Mindy alive and well, he is overjoyed as is Mindy, and their reunion is tearful and momentous. What Mork says to Mindy is just beautiful, and also, upon hearing this, it's even more profound knowing what had happened to Robin Williams himself. So there is truth within the form, and the magic of television sitcoms will live forever.

Thank you everyone! And keep watching classic TV!

"Thank you for being my family". The tearful Mary Tyler Moore as Mary Richards farewells her "family" in the finale for the iconic *The Mary Tyler Moore Show*.

Here's The Story
Early Examples of the Very Special Episode
1956 – 1969

"The Ricardos Visit Cuba" from *I Love Lucy*
Original Air Date: 3 December 1956
By Susan Leighton

I Love Lucy (1951–1957) was a groundbreaking show for the 1950's on many levels. It was the first multi-camera filmed sitcom before a live audience. This was something the American public at that time wasn't used to. Television was a relatively new medium and the notion that you could actually sit in your home and be entertained was amazing. Also, it gave families a chance to come together in the evenings and bond with one another. At the time that "The Ricardos Visit Cuba" premiered, the series had been on the air for six seasons and was an unqualified success. People would tune in to see America's sweethearts and to see what wacky escapades Lucy would get caught up in for the week. It was like visiting a friend's house and let's face it, that is what the Ricardos were. After all, we experienced the ups and downs in Lucy and Ricky's lives. We were there for the birth of their son. The trust was established. When you gain that intimacy with your viewing audience, then you can give them that Very Special Episode, because it is another layer in the relationship.

Cuba in 1956 was a paradise for tourists. Havana was one of the most popular vacation spots in the world. This was also pre-Communism and pre-Castro so relations between the U.S. and Cuba were at an all-time high. The idea that a Cuban man would marry an American woman isn't an issue today, however, back then times were not as progressive. In America, we were getting used to the cultural melting pot but mixed marriages were not prevalent like they are today. But in Cuba, which was very much the "old country," the idea of a mixed ethnicity union was still taboo. With deft humor, *I Love Lucy* decided to tackle this topic head on by having Ricky take Lucy back to Cuba to meet the man who raised him, his Uncle Alberto. This episode also took a look at both cultures.

Although women were still cooking and cleaning and birthing babies in the fifties, *I Love Lucy* depicted her world as being a partnership with her and her husband. However, Ricky's homeland had a very different view since its society was patriarchal. This is clearly evidenced with Ricky advising Lucy to always say, "Muchos gracias," to Alberto because he loves that. The entire notion that Lucy has to "please" Alberto in order to gain acceptance with Ricky's family despite bearing him a son and being married to him for 18 years is somewhat ludicrous when you look at it in the 21st century. Of course, from the get-go, we can clearly see that Lucy is going to be out of her element in this situation because she struggles with saying, "Buenos dias," while her son, Ricky, Jr. pronounces it perfectly. You feel sorry for her because she really does want to make a good impression on her husband's family because she realizes how important it is to him. After all, Alberto is more or less his father. When Ricky laughs at her attempts at

Spanish, she gets upset but he shrugs it off and says, "You have been making fun of my English for eighteen years." He makes that joke because he wants her to feel comfortable and he knows that she is extremely nervous.

When the plane touches down, the Ricardos head to their hotel where they prepare for the family reunion. Although Lucy looks radiant, she is still very insecure. While Ricky tries to assuage her anxieties, the doorbell rings and the parade of relatives begins. Everyone is pleasant and cordial but then Uncle Alberto makes his grand entrance. Immediately, the atmosphere in the room changes. It is like being on hand when royalty appears. Ricky presents him to his wife and all Lucy can manage to blurt out is "Hi." So, of course, Ricky quickly explains that she is nervous and tries to smooth things over but Lucy is in full overcompensation mode and ends up breaking Alberto's straw hat. Things are off to a rocky start and it is about to get worse. While Ricky draws everyone's attention to little Ricky who is adorable so that momentarily Alberto forgets what happened to his favorite hat. Meanwhile, Lucy is trying to hide behind the curtains. At this moment, we see how truly talented Lucille Ball is as an actress and a comedienne.

Her willingness to sometimes go "over the top" with her performances are not only daring but they make the "smaller moments" even more powerful. As she removes herself from the cacophony of people, we clearly see the pain and embarrassment all over her face. This is what makes Lucille Ball an icon. The ability to make people laugh at you, with you and then immediately go toward the opposite of the spectrum is a skill. Clearly though, she is the odd woman out. Although Ricky's mother accepts her, it is quite clear that Cuba is a male influenced society and women don't really have much of a say. Except in Lucy and Ricky's life that dynamic is definitely different because he is away from his roots. Ricky also experiences the not so subtle overtones of racism when Alberto remarks that he should have married a "Cubano." To which Ricky laments, but "I didn't fall in love with a Cuban girl." Even though Alberto compliments Lucy on her beautiful red hair and her looks, it seems disingenuous and somewhat patronizing what you would do to a favorite pet who was bothering you when you are busy.

However, she does the unthinkable. While trying to do her part and impress Alberto, instead of saying "Muchas Gracias," to thank him, she says "Mucha Grasa," which means fat pig. That is the straw that breaks the proverbial camel's back. The entire evening falls apart and just reinforces Alberto's prejudice toward Ricky's "Americano" wife. She only makes matters worse when she destroys his expensive Cuban cigars thus reinforcing that she is unsuitable for Ricky.

The next morning, the Mertzs drop by for a visit to see how the evening went. Lucy isn't her usual cheerful self; in fact, she is moping around. After she tells the pair about the gaffes she made last night, both Fred and Ethel insist that she will be forgiven. Wanting to take her mind off everything and escape for a bit, Ethel suggests a shopping trip. Now, you would expect that nothing could go wrong on a shopping spree but yet it does.

Feeling that buying Uncle Alberto a box of his favorite Cuban cigars would smooth things over, Lucy sets out to do that while Fred and Ethel continue exploring the city.

Upon entering the cigar shop, Lucy is immediately met by the proprietor. She requests (in rather poor Spanish) a box of Alberto's brand. The shopkeeper is more than happy to oblige. However, when Lucy goes to pay him, she notices that since she switched purses prior to leaving the hotel room, she doesn't have any money. She tells the proprietor that she will be right back to pay him and prepares to leave taking the cigars with her because in typical Lucy fashion, she is a little flustered. He perceives this as her trying to shoplift. They start wrangling over the cigars, the box crashes to the ground and Lucy steps all over the contents ruining the cigars infuriating the shop owner. Despite Lucy trying to explain that she wasn't stealing the items, he insists on calling the police because she is a crazy "Americano." Before he can dial the phone, Uncle Alberto enters and the two men start conversing. Lucy seizing the moment, disguises herself as one of the employees to avoid Alberto's detection. She starts rolling cigars while Alberto converses with the shop owner. Meanwhile, Lucy who has no idea what she is doing is making a mess of things as to be expected.

As the shopkeeper proceeds to tell Alberto about the thievery that took place, Ricky appears. He listens to the owner describing a "loco" redhead who was trying to abscond with an expensive box of cigars. A lightbulb goes off and Ricky wanders over to the table where Lucy is working. One glance at her and Ricky immediately knows that it is his wife. He proceeds to try and hustle Alberto out of the shop before she gets found out. After all, she sticks out like a sore thumb. Before Ricky can get his uncle out the door, Alberto notices the huge cigar that Lucy is making, intrigued he attempts to take a look at it. By this time, the shopkeeper is alerted and knowing that this is NOT the way a cigar should be rolled, sees Lucy in her disguise. Before he can grab her, she runs out the door with Ricky blocking the proprietor and his uncle is once again, without a cigar because of his nephew's incredibly inept "Americano" wife.

After all this craziness, it is the last night that the Ricardos will be in Cuba. Ricky is set to play the Casino Parisien. He takes his son with him to rehearse. Little Ricky will be making his drum playing debut on stage with his father's hit rendition of "Babalu." Lucy is worried that since she has to sit near Alberto, the night will be ruined. Everyone tries to assure her that won't be the case. It is pretty clear throughout the entire episode that no matter what she does it is never enough. But that is how prejudice works. It is pretty stealthy and covert. On the outside, sure, Alberto seems respectful but that is for appearances sake. In Spanish, he speaks his mind to Ricky. The duplicity is insidious and it can even be seen at work in today's political landscape. Sorry to think that in over 60 years, we still can't see beyond race.

At the nightclub, Lucy is seated next to Alberto. All seems to be going well. Ricky sings a song about being at home wherever he is no matter if it is Cuba or the U.S.A. The reason behind the tune is he is accepted in both places. "In Cuba, I'm a Cuban and in the U.S.A., I'm a Yank. Wherever I am, I'm at home." This is the teaching moment, the wrap up to the episode told in an innocuous way through song and entertainment. We get that message loud and clear. After he finishes, to rousing applause, Ricky gets serious and talks about leaving Cuba alone but he didn't come back alone. It is at this point, and he is a bit emotional, he introduces "his wife, a wonderful girl." When Lucy stands up and takes a bow, Alberto beams with pride. Now, he understands. He gets why his nephew loves her. Love has no boundaries. The heart is color blind and always will be. That is the universal language we all speak. While this is tied up in a nice, neat bow, *I Love Lucy* is from another era. Yes, it was troubled but at least through entertainment, we could come together and forget our struggles. Entertainment is for everyone no matter what race you are.

The iconic and legendary Lucille Ball. The queen of the American sitcom.

Relations between North and South America examined in "The Ricardos Visit Cuba" in I Love Lucy.

"Beaver and Andy" from *Leave it to Beaver*
Original Air Date: 13 February 1960
By Amanda Reyes

When one looks back on the sugarcoated nostalgia of 1950s television, family-centric sitcoms such as *Father Knows Best* (1954–1960) and *The Adventures of Ozzie and Harriet* (1952–1966) certainly make the list. But no other show seems to have had the cultural impact of *Leave it to Beaver*. The beloved series made its debut on CBS in 1957, and finished its run on ABC in 1963, mere months before the assassination of John F. Kennedy. It seems apt, as Beaver's childhood innocence now remains completely untouched by the tumult that was to come in the later years of the sixties.

The Beaver (Jerry Mathers) was a small boy growing up in an idyllic town named Mayfield. His real name was Theodore Cleaver, and he had an athletic older brother named Wally (Tony Dow), and two loving parents named June and Ward (Barbara Billingsley and Hugh Beaumont). The series was told through the perspective of Beaver's childhood wonderment, and therefore, problems were usually easy to manage, and could be solved in 30 minutes (if you count commercial breaks).

It is Beaver's untouched view of the world that made the show a classic. Sure, it's overly sentimental, but it is also genuinely funny and aside from the crisp and light dialogue, the series featured a number of clever sight gags that still tickle the funny bone. In the season three episode, "June's Birthday", Beaver buys his mother the most horrendous blouse, which June eventually wears to please him. In another season three episode titled "Tire Trouble", the brothers have a great time rolling a flat tire through town. And, of course in one of the series pinnacle sight gag moments, Beaver gets his head stuck in a gate in the season two episode titled "Price of Fame". All of these moments, along with many others, remain laugh out loud funny.

The main cast was terrific and they were supported by incredible recurring characters that were equally as comical and memorable. Beaver's first BFF, Larry Mondello (Robert "Rusty" Stevens) was a potentially troubled kid with an absentee father, and a monstrous appetite. He always found a way to drag Beaver down with him, and their adventures were uniformly amusing. Wally had his own crazy set of buddies, including, of course, the infamous Eddie Haskell (Ken Osmond) who played it very nice for the adults, but couldn't wait to create problems for Wally and his other friends. Lumpy Rutherford (Frank Bank) was a sweet, if not terribly smart kid, who was dedicated to two things – his car and his daddy, who just happened to be Ward's boss (and played by the great Richard Deacon).

The Cleaver's universe was simple and fun. They lived the good life in Suburban Paradise, and they believed in family, friendship and always having a homemade dessert after dinner. Because of this, critics regularly prescribed *Leave it to Beaver* as tone-deaf, or too sickly sweet to be thought of with much regard in terms of its social legacy. And to a degree, it's true. The Cleavers were so enveloped in living the American Dream they often found themselves unprepared when real issues crept into their sleepy neighborhood.

But, contrary to popular belief, the series did confront some concerns that were relevant to their audience. There's that time Beaver made friends with a kid from a broken home (season four's "Beaver's House Guest"), and there's the episode where Wally meets a girl and becomes so enamored with her older sister's married life, he considers forgoing college to settle down (season five's "Wally Goes Steady"), and one time Beaver accidentally insults his new Mexican friend, which allowed the Cleavers to explore the cultural gaps and tensions found within migrant families coming into a predominately white suburban space (season two's "Beaver and Chuey"). Each of these episodes expertly traverses possibly touchy issues with the solid guidance of Ward, the ultimate patriarch of fifties television.

Ward Cleaver was a nine-to-fiver, almost always in a suit, and known for his mild temperament. He kissed his wife as he went to work, and had another one for her when he came home. He always made time for his children, and while his kids could rattle him, he did his best to see things from their side. And it was here that some of the deftest writing in the series took place. Ward was a character who grew in small and human ways with each piece of advice he doled out to his loyal children. Because he was willing to alter his perspective he often saw the world in different ways, and his gentle mediation frequently ended with Ward giving a little advice to himself. So, while we saw the show through Beaver's eyes, we were also witness to Ward learning how to become a better father in the process.

However, Ward's devotion to his kids would sometimes lead him to attempting to shelter his children from the realities of life outside of Mayfield, when he should have had more faith in their ability to make mature decisions.

Such is the case with the season three episode titled "Beaver and Andy". A handyman named Andy (Wendell Holmes) approaches Ward for work, but Ward is hesitant to hire him because of a "problem" Andy had the last time he did odd jobs for the Cleavers. But Beaver has taken a real shine to Andy, because he tells great stories and knows how to tie a monkey knot. The two become fast friends, but Andy's "problem" is that he's in a constant battle with the bottle, and after the requisite commercial break, Andy finds himself asking Beaver to help him snake the family brandy.

Because June and Ward are so uneasy about explaining Andy's situation to their children, Beaver doesn't fully understand the severity of the situation, and he's easily hoodwinked by the pathetic drunk. When Beaver confesses that it was he who gave Andy the brandy, Ward is understandably upset. But, he soon realizes that the entire situation could have been avoided had he been more open with his son.

"Beaver and Andy" is poignant. Holmes is as tender as he is wretched as drunkard Andy. He appears to be on the verge of homelessness when he pursues work at the

Cleavers, but has such a dignified manner about him, it's hard to not instantly want to take him in. Ward feels much the same way, despite knowing better. Holmes would play three characters on the series – the other two were teachers – but it's here that he is most memorable, likeable and complex.

Andy tells Ward that he's been sober for several months, but through the course of the episode we see otherwise. Beaver finds an empty whiskey bottle in the bushes, and the drunk truly lowers himself to scum status when he seeks the Beaver's help as the shakes kick in. Even through the wary eyes of adulthood, Andy's plight is harrowing. It is only through the docile perspective of a child that Andy can truly come to terms with his situation. At the end of the episode, Andy returns to apologize to Beaver. In the process he heartbreakingly confesses that "An empty life and an empty bottle go pretty much together." It's a sad, dramatic beat that is also starkly realistic and brutally honest. Beaver takes the line with a grain of salt, absent-mindedly picking the mud off his shoes with a stick while he lets Andy clear his conscience. He accepts Andy, despite his flaws, and, therefore, so does the audience. We want to see their friendship go on and for Andy to get back on his feet.

Inevitably, there are two lessons learned here. One is that parents often underestimate their child's ability to understand serious issues. Keeping secrets from them leads to harm, and maybe they should put some faith into their little ones. The other, more important lesson is that people who hit rock bottom are still people and nothing good comes from judgment. Andy is able to open up to Beaver because he knows Beaver may ask some tough questions, but inevitably, he believes Andy is "a real neat guy." This is what makes Andy want to be better, and I trust he will be.

Certainly, there's plenty of white-picket-fence-softness to the series, but *Leave it to Beaver*'s quiet approach to important real-world problems is one of the many reasons the show remains not only watchable and enduring, but also wonderful.

An early representation of the Very Special Episode is found here in "Beaver and Andy" from Leave it to Beaver, *which dealt with alcoholism in a frank but compassionate manner.*

"Pine Lake Lodge" *from Mister Ed*
Original Air Date: 25 June 1961
By Lee Gambin

The premise of *Mister Ed* (1958–1966) is a simple one and stems from the likes of the popular 1950s Universal comedies in the *Francis the Talking Mule* series of films; here, a domestic horse converses with his human owner Wilbur Post (Alan Young) while everyone else around him are oblivious to his ability to talk. This is a sitcom that would come into the realm of the fantasy comedy series that were incredibly popular during the sixties including *The Munsters* (1964–1966), *I Dream of Jeannie* (1965–1970) and *My Mother the Car* (1965–1966).

The series would deliver a form of comfort escapist entertainment for decades as it would run in syndication and reruns, and develop a following of classic American TV fans who reveled in the likes of *Gilligan's Island* (1964–1967) and *The Brady Bunch* (1969–1974) as well as the rural-themed comedies such as *The Beverly Hillbillies* (1962–1971), *Petticoat Junction* (1963–1970) and *Green Acres* (1965–1971) – all of which would suffer at the turn of television's famous "rural purge". Among the many episodes of *Mister Ed*, there would be moments of tenderness and lessons learned, but not so much in the vein of the traditional Very Special Episode formula, which would ultimately become a phenomenon come the seventies, when television would "grow up", and varied shows as the aforementioned classic fun sitcoms would slowly make way for edgy and overtly socially aware series such as the shows spearheaded by producer Norma Lear, who would deliver the likes of *All in the Family* (1971–1979), *Maude* (1972–1978) and so forth. However, in "Pine Lake Lodge", an early episode of *Mister Ed* which would ultimately be a potential pilot in the making for a spin-off series (that never eventuated), the double issue of environmentalism and conservation as well as the plight of disadvantaged children sits at the core of what truly is a unique episode and one out of three attempts at backdoor pilots for the show.

It also serves as a foreshadowing aside to what was slowly developing into a trend in what would come in fruition in the seventies where animal-centric shows with an incredibly environmentally aware point of view and message, would be a majorly popular form of entertainment as seen in series such as *The Life and Times of Grizzly Adams* (1977–1978). The show has Wilbur and lovely wife Carol (Connie Hines) prepare to head out to spend some time away at Pine Lake Lodge, a rural retreat run by friends of theirs. Mister Ed's annoyance at this lays out some gags and because he is left behind this is an episode that doesn't feature him as much as usual, which makes the piece have a different tone. Also, further subversive commentary is made in regards to animal welfare when Ed is seen contacting the SPCA complaining about his "mistreatment" (not going along with Wilbur and Carol) and this may be in there as a joke, but it also could be read as a political statement, enforcing an ideology continually made in shows such as *Mister Ed* and then others such as *Gentle Ben* (1967-1969), that animals should be seen as equals to humans. The love and companionship shared between animals and humans in TV shows is a constant, and openhearted warm characters such as the critter loving Elly May Clampett (Donna Douglas) of *The Beverly Hillbillies* are poster children of animal rights – Wilbur Post is yet another example. When Ed calls out to Wilbur, "Drive carefully, you're all I have", the love and connection these two have is on display, and this is the heart of the show.

Bill Parker's (William Bendix) lodge is a resort that does relatively well (of course depending on the sometimes present wet weather which never helps) and he and Martha (played by Nancy Culp, who is best known to audiences as Miss Hathaway from *The Beverly Hillbillies* as well as starring in animal-centric movies such as *The Two Little Bears* (1961) and *The Night of the Grizzly* (1966)) are under the pump when they decide to help out in raising money and providing new furnishings for a local camp for under privileged children. This is the focal point and a continual topic of conversation for the episode – children who need help, a seldom seen issue or concern on television during the halcyon early sixties, especially in the sitcom format – and the bumbling but well meaning Bill promises to get "all the furniture those children need".

Bill's first idea is to get a friend to donate limber, but the pal shows no interest in helping. Bill goes out fishing and it is here where he gets the idea about using an old pine tree for furniture, assuming that an "act of nature" would cause the tree to fall by its own accord. Upon Wilbur and Carol's arrival, Bill tricks the gullible (and paranoid) Wilbur into chopping down the tree, and here a message is subtle, but there with the issue of commerce versus environmentalism as well as the law being broken all come into play. When Mr. Thompson (Will Wright), the owner of the land where the tree was once upright comes into the scene, the show shifts gears into a series of missteps, mistakes and miscommunications. Bill's initial confession to Mr. Thompson is turned around when it's learned that there is the opportunity to get off scot-free, however, Wilbur's conspicuous Hawaiian shirt gives them away and they are busted. Bill finally admits his guilt and protects Wilbur (a noble act), but Wilbur comes to Bill's defense by insisting that "Cutting down your tree is wrong, but the motive behind it is right..." Wilbur's speech is accompanied by maudlin pleading music, something that will become a standard come the golden age of the Very Special Episode, and when the surrounding characters pull together to buy the tree that has been cut down in an effort to pay back Mr. Thompson and carry forward with the wood being used for new furniture, the rights of children who have never had anything in their life becomes the main point of reference in what counts as a forerunner in the advent of the VSE.

The episode lends itself to being a message episode about children's rights, however, it says more about environmentalism in that it blurs the lines between ownership and commerce. It actually paints a picture of the man "protecting natural forestry" as a "bad guy", but his means behind his "That is my tree" is all about possession, personal principle and ego, it is not at all an admirable act of defending land and flora, but instead a bratty "That is mine, leave it alone!" mantra.

Mister Ed as a television sitcom truly does power through a message of animals being just as vitally important as their human counterparts, but essentially children during this period take precedence. Animals serve children, especially lonely alienated children who find it hard fitting in with fellow kids – and this is played out beautifully in the episode "Little Boy" where an unpopular youngster is thrown a party by Carol and where Mister Ed provides a platform for him to be celebrated, cheered and looked upon as a hero.

Mister Ed *would be one of the most popular in the quintessential escapist TV sitcoms of the sixties.*

"That's My Boy??" from *The Dick Van Dyke Show*
Original Air Date: 25 September 1963
By Nell Musolf

The Dick Van Dyke Show (1961–1966) was filmed in black and white, apt for the early to mid-1960's, an era when the world, for the most part, *was* black and white with very little variation into even the faintest shades of grey. Television was dominated by white characters in dramas, sitcoms and commercials. When African Americans were portrayed, it was seldom, if ever, in any kind of role that advanced a plotline.

The main character of *The Dick Van Dyke Show*, Rob Petrie, lived in that black and white world where his contemporaries were cut very much from the same upwardly mobile middle-class cloth. While the sitcom was one of the few to have regular characters who weren't WASPS but who, in fact, were Jewish, the cast was overwhelmingly white with the few non-white roles minor and fleeting. The people in Rob Petrie's world, for the most part, looked like him, thought like him, and acted like him. A groundbreaking episode in the 1963-64 season set out to change the status quo. Entitled "That's My Boy??", *The Dick Van Dyke* show's creator, Carl Reiner, took a very large step in the colorization of black and white television and he did so gracefully, intelligently and humorously, all trademarks of a man who wrote about life not only the way it was, but also the way it ought to be.

"That's My Boy??" was written by Bill Persky and Sam Denoff, veteran scribes for *The Dick Van Dyke Show*. The show opened with Mel Cooley as a dinner guest at the Petrie house when his wife was out of time helping her sister out after her sister had a baby. The writers used flashbacks as Rob told Mel about the chaotic events surrounding his son Ritchie's birth after Mel jokingly remarked that his new niece was so beautiful he was afraid the hospital might have given his sister-in-law the wrong baby. After a little prodding from his wife Laura, Rob, an extremely nervous first-time father, admitted that he suspected that they'd brought home the wrong baby after Ritchie was born.

Laura: Darling, why don't you start at the beginning?

Rob: Okay. You see, Jerry and I went to the hospital to bring Laura and Ritchie home. You know how hectic that first day can be.

Mel: Uh-huh…

Rob went on to explain how he became convinced the hospital gave his wife Laura and himself the wrong baby and that their baby had been given to the Peters family. The rest of the episode revolved around Rob finding "evidence" of the hospital's mistake (the nurse confusing rooms 203 and 208, Laura getting rice pudding instead of a blueberry tart and flowers from Dick and Betty Carter being delivered to the Petries to name a few). Reading the card from the Carters was one of the "clues" Rob zeroed in on as proof that the hospital had made a big mistake.

Rob: "Congratulations and much love… Dick and Betty Carter." Do we know a Dick and Betty Carter?

Laura: No. Maybe it's someone from your office.

Rob: No. The only Dick and Betty Carter I know are Phil and Edna Greenbaum.

Worried, but not wanting to upset Laura, Rob takes his next door neighbor and best friend, Jerry Helper, into his confidence. At first Jerry thinks Rob is mistaken but as Rob shares all of the mishaps that have occurred since Ritchie's birth Jerry quickly jumps on Rob's paranoid mixed-up baby bandwagon. Together they concoct a scheme to find out whether or not the baby lying in a bassinet in the Petrie's living room really and truly is a Petrie: they take an ink print of the baby's foot and attempt to compare it to the ink print on the baby's birth certificate.

Jerry, as a dentist and therefore more or less a scientist, studies both prints carefully.

Jerry: Rob… I would say… that that footprint and that footprint are from that baby!

Rob: You're positive?

Jerry: Yep!

Rob: That's what I was afraid of. Read the top line.

Jerry: Sex… male… name… Baby boy… Peters!

With Jerry's "testimony," Rob is convinced he has all the proof needed to swap babies with the Peters family, not something he wants to do but a task he feels must be done so that the "right" baby is brought up by the "right" family. Rob calls the Peters and explains the situation. To his surprise, the Peters agree to come over right away, not only to pick up the right baby but because they got Laura's aunt's dried figs by mistake. Rob breaks the news to Laura who is understandably upset.

Laura: Rob, we just got the wrong flowers!

Rob: You forgot the rice pudding and the blueberry tart pretty fast, didn't you? Not to mention the dried figs!

When the doorbell rang Rob ordered Laura to their bedroom but she refused to leave her baby in the hands of a man who is obviously half out of his mind. Rob opened the front door and the audience heard: "Hi, we're Mr. and Mrs. Peters." In stepped an attractive young black couple holding a basket of figs and smiling widely. Laughter ensued as the audience immediately saw there was no way the Peters baby could be mistaken for the Petrie baby. Rob, embarrassed, asks, "Why didn't you tell me on the phone?" to which Mr. Peters responded, "And miss the expression on your face?"

An interesting endnote was Rob remarking that perhaps the hospital had given them the wrong baby after all. When Laura expressed shock, Rob explained that while the Peters son was at the top of the class, Ritchie wasn't at all academically inclined. The subtle statement that an African American child could do better than a white child academically was also a subtle nudge that race didn't matter when it came to brains.

The premise was simple. The message packed a wallop. By introducing another obviously upwardly mobile young couple that happened to be African American, *The Dick Van Dyke Show* showed its viewing audience that, appearances aside, we are all the same. New parents are nervous regardless of race, new mothers are tired and new fathers are frazzled. As John F. Kennedy said, "Our most basic common link is that we all inhabit this planet. We all breathe the same air. We all cherish our children's future. And we are all mortal." *The Dick Van Dyke Show*'s "That's My Boy??" gave the same message, albeit very humorously.

What has changed after "That's My Boy??" aired almost sixty years ago? Practically everything. The civil rights movement, which was just beginning to pick up speed in the early sixties, really began rolling as the decade progressed. How blacks were portrayed in the media changed radically as well and it's safe to say "That's My Boy??" played a part in kicking off that change. Prior to "That's My Boy??" blacks in sitcoms were typically portrayed as either domestic help or comic relief or both. While sitcoms of the sixties treated black characters with a sort of restrained respect, those characters were never integral to a story's plot. "That's My Boy??" changed that. Other popular television shows of the 1963-64 season included *The Patty Duke Show* (1963–1966), *Petticoat Junction* (1963–1970) and *My Favorite Martian* (1963–1966). While an African American character might have appeared on any of those shows (although the likelihood of that happening on *Petticoat Junction* must have been slim to none), it is doubtful such a character would play the pivotal role Greg Morris had in "That's My Boy??"

Going forward five years to the 1968-69 television season and one sees a marked change in what was being offered to the viewing audience. *Julia* (1968–1971), a sitcom with an African American female lead, a groundbreaking event for blacks on white television if ever there was one. The year 1968 also saw *Mission: Impossible* (1966–1973) as a highly rated show and one Morris played a regular character on. Another hit from the 1968-69 season was *The Smothers Brothers Comedy Hour* (1967–1970), a sharp, witty, politically incorrect romp that would have been an impossible mission itself just a few years earlier.

Carl Reiner was justifiably proud of *The Dick Van Dyke Show*'s "That's My Boy??" episode as well he should be. Without preaching or hitting his audience over the head with a heavy handed message, Reiner managed to get his point across beautifully. Television was no longer black *and* white. It was the beginning of it being both, along with all other races, genders and people. The changes didn't happen overnight, but they started and nothing can ever change without taking that first step forward.

"Little Bamm-Bamm" from *The Flintstones*
Original Air Date: 3 October 1963
By Michael A. Smith

Seventeen days before this episode first aired, a child was born in Cleveland, Ohio. He never knew his birth parents as he was given up for adoption. A few months later that child found his forever family and, as of this writing, has gone on to live happily ever after. That child is me.

The subject of adoption is one that wasn't evident in the early days of television. In fact, thinking back to my childhood, the only character on television that I knew had been adopted was Ernie Douglas (Barry Livingston) on *My Three Sons* (1960–1972), who was officially adopted into the Douglas family in September 1965.

Normally, the addition of a new child on a television show was heralded. Ten years prior to Bamm-Bamm Rubble's arrival, television rating records were set when, on 19 January 1953, Lucy Ricardo gave birth to Little Ricky on *I Love Lucy* (1951–1957). But it took *The Flintstones* (1960–1966) to tackle the subject of adoption.

Following the arrival of Miss Pebble Flintstone, the new daughter of Fred and Wilma, their neighbors the Rubbles have become constant visitors. Wanting some time alone with his family, and jealous of how Pebbles has taken to Barney, Fred typically blows his cool and scolds the couple, meanly telling the Rubbles to "get your own baby and leave mine alone!" Upsetting, needless to say. At the time, *The Flintstones* was aired in prime time, and was made much more with adults in mind then children. I can't think of any other animated program where a couple's infertility was part of a punch line!

Barney and Betty go home and, that night, both wish on a shooting star and, though they don't reveal their wishes to each other, you know they each wished that they would someday have a child. Barney even breaks the fourth wall by asking the audience if they know what he was wishing for. The next morning Barney finds a basket on the stoop. Inside is a little boy and a note asking that he be given the chance of a good life by being raised in Bedrock. The boy's name, according to the note, is Bamm-Bamm. The Rubbles are curious about the name until they hand the boy a club that was also in the basket and he begins to slam it on the ground, yelling "Bam! Bam!" each time it strikes the ground and shakes the house.

Eager to share their joy, the Rubbles visit their neighbors and introduce Bamm-Bamm to the family. Everyone is smitten with the new arrival, especially young Pebbles, setting up years of animated hijinks. Things take a turn when it is discovered that another person wants to adopt Bamm-Bamm. Though the Rubbles are uneasy to learn that the judge presiding over the trial is the member of the family trying to adopt Bamm-Bamm, they are even more upset when they learn that the opposing attorney is none other than Perry Masonary – *The Flintstones* writers had a knack of taking familiar things and making them fit the stone age with a little "rock" wording; the opposing family in the adoption trial are named the Stoneyfellers. Will money win out over love? For a comedy program, there are very few genuine laughs in this episode. As if the Rubbles being left broken hearted wasn't serious enough, we also get a despondent Barney complicating suicide.

All's well that ends well when the Stoneyfellers learn they are expecting their own child so they just hand Bamm-Bamm over to the Rubbles, like they were returning an item to the store, unintentionally promoting the message that natural children are better than adopted ones.

Of course, I'm sure that wasn't the message the writer or producers of the show intended. And, thanks to this episode and those on other shows, adoption is no longer a stigma. I was one of the lucky ones. My parents adopted me before I was six months old. When I would question them about it, my dad would always tell me that I was special because, while most parents don't get to choose their children, he and my mother chose ME.

Today, most adoptions on television are presented positively. Lily on *Modern Family* (2009–2020), or Rachel on *Glee* (2009–2015) show that adopted children are wanted and loved. I should also note that both Lily and Rachel were adopted by gay male couples, which is also an important step in the right direction. From Alvin and the

Before The Simpsons, *the longest running animated series in prime time would be Hanna-Barbera's* The Flintstones. *A forerunner in the realm of the Very Special Episodes trend with the adoption themed episode "Little Bamm Bamm".*

Chipmunks to the Teenage Mutant Ninja Turtles… from Clark Kent to Princess Leia – adoption has come front and center. And we all have a little boy named Bamm-Bamm to thank for it.

For the curious, here is a list of some of the most popular adopted characters on television:

Diff'rent Strokes (1978–1986)	Arnold and Willis Jackson
Punky Brewster (1984–1988)	Punky Brewster
Heroes (2006–2010)	Claire Bennet
The Facts of Life (1979–1988)	Natalie Green
Felicity (1998–2002)	Julie Emrick
The Golden Girls (1985–1992)	Rose Nylund
Little House on the Prairie (1974–1983)	Albert Ingalls
Dexter (2006–2013)	Dexter Morgan

Not a bad bunch of people to hang out with – except maybe for Dexter!

Incidentally, I found my birth family when I was 45 years old. Ten brothers and sisters. And while I sometimes wonder what it would have been like to grow up with them, I wouldn't trade my parents for anything in the world.

"The Addams Family Meets a Beatnik"
from *The Addams Family*
Original Air Date: 1 January 1965
By Lee Gambin

The Addams Family (1964–1966) represents a multitude of various social constructs and does something magical with it all – it inverts what is considered conventional, questions and challenges the traditional value system, scrutinizes the reasoning behind normalcy, reconsiders the concept of familial unity, and satirizes the traditions of American culture both inside and outside of the constraints of television situation comedy. There are multiple reasons as to why The Addams' are incredibly important in the history of sitcom "seriousness" – not only are they one of the most loveable and supportive TV families ever to grace the small screen continually dealing with alienation from the so-called "regular community", but another major factor that showcases the sheer beauty of this "creepy and kooky" congregation is their openheartedness and willingness to accept absolutely anyone from any walk of life. The Addams' are the real deal – a genuinely loving, nurturing, comforting and non-judgmental group of misfits who come to represent the perpetual outsider living in a world dominated by paranoia, intolerance and moralistic prejudice.

Headed by the worldly, wise and wildly beautiful matriarch Morticia Addams (Carolyn Jones) and her forever doting husband Gomez (John Astin), the family are remarkably connected, completely devoted to one another and share an incredible sense of warmth, compassion, security, support, fun and respect for their fellow Addams. However, this unabashed and wide-eyed loyalty for one another is not only restricted for their "own kind", for the Addams' are endlessly trying to make the outside world feel welcomed. But because this adoring family lives in a cold and unfeeling world, they are shunned for the most part and ostracized from the supposedly "normal" folk. Outside of the Addams's decadent gothic homestead, there is massive hesitation and fear from most of their fretful and hysterical guests, and this is the case even here with "The Addams Family Meets a Beatnik", where a young man from an outsider subculture still feels alienated and is terrified by the likes of Morticia, Gomez and the rest of the gang – but not for long.

The proudly macabre Addams family go about their days completely carefree, happy within themselves, and not perplexed by insecurities or driven to mania from any kind of narcissism or egotism. Instead they are joyous, chipper and dedicated to each other's happiness and personal success. Interestingly enough, it is this elegant self-confidence, sense of community and mutual respect that makes them seem "bizarre" to the conventional mindset. For example, Morticia and Gomez are insanely in love and at the drop of a hat (or more specifically, at the drop of some French quip from the lips of Morticia), this highly sexed and incurably romantic couple will show their absolute desire and passion for one another, which is intensely different from the likes of fellow American sitcom couples during the early sixties. Their romantic devotion is so heartfelt and fiery that it is a rarity for the period. On top of that, gender roles are reconstructed (Gomez would be the first man to do dishes in an American sitcom; sleeves rolled up assisted by sharp tourniquets), age would simply be a number (Grandmama (Blossom Rock) and Uncle Fester (Jackie Coogan) would gleefully play in their household dungeon like a couple of youngsters) and children would be respected as freethinkers and artists (Wednesday (Lisa Loring) and Pugsley (Ken Weatherwax) forever in the throes of creativity – beheading dolls, sparking dynamite and so forth).

Opening with Uncle Fester posing for Morticia who paints him in a scene harking back to a decadent Shakespearean allusion, "The Addams Family Meets a Beatnik" is fundamentally a precursor to the advent of Very Special Episodes (VSE) in that it is a solemn detour from the usually laugh-heavy monster comedy. In the episode's final moments, there is a hush from the studio laughter and there is elongated spaces of dialogue (lengthy by sitcom standards) devoid of any humor and different in tone from other episodes. Here in this outing, the generation gap and the estrangement shared between stoic and gruff fathers and their wayward sons is examined and sensitively handled by the writers Henry Sharp and Sloan Nibley who give their heroic Addams family a job to do – which is bridging the gap and building harmony between stern old men and reckless young teens. Instantly the episode presents the affectionate togetherness and encouragement the Addams' are so good at with Gomez excitedly praising his wife's artistic talents. Along with this is Wednesday and Fester's conversation about her piggybank (a skull) which positions perceptive and wistful niece and wacky uncle as one in the same – a child and a child-like man; bonding their unity and mutual admiration for one another. When the family's day is interrupted by a big crash, they race outside to find a leather clad beatnik disheveled and injured, lying by the side of his turned over motorcycle. The disorientated beatnik Rocky (Tom Lowell) asks "Where am I?" and then upon seeing Wednesday's piggybank skull he answers himself "Forget dad I know!" Here, the morbid façade of the Addams family bangs out an instant response in Rocky – a young man who embraces a counterculture that rejects traditional American values, but who is more or less still "spooked" by the "mysterious and spooky" Addams family.

Nursed back to health, Rocky is confused by the "all together ooky" crew. He asks, "Are you cats for real?" to which Gomez responds, "Cats? Oh you mean Kitty. She's real alright!", making way for a wonderful appearance by Kitty Kat, one of the Addams family's most beloved pets – a full grown lion! Rocky shakes off the injury caused by his motorcycle accident and when he is asked about his living arrangements, he lets on that he does not exactly like his home life. This all follows up from right after he attempts to get his head around why Wednesday and Pugsley live in such a strange abode (Wednesday says "We love it here, it's nice and eerie"). The episode spends a lot of time with the Addams children and Rocky, connecting them thematically as the new generation – however, Wednesday and Pugsley are loved and nurtured, they are given a voice and permitted a place at the table, whereas Rocky is stifled by oppressive bourgeois society, as it is soon discovered that he is the son of a wealthy tycoon who wishes his boy to be "just like his old man". Where Wednesday and Pugsley are allowed individual thought, the freedom to be who they are and everlasting love and affection from their parents and the rest of the family, Rocky is lacking such essential support and guidance. When he confesses his disdain for his living arrangements to the children and explains why he wishes to run away, he asks them "Dig?" to which Wednesday replies: "Only graves". This beautifully composed macabre sense of humor that The Addams Family is so brilliant at, intercepts and rounds off a scene that could have quickly tipped into a preachy "the world doesn't get me" trope.

While the Addams children take an affectionate liking to Rocky, Gomez is keenly interested in his slang ("Morticia and I are fascinated with languages!") and is thrilled to hear his own children speak "beatnik". The cadence of Rocky's "daddy-o"'s and "I gotta split"'s sparks a fire in the enthusiastic eye of Gomez and this summarizes the aforementioned openheartedness of the Addams family who are continually courteous, eternally welcoming and forever the gracious host. They are also willing to learn and embrace varied cultures (and countercultures). Aesthetically, the Addams family are linked to beatnik and arts-centric culture in many regards – Morticia's musicality, Gomez's passion for Eastern philosophies such as yoga and so forth. The beatnik subculture would make an impression on varied films and television from Roger Corman produced horror/comedy outings such as *A Bucket of Blood* (1959) through to Spook the cool feline from Hanna-Barbera's classic cartoon series *Top Cat* (1961–1962). Morticia comments on Rocky's personality and its influence on the household: "He's bought charm and individuality into our lives, I wish we could keep him" and her observations are a poignant condensation on the idea of Rocky's subculture appealing to the Addams family who are the outsiders of all outsiders.

At the heart of *The Addams Family* is the importance of unique thought and expression, and the absolute necessity of tolerance and acceptance. This is all countered when Rocky's father Rockland Cartwright II (Barry Kelley) enters the scene and is painted as the enemy of individuality. Being a big important business tycoon, he is most definitely a caricature in the most classic sense (a heartless bully ready to turn on his son if his son won't play by the rules), but this establishes the generation gap in clear terms and without any unnecessary grey areas.

Helped out by Wednesday and Pugsley, Rocky comes to understand the dilemma facing these two kind hearted children. If Wednesday and Pugsley are perceived by the outside world as "strange" and "different", then the conventional world is at a loss. What Rocky discovers is the fact that these two spider and explosives enthusiasts have an aversion to lying making them honest, and possess an overwhelming sensitivity and sweetness that warms his jaded heart. Hiding from his father, Rocky ends up involving himself with the antics of the Addams children such as setting off hand grenades and is moved when they tell him that they have set up a birthday party for him. Touched by their tenderness, Rocky finally understands compassion and friendship while his father is repelled by the notion of his only son associating with such "riff raff". Bearing witness to the décor of the Addams house and accepting a light from Thing only to then do a double take, Rockland Cartwright II bellows "Where is that good for nothing son of mine?" which shakes up the Addams household who would never dare speak of their children in such a way.

Standing up to his father, Rocky makes a declaration: "These people are my friends, they're my kind of kooks, they dig me the way I am!" This is the soul of the episode and what brings it to the fore in the entire two season run of *The Addams Family* as a forerunner to the VSE phenomenon that would surface in more obvious and striking ways come the shows of Norman Lear such as *All in the Family* (1971–1979). While summarizing the issue of the generation gap – something that would be examined on mass during the period with the advent of the hippie movement drawing near, which would mark the first major divide between teenagers and their parents – the stoic stern gruffness of the cold unfeeling conservative elders pitted against the wayward recklessness of youth is a carryover from films from the previous decade before *The Addams Family* would entertain. Finally, in the closing moments of "The Addams Family Meets a Beatnik", Rocky's father thanks Morticia, Gomez and the others ("You people accepted the boy just the way he is") cementing the Addams family as a loving medium, bringing the generation gap to a close and bringing estranged father and son together. After Rocky and his son reconcile and overcome differences, the now centered well-adjusted youth bestows gifts to Wednesday, Pugsley and Uncle Fester before turning to Morticia and Gomez saying "Mr. and Mrs. Addams, you cats are alright."

The generation gap is examined with the forever welcoming Addams family – represented here by the children Wednesday (Lisa Loring) and Pugsley (Ken Weatherwax) – befriending a member of sixties counterculture in "The Addams Family Meet a Beatnik" from The Addams Family.

"The Indians Are Coming" from *The Beverly Hillbillies*
Original Air Date: 1 February 1967
By John Harrison

"There's gold in them there hills!" Or, in the case of *The Beverly Hillbillies*, Black Gold, Texas Tea... otherwise known as crude oil.

First broadcast on 26 September 1962 and lasting 274 episodes throughout its nine seasons, *The Beverly Hillbillies* was the unlikeliest of TV hits, though its premise was woven around the familiar fish out of water set-up, and the central family a clear riff on the phenomenally popular *Ma and Pa Kettle* series of hillbilly comedy features produced by Universal in the 1940s and 1950s.

Introduced by one of the more famous and memorable theme songs of its era ("The Ballad of Jed Clampett" by Lester Flatt and Earl Scruggs), each episode of *The Beverly Hillbillies* centered on the hijinks of middle-aged widower Jed Clampett (Buddy Ebsen) and his brood: beautiful daughter Elly May (Donna Douglas), elderly mother-in-law Daisy May "Granny" Moses (Irene Ryan) and Jethro Bodine (Max Baer Jr.), the brawny but half-witted son of his cousin Pearl. Eking out a pitiful existence in the Ozark mountains, Jed's life turns completely around when the small piece of land he owns is discovered to contain a rich reserve of crude oil, which he sells to the OK Oil Company for a whopping $25 million (the equivalent of a cool $205 million in 2020 dollars). Packing up his family and his meager belongings into an old jalopy, Jed heads for Beverly Hills and moves into the mansion next door to his greedy banker Milburn Drysdale (Raymond Bailey), who is always stressing about anyone other than himself getting their hands on the Clampetts' fortune.

For the most part, *The Beverly Hillbillies* stuck to mostly safe storylines in which the familiar sixties television plots and scenarios are dealt with, but "The Indians Are Coming", from the show's fifth (1967) season, provides an interesting early example of a Very Special Episode, not so much as in it deals with a controversial issue, but more in which it portrays a very familiar theme through the lens of a mindset that would be completely unheard of – not to mention culturally unacceptable – in today's moral climate.

The Native American has long been a staple of the Western genre, not just in cinema and on television but also within the pages of pulp magazines, paperbacks and comic books. Usually cast in the role of the savage villain, the depiction of the Native American began to evolve and mature as the 1960s wore on and people became more sensitive and appreciative towards people with different cultural and racial roots.

In "The Indians Are Coming", a simple boundary dispute with the Crowfoot tribe over Jed Clampett's land back in Bug Tussle has Granny convinced that war with the American Indians is on the horizon. When word gets out that Chief Running Wolf

(Stanley Waxman) and Little Fox (John Considine) are heading to Beverly Hills to sort out the issue face to face with Jed, Granny is not the only one who flies into a panic, with Milburn Drysdale convinced the visitors will try and bilk money out of his biggest client. While Granny has Jethro drive her around town in their jalopy, screaming "The injuns are coming" at the top of her lungs, Chief Running Wolf and Little Fox arrive in town and are revealed to be well-dressed and intelligent, successful businessmen, rather than the bloodthirsty savages that Granny and Milburn Drysdale have been expecting.

Predictably, there's lots of references to scalping, pow wows, palefaces, smoke signals and other Native American clichés throughout the episode, and Drysdale affects the simplified phony speech pattern with which they were often portrayed onscreen as having, particularly in the following passage of dialogue, when the banker is initially led to believe that the Crowfoot tribe have also struck oil on the land next to the Clampetts':

"Send a message to my red brothers. Tell them Milburn Drysdale, their friend, speak with straight tongue. Tell them send all black wampum to my bank, we put it in solid steel teepee, keep money safe for noble red brother."

Naturally, once Drysdale's long-suffering secretary Jane Hathaway (Nancy Kulp) informs her boss that the Crowfoots are in fact caught up in a dispute with the Clampetts over their land, he immediately changes his tune:

"What?! Why, those dirty, thieving savages! Call up the cavalry, this uprising must be put down!"

Drysdale further looks the fool when he greets the visiting Crowfoots while wearing the traditional feather war bonnet and garb of the Native American, banging away on a drum in his office while offering up worthless trinkets in an effort to fool and win over the visitors. Granny, meanwhile, continues to prepare for the inevitable injun attack ("Except for John Wayne, there ain't nobody that knows injuns like me"), insisting everyone in the Clampett household don wigs in order to fool the invaders when they try to scalp them. In order to placate Granny, Drysdale calls the head of a movie studio financed by the Clampett fortunes and orders him to organize a bunch of stuntmen to dress up as native Indians and fake an attack on the Clampett mansion, allowing Granny to emerge victorious thanks to her trusty shotgun (which Drysdale has somehow removed all the buckshot from).

The episode ends on a rather surprising note. As Granny sits on her rocking chair outside the Clampett home, exhausted by the battle she has just fought, she is approached by none other than John Wayne, one of the icons of the American western genre, playing himself. After introducing himself and advising that he had heard Granny had been asking about him, Granny simply looks up at the confused star and states: "Where was ya when I needed ya, John?"

One of the biggest American movie stars of the previous thirty years, Wayne's film career may not have been at its peak in 1967, but he still had stature as an undisputed cinema giant and a true icon of Americana. While Wayne regularly showed up on television variety and comedy shows and one-off specials (a highlight being his famous appearances on *Rowan & Martin's Laugh-In* (1968–1973)), he rarely lent his face to episodic TV, making his cameo on "The Indians Are Coming" even more of a surprise and a coup for the show's producers. Reportedly, the infamously hard-drinking Wayne agreed to the appearance in return for a fifth of Jack Daniels bourbon.

While director Joseph Depew started his career in the early 1940s and worked as an assistant or second unit director on a multitude of movies and television shows (including *The George Burns and Gracie Allen Show* (1950–1956), *Panic!* (1957–1958), *The Bob Cummings Show* (1955–1959) and *Petticoat Junction* (1963–1970)), his main directorial work was limited to a sole episode of *Don't Call Me Charlie* (1962–1963), along with an impressive 145 episodes of *The Beverly Hillbillies* (he was also an assistant director on a further 32 episodes).

Native beliefs and superstitions would continue to be an occasional theme in American sitcoms throughout the 1970s and early eighties, most notably in the *Brady Bunch* episode "Hawaii Bound" from 1972, where an old Tiki idol found by Bobby Brady supposedly brings bad luck to anyone who touches it, and in the *Diff'rent Strokes* episode "Burial Ground" from 1982, where Native Americans protest the plan by Philip Drummond (Conrad Bain) to construct a building site on top of an old Indian burial ground. The latter, of course, has been a popular trope in horror cinema and literature, most notably used by Stephen King in *The Shining* and *Pet Sematary* (along with their subsequent film adaptations), and Tobe Hooper's *Poltergeist* (1982).

The cast of The Beverly Hillbillies – *one of the most endearing classic sitcoms that would be based in a displacement sensibility, having our loveable but naive country folk living in "progressive" Los Angeles.*

Didn't Need No Welfare State, Everybody Pulled His Weight

1970 – 1973

"Sisters at Heart" from *Bewitched*
Original Air Date: 24 December 1970
By Alexandra Heller-Nicholas

Jane Elliott was a white woman teaching a group of young children at a school in Randall, Iowa, when American civil rights leader Dr. Martin Luther King, Jr. was assassinated on 4 April 1968. Randall was a white town, her students were white, the media coverage she watched on television that night was presented to her by white journalists. How, she asked herself, do I teach these kids about the magnitude and the horror of what has happened, about how bigotry and racism are destroying our country?

Her answer became known as the "Blue Eyes Brown Eyes" experiment. The next day at school, she asked the children what they think being a child with black skin might feel like and what racial discrimination means. Curious – as children always are – they said they'd like to find out. The next day, Elliott divided the children into groups according to eye color, making the blue eyed children superior and privileging with extra snacks, longer playtime and more access to playground equipment, and were told that it was appropriate for them to only play with other blue-eyed children, and to make sure they don't drink from the same water fountains as kids with brown eyes. The following day, the roles were reversed: it was the brown eyed children who were now superior, privileged, in charge. Elliott asked the children to write about their experiences, and these were published in a local newspaper before going national and leading to Elliott appearing on Johnny Carson's *The Tonight Show*.

America went wild: people at the time – as they are, to be fair, still now – outraged at the ethics of Elliott's experiment, but it simultaneously revealed how ingrained racism was in American culture more broadly. Elliott was ostracized at work and in her community, and of the many complaints *The Tonight Show* received, one notorious attack decried Elliott for her cruelty to white children who would no doubt be irreversibly damaged, stating it was different for black children because it was simply how things were: they were used to it. In 1970, Willian Peters produced a television documentary about Elliott and her experiment called *The Eye of the Storm* which made her even more famous as it was broadcast across the nation by the American Broadcasting Company. On Christmas Eve that same year – only months later – the popular sitcom *Bewitched* (1964–1972) screened their Very Special Episode, "Sisters at Heart".

The timing here is crucial. While the civil rights movement that exploded across the United States in the late 1960s was forever and indelibly marked by the assassination of Dr. King, the question of how to communicate the gross human rights atrocities that lay behind his murder to young children was one that polite White America was finding difficult to avoid. Rather than avoiding the subject, the team behind *Bewitched* decided to tackle the subject head on. Based on a story created by the tenth-grade fifth-period English Class in Room 309 at Los Angeles's inner-city Thomas Jefferson High School, the episode would go on to become one of the show's iconic star Elizabeth Montgomery's favorite episodes, and received the Governor's Award at the 23rd Primetime Emmy Awards the following year.

Like many "Very Special Episodes" of its era, "Sisters at Heart" opens with an uncharacteristic introduction to-camera by the show's star speaking as themselves. Making sure to mention the program's sponsor, Montgomery announces that "tonight's show was written in the true spirit of Christmas… My friends at Oscar Mayer and company and I feel it is a very special *Bewitched*, conceived in the image of innocence, and filmed with truth." The episode proper begins with an opening shot of a Christmas tree that pans down to reveal Montgomery's Samantha Stephens decorating it with tinsel as her daughter Tabitha (Erin Murphy) and little brother Adam (David Lawrence) sit happily beneath the tree. Samantha talks to Tabitha about what will that night be her first sleepover, reminding her to keep ixnay on the witchcraft-nay, but to otherwise look at it as "having a temporary sister for a few days". Eyeballing her younger brother, Tabitha pines for a real sister, kvetching that Adam broke her jack-in-a-box. Once again, even in these early moments *Bewitched* reminds us that the patriarchy is ruled by white destructive assholes. Tabitha's guest arrives, Lisa (Venetta Rogers), who is a little older than Tabitha. The younger girl is thrilled with her "temporary" new sister, despite struggling to pronounce the word "temporary". Lisa's doting parents Dorothy (Janee Michelle) and her husband Keith Wilson (Don Marshall) – the latter a colleague of Samantha's husband Darrin (Dick Sargent) at the McMahon and Tate Advertising Agency – leave Lisa in Samantha's care as Larry Tate (David White) mentions an important client, Mr. Brockway (Parley Baer), who is soon revealed to be the potential source of a one-million dollar advertising contract. Lisa and her family are black, so the scene concludes complete with light-hearted jokes about how wishing for a "white" Christmas might not be ideal scenario for everyone in the room.

As Darrin earnestly plugs away at the much-desired account, the latter is revealed to be a privileged white man child: before demanding milk and cookies from his weary secretary, he tells her he wants to make a surprise visit to the Stevens household to make sure there are no "skeletons rattling around the family closet" before signing the contract. In any other *Bewitched* episode this would no doubt lead to fears concerning the revelation that Samantha and Tabitha are witches, but in this particular episode, more real-world forms of discrimination take center stage.

Sitting with their coloring books and pencils at the Stevens' kitchen table, Tabitha casually noting that the girls they are coloring can't be sisters if they are not the same color. Instantly sensing bullshit, Samantha's eyebrows are raised – immediately sensing the bigger picture at stake here – as Tabitha explains that she learned this from a girl in the local park who told her and Lisa that they she couldn't be sisters because they had different color skin. Referring to this girl as "a big dope", Tabitha confesses to her mother that she almost did some "magic" on her, sending Samantha into her usual paroxysms of anxiety lest the family secret of female empowerment become public knowledge. Samantha frantically lures Tabitha out of the room, but not before Tabitha reminds Lisa "don't forget we're sisters, no matter what anyone else says".

While they are out of the room, Lisa answers the door to snooping dogshit racist Mr. Brockway, seeking as he is to confirm that all is above board in the Stevens household. Seeing Lisa, his eyes bulge at the thoroughly pleasant young girl who has the audacity to have a skin color different from his own. Assuming she is the daughter of the housekeeper because he is – again – a dogshit racist, when Lisa says her father works for McMahon and Tate and that Tabitha is her sister, Mr. Brockway assumes Darrin has a black daughter and almost passes out in horror at the idea that Darrin might be married to a black woman.

Arts and craft continue to keep the girls occupied, Tabitha wholly incapable of keeping her witchcraft in check as she magically removes spilled white paint from Lisa's cute little 1970s frock. In the process, however, she accidentally turns Lisa white – blonde hair, pale skin and all. Satisfied with her error, Tabitha is pleased that they can now really be sisters because – according to the logic of the local playground racist – they have the same skin color. Comforted by this pigmentational evidence of true sisterhood, Tabitha spills the beans about her dark secret to her "sister", and despite Lisa's doubt that witches are real, seeing herself as a little white girl in the mirror is all the evidence she needs for confirmation of Tabitha's supernatural prowess. Turning Lisa back to her usual appearance to demonstrate what witches can do, the lesson is one the younger girl uses to demonstrate how untrue the stereotypes are: witches don't have warts on their noses, and they don't ride broomsticks (the animated opening credits of *Bewitched* aside, of course). To her friend's surprise, further demonstrations of Tabitha's skills include her turning herself into a little black girl – dark skin, dark hair – and then back. The two girls dream of finding a way that they could still be recognizable to their mothers (thus avoiding the full blackface/whiteface transformation) but somehow visibly be the same. Then Tabitha has an idea.

Meanwhile, the embodiment of conservative while male anxiety Darrin once again berates Samantha for what he assumes is someone from her family of outsiders losing him the Brockway account after the latter's surprise visit and his decision that Darrin is not appropriate for such a high-value contract. Samantha stands her ground and says he did not visit to her knowledge, but before they have time to continue the conversation Lisa and Tabitha reveal their solution: thanks to a bit of good old-fashioned nose-wiggling on the latter's part, Tabitha is a little white girl covered in black spots, while Lisa is a little black girl covered in white spots. Dismissing it first as "wishcraft" instead of "witchcraft", Samantha discovers the permanence of the polka dot pigmentation when Tabitha confesses to being incapable of changing them back.

In her usual unflappable, perky style, however, Samantha's not bothered (explaining it to the eternally thick-headed Darrin), while Tabitha wants to consciously reverse the spell, her subconscious is so determined for she and Lisa to be sisters that she just can't do it. Unsurprisingly perhaps, Darrin suggests corporal punishment because a) it's the 1970s, and b) he's an asshole. But Sam won't stand for it. Enter Larry Tate: insistent on keeping the Brockway account, he wants to find out why Brockway thinks Darrin is unstable, and has the great idea that they'll have the office Christmas party at the Stevens house. Brockway is perversely fascinated with the idea of an interracial couple, the entire event putting the pressure on Samantha and Tabitha to reverse the spell. Darrin in his infinite wisdom decides the only option is to kidnap Lisa and flee the country; somewhat glibly, Samantha explains to him that their best bet might be to tell the truth, that as witches she and Tabitha are members of a minority group and it is this that caused the problem.

Neither of these will cut it, of course, so all hope – again – depends on the off-screen witchdoctor Dr. Bombay coming through with a solution in spell-form. Which he does, but not before Brockway turns up with a black doll for Lisa, a white doll for Tabitha and a panda (black *and* white) for Adam, because Brockway says he was unsure of that child's background. Realizing that Brockway thought Lisa was his daughter as the party begins, Darrin realizes Brockway's mistake, Dr Bombay's spell reverses Tabitha's magic just before Lisa's mother Dorothy enters Tabitha's bedroom. But this is only after Tabitha allows the spell to work, having accepted that their different skin color doesn't make her and Lisa's relationship any less solid. This is caused by a short but central speech from Samantha:

Sisters are girls who share something. Usually the same parents, but if you share other things – good feelings, friendship, love – the way you two do, well, that makes you sisters in another way.

Downstairs, Brockway is thrilled to realize that Darrin's marriage is not "mixed" and tells Larry he's very happy to welcome Darren back to the contract. Larry – totally against character – realizes that he's dealing with a racist, and tells Brockway that he doesn't want the contract, even though it's a million dollars. Brockway insists "you've got me all wrong – some of my best friends are negroes!". At this, Darrin uncharacteristically permits Samantha a little moment of witchcraft; her nose wiggles and Brockway sees everyone (including himself in the reflection of a mirror) in blackface. He smiles awkwardly, confused, and leaves clumsily. Larry asks what that was all about and Sam smiles, saying "I think Mr. Brockway is dreaming of a Black Christmas".

The conclusion finds Lisa and Tabitha's families exchanging gifts under the Stevens' Christmas tree; idyllic, happy and – in this moment of sitcom idealism at least – equal. Mr. Brockway, solemn, appears at the door and speaks of an epiphany after a sleepless night: "I found out I'm a racist ... oh not the obvious out-in-the-open racist, I was a sneaky racist. I was so sneaky I didn't realize it myself." The acknowledgement and apology is met with the approval of both Lisa and Tabitha's families, and he is invited to share Christmas dinner with both families.

Like Jane Elliott's "Blue Eyes Brown Eyes" experiment, much of "Sisters at Heart" would not stand up to the scrutiny of today's assumptions of what's acceptable and what is not, but the arrogant temptation to position ourselves somehow outside of history and condemn historical phenomenon as that old liberal chestnut "problematic" from our present-day high-horse does a gross disservice to the genuine spirit that drove both of these remarkable events. Whether they'd cut it by today's standards is not the point; they tried – from a genuine place of wanting to change the ugliness of the world they lived in – to communicate something fundamental about our shared humanity, and the abomination that is rejecting that in the name of bigotry, intolerance and hate.

"Sisters at Heart" and "Blue Eyes Brown Eyes" are of their time, sure, but that was – to state the obvious – when they were conceived. As historical moments that speak to an extraordinarily volatile and difficult moment of socio-cultural transition in the United States they are intriguing case studies. Today, almost half a century later, as neo-Nazism is increasingly on the rise in the mainstream and discriminatory violence and extremist, bigoted political leaders drive policy and mass-cultural discourse across most of the Western world, perhaps it's time to stop condemning the past for trying when we have learned so little from the very basic lessons they tried to teach us.

A vitally important Very Special Episode, and conceived by students of a public school wanting to discuss interracial friendships, "Sisters at Heart" from Bewitched *dissected prejudice but most importantly brought black and white friendship to the fore, empowering children to see beyond race, whilst teaching bigots a very necessary lesson.*

"Where There's Smoke" from *The Brady Bunch*
Original Air Date: 8 January 1971
By John Harrison

Although it premiered during the final year of the 1960s, *The Brady Bunch* (1969–1974) would become much more known for its enduring place on the 1970s cultural landscape. Like many episodic shows, it took *The Brady Bunch* a season before it really started to gel and the characters found their feet and the young cast developed some confidence and natural interaction with each other. By the time the classic episodes of *The Brady Bunch* really started coming in thick and fast, the sixties were over and the matriarch and patriarch of the Brady tribe, mom Carol (Florence Henderson) and dad Mike (Robert Reed) were the flared-panted, big-collared and sexy television parents of the new decade, a role they played upon right up until the end of their notorious *Brady Bunch Hour* variety show in 1977. Though I loved my parents and family, when I was a kid I had a secret wish to run away to the United States and be adopted by the Bradys so I could share in their perfect little slice of the American dream, a suburbia that was free of crime, where money never seemed to be an issue, and every year started with a trip to the Grand Canyon or Hawaii.

In the perennially Sunshine Day world of the Bradys, life problems rarely got any more serious than trying to win an audition spot on Hal Barton's Saturday morning TV variety show, or hoping a stray football-induced bump on the nose will heal in time for the big date. Beyond the first episode, the six kids never seemed to miss or reminisce about their real mother or father (Mike Brady was a widower and, though initially written as a divorcee, the fate of Carol's first husband is never officially stated, though it is assumed she is a widower also).

Occasionally, however, *The Brady Bunch* would punch a hole in that fourth wall and let a dark cloud of real life come through for a brief moment. One such episode was "Where There's Smoke" from the show's second season (1970–1971), in which the subject of cigarette smoking takes centre stage. When oldest Brady brother Greg (Barry Williams) is approached by happenin' school rock band The Banana Convention and offered the chance to fill-in on guitar for the upcoming dance, the grooviest Brady doesn't want to come off as unhip when band leader Tommy (Craig Huxley a.k.a. Craig Hundley) offers him a cigarette, right there on the grounds of Fillmore Junior High! Of course, younger sisters Jan and Cindy Brady (Eve Plumb and Susan Olsen) happen to be leaving school at the same time and spot Greg trying to keep his cool while coughing up his lungs in-between drags on his stick.

Naturally, after Jan and Cindy tattle to big sister Marcia (Maureen McCormick), who in turns tattles to mom and dad, the shock of Greg smoking reverberates throughout the entire Brady household, though Mike and Carol actually show quite a bit of understanding when discussing the issue with their son and deciding on his punishment. Mike admits that he himself also tried smoking when he was younger (though Carol is quick to point out that this was when "we didn't have all the evidence that we do now"), and when Greg appears to be genuinely remorseful about trying the evil tobacco in the first place, he is let off without being grounded or having his allowance taken away from him! It's a nice way of dealing with the situation and the lesson learned, though doubts about Greg's honesty are soon raised when a packet of Valiants falls out of his high-school jacket in front of mom and her militant anti-smoking campaigner friend Mrs. Johnson (Marie Denn), who also happens to be the mother of Greg's bandmate Tommy. While Greg scratches his head wondering how the cigarettes made their way into his jacket, reliable housekeeper-cum-detective Alice (Ann B. Davis) soon deduces that Greg has, in fact, picked up the wrong jacket, and it was Tommy's identical jacket that he came home wearing, unaware of the contraband hidden in one of its pockets. While Mike and Carol's faith in Greg's honesty has been rewarded, poor Mrs. Johnson is left to deal with the fact that her own son is hooked on the very thing she is so outspoken against. Carol, always happy to do her part for the community, decides to help raise awareness of the issue by joining Mrs. Johnson's anti-smoking group.

"Where There's Smoke" was one of six episodes of *The Brady Bunch* to have been written by David P. Harmon, a veteran who at the time already had nearly two decades of television writing behind him. Though some of his other *Brady Bunch* contributions include some entertaining episodes (such as "The Grass is Always Greener" and "The Fender Benders"), "Where There's Smoke" is easily the highlight of Harmon's work for the series. Among the many other classic television shows which Harmon wrote for are *Gilligan's Island* (1964–1967), *Star Trek* (1966–1969), *Hawaii Five-O* (1968–1980), *Mod Squad* (1968–1973) and *Starsky and Hutch* (1975–1979). The director of "Where There's Smoke", Oscar Rudolph, was also a television veteran with shows like *Gidget* (1965–1966), *I Dream of Jeannie* (1965–1970) and *The Flying Nun* (1967–1970) under his belt, not to mention 35 episodes of *My Favorite Martian* (1963–1966) and 36 episodes of *Batman* (1966–1968). Rudolph, who would eventually direct 27 episodes of *The Brady Bunch*, also helmed the Sam Katzman-produced rock 'n' roll films *Twist Around the Clock* (1961) and *Don't Knock the Twist* (1962).

Of course, in an era when illegal drugs like marijuana and LSD were enjoying widespread use by so much of the world's youth culture, tackling a subject like tobacco in 1971 seems almost antiquated and more akin to the short classroom social guidance films of the 1950s. To that end, "Where There's Smoke" actually hints at the existence of something more sinister when Tommy reassures a reluctant Greg with "Hey man, they're just plain cigarettes", when he is offering him one of his smokes. It's quite strange to hear even a veiled reference to marijuana on a show as homogenous as *The Brady Bunch.**

Apart from the regular cast, there are a couple of interesting guest spots and supporting roles in "Where There's Smoke". Marie Denn, who plays the stern Mrs. Johnson, made her screen debut as diner waitress Marge in Ray Dennis Steckler's classic low-budget Hollywood rock 'n' roll flick *Wild Guitar* (1962), and also appeared in Barbara Peeters' biker film *Bury Me an Angel* (1971) along with *Night of the Demons* (1988) and lots of episodic television shows. As someone who has long admired Stanley Kramer's remarkable adaptation of *Bless the Beasts & Children* (1971), it is great to see Bobby Kramer, who played Lally 1 in that film, show up in "Where There's Smoke" as Johnny, one of the members of The Banana Convention. Craig Handley (later Huxley), who plays the smoker and clear bad influence Tommy Johnson, has also had a rather interesting career. While he appeared in many of the usual episodic TV shows at the time, including *Bewitched* (1965–1968), *Adam-12* (1968–1975), *Kung Fu* (1972–1975) and *The Waltons* (1971–1981), Huxley retired from acting in 1977 after an appearance on *Kojak* (1973–1978), changed his surname and started his second career as a composer and electronic musician, though rather than reform The Banana Convention he stuck to working on the soundtracks for an impressive array of genre films and television shows. *Prophecy* (1979), the Marjoe Gortner classic *When You Comin' Back, Red Ryder?* (1979), *Cat People* (1982), *Friday the 13th Part III* (1982), *Total Recall* (1990) and *Se7en* (1995) are just a few of the films to feature his musical talents, not to mention a number of the *Star Trek* (1979–2016), *Alien* (1979–1997) and *Back to the Future* (1985–1990) films as well as many episodes of the original *Battlestar Galactica* (1978–1979) and *Walker, Texas Ranger* (1993–2001). His more recent work includes *10 Cloverfield Lane* (2016) and Seth MacFarlane's *Star Trek* satire *The Orville* (2017–).

Though it still reflects some of the lingering late-sixties elements of the first season, "Where There's Smoke" certainly rates among the first real noteworthy episodes of *The Brady Bunch*. Aside from talking a more serious issue than usual, the episode also marks an important step in the characters and the cast expanding upon their acting roles and using the series to launch a lucrative side career as singers and live stage performers. What started in "Where There's Smoke" as Greg sitting on his bed picking his electric guitar while gently singing "Clowns never laughed before, and beanstalks never grew …" would soon grow to encompass singing and recording careers both on the show and in real life, for the Bradys as both a group and as solo artists. It was another aspect to the series which helped give it a unique appeal and a reach that extended beyond the limits of the TV tube.

*In his highly enjoyable 1992 memoir *Growing Up Brady*, Barry Williams would recount an incident where he was called into the studio on his day off in order to shoot an additional scene for the fourth season episode "Law and Disorder", which originally aired on 12 January 1973. Unfortunately, Barry and some of his friends had been smoking pot for the very first time at his house that afternoon, resulting in the actor being very stoned when he arrived at the studio to film the sequence, which involved Williams pumping up a tyre on his bike as his dad arrives home with an old boat tied to the roof of his station wagon.

"Judging Books by Covers" from *All in the Family*
Original Air Date: 9 February 1971
By Lee Gambin

What would be the fourth episode of the controversial and much loved sitcom *All in the Family* (1971-1979), "Judging Books by Covers" was one of the earliest depictions of gay civil rights in the history of American television comedy, and it would come out two years after the formation of the Gay Liberation Front, an activist group dedicated to protecting the rights of gay people across the board. The episode would be met with critical praise as well as the standard controversy and uproar from conservative audiences not for its depiction of gay characters as cartoons, but because the real homosexual of the piece was a "man's man" – a beer guzzling, sports loving, ex-jock, blue collar real man. Therefore, this episode that has affable bigot Archie Bunker (Carroll O'Connor) realizing that his best pal for many years is the genuine article "fruit" that he positions his judgment on to another guest character, Roger (Anthony Geary), a friend of his daughter Gloria (Sally Struthers) and her husband Mike (Rob Reiner), who is flamboyant and expressive (read: homo in the eyes of the prejudiced Archie).

The issue of masculinity and the changing perceptions of gay men (that they do not have to be mincing and queenie) is something that propels the message of this episode at full force, and when the theme song aments a time when "girls were girls and men were men", this is being challenged, in that masculine men can most indeed be attracted to other men, and seemingly effeminate "pansies" could in fact be fervent heterosexuals.

Gloria and Mike's friend Roger dresses flashy, speaks in a hyper-excited manner and is offbeat and way out for the likes of Archie, who has also had his fair share of his daughter and son-in-law's pals who are "fringe dwellers" such as hippies and feminists and so forth. Here however, Roger is a person who irritates Archie more than any other simply because he believes him to be gay and quite possibly, after the long line of hippies and feminists that are "forced into his life" via the way of Gloria and Mike, the gays are just the worst of all. Even the opening sequence that has Gloria and Mike prepare a nice lunch for their friend is a statement on difference in that they have cashews on hand instead of peanuts and smoked salmon instead of tuna. These are poor working class people who want to impress their worldly friend Roger, paying an extra few cents more for a guest who is cultured. This enraged Archie who equates phony classiness with queerness, and when he finds out who is coming over, he barks "Roger the fairy?"

President Nixon's outrage about the episode became a thing of pop-cultural legacy – he famously made a recorded statement that he turned on the television only to see such a "disgusting display of immorality", in that what enraged him so much was the fact that the show presents the homosexual as a "regular Joe", someone that a guy like Archie Bunker (or Nixon for that matter) could hang out at a bar with and down a few beers with. In Nixon's viewpoint, homosexuality was meant to remain either a joke or something to condemn, but Norman Lear and his wonderful writers present something profound and intelligent – we laugh at Archie's ludicrous ideas on what it means to be a man and what it means to be heterosexual and we also laugh at the fact that flamboyance and sensitivity and even cultured worldliness and class is something that exists upon its own merits or complexities and have nothing in regards to dictating one's sexuality.

Archie despises Roger simply because Roger is considered an "off-horse", and he even says "we don't need any strange little birdies". Mike makes a point explaining that "Just because a guy is sensitive…" that it doesn't meant that his sexuality is to be questioned, that artistic flair or emotional intelligence is just part of the fabric of a person and nothing to do with what his penis gets hard to. Archie's comeback is both hilarious and an insight into his stupidity (which of course is the basis of his hilarity as a character) – he says "a guy who's a fag is a queer", which is followed by a bunch of slurs made including a reference to England being referred to as a "fag country". While Roger is flamboyant, dresses colorfully and is hyperactive loaded with enthusiastic observations, there are means for his excitement. He has just returned from Europe being the worldly man he is, and he is trying to share his experiences with the Bunkers. The show also probes the notion that effete men are intellectual and "real men" are hard working and stuck in a rut – one is allowed to have "free time" to be gay and promiscuous, whereas the latter is meant to be married, settled and devoutly heterosexual. Hunting and sport are established as being "real man activities" and championed by the likes of Archie, who harbors a relentless disdain for gay men – something that remains a constant throughout the series, which is an interesting take in which this is a show devoted to "messages" and the Very Special Episode formula (in many ways the series would set that model in the realm of the American sitcom) but doesn't need to have its main stay characters grow or learn in the long run.

In "Judging Books by Covers" from All in the Family, *Archie Bunker (Carroll O'Connor) comes to realize that his "manly" friend Steve (Philip Carey) is actually gay, shattering his belief that only effeminate men could possibly be homosexual.*

At Kelsey's Bar, a place of "real average Joe men", there is an opening discussion on striking, which is a fascinating point of conversation in that here we have these guys talking about socialist ideals which is odd for a group of varied conservatives. The talk then shifts to conversation about a Swedish sexploitation film with sexy women and this makes Archie uncomfortable too, which is an insight into his all-rounded conservatism. Eventually, we get a moment of Archie at ease, where his almost obsessive admiration for his ex-footballer friend Steve (Philip Carey) – a real man who is big and broad and strong – becomes the focal point. Archie believes Steve would be fighting off women who would be throwing themselves at him, but Steve later explains that Archie has to face the fact that he has never seen him with a woman at all. Strange bedfellow perceptions are cemented when Archie sees that Steve and Roger know each other, as it is learned that Steve runs a camera store (much like openly gay governor Harvey Milk) and Roger is a regular customer.

The bartender's homophobia comes into play here and he expresses his disdain for "sissy fags", but he's OK with Steve's sexuality because Steve's masculinity is a nice closeted way to be gay – therefore, his bar Kelsey's won't "attract that kind". Masculinity and the perception of gender conformity is ultimately passing (passing for straight) and therefore, that is tolerated, but the likes of Roger (who ironically is heterosexual) is a no-no for a place like Kelsey's. This insight is telling about the period where groups such as the Gay Liberation Front and others were entering public domains discussing queer politics and gay rights. One major point of conversation was the fight to insist that gay men were human beings and not sissy caricatures that Hollywood had perpetrated for decades. Activists within the gay liberation movement would argue that gay men in the political movement would start to attack the role of effeminate men in order to breakdown the stereotype that heterosexuals saw as the supposed "norm". However, the irony here is that drag queens were ultimately the first to bring homophobia to its knees and demand respect, however they were being looked upon by fellow "conservative gay libbers" as detrimental for the movement.

Mike outs Steve in anger over Archie's constant belittling of Roger, and in fervent denial, Archie remains desperate to ensure that Steve is a "real man" – his forced admiration of his strength and physique reinforcing such a desired belief. Archie's confusion as to what gay men are like is the core component that drives this episode, and this is what also upset the likes of President Nixon, but impressed activist groups desperate to ensure that the straight world understood that homosexuality (like heterosexuality) came in all shapes, sizes, colors and personality types. When Steve gives Archie a big punch goodbye, Archie remains skeptical of Steve's queerness ("If that's a punch of a fruit…"). Archie leaves the bar in disbelief and we are left with a bigoted principal character who will forever have a hard time understanding gay people.

Steve coming out was a major big deal for gay visibility on American television, it not only was provocative and essential, but it also made an impression on the world of gay rights. Decades later, "The Puppy Episode" from *Ellen* (1994–1998) would have its star (lesbian comedienne and actress Ellen DeGeneres) come out openly on air in an episode devoted to outing her character as well as being an in for DeGeneres to be happily outed as a successful and thriving gay woman working in major mainstream television. However, for the most part, gay characters coming out in American sitcoms were usually relegated as the guest spot who was never heard of before and never heard of afterwards – in and out to serve an episode and its message of either ridicule or acceptance (or both). In "Double Date" from *Blossom* (1990–1995), Joey (Joey Lawrence) is shocked to discover his pal on his baseball team has a crush on him and has been writing him letters declaring this crush. Repulsed by his friend outing himself, Joey is guided by his brother's black girlfriend who compares racism to homophobia of which Joey listens and understands. Joey learns that being gay is natural and healthy and just as natural and healthy as being straight because race is brought into the picture which is something that Joey completely understands and is respectful of. The final moment of the episode has Joey "rescue" his friend from a homophobic bully and all is right in the world.

When we look at gay characters in the Norman Lear universe, "Maude's New Friend" from *Maude* (1972–1978) is a perfect example of giving complexity to the issue where the man in question, an urbane smarmy author, is the object of disdain for Walter (Bill Macy) because he is a jerk. Maude (Bea Arthur) of course claims that this is Walter displaying homophobia, but this is not the case, instead it is Maude's overbearing liberalism that actually is the nuisance here, in that it paints a picture of her gay friend as "her personal homosexual". Lear's shows dissect these issues of gay and straight relations with an interesting multidimensionality that would soon inform other shows to come, such as the *Designing Women* (1986–1993) episode "Suzanne Goes Looking for a Friend" among others.

Archie Bunker (Carroll O'Connor) sits in the foreground, completely "put off" by his daughter Gloria (Sally Struthers) and her husband Mike's (Rob Reiner) friend Roger (Anthony Geary) who he feels is "not quite right" and a "pansy" in "Judging Books By Covers" from All in the Family, *one of the earliest TV explorations of male homosexuality.*

"Road Song" from *The Partridge Family*
Original Air Date: 26 February 1971
By Matthew Krause

In 1965, a psychedelic/bubblegum pop group called The Cowsills was created in their garage and began performing Beatles covers at Bannisters Wharf in Newport. The group consisted of five siblings aged six to mid-teens, and while filling regular gigs, they also managed to release a handful of original singles via JODA and Philips Records. By 1967, The Cowsills would be signed to MGM Records, with their mother Barbara joining the act. The band enjoyed a couple of hit singles: "The Rain, the Park & Other Things," which reached number two on the Billboard Hot 100, and "Indian Lake" peaking at number 10 the following year. Despite the requisite drama with both label and manager, the group still managed to play roughly 200 gigs a year from 1968 to 1972.

It was at the outset of the band's salad days that their story caught the eye of Canadian screenwriter Bernard Slade. Slade sought to feature The Cowsills in a weekly sitcom, but after teaming up with TV producer Bob Claver, the idea was quickly abandoned. Both men realized The Cowsills had become too old for the roles as written in Slade's spec script, so the idea was modified to tell the tale of a wholly fictional family band, with musical film veteran Shirley Jones (*Oklahoma!* (1955), *Carousel* (1956), *The Music Man* (1962)) signed on to play the widowed matriarch.

In this way, *The Partridge Family* (1970–1974) was born. In the season pilot premiering 25 September 1970, a quintet of musical siblings – handsome teen idol Keith Partridge (David Cassidy), his girl-next-door sister Laurie (Susan Dey), precocious preteen brother Danny (Danny Bonaduce), and younglings Tracy (Suzanne Crough) and Chris (Jeremy Gelbwaks in season one; Brian Forster seasons two-four) – persuade their mother Shirley to sing vocals on a pop song they're recording in their garage. The result is lighting in a bottle, which inspires ambitious Danny to track down a manager, Reuben Kincaid (Dave Madden). Kincaid reluctantly signs on and promotes the song to the Top 40 charts, which turns the Partridges' hobby into a career. The gang buys a 1957 school bus, gives it a wild paint job, and soon they are off to Las Vegas for their first gig at Caesar's Palace. Hilarity ensues for four seasons.

Throughout the course of its run, *The Partridge Family* opted for the lightest of tones. After all, the band that inspired the show, The Cowsills, had established itself as wholesome, accessible, and familiar, with the ubiquitous chaos of touring kept safely behind the scenes. *The Partridge Family* cultivated a similar image. Story complications mostly arose by contrasting the mundane glitches of day-to-day suburbia with the tension and disarray of life on the road. Humor was derived from the character quirks of the children – Keith's teen boy hormones, Laurie's teen girl insecurities, Danny's precocious avarice – with mom Shirley providing the rudder. Every episode included at least one Partridge Family song, sometimes performed by the band in concert, sometimes played over a montage of events to consolidate the action. The result each week was an innocuous half-hour of escapist confectionary, low on crises and heavy on fun.

Not surprisingly, when The Partridge Family tackled the story of a teenage runaway midway through the first season, it took the easiest route possible. No weighty conversation about runaway statistics or the evolving runaway crisis (even in 1971, one in seven teens would run away from home at some point in their lives), no glaring examination of the kind of toxic home life that might compel a teen to run, and any mention of the consequences of life on the street is made in the blandest ways possible. Perhaps most egregious is that everything comes out clean and pretty in the end, thanks to a few well-placed words by Shirley Partridge. This is The Partridge Family, after all, not Agnès Varda's Vagabond (1985).

"Road Song," the episode in question, opens in media res, as most first season episodes do. The Partridges, along with manager Reuben, are on tour, dining in a greasy spoon in New Mexico. Laughs are mined via some modest gross-out humor – a waitress (Yvonne Wilder) keeping tally of the flies she's killed, Danny complaining that his PB&J is greasy, and Laurie noting that her gravy has hardened – but things take a turn when teenage Maggie Newton (Laurie Prange) walks in. Recognizing the Partridges, Maggie asks for a ride to Albuquerque. Of all the family, Keith seems the most interested (David Cassidy's trademark leer as the character pops up for all of ten seconds), but Shirley quickly gives in as well. Once on the bus, Maggie spins yarns about feasting with Native American tribes, befriending Basque shepherds in the desert, and ironing the Maharaja's turbans ("She should have Lloyds of London insure her imagination," Reuben mutters). But Maggie's tall tales are the least of the Partridges' concerns. For the next 48 hours, Maggie will move in and out of the family's lives, keeping Shirley and company at arm's length while staying one step ahead of a local Sheriff (Harry Hickox).

When the Partridges stop in Kumquist, a fictional New Mexico town modeled after the old west, Shirley seeks answers with the local authorities. Here, she learns that Maggie is a runaway. After the death of her mother, Maggie was sent to Nebraska to live with her grandparents. Maggie's pattern has been to run away every couple of weeks and hitchhike to Albuquerque, where her widowed father (Sandy Kenyon) lives. So far, Maggie has never made it to Albuquerque; local authorities always manage to intercept her outside city limits and return her to her grandfather (Ian Wolfe).

Enter Shirley Partridge to make everything right. Which she does, in just under twenty-five minutes.

Given the soft-pedal tone of the series, it's hard to tell why Bernard Slade chose a teenage runaway as the subject of an episode. Directed by Alan Rifkin and written by Dale McRaven, two TV comedy warhorses with classic credits dating back to the early

1960's, "Road Song" has the same airy lightness of most Partridge Family adventures. The episode premiered in February 1971, the same year the teen runaway crisis would reach such proportions that the National Runaway Safeline would be established. One would think the gravity of the runaway crisis might be worthy of more thoughtful attention. But alas, The Partridge Family was a different animal, a more family-friendly venue, and perhaps not the best place for such meditations.

As such, "Road Song" suffers by taking the easy path. Instead of a child with the kind of home life issues that compel teens to run away (incest, abuse, etc.), we have Maggie, an unhappy teen who just wants to be with her daddy. Once Shirley Partridge reunites Maggie with her father, the grandfather (who refers to Maggie's dad as a "weasel in a chicken coop") angrily objects, giving Shirley the opportunity to calm the waters in seconds ("I think you could [lose her]," Shirley intones, "but you don't have to," inspiring the grandfather to lose all anger and embrace the hated son-in-law).

The closest "Road Song" comes to the real terrors of runaway life is an awkward visual that doesn't really land. During the family's stopover in Kumquist, Maggie steals away, and Danny sneaks out to find her. Danny runs into a cowboy (Dick Wilson, Mr. Whipple in the Charmin commercials) and states he is "looking for a girl." The cowboy summons a scantily-clad showgirl who wraps the terrified Danny in her arms and tries to pull him into the shadowy recesses of a saloon. Moments later, during the requisite musical montage (the gang searches for Maggie as "Point Me in the Direction of Albuquerque"

The counterculture and youth idealism as well as the need for freedom is explored in various episodes of The Partridge Family, *but here in "Road Song" it is treated with a decidedly serious tone.*

plays over the soundtrack), Reuben runs into the same showgirl, who wraps him in a headlock and manages to drag him into the same saloon. Reuben's struggles suggest that the showgirl is a prostitute (the laughing cowboys witnessing the event give the scene a creepy "gang rape" quality), and the reality that many teenage runaways turn to prostitution in order to survive gives the sight gag a disquieting ambiance.

As a traditional Partridge Family episode, "Road Song" is barely passable. Its laughs are clumsy and unearned, and it features one of the least-memorable songs in the Partridge Family discography. As a Very Special Episode, it's almost blink-and-you-miss-it. The gang's ubiquitous antics, a goofy Scooby Doo-esque foot chase in the desert, and the sense that Maggie is never in any real danger undermine the potential for a powerful and groundbreaking statement. It's too bad, because "Road Song" could have been The Partridge Family's moment to shine, to take its narrative into challenging new territory and secure the shows place as classic culture-shifting TV. Instead, "Road Song" is a short-lived distraction, and The Partridge Family remains more memorable for its nostalgia than its courage.

"Gloria Discovers Women's Lib" from *All in the Family*
Original Air Date: 23 March 1971
By Lee Gambin

The second wave feminist movement, spearheaded by politics involving the laws of the body (contraception issues, the right to abortion et al), equal pay, the rights of women in the workforce and the unity of the gender balance, influenced popular culture in its depiction of sexual politics and the right to an independent voice and attitude for female characters – and the American television sitcom was not immune. Writer/producer and television legend Norman Lear set to explore feminist issues in his hit TV sitcom *All in the Family* (1971–1979), and the first outing for such matters was depicted in the episode "Gloria Discovers Women's Lib" – a multi-layered piece of writing and a captivating examination of Sally Struthers' creation Gloria Stivic (née Bunker) as a young woman growing intellectually and politically.

Opening in the Bunker kitchen with Gloria preparing Sunday breakfast with her cheery dutiful mother Edith (Jean Stapleton), the episode delivers its starting point as a clear presentation of "women's work", however it uses this platform as a canvas for creative expression and as a place to discover secret gifts. Edith is being guided by her libertine daughter and breaking age old traditions of prepping her usual breakfast – so a tiny revolution is happening in this humble kitchen. Gloria asks her mother what it feels like "being creative again" – a lovely indication that Edith, before being married to the oppressive Archie (Carroll O'Connor), was once a woman who had a life before matrimony and motherhood. Edith of course is a character who is deep and with sincere warmth and dignity, and even though she rushes off to fetch Archie his beer or dinner, she is her own woman, and this episode also examines that, as well as providing a narrative ploy for Gloria's newfound liberation. The sequence here in the kitchen would be a forerunner for an episode of *The Simpsons* (1989–) entitled "Separate Vocations", where Marge (voiced by Julie Kavner) and Lisa (voiced by Yeardley Smith) have a conversation about being able to be creative in domestic duties. The scene unfolds lovingly – Gloria loves that she and her mother are close ("Working with you and talking") and her love for her mother is epitomized with "we're talking like friends". Edith complies with this in her words of wisdom that are clouded by naivety ("we worked ourselves up from mother and daughter"). While the two women enjoy "creative cooking" and Edith protests that it is a cheerful change, there is an inspired sense of women wanting to break the monotony of the humdrum, and in doing that, there would be a change in the interpersonal domestic culture.

The generation gap would be a point of reference in *All in the Family*, and in an earlier episode "Mike's Hippie Friends Come to Visit", this would be the core component. In that piece, Archie's son-in-law Mike (Rob Reiner) has his unmarried friends come stay over and this enrages Archie, who has no time for what he considers "sinful, sleazy, filthy hippies". Here, the early seventies, being a time of generational transition and generational divide, is expressed in a situation comedy format, and although the sexual politics of couples who are free from the commitment of holy matrimony does skim on the issue of women's liberation, it is more about sex and free love rather than independence for the female component of couples. Here in "Gloria Discovers Women's Lib" the role of women and how feminism would influence the culture is put to the test, and as progressive women are represented by Gloria's passionate and dedicated plight, the concern is complicated by the older generation of women who may be "left behind" who are here represented by Edith. Interestingly enough, Norman Lear's favorite show would be his creation *Maude* (1972–1978), a hugely popular spin-off of *All in the Family*, and Lear's love for Bea Arthur as an actress would be a major point as to why he cherished that particular show above the others. Also, the feminist attributes of *Maude* were appealing to him, being a feminist himself and being married to a major player in the movement. Maude's visit to the Bunker household would be an integral part of the *All in the Family* structure (not only because it inspired the spin-off) but because it provided Archie a major rival who would be an extension of Gloria's enraged feminist diatribe that would be depicted in a more mature and middle class demeanor.

Archie ultimately finds women's liberation a nuisance, and when he comes to understand that his daughter is reading feminist literature it angers him. He is more perplexed and annoyed that Gloria has inspired Mike to read the same books, which prompts Archie to make a bold statement that he sees feminism as a disease. The first major battle in this episode is situated over the dining table – a place that the series would feature prominently as a focal point, whether the Bunkers are eating (shuffling plates from here to there) or arguing about some political concern be it race, gender, the Vietnam War or whatever. Here, Gloria protects and defends her mother, yelling at her father "you're choking her spirit!" In this summary we clearly get the picture that there is a major need for Gloria wanting women to realize their full potential (something epitomized here in her concern for Edith), but this is countered by Mike's attitude which renders Gloria on her own in her feminist principles. She is essentially betrayed by her husband who is supposedly leftist and a liberal thinker – and eventually, as yet another spin-off from the series evolves entitled *Gloria* (1982–1983), he will break her heart by having an extra-marital affair leaving her a single mother trying to make ends meet on her own.

Mike's stance on women here in this early representation of the trajectory of the Gloria/Mike relationship is dubious. He doesn't think that women have it as bad as blacks, Chicanos, Polacks, Jews and whoever else. Gloria stands up to Mike and his hypocrisy, calling out that his leftist politics leaves out caring about women's rights which leads into her inspired and emotional speech about rising against her oppressors – that she (representing white feminists) shall join forces with her black and Chicano (and every other) sisters and fight the patriarchy. Within her speech she tears up and admits that she might not know what she's saying and this is a great indication of a woman purely beginning to understand her own true potential and importance in a world that sees women as second class citizens. As she races upstairs crying – angry and determined to remain an independent thinker – Archie brings the feminist war cry to a halt by thinking that Gloria's anger is because of PMS. His sexism is astounding, but it is there to point out his endless buffoonery, however, Gloria's rage that turns to an emotional water works is there to point out that even liberation can be a terrifying and upsetting thing. This is what makes the episode all the more endearing and interesting – as well as having a character like Mike exposed as a bigot himself.

Gloria's expressing herself upsets Mike, who remains self-obsessed and solely concerned with his grades. He is unresponsive to Gloria's need for independence and how important gender equality is to her. Mike's blunt sexism is in many ways akin to Archie's – Mike just conceals it better with flowery academic lingo. The roles of men and women are touched on here and the impact of the mindset that problems of men are more important than women's is evident. In the second major confrontation piece of the episode, even the constitution is mentioned where "all men are created equal" sits in the Declaration of Independence and exposes the inherit sexism in America's culture. When all the yelling reaches its climax, Gloria decides to leave and her leaving is a good representation of the authenticity of Norman Lear's intentions – that feminism is serious and needs to be taken seriously, or so-called progressive men can lose their wives.

When Gloria returns, more complex personal politics arise, and thankfully, the writing and the inspired performances from the cast, inject the episode with a truly human heart. Instead of opting for a black and white idea of women versus men or a dull battle of the sexes saga, "Gloria Discovers Women's Lib" hammers in a very truthful and nurturing message of togetherness and true equality. Gloria comes home and tells her mother that she had been missing Mike. Crying in Edith's arms there is a carefully plotted ethos here that as much as women want their independence and freedom, there is also the need of companionships and love, a sturdy and heartfelt dissection of sex roles and the politics of equality. Edith's own liberation is also expressed here (and she shall overtly develop throughout the series and become obviously independent and strong-minded in such later episodes) with her profound question "how do you know that what you see is all there is?" Edith has a secret power, and that is holding a family unit together – something far more important than anything Archie could ever say or do. When Mike's grades arrive, they are good, but they mean nothing if he can't share it with Gloria. Essentially, he needs her more than she needs him and the equality war is summarized by the duo being integral for one another. However, what could be a serene ending erupts with Mike ruining a truce by calling the equality something that solely exists in the couple's bedroom (linking sex with togetherness, but nothing more) Here, male chauvinism and feminism come to war, and even though (through sex) peace eventuates, the battle persists.

"Cousin Maude's Visit" from *All in the Family*
Original Air Date: 11 December 1971
By Michael Barrett

The Guest Relative: One of the hardiest tropes in sitcoms, and one conducive to Very Special Episodes. Often serving as a showcase for a special guest star, the visiting relative can be found with varying frequency in sitcom history.

The pioneering 1950s series *The Goldbergs* could have hardly existed without regular visits from relatives. *Bewitched* (1964–1972) relied heavily on recurring wacky relations. *Family Ties* (1982–1989) made hay out of visits from Steven Keaton's dying father (John Randolph) and divorcing brother (Norman Parker), while Elyse weathered visits from her sister (Karen Landry) and her alcoholic brother (Tom Hanks).

Other shows were more self-sufficient. *I Love Lucy* (1951–1957), which was the #1 series on the air for four of its six seasons (and the other two seasons were #3 and #2), only indulged two Guest Relatives. One was "Lucy's Mother-in-Law" (played by Mary Emery on 22 November 1954), and the other was Tennessee Ernie Ford showing up as Cousin Ernie (actually Lucy's mother's "friend's roommate's cousin's middle boy") in a two-part visit (1 and 8 April 1954), thus combining the Guest Relative with a variant of the Guest Celebrity as Himself. He'd make a third appearance on the Ricardo's trip to California. In fact, this series made up for its lack of relatives by entertaining a whole season of Guest Celebrities in the California sequence.

Similarly, the cultural and ratings powerhouse known as *All in the Family* (1971–1979), which was the #1 show on TV for five consecutive seasons (on Lucy's network, CBS), felt little need to indulge the Guest Relative. As with earlier landmarks *The Honeymooners* (1955–1956) and even *I Love Lucy*, *All in the Family* could feel at home with its four main characters in a room, bouncing off one another reliably. A penetrating analysis awaits to be written comparing and contrasting Alice Kramden, Lucy Ricardo and Edith Bunker as types of the patronized housewife who's smarter than her husband, but we digress.

Although *All in the Family* did have its gallery of recurring neighbors and its guest stars, including one prominent example of the Guest Celebrity as Himself (Sammy Davis Jr. in "Sammy's Visit", 19 February 1972), the series only brought one Guest Relative on stage: Cousin Maude, who would never consent to be a patronized housewife. In her household, she did all the patronizing.

Maude was conceived as a foil to Archie Bunker simply by being his inverse or complement. He was a man, she a woman. He was conservative, she liberal. Their one commonality was a fearlessness about being loud and argumentative. It would never have worked if he was rude and overbearing while she was meek and polite. That's no way to stage comedy, and anyway the writers were making the point that it was possible to be abrasive and liberal just as easily as abrasive and conservative.

This had the added wrinkle of making Maude generally in the right, at least as far as Norman Lear and his writers were concerned, for a woman who was right often had to make her point loudly and repeatedly in the era when "women's lib" had become a catchphrase. That much hasn't changed. We don't talk about "women's lib" anymore, but nevertheless, she's persisted.

Maude showed up in the second season's 12th episode, "Cousin Maude's Visit" (11 December 1971), directed by John Rich from a script credited to Philip Mishkin, Michael Ross and Bernie West. *TV Guide* ranked this at #9 in a 2009 list of Top 100 Episodes of All Time.

Cousin Maude (Bea Arthur) arrives to help a Bunker family bedridden with flu. The sense of family affection between Edith and Maude is one of the episode's minor joys and helps immeasurably to make us like Maude. We also like that she's arriving as an angel of mercy, if an often acerbic one. Indeed, Arthur would play an acerbic angel on a special one-hour "season recap" of *Soap* (1977–1981), as she gets to decide if the late Jessica Tate (Katherine Helmond) can return to Earth to see how the previous season's plotlines work out.

Maude is identified as Edith's cousin, if only vaguely. We never learn if she's the daughter of Edith's uncle or aunt, or whether on the maternal or paternal side. These picayune details don't seem to matter any more than they did with Lucy's Cousin Ernie. What's more important is that Maude is named as a witness to Edith's first meeting with Archie, when he made her laugh by sticking straws up his nose and pushing his hand into her sundae. Maude said it was the most disgusting thing she'd seen since her little brother heaved up his lunch at his confirmation, and Archie hadn't gotten along with her since.

When she first barges into the Bunker home and Archie tries to block her entrance, she makes a hand gesture that's staged in such a way as to be hidden from the camera. Then she brushes past him as he stares in astonishment, leaving viewers to conclude that she flipped him the bird, which still wasn't possible to show on TV.

While Archie insults and bullies everyone else, only Maude matches him, already in full mastery of Arthur's pauses and deadpan zingers and turns to walk away. In the morning, she tells him: "Listen, Archie, I'm not going to let you upset me. I'm only here because of Edith. The fact that you happen to be here with her is beyond my control, like any other freak of nature. [Arthurian pause] Now you can either come to the table and eat, or you can lie there and feed off your own fat. [Longer Arthurian pause] And if you choose the latter, you can probably lie there for months." [Turn and walk away]

Nobody else, not even Mike, could hand Archie that level of withering contempt, and it's one reason *Maude* created such a sensation. As Norman Lear wrote in his memoir *Even This I Get to Experience* (2014), "we wanted someone to clobber Archie as he'd never been clobbered before." The script presents a draw between these two mighty mouths as they argue over recent American history from FDR to Nixon, touching on many points amid acid one-liners and Archie's malapropisms. Even though Maude's grasp of facts is more accurate (e.g., Yalta instead of Gibraltar), Archie gets the last word and feels he's won; this is typical of the show's balance.

The other reason for *Maude*'s success is Arthur's confident performance as what Archie calls "a singing stormtrooper." Born Bernice Frankel, Beatrice Arthur was a tall and powerful stage presence with a husky, smoky voice that must have been useful in her role as a Staff Sergeant for the U.S. Marine Corps Women's Reserve during WWII. After she decided to go into acting, she gained attention as Lucy Brown in Marc Blitzstein's 1954 revival of Bertolt Brecht & Kurt Weill's "The Threepenny Opera", for which Lotte Lenya won a Tony. Other future sitcom stars in that production: Charlotte Rae, Edward Asner, John Astin and Jerry Stiller, with Jerry Orbach for good measure. (Oh, for a time machine!)

In 1964, Arthur was Yente the Matchmaker in "Fiddler on the Roof", and she won her own Tony as Vera Charles in the 1966 musical "Mame" (that time machine again, please). The latter production was helmed by her then-husband, legendary Broadway director Gene Saks. She'd reprise that role in the 1974 film version, which was at least one piece of casting that film got right.

Lear had spotted Arthur in a 1955 off-Broadway revue and arranged her TV debut on *The George Gobel Show* (1954–1960) so he knew her well when he telephoned her to request that she play Maude. Lear wrote: "She mirrored the most profound understanding of the foolishness of the human condition. It wasn't anything she thought about, it wasn't anything she could talk to you about, it wasn't anything she knew, but her reaction to the bullshit in ordinary life was a gift to the character and contained a degree of truth-seeking madness that got to me and wrung me out. The madness originated in the woman, the actress."

Although some sources speculate that Maude was partly based on Lear's wife Frances, a more direct source is in the BBC sitcom *Till Death Do Us Part* (1965–1975), the basis for Lear's series. The final episode of the third season, "Aunt Maud" (16 February 1968) focuses on the wife's sister, played by Ann Lancaster (and note the slight difference in Maude's spelling), who arrives to tend her ailing sister and constantly argues with reactionary paterfamilias Alf Garnett. Although this episode doesn't survive except as an audio recording, it clearly has much in common with "Cousin Maude's Visit", including discussions of other men Edith might have married.

Before the episode finished its broadcast, CBS programming chief Fred Silverman called Lear and said "That woman should have her own show." Lear's answer: "What a great idea!" So the character returned in the season finale, called simply "Maude" (11 March 1972). As written by Rod Parker and directed by John Rich, this episode functions as the practical pilot for the spin-off of the same name, which was already scheduled to debut that fall.

The plot finds Archie and Edith repaying Maude's visit by showing up at Maude's well-appointed home in Tuckahoe, New York. That's in Westchester County, a stone's throw from the Petries in New Rochelle of *The Dick Van Dyke Show* (1961–1966). The occasion is the wedding of Maude's divorced daughter Carol (Marcia Rodd) to a Jewish groom, but that event doesn't transpire.

Carol, along with Maude's husband Walter Findlay (Bill Macy), neither of whom were mentioned in "Cousin Maude's Visit", are introduced here and both would be retained in the spin-off, although Adrienne Barbeau would play Carol in the series. This episode also explains that Walter is Maude's fourth husband – which is fast work, considering that "Cousin Maude's Visit" only presented Maude as a widow of two husbands. The names and fates of the husbands got shuffled.

In the world of Guest Relatives who get their own shows, such confusion and retro-fitting isn't uncommon when nobody thought in terms of a spin-off before suddenly having to develop one. Even so, the cases of amnesia can be striking. On the fourth season of *The Mary Tyler Moore Show* (1970–1977), the episode "Rhoda's Sister Gets Married" (29 September 1973) featured Liberty Williams as Rhoda's younger sister Debbie, with Nancy Walker and Harold Gould as their parents. By the time Rhoda got her own spin-off in the fall of 1974, the parents were the same but Debbie and her marriage had been erased from living memory in favor of younger unmarried Brenda (Julie Kavner), who sort of became the show's new "Rhoda" as Rhoda became the show's "Mary Richards".

If Rhoda could replace one sister with another while keeping the same parents, it was a piece of cake for Maude to acquire two more husbands, a divorced daughter and a grandson. And it still wasn't clear what family tree connected her to Edith.

The modified history of Maude's husbands produced the historically interesting result that, while Maude was married, she became the first divorcee to star in her own sitcom. Vivian Vance had played the divorced Vivian Bagley on *The Lucy Show* (1962–1968), also a TV first, but we must note that it was never "The Vivian Show". For those keeping track, the first sitcom to open with a husbandless divorcee was the short-lived *Diana* with Diana Rigg in the fall of 1973, then Susan Harris' even shorter-lived *Fay* with Lee Grant in September 1975, followed two months later by Lear's *One Day at a Time*.

As it proved, Maude's spin-off wasn't shy of Guest Relatives. Between blood relations and the various characters' ex-spouses, quite a few showed up. In a nod to TV history, Maude even hosted her own sharp-tongued "Maude's Aunt" (7 March 1977). Aunt Lola was played by Eve Arden, a Bea Arthur prototype in her sardonic tone and mastery of timing. She'd starred in a pioneer sitcom about a single working woman, *Our Miss Brooks* (1952–1956), although it finally capitulated to marrying her off. That was the series' "happy ending" and there'd be no question of divorce. As the 1970s Virginia Slims ads used to say while promoting their cancer sticks, "You've come a long way, baby."

Meanwhile, audiences responded to *Maude* in much the same way that her theme song spoke of Isadora Duncan: "the first bra burner – and you're glad she showed up."

No matter how the connection to Edith Bunker was made, everyone – except Archie and those like him – was glad when Maude showed up. The series would be in the Top Ten during the first four of its six seasons, and a lot of sitcom history was made along the way.

When the Bunkers fall sick, the left-wing liberal Maude (Bea Arthur) comes to take care of them, much to the bigoted and conservative Archie's (Carroll O'Connor) disdain in "Cousin Maude" from All in the Family.

"Edith's Problem" from *All in the Family*
Original Air Date: 8 January 1972
By J.R. Taylor

"Hey, Arch," says Michael Stivic, "look at this weather you're gonna have! Orlando, Florida – high of 84 degrees!"

You wouldn't expect a classic episode of *All in the Family* (1971–1979) to start with a weather report. The legendary sitcom made headlines by courting controversy as Archie Bunker displayed his regular guy conservative beliefs amid all kinds of taboo subjects. *All in the Family* took on integration, premarital sex, gun control, and even had a touching series of stories about transgendered gal Beverly LaSalle.

But one of the show's most acclaimed scripts came with a bizarre subplot. "Edith's Problem" was one of the first shows to address the then-touchy issue of menopause. The end of a woman's menstrual cycle had previously been referred to as simply "the change." New hormone therapy, however, had become tied into the feminist movement as a liberating development that mixed the personal and the political.

So, of course, did *All in the Family* – but the story of Edith Bunker's own liberation has the backdrop of a trip to Walt Disney World in Orlando. Archie's so excited that he doesn't even argue with his son-in-law's take on the weather. Edith was originally excited, too, but Archie tells Mike and his daughter Gloria that "a funny thing happened."

"I come in and I said, 'Edith, the lodge is springing for a special charter flight down there for the weekend, you know. So she starts jumping up and down laughing, and then – I think it was about the third jump – she come down crying… that's screwy even for your mother.'"

Archie has to be reminded that Edith's still out shopping for dinner. She comes through the door to a typical Archie greeting: "There ya are. Gee, we're waiting here. We're starving!"

Edith's response is atypical. "Don't you rush me, Archie Bunker!" she declares. "You'll get your dinner on time! You always get your dinner on time. And don't you forget that, neither!"

Then she's just as dismissive of Gloria. Archie sincerely tries to reach out, attempting to figure why his wife is upset. Edith isn't interested, though, replying: "If you're asking for a fight, you're going to get one!"

"Leave me alone, damn it," she adds while going into the kitchen. That leaves the audience as shocked as poor Archie, who asks: "Did she really say that?"

The entire family is only more confused when Edith then swings back through the swinging door with a mood swing – carrying Archie a beer and saying, "It's so nice to be home!"

A confused Edith assures everyone that she's feeling great and is "all set" and "looking forward" to her upcoming trip down to Florida. Archie is eager to show Edith a magazine with "a whole article in here, Edith, on Disney World here."

(This is a good time to note that Disney World gets a lot of love here. The darkest moment is when Archie boasts that a good pal of his "wants to go to Disney World to die!" Other moments almost turn the sitcom into a proper infomercial for the newly-opened theme park. There's certainly some chance that a few *All in the Family* insiders enjoyed the early months of Disney World with some compensated stays.)

Mike distracts Archie with a debate about Mickey Mouse, while Edith suddenly gets upset over how the house has gotten hot. Archie sees that the living room window is already open, and they start arguing about the electricity bill – ending with Archie's catch phrase of "Stifle yourself, Edith!"

This time, however, Edith doesn't go along: "Oh, that's a terrible thing to say… how can you say that to me?" She runs crying back into the kitchen.

"After 23 years of stifles," marvels Archie, "the dingbat turns on me!"

Archie decides he's going to step out to borrow some suitcases for the vacation. Gloria tells Mike to go along, too, as Edith comes back from the kitchen crooning, "I'm in the mood for love…"

Fortunately, Gloria has been looking at the kind of magazine that Archie and Mike don't bother reading: "There's an article here that I think applies to you. It explains why you've been having those hot and cold spells lately… don't you see? The forgetfulness, the hot flashes – it's the change of life!"

This is bad news for Edith, who still believes in the old unenlightened ways. She's thinking that she's too young for menopause to happen. "And when it does," Edith adds, "it can turn you into an old woman!"

"It's a natural, beautiful time of life," assures Gloria. "There's nothing to worry about. It says right here, nowadays, with simple hormone treatments, there are no unpleasant manifestations."

"Well," counters Edith, "my Aunt Elizabeth went through this and she didn't get manifestations. She got a mustache… When Archie hears about this, he ain't gonna love me no more!"

The generation gap is also acknowledged by Edith's shame at having to learn this belated fact of life from her daughter: "Imagine you having to tell me what's wrong. When I was a young girl, I didn't know what every young girl should know. Now I'm going to be an old lady, and I don't know what every old lady should know!"

Edith tries to put on a brave face as Archie and Mike return with the luggage – only to melt down over the black bags. "Black is for funerals, not a vacation!"

Archie tries to calm her down with another pitch for Disney World. He reads from the brochure to a protesting Edith, who finally says: "Stifle!"

The response is like when Zira first speaks in *Escape from the Planet of the Apes* (1971). Edith keeps going, too, screeching: "We ain't going to Disney World, or any other world!"

A commercial break finds Archie and Gloria at a diner after he's been talked into a visit with Edith's gynecologist. "Mom's alright, isn't she?" Gloria asks. "The doctor didn't say that she was going through anything more than menopause?"

Archie confirms that the "groinecologist" said Edith's health was fine, but he wasn't happy about having the conversation. "It's important that you understand about this time in Ma's life," insists Gloria.

"I ain't understood no time in your mother's life!"

"You're just gonna have to be patient and extra nice to her for the next couple of weeks," Gloria explains. (Medical experts might disagree, but we'll get to that later.)

Meanwhile, Mike and Edith are back home, with the mother-in-law trying to avoid the topic. "I feel like I'm starting off to the old folks' home, and that's probably what that doctor is telling Archie right now!"

She runs upstairs right before Archie and Gloria return. Mike asks what the doctor had to say. "Menopause is a tough time to be going through," Archie explains to Mike, "especially for nervous types, so he prescribed these here pills. I gotta take three of them a day."

Archie adds that he brought home some pills for Edith, too, which provides some education for the folks at home.

"These are hormones," Archie explains. "Hormones are pretty hot stuff, you know. They do a kind of, what do you call, realignment job there on your glands, since your mother-in-law's glands don't know which way they're going. And neither does she… Until these here pills take effect, you're going to be looking at Super Dingbat!"

Archie also complains that the doctor told him to be patient with Edith, and not to argue. He was happier about the hormones. That sets up a stretch where Archie tries desperately to appease Edith. He even throws in a *Twilight Zone* reference after learning his wife has used the daily newspaper's sports section to line a garbage can: "That's alright, Edith. That's a good thing."

All of that effort sends Edith crying to the kitchen again – and for good reason this time, as she explains to Gloria: "He don't mind the pot roast burning up. He don't mind the sports section in the garbage pail. He ain't talking to me! He's talking to some old lady!"

All of this sets up one of *All in the Family*'s finest contradictions. A lot of good Leftists couldn't understand how Archie Bunker quickly became such a beloved figure. As seen here, the ignorant dock worker is about to have to defy the experts who were supposed to make him all liberated. The episode's big turning point comes when Edith suddenly decides that she's not going to Florida – and tells Archie they're going to Scranton, Pennsylvania, to visit her cousin Emily.

Archie tries to go along by talking about how much he likes Emily's family, but snaps about halfway through. "I can't believe a word of anything I'm saying around here! This ain't natural… the only way you're gettin' me to go to Scranton is if some screwball hijacks the airplane! I know all about your women's troubles there, Edith, but when I had the hernia that time, I didn't make you wear the truss!"

Damn. The audience feels kind of bad about this – but it looks like *All in the Family* wasn't so liberal that it didn't believe in the occasional shock treatment. To the surprise of everyone, Edith is thrilled to have Archie lay down the law.

"He don't think I'm old," Edith tells Gloria. "He loves me!" Then she has another temper tantrum, which leaves Archie sighing, "Uh, back to the groinecologist!"

There's still a happy ending, though. "Edith's Problem" is like any VSE, with Menopause just another special guest that we'll never see again. It was only the 15th episode of the second season, but producer Norman Lear knew that the audience wasn't tuning in to see Edith telling Archie to stifle it. Even revolutionary sitcoms have a status quo to maintain.

So, despite menopause being able to go on for decades, the gynecologist is proven correct about Edith just needing a few weeks to get back to normal. That allows the episode's final seconds to feature Gloria and Mike opening the door as Archie and Edith return triumphantly from the new Happiest Place on Earth. They're even sporting Mickey Mouse ears.

You don't see it at the time, but Archie also has a Disney World shirt in his luggage that he'll wear a few times. There may have been a little kickback involved there, too. We'll probably never know – but if credited writers Burt Styler and Steve Zacharias sold out to Disney, they did it in an Emmy-winning fashion.

"Maude Meets Florida" from *Maude*
Original Air Date: 26 September 1972
By Lee Gambin

From the eighties onward, interracial friendships in television became the norm – one must think of sitcoms for instance such as *Punky Brewster* (1984–1988) and *Diff'rent Strokes* (1978–1986), and this social wonderment would more than likely be helped by varied works and as seen in various media that had paved the way. For instance, the rock musical *Hair* from the late sixties would feature white and black people on stage as pure equals and films such as *The Defiant Ones* (1958) presented the unity of race in a solid and stirring manner. However, before *Hair*, stage musicals such as *Show Boat* featured the solidarity shared between white and black people as a principal narrative point, and films such as *The Flame of New Orleans* (1941) – which had Marlene Dietrich and Theresa Harris as a pair of opportunistic charmers trying to get ahead in the world – showed us that the color divide can be blurred. But in the latter mentioned cases, the black characters would be in service to the white characters – even if they were respected and loved by their white counterparts, they were employed by them. Fast forward to the seventies and in the realm of Norman Lear driven television, the hit series *Maude* (1972–1978) presents a scrutiny on race relations and delivers a hilarious example of overbearing white liberalism going head to head with black sassy smarts cemented in the fabric of the white employer/black employee relationship.

Bea Arthur's Maude Findlay is ultimately the polar opposite to Carroll O'Connor's Archie Bunker from *All in the Family* (1971–1979); where he is a bigoted buffoon, she is a bleeding heart liberal completely devoted to ensuring that she is forever on the "right side" of political correctness. However, what makes these two iconic characters so wonderful is their complexity and vulnerability, as well as what makes them hilarious to watch: we laugh at Archie's ridiculous prejudices because he is so terrified about progress and reality, and we laugh at Maude because her over the top attempts to reinforce leftist attitudes are just as obnoxious. When Maude goes on about her background being very working class, she also revels in taking in cocktails mid-afternoon since her middle class life with her most recent husband Walter (Bill Macy), who has done pretty well for himself with his hardware store, has allowed her such privilege. The Findlays are the epitome of white American middle class sensibilities and a couple who can afford some frills, such as having a domestic tend to menial duties such as cleaning.

This early episode from the first season of *Maude* opens with our titular heroine – a woman compared to the likes of Lady Godiva, Joan of Arc and Betsy Ross in the theme song – preparing to meet a new maid that she has just hired. In preparation for the maid's arrival, Maude frantically cleans the house, which in itself is a joke: cleaning up for someone who is going to be paid to do just that. With a subplot that involves Maude's take on Walter's handle of her grandchild Phillip (Brian Morrison), the only child of Maude's single daughter Carol (Adrienne Barbeau), the episode establishes everybody's stance on Maude's jaw dropping embarrassing white guilt that will eventually drive the maid in question, the earthy and brilliant Florida Evans (Esther Rolle) crazy.

Carol is a single mom and hard done by, forced to live with her mother, she is also the show's anchor of reason and sparkling intelligence, measured and always calling out her mother's overbearing liberalism. Maude insists to her that "we do not say 'maid'" and Carol confronts her with "I suppose we're getting another black housekeeper" forcing her mother to look at her obsession with trying to do good, but ultimately coming across as cringeworthy in her social justice carry ons. Carol tells her "You see black and you melt" to which Maude disagrees, followed by the excellent line that summarizes white guilt: "A black man says 'Hello', and you say 'Sorry'!" Maude denies such observations, but as soon as Florida enters the scene, we get the sense that Carol is most completely correct.

Florida Evans is an instant hit, not only with the mix of the characters already established in *Maude,* but also with critics and audiences. She arrives already ribbing Maude with "I heard you all the way from the bus stop", commenting on Maude's volume (Maude and Walter would have the loudest fights in the history of television) and with that also showcases her lady like politeness referring to Carol as "mam". Maude is shocked by this and insists that everyone know one another as their first name, however Florida's comeback counters this by insisting that Maude call her "Mrs. Evans" generating roaring laughter from the studio audience. Carol and Florida get along beautifully; they understand each other and an instant friendship is made ("I like you Florida, you're funny" "Thank you honey"), but Maude is so detached from the world even though she feels that she has the finger on the pulse of it and is obsessed with making sure that black people love her that she misses the point – she doesn't see Florida as a person, but as a representation. Although Maude wants Florida to feel like one of the family, she undermines the position that justifies her being there; that is, to be a housekeeper and to get on with her work. What makes the initial meeting of these powerhouse women so wonderful to watch is knowing that Bea Arthur and Esther Rolle were loving and loyal friends. Their beautiful chemistry and how they work together as two masters of their craft (acting and comedy) is a wonder to unfold in front of one's eyes, and the sense of these two truly being bosom buddies is the icing on the cake.

Florida's sharp sass and her pride in that she works on her own merits is a testament to her intelligence and wit, while Maude's display of well-meaning good intention and the absolute pure dedication to ensuring that there is true equality between the races is a marking of her strength as a human being – even though she might go around it the wrong way. "It's your fawning over her that's the problem" remarks Carol, while Maude speaks for Florida and really has no need to. When she refers to her as an old fashioned pre-liberated Negro it comes with her wishing to "teach" Florida a newfound sense of self-respect here, the white liberal tries to enlighten and empower the black working class. While Maude screams about the rights of black people, Florida praises the notion of respecting the "privacy of the individual" and this is summarized in the issue of Maude insisting Florida walk in and out of the front door because using the back door has archaic racial overtones, suggesting that black people were not "good enough" to use the door that hits the main street of address. Florida wants to use the back door because it's quicker to the bus stop to get home, but Maude is outraged by such a "regressive" response. In a fantastic quip, Florida refers to Maude as the N.A.A.C.P – an organization renowned from protecting the rights of African Americans.

Maude would get a serving of "butt out white liberal pro-black person" in a follow up episode devoted to Florida entitled "Florida's Problem" which introduced Florida's husband Henry (John Amos) who would eventually evolve into James Evans in the spin-off sitcom *Good Times* (1974–1979), which was made possible because of the popularity of Esther Rolle in *Maude*. In that episode in question, Florida sides with Maude as a fellow woman, and the race issue is sidelined and becomes an issue of men versus women. Maude and Florida's charged relationship is also one fueled on absolute respect, admiration and love for one another – as Carol points out in "Maude Meets Florida" the two bawdy broads are not at all unlike one another.

Harking back to what is originally mentioned in this essay is the fact that Maude has hired Florida as a maid, but is she really that desperate for domestic help? The question of Maude hiring a black maid just so she can have a "black friend" that she sees regularly pops up and in many ways it doesn't matter once the two characters share screen time throughout the early run of the series. Eventually Maude would definitely need a maid and Florida's replacement would be the kooky British white housekeeper Mrs. Naugatuck (Hermione Baddeley). Florida snaps "What do you mean improve myself?" in response to Maude wanting Florida to be proud and wanting to be an "equal". Florida likes the way things are and wants to simply do her work, and in her eyes, she is more than equal to the easily agitated, screaming Maude. When it comes time for "Florida's Goodbye" in the second season, which would pave the way for Florida/Rolle to star in her own sitcom *Good Times*, we get the wonderful sense that Maude and Florida are far more than employer and housekeeper – they are more certainly good friends, and more importantly soul sisters.

A black/white TV friendship that did not rely on housekeeper and home owner as its backbone was the glorious union shared between the eternally loving Edith Bunker (Jean Stapleton) and feisty fun loving Louise Jefferson (Isabel Sanford), who showed America what it could be in *All in the Family*. If the bigoted and angry Archie and George Jefferson (Sherman Hemsley) represented what the United States was – loaded with prejudice and disdain – then the friendship of these two women came to represent what could be. In a switch of race and class as seen in *Maude*, here, Louise is a black woman who gets to be wealthy and "move on up", while Edith, the white woman remains poor in a low class neighborhood. Louise outclasses Maude, while Florida and Edith share the financial struggle that Norman Lear proudly examined on network prime time TV. However, the friendships shared between these four women transcended both class and race, and what we are left with are beautiful women who have found one another even if their husbands are completely devoid of understanding or tolerance.

In the *All in the Family* episode "The Jeffersons Move On Up" (which would be the backdoor pilot for *The Jeffersons* (1975–1985), another spin-off, like *Maude*, of *All in the Family*) Edith asks Louise "Did I ever tell you I loved you?", to which Louise replies "Every minute we spent together", and this is what these TV friendships are about: unity, solidarity and tenderness.

Queens of TV: Esther Rolle and Bea Arthur, out and about and taking a moment from their work together on Maude *(which would spin-off* Good Times, *a starring vehicle for Rolle).*

"Gloria and the Riddle" from *All in the Family*
Original Air Date: 7 October 1972
By Lee Gambin

By 1972, the second wave feminist movement was fully in the public consciousness and cultural and political awareness of women's liberation was something that was documented in living rooms all across the globe. Norman Lear, the creator of *All in the Family* (1971–1979) (as well as its spin-offs such as *Maude* (1972–1978)), would also introduce the world to the Bunker family who were made up of conservative bigot Archie (Carroll O'Connor), long suffering openhearted Edith (Jean Stapleton), liberal and assertively leftist Mike (Rob Reiner) and possibly the most complex of them all, Gloria (Sally Struthers), a young woman caught in the cultural turbulence of seventies America. Norman Lear had gone on record in an interview conducted by actress and activist Whoopi Goldberg that if there were a character he was most like in his diverse universe, it would most likely be his invention Maude Findlay (Bea Arthur), the overbearing liberal who is so pro-everyone (women, black, Latino, gay etc) that sometimes her good natured leftist passions turn her into a buffoon (as laughable as Archie with his right-wing tirades). Lear has feminist ideals, and a lot of Maude Findlay was also based on his wife during the core period of his television career, Frances Lear, an activist, author and renowned women's liberationist.

However, whereas Maude was aggressively eager to prove her political agenda endlessly in the outstanding series centered on her relationship with the world both at home and outside of it, Gloria in *All in the Family* seems to struggle with her feminist leanings in that she has more adversity pushed in her way. Gloria comes from a poor family, she has very basic education, she has married young, she has to work a low paying job in retail, she is consistently making personal sacrifices for her student husband and she has a major obstacle in that her father is the most anti-feminist person she will possibly ever know. In "Gloria and the Riddle", the blonde sweetheart fights for her rights as a vocal feminist in a household that seems to either ridicule the ideology or not see value in it.

The opening conversation between Edith and Gloria begins with talk about Archie, and when Gloria attempts to tell her mother the riddle her feminist friend told her, she is interrupted by Edith rushing off to see to the breakfast for Archie. Here in this opening sequence, we understand the prescribed "place" for Edith, that she is there to ensure that Archie is happy and that her endless servitude to her husband is never interrupted and that ritual and family tradition are upheld. Entering the scene is Mike, who is under great stress and moans like a man-child when his favorite shirt has been rendered buttonless since being put in the wash by Gloria. He barks at her "Didn't I tell you to fix it?", and the defiant Gloria responds with "Sew it on yourself!" She adds:

"Where is it written down that a woman has to do all the sewing?" and the role of women and the role of men is examined in a tiny splice of screen time, but profound in its message. Mike may consider himself a liberal and care about the rights of blacks and other minorities, however his stance on feminism is something that needs thorough scrutiny in that he still has old fashioned beliefs as to what women are supposed to do. When Mike's cry of "You're my wife!" bellows out through the rickety walls of the shabby Queens home, there is an understanding that this is a relationship that is not without its issues or concerns. Gloria is liberating herself from being conditioned, and that is what this episode examines – the concept of how everyone, both women and men, are systematically prescribed certain roles and cultural understandings (and misunderstandings). Gloria clearly states early in the episode that if she wants to do something then she will do it, but she will not do it simply because she is expected to do it because she is a woman. Throughout the series, her father Archie refers to her as "little girl", an interesting choice of pet name for her, in that it both serves as an oppressive put down as well as a desperate cling on to hold onto something that renders the young lady as someone who will always be "daddy's little girl". Also, Gloria herself is a character not without her infantile mannerisms – in some episodes she would don Shirley Temple style hair, she whines and cries like a baby and matches her father's juvenile raspberries to a tea. However, her intelligence is burning and sharp – this is no "dumb blonde"; here is a wise beyond her years woman, sensitive to the harsh cruelty of a world that looks down on her and misjudges her.

Archie complaining about breakfast jettisons Gloria's anger ("We're just paid servants!"), and while the cantankerous taxi driver head of the household questions Mike's manhood when the young Polack tries to sew the button on his shirt himself (but injures his finger in the process), Gloria asserts her feminist leanings by teaching her father about the origins of "male chauvinist", eschewing some great jokes from the naïve Edith about the historical French officer Chauvin. The episode introduces Tammy Robinson (Patricia Stitch), an out and proud feminist character, who is influencing Gloria and helping her along the way into finding independence through the women's liberation movement. Tammy is an exceptionally well written character in that she is not at all two dimensional, she is not only intelligent and stoic in her political beliefs, but she is also compassionate and warm. She also surprises Archie in that she shares his love for big band musicians of the thirties and forties, and in many ways Archie admires that aspect of her, but still finds it hard to accept her feminist principles because they just do not sit well with his own take on the place of women in the world.

Into the fold comes the titular riddle of the piece, which basically when summarized discusses the issue of women being respected and regarded as surgeons in the medical field. When the riddle is delivered by Gloria, the entire clan cannot figure it out, and with Archie the most affected by being baffled by something a woman has put to him, it sends him crazy and heading over to Kelsey's Bar for drinks with the boys where he tries it out on his pals. Needless to say, none of these men can figure it out either. With the show powered by inspired and hilarious writing, including Edith's wonderful rant about seeing a production of *Peter Pan* sparked from Archie talking about "female fairies" (a dyke joke in hiding) in response to disdain over Gloria joining a feminist group, the gags cement a thoughtful expose of sexist attitudes towards women that seem to be institutionalized. Even when Archie spits out: "Nobody is listening to you, Edith", his sentiment is clear even in this throwaway joke. Archie's primary disgust in women liberationists is that they don't want to simply be wives and mothers and yet the way he talks to his own wife (and mother of his daughter) is disrespectful and without any care of potential repercussions.

An extension of his bigotry comes from when Mike drops his hushed sexism for a moment and makes the statement "Women make some of the finest leaders there ever were", which ends with Archie's anti-Semitic remark and then an anti-Indian quip that is both hilarious and yet telling. Gloria summarizes this perfectly: "He's a result of centuries of conditioning". When she and Tammy follow this up reading religious doctrine from Christian, Jewish and Islamic scriptures that attack women, we understand that oppression is a serious thing. Archie may not see it, but many women watching the episode cheered on Gloria and her struggles as a young working class girl fueling her liberation with the advent of a movement that gave her strength.

Religion stays on topic in regards to feminism for a moment (Norman Lear's team of writers thoroughly understood how to cover all aspects of social change and questioning, and also did it with complexity and not painting things in clean blacks and whites) where Mike makes the gag: "When I hear things like that I thank God I'm an Atheist" and it is discovered that Tammy goes to church but doesn't believe everything that church says. As aforementioned about Lear's writing staff, this addition to her character makes her more interesting – she may be Christian but she is devoutly feminist (here in *All in the Family*, you can be both). Abortion laws are mentioned with Gloria's stance being "men have no right to tell a woman what they can do with their bodies" and that is controversial subject matter for Archie who hates the very notion of abortion being a topic of conversation on a Sunday.

Finally, after much head scratching over the riddle, the loveable Edith works it out: "The surgeon was the boy's mother!" What is so lovely here is that the young ladies Gloria and Tammy applaud Edith and are so happy their elder gets it; here Edith Bunker has championed the feminist movement without even knowing she has. With supposedly liberal Mike's own sexism realized ("We have all been conditioned to believe that only men can be surgeons"), Gloria is able to shine and grow as a young woman who can make her own mind up and feel empowered by the fact that women can do whatever they want in America of the seventies.

"The Puerto Ricans Are Coming" from *Sanford and Son*
Original Air Date: 10 November 1972
By Dennis Capicik

According to the U.S. Census Bureau from 2016, Puerto Ricans accounted for roughly 1.7% of the population in the United States, and to this day, one of the largest demographics remains in New York City. Although Harlem was – and is – still considered a predominantly African American neighborhood, East Harlem (more commonly referred to as Spanish Harlem or *El Barrio*) has always been a real melting-pot of ethnicities, mainly comprising Jewish, Italian, and later, Puerto Rican immigrants, who, following the Jones Act in 1917, which established Puerto Rico as a U.S. Commonwealth, Puerto Ricans began to migrate to the United States in vast numbers. As a result, over time, East Harlem became the largest Latino community in New York City.

This influx of immigration and the everyday struggles the Puerto Ricans faced eventually became the impetus for Leonard Bernstein's and Stephen Sondheim's 1957 stage musical *West Side Story*; then later, in 1961, Robert Wise's and Jerome Robbins' cinematic adaptation, which remains an expertly-choreographed, eye-popping musical that is both brilliant and highly influential. But at its core, it is a film about intolerance.

Puerto Rican culture is once again placed in the spotlight in this VSE of *Sanford and Son*, and despite the comedic context, features another convincing condemnation of racial prejudice and ignorance, something which, unfortunately, even today, continues to be a deadly serious issue not only in the United States but the world over.

Cantankerous as ever, Fred Sanford (the inimitable Redd Foxx) is becoming increasingly annoyed because "some stupid jerk" who bought the once-vacant property next door, continues to make a bunch of noise. As he hopelessly tries to finish a crossword puzzle, Fred asks his son Lamont if their new neighbor is a "brutha", and of course, being far more open-minded, Lamont frustratingly responds, "What difference does *that* make?! Good neighbors come in *all* colors!" But Fred obviously doesn't think so, especially when he finds out his new neighbor is Puerto Rican ("That's it! There goes the neighborhood!"). Sure enough, Lamont chastises him immediately for this comment, but Fred vehemently replies, "Puerto Ricans run-down every neighborhood they get into! Look what they did to Harlem!" Even though Lamont and Fred's long-time if rather dim-witted friend Melvin (Slappy White) agrees that "Harlem was a ghetto long before any Puerto Ricans moved in", Fred uses this as a springboard to prove his point that Harlem was in fact a "paradise" before the Puerto Ricans' arrival.

While it's never made clear, perhaps the "paradise" Fred's referring to is the "Harlem renaissance" when, in the years prior to the Great Depression, Harlem and its African American population had been thriving both culturally and economically. Following this once-prosperous social climate within the Harlem community, which remains influential to this day, the neighborhood began to feel the effects of both the Great Depression and the aftermath of World War II, when it was crippled by a number of socioeconomic difficulties, which lasted until well into the seventies. High unemployment rates, dilapidated tenements (which led to ongoing rent strikes throughout the neighborhood), race riots, drugs and even gang warfare were just a few of the struggles that plagued Harlem for decades. Harlem was no longer a "paradise", but a neighborhood striving to find its identity once again amidst an ever-changing – and deteriorating – social climate beset with racial discrimination, police brutality, barely-livable housing and an escalating cross-cultural contempt among its many different ethnicities, an attitude which Fred Sanford – however foolishly – still harbors many years later with his resentment towards the Puerto Rican people and culture.

Even though Lamont tries to calm Fred's hostilities ("You're gettin' yourself worked up all over nuthin'!"), Fred's tirade against Puerto Ricans is relentless, especially when it revolves around Harlem (which further illustrates the importance and impact this former cultural mecca had on America's African American citizens). In one rather ridiculous yet hilariously silly monologue, he offers his thoughts on Harlem's cockroach and rat infestations. "Before the Puerto Ricans moved into Harlem there was not one cockroach in Harlem. *They* brought 'em there!" And then he goes on to explain that they also brought all the rats into the neighborhood in order to "kill all the Puerto Rican cockroaches!" Even as he learns his new neighbor's name, no insult is spared, "Julio Fuentes?! That sounds like something you get from drinkin' their water!"

Making his *Sanford and Son* debut as Julio Fuentes, Gregory Sierra is a prolific actor who has appeared in countless TV shows over the past four decades. Outside of his memorable role in *Sanford and Son*, he is perhaps best-known for his role as Det. Sgt. Chano Amenguale on *Barney Miller* (1975–1976), but he also appeared in numerous films, including Ted Post's *Beneath the Planet of the Apes* (1970), Franklin J. Schaffner's *Papillon* (1973) and John Guillermin's *The Towering Inferno* (1974). Sierra is excellent throughout his tenure on *Sanford and Son*, delivering plenty of youthful idealistic energy into his role, and, along with Lamont, plays well alongside Fred G. Sanford's set-in-his-ways, cranky 'ol codger main character.

When a goat wanders into Fred's living room through an open door, Fred is immediately startled, and begins to feign the expected heart attack, but this goat turns out to be Chico, Julio's pet goat (or as Fred so eloquently puts it, a "Puerto Rican poodle"!). Not the best of introductions, Lamont tries to lighten the mood when he offers some food for thought: "How'd you like it if the guy next door turned against people from Africa?" But Fred offers one of his typically selfish responses, saying, "I don't care, as long as they don't turn against people from St. Louis!" Tensions escalate quickly, but Julio, in his pet goat's defense, quips, "I would rather live with a young goat that gives milk than an old goat who gives trouble!"

In spite of the "bad vibes", Julio feels that Fred isn't such a bad "*chamaco*" (i.e., "kid") and offers a most sincere, heartfelt apology for not coming over in the first place to properly introduce himself. As a token of his appreciation and to quell the tensions, Julio attempts to gift him with some homemade goat's milk cheese. Even then, however, Fred remains steadfast in his pigheadedness. "I only like *American* cheese, and you can't get American cheese from a Puerto Rican goat!" At this point, Julio has had enough and admits, "You are an impossible person, Mr. Sanford! Like a fool, I tried to be your friend, but you refuse! *E También*! You will not see me around here again! You *sangano* ['jackass']!"

In hopes of having Julio removed from his newly-purchased property, Fred launches a complaint ("His place is unfit to live in!") with the county building inspector (Larry Blake) because he doesn't "want the beauty of his community destroyed!", but Fred's underhanded scheme backfires when Julio receives a "Citation of Neighborhood Improvement" from the county of Los Angeles for contributing to the betterment of his community; Fred, on the other hand, receives a $200.00 fine for a number of building code violations on his own property. A fitting comeuppance indeed!

Although Julio has already – however unsuccessfully – attempted to ingratiate himself with Fred, in yet another neighborly gesture, Julio brings over a further culinary delight to help placate the situation. This time, instead of cheese, it is one of Fred's very favorite dishes ("Spare ribs, candy-sweet potatoes and mustard greens!"). Earning his immediate respect and gratitude, Fred and Julio become instant "*amigos*", and when Lamont asks where he learned to cook like that, Julio, rather excitedly, replies, "I learned all that while I was living in New York! I lived in Harlem, you know!" Sure enough, Fred happily responds, "If all Puerto Ricans were like you, Harlem would be a *paradise*!"

In spite of the pair's newfound friendship, Julio and Puerto Rican culture in general remained the butt of many a joke in such later episodes as "Julio and Sister and Nephew", wherein Fred facetiously implies he has a disease called the "creeping *cucarachas*" to avoid looking after Julio's nephew; and in "Watts Side Story" (which further establishes the enormous influence of Wise's film), Lamont is dating Julio's sister María (Migdia Skarsgard Chinea) and is besieged by both Fred and Julio's mother (Alma Beltran) for their interracial affair, in yet another episode that confronts racial prejudice head-on.

Demond Wilson and Redd Foxx as Lamont and Fred Sanford in Sanford and Son, *an American reworking on the BBC's* Steptoe and Son.

"Maude's Dilemma" from *Maude*
Original Air Dates: 14 November 1972 (Part 1) and 21 November 1972 (Part 2)
By Lee Gambin
With Very Special insight from actress Adrienne Barbeau

One of the most groundbreaking of Very Special Episodes in the history of the phenomena and the most widely discussed and controversial would be "Maude's Dilemma" from the Norman Lear produced series *Maude* (1972–1978) – a sitcom about a feisty, strong minded, highly opinionated liberal as played by the force of nature that is Bea Arthur. This episode would find its genesis in the foundation of a competition of sorts – health care activist group Zero Population Growth had announced a prize sum of ten thousand dollars for comedy series and variety shows to come up with comedic takes on how to combat over population and the issues that come with that. Writers on the show came up with the issue of vasectomy, but Lear opted for abortion – something that was seldom brought up in conversation and most certainly never discussed in depth on a television series. There had been illegal abortions occur on soap operas prior to this double episode of *Maude*, however to have the central character in a comedic arena openly discussing a woman's right to choose was a brave and solid decision from Lear, his team and the legendary cast who would speak the highly political, but more importantly very human and very honest, words that would generate and spark debate across America.

The episode opens with an open feminist conversation as the focal point with single mother Carol (Adrienne Barbeau) and housekeeper Florida (Esther Rolle) dissecting the question of the title of "Ms.", something that liberated women of the second wave feminist movement would adopt as a way to establish an inroad with men in regards to marital status. Of course, the feminist periodical "Ms. Magazine" heralded by leading voice of the movement Gloria Steinem was making a profound impact on the culture of the seventies and a series like *Maude* was a terrific extension of all of this. The episode then explodes with vibrant agitation and anger only ever done splendidly by the super talented Bea Arthur who storms into the scene mighty pissed off. She storms in hitting herself as if in a state of self-punishment, which is comical of course but in retrospect there is something pretty dark going on there when you consider horrific methods women had to resort to in order to abort pregnancies prior to the medical practice becoming rightfully legal.

Maude finally confides in her best friend Vivian (Rue McClanahan) and their friendship is referred to as a "sisterhood", therefore more feminist tropes paint the picture of this brilliantly crafted and constructed double episode. The writing and performances and the way in which the first episode and especially the opening moments ring out hilarity and full throttle comic excellence is a testament to the VSE at its best being a construct that begins with the familiar (comic) and then evolving into something else (dramatic). When Maude tells Vivian of her pregnancy, actress Rue McClanahan gets to play off the response with a cheekiness and masterful command, and it matches the audience's response, however, as much as the episode begins with all the comical aspects of Maude being pregnant in her more "senior" years, later it will drive in seriousness at the helm of Carol and her concern for her mother's health and her advice on how abortion is now a safe and legal and healthy option. Florida's response to the news is also incredibly admirable: "If you're sorry, I'm sorry" – emphasizing pure empathy. The show will then tackle the truth of the matter, that abortion is now an option for women legally, and that women are in charge of their own bodies, regardless of what state or church says or judges, and that conservatives need to keep out of the way of a woman and her body and what she chooses to do with it.

Gloria Steinem, Betty Friedan and leading feminists rally for the women's movement, and a TV sitcom like Maude *reflects a lot of the same sentiment.*

The legality of abortion and having to tell husband Walter (Bill Macy) are the two components that bring the first part of this two part VSE home and while neighbor Arthur (Conrad Bain) is more excited to see Walter's expression when he hears the news, while Carol voices her anger at how women are treated when the issue of the pill is brought up and she even poses the question of when men will take responsibility of birth control. Carol's point about overpopulation is made clear and when Walter finally enters, he is initially ignored but then comes to understand that there is news to be shared. Maude has something to tell him and his first response is anxiety about his car. This enrages Maude ("Not Maude are you sick? Maude are you unhappy?") as concern about the car is more important than her well-being (another aside to the feminist argument, that women are neglected and seen even secondary to automobiles), but Walter comes through and asks what it is that is upsetting Maude, when she tells him, he chokes on a chicken bone, and Macy's handle at physical comedy takes the floor.

But it is Carol's incredible speech and advice for Maude that truly is the star of this first part of this super important VSE. Carol sees that her mother's "late in life" pregnancy is clearly distressing her, and so she offers support that is both warm and compassionate but also a war cry for women celebrating that finally abortion laws have come into play and they can choose what they want to do with their bodies without guilt. She reminds her mother that the procedure is not what it was like back when she was growing up and Carol's loving insight even has Walter being impressed and leads him to an honorable decision to consider having a vasectomy (men's response to birth control). By the end of the first part, Walter expresses his love for Maude by telling her "Whatever you decide", symbolizing a man ready to stand by his woman in her decision.

But of course the complexities of the piece and the treatment of the issue at hand are not so cut and dry. The beginning of the second episode has Carol convince Maude not to have the baby and to not feel guilty nor be afraid of making that decision. It is also made clear that Maude is a character who strongly supports the right to choose agenda, however, being pregnant changes her clear principles there – she is confused by the notion seeing that she is now in this predicament. This is a great choice by the writer Susan Harris (who will of course later created legendary shows such as *Soap* (1977–1981) and *The Golden Girls* (1985–1992)) who powers the script with the complex multi-dimensions it needs in order to both paint up Maude's politics as not so black and white when the matters at hand are so personal and close to home. Shockingly, Maude explains that she will have the baby, and while Carol worries that it is risky at her age, Maude believes that Walter wants the baby because he never had the chance to be a father. Much protest from Carol sends Maude into a retelling of her impoverished backstory where she explains that her poor background, raising Carol, was what gave her trepidation in having another child now later in life, but now with some money behind her with Walter, the possibility of a baby isn't so nerve wracking.

Another addition to this story is the introduction of the neighborhood friend Lorraine (Elisabeth Fraser) who has a bunch of kids and in her late thirties, approaching forty, she is pregnant again and very happy to have the child ("What's another baby?"). This character was a prerequisite from CBS for Susan Harris to write in, as a somewhat "opposing view", presenting a woman not in her twenties who was happy to have a baby "later in life". The character's messy existence does not at all suit Maude, who is independent from the rearing of children and quite happy about that, even though she makes a terrific and passionate grandmother to Carol's son Phillip (Brian Morrison).

The episode finally positions Maude and Walter in a pit stop that has them both not truly knowing what each other want, and its treatment of the male perspective is hilarious because it comes from a place of fear, anxiety and reluctance to help. Walter and Arthur's discussion at the bar is centered around talk on vasectomies and a friend Harry (Robert Mandan) makes a brief appearance as someone who has had the procedure and is enjoying a very healthy active sex life with his wife, ensuring Walter that "nothing changes" when you have the operation. Incidentally, actor Mandan would appear in a future episode of *Maude* entitled "Maude's New Friend" about Maude's newfound friendship with a gay author who is obnoxious and cruel to Walter causing the cast of characters to look into their own personal hang ups (notably Maude who comes to understand her overbearing liberalism can actually be as offensive as outward bigotry). But Mandan's character here is "what could be" in the case of Walter actually following through with a vasectomy which would ensure no more worry about unwanted pregnancy in their "autumn years" – seeing that the pill does not agree with Maude (as stated early on in the first episode).

The last sequence in Maude and Walter's bedroom is the climactic moment that speaks volumes and touches a nerve. Walter never wanted to be a father; here is a confession he makes where he refers to fatherhood as an "ambition", something that

The revolutionary "Maude's Dilemma" from Maude: *Maude (Bea Arthur) gets some daughterly comfort from Carol (Adrienne Barbeau) who explains to her that having an abortion is not the terrifying procedure once known to women Maude's age.*

he never had the drive for ("I do love kids, but they don't have to be mine"), and once again, he makes an excellent step-grandfather to young Phillip. He also admits "I think it would be wrong to have a child at our age", to which Maude tearfully agrees. When he then confesses to not having a vasectomy, Maude doesn't mind, the object of conversation here is the concern of having the baby or not and committing to an abortion. Maude has made up her mind, she wishes to take Carol's advice and take control of this unwanted pregnancy and terminate it – a powerful statement made by a television character which would spark conversation across the United States and also generate a lot of hatred from conservative groups who would send in letters, death threats and organize pickets. Feminists of the period championed the episode and its stance – most notably for the conversation had between wife and husband in their bedroom sitting on their bed talking about such private and personal matters, and that the decision was all coming from the wife. Maude tearfully asks "Tell me I'm doing the right thing" – a question that humanizes the freedom of choice amendment, making the political personal. Walter's reply is one of tenderness and understanding, also furthering his newfound understanding of a woman's right to choose, he says "From the privacy of our own lives, you're doing the right thing." This reinforces the stance of good men who will stand by the women they love in whatever decision said women make. The episode ends with Maude declaring an undying love for her husband: "I love you Walter Findlay."

Initially, Norman Lear opted out of the idea of Maude having a false alarm or a "phantom pregnancy" as he felt that would lend itself to great jokes, yes, but also be an easy out, and something that would not possibly hit as hard with the same impact. Also, miscarriage was another issue that he strayed from seeing that his series *All in the Family* (1971–1979) dealt with that in the tearjerker Very Special Episode "Gloria Has A Belly Full", where Gloria (Sally Struthers) falls pregnant but loses the baby – an episode that will end with her crotchety father Archie (Carroll O'Connor) finally showing us that he is in fact sensitive and human, mournfully tending to his daughter who painfully suggests that she "didn't do a good job, did I daddy?" In that episode, we feel the sense of loss of miscarriage and it carries through from the emotionally aware characters like Gloria right through to the hard as nails tough guys like her old pops Archie, and here in "Maude's Dilemma", the struggles of a character as equally fiery as him, here in the guise of Maude Findlay, the concept of having an unwanted baby is an inversion of the matter: that older people are not equipped to handle the long years of responsibility of child rearing. Maude is also a dedicated careerist, and as the series progresses she would involve herself in the world of politics, with the series ending with her entering the professional arena of this world, and even meeting a younger variant of herself which would solidify an interesting point that the series makes: that there are women out there, young and old, who think and act like Maude.

A woman's right to choose what happens to her body becomes a major focal point in the Second Wave feminist movement and is reflected in the special double episode "Maude's Dilemma" from Maude.

ADRIENNE BARBEAU: Up until the time I did *Maude* in 1972, I had been on stage. I never watched television. I didn't know what was going on. I had no frame of reference. I [became] aware as we were filming *Maude* that it was very special. Once I came out to L.A. and started doing the show, then I was introduced to *All in the Family*. But I didn't realize how important it was in the beginning. I remember thinking this at one of our first table reads. We'd get a script a week before we were going to film it and we would read it, and then the writers and producers would go back and rewrite what didn't work. I remember probably around the third week in sitting there and thinking, 'Oh my gosh! I am sitting here with a genius! I've never met a genius before!' and that was Norman, of course, because [he] knew how to make something work. He didn't always write the scripts from scratch, but he knew what they needed to make them so viable. The reason I think that *All in the Family* and *Maude* and then all of Norman's shows that came after were so successful was we had a point of view, we were making a social statement, but we were making it with laughter and humor, and people kept coming back. We weren't hitting anyone over the head with our philosophies. [But we dealt with] issues that had never been addressed before. I believe that Maude ... was the first divorcee single mom that I am aware of on television at the time. Maude's character had been married and divorced three times and was on her fourth marriage! I mean, you didn't see that. And of course, the topics that we dealt with. The Broadway and off-Broadway stage were breaking open and exploring things that had never been seen on stage before, and we were doing the same thing on television. We were coming out of the sixties; there had been a lot of upheaval in the culture and Norman had grabbed onto that and unfortunately most of those shows if they were to air today would be as current as they were then because in many ways our society has gone backwards. [My character] Carol was sort of the straight man. I was there to give the information and to counter Maude. I think they hired me because they realized Bea (Arthur) and I did not have the same approach to humor. We didn't have the same delivery, but I could stand up to her and still be funny and likeable, I hope. I was an actress, and I was just coming off of Broadway, and I got this television show, and I had never done television. So when I arrived, I was really sort of finding my way in a new medium, and just trying to figure out how this was all done. What Carol gave me though – the media started turning to me as a spokesperson for the issues that we were dealing with. It was the height of the Equal Rights Amendment movement. Roe v. Wade had just been passed, and so first-trimester abortion was legal in the land. Up until that point I had been an actor trying to get my career going, just dealing with life on a much more limited basis, I guess. And all of a sudden it was like, 'wait a minute. Okay. We're dealing with some life-changing issues here!' And I had to figure out how I felt about all of them. Fortunately, I was right in step with Norman. I ended up spending my hiatus working at a women's low-cost health care clinic providing first-trimester pregnancy terminations. I became a radical! Maybe as a result of doing *Maude*.

It made me examine my own feelings. And up until that point, I suppose I voted, but I don't even remember! You know we never really discussed [Carol's activism]. She was very active. I don't know if at that time she was active in PETA, but she was very involved as an animal rights person. We got a lot of negative mail. I think I've read in places [that] Bea got a lot of antagonistic mail when we did the abortion episode. I really can't speak for Bea. What she was concerned about was making every episode as good as it could be, and if that meant her giving over lines to another character because she thought they would be funnier coming from one of the rest of us in the cast, she was the first person to do that! She was one of the most incredibly giving actors I have ever worked with. Professional. And I took it all for granted at that time, so it is hard for me to really be specific because I just thought that everybody was like that. We all came from the theatre, but Bea was the first one in the rehearsal hall. She was the last one to leave. She was the first one to get up from the table and welcome a guest actor. She knew her lines before any of the rest of us. Someone later said they thought that she had a photographic memory. We would do a televised dress rehearsal. It wasn't even called that; we would do [the first show] at 5:30 with an audience. We did it straight through; everything memorized – just like a play. While we were having dinner, the writers and producers were rewriting. If this joke didn't work or that dialogue didn't make sense, if we were too long and they needed to cut the episode; if the blocking wasn't working. And then they would bring their notes to us as we were eating and we had to memorize a lot of changes. And Bea, she knew them in an instant! There was just no question. I didn't realize how exceptional that was until I went off to do other television work and all of a sudden I thought, 'wait a minute! You mean not everybody is as professional and as wonderful to work with as Bea is?' I really don't know what went on between her and Norman and what her input was in terms of the social significance of what we were doing

We started working on the [abortion episode] in July of 1972, and it didn't premiere until September of 1972. We shot the first episode of the abortion segment somewhere between July and September, but the network refused to allow us to shoot the second one until they saw the numbers for the show. And had the show not been a success we would have never aired the first one. Then, of course, when it did air [many] stations refused to air it! It did not air in the South or wherever. So that comes back to the fact that we were successful not because we were dealing with these issues, we were dealing with these issues with humor that allowed audiences to want to keep watching. I've talked about this in my memoir. Prior to 1972 – it would have been back in 1966, let's say. I helped a girlfriend get an abortion because they weren't legal in those days. I was working for someone who had contacts. But I sat with this friend as she went through – not the procedure – but immediately after when she miscarried, and it was a horrendous experience! If I had never thought about abortion prior to that, seeing what this woman went through certainly set me on a path of fighting for a woman's right to choose! And then when I did come to L.A., I started working in this little-cost health clinic providing counselling and helping the doctors, and they were doing, what was then, finally, a legal procedure. Roe v. Wade was already the law of the land. I may not have been working at the clinic when we shot this, but those words came from a deep place in me, I'm sure that I didn't have any trouble finding the reality for myself. Carroll O'Connor suffered greatly because his character was a hundred and eighty degrees on the other side of his personal philosophy. I know it was hard for Carroll to say some of the things he had to say. I was so in-step with what they were writing for Carroll. And probably because they wind up in television. You end up writing for the actor. You hear the actor's voice. I was just proud to be doing [the show]. I liked Esther (Rolle) as a person. She was a wonderful actress! So that was all easy! Everything I did I had a reason for doing it. Did I ever ask myself should I do this or this? So maybe it isn't a good thing to do? No. Everything has always been pretty clear to me. Some things I have done because I needed to do them because I needed to pay the bills! I had done some things that are absolutely

God awful! But I did them because I wanted to go to Moscow. I would never think to myself 'Oh, I'm sorry I did that.' There were a couple that were really hard to do. Specifically in terms of *Maude* I certainly didn't feel uncomfortable about anything we were doing, or I was doing.

The reason that drama worked on *Maude* is because the comedy worked. But that has nothing to do with me. That has to do with our writers and they were brilliant! I think with the comedy we weren't hitting anyone over the head with the message. We were making it palatable because we were using comedy to do that. I learned so much doing *Maude*. In the first place, I had never done television, and when we first got here, none of us had really done much television. But I immediately went 'Oh my God! I'm surrounded by people who are more talented and who know the medium'. It took me a while to find my way, and had it not been for Norman, I think anybody else would have fired me the first week because I was nervous. I wasn't working to my best, and I remember Norman saying to me 'Look if you don't trust yourself, trust me. I know you're great! Just relax and do the work.' So Norman gave me my career in many ways. You know if I had stayed on Broadway, who knows, it would have been a whole other thing. Not only did he hire me, but he stayed with me for those first couple of weeks! Especially in today's television market, if you do the first read through and you don't land with every joke, they're replacing you! The next day Norman stayed with me. So he gave me my career and then, of course, because *Maude* was so successful, that brought me to the nationwide viewing audience. And then I learned so much of what I know about comedy from working with Bea and Conrad (Bain), and Bill (Macy) and all of them, but Bea... there are times now and I hear myself deliver a line, and I think 'Oh my God. There she is!' That's Bea's timing! Nobody had timing like her. Nobody could hold it for a laugh like she could and she was just fearless. It just rubbed off on me, I think. It was a family for six years. It was a joy to go to work. It was my beginning. The only thing that she (Bea) may have been aware of was that she taught me how to cook a hard-boiled egg! Because Bea used to cover her hard-boiled eggs with Tabasco sauce and that is still how I eat my hard-boiled egg!

In regards to more groundbreaking work, the horror TV movie *Someone's Watching Me!* (1978) makes me proud because I believe that was probably the first gay woman on television. I can't think of anybody else, and no one has come forward to say. But it was just like yeah, take him for granted. That's the way it is, and it was the way he handled it. It was just spot on! By the time I did *Someone's Watching Me!*, I had a pretty large body of television/film work. My first TV movie was *The Great Houdini* (1976). Up until that point I had done stage, and I had done half-hour sitcoms which were shot like a stage play, you know, four cameras, straight through, everything memorized. So, I show up to do my first scene in *The Great Houdini*, and we do the master, and I went back to my dressing room to do the next scene because I didn't know about close-ups! The stage manager or the A.D came to the dressing room and said 'Okay, we're ready for the coverage!' I thought 'Coverage?' So I didn't know anything about that technique. But I learned what I needed to know about television acting as opposed to stage acting. In the early days of *Maude*, I learned to bring it down. John Carpenter gave me one of those electric light bulb moments in terms of acting, when we were doing *Someone's Watching Me!* We shot the first scene – I doubt that it was the lesbian reveal scene, but it may have been. John came up to me and said, 'That was great! It was just great! Do less.' And I said 'What?' and he said 'Do less. Just do less.' And all of a sudden I thought, 'Oh, of course! That's it! You're not acting for the theatre. You're not even acting for the audience for *Maude*. Do less.' And it may very well have been that scene, which is why that scene worked so well. I don't know, but I've carried it with me for the rest of my life! Until I got to *Creepshow* (1982) and then there was George Romero saying 'Oh no, you can go bigger! You can go bigger!' I owe all of that to George! You know, he just kept saying 'Yeah! Go for it. Go for it!' I'm thinking, 'Oh my God! You're not supposed to act like this in the movies!' Paul Michael Glaser played Houdini, and Vivian Vance was Houdini's mother, and Sally (Struthers) was his wife, and I was his mistress. I pretty much show up and do the work. I don't philosophize about it a lot.

Actress Adrienne Barbeau who starred as savvy single mother Carol Traynor in Maude *would become political due to her involvement in the series. She would help open a free clinic for women and be a spokesperson and activist in the women's movement.*

"Bobby's Hero" from *The Brady Bunch*
Original Air Date: 2 February 1973
By John Harrison

The fourth and penultimate season of *The Brady Bunch*, which originally aired between September 1972 and March 1973, is widely considered to be among the most consistent and memorable of the show's five-year run. It's certainly hard to argue with a season that starts off with the classic three-episode Hawaii storyline, in which the Brady clan tag along with Mike on a business trip to the islands, where local superstitions and an old tiki idol ultimately lead to an encounter in an dank cave with guest star Vincent Price. Other memorable episodes from this season include "Fright Night", "Greg Gets Grounded" and the infamous "The Subject Was Noses".

Another undoubted highlight of season four is "Bobby's Hero", in which the subject of unhealthy hero worship and the potentially harmful effects that playing with toy guns might have on an impressionable and developing young mind come into focus. An even more contentious issue today, in 1973 it was still considered a pretty normal part of a boy's childhood to play shoot-'em-up games with toy guns (if you were a girl playing gun games at the time, then it may have raised the brow of the school social guidance counsellor). Just about every television cop series at the time had some sort of official toy gun produced as a merchandising tie-in, and cap-firing western revolvers and full-size plastic machine guns which shot sparks out of its barrel were still popular toy and department store items. But there were signs that opinion was starting to change. The Vietnam War had brought the ugly reality of combat and gunshot wounds into the American living room in full dying colour, sparking an increased level of concern over the potential effects of television violence on the young. And just a couple of years earlier, the popular G.I. Joe 12" action doll stopped being an armed combat soldier and was re-invented as a rugged adventurer (with life-like hair and kung-fu grip), after its manufacturer Hasbro became concerned over toys glorifying war.

In "Bobby's Hero", youngest Brady boy Bobby (Mike Lookinland) raises the concerned eye of the school principal when he submits an essay on his hero, notorious western outlaw and killer Jesse James (1847–1882). While most kids go through a brief phase of harmless anti-hero worship, Mike and Carol are having none of their son's current fixation, and they demand he ditch the Jesse James adulation immediately and find a more wholesome American hero, like George Washington or basketballer Wilt Chamberlain, to look up to and emulate. Bobby finds it hard to abandon his cap gun-totin', black cowboy hat-wearin' ways, raising Mike's particular ire when the gun goes off under the dinner table while the Brady's are saying grace (over what looks like a meal of frozen pizza, lettuce leaves and milk). When Bobby pleads with his parents to be able to stay up past his bedtime in order to watch the (fictional) movie *Jesse James on the Vengeance Trail* on TV, Mike and Carol are initially appalled, but eventually relent in the hopes that the film's notorious violence will show Bobby once and for all that Jesse James was not a man to look up to. Unfortunately, the old black and white movie has been severely trimmed for its television broadcast, and with all of the violence cut out it leaves Jesse James looking like the most well-mannered, peaceful outlaw in the west.

It's only when Mike tracks down a local elderly author named Jethroe Collins (Burt Mustin) and invites him into the Brady home that Bobby starts to realise what sort of a man Jesse James really was. While Bobby is initially excited to meet the author of the book "The Real Jesse James", his enthusiasm is quickly dampened when Mr. Collins tells the boy that his own father was shot – in the back – and killed by Jesse James himself. That night, as Mr. Collins' words ring in his ears, Bobby has a terrifying dream in which he is on a train back in the wild west, watching on in horror as a smiling Jesse James (Gordon DeVol) robs and shoots dead his entire family (in much the same way in which Mr. Collins describes his own father's death).

"It was the worst dream in the whole world", Bobby tells his brothers Peter and Greg after his screams wake them up, before he sheepishly turns in his cap guns to mom and dad. "I don't ever want to see another gun again" he tells his parents, proud that their youngest son has finally seen the ugly truth behind the myth that is Jesse James, as Bobby trots out of the room in search of a new and true American hero.

Underneath its laugh-tracked, almost impenetrably-safe Brady Bunch veneer, "Bobby's Hero" is quite a forceful and effective piece of work, at least within the confines of its format. The scene with Jethroe Collins really has a somber undertone and an almost documentary-like feel to it, due in large part to the earnest performance of Burt Mustin (who was well into his sixties when he made his acting debut in 1951 after a long career as a salesman). The dream sequence which follows Bobby's talk with Mr. Collins also creates quite a disturbing and nightmarish impact, thanks to the surrealism of the production design (with the train carriage made out of painted cardboard like a high school play set), and the performance by Gordon DeVol as Jesse James, grinning maniacally as he shoots the entire Brady family dead despite the cries and pleas from Bobby.

Naturally, the influence which the media has on glorifying crime and violence is directly touched upon in the scene where Carol and Mile attend Bobby's school and talk to his principal, Mr. Hillary (Richard Carlyle).

"Look what's happening today", the school head tells them. "The press writes stories about gangsters and skyjackers, they make them seem very glamorous in the eyes of the children."

"Today's criminals will probably be tomorrow's folk heroes", is Mike Brady's insightful reply.

Interestingly, while both books and movies are signalled out as a misleading and corruptive influence on youth, television, the very medium for which *The Brady Bunch* is made and one that at the time was infinitely more influential than books or movies, is never actually mentioned by name. It would seem the network and/or the producers of *The Brady Bunch* did not want to risk any of their advertising dollars.

Another reason why "Bobby's Hero" comes across so well is the assured direction of Leslie H. Martinson, who mostly worked in television but also directed a number of interesting features including *Hot Rod Girl* (1956), the John F. Kennedy wartime biopic *PT 109* (1963), the sexy espionage adventure *Fathom* (1967) with Raquel Welch and, an undoubted high-point of his career, the 1966 *Batman* movie based on the TV series starring Adam West and Burt Ward. Martinson would ultimately end up helming six episodes of *The Brady Bunch*, including the season five classic "The Cincinnati Kids", which was partially filmed at the then-new King's Island amusement park in Ohio (*The Partridge Family* (1970–1974) had also filmed an episode there the previous year).

With "Bobby's Hero", Leslie H. Martinson, along with writer Michael Morris, managed to deliver a rare episode of *The Brady Bunch* that flirted with some genuine darkness and tackled a topic that was legitimately controversial at the time, while presenting it within a format and tone that remained true to the show's idyllic feel-good American fantasy family values.

In "Bobby's Hero" from The Brady Bunch, *Bobby Brady (Mike Lookinland) has a nightmare involving his entire family gunned down by notorious figure of the West, Jesse James, someone that he had once idolized.*

"Rated X" from *Sanford and Son*
Original Air date: 16 March 1973
By Dennis Capicik

Throughout the sixties, the motion picture industry in Hollywood was in a constant state of flux. This, by decade's end, eventually led to the collapse of the studio system, as symbolized by a couple of ambitious, high-profile and exceedingly costly flops: Joseph L. Mankiewicz's now-infamous, ancient Egypt-based "biopic" *Cleopatra* (1963) and Anthony Mann's sumptuous classical era historical drama *The Fall of the Roman Empire* (1964); epic in scale, scope and grandeur but also equally thoughtful in their approaches to the material. At the time, audiences – in particular U.S. audiences – were still craving something "different": films that would better reflect the monumental changes going on in the world during a socio-politically volatile period when presidential assassinations, the Civil Rights and Women's Liberation movements, the ever-ongoing Cold War and the war in Vietnam, and endless anti-war protests were all dominating the international headlines. With the eventual abolishment of the Motion Picture Production Code in 1968 and a wave of younger, independent filmmakers about to take over Tinseltown, the so-called "Golden Age of Hollywood" was fast coming to an end. This new Hollywood – or "Hollywood New Wave," as it's sometimes referred to – was typified by such counterculture films as Arthur Penn's *Bonnie and Clyde* (1967), Dennis Hopper's *Easy Rider* (1969) and John Schlesinger's X-rated – but Academy Award-winning nevertheless – *Midnight Cowboy* (1969), all of which not only better reflected the tumultuous times of the sixties, but also helped pave the way for more mature, adult-oriented (up to and including XXX-rated) material.

With the formation of the Motion Picture Association of America and their new rating system, which also included the non-copyrighted "X" rating, filmmakers were finally allowed the opportunity to more freely realize their visions and at the same time buck the status quo represented by The Establishment, thus resulting in a number of bold and inventive films. These included, as only a few select examples, such trailblazing works of cinema as Haskell Wexler's *Medium Cool* (1970), Stanley Kubrick's *A Clockwork Orange* (1971), as well as even lower-budgeted but equally influential films like Melvin Van Peebles' *Sweet Sweetback's Baadasssss Song* (1971), all of which were controversial for being slapped with X ratings upon their initial releases. This new permissiveness was also prevalent in – and was quite likely even largely pioneered by – the "sexploitation" film industry, wherein for decades moviemaking mavericks such as Dan Sonney, David F. Friedman and Harry Novak had and continued to push the boundaries and further stress the envelope of what was deemed "acceptable" viewing for discerning modern adult audiences. But it was Bill Osco's and Howard Ziehm's *Mona* (1970) and Gerard Damiano's *Deep Throat* (1972) – "skin-flicks" that depicted actual onscreen sex but had honest-to-goodness *plots* too! – which, after first warily dipping their toe in, really took the plunge way over their heads into formerly-uncharted cinematic waters (it was the so-called "Permissive Era," after all!). Spearheaded primarily by that latter film just cited, this new trend, which was memorably tagged "porno chic" by New York Times critic Ralph Blumenthal, swiftly rose to transcend the form's lowly, stigmatized underground origins and initiated an aboveground – mainstream, yet – interest in pornography by the general public (even many a long-established "A"-list celebrity, including beloved singer-actor Sammy Davis, Jr., openly embraced and celebrated the sudden newfound social acceptability of "blue movies," which could now be attended without stigma (even by those not wearing dirty raincoats!).

This new interest in sexually explicit films even resulted in serious write-ups by "respectable" mainstream film critics and held a fascination for many viewers of the time, as depicted in Fenton Bailey and Andy Barbato's 2005 documentary *Inside Deep Throat*. "There was something *exciting* about pornography!" exclaimed celebrated novelist Norman Mailer, and this fascination with the meaty mechanics of the sex act(s) came to permeate the very fabric of American culture, which, much like the Hollywood New Wave, was yet another – albeit short-lived – development in the ever-changing tides of the American film industry.

Produced and aired at the height of the Porno Chic craze, the *Sanford and Son* (1972–1977) episode "Rated X" is quite unique for a VSE and, although executive producers Norman Lear and Bud Yorkin were no strangers when it came to tackling controversial subject matter on primetime television, *Sanford and Son* was, for the most part, generally a lighter affair. Brimming with frequent, well-timed laughs, *Sanford and Son* was actually based on *Steptoe and Son* (1962–1974), an enormously popular British telly series about an ever-bickering father-and-son team of junkmen living and working in West London. Transposing the same basic premise to Watts – a notoriously dangerous neighborhood in Los Angeles – and casting iconic comedian Redd Foxx as the cantankerous Fred Sanford and Demond Wilson as his son, Lamont Sanford (the eponymous roles originated, respectively, by Wilfrid Brambell ("Albert Steptoe") and Harry H. Corbett ("Harold Steptoe") on the long-running Britcom). As with the Steptoes, the Sanfords' constant rivalry, in-fighting and relentless witty smartassery remained the foundation and backbone of the show. However, unlike Lear's other smash-hit shows *All in the Family* (1971–1979), *Maude* (1972–1978) or *Good Times* (1974–1979) – which, while all were situation comedies, definitely had the propensity to get deadly serious when they wanted to – *Sanford and Son* rarely flirted with VSE's. Which is what makes "Rated X" particularly noteworthy and, at the same time, it remains one of the few mainstream sitcoms of the time ever to tackle the sudden inundation of readily-accessible pornography, which at the time had attained a previously-unheard-of level of social acceptability.

Along with his close friend Rollo (Nathaniel Taylor), one of the show's many colorful recurring characters, Lamont is preparing for an interview for "one of them low-budget films" in the hopes of getting cast, but 'ol Fred is quick to respond with his usual condescension and ridicule ("Your head is *empty*! Rollo and Hollow!"), even though this so-called "independent film company" pays fifty bucks per day. Eager to be "discovered," during what Lamont and Rollo refer to as the "Golden Age of Filmmaking for the black man", Fred remains stubbornly doubtful, even though "Studios out in Hollywood is comin' out with black films faster than cars comin' off the assembly line." Of course, Lamont and Rollo are referring to the sudden surge of what have since become affectionately known as "blaxploitation" movies that proliferated on cinema screens during the early seventies. As much as these films are now revered among more "hip-to-the-scene" cineastes, Fred opines otherwise (his typically disparaging remarks include, "Yeah, and from what I've seen of some of them, you oughta send 'em back for corrections, like they do them cars on the assembly lines!"). In a wonderful – and greatly appreciated – rant that any film aficionado can relate to, Fred goes on to reminiscence about the "old days" when "movies were movies and stars were stars. Louise Beavers, Rex Ingram and Lena Horne. Nowadays, any fool they cut loose from a football team, right away they stick them in front of a camera and call it a movie!" But it's exactly this kind of creative casting that illustrated the changing times in Hollywood, where former NFL (National Football League) players such as "Big" Jim Brown, O.J. "The Juice" Simpson and Fred "The Hammer" Williamson had recently become bankable box-office stars. As Lamont so adroitly points out, "Black is very profitable right now!"

The episode was written by Ilunga Adell, a prolific TV writer who penned a total of 14 *Sanford and Son* episodes, including "Have Gun, Will Sell", which not only dealt with such contentious issues as illegal gun ownership and racism, but also introduced Rollo, who is always portrayed as a rather lovable ne'er-do-well schemer trying to get ahead; a character trait which is once again on display in "Rated X" (e.g., "This is our passport out of the valley of the shadow of poverty!"). Although Rollo is constantly looked-down-upon and regarded with suspicion by senior Sanford Fred for his possible criminal affiliations and activities, the irresistibly tempting allure of potentially becoming a "movie star" also gets the better of Fred. This is after he reads the want-ad for himself (it promisingly specifies, "No previous experience needed"). In a playful bit of improvisation, Fred even imitates Ronald Colman's and Charles Laughton's respective – now-legendary – performances from Frank Lloyd's *If I Were King* (1938) and *Mutiny on the Bounty* (1935) while he practices his acting chops in front of a mirror.

Dressed to the hilt like some big-time pimp straight out of Michael Campus' *The Mack* (1973), Fred subsequently shows up at a meagre production office, where he's greeted by a stereotypical sweaty, cigar-chompin', penny-pinchin' movie producer (Ralph James, best-known as the voice of Orson on *Mork & Mindy* (1978–1982)), who is first seen excitedly counting money in a miserly manner at his desk. Along with his director Don (Jack DeLeon), the producer believes Fred would actually be a perfect casting choice for use in the harem scene ("Wouldn't he be *delicious*?!" exclaims Don) as they continually stroke Fred's already overinflated ego ("You're absolutely *perfect* just the way you are!"). After being told to go wait in the next "room" – which is actually nothing more than a storeroom containing some lighting equipment, a 16mm camera and a dingy, ratty old bed – it soon becomes apparent just what *kind* of movie it really is when the "actors" are instructed to remove their clothes and given a "script" to read ("It's basically skeleton. We do a lot of improvisations!"). After perusing the first few pages, all three become increasingly concerned until Fred asks with some nervousness, "Sayyy, what kind of movie *is* this?! Ain't nobody got no clothes on!" However, just as they are about to leave, the place is raided by the vice squad and everyone is arrested for taking part in the production of a porn film, a development which cues the now-infamous feigned heart attack by 'ol Fred ("I feel a *big* one! I'm comin' to join ya, Elizabeth! Do you hear that? But shut your eyes honey, cause it's a nudie rap!").

Eschewing the grittier nature of the somewhat messy scenario they've gotten themselves into, the accused pornographers' jail-time is mostly played for laughs, including one of the episode's funnier moments when Fred – in all seriousness! – asks Rollo where the men's room is. But before Rollo can even answer, Taylor as Rollo can barely keep a straight face when the studio audience bursts out in laughter as well, allowing him the necessary time to gather his composure and answer him, "Turn around and aim yourself in *that* direction!" while pointing to the exposed toilet in the corner of their shared cell. Fred's uneasiness during his taste of prison life is further exacerbated by Don, the foiled blue movie's director, who is in the next cell over and goes on to proposition Fred after offering him a cigarette through the bars ("It could get very *lonely* after a few weeks!"). Upon demanding their obligatory single phone call in the hopes of obtaining a writ of *habeas corpus*, Lamont phones the bible-thumping Aunt Esther (LaWanda Page) – one of the show's most popular characters – to come and bail them out of jail. But, even after they're exonerated on all charges, Aunt Esther asks the fuzz to keep them locked up for the time being, because "these heathens ain't gonna stand still and listen to this!" as she then goes on to read them a pertinent passage from the Bible, much to their disdain.

Even as pornography was gaining mainstream popularity and semi-legalization in the United States during this time, legislation varied from state to state on what was deemed obscene, a fact which Fred, in his naivety, is quick to realize while skimming through the entertainment section of a local newspaper. He is shocked by the amount of "porno movies" that are currently playing, some of whose titles and taglines he reads aloud to Lamont: *Nurses' Night Out* ("Frank, daring and bold!"), *Sweets from Sweden* ("No one under 40 admitted!") and *Sex on the High Seas* ("The story of a man, a woman and a fish!"); all of which are, of course, made-up titles, but their inclusion does accurately illustrate the kind of exploitation chutzpah used to advertise these sorts of films back in their long-gone heyday. Young Lamont agrees with his father that, "A lot of people are gettin' pretty uptight about them pictures, Pop. They've been condemned in a whole lot of places!" This prompts Fred to ring up the Paradise Theatre and mutter under his breath, "What happened to them old family movies like Mickey Rooney and them Andy Hardy pictures, stuff like that?!" Although, after phoning the Paradise ("It shows *what*?!"), Fred's attitude changes soon enough, but before he can leave the house, Lamont gives him a dirty look as he admits with some embarrassment, "Well, I gotta go down and *see* them before I can condemn them!", which remains a fitting conclusion that not only illustrates some people's hypocrisy regarding such provocative issues, but also reiterates the importance of having the freedom to choose as opposed to being subjected to enforced governmental censorship.

"Gloria the Victim" from *All in the Family*
Original Air Date: 17 March 1973
By Lee Gambin

Possibly the first time the issue of sexual assault and attempted rape would make its way into the realm of American situation comedy, "Gloria the Victim" from *All in the Family* (1971–1979) is an outstanding achievement in writing as well as performance most notably from Sally Struthers as Gloria Stivic, the golden haired sweetheart who is active in social causes but not without her own sensitive insecurities and vulnerabilities. Gloria is a multi-dimensional character who sits proudly in the Norman Lear TV universe mix and her overriding arc throughout the series is a tenderly conceived one that stretches from liberal minded independent working class girl to nurturing and adoring mother struggling to make ends meet alongside her social justice dedicated husband Michael. However, from the original series and right up to season three where this episode would hit, Gloria is a character constantly at war with her father, the bigoted and small minded Archie Bunker, while also trying to mediate and find some kind of reckoning point between him and her left leaning husband. So, when an episode brings Gloria's own personal dilemma to the fore, the attitudes and politics of the two men in her life are rendered silly and incidental, when she faces something as harrowing as nearly being raped on the mean streets of New York. Therefore, Gloria as a person as well as an entry in the vast complexity that is the Norman Lear-scope is a character that deserves recognition as one of those great ingredients whose core focal point in "issues based situation comedy" is treated seriously and perfectly suited to the advent of the Very Special Episode.

Archie Bunker's take on rape is also a primary example of insightful writing from Don Nicholl as well as husband and wife team Austin and Irma Kalish, where his absolute embarrassment of even mentioning such a thing shines a light on even more idiocy from this buffoon among men. Rape and sexual assault is a concept he truly cannot understand or want to even acknowledge, and even when it happens to his own daughter, he is torn from being sensitive to her trauma and prefers to intercept the space that holds shame and inappropriate conversation. This is something that would not be closely associated with an era championed by the theme song ("… those were the days") that he and wife Edith introduce us to before each episode unfolds. In "those days", this kind of horrible thing was just not discussed, and this is something examined later in the episode when Edith recounts her own sexual trauma as a young girl. While Archie opens the episode with poking fun at Michael's seemingly endless hunger and overeating habits, he also makes his first interaction with Edith one of berating and condemnation. His first comment to her in this episode is the trademark "Will you stifle yourself?" which is a suited condensation of his thoughts on women and how they need to remain quiet and without a voice. Archie later groans and looks as though he has suffered some kind of stomach cramp when Gloria later explains to the visiting police officer (Charles Durning) that she had once posed nude for a male artist friend during the faux interrogation sequence that carries the majority of the episode.

Gloria's entrance breaks the mood of the episode as we the audience who has come to know and love her see that she is not herself; she is distressed and even refuses to kiss her husband hello. This is a tell-tale sign to Michael (and to us) that something is wrong, as this is a couple constantly showing affections to one another (kissing, groping, cuddling etc), much to Archie's disgust. This usually very romantic couple has a dark cloud hanging over their heads at this point and as actress Sally Struther's remarkable performance dictates, her Gloria is not in a "good place". While she fends off obnoxious pleas from both her husband and father (Gloria having to take on the responsibilities of her husband's studying and constantly under the nagging nuisance of her right-wing pops), she makes mention of not wanting to come home to a "jungle" when there is already "a jungle on the streets". Her use of "jungle" as an expression of a place of danger is an acute testament to New York City during the rise of the recession and in the wake of the 1970s – something sometimes romanticized but often presented as a deadly terrain in many films of the period detailing vigilantism, street crime, gang culture and also rape.

Michael notices that Gloria is not wearing her own clothes and it is learned that she had borrowed some from her friend Trudy. The evocation of an image of Gloria having her own clothes soiled at the hands of a would-be rapist springs to mind as she erupts into a frenzied rage, screaming about dirt and about uncleanliness. At the time of the episode's airing, rape and sexually orientated crimes would primarily go either unreported or not followed up by police officials, and this was ultimately to do with the issue of guilt, shame and the fear of not being believed. Norman Lear and his team of writers would not tip toe around that concern – they would face this head on, and with the help of Sally Struthers who would bring so much truth to this episode and its towering power, that horrendous idea of "not being believed" would be dished out with great gusto and strength. The culture of rape and the misogynistic diatribe of even asking "did that really happen?" is fundamentally dissected within the episode and how it reaches varied spectrums of conversation. When Gloria needs to talk to her mother about such an awful encounter, it is a warranted choice because women can feel they can come to other women (but not always) in this dire situation. Also, what *All in the Family* does so well is deliver female-centric points of conversation with upmost seriousness that sometimes is allowed to step aside from the pandering comedy. The many conversations between Edith and Gloria in the kitchen throughout the series have been some of the strongest moments in the show – and they can be serious in tone such as this one, or pure magic as far as an eruption of screaming and hollering about the banality of life made life altering or evidently meaningful.

The death of innocence sits at the heart of their conversation here; Edith is reminded of when Gloria was a little girl (something that Archie continues to call her, as part semi-affection but mostly as a point of condescension), and she makes mention of how she taught her how to make gingerbread men. Gloria glares into space and makes a poignant and remarkably sad statement: "There are no gingerbread men anymore, ma." There is a solemn longing here for Gloria missing the purity and innocent pleasures of childhood, and all through the series, Gloria does seem to hold onto her childlike wonderment (which at times can devolve into downright screamy hissy fits), but here Edith acknowledges the end of innocence with "You're a grown up lady now", which in turn upsets Gloria – facing adult responsibilities and also the fact that men can be vile rapists, eager to take advantage of a situation. Her recount of nearly being raped makes mention of nearby steelworkers making comments and whistling at women as they cross the street (an indication of "tolerated sexism and the objectification of women") and then leads into Michael's advice for her not to walk through those parts, because she doesn't like being sexualized by such grotesque men. She explains to her mother that thinking it was Saturday and no one would be working, that she would be safe from such grubby behavior, however it proved to be a decision that would lead her to sexual assault. In a swift stroke of writing genius – and given power by Jean Stapleton's masterful delivery – Edith is confronted by the ugly truth and tries desperately to distract Gloria as well as herself with mundane talk about a friend of hers getting a new sofa. Edith's longwinded detracting and digressive anecdotes that are staple in the grand tradition of running gags in *All in the Family*, turn into something else here – they become a protective shield from having to deal with harrowing horrors. Edith's fear of her daughter being subject to such a violent act pushes her to help the men understand what has happened, but ultimately it is Gloria's personal battle with inner-guilt that suppresses a breakthrough. Gloria's breakdown in her mother's arms is an image unto itself that summarizes the Very Special Episode phenomenon, and when Michael's first thought is that Gloria got mugged – prompting Archie to ask about mugging – we get a clear picture of how men react compared to women, in dealings of this kind.

Gloria fainting at the hands of the assailant (ultimately saving her from being raped) is addressed in an extreme close-up, something that the series would introduce to episodes detailing dark subject matter, and the graphic content – the talk of the attempted rape – is treated with sincerity and an earnest reasoning with the audience to truly understand such an ordeal. Archie's queasiness at the word "rape" and his reaction is classic Bunker, however, he does remain quiet during Gloria's initial account and utters "Thank God for that" when he realizes that she was not raped. Archie has shown rare moments of tenderness, most notably when it did concern Gloria, for instance in the episode "Gloria Has A Belly Full" where he is finally excited that his little girl is going to be a mom, only to learn that she suffered a miscarriage. "I didn't do a good job did I, daddy?" mournfully cries Gloria, while Archie comforts her, holding her hand, attempting to tell her that he loves her, but letting her nod her head in full understanding.

In "Gloria the Victim", Archie is relegated to traditional unfeeling, insensitive Archie Bunker along with his classic mispronunciations ("Jack the Raper") and constant insults to Edith ("He could attack you, them guys don't care who they grab!"). Edith of course would face her own rape attempt in the two part Very Special Episode "Edith's 50th Birthday", which would carry story elements from this within its narrative fabric. As Archie reports Gloria's attack – he sees rape as being something to be embarrassed of, while the frightened and rattled Gloria holds resistance to contacting the police. Legendary character actor Charles Durning steps in as the hardened copper, and along with his hard edge would be status reports within his dialogue – he will spout out statistics detailing rape reports of the early seventies and the unsettling fact that most defense attorneys get rapists off and assist in their freedom. Durning's officer (a man completely cynical when it comes to lawyers) plays up a courtroom situation and grills Gloria bringing up what she was wearing, if she was flirting with men on the street and even the fact that she posed for an artist friend in the nude (which was the storyline for the episode "Gloria Poses in the Nude"). Durning's grilling leads Gloria to race to her mother where Edith's story about a double date in her early teen years grows into something telling about the situation at hand when it comes to society's viewpoint on talking about rape. Edith explains that she was pressured into sex (the only way Edith Bunker could tell such a story) and she also explains how she escaped ("My father taught me two things") – she kneed the sleaze in the testicles. The concept of conversations about girls being attacked to prevent it happening again would be a bookended theme in "Edith's 50th Birthday" when Gloria insists her mother report her attempted rape to the police, even though it is distressing and horrible to recall. From a male perspective, "Gloria the Victim" calls upon Michael's outrage at this situation (where women are not believed and rapists are free to roam the streets) but then his insensitivity to broad feminist theory and women's liberation is something examined in "Gloria Discovers Women's Lib" (therefore, Michael is not exactly a pure point of reference to a solution or empathy). In fact, something that happens in "Gloria the Victim" that is so subversive in its telling of the treatment of rape victims is that Gloria's inner turmoil is at one point sidelined when there is flippant and inane conversation about hot dogs involving not only Archie and his neighbor Jefferson, but also the policeman. It is indicative of how the world ignores or doesn't believe women who have been sexually assaulted. Television would take on such a subject with a made-for-TV movie entitled *The Rape of Richard Beck* (1985) where Richard Crenna as the titular police officer who is completely dismissive of women and their tales of being raped is raped himself and then becomes an activist protecting those assaulted. This Movie of the Week would definitely owe a lot of its progressive ideologies to something like "Gloria the Victim" which was not shy in dissecting and scrutinizing the issue of women "asking for it". *The Rape of Richard Beck* does something profound – it makes men understand rape and what rape does to women, so, when Archie rants about "taking care of our own", we get that sense of men not wanting to take responsibility for "women everywhere". Here is another issue tackled by "Gloria the Victim", men seem to rather just look after the women they know (or more correctly, the women under their roof), while Edith in all her infinite wisdom that is constantly poo-pooed and dismissed by the likes of Archie, prompting her to race off and "happily" grab him his beer or sandwich, explains to America that talking about rape and these kind of experiences can help others. While Archie carries on about only helping "his own", the camera zooms in on Gloria quivering in fear – and we all come to understand that she will live with this forever.

The coda for the show has the family sitting at the dinner table about to dig into hot dogs (ordinary sized hot dogs, much to Archie's annoyance who has been longing for the foot long hot dogs throughout the episode). Here we find Gloria seemingly fine and unaffected. This closing pre-end credits moment assures us and reinforces the very nature of the American situation comedy, that by the end point, characters' trials and tribulations will be resolved (in a satisfying manner or not) and that things can be completely as they were come "next week's episode". However, having this follow an unsettling close-up image of Gloria trembling and unsure of what will happen in court (something that is not discussed again) assures us that sitcom turf and tradition can ultimately be a band-aid solution to a deep rooted problem that sits at the heart of a character who will face such an ordeal again, and in turn, bring it up once more. When "Edith's 50th Birthday" aired, the nation was shocked to bear witness to a sexual assault on one of America's favorite TV moms, while here in "Gloria the Victim", an off-camera occurrence seemed to be a precursor (or a terrible taste) of horrors yet to come and therefore not as monumental. This does not weaken the power of "Gloria the Victim" whatsoever – as this is a tremendously good piece of writing and an incredible platform for Sally Struthers and her dramatic ability – but it does suggest that the American sitcom was still heavily influenced by prime time TV drama that dealt with rape and sexual assault on a regular basis and that more of a visceral representation of such nastiness would be necessary in order to tap into the universal psyche of an audience not ready to deal with it in the realm of comedy.

Gloria Stivic (Sally Struthers) is comforted by her mother Edith (Jean Stapleton) after being sexually assaulted in the groundbreaking "Gloria the Victim" from All in the Family.

"Walter's Problem" from *Maude*
Original Air Dates: 11 September 1973 (Part 1) and 18 September 1973 (Part 2)
By Lee Gambin

Casual drinking and social drinking would raise concerns in the arena of television drama when something tragic arises as a symptom of it becoming an issue. In the world of the American sitcom, alcoholic characters would generally be an additive component who would step in, have their "secret" revealed, cause a problem then seek help or not. However in "Walter's Problem", a lead character – here in Walter Findlay (Bill Macy) – would get caught in a web of obsessive drinking that arises from the complacency of being a man of the "after work drink" generation, who would probably never see his drinking as an issue at all. The series of *Maude* would take place primarily in the living room which would feature a bar prominently to the side, just before the entrance to the kitchen. Drinking is absolutely commonplace throughout the series run, with not only cocktails being made when guests arrive, but just for Maude (Bea Arthur) and her husband to unwind and drink to get through whatever the daily problem at hand would be at the moment. "Walter's Problem" flips this innocuousness on its head and forces not only the characters to respond but also the audience – while drug abuse runs rampant on television as a social ill, the concern for casual drinking being taken for granted becomes a focal point for this episode which in turn has a component of the primary audience seeing this firsthand.

Maude wakes up groggy after a drunken party and the two part episode opens with her thinking she's been talking to Walter in bed. Shocking her system, Walter enters the room nursing a hangover eschewing a roar of laughter from the audience as it turns out that it is their neighbor and friend Arthur (Conrad Bain) who is in bed with Maude. Jokes aside, one of the first lines uttered from the hungover Walter is "Sorry about last night", which ultimately sets the mood of this two part Very Special Episode. It has a loaded sensibility in that it packs a punch commenting on mistakes made whilst drunk and the repercussions of such mistakes. Works such as *Days of Wine and Roses* (1962) and *Who's Afraid of Virginia Woolf?* (1966) would use casual drinking that would take a dive into harrowing examinations into alcoholism terrified audiences and here in the medium of the American TV sitcom, it would serve the same purpose. Just as the leads in *Days of Wine and Roses* lose a grip of reality and become shambles of themselves, shattered by destructive boozing, in "Walter's Problem" the state of the house and the juvenile behavior such as obscene phone calls and playing darts with a picture of Maude's mother as a target are an indication that these people – these supposedly sophisticated and intelligent middle class adults – are under the spell of alcoholism without knowing it. It even changes their personalities such as Walter snapping

"I'm not hostile" to have Arthur respond with "Only when you drink, Walter". While the fun of drinking is made an example by Walter and Arthur's vaudeville style musical performance for Maude, Walter drinking first thing in the morning is an indication that he is the character that has it worst.

Maude's single mother daughter Carol (Adrienne Barbeau) expresses her concern throughout the episode but also summarizes her mother's age group in terms of addictions: "Your generation is the cocktail generation." She goes on to explain that there are "Twelve million alcoholics in America" and the concern of social drinking turning into something malevolent is pretty much at an epidemic level. Carol tests Maude and in turn, Maude and Arthur try and give up drinking for a month with Arthur using his professionalism in his position as a doctor to tell Maude that Walter actually has a drinking problem – this is something that comes into play in "Walter's Crisis" where Arthur helps Walter out during his breakdown and suicide attempt. The character of Arthur, as much as he is an antagonist for Maude (he being conservative and she being the bleeding heart liberal) is someone who deeply cares for Walter, their friendship being one of the most endearing ingredients in the show. Carrying through here is a moment where Arthur makes a deal with Walter to stop drinking (involving money) but when Walter meets up with Arthur at a favorite watering hole, he spikes his Shirley Temple and gets drunk.

The set up for something that will eventually spell out disaster comes in the guise of Carol bringing her young son Phillip's (Brian Morrison) birthday present home. What is happening here is a trope commonly used in sitcoms where something that is meant to be joyous and wholesome (like a child's birthday party) will be ruined by the character who is going through the Very Special Episode saga (here being Walter and drinking). But the show tackles Maude's drinking as well, it suggests that she too is someone who takes her breezy boozing for granted, but it is in no way as problematic as Walter's, who after coming home drunk doesn't set off a fight (a rarity for Maude and Walter whose screaming matches are television iconography) but instead lead into a suggestion from Maude that they become "a drinking couple" and that drinking is "a way to forget" (a common reason for chronic drinkers who are haunted or trapped by personal responsibility). When Carol leaves to get more birthday trimmings for Phillip's birthday, a drunken Maude decides to decorate his cake as a surprise and she and Walter, who is even more intoxicated than she, attempt to design their grandson's cake.

What opens as a comical slapstick effort of drunks trying to decorate a cake turns into something grim and devastatingly dark. Maude admits that Walter's mood changes when drinking ("Well you are different, Walter!") which gradually builds into a heated argument with Walter spewing out hateful outrage at his wife, we feel his pent up rage ("I look at you and all I see is resentment!") and defending his alcoholism ("I drink coz I like to!") and then finally grilling Maude ("Answer me Maude?!") which erupts into violence – he slaps her.

How the audience responds is what is truly telling about this and what impact it leaves. When audiences are so used to seeing a TV couple scream at each other in a comical sense episode after episode they become disarmed when it eventuates into an onscreen slap. This is when the audience may turn on a much loved character or at least be thrown by them and never know whether to trust them again. Walter's breakdown after slapping her sends the first episode of this two part venture into somber and also sobering terrain, with Maude comforting her broken husband, holding the shaky wreck of a man in her arms insisting that "It's just a little problem, we'll lick it together." Actor Bill Macy recalled how slapping Bea Arthur really upset him and he cried in an on camera interview when discussing this.

The second episode opens with Carol noticing Maude's black eye ("What happened to your eye?") and in grand Bea Arthur/Maude style her response is "I walked into a chocolate donut". Maude's attitude towards Walter hitting her is not at all one of fear or depression, it is buried underneath an onslaught of jokes which is Maude's defense mechanism and something that she uses to cope. In a sense, Maude's attitude is a summary of how the Very Special Episode sometimes deals with serious matters; it pits the ugliness of human nature against the routine set ups and gags and sometimes doesn't necessarily understand how to manage them as mutual entities that should coincide rather than be jarringly opposed. More gags come thick and hard such as Florida's (Esther Rolle) line which is racially flavored: "If black is beautiful than that's exquisite", of which she follows up with a sobering comment being "You walked into a door, right?" What this examines is a commonplace excuse a lot of audiences had come to know when popular culture tackled serious subject matter such as wife battering. The women in the piece who aren't Maude (Carol and Florida) are not at all impressed and don't see the slap as "light" and Carol's anger towards Walter is overt while Florida scrutinizes his wrong doing with another racially flavored snipe: "How's the Great White Hope?", a clear reference to the film about the black boxer but inverting it to reflect Walter's whiteness and pathetic action against his wife.

Spousal abuse as a result of drinking is something that pops up in some television movies and dramatic series, and it would come out more so in sitcoms come the nineties in shows such as working class-centric shows such as *Roseanne* (1988–1997) and *Grace Under Fire* (1993–1998). Alcoholism and what comes from it would be the umbrella thematic link that propels a lot of what makes up Sam Malone (Ted Danson) in *Cheers* (1982–1993), and also pops up in multiple episodes – which of course makes sense seeing that the long running much loved show is set in a Boston bar – and if it popped up as a teen outing that could get young girls into trouble as seen in "Story with a Twist" from *My Two Dads* (1987–1990), it was a cautionary tale but not as complicated or probing as what the Norman Lear shows tackled. But it is Walter's self-hatred in this VSE from *Maude*, his absolute disdain in himself for doing such a vile act, that is something that overrides the issues of alcoholism and domestic abuse. His self-doubt and inner rage is something that comes up as an issue in "Walter's Crisis" which features a heated moment in the hospital room keeping the suicidal Walter where Maude screams at him to "Stop it!" The chill-inducing moment there is replicated here but not with the desperation of Maude, but with the innocence and trusting love from Phillip.

Walter's issues at work drive him back to the booze and a clergyman, who is also a recovered alcoholic, drives in the facts, ultimately standing in as a voice of reason and social insight. Most importantly is his provided information that alcoholism is a disease – something that would become a newly understood fact, and something that would be furthered in comprehension as major stars would come out explaining that their desire to drink was something they were born with, like a predisposed genetic condition. Despite efforts to stop, Walter returns drunk once again and when he goes for yet another drink, he notices that all his booze is gone. Maude confesses that she gave it all away and then desperately tries to hide the drunken Walter – trapping him in the closet – from Phillip who has had his mother Carol threaten to leave ("No place for a child"), protecting her son from an unstable step-grandfather. This is what drives the episode home in regards to how Walter realizes what he may lose. When Phillip sees his drunken step-grandfather and tells him he loves him it breaks Walter's heart and he throws the last drink he will have (for this episode at least) right through the kitchen window. For this doubler, Walter is "cured", with a coda showing him healthy, energetic, full of life and so forth. However, before the coda, Maude considers a drink, but then tips it into the sink – for Maude, booze is also a demon she can live without. However, of course, as it is with a lot of Very Special Episodes dealing with central characters going through an ordeal that could be life changing, the old habits come back without any dire consequence, as Walter (and Maude) will go on drinking without the heavy and grim results.

Going through so much, including hell and back, Walter (Bill Macy) and Maude (Bea Arthur) Findlay remain at one another's throats, but sincerely love each other. Walter would go through multiple character downfalls, such as a suicide attempt and a deep dependence to alcohol throughout the seasons on Maude.

"Maude's Musical" from *Maude*
Original Air Date: 13 November '973
By Michael Barrett

With Very Special insight from actress Adrienne Barbeau

Many a sitcom has fashioned episodes from the grand tradition of Putting on a Show. These theatrical, song-based outings function as a change of pace while giving regulars with musical backgrounds a rare chance to strut their stuff.

While some series, like *I Love Lucy* (1951–1957), featured performances on a regular basis, other shows brought out the trope once or twice, often on the pretext of raising money for charity, or to compete in a talent show or stage a Christmas pageant, or, in the case of *Gilligan's Island* (1964–1992), to impress a show-biz mogul (Phil Silvers) with a musical version of *Hamlet* (the 3 October 1966 episode "The Producer"). *The Mothers-in-Law* (1967–1969), produced by Desi Arnaz and using several of the *I Love Lucy* writers, seemed to devote half its final season to Putting on a Show, the better to dispense with inventing one more wacky plot.

Over her show's six seasons, Maude (Bea Arthur) several times Put on a Show that usually threatened to be a disaster, from "The Telethon" (20 January 1975) without a cause to the all-woman "Tuckahoe Bicentennial" (9 February 1976) to "Musical '"78 28) January 1978), a fund-raiser for a child who's not actually sick. Before them all came "Maude›s Musical."

"Maude›s Musical" finds Maude directing a high school charity show that apparently won't star any high school kids. The surprising theme is "a tribute to burlesque," which serves two functions. First, it allows the episode to nod at forgotten routines like the prostitution skit "Meet Me Round the Corner in a Half an Hour" or the 1920 song "Lena from Palesteena." Such nostalgia showed up now and again in Norman Lear's series; indeed, nostalgia was embedded in the opening theme songs of both *Maude* (1972–1978) and *All in the Family* (1971–1979).

As one example, "Cousin Maude's Visit," the episode of *All in the Family* that introduced Maude, had included gratuitous dialogue in memory of Ish Kabibble, a comedian on the radio show "Kay Kyser's Kollege of Musical Knowledge." Neither Mike (Rob Reiner) nor Gloria (Sally Struthers) had heard of it, and the effect was of the elders instructing them, along with any ignorant viewers, on this bit of American pop culture. That same instructive-nostalgic impulse is at work in "Maude's Musical."

Second, the topic allows Maude and her regular foil, the conservative Arthur Harmon (Conrad Bain), to argue about whether the subject is appropriate or whether, as "bluenose" Arthur thinks, it's "poppycock" and "creeping smut." Even though burlesque is an emphatically old-fashioned form of comedy, moribund in 1973, Arthur's dialogue somehow links it to the morality of contemporary TV shows, and thus Arthur and Maude are implicitly arguing over *Maude* itself and its controversial language and topics.

Of course they don't mention the show they're in; that would be going too far. Instead, Arthur cites an episode of *The Mary Tyler Moore Show* (1970–1977) in which Mary goes on a date and doesn't come back all night, and "as Mary Tyler Moore goes, so goes America." (That would be "Just Around the Corner" on 28 October 1972, where we also learn that Mary takes birth control pills in what's probably a sitcom first.) Arthur also complains that Marcus Welby treated a homosexual, which causes Maude to ask, "Really? To what?"

She declares that their show is "a tribute to burlesque, not *The Waltons*," and thus the survey of the range of contemporary television seems pretty complete. She also asserts that "burlesque has been family entertainment for almost two thousand years." Maybe she's referring to Roman playwright Plautus, who inspired Stephen Sondheim's "A Funny Thing Happened on the Way to the Forum." That would explain why a chorus chirps that musical's "Comedy Tonight" in the opening minutes of this episode, thus implying a long historical case for ribald comedy.

Arthur finally drags in a reference to "hardcore porn" and that year's 4-5 ruling in the Supreme Court case of Miller v. California, which allowed local communities to define standards of obscenity. Arthur welcomes this, although one practical result of that case is that defining obscenity by the Court's "three prongs" actually became harder than before.

When Arthur, as a member of the school board, threatens to shut down the production, Maude saves the situation with a compromise. They're already performing a patriotic opening song, written by Arthur, about America as a "melting pot" with beautiful women from around the world, including Miss Africa played by Florida (Esther Rolle, impersonating Maya Angelou's nightclub phase), Miss Asia embodied inaccurately by Carol (Adrienne Barbeau) in a Thai head-dress, and, with not inappropriate symbolism, the statuesque Maude as the Statue of Liberty. This became an iconic image for the series.

Now, to end the stalemate, Maude agrees that Arthur can perform his WWII song to "elevate the tone." The moral is that bluenoses want to be stars too.

So this episode makes the requisite nod to a controversial subject by speaking against censorship of "offensive" comedy, putting this outing in the tradition of episodes on that topic. A more famous example is «Itchy & Scratchy and Marge» (20 December 1990), from the second season of *The Simpsons* (1989–). Marge becomes a crusader against cartoon violence with ambiguous results; TV cartoons become so sanitized that children actually go outside to play. Then her neighbor (named Maude!) feels empowered to crusade for putting pants on Michelangelo's David.

Ten years earlier, *The Associates* (1979–1980) ended its run before 13 episodes, but Stan Daniels and Ed. Weinberger received Emmy and Writers Guild nominations for "The Censors" (10 April 1980), in which a slapstick, saucy *Three's Company*-type sitcom (starring guest John Ritter) gets so revised to avoid being offensive that the result comes across as dumb and unfunny. This episode's insight cut very close to TV's funny bone.

In between came "Clean Up Radio Everywhere" (12 April 1981), an episode of *WKRP in Cincinnati* (1978–1982) in which bumbling radio station manager Arthur Carlson (Gordon Jump) initially agrees with the request of a Jerry Falwell-esque preacher (Richard Paul) that songs with "offensive" words be removed from the playlist. Carlson ends up drawing the line at John Lennon's "Imagine," saying "First you censor a word, and then you censor the ideas."

Still, "Maude's Musical" isn't really about censorship except in a token way, and notwithstanding the series' own status as a taboo-breaking "offensive" comedy. It's about performance, from Carol's belly dancing to Maude – or is it really just Bea Arthur? – belting out "Hard Hearted Hannah" to general applause. Arthur would reprise this song for *The Golden Girls* (1985–1992) on "Journey to the Center of Attention" (22 February 1992).

In a scene both joyous and politically loaded, Maude and Florida perform "Me and My Shadow," introduced by Al Jolson in 1927 and sung by countless artists since. 1970s viewers would most likely associate it with Frank Sinatra and Sammy Davis Jr. making a then-hip joke of Davis as the shadow.

Maude, ever insisting on her liberal credentials, reverses the joke by casting herself as the shadow. She's making a point while pretending not to because "it doesn't matter." Taking up her logic and perhaps goading her, Florida argues that if it doesn't matter, then Florida could be the shadow. Maude is reduced to asking who would know the difference in their poor lighting, and Florida replies "The shadow do." This combines two old-time references: a catch phrase from "The Shadow" radio series and a catch phrase of African American performer Fats Waller: "One never knows, do one?" It's more pop culture instruction.

For the record, IMDb informs us that this classic song has shadowed many a sitcom, including *Make Room for Daddy* (a.k.a. *The Danny Thomas Show*) (1953–1965), *The Jack Benny Program* (1950–1965), *The Dick Van Dyke Show* (1961–1966), *The Brady Bunch Variety Hour* (1976–1977), *All in the Family* (sung separately by Archie and Edith in "Archie and the KKK"!), *M*A*S*H* (1972–1983) and *Mr. Belvedere* (1985–1990). Nell Carter and Joey Lawrence perform it on "Joey: Part 2" (3 November 1983), an episode of *Gimme a Break!* (1981–1987), written and directed by *Maude* alumni, including Hal Cooper, director of this very same *Maude* episode.

The most resonant recycling of this song, however, is on "Walter's Crisis," a three-part arc in the fifth season of *Maude*. Walter sings it, pausing to emphasize "nobody's there" as he climbs the stairs with the air of a drunken man. They're his last words to Maude in the episode; the next time she sees him, he'll be unconscious from a drug overdose.

The final song, Arthur's "We're Going to Hang Out the Washing on the Siegfried Line," becomes a sensation when, without his knowledge, Carol bumps and grinds behind him. This stunt refers directly to the great *I Love Lucy* episode "Ethel's Home Town" (31 January 1955), set in Albuquerque, New Mexico. While Ethel (Vivian Vance) performs "Shortnin' Bread" to an audience that imagines she's a star, her husband and the Ricardos literally upstage her with antics behind her back.

Although it's no great role, vaudeville star Joey Faye appears as Mousie, an old burlesque trouper in yet another example of connections to the forgotten past. Faye, who claimed to have invented the classic "Slowly I Turned" routine, also played a forgotten burlesque star in «Good Old Burlesque» (20 February 1961), an episode of *Make Room for Daddy*. One of that series' many Put on a Show moments, it featured Danny reviving classic burlesque routines to help out the guest.

The numbers are staged by Tony Mordente, at this point transitioning from a prominent TV variety choreographer to a prolific director of both sitcoms and dramas. Music consultant Ray Charles (not the singer), a big name in TV variety and specials, worked with Perry Como, Bob Hope, Bing Crosby, Julie Andrews, the Muppets and repeatedly for the Kennedy Center Honors; he released many "easy listening" records as The Ray Charles Singers. The arranger and conductor was Bob Alberti, who worked regularly with Bob Hope and would return for "Musical '78."

"Maude's Musical" is one of five episodes credited to writer Woody Kling, who had written for several seasons of *The Carol Burnett Show* (1967–1978). The son of a newspaper cartoonist, Kling began his TV career as writer for the first season of Milton Berle's *Texaco Star Theatre* back in 1948–1949, the series credited with dramatically increasing the sale of TV sets. Before becoming "Mr. Television," Berle had been a star in vaudeville but really not burlesque.

The inherently nostalgic nature of this episode must have appealed to Kling, who virtually sidelined any concept of plot in favor of an old fashioned variety revue. Here's an episode that makes up-to-the-minute topical references while harking back to styles of comedy that many of its viewers would never have seen or only dimly recalled. One of the paradoxes of Lear's shows is their commitment to the present historical moment while looking kindly upon the past. Perhaps those who work in comedy know only too well how quickly they risk being forgotten.

> **ADRIENNE BARBEAU:** My favorite moment for Carol – and the only reason I know this is because I had just done An Evening With kind of one-woman show at the theatre here in L.A.. The producers had asked me to put something together. So I had to look at a lot of footage. It's hard for me to watch the Maude episodes because I hated my hair and I hated the wardrobe. But I was looking for something. I think one of my favorite moments for Carol was the dance sequence [where] Walter is in bed, and I am singing 'Fever.' I'm doing some sort of a belly dance or something, and Walter is saying 'No, this isn't going to fly!' And there was one that we did [and] we're all waving flags and singing. But this one, maybe it was a talent show? [In the scene] I'm singing 'Fever', and Walter is a patient in the

bed, and I am a nurse, dancing around and we're mugging and just having a good time. That was one of my favorite episodes for her. And then I do love the speech that she gives to Bea in the abortion episode.

"Edith's Christmas Story" from *All in the Family*
Original Air Date: 22 December 1973
By Michael Varrati

More than just a landmark American sitcom, All in the Family (1971–1979) is, in many ways, *the* American sitcom.

While it's true that there was a proud tradition of half-hour situational comedies long before the Bunkers came along, the show's exploration of the nuclear family grappling with the generational divide allowed *All in the Family* to venture into territories other programs previously dare not tread.

In the era before the show's 1971 debut, it was not uncommon to see television series confront the battle of the sexes or the challenges of keeping a home in order, but rarely did such narratives buck the status quo. Such popular fare as *Leave it to Beaver* (1957–1963) and *The Dick Van Dyke Show* (1961–1966), while entertaining and groundbreaking in their own right, traded in the power of Americana, and guaranteed that all would return to a state of wholesome, familial goodness before the end credits rolled.

But as the sixties gave way to the seventies and the specters of Vietnam and Nixon's White House loomed large across the cultural landscape, it became apparent that returning to the status quo of familial goodness was going to be increasingly tricky. A generation steeped in "traditional values" was raising the next who was automatically suspect of those same core beliefs, caused by watching friends be whisked away to a war they barely understood. The wholesome lessons of Dick Van Dyke, Donna Reed, and the tenets of being a good neighbor seemed inconsequential in an age where the national guard was opening fire on college students on our own soil.

It was now part of the national discussion: Even if there was love at home, there was also division.

When Norman Lear and Bud Yorkin introduced *All in the Family* to audiences in January of 1971, there were some who immediately hailed it as bringing "reality" to primetime TV. The inference being that the titular family of the show was going to directly tackle the issues of the day… and for the most part, what was reflected on screen was not too far off from the shifting world outside. Of course, it being a sitcom, *All in the Family* still did so mainly from a place of well-intentioned comedy.

With Archie Bunker, the series established a perpetual curmudgeon and patriarch who was constantly at odds with his progressive progeny, namely his feminist daughter Gloria and her counterculture influenced liberal husband Michael. Presented as an uneducated, yet outspoken bigot, Archie would run afoul of issues that had heretofore not been seen on American TV, such as homosexuality, race relations, women's liberation, and much, much more.

Even as Archie made his loud opinions known to Gloria and Michael, his sweet, but often naïve wife Edith would serve as the intermediary to the family's discord. And, much like the sitcoms of yesteryear, even though the subjects were often heavier, things tended to wrap up nicely before the end.

Still, even with such weighty material being played for laughs, the message was clear: Discord in the world meant discord at home, and by examining those differences, perhaps healing could eventually begin. After all, if Archie Bunker, despite his stubbornness, could learn and the family could still come together with love, then maybe the viewing audience, at political odds with people under their own roof, could do the same.

While the show did have the tendency to generally deal with the macro issues of the world with some brevity, the genius of its construct was that it quite frequently handled the micro with a measure of respect and gravity. The inference being, of course, that often the things that occur within our own homes tend to have the most impact on our day-to-day lives.

Few episodes of *All in the Family* display this careful consideration more than "Edith's Christmas Story." Aired on December 22, 1973, this holiday-centric story finds the Bunkers four seasons into their television tenure. By this point, audiences were well accustomed to the show's brand of humor and the characters had ingratiated themselves into the larger zeitgeist.

That's why this particular episode has such impact, because by this point in the show's legacy the characters on *All in the Family* had done what good sitcom families ought: They became part of our own.

"Edith's Christmas Story" opens innocuously enough, kicking off with a B-plot that has Michael and Gloria goofing around with some novelty glasses, leading to an escalating gag that causes Archie to be put-off because he was planning to pull the same joke. It's a playful moment that allows the cast to indulge in the comedic hijinks the audience expects. Carroll O'Connor, Rob Reiner, and Sally Struthers (Archie, Michael, and Gloria, respectively) make a meal of the scene, and are given an extra push of pizazz by Betty Garrett and Vincent Gardenia, who play the Bunkers' next door neighbors Irene and Frank.

It's a whimsical scene that suggests this Christmas episode is going to be rife with merriment.

However, the arrival of Edith (played masterfully, as always, by the iconic Jean Stapleton), home from a doctor's visit, reveals that maybe there's more to this Christmas than the façade of tinsel and lights.

Sensing something is off about her mother, Gloria confronts Edith in the kitchen, who in turn reveals that her doctor found a lump in her breast. As the two women reel at this development and what it may potentially mean, Edith issues a firm request: Archie must *not* know.

As Edith goes through the personal journey of confronting her own mortality, all the while trying to keep the news from her husband, the viewing audience is suddenly presented with a new perspective on a familiar face. For a character who weekly often served as a comic foil or pastiche, Edith's plight now made her deeply and relatably *human*. In many ways, that's the power of this episode, and by proxy, the sitcom itself. We invite these people into our homes and, as mentioned, allow them to become part of our family. To present Edith with this unexpected and tragic uncertainty strikes a chord, because in many ways, we know her, and she is one of our own.

As Edith struggles with her now undetermined future, she is approached by Irene, who shares a story of her own fight (and eventual victory) with cancer. It's a tender and powerful moment that speaks to the indiscriminate nature of illness, and how it will invariably effect all of our lives in some capacity, if it hasn't already.

Through Irene's past and Edith's present, the audience is reminded that there are many things that are out of our control, but we don't have to face things alone. Despite this, Edith maintains her policy of keeping Archie out of the loop, mainly because she believes that her husband already has too many stressors and cannot handle another.

However, as tends to happen with sitcom schemes, Edith's plan of Archie's non-involvement crumbles when Archie, suspicious of Edith's skirting him, confronts Michael. Initially, Archie believes that Edith is merely evading him so that she can buy him a really swell Christmas present (a fishing rod, to be exact), but eventually the truth comes out.

Rushing to the hospital where Edith is having a follow-up procedure, Archie parks himself bedside to be there when his wife wakes up. As expected from the show and its tone, the initial reunion of the spouses has some comedic beats, but what follows is deeply emotional and some of the most developed pathos Archie receives over the course of the entire series.

Gently admonishing Edith for not revealing her health scare, Archie shares that *of course* he'd want to know what was going on with her, other stresses or no. The duo share a tender moment where they reflect on the importance of the bond of love and family, and what it means to be there for one another, regardless of all else.

In the end, it's revealed that Edith's cancer scare was merely that: a scare. The lump in her breast was a benign cyst, and the final comedic punch is that Edith's stay in the hospital is based upon the fact that she broke her ankle during a jump for joy at discovering she was cancer-free.

While the show can't resist returning to its humorous roots after treading into such serious territory, "Edith Christmas Story" ends on a note of companionship and togetherness that resonates long after the episode's 30 minute runtime. Ultimately, it's the quiet emotion and very personal themes that make this particular episode of *All in the Family* a success. While the show's humor so often dealt with culture wars and generational divisions, "Edith's Christmas Story" cuts to the quick and makes the issue a deeply personal one. It's a story of taking stock and valuing the people in our lives, despite our differences, because the people who care and are there for you may not always be.

All in the Family was often praised for its ability to highlight the things that go on in the American home with an acute eye, but rarely did it deliver such intimate fears or personal stories. That the episode is framed against Christmas is no mistake, as Americana dictates that Christmas is a time of unity and togetherness. However, the show being what it was, even this traditional notion is turned on its head. Unity and togetherness are not assured and only happen when we actively work together to be there for one another. For the briefest of moments, while spiraling with the news of her own tragedy, Edith wanted to shut people out, but it was ultimately those around her who helped her through… including the person she least suspected.

"Edith's Christmas Story" is a significant moment in *All in the Family* history not because it challenged the status quo or bucked the zeitgeist, but because it was a solemn (and occasionally funny) reminder that if we don't start at home and care after those under our own roof, how can we ever begin to care for those out in the world at large?

Help and love can sometimes come from unlikely places, but you won't know until you ask.

In her time of need, Edith's family pulled together, and it made not only for powerful television, but a moment of significant introspection for viewers: Despite the differences we may have with those in our lives, would we do the same?

Though Archie and Edith would weekly warble about the glory of days gone by, the message of this episode is clear, it's only by being there for one another today that we are assured a tomorrow.

… and that's not just the power of Christmas. That's the power of the Bunkers.

Not Gettin' Hassled, Not Gettin' Hustled

1974 - 1977

"Kelly's Kids" from *The Brady Bunch*
Original Air Date: 4 January 1974
By John Harrison

While it may not be among the most loved or well-remembered episodes of *The Brady Bunch* (1969–1974), "Kelly's Kids" was undoubtedly one of the most interesting moments from that series, where the subjects of adoption, racism and mixed-nationality families (still quite controversial and taboo subjects in many parts of 1974 America) are tackled, though with the show's usual candy-coated approach. The episode was in fact planned as a pilot for an offshoot television series of its own (to be titled, of course, *Kelly's Kids*). The concept didn't pan out, and "Kelly's Kids" became just another, albeit somewhat odd and out of place, episode of *The Brady Bunch*'s fifth and final season.

In "Kelly's Kids", the main focus of the story is not on the Bradys but on their good friends and nearby neighbors the Kellys. Ken Kelly (Ken Berry) and his wife Kathy (Brooke Bundy) are a married couple of around the same age as their good friends Mike and Carol Brady (Robert Reed and Florence Henderson). Though happy and very much in love, Ken and Kathy's inability to start a family leaves them with a large vacuum in their lives, so one afternoon they arrive at the Brady household and inform Mike and Carol that they have decided to adopt a small boy. Matt (Todd Lookinland, Mike's younger brother) is a typical all-American eight-year-old boy whom the Kelly's rescue from the local orphanage and bring into their home, giving the kid his own room complete with brand new skateboard and slot car set (toys – the best way to win a young kid's love).

While Matt clearly loves his new digs and the love and attention given to him by his adoptive parents, he misses the companionship of the kids he left behind at the orphanage, especially his best friends Dwayne (William Attmore II a.k.a. Billy "Pop" Atmore) and Steve (Carey Wong). Before you know it, Ken and Kathy are back at the orphanage and adopting both of Matt's best buddies – one of whom is a Black-American and the other an Asian-American – with the apparent casualness and ease of picking out some new outdoor furniture. Unfortunately, not all of the Kelly's neighbors are as hip and accepting as the Brady Bunch, and the three kids overhear nosey biddy Mrs. Payne (Molly Dodd) complaining to Mr. Kelly about the noise his instant new family are making, clearly insinuating that their mixed races mean certain trouble. Dejected and not wanting to cause more trouble for the nice people who adopted them, the Kelly kids decide to run away from home, but only get as far as the Brady's backyard, where Greg Brady (Barry Williams) discovers them asleep on the patio (Greg strutting his way to the back door as if he's just gotten to first base with a Westdale High School cheerleader). A cup of hot chocolate from Mrs. Brady and some strong comforting words from Mike keeps the three boys around long enough for Ken and Kathy to arrive and assure them that they are family and they are loved, no matter what some stickybeak neighbor has to say.

When we see the Kelly kids for the last time, they are enjoying some playtime fun with the Brady siblings in the Bradys back yard, while the Brady and Kelly parents are indoors congratulating themselves on solving yet another life dilemma in under twenty-five minutes. The episode ends with the parents sharing a laugh after Ken and Kathy show Mike and Carol a copy of *The Three Musketeers*, their boys' favorite book and inside which they have coloured-in a drawing of the Musketeers, giving one a black face and another a yellow face.

Though we know now that "Kelly's Kids" was what the industry calls a "backdoor pilot" (using a popular show to try and launch a new standalone series), watching the episode as a kid was always a confusing experience. How come the Bradys were hardly in it? Who were this new family and kids and where did they suddenly come from? And why make such a big deal out of them if they were never going to be seen again? Of course, if the "Kelly's Kids" episode had successfully spun-off into its own series, it would have been easy to understand the connection. But as it stands, it's like watching an episode of *The Brady Bunch* through some distorted kiddie-level *Twilight Zone*-esque lens. Some kids at the time must have watched it and scratched their heads, wondering if the kids who played the Bradys were too sick to appear or had quit the series.

It's highly likely that the "Kelly's Kids" concept was developed to play off the apparent humor generated by three boys of mixed races living under the one roof, rather than through any serious desire to confront and combat racism. This is still an episode of *The Brady Bunch*, after all. The deepest any conversation on the subject goes is when Ken tells Carol and Mike: "The fact that Dwayne is black and Steve is Oriental surprised us a little bit at first, but what difference does that really make?" But the ignorance behind racism is effectively represented by the "concerned" neighbor (though even here, it is first established that Mrs. Payne is unhappy with just a single white boy moving in next to her, perhaps in an attempt to depict her as just as racist towards whites as blacks or Asians). In fact, perhaps the most provocative moment in the episode is not any comment regarding racism but more the clear reference to urination and bedwetting, when Steve worries about Dwayne drinking a glass of milk before bed, as they share a bunk and Steve sleeps on the bottom.

Cast as Ken Kelly, Ken Berry was a successful and very familiar face on American television, guest starring on an abundance of popular sitcoms and drama shows, but perhaps best known for his lead role of Captain Wilton Parmenter on *F Troop* (1965–1967). Also an accomplished tap dancer who grew up worshipping Fred Astaire and Gene Kelly, Berry manages to showcase his dancing talent in "Kelly's Kids", when he dons a hat and cane for a little soft-shoe demonstration in front of his new boys. Playing his wife Kathy, Brooke Bundy was another familiar face who turned up in a long list of television shows going back to *The Donna Reed Show* in 1962. By the eighties she was appearing in exploitation and horror fare like *Mission Kill* (1986), *Stewardess*

School (1986) and *Beverly Hills Bodysnatchers* (1989). She also played the character of Elaine Parker in *A Nightmare on Elm Street 3: Dream Warriors* (1987) and *A Nightmare on Elm Street 4: The Dream Master* (1988).

"Kelly's Kids" was one of only two episodes of *The Brady Bunch* to be written by the show's creator and producer, the legendary Sherwood Schwartz (the other episode being the pilot, "The Honeymoon"). It was clearly Schwartz who was behind the *Kelly's Kids* concept, perhaps realising that *The Brady Bunch* was likely in the throes of its last season and looking to use it as both a testing ground and a springboard for his new series. Though *Kelly's Kids* would not eventuate as originally planned, Schwartz would resurrect his original idea in 1986 with *Together We Stand*, a sitcom starring Elliott Gould and Dee Wallace as adoptive parents to an ethnically diverse range of children. After six episodes, *Together We Stand* was re-tooled (without Gould) as *Nothing Is Easy* until the series was cancelled after nineteen episodes.

In what would be a failed backdoor pilot, "Kelly's Kids" from The Brady Bunch *had pals of Carol (Florence Henderson) and Mike (Robert Reed) Brady adopt three orphaned children, one white, one black and one Asian in an episode that tackled not only race, but parenthood and the importance of togetherness and family.*

"Gloria's Boyfriend" from *All in the Family*
Original Air Date: 2 February 1974
By Lee Gambin

For the most part, dramatic TV series of the seventies and eighties would take on various issues facing characters with intellectual disabilities or learning difficulties rather than situation comedies. Whether they be medically inclined shows such as *Quincy, M.E.* (1976–1983) or crime-centric entries such as *Murder, She Wrote* (1984–1996), the topic here would rarely see the light of day in the realm of episodic comedy. However, in a groundbreaking episode of the always thought provoking *All in the Family* (1971–1979), this is highlighted and brought to the fore with astounding sensitivity, intelligence and dignity. With an opening that features cantankerous Archie (Carroll O'Connor) and fiery liberal Mike (Rob Reiner) having to fix a door by using a wood shaver to carve the width down, the episode builds itself up with a heated notion that people with intellectual disabilities are completely misunderstood but will somehow prove themselves as worthy as their mentally "capable" peers. When the audience realizes that the blade on the wood shaver doesn't seem to work, it is a perfect set-up of what will eventually turn out to be a clear indication that Archie is reigning king of buffoons and a character by the name of George (Richard Masur) will come out on top, figuring out the mechanics of the tool and beating Archie at his own game. Funnily the set-up, pay off and entire overstretched sequence is similar to a moment where the "bimbo" and simple-minded Kelly Bundy (Christina Applegate) works out how to erect a complicated work bench while her father Al (Ed O'Neill) is perplexed by it on an episode of *Married… with Children* (1987–1997) many years later.

George, the local box boy at Ferguson's market, is an intellectually handicapped young man who takes a liking to the lovely Gloria (Sally Struthers) who not only treats him as an equal but also admires him and is his trusted good friend. While her incorrigible father refers to him as "George the nutcase" and her left-wing husband Mike refers to him as being "retarded" and seems to also only see his "disadvantages" (even though he spends the entire episode defending him), Gloria sees George as a gifted and wonderful person. Her mother Edith (Jean Stapleton) is much the same, and mother and daughter even make George laugh but more importantly make him feel respected and needed. George is sensitive and sweet and his crush on Gloria is one solely based on the fact that she sees him as her equal – when he helps her with the groceries it makes him feel useful and important and when he mentions that he is grateful of her treating him so kindly he makes a profound comment on it all by remarking: "You talk to me."

In what could be considered the most telling opinion here is the fact that George, and millions of people that he comes to represent here in this episode, don't feel that "regular" folk converse with them as human beings. Instead, they are mistreated, ignored, shunned, ostracized, put upon, feared or pitied, all of which is tiring and offensive.

The other factor is the Mike-syndrome, where liberals overcompensate with their leftist leanings that come across as guilt-driven empathy, which perceptive people such as George can pick up, and which is just as obnoxious. Interestingly enough, this kind of social thought is expressed in the 1973 episode "The Games Bunkers Play" where Lionel Jefferson (Mike Evans) finally snaps at Mike, telling him he can talk to him as "Lionel" and not as a "black man". In the same episode, the eternally cool Lionel expressed his love and admiration for the eternally gracious Edith who he says has always treated him with respect and great decency. In "Gloria's Boyfriend" the same principle can be examined – the fact that Gloria doesn't see George's "disability", she only sees "George", hence promoting a lovely message that the world needs more of her and less of her bigoted father (who doesn't change by the episode's end). This factor is a sublimely brave decision from the writers and producer Norman Lear, in that Archie Bunker is not a character whose opinions will change at the end of the episode, even if he is proven wrong and is fundamentally wrong.

The way Archie talks to George is painfully condescending, treating him like every other "minority" that the cigar chomping conservative "has to deal with". Archie's personal feelings on people with intellectual disabilities are linked to his opinions on gay people, black people, Latino people and so forth, and much like these social groups, there is a cry to be treated as individuals and to be treated with decency and respect. On top of all this for George is the fact that he wishes to feel that sense of independence that a lot of other people take for granted. Also, upon watching the episode by this time in the series' run, the theme song would be taken for granted. However, the lyric "Everybody pulled his weight" is something that inadvertently makes a statement about George just wanting to do that: to feel as though he is contributing.

This is a common plight for other characters in TV history with handicaps from the spunky Corky (Chris Burke) who has Down Syndrome in *Life Goes On* (1989–1993) or the wheelchair-bound singing student Artie (Kevin McHale) in *Glee* (2009–2015). Of course in TV sitcoms disabilities in all shapes and forms have been explored and scrutinized from Arnold (Gary Coleman) befriending Kathy (Melanie Watson) a young girl afflicted with osteogenesis imperfecta in the episode "Kathy's Olympics" and a former athlete now a paraplegic in "The Gymnasts" on *Diff'rent Strokes* (1978–1986), through to Rose's (Betty White) romance with a dwarf in "A Little Romance" and Blanche's affair with a man in a wheelchair in "Stand By Your Man" on *The Golden Girls* (1985–1992). Not to mention the exquisite Geri Jewell, a comedienne and actress with cerebral palsy who made a massive impression as a semi-regular on *The Facts of Life* (1979–1988).

As far as intellectual disability went on television, the wildly important movie of the week *Bill* (1981) starring Mickey Rooney would make a huge impact, and Rooney's performance as a mentally handicapped man would spark a keen cultural interest in advocacy for the rights of these people. Dennis Quaid as the sympathetic good friend and filmmaker would help to inspire intellectually "capable" counterparts to move forward and look beyond limitations which is something that the excellent *Punky Brewster* (1984–1988) episode "The Gift" does so well. The eponymous Punky (Soleil Moon Frye) is a champion of the underdog, and being one herself, is not willing to take social oppression lying down. When she befriends an intellectually handicapped young woman Linda (Bonnie Urseth) who works as a janitor at her school, Punky learns about mental disability but empowers the custodian with important factors that make her wonderful. Eventually, Linda wows everyone with her musical talent come the end of the episode, which is a common trope that shows dealing with these issues adopted.

George in "Gloria's Boyfriend" is much like Linda in "The Gift" from *Punky Brewster* in that he is talented and also lucky enough to have supportive friends. Gloria's open heart and loving nature and Edith's sweet response to George's disposition ("It's nice that he's always smilin', he's always happy") show us that the world is not only made up of good people, but it's also made up of people who choose to see goodness. When George helps Gloria reach high cabinets by lifting her up, it causes concern for Archie who thinks that the young man has lascivious feelings for his "little girl", but Gloria angrily defends her friendship with George ("That's right Daddy, we're friends!"), and in turn protects George's honor. Archie's fear of George being sexually attracted to Gloria leads into Mike's comment that both smashes stereotypes but also somehow gives them a tangibility when they may not be so obvious: "Retarded people have no more of a sex drive than anybody else!"

The episode gets heated when it lets George get angry. When he protests: "You're making fun of me!" there is a great sense of George's pain made, and when the audience comes to understand that George fully comprehends the world's opinion on him as represented here by Archie's bigotry, it is powerful television. Another great factor in this piece is the addition of George's father Pat (Joseph Mascolo) who is not only protective of his son but has strong opinions that young people with intellectual disabilities are not given vocational opportunities and that if they were they'd be excellent at their prescribed jobs. Archie insensitively asks Pat why he doesn't put his son in a "home" and Pat's push for George to make it on his own counters such an unenlightened query. Pat also provides traditional Very Special Episode exposition and clinical information on the reasoning behind George's disability and here the cause is said to be anoxia, a condition where not enough air circulated as George was being born, causing him to grow up with learning difficulties. But this is a side point, and completely unimportant. What is fundamentally vital here is the premise of George being allowed to be himself and to be self-sufficient. When he is compared by his father to his off-screen brother who is a lawyer, there is no competition in favor or anything of the sort, it is simple fact – and an insight into these kinds of things not being inherited or linked to familial genetics in any way. However, bringing up a lawyer son in comparison to a mentally handicapped son paints a picture of how success is measured.

George summarizes this reasoning with returning to the Bunker household with a placard a considerate teacher gave him when they saw that he was being picked on by other boys in his class. The placard reads: "Every man is my superior in that I may learn from him" – something that touches the entire household, most notably Mike who may learn that even being a leftist socially conscious liberal might not be a clear cut "in" on being a good, decent human being. With George feeling good about himself and Gloria reinstating her pride in him, the final line from the guest character who is the basis of the issue at hand is an inspired piece of writing: George says, "Don't worry about it Mr. Bunker, sometimes I get things backwards too." What this line truly tells us is that Archie's ideology is a backwards one – it is reductive thought, regressive and unenlightened and here it takes an insightful commentary from a character who is deemed supposedly "simple".

"The Tax Audit" from *Maude*
Original Air Date: 12 February 1974
By Michael Barrett

We sometimes hear the assertion that topical or "socially relevant" sitcoms tend to "date" more badly than those dedicated to old fashioned escapist apolitical entertainment, such as shows about air-headed women or jolly ethnics. The reality seems to be that just about every sitcom becomes more fascinating with age, if not always funnier. And now that decades have passed since the first wave of relevant sitcoms, we can recognize that their hot-button topics haven't dated at all, unfortunately.

From the second season of *Maude* comes "The Tax Audit," which uses only three of the regulars: Maude (Bea Arthur), her husband Walter (Bill Macy), and Arthur (Conrad Bain), one of those sitcom neighbors who stroll into houses without knocking because it would take valuable time and it's just an open set anyway.

As the episode begins, Walter is distraught because he may have fudged a little on the taxes for his appliance store, and an Internal Revenue Service auditor is arriving any minute. Maude sweeps into a theatrical speech: "Oh Walter, where does it all end? What has happened to the moral climate in this country? Is there no--is there no difference between right and wrong? Sure, it starts small, stealing from the cookie jar and copying answers on final exams, now cheating on your income tax. Walter, before you know it, if you're not careful, you'll have a really big job in Washington."

When the little auditor, Harvey Clarke (Larry Haines) arrives, he seems vaguely familiar to Maude, but only when she spots his wrist tattoo does it come rushing back to her. Taking Walter into the kitchen, she whispers that Clarke tried to rape her. This gets a laugh from the audience, probably a nervous one because viewers are familiar with Maude's theatricality and also because this topic is so unexpected and "outrageous" in the context of a sitcom.

The laughs continue as Walter responds in amazement that he only turned his back for a second to hang up the man's hat. "Not now! 31 years ago!" says Maude. Their lengthy dialogue and increasingly loud argument will feature this continual interdependence, the comic asides puncturing the serious moments while the serious moments puncture the comedy. It's a weave impossible to separate, but what sticks with viewers is Walter's tendency to question or trivialize while Maude continually asserts the seriousness of the situation.

She relates a story of attending a dance in Boston during WWII, when she was 17, and of parking at the Bunker Hill Monument with a sailor. The next thing she knew, she was struggling against him and escaped when her shoe broke his windshield. She fled home in her torn dress, only to be blamed by her father, who called her "terrible names" and kept her in the house for six months.

"When I was fighting desperately to keep my clothes from being ripped off me, Ish Kabibble was singing 'Don't Sit Under the Apple Tree,'" says Maude. Walter says, "Ish Kabibble?" and Maude answers, "Walter, I was fighting for my life, I didn't have time to switch stations!"

Here's not only an example of winding comic details inseparably into the narrative, but of the show's penchant for nostalgic references. In Maude's debut appearance on *All in the Family* (1971–1979), she and Edith Bunker (Jean Stapleton) had already discussed the career of Mr. Kabibble, clearly cited on account of his peculiar name. Maude had disparaged his humor; in retrospect, the series may finally have explained Maude's aversion to him.

When Walter tries to reassure her that at least "nothing happened," Maude responds, "Because he didn't finish what he started out to do, that wipes the slate clean?" When he says she's "making a mountain out a molehill," she really sets off: "Assaulting a woman, Walter, is not a molehill, nor are her feelings about it. They are her most precious possessions and they should be treated with dignity and respect, but I wouldn't expect you to understand that. You're a man."

"What a lousy thing to say!" he shouts.

All boxes get checked off swiftly and thoroughly, from "are you sure?" to "hysteria" to "what were you doing there?" From her own husband, who fears upsetting the auditor, Maude runs the gauntlet of blames, equivocations, condescensions and dismissals with which today's viewers are familiar from contemporary TV shows, such as Senate hearings. Walter may be headed for a really big job in Washington.

To refresh Clarke's memory, because it seems the incident has passed from his mind, Maude re-enacts it on the couch with roles reversed, and viewers are treated to the surprising and liberating slapstick of Maude grabbing the mortified man's breast and pushing him down on the couch. It's vulgar, funny and shocking all at once, and it's the kind of action possible only in a daring comedy.

It's also an example of play therapy or drama therapy, where patients enact role reversals and ritualistic rewrites for the sake of catharsis. Another acute psychological gesture finds Maude rushing to the refrigerator and grabbing some garbage to eat as she becomes increasingly upset with Walter.

This version has a happy ending in which Clarke states that his memory of events is somewhat different, but he apologizes and says he tried to apologize at the time. This apology is exactly what Maude needs to hear in order to have 31 years of sour memory lifted from her shoulders. She also allows herself to be flattered by his remark that she was a "sexy dish" who hasn›t changed.

Walter is less happy when presented with his tax adjustment. "How do you like that?" says Maude. "What he tried to do to me 31 years ago, he just did to you today." This is among many examples of how Maude alluded to words the censors wouldn't allow her to say, a strategy of the show's will to shock into laughter by referring to its boundaries. Sometimes it pushed against the boundaries and tweaked them, as with Clarke's man-breast.

This is Bernie Kahn's only script for *Maude*. Kahn is one of the subjects of the 2003 video documentary *Funny Old Guys*, about a group of elderly Jewish TV writers who tell jokes and reminisce at weekly lunches. His output specializes in the fanciful and fantastical: *My Favorite Martian* (1963–1966), *The Smothers Brothers Show* (1965–1966) (the sitcom where Tom is an angel, not their variety show), *My Mother the Car* (1965–1966), *The Addams Family* (1964–1966), *Get Smart* (1965–1970), *The Second Hundred Years* (1967–1968), *The Ugliest Girl in Town* (1968–1969) (a cross-dressing show), *Bewitched* (1964–1972) and *My World and Welcome to It* (1969–1970), the wonderful partly-animated series inspired by James Thurber.

He and co-writer Lila Garrett shared Writers Guild nominations for *Get Smart* and *My World and Welcome to It*, and they contributed to the Disney movie *The Barefoot Executive* (1971) about a chimp. Oh, he also wrote Saturday morning cartoons like *Super Friends* (1973–2011) and *Valley of the Dinosaurs* (1974).

None of this signals a likelihood that Kahn would write for *Maude*, much less such a premise. We'd rather expect him to write "The Flying Saucer" (26 September 1977), the series' only brush with the fantastic – and topical even so.

And yet, IMDb says Kahn's previous sitcom script was "Alice's Wild Oat" (3 October 1973), second episode of the quickly-cancelled *Bob & Carol & Ted & Alice*. Inspired by Paul Mazursky's 1969 film, this series tried to cover sexual topics. The logline for Kahn's episode says, "When an attorney who's been indicted for tax fraud shows up on the front page of the paper, Alice admits to Ted that she lost her virginity to him." Hmm, this combines tax fraud with a wife telling her husband of a long-ago sexual encounter, though of a different nature. Coincidence?

"George" from M*A*S*H
Original Air Date: 16 February 1974
By Samm Deighan

One of the highest rated and most popular shows in American television history was undoubtedly *M*A*S*H* (1972–1983), a situation comedy about the doctors, staff, and patients of the "4077th Mobile Army Surgical Hospital" made for CBS. Short for Mobile Army Surgical Hospital, *M*A*S*H* began as a comedy, but took an increasingly serious turn throughout its 11-year run. Set in a camp in South Korea, during the Korean War – which lasted from 1950–1953 – *M*A*S*H* was a clever way for series creator Larry Gelbart and its numerous other writers to critique the Vietnam War, which was ongoing at the time. Though it was less scathing and ribald than Robert Altman's 1970 feature film of the same name, which it was inspired by, the 25-minute long episodes could be quite dark and confronted a range of issues within American society.

Altman's film can be said to be an open criticism of the Vietnam War, whereas the creators of *M*A*S*H* had to be more careful and much more subtle with its anti-war message, though this gradually changed throughout the series. A symbolic example of this difference is in the theme song: while Altman's film features the theme "Suicide is Painless," by Johnny Mandel and created specifically for the film, the television show only includes it in a brief, instrumental form during the opening credits. *M*A*S*H* often approached its social criticism with humor, which was frequently quite sexual in nature (and the show was one of the first on television to present some nudity), as a way to deal with violence, death, and the relentless trauma of war. The show also presented characters with widely differing viewpoints in discussion with each other as a way to question the war and explore issues related to it – and more broadly to American society.

Episode 22 of season two, titled "George," which aired in February of 1974, is a key example of this formula. A soldier, Private George Weston (Richard Ely), is brought in for surgery and Captain Pierce – better known as Hawkeye (Alan Alda), a sarcastic surgeon and the show's primary protagonist – notices that Weston is covered in bruises, which are unlikely to have come from his war-related injury and the doctors assume that perhaps he's been fighting. Major Frank Burns (Larry Linville), the conservative, often dog headed second-in-command at the hospital for the first half of the show's run, remarks that Weston must be a hero, as he has been wounded in battle several times, but notes that he should reprimand the Private for fighting. When conscious, Weston confesses to Hawkeye that he is gay and was beaten up by other soldiers for drunkenly confessing that fact to his unit.

Hawkeye and Trapper – Captain John McIntyre (Wayne Rogers), effectively Hawkeye's sidekick and close friend for the first three seasons of the show – discuss Weston's sexually in a positive, tolerant light. Soon though, Burns hears a rumor that Weston is gay and moves to have him dishonorably discharged; all Weston wants is to be sent back to his unit as soon as his injuries have healed, so he can resume fighting in the war. Outraged that Burns is trying to have Weston discharged, Hawkeye and Trapper argue with him and try to change his mind. When this doesn't work, they hold a mock argument in which Trapper appears to agree with Burns. The false rapport between Trapper and Burns allows Trapper to trick Burns into admitting that he bribed his way through a medical school exam. Hawkeye and Trapper are thus able to blackmail Burns into putting an end to his plans for Weston's dishonorable discharge.

"George" was an incredibly daring episode for the time and works as both a critique of the military and also of American society in general. There were few, if any, positive depictions of gay characters on television in the seventies. Anyone openly gay was not allowed to serve in the United States military and the public announcement of Weston's homosexuality would have been enough to proceed with the dishonorable discharge: a sentence with far-reaching economic, social, and personal consequences. Burns says that because he is gay, Weston is "sick" and "not normal," a belief held by many people in mainstream America with few positive cultural examples of homosexuality. This was obviously beginning to change, as can be seen in the supportive dialogue between Hawkeye and Trapper, clearly the show's protagonist. Burns, on the other hand, was often represented as a close minded bigot, becoming more openly antagonistic and even villainous throughout his run on the show.

Directed by series producer and frequent director Gene Reynolds and written by John Regier and Gary Markowitz – their first for the show, though they would return to pen two additional episodes – "George" is notable for its lack of jokes at Frank's expense, though earlier episodes of M*A*S*H do occasionally feature gay jokes and mild homophobia. But in "George," the only vague, stereotypical "effeminate" behaviors – such as painting a woman's toenails and being unable to throw a ball well – are attributed to Hawkeye throughout the episode, not Weston. Burns is also the butt of jokes – and even more so, derision – because of his views about homosexuality. Weston is not on screen for much of the episode's running time, but he's portrayed heroically. He has been repeatedly wounded, beaten up by his own men, and still wants nothing more than to return to active service, because he believes that now, more than ever, he has a moral obligation to serve.

Contemporary audiences may note that Weston doesn't have a major presence in the episode and we don't spend a lot of time getting to know him – he is depicted injured and in surgery, and then in recovery, when he speaks matter-of-factly to Hawkeye about his sexuality and the incident with his unit. His presence is really a way to allow Hawkeye and Trapper to have a dialogue with Burns; they are unable to change his mind, but raise important issues about individuality, a key American social value, and question what "normal" really means. This idea of "normal" behavior is repeatedly questioned throughout the show, often as Hawkeye and the other *M*A*S*H* personnel attempt to come to terms with war trauma and their ongoing experiences in South Korea. While Hawkeye often deals with this through humor, the show was not afraid to explore issues of madness, post-traumatic stress disorder, and mental instability as an inevitable by-product of exposure to violence and war. "George," of course, is less specifically a war protest episode and more a portrait of changes mores within American society and remains an example of how boldly the show was willing to confront taboo issues – it's still surprising to think of a military-themed situation comedy as being one of the first cultural platforms to confront gay bashing, a feat made even more impressive by the fact that *M*A*S*H* was on network television with an audience of millions of Americans.

"Lt. Preston of the 4th Cavalry" from *The New Dick Van Dyke Show*
Original Air Date: 1974
By Rachel Bellwoar

"Lt. Preston of the 4th Cavalry" was supposed to be the season finale for the third season of *The New Dick Van Dyke Show* (1971–1974). Had it aired, it would've been the series finale but, in the end, it wasn't until the show ran on syndication that the episode ever saw the light of day.

What could've been so terrible that CBS parted ways with Carl Reiner (who created *The New Dick Van Dyke* and the old one, starring Mary Tyler Moore) rather than agree to his demand that the episode not be pulled? The series could've continued but Dick Van Dyke's contract was up and since Reiner wasn't going to produce, he decided to leave his Dick Preston days behind him.[1]

It all came down to a storyline where Preston's daughter, Annie (Angela Powell), walked in on Dick and his wife, Jenny (Hope Lange), having sex. The title of the episode paints a picture of a soldier coming home from the war, but Dick's only been gone a week, for a role where he's playing a soldier.

Right away you get a clear picture of how close this family is from the fuss they make over reuniting. Annie draws a sign to welcome him home, with every intention of waiting outside and giving it to him. She only comes back in when he calls on the phone, to tell them he's going to be late.

This is the call that gets the ball rolling for Annie opening her parents' bedroom door by mistake. When she expected her dad, she knew where to be for his arrival, but the phone call throws everything off. Dick wasn't just expected home. He needed to be home in order to make a father-daughter banquet he'd promised Annie they would attend. Once that's out of the picture, Dick doesn't have a deadline, so when Jenny asks him when he'll be home, the best he can do is guess by the time Annie finishes school the next day. There's nothing that holds him to a specific time anymore (and even when there was, it didn't matter). Unless Annie camps out in front of the house, the window for his arrival has gotten too big for her to personally greet him. Dick later finds the sign she made for him in the kitchen, her excitement to give it to him having fizzled out.

Dick thinks this means she must be angry at him and, given how guilty he feels, you can understand why he'd blame himself. Anytime someone on a sitcom waits to the last minute to get home it's inevitable that something will happen to make them late. The writing was almost on the wall and had the episode gone in a more obvious direction, it would've centered around Dick trying to make it up to his daughter.

---

1 Ingram, Billy. "The New Dick Van Dyke Show, Part Two." TVparty, <www.tvparty.com/new van2.html>.

Jenny claims Annie took the disappointment well and there's nothing on screen to contradict her. If anything, Annie seems too forgiving, which is why you're inclined to doubt her story. As audience members, though, we also have the advantage over Dick, of knowing what really happened, and that Annie's silence isn't because she's mad but because she's embarrassed.

Since Annie's not going to say anything, it's up to Dick and Jenny to investigate the subject further. What's refreshing about this episode (and the reason CBS probably shelved it) is it doesn't avoid having uncomfortable conversations. Talking about sex, especially with one's parents, hasn't stopped being awkward in the forty-five years since *The New Dick Van Dyke Show* aired. Network TV has a history of being conservative in this area, too. You only have to look at the sleeping arrangements of married couples on early sitcoms to see how much times have changed. As Neil Pond notes in his article, "Sleeping with the Stars," "Hollywood's notoriously strict Hays Code prohibited the depiction of men and women in bed together for decades",[2] and when you look at it that way it's no wonder CBS considered "Lt. Preston of the 4th Cavalry" unfit for broadcast.

However, when you look at how the episode actually depicts the incident, everything's implied. You're not allowed to see what Annie sees. If the scene were filmed today you might hear noises coming from the bedroom, as a way of letting adults know what Annie was about to encounter, but both later, when we know why Annie's upset and her parents don't, and in the moment, everything caters to Annie's perspective.

That means instead of sounds, there are musical cues by Allyn Ferguson and Jack Elliott to let us know something's happened. Change the context and these cues could be suggestive of anything but given how Dick and Jenny were acting in the bedroom just beforehand, when Dick surprised Jenny by arriving home early, the location (their bedroom), and Annie's body language, it's safe to assume Annie saw them having sex. Another benefit of having the cues not be directly sexual is they reflect Annie's lack of understanding at what she's witnessed. The first sounds you hear, when she opens the door, are two chimes, implying surprise and curiosity. Annie didn't know her dad was home yet, so it makes sense that her first reaction would be one of happiness to see him, but then comes the low, sliding sound of horror, timed to Annie shutting the door behind her.

Annie's silence and desire to walk away, unnoticed, is another giveaway that what she saw was her parents having sex and this is confirmed officially in the next scene when Dick and Jenny are shown lying in bed together. The comforter's pulled up tastefully, so the only body parts visible are their bare shoulders, but it's enough to tell you they're naked underneath. All in all, it's a chaste scene yet, to acknowledge CBS' concerns, if not condone them, sex wasn't something all sitcoms acknowledged. Sex could be hinted at but there was usually a sense of deniability around the act, where logically that's what was going to happen, but you never knew for certain. TV was supposed to be scaring teens away from intercourse, not showing it in a positive light, yet Jenny and Dick never

---

2   Pond, Neil. "Sleeping with the Stars." *Parade Magazine*, 20 Jan. 2019, p. 9.

pretend they were sleeping. They don't realize right away that Annie walked in on them (that requires some detective work) but, once they do, they never consider lying to her or making out like there's something shameful about having a healthy sex life.

What they do question is how they should approach Annie about it, and what is particularly great about this episode (as written by Reiner, Sybil Adelman and Barbara Gallagher) is that Dick and Jenny make all of their decisions together. Instead of going for cheap laughs and having one or the other try and resolve the issue on their own, Reiner, Adelman, and Gallagher show two parents working as a team and doing everything in their power to make sure they don't say the wrong thing.

Co-parenting is always important, but it's not something you can take for granted, especially where a topic like sex is concerned. Often the conversation gets split along gender lines. If it's a son, the father talks to him. If it's a daughter, the mother. Since Annie's so young, it's a matter of how much to say, too. Dick and Jenny likely thought they still had time to give Annie the birds and the bees talk (as represented by the way Dick plays with Annie's pigtails, as if wanting to preserve her innocence). At the same, they want to make sure Annie's comfortable, which is why they take gender into consideration at all. Dick agrees to find out whether Annie really saw them together, and Jenny agrees to take over, should her answer be "yes." Rather than take Jenny's out, and not participate in the conversation, though (and he could've done that, in good conscience, and the episode would've been fine), Dick makes sure to make himself available, too, by first giving Annie her privacy and then showing up at the end, to give Annie a chance to ask him questions.

It's easy to build these conversations up in your head, but the whole thing ends up being a lot more painless than Dick or Jenny expected. Considering how tempting it must have been, to ignore the situation and hope it went way, Dick and Jenny are rewarded for their direct approach, both in the immediate change it brings to Annie's demeanor and in ensuring Annie knows she can come to them in the future. As it turns out, the reason she was really upset was she thought Jenny might be pregnant (a direct example of how not having these conversations with your children, or TV shows willing to show parents how to broach these conversations, can lead to misinformation, not prevention). By establishing an open dialogue, the Prestons save themselves a lot of grief and it's all because they were brave enough to ask questions, instead of suffering in silence.

"The Manuel Who Came to Dinner" from *Chico and The Man*
Original Air Date: 27 December 1974
By Kevin Nickelson

"I guess because the shows were activist in their own way – the marriage of my public activism and my career activism, you know – people understand me very well. They also understand there's a very strong bipartisan part in all of this." – Norman Lear

If Norman Lear was busy shining a light on the African American life experience through the small screen, James Komack was building a spotlight of his own and aiming it squarely in the direction of the Hispanic community. Komack had quite the *résumé* before *Chico and the Man* came flickering to life on 13 September 1974. He'd already had success with three seasons of *My Favorite Martian* (1963–1966) as well as *The Courtship of Eddie's Father* (1969–1972) before giving viewers a peak into the lives of the young hotshot mechanic Chico Rodriguez and the old codger garage owner Ed Brown. But Komack did not have the ordinary rise to fame as a writer. In fact, he started out his professional life as Jimmie Komack, bit and supporting actor on fifties western TV chestnuts as *Zane Grey Theatre* (1957–1961) and *Wagon Train* (1957–1965) as well as roles in the 1958 film version of the musical *Damn Yankees* and Frank Capra's sparkling comedy-drama *A Hole in the Head* (1959).

Komack's first writing gig was a 1961 episode (called "Size 10") of *The Barbara Stanwyck Show* (1960–1961). One could say Komack received two big breaks that catapulted him to success. First, it was writer and series creator John L. Greene who tabbed Komack to produce and write for Greene's series *My Favorite Martian*, popular enough at the time to garner three seasons of production and has gone on to TV and cult status to this day. Two, Komack received advice from the legendary Sherwood Schwartz (of *Gilligan's Island*, *Brady Bunch* fame) that may have helped him most of all. Schwartz was script consultant/head writer on *Martian* and made the following observation in his book *Brady, Brady, Brady: The Complete Story of the Brady Bunch as Told by the Father/Son Team Who Really Know*: "Jimmie was gifted but he wrote scenes that were overly long and kept going beyond their value to the story. He needed control. I told him about my 'diagram' system, which I demonstrated by applying it to one of his scripts. Jimmy was really excited about my 'method'. He said he was going to use that on every script he wrote from then on. In fact he asked me if he could have that sheet of paper. I said, 'sure.' It was just a sheet of typing paper that I divided into boxes like I always did." It's a method to suggest breaking down the script into Act One and Act Two sections, allowing for commercial break insertion and story flow within a twenty-one minute or so sitcom format.

Komack long credited this advice for helping him create pilot scripts on *Courtship* and *Chico* that helped sell those properties to the network. He may be overly simplistic and modest in this "telling" of how he got those shows off the ground. A writer also has to have a solid, inventive, at least somewhat original premise and interesting characters. But one gets the idea here that Komack was never the cheerleader for himself and would rather just let the work speak for itself. With *Chico*, it did in volumes. The gulf difference in understanding and lack thereof between the Hispanic and Anglo populations in the United States has varied in size over the years but closure remains a work in progress. It is that very potent issue that Komack made central to his theme for the show. He took something of a huge risk in launching this series. Though the show was not the first to feature a Hispanic lead character (we all remember *I Love Lucy* and Ricky Ricardo in the 1950s), it was the first to deal more realistically with the day to day struggles of Latinos within a working class milieu. Komack wanted a platform to be able to tell of the issues of the day through the eyes of one young man, Chico Rodriguez, as he navigates the obstacles of being single, financially strapped and a member of an ethnic minority who does not have the benefit of white privilege. His stout pride, on occasion, proving to be its own obstacle. On the other side of the generational and civilizational coin in the series is the owner of the auto repair garage Chico goes to work for named Ed Brown, a senior citizen-aged white male Korean War veteran who's squandered whatever advantage white privilege offered him. Wisened, bitter and oh-so-crusty, he is the burn out who first resents Rodriguez' constantly positive attitude only to discover just how much he needs to draw from that energy to save himself from mentally dying much sooner than he truly wishes.

This is the tale of two people who find each other and, without seemingly wanting it on the surface, need to lean on each other if they are ever going to make it through living beyond the next day. Along the way, one side gets a true view of how the other lived to get to the point where they are currently. Plumbed out of the huge assortment of engrossing, edgy and funny stories *Chico* generated are two episodes that stand as prime examples of the uniqueness the show illuminated each week. The first is one from late in season one, called "The Manuel Who Came to Dinner". In it, Chico comes to see a rivalry in full evidence between Ed and an old friend-turned-enemy Manuel Guerrera. As the young man hatches a scheme to bring the pair together again, he discovers that the falling out came as a result of Ed's son and Manuel's daughter wanting to marry and the elders taking issue with an interracial marriage. All of the fears and racial divide are exposed briefly for all to see. Though the obligatory positive resolution is never far away (can't have an ugly downer ending for a sitcom, even with the dramedy in full force during the seventies), the journey to the revelation is well-handled and remarkably adult in frankness. It examines equally Manuel's reluctance to have his son marry someone outside their culture as it does the fear of being different that Ed exhibits and interjects between his daughter and her fiancé. Both reluctantly admit their parts in the feud (and, in a way, their own personal failings) by the fadeout. I appreciate, especially, that Chico seems to be written as the bystander in all of this, almost seen as a student in a pseudo-human condition/biology hybrid study class, observing two guinea pigs being dissected by life to find the root cause of the racial divide cancer the duo are riddled with.

As I ended my viewing of this episode I remembered that old adage about a person viewing the grass as greener on the other side of the fence. I think James Komack took a look at the crisp green blades Norman Lear was growing in his yard and said to himself "my grass is just as green here. But, maybe with a bit of advice on the right manure, weed killer and the perfect mower, mine can stand out just a bit differently from what Lear is growing in his!"

The Chicano experience as presented in Chico and the Man – *a sitcom whose heart is summarized by the back and forth banter shared between the charismatic and ambitious Mexican/Puerto Rican mechanic Chico Rodriguez (Freddie Prinze) and his cantankerous white boss Ed Brown (Jack Albertson).*

"Rhoda's Wedding" from *Rhoda*
Original Air Date: 28 October 1974
By Susan Leighton

"Rhoda's Wedding" was a Very Special Episode that turned into a bona fide network event. When the show aired on October 28, 1974, it was the second highest rated program in television history. The number one show was the classic *I Love Lucy* (1951–1957) production when Lucy gave birth to Little Ricky.

It really isn't surprising when you think about it because Valerie Harper endeared herself to audiences around the world as Mary Richards' best friend on *The Mary Tyler Moore Show* (1970–1977). For those of us that grew up during the seventies, Rhoda Morgenstern was that neighbor or co-worker that we shared a couple of laughs with, a comfortable, familiar face. So, her marriage to Joe Gerard (David Groh) would have to be an affair to remember.

Every one of the "Big Three" networks were rushing around trying to come up with the quintessential "event" show since James L. Brooks and Allan Burns set the benchmark. According to writer Barbara Gallagher (*The Mary Tyler Moore Show*, *The Bob Newhart Show* (1972–1978) and *Maude* (1972–1978)):

> We were in one of the development meetings show by show on the West Coast. Jimmy Komack and Nick Arnold were there to discuss future episodes of *Welcome Back, Kotter* (1975–1979). It was the Kotter and his wife were pregnant episode which was going to be a big event. When Fred (Silverman) mentioned quadruplets Jimmy and Nick went into shock. They were trying to convince Fred that it might be a bit over the top. So, Fred went around the room asking everyone what they thought. I was quiet. He looks at me and says 'you... the mute over there, what do you think!' I said "Rhoda's Wedding". And without missing a beat Fred looked at Jimmy and said 'okay, twins'. They were so relieved. Next day on my desk was a huge vase of flowers and the card read, 'These were left over from "Rhoda's Wedding". Thank you, thank you, thank you!' It was signed Jimmy and Nick. I laughed out loud.

The reason why "Rhoda's Wedding" was such a monumental success was because she was so relatable. Her problems were similar to the viewing audience's dilemmas. Every single person knows what it is like to go on disastrous date after disastrous date. Rhoda Morgenstern was not Farrah Fawcett. She was a real woman in every sense, not some manufactured Hollywood version of femininity. That is why we loved her. When she found Joe, much like a beloved friend that has finally found her mate, we were genuinely happy for her.

This episode was also a reunion with her old castmates from *The Mary Tyler Moore Show*. Yes, this was specifically done for ratings but for fans, it was more than that. One of the many explanations of why both series were consistently in the Top Ten was not only the stellar writing but the dynamic between the actors. It is rare to capture lightning in a bottle but Grant Tinker and Mary Tyler Moore, the entities behind one of the best television production companies of all time, MTM Enterprises did just that by assembling some of the finest thespians in the business.

For "Rhoda's Wedding," it was great fun to see Valerie Harper back with Mary, Ed Asner, Gavin MacLeod, Georgia Engel and Cloris Leachman. You get the sense watching them interact on screen together that they enjoyed one another's company in the real world and it translated into pure magic. The relationship between Mary and Rhoda is ideal. Two females, not competing with one another but forging a strong bond not unlike sisterhood is always great to witness. These best friends were there for one another through terrible blind dates and all of life's ups and downs. Rhoda loves her family but Mary is special. For Mary, Rhoda is her "one."

It was extremely important that Mary liked her choice for a spouse and that Joe liked her best friend. In some ways, Rhoda looked up to her pal and to have her approval meant the world. When the two met originally, they clashed. Mary was a kind, excessively polite Midwesterner with an overwhelming optimistic attitude while Rhoda was your typical blunt, outspoken New Yorker. Rhoda coveted Mary's apartment because it was larger and she was living in an attic loft. However, they got to know one another and they became the yin to each other's yang. Throughout their individual problems like Rhoda losing her Bloomfield's job and eventually getting a divorce from Joe, Mary was there for her. However, not all was perfect in their relationship. After both shows went off the air, the two actresses reunited for a made-for-TV movie, *Mary and Rhoda* (2000).

For those of you that remember, after Rhoda's divorce from Joe, she re-entered the dating scene. At the same time, she was trying to establish her window dressing venture which didn't pan out so she took a position with a costume company. Unfortunately, she moved on from that job and became a photographer. This is where she met her second husband, Jean-Pierre Rousseau. Mary didn't like him at all and this caused a rift between the two friends after a particularly harsh argument. The pair reconnected in *Mary and Rhoda* and re-established their affectionate bond.

Another example of terrific onscreen chemistry was between Rhoda, Brenda (Julie Kavner) and their mother, Ida (Nancy Walker). The brilliant Nancy Walker was a wonderful comedienne who everyone fell in love with as the nosey but loyal housekeeper Mildred on *McMillan & Wife* (1971–1977). Ida was your typical meddlesome mother who only wished for the best for her two girls but ended up being overbearing and interfering. As much as she infuriated Rhoda and her sister, the pair fiercely loved their matriarch. She laid a guilt trip so heavy on Rhoda who wanted a simple courthouse wedding that she ended up changing her plans to accommodate her mother's vision which was a huge affair in her parents' apartment. As with any comedy, the logistics of this event turned out to be one of the comedic moments of the episode when Rhoda had to literally ride the subway to her destination in her wedding gown.

Julie Kavner (who most people today would recognize as the voice behind Marge Simpson) was very endearing as Rhoda's self-conscious sibling, Brenda. James L. Brooks enjoyed her work so much that is why the two ended up pairing again a decade later for his animated venture, *The Simpsons* (1989–). While she doesn't have a huge part in "Rhoda's Wedding", the scenes between the two actresses are very touching since Brenda is having a hard time getting used to the fact that Rhoda will no longer be her roommate. Rhoda is deeply devoted to her sister and is almost like a second mother. Even going so far as to do her make-up for the nuptials.

Although Rhoda's dad, Martin had a relatively small role in the episode, it is definitely one worth mentioning. Veteran actor Harold Gould (*The Sting* (1973), *The Golden Girls* (1985–1992)) had one of the most poignant scenes in the show. Before he walks Rhoda down the aisle, he feels as if he has to say something to her, impart some sort of wisdom but he doesn't have anything. At least, he doesn't think so. But then, he launches into a little speech that is guaranteed to bring tears to viewers' eyes:

> Fathers. You come home late from work; the kids are all asleep. You never get the chance to see them enough. By the time they're old enough to stay up late so you can see them, they don't want to stay home. Then comes the time when you can't stay up late enough to see them when they come home. So, Rhoda… I just want to say, it's good. It's good to see you.

Very Special Episodes are a lost art in today's world. Crossovers like "Rhoda's Wedding" exist but none have the impact where they become event television. Shows featuring realistic relationships between everyday people don't seem to exist anymore. Sure, *This Is Us* (2016–) and *A Million Little Things* (2018–) attempt to duplicate real life but there is always so much exaggerated drama that it becomes impossible to relate to any of the characters or situations. At one time or another, viewers could identify with Rhoda. Who hasn't lost their job, been annoyed with their parents or had a significant other? Even if the circumstances were exaggerated like Phyllis (Cloris Leachman) forgetting to pick Rhoda up for her wedding so she had to hoof it, take the train and run across Manhattan, it is still in the realm of possibility.

The characters were also like people we would know in the real world. Mary worked for a television station but she wasn't Katie Couric. There was no divide between the "haves" and "have nots." Plus, we all have a Mary in our life or a Rhoda. We may even be them. This is why audiences were so willing to let this show into their homes week in and week out. There is a reason why "Rhoda's Wedding" is one of the highest rated programs in the history of the small screen. It is an example of popular culture at its zenith. When we could escape from the problems of the day and have some fun with characters that are like our friends. The invitation to Rhoda Morgenstern's nuptials was one that everyone RSVP'd to and was glad to attend.

The event of a lifetime – "Rhoda's Wedding" from Rhoda *had our Jewish working class heroine Rhoda Morgenstern (Valerie Harper) finally land the man of her dreams, but the trek to make the wedding would summarise life's uncertainty for this loveable character.*

"Archie the Hero" from *All in the Family*
Original Air Date: 29 September 1975
By Jake Wilson

Morning in the Queens home of Archie and Edith Bunker (Carroll O'Connor and Jean Stapleton). Their son-in-law and neighbor Mike Stivic (Rob Reiner) has dropped by to use the bathroom, the one at his place being occupied by his pregnant wife Gloria (Sally Struthers). He strolls into the kitchen in a robe with a towel over his shoulders, helping himself to coffee. Edith is busy making buttermilk pancakes, in preparation for Archie's arrival home from an all-night shift as a driver for Munson's Cab Company. When Archie comes in, he's in a good mood, bursting with pride at a heroic deed he has just performed. "You delivered a baby?" guesses Edith, still with her daughter's pregnancy on her mind. Shrugging this off, Archie launches into the tale of how a "big, tall, beautiful-lookin' classy dame" collapsed in his cab, and how he revived her through mouth to mouth resuscitation – all of which he acts out in elaborate mime, much to Mike's amusement.

Keen to have his heroism known far and wide, Archie urges Mike to phone the local paper with the story; he can't do it himself, he explains, because "heroes are s'posed to be shy". Mike politely declines, pointing out that he is unable to vouch for Archie's account first hand; he heads back next door, still in his robe. Archie then goes upstairs to the "library", leaving Edith to greet an unexpected visitor: the "classy dame" herself, Beverly LaSalle (Lori Shannon), who has just been discharged from hospital and wants to thank her savior in person. When Beverly shows up on the Bunkers' doorstep, her appearance is striking but not startling: a large, self-possessed woman in orange, with a bouffant, a black scarf and a general air of matronly goodwill. Even her swaying walk and exaggerated way of clutching her bosom do no more than hint at the truth, which emerges after she blames her collapse on exhaustion brought on by performing three shows a night. "Are you in show business?" Edith asks eagerly. "Yes", says Beverly, letting the cat out of the bag. "I'm a female impersonator."

Up until now, the studio audience have seemingly been uncertain what to make of Beverly; as realization sinks in, all hell breaks loose on the soundtrack, Edith's gob-smacked expression giving the shrieks of laughter time to subside. "Ain't that interesting!" Edith eventually manages, while Beverly beams encouragingly and flutters her eyelashes. In many respects, this was business as usual for *All in the Family* (1971–1979) – the original "message" sitcom, in which the bigoted Archie was forced to confront his prejudices week after week. Still, "Archie the Hero," directed by Paul Bogart, ranks as a historical landmark, the first prominent appearance of a professional drag queen on American television (though drag had long been a staple of TV comics such as Milton Berle). Shannon, otherwise known as Don Seymour McLean, was a screen newcomer cast on the strength of her performances at the celebrated San Francisco drag club Finocchio's; she would go on to guest-star in two subsequent *All in the Family* episodes, achieving a measure of nationwide celebrity before her early death in 1984.

Strikingly, the show refuses to present Beverly as a bizarre curiosity (as she showed in a 1982 TV appearance, Shannon was capable of far more flamboyance in her own drag persona). Far from being the butt of the joke, she serves as a "straight woman" of sorts, a foil for the comic naivety of Archie and Edith. By her account, Shannon was permitted to make changes to the script of "Archie the Hero," credited to regular series writers Lou Derman and Bill Davenport; as a performer, she exercises a degree of authorial control over her scenes through her coy smiles and ironic glances, expressing various degrees of supercilious bemusement. What she brings to the show might paradoxically be described as an authentic sense of camp which threatens to break the fourth wall, hinting at a sophisticated understanding no more available to the audience than it is to the Bunkers.

Too pure of soul to pass judgment, Edith nonetheless struggles to grasp the concept of a female impersonator. "Who can imitate a female better than a lady?" she asks, anticipating Blake Edwards' *Victor Victoria* (1982), and subsequent theories of gender performativity, by a number of years. Arriving back downstairs, Archie in turn accepts his charming visitor at face value, reaching out to take her hand as she presents him with a fifty-dollar bill as a token of gratitude: "I never say no to a lady." "I'm no lady," Beverly archly confesses. But even now Archie misunderstands, smirking as he congratulates himself on his tolerance: "How you earned this fifty is no business of mine." With the situation veering out of control, Beverly is obliged to make things plain, letting her voice drop by an octave as she removes her wig; the camera closes in on Archie's horrified reaction as we go to a break.

Later the same day Mike is back in the kitchen with Edith, who continues to puzzle over the strange visitor. "I would never have guessed she was a man until she took his hair off. I mean, until he took her hair off. Well, anyway his hair came off and there she was, a man." Mike chortles over his father-in-law's misfortune: "I can imagine the look on Archie's face." "It was kind of like the look he had on his face when he first met you," Edith tells him artlessly. Mike's expression clouds, as if he were recalling his own less than manly attire in the previous scene. The parallel between Mike and Beverly as "feminine" characters is reinforced when Archie enters and Mike leans in, mockingly, for a kiss of his own. Archie predictably fumes; Edith tries to sooth him, pointing out that lifeguards routinely give mouth-to-mouth resuscitation to both men and women. Archie is unconvinced: "Lifeguards' victims is always wearing bathing suits, so lifeguards know who they're mouth-to-mouthin'. This freak took my breath under an assumed sex." As the spokesman for enlightened liberalism, Mike weighs in on the debate, pointing out that Beverly, under the surface, could be just a regular guy: "It just so happens that the majority of transvestites are heterosexual."

As usual for the show, Mike serves as a voice of reason but a faintly suspect one: his argument carries a whiff of homophobia (he echoes Archie's use of the word "fag", for modern viewers the episode's most shocking element) and depends on conflating Beverly's profession as a drag queen with transvestism offstage. In truth, the show itself is somewhat guilty of this conflation: repeatedly, the plot requires Beverly to "pass" as a woman – something an actual drag queen would be unlikely to attempt – before switching identities at the crucial moment. It is telling, in this light, that the phrase "drag queen" is never uttered; nor is the question of Beverly's sexual orientation resolved either here or in Shannon's subsequent guest appearances, though *All in the Family* had separately tackled the "issue" of homosexuality more than once. With only superficial irrelevance, Edith comments directly on the matter of enforced silence, recalling how she once sat on a jury and was told not to talk about the case: "Tick a lock," she says, miming zipping her mouth shut. Irritated by her prattle, Archie improves on this: "Tick a lock and swallow the key."

Archie himself has followed this advice, in that he has swallowed the key to his own neuroses: his trademark malapropisms illustrate the difficulty he finds in justifying a bigotry transparently rooted in repression. Even the most innocent public display of affection makes him uncomfortable, as we see when Edith tries to kiss him in front of Mike; similarly, his hostility towards Mike appears to stem from his inability to accept that his adult daughter – whose off-screen pregnancy haunts the episode – has a sex life. Archie seems to fear that he himself is not "normal", an anxiety which may be justified considering the many attributes that set him apart from other men: his extreme naivety and gullibility, his struggles with language, and his streak of paranoid imagination especially where bodies are concerned. (Edith, who is not altogether normal herself, understands this side of her husband well and loves him for it.) In restoring Beverly to consciousness, he equally restores his own self-esteem, giving himself a respectable motive for an erotic impulse that would otherwise be a source of shame. When the truth comes out he is doubly humiliated, the deeper shock being one that neither he nor the show can face head-on: not merely that he "kissed" another man but that, however unwittingly, he enjoyed it.

Archie's argument with Mike is interrupted by a dismaying phone call: Munson has spread the word about Archie's heroism, which has sparked the interest of the *Long Island Press*. When Archie ducks out to his local watering hole, he finds that the story has arrived there too, the leering bartender Kelsey (Bob Hastings) assuming that Archie must have "got a big kick" out of rescuing a woman in this fashion. In response, Archie rehearses what has become his official line, that he was motivated strictly by duty rather than desire: "This was a human being in trouble. Stretched out like a dead fish." Kelsey is incredulous: "And you kissed *that*?"

Munson (Billy Halop) now enters, accompanied by Jim Kitchener (Sandy Kenyon), the reporter sent to investigate the story. Hoping to bluff it out, Archie panics when Beverly herself enters soon after, still in full drag and bearing complimentary tickets for her nightclub performance later in the evening. Archie pulls her aside, begging her not to blow his cover: "These guys here, they aren't liberal thinkers like you and me." Beverly seems willing to play along but deliberately or not, soon gives the game away once more. Heading into the men's room to "use the sandbox", she crosses paths off-screen with Jim, who emerges flabbergasted but in no doubt about what he saw. When Beverly emerges in turn, this cues the episode's most striking shot, which positions her in the right foreground with her back to the camera; we share her perspective on the four men clustered at the bar, who stare back at her in united mistrust. The show's "normal" way of seeing has momentarily been reversed, allowing a direct illustration of what homophobia looks like to its victims – a gesture all the more powerful in the context of a multi-camera sitcom largely eschewing point-of-view shots.

The moment also marks the culmination of the string of "bathroom" jokes which structure the episode, beginning with the dialogue between Mike and Edith (in which the possibility that Gloria is suffering from morning sickness is skirted rather than directly broached). That "bathroom" is a euphemism for "toilet" links this exchange with two later, more openly vulgar jokes: Archie says that he learned the technique of mouth-to-mouth resuscitation from a poster in the "john" at work, and when he departs for the "library" the implied meaning is obvious even before an off-screen flush removes all doubt. As both these jokes imply, Archie's repression defines him as an "anal" character, the crudity and confusion of his language standing in for the "dirt" he seeks to expel. This is further brought home when he buys a bottle of mouthwash to expunge the taint of contact with Beverly – a reversal in itself, with the mouth rather than the anus viewed as soiled.

Again, some portion of this repression extends to the show itself. Bathrooms, according to the TV conventions of the 1970s, could be alluded to but not shown: their importance here derives precisely from this taboo, which lets them serve as receptacles for the unrepresentable realities of the body. Significantly, another euphemism for "toilet" is "closet", as in "water-closet"; the phrase "coming out of the closet," popularized in the early 1970s, carries a hint of this meaning given the longstanding use of public toilets as venues for gay sex. Beverly, then, has "come out" in more than one sense and Archie too must resign himself to public exposure.

That is, until Beverly saves the day: having consented to an interview with Jim, she improvises a new version of events, in which she received the kiss of life not from Archie but from an anonymous "truck driver". Archie is off the hook: the story is over, and so, seemingly, is any possibility of him rethinking his homophobia. Yet this ending remains ambiguous, especially since the episode as a whole rests on a similar cover story, with many questions left unresolved. What was Beverly doing in full drag in the middle of the night at Kennedy Airport, where Archie says he picked her up? Is it plausible that she could have stopped breathing simply from exhaustion and if not, was Archie's intervention strictly necessary? And what exactly happened at the hospital, where she was presumably examined then quickly discharged?

What is clear, at any rate, is that Archie and Beverly share a secret: Beverly's final smile is one of complicity, indicating that she knows full well what it means to have something to hide. This time, it is she who reaches out and takes Archie's hand, making him wince at the firmness of her grip. In a sense, she has triumphed: her identity is out in the open, leaving Archie as the one in the closet. Tick a lock and swallow the key.

Archie Bunker (Carroll O'Connor) saves the life of female impersonator and soon-to-be good friend of the Bunkers, Beverly LaSalle (Lori Shannon) in "Archie the Hero" from All in the Family.

"Discovery" from *Barney Miller*
Original Air Date: 30 October 1975
By Jessie Lilley

Before I begin, I wish to note that one would be hard-pressed to find a finer ensemble than that of the original *Barney Miller* (1975–1982) cast. The veteran performers, headed up by the incomparable Hal Linden in the lead role, offer huge presence and exquisite timing. The writers on the show played to the strengths of each actor in turn and the episodes hammer along non-stop until the credits roll. It was and remains my go-to example of brilliance in comedy and a model for sitcoms. And now, let us analyze "Discovery". We begin with the discovery by Fish that the payroll department killed him and as a result, they did not cut him a paycheck. Barney, nodding sagely, suggests that "It's probably a mistake." Abe Vigoda as Fish does one of his patented slow takes and we're off to the races. The usual banter about odd colored coffee, typewriter ribbons and other daily trials comes and goes, and then we get to the meat of the episode.

Bear in mind that this show originally aired in 1975 when men in the U.S. wore mustaches to cement their machismo and cover the fact of their true sexuality. Queer jokes were in style and "fairies" were the subject of ridicule. At a time when the LGBT community was stretching its wings and standing up for its rights, the established culture was doing everything possible to turn their collective back on this reality. Gay bashing was the order of the day and in typical American fashion, no one wanted to get involved. A handful of television shows stood up for the gay community. *Barney Miller* was one.

As the squad tries to convince Fish that he is not dead, two gay men enter the room. Darryl Driscoll (Ray Stewart) is clearly unhappy with this and notes that "This is enemy territory." His companion Marty Morrison (Jack DeLeon) replies, "Don't be ridiculous, these are my friends!" Wojo (Maxwell Gail) is openly hostile to the men noting that gays make him nervous, but the ever-philosophical Yamana (Jack Soo) notes that "It takes all kinds to make a world. That's why we're not all Chinese."

The men meet privately with Barney and the reason for the visit is revealed. It seems that Darryl was recently arrested but charges were never brought to bear. In fact, he was never brought to the precinct house. Instead, he found himself being shaken down. The arresting detective, claiming to be a member of the 12th Precinct, told him to pay $50 and he could go. Barney is stunned at the possibility that one of his men was guilty of extortion. Our victim says, "All I know is that I was given a choice. Either pay through the nose, or bleed through it." Barney shows Darryl around the squad room but he is unable to identify the shake-down artist. A report is filed about an imposter while the two complainants look through the photo IDs of every person employed at the 12th.

Wojo – always a tad slower than the others on the squad – is still obviously uncomfortable being in such close proximity to Darryl and Marty. He questions his own sexuality and asks Barney if he has not done the same. Barney replies no and leaves Wojo worriedly pondering his own response. As usual. He asks Soo what he thinks about homosexuality and Soo states quite simply, "It's none of my business." During all this, Harris (Ron Glass) and Amenguale (Gregory Sierra) have collected a probable attempted suicide. A divorced man who lives alone whom Marty spots as a fellow traveler. He offers the fellow, a Mr. Buckholtz (Philip Sterling), a smoke and talks to him about his own suicide attempt in his teens. Buckholtz proclaims that there is nothing "wrong" with him, "I'm a perfectly normal man!". Enter the folks from Bellevue (NYC's legendary psych hospital) come to collect him.

While Barney and the Bellevue attendants try to coax Mr. Buckholtz out from under a desk, a Manhattan South detective sergeant named Forbes (Paul Jenkins) arrives

The cast of Barney Miller. *The sitcom would focus on the efforts of the fellas from the 12th Precinct Station House in Greenwich Village.*

with a man in tow who is immediately identified by Darryl as the man who rousted him the other evening. When asked where he was found, the DS says he was right outside a gay bar on 2nd Avenue, stating, "I just walked out and *he* grabbed *me*." Wojo is stunned to realize this man too, is gay. He collects Darryl to act as witness for the collar and Marty crows, "I told you they were human!"

Mr. Buckholtz, in the meantime, has agreed to go to Bellevue as long as he doesn't need to go in a straight jacket. At the end of the day, Wojo is requested by Forbes to consult on the shakedown arrest. He doesn't want to go and Barney tells him not to jump to any conclusions. When asked if he thought there were any "funny" cops in the department, Barney replies, "You mean cops with a sense of humor?" Wojo leaves for Manhattan South, but declares that he won't stay long. "Discovery" is an attempt to "humanize" homosexuals to the viewing public much in the same way Marty tried to humanize cops to Darryl. Sadly, Barney's non-concern doesn't sway Wojo's discomfort, probably any more than the show's viewership. Fear is a driving force in humans, and this episode shows several versions of that emotion. Fear of difference, fear of self, fear of life in general. While not a particularly powerful episode, "Discovery" nonetheless made the attempt to open the eyes of viewers to reality.

I will now take this opportunity to grind on one of my pet peeves. The term "race" is used incorrectly in our language. We refer to the African race, the Asian race, the white race … no. In fact, these are ethnicities. The definition of race is something else entirely. We are – all of us – the Human Race. As Soo pointed out early on, "It takes all kinds…" Imagine how boring life would be if we all agreed, all looked and acted the same, homogenous. What a ghastly thought. No, I agree with the French. *Vive la Différence!*

"Maude Bares Her Soul" from *Maude*
Original Air Date: 10 November 197
By Michael Barrett

All in the Family (1971–1979) and *Maude* (1972–1978) were so comfortable with their characters that they sometimes broke an episode down into a "two-hander" with only two characters in a room to carry the whole episode. This groundbreaking fourth season episode of *Maude* went one step further by functioning as a one-woman monologue for Bea Arthur. The only other actor on stage, Gene Blakely, plays the psychiatrist without showing his face and without saying more than "mm-hmm."

Maude begins by displaying amazement that she, Maude Findlay, should be seeing a psychiatrist just because she's "slightly depressed." This expresses the lingering cultural stigma embodied in the old joke that anyone who sees a psychiatrist should have their head examined. That prejudice was giving way, especially as such therapy was a relatively affluent proposition; Maude jokes about what she's getting for fifty dollars an hour.

The two halves of the episode parallel each other. Both begin with Maude pacing the room until she finally settles on the couch in the middle of the space. As overhead shots dolly in to tearful close-ups, Maude comes to opposite conclusions about her father and differing interpretations of why she stopped kissing him goodnight.

Her first interpretation of their relationship involves lack of love or engagement on his part, and concludes with her remembering the lyrics to "Where or When," her father's favorite song. In the second half, she remembers a display of love she had put out of her mind, so that she now blames herself for withholding her love from him. She believes this affects her relationship with her husband Walter.

Maude's negative memories of her father, and the nature of memory itself, had been addressed in the second season episode "The Tax Audit," as discussed in an earlier essay. In Norman Lear's sitcom world, the free association of self-analysis seems to recur to the father rather than the mother, as shown by Archie's revelations of physical abuse and his insistence on defending his father when he and Mike are locked in a storeroom in "Two's a Crowd" (12 February 1978) on *All in the Family*.

The tricky nature of memory and how we interpret our lives is another recurring theme of these series. For example, both had *Rashomon*-like episodes in which the regulars enacted wildly differing flashbacks on the same events: the brilliant "Everybody Tells the Truth" (3 March 1973) in the third season of *All in the Family* and "The Case of the Broken Punch Bowl" (5 January 1976) later in this season of *Maude*.

Also this season, Maude nearly divorced Walter (Bill Macy) as she unsuccessfully ran for State Senate in a five-episode arc that feels like a trigger for her visit to the analyst, and she would finally have a concrete reason for psychiatry when diagnosed as manic depressive (today called bipolar disorder) in the two-part "Maude's Mood" (26

January 1976 and 2 February 1976). It may or may not be a coincidence that Norman Lear's then-wife Frances Lear, as discussed in her 1992 memoir *The Second Seduction*, received the same diagnosis a few years earlier.

Like "The Analyst," "Maude's Mood" was scripted by Jay Folb. Is it another coincidence that Folb's two-year stint as a story consultant on *M*A*S*H* oversaw episodes highlighting the minor recurring character Dr. Sidney Freedman (Allan Arbus), including one where he treats Hawkeye (Alan Alda) for sleepwalking and nightmares ("Hawk's Nightmare," 21 December 1976) and "Dear Sigmund" (9 November 1976), in which Freedman takes center stage in narrating the week's events by writing an imaginary letter to Freud?

As we've noted, the pricey nature of psychotherapy often limited its access to those in some degree of luxury. Hollywood writers and producers were part of the cultural vanguard in experiencing therapy and reporting their findings to the middle class mainstream.

In the sixties, sitcom shrinks still implied something fantastical, untrustworthy and witch-doctor-y about the mumbo jumbo. In *I Dream of Jeannie* (1965–1970), NASA psychiatrist Dr. Bellows (Hayden Rorke) is the regular antagonist who must be constantly fooled. When we also consider the villainous yet incompetent Dr. Zachary Smith (Jonathan Harris) of *Lost in Space* (1965–1968), we must admit the space program had an awful record with head doctors.

On *Bewitched* (1964–1972), Darrin (Dick York) has a session with no less than Sigmund Freud (Norman Fell) in "I'd Rather Twitch Than Fight" (17 November 1966) and finds himself subjected to psychiatry again in "No More Mr. Nice Guy" (23 March 1967). In both cases, he had mother issues – his wife's mother, Endora (Agnes Moorhead), was causing his problems.

On *The Addams Family* (1964–1966), an alarmed Morticia (Carolyn Jones) consults a child psychiatrist (George Petrie) when little Pugsley (Ken Weatherwax) shows distressing signs of wanting to join the Boy Scouts and raise a puppy ("Morticia and the Psychiatrist," 25 September 1964). Another child psychiatrist, this time German (Harvey Korman), is consulted to determine whether *The Munsters* (1964–1966) are imaginary ("Yes, Galen, There Is a Herman," 10 June 1965).

On *The Dick Van Dyke Show* (1961–1966), Rob lays on the couch for "The Brave and the Backache" (12 February 1964) to find out if his health issues were psychosomatic, and he unearths a childhood memory of when a bully made him afraid of being a sissy. He consults the shrink again – with a different surname but played by the same actor (Ross Elliott) – when he sees a flying saucer in "Uhny Uftz" (29 September 1965). (This event has a more mundane resolution than when Maude sees "The Flying Saucer" on 26 September 1977). Whatever his surname, this doctor is very reasonable, helping lay the groundwork for the growing acceptance of psychiatry.

Dramas, or at least medical soaps, made better efforts at normalizing and middle-classing psychiatry, even though the first medical series on the topic, *The Eleventh Hour*

(1962–1964), devoted its first season to the treatment of criminals. That is, the show made a case for its social use among the marginalized before switching to swankier private practice in its second season. While that series shared a crossover with *Dr. Kildare* (1961–1966), the one-season *Breaking Point* (1963–1964) was spun off from Kildare's rival *Ben Casey* (1961–1966). 1971 saw the short-lived *The Psychiatrist* with Roy Thinnes.

By the 1970s, analysis had been rendered more mainstream by *The Bob Newhart Show* (1972–1978), though its hero was technically a psychologist. What's more important is that his patients' problems weren't presented as a unique and serious crisis in their lives but as part of an ongoing lifestyle of depression and insecurity and neurosis, which more closely approximates the real world.

It was against this background that Maude made her initial visit to an analyst, little anticipating the psychic break that happens several episodes later, courtesy of the same writer and director. Some later sitcoms followed Maude's example in using mental breakdown as tour de force showcases for Very Special Episodes. Possibly the most famous is the one-hour "A, My Name Is Alex" (12 March 1987) on *Family Ties* (1982–1989).

If we have time for what seems a digression, the clinical revelations of "Maude's Mood" are initially disguised by a fact they end up overshadowing: that it falls into the grand sitcom tradition of Guest Celebrities. In this case, Henry Fonda appears as himself, thus harking back to "Maude Meets the Duke" (9 September 1974), in which John Wayne leaves Maude tongue-tied and starstruck after she'd blown up at the prospect of having such a prominent conservative in her house.

To digress further, Wayne's appearance links *Maude* to both *I Love Lucy* (1951–1957) and *The Lucy Show* (1962–1968), which both had episodes titled "Lucy and John Wayne," which aired on 10 October 1955 and 21 November 1966. As in *Maude*, these plots exploit the Celebrity Guest as Himself before a flabbergasted heroine. We tend to think of Lucy and Maude as separated not only by decades but virtually on separate planets, though *Here's Lucy* (1968–1974) was contemporary with *Maude* and on the same network. One type of show is escapist slapstick, we think, while the other is relevant and political.

Not so fast. Both *Maude* and *I Love Lucy* are about loud, argumentative housewives at loose ends, constantly pursuing various projects as outlets for their energy. And even though Maude is the more enlightened person in a more liberal age, for every time that Ricky threatens to spank Lucy, there are occasions when Walter loses his temper and bellows "Maude! Sit!" whereupon Maude demurely sits.

More relevantly, both series fall into what I call the Chaos mode as opposed to the Order mode. In this sitcom taxonomy, some shows dwell in a natural state of Order, rippled briefly by the week's problem, which can be handily addressed in a sane and sensible manner. Such are most of the polite or gentle family sitcoms, and they end with everyone happy and smiling. We watch these shows to be reassured that the world is in its proper order.

By contrast, other shows dwell normally in Chaos, and any solution reached to this week's problem is temporary. Such shows end on punchlines where a fresh form of Chaos erupts and everyone starts running and screaming at once. We watch these shows to anticipate and enjoy the frantic.

When Chaos shows focus on women, as in *I Love Lucy*, *Bewitched*, *I Dream of Jeannie* and *Maude*, we fully expect these women to assert their power to the dismay of everyone around them. If they behaved politely and followed the rules laid out for them by men, there'd be no show. It's true that *Maude* is the example most assertive of contemporary politics, especially gender politics, but this factor is well grasped in the other shows too, if more understated.

But no matter how many times Lucy got called crazy by her husband or neighbors, nobody believed for a moment that she had a mental illness, nor would Lucy ever devote an entire episode to a long dark night of the soul. Here are the areas where *Maude* differs sharply, and now you see why this wasn't really a digression.

"Fonzie's New Friend" from *Happy Days*
Original Air Date: 25 November 1975
By Lindsay Hallam

To speak of 1950s America is to conjure up specific images: white picket fences lining suburban streets, Dad mowing the lawn while Mom is in the kitchen making apple pie, teenage boys in letterman jackets and girls in poodle skirts dancing to pop music coming from a jukebox in the diner after school. The war is over, there is a car in every driveway, a boy for every girl, and a bright future ahead. What a time to be young.

But look at bit closer and things become complicated: there is an underlying paranoia breeding mass conformity. Nuclear families live in fear of nuclear war, of reds under bed, of men with their fingers on the button, of terror in the skies. Women begin to see that their beautiful homes are really beautiful prisons, men buckle under the pressure of being shackled to the soulless 9-5, and their kids realize that only rebellion and revolution can stop them from meeting a similar fate. But the social upheaval of the 1960s did not lead to the Age of Aquarius but to assassination and senseless wars, government corruption and mass disillusionment. And so, by the time the 1970s rolled around those bygone days suddenly began to take on a certain sheen, and the rosy glow of nostalgia descended.

Happy Days (1974–1984) plays right into this nostalgia, debuting in the midst of the Watergate scandal and ending slap-bang in the middle of Ronald Reagan's presidency. Created by Garry Marshall, whose previous show *The Odd Couple* (1970–1975) had been a resounding success, the 1950s setting was partly due to a need to get around network restrictions, which created constraints when attempting to present what Marshall hoped would be a somewhat believable representation of teenage life. As Marshall explains:

> I couldn't figure out how I could do a realistic comedy about young people today and avoid drugs and avoid the sexual revolution, because I know they wouldn't put that on television. So I said, what's the use? It's not real, people are gonna watch it and say: 'Baloney, that isn't real life.' Then it crossed my mind – how can I beat this? I can do it if I push it back in time – to the fifties. If I'm not doing drugs, and I'm not doing the sex things, then the audience will buy it and they'll say: 'That's right, it's not today, but that's the way it was.'[3]

The show had begun its life as a failed pilot, which originally aired as a segment on *Love, American Style* (1969–1974). The pilot had starred Ron Howard, who was well-

---

[3] McCrohan, Donna. *Prime Time, Our Time: America's Life and Times Through the Prism of Television* (Prima Pub. & Communications, 1990).

known to audiences from his previous role as Opie Taylor on *The Andy Griffith Show* (1960–1968). Howard had been on America's screens since the age of four, and was now making the awkward transition from child star to teen idol. Somewhat gangly with red hair and freckles, Howard perfectly suited the role of the innocent, all-American teenager Richie Cunningham, helped through the usual trials and tribulations of adolescence thanks to his loving and supportive parents Howard (Tom Bosley) and Marion (Marion Ross), and the guidance of cool guy Arthur "Fonzie" Fonzarelli (Henry Winkler). Based on his performance in the pilot, George Lucas cast Howard as the lead in his film *American Graffiti* (1973), which in turn helped *Happy Days* get picked up by ABC. As Marshall stated, "I had created *Happy Days* in the early seventies, but nobody wanted it until after the play *Grease* and the movie *American Graffiti*."[4] However, unlike *Grease*, *Happy Days* delivered a more sanitized version of the fifties, with all teenage sexual activity never venturing beyond first base.

For its first two seasons *Happy Days* was filmed using a single camera and a laugh-track, with a focus on smaller character moments rather than broad laughs. Unfortunately, ratings began to slump, and so changes were made to the show in its third season in an attempt to garner a larger audience. The set was retooled, and filming moved to a three-camera setup in front of a live audience. The opening credits now ran with a *Happy Days* theme song, replacing the Bill Hayley and the Comets song "Rock Around the Clock" that had played previously. The character of Fonzie was increasingly foregrounded, moving into the Cunningham home in a room above the garage. More emphasis was given to jokes and catchphrases (notably, Fonzie's catchphrase, "Sit on it"), and Fonzie became known for his motorcycle stunts (culminating in the infamous "jumping the shark" scene in season five).

"Fonzie's New Friend" comes right after these changes, halfway through the third season. It is significant, though, in that it is one of the few times the show confronted the fact that, for many Americans, these had not been happy days at all. The 1950s had been a time of great injustice and outright racism, with parts of the nation still segregated and many of its citizens denied basic rights and equality. Racism had been tackled in an earlier episode in the show's first season, "The Best Man", in which the Cunninghams were confronted with the racist attitudes of both their neighbors and the police after Howard is visited by an old Army buddy Fred, an African American. Members of the Cunningham family themselves even grapple with their own prejudices; in one scene Marion confesses to Howard that she feels discomfort at the thought of them being the only white couple at Fred's upcoming wedding, where Howard will

---

4   Marshall, Garry. "From the *People* Archive: Garry Marshall on *Happy Days* and the Day He Discovered Robin Williams" (*People Magazine*, 20 July 2016) ≤https://people.com/movies/garry-marshall-on-the-success-of-happy-days-and-the-discovering-robin-williams>.

serve as the Best Man. Only by coming to terms with her own deep-rooted racism does Marion begin to change, later offering to host the wedding in the Cunningham's own home, much to the chagrin of their white neighbors.

Similarly, "Fonzie's New Friend" does not shy away from showing the main cast as often being guilty of racial insensitivity and prejudice, the realization of which then leads to growth and progress, albeit on a small, localized level. The episode opens at Arnold's diner, as Richie attempts to ask a girl, Lois, to his party on Friday night. As Richie bumbles his words he is interrupted by Fonzie, who tells Richie he has found a drummer for his band, a new guy in town called Sticks Downey. Fonzie says Sticks should be stopping by, and when asked how they will know him, Fonzie declares that he is "about your age, only cool." This statement sets up a running theme in the episode, in which Fonzie's view of the world, where the only division is between those who are cool and those who are uncool, is shown to be out of touch with the cold, hard reality of the time. Usually in the show Fonzie's coolness takes on the aspect of a superpower, most clearly expressed in his uncanny ability to make jukeboxes and other appliances start or stop just by touching them, but here these powers prove inadequate when faced with something so ingrained as racism.

Fonzie leaves after telling Richie to be confident, so Richie strides back to Lois and her friend, Meralee: "Hold it, dollface. How'd you like to do yourself a favor and go to a swinging bash over at my place?" Lois accepts, but only if he can find a date for Meralee. Meralee states that she doesn't want another "joke date", having previously been set up with kids, old men and poodles, so Richie promises her a date with Sticks. As Richie assures Meralee that Sticks is "cool" (having been designated so by Fonzie), a wide shot shows Sticks (Jack Baker) stroll into Arnold's. As Sticks introduces himself to Richie, Meralee staggers backward in shock, and Lois tells Richie, "That's not very nice!" as she drags Meralee away, insinuating that they believe that this is yet another "joke date".

While the reactions of Lois and Meralee reveal their bigotry in a very blatant manner, Richie, Potsie and Ralph hardly come across any better in their treatment of Sticks, who, in an attempt to relate to him, fall back on lazy, outdated and racist stereotypes. Sticks' response to their seemingly endless stream of tactless remarks is to make a joke out of it: after Ralph suggests they should play basketball sometime, Sticks retorts, "I don't play basketball, my hands get too slick from eating all that fried chicken!" One gets the sense here that this is something that Sticks has had to deal with many times before, as it falls to him to point out how ridiculous and offensive these comments are, as the boys (and by extension, members of the audience) are completely unaware of this.

Eventually these misunderstandings are put behind them, with Sticks agreeing to play in the band after Richie finds him a date for the party. But just as it seems to all be falling into place, Ralph and Potsie hear that no one plans to show up to the party because Sticks and his date Kathleen will be there. Potsie explains that the kids down at Arnold's "think that there's only two kinds of people: white and colored." Fonzie counters this with his own worldview: "There are two kinds of people: cool and nerds, and the people down at Arnold's are nerds."

The crux of this episode is the realization that even Fonzie's coolness cannot overcome such entrenched and systemic racism. Fonzie goes to Arnold's and demands everyone raise their hands to show they are coming to the party, but once he leaves one of the kids asks everyone there "How many of you were told by your parents that you better not go to that party?", to which everyone raises their hands again. In moments like this *Happy Days* actually breaks through the fog of 1950s nostalgia that the show often falls into, highlighting the overriding conformity of the time, as the kids choose to follow their parents rather than someone from their own generation who opposes these views. The civil rights movement and the youth protests of the 1960s are still years away, and this episode demonstrates how the prevailing racist attitudes of the time were instilled from one generation to the next. Potsie's earlier assertion that the kids at Arnold's believe that there are "two types of people" clearly comes from what they have been told by their parents, and not even their collective idolization of Fonzie's coolness can break the cycle.

Thus, this episode contains within it the revelation of a rather uncomfortable truth: all those nice white kids we see hanging out at Arnold's week to week are completely free to enjoy their "happy days" because the real injustices of the world do not affect them. If they are ever confronted with these inequalities, they will not question them or fight back. The ultimate irony of it all is that the turmoil of the 1970s, which so many viewers were trying to escape from, directly stems from the very period they feel nostalgic for.

The episode ends with the party itself, as Richie slowly realizes that no one is coming. Fonzie refuses to believe that his influence is not enough to change everyone's mind, stating that all he has to do is go to Arnold's and "snap my fingers". Always the paternal voice of reason, Howard takes Fonzie aside to provide a tough lesson: "Prejudice is stronger than cool… you see, prejudice had a big head start. It started with the cavemen. Cool's only been around since Benny Goodman." Although Fonzie cannot change the minds of all the kids in town, he is still able to provide some words of advice to Richie, who, incensed by the whole situation, declares that he has every right to have "colored people" at his party. Fonzie admonishes Richie for making this about himself, saying he shouldn't ask Sticks to stay just "to prove something", but because he likes him as a person. Sticks isn't there as a token gesture, but because he is part of their band, and a new found friend.

The episode concludes on a bittersweet note, with Richie determined to continue the party with this band of outsiders. They are further joined by Arnie (Pat Morita), the Japanese owner of Arnold's, who proclaims that he is "not like those kids back at Arnold's who are afraid to come out… what do I care what my parents think?" "The kids at Arnold's" have become an emblem of mainstream white America, scared into conformity and prejudice. The presence of Arnie in this scene (one cannot help but think of how just a decade before the show was set, Japanese Americans were being interned in camps) brings together a diverse set of characters not just of different races, but also ages, classes and backgrounds. It should also be noted that the theme of the party, a Hawaiian luau, is one of inclusion and diversity, devised by Richie as "a really cool welcome to Hawaii to the state of the union". The episode ends as they all join together to dance as Richie's band plays a song, in an act of defiance and joy. Those kids at Arnold's sure are missing out on one cool party.

The cast of Happy Days. *Presenting the halcyon days of 50s America,* Happy Days *provided a 70s sensibility for a decade that kept certain concerns deeply hidden and not up for conversation. However, this sitcom would address these issues, with a sensitive and loving hand.*

"J.J.'s Fiancée" from *Good Times*
Original Air Dates: 6 January 1976 (Part 1) and 13 January 1976 (Part 2)
By Dennis Capicik

Even during the so-called "permissive" seventies drug abuse still remained one of the least-talked-about topics on American television. However, in the eighties, at the height of the Reagan administration, Ronald Reagan and First Lady Nancy Reagan brought the "War on Drugs" back into the public consciousness following President Richard Nixon's original – and unsuccessful – drug campaign from the early seventies. Highlighted by the unforgettable slogan "Just Say No" Nancy Reagan made numerous public service announcements, appeared on talk shows and even put in a guest appearance on *Diff'rent Strokes* (1978–1986) for the Very Special Episode "The Reporter". So in that respect, it shouldn't be any surprise that a number of VSE's – such as the "Thank God It's Friday" episode from *Growing Pains* (1985–1992) and "High Anxiety" from *The Golden Girls* (1985–1992) – began exploring this formerly taboo subject with seemingly unending regularity.

Prior to this influx of drug-related VSE's, one of the earliest sitcoms to tackle the subject was *Good Times* (1974–1979), yet another groundbreaking show developed by television giant Norman Lear. Focusing on a poor African American family headed by Florida and James Evans (Esther Rolle and John Amos, respectively) and their three children J.J. (Jimmie Walker), Thelma (BernNadette Stanis) and Michael (Ralph Carter), *Good Times* was the first American sitcom that primarily focused on life in the inner city, and it was able to bring to light – at least to primetime mainstream TV audiences – some of the issues that continue to plague the "ghettos" of America, including poverty, unemployment, racism, gang violence, drug trafficking, and of course, substance abuse. While never made explicit, the show took place within the high-rise Cabrini-Green housing projects of Chicago, which is where Eric Monte, one of the show's co-creators, was brought up, so he was undoubtedly very well aware of the daily struggles and illicit temptations of growing up in such a tough and impoverished neighborhood. Of course, like Lear's seminal *All in the Family* (1971–1979), *Good Times* was also unafraid to delve into any number of controversial topics, which, more often than not, weren't easily resolved (or not at all); a pretty bold move for a mainstream television show.

Following "J.J. Is Arrested" and "J.J. and the Gang", two earlier and equally-important "two-part" episodes in the show's history, "J.J.'s Fiancée" remains one of the many extraordinarily forthright and controversial episodes in this long-running show. Earlier in the decade, drug abuse was declared "Public Enemy No. 1" by President Nixon, but his "War On Drugs" failed miserably and merely demonstrated the impossibility of fighting this crisis, which in this particular instance is very perceptively summarized throughout this rather devastating two-part VSE.

It's the night before prom, and J.J. is eager to introduce his new girlfriend Diana Buchanan (Deborah Allen) to his parents, who merely regard this new girl as just another of his "brief encounters in the night", but, with a big, wide-eyed grin, J.J. happily confirms it's one of the "accidents of love". However, Thelma thinks something isn't right and warns J.J. that "she's very strange sometimes." However, J.J., who is blinded by his love for her, remains blissfully unaware or simply refuses to acknowledge some tell-tale signs that *something* isn't quite right with the girl of his dreams ("Cupid has shot me with the zip-gun of love!"). Taking everyone by surprise, J.J. and Diana announce their plans to get married, a premature decision that is met with consternation from both sets of parents ("You wanna run that by me again?!" exclaims James), who deem them "too young and irresponsible" to take such a major step. Determined to win over his parents, J.J. ensures he can manage as the "breadwinner" with his job at the Chicken Shack, but James, clearly not wanting his son to make the same mistakes he made, declares, "You got to bring home the whole loaf, not just the crumbs!"

Always portrayed as the family jokester, Jimmie Walker's wise-crackin'/trash-talkin' character J.J. became – not surprisingly – one of the show's comedic focal points, and his now-infamous exclamation "*DY-NO-MIIITE!*" became THE catchphrase of the era (right up there with lollipop-sucking Telly "Kojak" Savalas' "Who loves ya, baby!"). Conversely, many of *Good Times*'s early VSEs in fact centered around J.J., which not only allowed his performer Walker to display his dramatic chops, but endowed his character with more depth and authenticity. Unfortunately, unbeknownst to him, Diana is in the clutches of a serious heroin addiction, which is hinted at throughout the episode with her fidgety, anxious behavior, and then later, when she's seen stealing money out of her mother's purse. At first, Diana is presented as a normal girl "from a nice family" who even wears a very conservative, almost prudish dress to her prom – no doubt to try and appease her parents – in an attempt to keep up her "good girl" façade, so when she balks at the idea of eloping ("I can't elope! That's pretty wild! Eloping is a serious thing!"), it makes for an interesting paradox, given that she herself is involved in something far more serious, but it also demonstrates the intense power of denial that most drug addicts succumb to *and* contend with on a day-to-day basis, as well as how anyone can succumb to addiction – including a good girl "from a nice family". At the end of the episode, the extent of her habit is jarringly illustrated when, following a heated argument, Diana runs into Thelma's room, wedges a chair behind the closed door and, as she begins to roll up her sleeve, the camera slowly zooms in on her as she wraps a rubber tourniquet around her arm, much to the shock and disbelief of both the viewer *and* the studio audience.

While Part One definitely ends with a jolt, viewers are given a little respite at the start of part two. Beginning immediately after Diana's outburst, she exits the bedroom feeling exuberant and full of renewed energy; a complete about-face which surprises even her mother. "Just one of my headaches. I took some aspirins and they really do a job!" she exclaims happily and whose rather blasé comment – quite surprisingly – even elicits laughter from the studio audience! Brimming with confidence, Diana is now adamant about eloping ("We just *do* it!") instead of going to the prom. In an ensuing scuffle, however, J.J. mistakenly takes Thelma's purse instead of Diana's, which leads Thelma to not only discover that Diana and J.J. never arrived at the prom but also Diana's dirty little secret as well. This simple-but-brilliant plot device skillfully sets up the rest of the episode, which not only leads into the inevitable familial crisis, but also sheds light on the fallout of addiction when, stranded in a motel across the state line, Diana has no way of getting her fix.

"Man, you talkin' about *trouble*?!" exclaims Diana's father Fred (Sonny Jim Gaines), to which he answers, "We got it! Two junkies marryin' each other!" Beginning with anger and pointed accusations, the situation soon descends into sadness and an air of hopelessness as Diana's mother Lucille (Marie Moore), greatly saddened by the revelation that her daughter is a junkie, breaks down. As the camera slowly pans onto Lucille's concerned face, she delivers one of the episode's finest, most-heartfelt monologues: "All those 'headaches' of Diana's. It wasn't just the headaches, it was more than that. I've noticed changes in her lately. She's been real edgy, nervous… Well, I know as a mother, I should have sat down and tried to talk to her and try to find out why. But I didn't… I was hoping it would go away." James, on the other hand, expresses the impossibility of the situation in an altogether different light when he candidly remarks how the pushers "slip the kids free pills, and then when they get 'em freaked out, they push 'em onto the *hard* stuff!" While rummaging through Diana's purse, Lucille finds a phone number scrawled on a piece of paper, which James, who has the obvious street smarts, deduces must be her pusher's contact. But even James is completely baffled when a young boy, no more than ten years old, shows up with Diana's fix. Shocked and concerned, the mouthy kid (Edward Crawford) quickly retorts, "Whaddaya expect? Popeye?! *The French Connection*?!" In the space of three minutes, this self-assured street kid just about sums up the ridiculousness of trying to combat the drug crisis, which still rings true today. "I just deliver! I get it from this dude who gets it from somebody else, who gets it from the boss-dude. And this I know for sure, the boss-dude *don't* live in the projects!" This declaration even prompts a wholly appropriate "Right on!" from the studio audience. Even as James threatens to flush his "stuff" down the toilet, the kid boldly proclaims, "Hey man, it's cool, it's cool… There's more where that came from." And then, as Florida contemplates calling the police, the kid confidently proclaims, "Go ahead lady, call the fuzz! What can they do? Juvenile court is so crowded, I'd be forty before my case comes up!" The utter futility of the situation is, however briefly, enlightened by James' impassioned speech, and this is the sole glimmer of hope the episode even *tries* to put forth: "In 1961, President Kennedy said, we'd have a man on the moon by '70! And we did it! Now you can't tell me that the country that can put a man on the moon can't stop dope traffic?! I don't believe it!"

Later, at their motel getaway, J.J. and Diana are continuing to plan their wedding with the help of the motel's rather shady owner (Philip Baker Hall), which is far from the marriage they initially envisioned. To make matters worse, Diana quickly realizes that she doesn't have her purse and begins to lose her nerve as she curls up on the bed and nervously mutters, "Oh J.J., you don't know what you did." When they realize there is a three-day waiting period before they can get married, Diana's frustration and anger intensifies ("We can't stay here for three days! I can't go that long without my…"), after which she locks herself in the bathroom. Meanwhile, J.J. calls home to let his parents know they're alright, and in another beautifully poignant moment, J.J.'s mom hesitatingly tells him the truth about Diana. Naturally enough, J.J. assumes this is merely another ploy to prevent the smitten youngsters from getting married ("You guys will do anything to break our marriage up!"), which annoys him no end, so he calls out for Diana to come and prove them wrong. When she doesn't answer, he enters the bathroom, and much to his horror, finds her gone. As he briefly stares at the billowing curtains in the open window, J.J. slowly turns around and walks back over to the phone, which is sitting off-the-hook on an empty bed. As he sits down next to it, his Dad repeatedly calls out over the phone, "Junior? Junior? Come on, answer me, son…"

The cast of Good Times. *Developed by Norman Lear, the sitcom would position a black family as the focus, living their lives, struggling in the ghetto and facing multiple issues such as drug addiction, street violence, gang warfare, racism and much more.*

The camera then moves in on the stunned and overwhelmed J.J.'s face as the picture slowly fades to black.

Even though James does offer a smidgen of optimism earlier in the episode, seldom has a sitcom had the audacity to end in such a startling and disheartening manner, especially given that it's a two-part episode, which requires a greater emotional investment from the audience, who originally had to tune-in over a two-week period. Upheld by a number of engaging principal performances and superb writing, which deftly handles the sensitive material, it's made abundantly clear by the episode's end that, when it comes to tackling this still-ongoing problem which blights human lives the world over, there are no easy answers. Nowhere is this more cleverly depicted than in that closing shot of the devastated J.J.'s anguished face as he stares off into nothingness. Being that he's typically perceived and portrayed as such a carefree soul, his utter devastation only adds further resonance to the theme of lost innocence, which at this poignant moment in the two-parter's decidedly downbeat resolution provides stark, bleak contrast to the show's catchy, upbeat opening ditty.

"Maude's Mood" from *Maude*
Original Air Dates: 26 January 1976 (Part 1)
and 2 February 1976 (Part 2)
By Dennis Capicik

With Very Special insight from actress Adrienne Barbeau

Following "Maude Bares Her Soul", an earlier and equally extraordinary episode of *Maude* (1972–1978), which showcased Maude (Beatrice Arthur) performing a remarkable 22-minute monologue at her psychiatrist's office, wherein she revealed all of her fears and anxieties about her marriage, her childhood and even about growing old, writer Jay Folb took the opportunity to delve further into the title character's state of mind with "Maude's Mood". This episode featured yet another startlingly honest and gutsy performance from Arthur as she comes to grips with the realization that she suffers from manic depression – a.k.a. bipolar disorder, as it's more correctly referred to these days.

Along with miscarriages, mental disorders – understandably enough, considering their intensely personal nature – remain one of the *least* openly-discussed subjects among the general public; such subjects are often met with awkward misunderstanding, or even outright negative responses. In more recent decades, discussing dysfunctions of the mind (often caused by chemical deficiencies) has become much more acceptable in the mainstream. Some stigma, unfortunately, still remains for many people, which is why this two-part VSE of *Maude* remains so exceptional, and it was way ahead of its time when first aired. It's both realistic and sensitive in its approach, emphasizing all the initial denial, frustration, anger and eventual acceptance of living with a mental illness. Most importantly, it successfully breaks down the negative attitudes surrounding the issue, many of which biases are still commonplace even today, especially in less-developed cultures.

In the hopes of getting famed Hollywood actor Henry Fonda to run for the presidency of the United States, Maude has set up the HFP ("Henry Fonda for President") Headquarters at her Tuckahoe, New York home, and recruited most of her family and friends to help out with the campaign. As Maude's daughter Carol (played by future "Scream Queen" Adrienne Barbeau) and her best friend Vivian (Rue McClanahan) stuff envelopes with campaign pamphlets, Vivian's husband Arthur (Conrad Bain) is the first to mention that "She's got half of Tuckahoe working on this silly project of hers," but despite this difference of opinion, Maude's enthusiastic energy and persuasiveness proves highly infectious among her supporters. But when Maude's husband Walter (Bill Macy) brings home their latest phone bill – totaling an astronomical $1643.00! – Walter is beside himself and resorts to *literally* banging his head on a table. Infuriated, he remarks, "I've seen Maude get excited about her wild ideas before, but this time…

I bet she doesn't sleep four hours a night. She's either writing or phoning or planning meetings!" To which Carol rather nonchalantly replies, "You know her, she's had these super highs off-and-on since I was a kid." In still another all-too-realistic reaction, Vivian commends Maude's dynamism during these "super highs" without even giving it a second thought, innocently shrugging off the possibility that a potential crisis may be in their midst. Right on cue ("*Ta da!* Bring it in boys!"), Maude makes a grand entrance with the official "Henry Fonda for President" campaign poster, whereupon, thanks to the exaggerated sense of jubilation brought on by her mania, she proceeds to tip the delivery guys a whopping fifty bucks! Then, just as suddenly, she explodes into a fit of anger, yelling, "CAROL!!! You've stuffed the envelope incorrectly! I've told you, I don't want Mr. Fonda's face folded!"

Efficiently written with plenty of snappy dialogue, this brief opening skillfully establishes many of the potential warning signs usually associated with bipolar disorder. Even more importantly, it also very accurately presents most people's confusion and frustration when confronted with some of these (as-yet-undiagnosed) telltale symptoms, which are simply put aside or ignored altogether. But thankfully, in this instance, Walter, Carol and Arthur decide to visit Dr. Herbert Lester (Tim O'Connor) for some advice. Upon their arrival, Dr. Lester, who had seen Maude previously, already suspects what may be going on when he remarks, "You think she's gone overboard, eh?" But Walter is still in denial when he emphatically declares, "Maude may be driving me up the wall, but she's *not* crazy!" which is a common response, only to have Dr. Lester calmly reply, "She may need a little help." In a very straightforward and reassuring explanation, he talks about normal, everyday emotional highs and lows and that "manic depressives are people with a chemical imbalance in the blood, and there may be 20 million Americans who suffer from some variation of the same disorder." Once again, it becomes understood that, despite Walter's continued denial, it is in fact a very real, if wholly controllable, mental illness.

Originally appearing as Edith Bunker's (Jean Stapleton) cousin Maude on the season two *All In the Family* episode "Cousin Maude's Visit", Maude turned out to be one of Archie Bunker's (Carroll O'Connor) most memorable adversaries, a "bleeding heart liberal" who continually clashed with Archie's conservative working class viewpoints. Just like Archie, she too was as stubborn and opinionated as he was; a perfect symbolic representation of a highly divisive United States. While Maude has always been presented as being open-minded and full of energy (both admirable character traits), her impulsiveness and at times sudden angry outbursts are behaviors that could be considered consistent with Dr. Lester's above diagnosis, and such a development was audacious indeed for the lead character in a mainstream sitcom.

Furthermore, it firmly establishes that, even on TV, nobody is perfect. Incidentally, later that same year, Daniel Petrie's much-lauded two-part TV movie, *Sybil* (1976), based on Shirley Ardell Mason's highly-documented – and later controversial – multiple personality (or dissociative identity disorder) diagnosis and Flora Rheta Schreiber's

1973 book *Sybil: The True Story of a Woman Possessed by Sixteen Separate Personalities* (1973), debuted on network television, featuring stellar performances from both Sally Field in the title role and Joanna Woodward as Dr. Cornelia Wilbur. In an interesting – and no doubt intentional – role reversal for Joanne Woodward, she had previously starred as the woman who suffered from multiple personal disorder in Nunnally Johnson's celebrated *The Three Faces of Eve* (1957), which earned her an Academy Award for Best Actress. Much like "Maude's Mood" and even "Maude Bares Her Soul," *Sybil* was yet another daring and thoughtful portrayal of a woman's daily struggles – and subsequent therapy – as she gradually comes to grips with her mental illness.

Making considerable headway in his political campaign, Maude manages to secure no less than Henry Fonda himself to make a personal appearance at her Tuckahoe home. Of course, it's soon revealed that she lied to his agent about the *real* reason for her wanting him to visit! Even more alarming, she prepaid a $5,000 deposit against a total $20,000 guarantee for his appearance, a reckless act which leaves Walter flabbergasted. When he snaps, "She's practically wiped out our bank account!" Carol, sounding ever-more-worried, remarks, "Dr. Lester was right, Mother's got a *terrible* problem!"

However, Maude persists in her folly, and to the delight of everyone (the studio audience included!), Mr. Fonda appears on her doorstep a few days later, looking a little confused as he searches for the nonexistent "Tuckahoe Community Theatre" whereat to perform his one-man Darrow show (a reference to Fonda's 1974 made-for-TV movie *Clarence Darrow*, directed by frequent *All in the Family* director John Rich). When Maude reveals her wish to nominate him for the presidency, Mr. Fonda jokingly replies, "Jimmy Stewart put you up to this, right?!" However, it quickly dawns on him that Maude is in fact serious as she begins trying to convince him otherwise by gushingly praising his performance in the aforementioned telemovie. "I saw you play Clarence Darrow and I was overwhelmed by the way your earthiness, and your honesty and your integrity came shining through!" At which he cheekily replies, "I also played Jesse James' brother!" (he is of course referring to his character in Henry King's 1939 film *Jesse James*, wherein he co-starred alongside Tyrone Power (who played Jesse). Fonda reprised his now-iconic role as Jesse's bro in Fritz Lang's 1940 follow-up, *The Return of Frank James*. Incidentally, the name of his consummately villainous, mononymous "Frank" in Sergio Leone's *Once Upon a Time in the West* (1968) was undoubtedly inspired by the same far-less-reprehensible character).

Maude continues her gushing praise of Fonda in vain but, as he prepares to leave, he makes his intentions very clear: "I'm positive you can do anything you set your mind to do, but I do not wish to become the President of the United States. And, because I am so sure that you can do anything you set your mind to, if you do succeed in getting me nominated, I will *not* run!" Devastated, Maude is beset by anger and disappointment, but Walter still believes he can "snap her out of it just like that!" However, as he takes her into his arms, she breaks down completely and begins to sob. "I'm so tired… I did everything wrong, Walter. *Everything!*" As the episode comes to a close, Walter tenderly replies, "I'm sorry I didn't see it sooner." It's a wonderfully poignant, perfectly-achieved moment, which not only illustrates the unsteady balance of the disorder when left uncontrolled, but Walter's deep and heartfelt love for his wife.

Despite Maude's breakdown ("Maude gets so depressed, she has to go to bed for two days!" remarks Arthur), her campaign remains fully in motion as part two of "Maude's Mood" begins. Following unwilling candidate Fonda's unexpected visit to Tuckahoe, word had gotten out quickly, and now Maude is in preparation to be interviewed by Barbara Walters. Even though Walter attempts to talk her out of it, she answers him angrily, "You see the psychological problem! You see the psychiatrist!" Afterwards, she condescendingly remarks, "Frankly, Scarlett, I don't give a damn!" But Walter, recognizing this infamous quote from *Gone with the Wind* (1939), responds with equal wit by saying, "You're in the wrong movie, Maude! But if you ever want any help, all you have to do is whistle. And you know how to whistle, just pucker-up and *blow*!" – which is, of course, a direct (and fitting) quote from Howard Hawks' Bogart and Bacall romantic comedy *To Have and Have Not* (1944). Yet Maude's denial continues unabated ("Every time I turn my back, this place turns into a *madhouse*!" exclaims Walter). But even Maude's best friend Vivian also expresses her concern after reading Nathan S. Kline's book *From Sad to Glad* (1975) ("Depression. You can conquer it without analysis"). "I have such encouragement for Maude. I stayed up all night reading this wonderful book, and it fits Maude's case exactly! Her violent swings from high to low, and how she spends money like water, and how she's so unpredictable… like suddenly getting romantic right in the middle of an argument!"

As the furor surrounding Henry Fonda's candidacy increases, Maude receives a telegram from Mr. Fonda that he is "emphatically *not* a candidate," which, despite her already having heard it before directly from his own mouth, once again leaves Maude completely devastated. Soon after, it comes to Walter's attention that Maude – possibly mistakenly? – had authorized withdrawals from their grandson Phillip's (Brian Morrison) college fund to finance her foolish venture. This ends up being the last straw for Walter. "That *does* it!" he exclaims. "We broke our backs for eight years saving that money for Phillip!" Amid all the commotion, however, Phillip takes time to console his grandmother, which eases the tension considerably. "You're quite a guy, Phillip," says Walter. "Your grandmother needed a little love just then." After some further introspection, Maude agrees to visit Dr. Lester first thing in the morning. In a nice comic touch, she suggests to Walter that they should further ease the tension with a little lovin' atop the kitchen table ("Since I'm still on cloud nine, why don't we take advantage of it?!").

Moving ahead six weeks, Dr. Lester comes over for dinner and, as Maude and her maid Mrs. Naugatuck (Hermione Baddely) are preparing their meal, Walter is keen to know how everything is going. "The medication seems to have stabilized her moods," explains Dr. Lester. "Now we can get at the *real* causes." This is yet another example of Jay Folb's dedication to getting all the details right, and it's understood that medication alone will not "fix" the problem; an idea which, even in today's world, is a common misconception (as seen in the countless pharmaceutical ads on American television). Throughout "Maude's Mood", barriers are repeatedly broken down, and even though she is left forever changed by the experience, a person living with such a diagnosis can nevertheless still lead a normal, meaningful life. "Maude is a forceful, dynamic person but she's at an even keel now. Not any more of those extreme high and lows," explains Dr. Lester as Maude exits the kitchen while berating Mrs. Naugatuck for attempting to "deep fry a leg of lamb." With a slight smile on his face, Walter reacts thoughtfully: "You're right. She's back to normal." Indeed she is!

ADRIENNE BARBEAU: I haven't seen the documentary about Norman Lear, but I knew Bea was modelled on Norman's ex-wife Frances Lear. And definitely the episodes we did involving manic depression which now, of course, is bipolar but that was something that Frances Lear did suffer with. Just as a little personal story that came out of it, I had started dating a fellow who came out of the state, so I didn't see him very often. When I first met him, he was just the most remarkable, charismatic gentleman. Then as we started to get to know each other, I realized that he was suffering, he had physical pain, he had difficulty with sleeping, he had mood swings, he even talked about suicide at one point. And after about two months of being in his company, I realized that some of what he was exhibiting were the same symptoms that we had dealt with in the episodes where Maude is promoting Henry Fonda for President, and we finally come to realize that she's suffering with manic depression. Frances Lear's doctor was our technical supervisor on those two episodes. He had written, at that time, the only book on manic depression. I believe it was called *From Sad to Glad*. But he was the leading doctor working with pharmaceuticals/working with patients who were suffering from manic depression. When I recognized this about my friend, I called him – he was in New York – and I explained to him, and he said: 'Let me talk to him.' And he spoke to him on the phone, and when they hung up, my friend said to me 'That is the first person who has ever said anything that has led me to believe he had an understanding of what I was going through.' Up until that point, all the doctors had said 'Oh you're nervous? Take a Valium. You can't sleep? Take a sleeping pill.' No one was dealing with him. So we flew to New York and met with this doctor, and he diagnosed my friend and got him on medication. And after three or four years of thinking he was crazy and being suicidal, suddenly he had a diagnosis and help and changed his life completely. So those episodes on *Maude* were life transforming for my friend, and I would assume for other people. When we were doing the work, I at least was just wanting to make it as good as possible, and proud to be in shows that weren't just about pratfalls or getting stuck in garbage cans or something and not having it affect society. But it wasn't until I would say these last ten years when I have started doing autograph signings at the conventions, the horror conventions and the comic conventions that I have had so many people come up to me who say that that show changed their life! I still remember one man coming up to me saying 'That was the first time I ever saw a family portrayed, that was yelling at each other and still loved each other because we didn't have that in my family. I didn't understand that there could be anything besides just the yelling.' I've had many women come up to me and say that Carol gave them a roadmap for how to be as young or teenage girls/gay women or lesbian women, who were trying to find their place. It's been incredibly gratifying! Since then, at the time I wasn't thinking we're changing the world.

"J.J. in Trouble" from *Good Times*
Original Air Date: 3 February 1976
By Emma Westwood

In this Very Special Episode of *Good Times* (1974–1979), the parents are taken out of the picture (the excuse being their attendance at Aunt Rose's wedding across the weekend) – a smart way of concurrently signaling the viewing adults to also "leave the room" and create a "kids only zone" for this show to unfold. Why do this? The discussion is going to turn to the rather awkward subject of sexually transmitted disease and, if there are no adults present, then, hopefully, the kids in the audience will stay glued to the TV and take heed, rather than tuning out and turning off in embarrassment.

The writers of *Good Times* use the eldest Evans' child, J.J. (Jimmy Walker) as the conduit for this rather delicate storyline. J.J. sees himself as something of a ladies' man so immediately jumps at the opportunity when an ex-girlfriend, Mary Ann Thomas (Ta-Tanisha), asks if she can come around and see him. He makes sure his younger brother Michael (Ralph Carter) and sister Thelma (BernNadette Stanis) are out of the apartment because he mistakenly thinks Mary Ann, who is now dating the captain of the football team, is coming around to rekindle the "good times" they shared. Instead, she has a big surprise: "I've got VD and you're the one that gave it to me."

The use of the term VD (short for "venereal disease") is an interesting one, given it's a catchall (pardon the pun) phrase that fails to detail any specifics. The dictionary definition of VD is "a disease typically contracted by sexual intercourse with a person already infected; a sexually transmitted disease" with illnesses falling under this umbrella including chlamydia, herpes, gonorrhea, syphilis and even HIV/AIDS (although the AIDS epidemic, while in its infancy, was yet to become a matter of widespread public concern until the 1980s). It's probably safe to assume the writers chose to use the term VD, rather than expound on the details, so not to cause any further alarm within an audience that could extend to young children. Similarly, there is no talk of VD symptoms or the showing of any explicit or uncomfortable imagery.

It takes a while for the reality to hit home. J.J. talks to himself as a way of processing it all: "I can't believe this is happening! I mean, this only happens to other people. Wait a minute... to other people? I AM other people!" Right off the bat, the dialogue tackles a big misconception around venereal disease: this only happens to someone else. It also does so by refusing to slut shame, opting to inflict the "good girl", Mary Ann, with the condition ("sweet little Mary Ann Thomas," as Thelma calls her).

Given VD attacks people in a non-discriminate manner, the show also wisely steers clear of making any racially specific statements. Nevertheless, it's still important to note, even as late as 2002, gonorrhea ranked first among notifiable diseases with the largest racial disparities in the U.S., with a black/white ratio of 24:2.[5] Given this statistic, we can safely assume the producers of *Good Times* identified this issue as a serious one with specific consequences within the African American community.

J.J. gives voice to the shame people feel around sexually transmitted diseases when he asks himself why it couldn't have been something else, like the mumps or measles. Then he says he needs to talk to someone about it but, when he picks up the phone, he slams it down because his shame prevents him from talking. In a panic, he thinks the disease is "going to his head" and making him crazy, which shows how little J.J. knows, even though he's 18 years of age. Ironically, it takes the youngest of the Evans clan, Michael, only a moment to clock the page J.J. is consulting in the family medical reference book and then to ask him, "Do you have VD?"

The scriptwriters embrace the progressiveness of a new generation when they give Michael – who, incidentally, is the more mature of the two brothers, despite his years – an opportunity to educate the audience, along with J.J. and Thelma, about VD. Michael's learnt all about it in a sex education class at school and he provides vital information that also addresses economic realities when he says VD is 100% curable and "the public health department gives free treatment in every major city in the country." Michael also emphasizes the importance of getting treatment because, while the symptoms may go away, the disease will stay with you and that can lead to other major illnesses, even death. He broaches the shame and fear of retribution, which is why so many teenagers choose not to seek treatment, when he points out, "a doctor can treat anyone over the age of 11 for VD without their parents' permission."

Michael also imparts a thinly veiled warning against underage sex: "Don't do the crime if you cannot do the time." It's a brief warning, without proselytizing, but it's there to play on the conscience of those in the audience who choose to hear it.

The Evans kids arrive at the VD clinic and are immediately confronted with the fact that disease can affect everyone and anyone. Males and females – black and white – sit patiently waiting to be seen by the doctor. When J.J. is awkward about saying "VD" to the white, female nurse, she remarks, "That's nothing to be ashamed of."

One of the patients in the waiting room is Jay Leno – around 15 years prior to his *Tonight Show* hosting gig – who also asks J.J., "What are you here for?" J.J. lies: "A cold." "A cold?" questions Leno's character. "That's funny – everyone else is here for VD." J.J. looks around and sees the everyday people surrounding him. Leno confirms, "A germ's a germ, ain't it? I mean, what's the difference between VD and your cold?"

When J.J. finally gets to see the doctor, he is a black man, which is a tactful approach by the screenwriters, given subjecting J.J. to white authority at this point could

---

5   Aral SO, Fenton KA, Holmes KK. Sexually transmitted diseases in the USA: temporal trends. *Sex Transm Infect*. 2007; 83(4): 257–266.
    doi:10.1136/sti.2007.026245
    <https://www.ncbi.nlm.nih.gov/pmc/articles/PMC2598671/>.

undermine the message. J.J. is surprised when the doctor greets him with a thanks for coming to the clinic. He effectively finishes the lecture that Michael began.

Doctor: "You'd be surprised how few people who suspect they have VD will even seek treatment. VD's the biggest problem with kids around your age."

J.J.: "But I thought it was an older person's disease."

Doctor: "Oh no, not at all – the next biggest group to get it are kids younger than you. As a matter of fact, it's so out of control now that one out of five high school students will get VD before they graduate… And it's not the bad guy disease anymore either. Anyone can get it and they do."

This episode concludes with a plot twist: J.J. doesn't have VD – so how did nice Mary Ann get it? Mary Ann doesn't want to admit to the inevitable that it was passed to her from her football-playing fiancé. She doesn't want to believe that the man she is planning to marry may be sullied in any way, and she doesn't want to create a shameful wedge in their relationship by telling him. But she needs to tell him. As Thelma so rightly points out, "The worst thing you can do is NOT tell him." And the worst thing the audience can do is to not learn from J.J.'s misfortune.

"The Interview" from M*A*S*H
Original Air Date: 24 February 1976
By Samm Deighan

M*A*S*H (1972–1983) is certainly notable for its willingness to confront social issues and to protest the then ongoing Vietnam War, but the show was innovative not only for its approach to content, but to form. In general, it could be described as a situation comedy, though it became more of a drama as the seasons progressed, tackling quite serious and even dark subject matter that culminated in the mental breakdown of the protagonist, Hawkeye, during the show's feature-length conclusion, "Goodbye, Farewell and Amen."

Generally speaking, episodes followed a standard sitcom format – focusing on storylines that followed the key characters, with narration of the contents of letters characters have written home. The balance was between comic episodes and more serious ones, and even more than the 1970 film, the show was required to gently, more subtly approach the issue of political protest. The medical characters were often presented in contrast to the military characters, leading to healthy – and often hilarious – debates between the two sides, with an emphasis on pranks particularly in the early seasons of the show. These debates questioned the role of war in American society, an unspoken but obvious critique of the Vietnam War and the Cold War.

Episodes that played with the sitcom format were often daring with their presentation of subject matter, such as "Dreams," featuring the dreams of various cast members, or "Life Time," which presented an episode in so-called real time. One episode that experimented with format while also daring to challenge war directly was "The Interview," which stripped the show's occasional laugh track completely and rejected its standard narrative format. Aired in February of 1976 – months after the end of the Vietnam War – as episode 24 of season four, "The Interview" is less like a conventional episode of *M*A*S*H* and is essentially a mock news segment. A news correspondent (Clete Roberts) interviews many of the central cast members, asking them about their experience with the war. This was the final episode for Larry Gelbart, the show's creator, and features some frank and occasionally shocking dialogue (at least by the television standards of the day).

There is a realism to the episode that seems to borrow from the neorealist cinema of the fifties and sixties and this episode, perhaps more than any other in the show, is at home with a lot of the New Hollywood Cinema of the late sixties and early seventies. The episode is in black and white, which makes it feel a little bit like a John Cassavetes film. Dialogue feels improvised – which some of it apparently was – and characters accidentally curse, look directly at the camera, or seem self-conscious and uncomfortable about being interviewed on film. The interviewer, Roberts, was an actual news correspondent who reported on the Korean War – a detail likely lost on contemporary fans revisiting the series, but it must have added an unsettling layer of realism for anyone watching *M*A*S*H* when it was initially broadcast. But unlike a conventional news broadcast or war reporting, the questions are deeply personal, asking characters like Hawkeye or B.J. Hunnicutt (Mike Farrell) how the war itself makes them feel. Do they miss home? What do they fear?

In the modern era of CNN and uninterrupted political and military reporting, it's difficult to imagine military personnel being interviewed about such personal subjects – and even more difficult to imagine them giving anything other than a guarded, canned response that would be approved or even written by a PR person before the interview. This is a particularly interesting example of how *M*A*S*H* was often meticulously well researched as regards to historical detail about the 1950s and the Korean War, but was frequently more interested in anachronisms that allowed the show to comment on life – and war – in the seventies. This running theme through the show is a testament to its power and perhaps explains its continued popularity and influence. It became less a show about the Korean War and more generally about the evils of war and military intervention.

By 1976, public sentiment had largely become anti-war, but it's still jarring to hear some of the characters speak so openly about the evils of war and their ambivalence about belonging to the military. For example, in "The Interview," Hunnicutt described himself as a civilian who has been "temporarily misassigned." One of the key character conflicts in *M*A*S*H* was between medical and military personnel, which this undercuts, with the military characters towing the company line, not because they have to, but because of their loyalty to and strong belief in the institution. On the other hand, other characters speak with horror and pain about the realities of war: about turning away orphaned children because there isn't enough food to go around, for example. The quick pace of "The Interview" allows the episode to cover a lot of ground in its short running time, where characters discuss everything from what they miss most at home to subjects like the presence – and effectiveness – of female nurses in a battle zone.

One of the most gut-wrenching replies comes from resident priest Father Mulcahy (William Christopher), who imparts the horror of war in an all too visceral sense. Roberts asks various characters if they have been changed by their experience in Korea. Mulcahy replies, "When the doctors cut into a patient, and it's cold – the way it is now, today – steam rises from the body. The doctor will warm his hands over the open wound. How could anybody look upon that and not feel changed?" Hawkeye, likewise, is among his angriest in this episode. Though he speaks highly of his colleagues, he mocks the Trumans, and says that war is crazy and being there day in and day out is a struggle to remain sane. This can be read as a foreshadowing – even unintentional – of the series finale, where he suffers a mental breakdown, but his bitterness is all-consuming in this episode in particular, with his trademark humor nowhere to be found. Even hospital commander Colonel Potter (Harry Morgan) – a fair character throughout the later seasons but one who is always loyal to the military – remarks that "not a damn thing" will come from the war and the countless lives lost. The tone of the episode is deadly serious, and various characters' assertions that "war is just killing" and "there's always terror to fall back on" are haunting to hear, even 40 years later.

"The Big Move" from *Good Times*
Original Air Dates: 22 September 1976 (Part 1) and 29 September 1976 (Part 2)
By Emma Westwood

Traditionally, a television series will end any given season with a cliffhanger to keep viewers on tenterhooks across the summer ratings break, waiting eagerly for the next season to hit the airwaves. The legendary "Who shot J.R.?" catchphrase from *Dallas* (1978–1991) – referring to the whodunit mystery of J.R. Ewing's attempted murder in the third season 1980 finale, "A House Divided" – is a perfect example of a classic storytelling device that has lost its punch in these days of streaming, downloading and binge-watching. With *Good Times*' "The Big Move", however, the "cliffhanger" (although not so much of a cliffhanger as a gut-wrencher, in this specific example) would occur at the very *beginning* of the fourth season in a surprise two-parter that ripped the rug out from under the Evans family and floored audiences in the process. This Very Special Episode sits at the beating heart of *Good Times* (1974–1979), not just in terms of the on-screen narrative but also as the fulcrum on which the show's production history hinged, with this significant juncture occurring roughly midway through the show's lifespan.

By the time this episode of *Good Times* went to air, the creative differences between the show's lead characters – Esther Rolle as Florida Evans and John Amos as James Evans – and the show's producers, including creator Norman Lear, had been played out in public. As a spinoff from *Maude* (1972–1978), in which Florida Evans was popularly featured as Bea Arthur's maid, *Good Times* was intended to center on meaningful, socially conscious content based around the family unit of James and Florida, but was being railroaded with the rise of Jimmy Walker's character of J.J. Both Rolle and Amos felt the original intent had been lost in J.J.'s wisecracks and general buffoonery.

Somewhere between the third and fourth seasons, Amos' relationship with the producers reached an irreparable boiling point and, consequently, he was swiftly written out of the show, never to appear again, not even in flashback. As a result, the beginning of the fourth season, "The Big Move", opens with a climax that would usually be reserved for the season end but, nonetheless, gives the writers plenty of juicy narrative fruit to be dissected across forthcoming episodes. Rather than "Who shot J.R.?", the question insinuated here is "How will the Evans family cope?"

As the screen fades up on part one of "The Big Move", Florida and her daughter, Thelma (BernNadette Stanis), dance around their Chicago housing project apartment singing the lyrics "Mississippi, here we come, right back where we started from", which they've reworded from the Al Jolson hit of 1924, "California, Here I Come" – itself a "grass is always greener" ditty about an imminent homecoming to a southern state.

The inclusion of music in *Good Times* is always very pointed, another example in this Very Special Episode being the appropriately named "Movin'" by Brass Construction, which acts as the funky soundscape to the Evans' going away party held by their much-loved neighbor, Willona Woods (Ja'net DuBois). But then also inadvertently, and incongruently, the track accompanies the realization of all the party guests that James has been killed, as Florida reads a telegram from Mississippi.

While the Evans women dance gleefully and wave their hand towels, there is a bittersweet nature to their celebration – something in which the entire *Good Times* series is steeped – that of making the best of a crap situation. In this case, their farewell to Chicago and return to Mississippi is because James gets offered a share of his uncle's garage business, which promises greater stability and financial opportunity or, as Florida puts it by way of Martin Luther King Jr., "Free at last, free at last!" The irony that a return to the Deep South elicits a cry of "Free at last" is not lost.

While Thelma exclaims how great it is going to be for them in Mississippi, we can't help but surmise why the Evans family left Mississippi in the first place. The heartland of Confederate country (the second southern state to declare its secession from the United States of America on 9 January 1861), Mississippi represents pain, suffering and slavery to Black America. For the Evans family to celebrate their return, in a belief that things are going to be better, suggests a sad cycle of poverty and privation in America, where blacks and other racial minorities are unable to break the generational chains and rise beyond what has been deemed their lot in life. Florida even realizes it too, and she tells the children that when she left Mississippi, they still had separate facilities for blacks and whites. Whether consciously or not, when she says, "Wouldn't it be awful if, on our way down to Mississippi, we met some sisters and brothers on their way to Chicago, and we both said, 'Go back, go back!'?", she perfectly encapsulates that cycle. The Evans family may flourish with the opportunities that James' new business could bring but we know that is highly unlikely, and the events of this episode seal that fate anyway.

Part one of "The Big Move" fades out on the faces of Florida hugging her youngest son, Michael (Ralph Carter), as reality sinks in. The end credits come up but, rather than play the *Good Times* theme immediately, there is a five-second pause on the first of the end credits – a moment to let it sink in for the viewers – before the very recognizable, cheerful gospel strains of the *Good Times* theme can finally be heard.

When we return for part two, the mood is decidedly different to part one, having swapped the vibe of the going away party for a gathering of a very different kind: James' wake. As is consistent with the staging of live studio audience sitcoms, we skip the funeral and, instead, are brought back to the family apartment, which is where most of the dramedy of *Good Times* takes place. The lack of external scenes is likely a budgetary and logistical consideration, but it also serves diegetically to show that the most profound things can take place within the four walls of the home.

Willona, dressed in black, opens the door to an older lady, Wanda (Helen Martin) who is wailing but, when told that the Evans family are yet to arrive back from the funeral, manages to turn off her tears like a tap. That's the theme of part two – grief, and how different people not only process but also display their grief in varied and sometimes contradictory ways. Given that one of America's first, black TV families had just lost their dad, we cannot underestimate the grieving the *Good Times* audience was experiencing at the time. Television in the 1970s was still in its infancy and the hours every week that people would spend with on-the-box personalities meant a level of rapport beyond that of cinema. For viewers, James' death had come out of the blue and, for the majority of this episode, we're given little to no information about his death either – just a passing comment that it was in a motor vehicle accident.

While the shock of his death forms much of the drama behind part two, the soul of the episode sits with Florida and her means of processing James' passing. Florida, as the widow, is a model of stoicism and fortitude. She is the stereotypical strong black woman who has weathered more than her fair share of storms. At one point, when J.J. offers to help her clean up the house, she insists, "J.J., I said I don't need any help", which demonstrates how pulling up her socks and getting on with it is Florida's way of coping. But her kids don't understand her, particularly Michael and Thelma who are lashing out with anger and despair respectively in trying to process the loss of their father. In a strange role reversal, the usually irresponsible J.J. takes on a more mature stance, putting forward the insightful observation of his mother: "I don't know why she ain't crying but I know she's suffering more than any of us."

The running joke in part two is the number of hams being offered as gifts of condolence. Why ham is consider the appropriate offering for this occasion appears to be lost on everyone, although it does allow for a couple of Jewish jokes, and for Willona to sing an impromptu ham song – "Come and get your ham or get your hams out the house!" Florida claps along to Willona's song, much to the family's disdain. When Michael and Thelma directly tackle Florida about what they see as her weird behavior, she says, "People have always acted this way – it's part of your heritage. Back in Africa, folks marked the passing of a loved one by running up, tapping on the drums, singing and dancing. They don't mourn the death, they celebrate the life." But Michael retorts by saying, "Ma, we don't care about the old days" and Thelma supports him by admitting, "We want to know what's happening now!" This is as much about generational divide as about how Black America may be descended from Africa but Black America has very much developed into a people unto its own.

Part two of "The Big Move" works so well because it enables Americans to grieve, and does so without histrionics and overt sentimentality. It looks at the many faces of grief and concludes that, while the methods of some might be confusing to others, there is no right or wrong where death is concerned. It concludes with a superbly poignant eruption of emotion when Florida, cleaning up her kitchen, drops a bowl and screams, "Damn, damn, damn!" As tough as Florida may be, she is unable to contain the pain that erupts inside her. But, by showing her children that she feels the same as them, the Evans family are able to come together again in a four-way embrace.

The episode poetically ends – no mushy song, no nostalgic flashbacks. Some fans wanted more from this ending but there is genius in the subtlety of the show's decision here, and its refrain from milking an already emotional high point. As the *Good Times* theme song goes, "Keeping your head above water, making a way when you can", and so will the Evans Family for at least another two and a bit seasons.

When the sitcom needs to move on: "The Big Move" from Good Times *had a shift in structure with star John Amos deciding to take leave and therefore having his character of James Evans killed off. Here, Esther Rolle as matriarch Florida Evans, hears the news of his passing, shifting the series into its next wave.*

"Quarantine" from *Barney Miller*
Original Air Dates: 30 September 1976 (Part 1)
and 7 October 1976 (Part 2)
By Shawn Macomber

"The human comedy is always tragic but since its ingredients are always the same – dupe, fox, straight, like burlesque skits – the repetition through the ages is comedy," the great if bafflingly under-loved Greenwich Village novelist Dawn Powell wrote in her posthumously published diaries. "The basis of tragedy is man's helplessness against disease, war and death; the basis of comedy is man's helplessness against vanity (the vanity of love, greed, lust, power)."

And so it is with the first three episodes of the third season of *Barney Miller* (1975–1982), in which the sweet and genial foibles, vanity, and plainclothes burlesque of the detectives working out of New York City's 12th Precinct – also based in Greenwich Village, if you like a bit of serendipitous symmetry with your literary allusions – are thrust into confrontation with "helplessness against disease, war, and death" rather than the usual chill petty crimes and easygoing banter.

In the season three premiere, "Evacuation," Detective Stan "Wojo" Wojciehowicz (Max Gail) pulls a short tour as the Public Information Officer for Manhattan South. In less conscientious hands it seems as if the gig would be a glorified vacation. Wojo, on the other hand, digs into the city handbook *Procedures in the Event of Civil Disasters* and realizes there aren't really any procedures in the event of civil disasters. How, he begins to ask himself, will city residents packed into a very small landmass like sardines possibly escape and/or survive a major crisis?

Wojo manages to freak out Officer Callahan (the late, extraordinarily great Kenneth Mars), but no matter how many apocalyptic scenarios he conjures up – a tidal wave of sewage flooding the streets; earthquakes; a thermonuclear device – the rest of the unit responds to hypothetical tragedy with typical wisecracking comedy.

"We're all sitting ducks," Callahan muses. "Trapped here on an island."

"It's better than the South Bronx," Captain Barney Miller (Hal Linden) shoots back.

By episodes end, the emerging moral seems to be that some events are too enormous and unfathomable for one man to solve during a four-day stint as a Public Information Officer. You've got to focus on your own tiny patch of influence if you don't want to go completely mad: Think globally about extinction level events, sure, but act locally. "Wojo, you're getting obsessed with that [handbook]," Miller says. "Now will you put that thing away and get to work on something you can do something about?"

And so he does. Yet in the very next episode the stakes are raised by taking the threat from macro to terrifying micro. Which is to say, in the two-parter "Quarantine," the "helplessness" that in a way floated up somewhere in the celestial firmament in "Evacuation" kicks in the precinct door and puts its feet up on the desk.

Here's how it begins: It's an average – if extremely hot – day in Barney Miller's familiar fiefdom. Detectives Phil Fish (Abe Vigoda) and Ron Harris (Ron Glass) are comparing and contrasting the latter's hot weekend date with the former's ice cube marriage while nearby Detective Sergeant Nick Yemana (Jack Soo) processes a prostitute. Miller himself is eager to wrap up the day and head to the Jersey Shore with his not-yet-estranged wife Liz. Everyone, it seems, has a magnet drawing them out of the precinct and into their real, separate lives.

Alas, there's a Chekhov's gun-adjacent principle often at work in television dramas and comedies: If a character has absolutely fantastic plans they cannot stop dreamily talking about, those must be at some point shot down. Here the metaphorical firearm comes in the form of one sweat-drenched Philip Dupree – David Darlow, who would later appear in a season six episode simply as "Burglar" before going on to low-key Hollywood success with roles in *Miller's Crossing* (1990), *The Fugitive* (1993) and *Road to Perdition* (2002) – collared by Wojo in a warehouse pilfering a box of radios. The man's got a passport with stamps from seemingly every unstable country in the world and is complaining of a fiery fever. He collapses, a doctor comes in, does a few doctorly things, and promptly quarantines the building because of potential smallpox exposure.

Today, of course, smallpox is an exotic and distant disease – though there is reason to believe our complacency and growing skepticism of its vaccine could soon engender a most unpleasant modern-day re-acquaintance – but it is important contextually to remember that "Quarantine" aired a full four years before the 33rd World Health Assembly declared the disease officially eradicated on May 8, 1980. Though humanity had been battling smallpox since *at least* the 3rd century BCE, in the 20th century alone, according to researchers at Saint Louis University, the disease is "estimated to have caused between 300 million and 500 million deaths."

In short... *no bueno.*

At the opening of the concluding second episode we find a heterogenous gaggle of human beings thrust together under the looming shadow of tragedy: Miller's crew. The prostitute. The doctor. A beat cop with a chip on his Napoleon complexed shoulder over his failure to be promoted to detective. A gay couple straight out of central mid-1970s casting (Ray Stewart, Jack DeLeon) that popped in at the worst possible moment to ask Miller to help them get probation waived for an old shopping lifting charge lifted so they can move to the promised land of San Francisco (see!), and crusty old Inspector Frank Lugar (James Gregory; *Beneath the Planet of the Apes* (1970), *That Girl* (1966–1971)) who asks Miller of said gay couple that are now his effective short-term neighbors, "Where'd you pick up the Lavender Hill Mob?" (Speaking of context, this was seven years after the Stonewall riots, but four years before sexual activity between same-sex couples would be legal and thirty-five years before New York legalized same-sex marriage.)

If this were an episode of *The Twilight Zone* we'd clearly be trending towards "The Shelter" or "The Monsters Are Due on Maple Street" territory. In the former's exit narration Rod Serling opines, "for civilization to survive, the human race has to remain civilized" – which perhaps expects too much. Whether it's a nuclear bomb instantly incinerating ten million urban dwellers or an invisible virus stalking one isolated building in that same city, we are by design vulnerable creatures constantly tempted to negate our lives with attempts to eliminate vulnerability. That is our folly, our embrace of tragedy.

Barney Miller takes a different, more stoic approach – a tack not unlike the one embodied in Marcus Aurelius famous maxim, "Death smiles at us all, but all a man can do is smile back." In other words, a dark force tries to press the quarantined into tragedy, but they overcome it by allowing the vanity of existence to feed and nurture the human comedy.

"You keep your body in shape," Wojo tells a cornered Fish. "You take vitamins, eat the right foods. And then some germ comes along and kills you."

Fish's clap back? "You see why we don't talk more often?"

There is something comforting about the way the group doesn't trade its petty squabbles and wisecracks and internecine office feuds and fecund sexuality – literally every dude in these episodes at one point or another fears the sophisticated gays in their midst may be picking up vibes he is (latently) putting down – for long, morose meditations on existential philosophy. Even when Harris begins talking in his sleep amidst the throes of a nightmare, he's not yattering on about smallpox but, rather, Miller's management style.

"You know, I remember what my great grandfather said just before he died," Yamana says. "He said, 'Though one may conspire to delay the moment of one's death…'"

"Yeah?" Wojo asks, eager for esoteric wisdom.

A beat. "That's as far as he got."

It's a punchline, sure, but also a legitimate piece of insight: We do not know – cannot know – what lies beyond the veil. There is no need to preoccupy one's self with death because it is a certainty. What's the use of, say, thinking about blinking? Focus on it and you'll never actually see anything. "Quarantine," if we consider it on a "meta" level, encourages us to imagine what we'd rather immerse ourselves in: The tragedy of creeping death or the laughter of life.

"Death smiles at us all, but all Barney Miller can do is roll his eyes and get us to laugh uproariously back."

"Walter's Crisis" from *Maude*
Original Air Dates: 11 October 1976 (Part 1), 18 October 1976 (Part 2) and 25 October 1976 (Part 3)
By Michael Barrett

In the 1970s, sitcoms became dangerous. If viewers tuned in for reassurance and repetition of the conventions, the ground was shifting beneath their feet and, to mix metaphors, all bets were off. This wasn't true of every sitcom, of course, but it felt true of the top-rated ones that were redefining the genre.

One of the conventions is that regular characters don't die. That went out the window with "Abyssinia, Henry" (18 March 1975), the third season finale of *M*A*S*H* (1972–1983). With its Korean War setting, this series had already become the deathiest sitcom ever, but this particular episode saw Col. Henry Blake (McLean Stevenson) written out in a "feel good" way by having his character sent home, thus fulfilling what viewers already knew – that Stevenson was leaving the series. Then the final scene announced Blake's death. It seemed gratuitous and cruel, and also credible and appropriate to the wartime context.

Technically, he wasn't the first sitcom regular to die. When Jean Hagen left *Make Room for Daddy* after three seasons, the show changed its title to *The Danny Thomas Show* (1953–1965) and explained with infinite delicacy that her character, Danny's wife Margaret, had died. It was handled so smoothly that, as the show continued for several more seasons, viewers mostly forgot it, such that it seemed hardly to create a ripple in sitcom history, so in accord was it with the gentle era of family sitcoms. Henry Blake's shocking and violent death was a different matter.

When "Walter›s Crisis" began its three week arc on *Maude*, not only was Henry's death still a recent memory, but fans of Norman Lear's series had just suffered through the even more pertinent death of James Evans (John Amos) on *Good Times* (1974–1979) only the previous month (22 September 1976).

Therefore, when part two of "Walter's Crisis" ended with Walter (Bill Macy) overdosed on sleeping pills, his eyes open and unresponsive, and the closing credits began in blank silence, shocked viewers had no reassurance that Walter would survive. The rules were being rewritten as we watched.

Each of the three parts, by different writers, has a slightly different feel. Part one opens at a tourist restaurant in Acapulco, where the Findlays and their friends, the Harmons, are on vacation. Amid much byplay and even a bit of music, Walter receives bad news about a bank loan to open a second Findlay's Friendly Appliances store.

The second half of the episode has them back home in Tuckahoe, where a careless attorney (Dick Van Patten) explains that Walter must declare bankruptcy to cover his debts – on the same night he's receiving an award for Businessman of the Year. The other business owners at the dinner stood to make lots of money from Walter's new store, and now they'll be paid ten cents on the dollar.

Here's probably the first hint on any American sitcom that something's wrong with this system, especially when the lawyer apologizes for his wife's insensitivity because she doesn't understand things like this. "We're rich," he explains. Walter says he'd believed Washington's announcements about the thriving economy. "You can't believe everything you hear," says Maude. Barbs like this, alas, haven't lost their thrust.

While part one went from Mexican frolic to political and business satire, part two basks in Walter's humiliation as he cannot find a job because he's too old. Maude tries to make him feel better by seducing him, but he recoils at the sympathy and disappears. She thinks he's drunk when he shows up carrying a duck, but when he sings a bit of "Me and My Shadow" and disappears up the stairs, things take a very ominous turn.

Part 3 finds Walter in the hospital telling Maude, "Yesterday I said to myself here I am worrying about being bankrupt, worrying because I can't find a job, worrying because there's no hope for the future. Why the hell am I killing myself? That's when I decided to kill myself." The episode ends with Maude and Walter reaffirming their love while Maude can only assure him that everybody's afraid but most people don't admit it to each other.

Meanwhile, we get a dose of hospital satire. A nurse (Helen Page Camp in one of six unrelated appearances on the series) tells Maude that her own husband was admitted to this very hospital with shingles the previous day and is now in intensive care because a nurse gave him the wrong medication. "That's terrible!" says Maude, and the nurse says, "I know, but I can't blame her. I've made the same mistake myself."

This humor matches movies such as *The Hospital* and *Such Good Friends*, both from 1971. The latter features a man who's admitted for a minor procedure and goes into a coma, leading one doctor to state, "Hospital care only really becomes adequate when a patient's life is in danger. Otherwise it's so poor that we must wonder not why so many die but how so many survive." Unfortunately, some of us can report that this vision also remains as relevant as ever. A hospital is no place for sick people.

If death had become a real possibility on sitcoms, "Walter's Crisis" became the first warning shot that even suicide wasn't necessarily off limits. In the 21st century, a recurring character on *Scrubs* (2001–2010) named Ted (Sam Lloyd) actually had suicidal tendencies built (comically) into his personality.

The deaths or near-deaths of regular characters can be placed in a wider context of how sitcoms handled death. Most didn't foreground it in any way, of course, but there were exceptions. Jack Benny's classic Christmas show, repeated several times on radio and made twice for TV›s *The Jack Benny Program* (1950–1965) ("Christmas Shopping Show" of 15 December 1957, and "Jack Does Christmas Shopping" of 12 December 1954) ends with the frazzled store clerk (Mel Blanc) blowing his brains out behind the department store's Christmas tree because of Benny's constant demands. "Such a shame, he was so young," says Benny, before removing his change from the cash register.

This very acid commentary on Christmas and shopping belonged to Benny's special brand of dark, anything-goes, unsentimental and neurotic humor. In another radio remake, "Jack's Lunch Counter" (20 February 1955, then again as "Lunch Counter Murder" on 4 December 1960), Jack is even called upon to shoot guys dead. The amorphous, free-wheeling, self-conscious nature of the series allowed this.

Benny's humor would be replicated on *Seinfeld* (1989–1998), which was also capable of serving death devoid of any warm fuzziness. Both shows focused on urbane Jewish stand-up comics, as "themselves," who were seen performing their act and living their lives, being the straight man in a gallery of neurotics and being supremely neurotic themselves, engaging in running gags and catchphrases, being "existential" and "about nothing" while indulging screwy twists, and always aiming for the laugh. It's a temperament that eschewed Very Special Episodes, and in retrospect we can see how timeless was Benny's attitude.

With the shining exception of Benny and sketch satirists like Sid Caesar, TV comedy tended to avoid death and certainly making light of it. True, the WWII antics of *Hogan's Heroes* (1965–1971) and *McHale's Navy* (1962–1966) sometimes permitted enemy deaths without pausing for emotional resonance, but there was a war on.

The real groundbreaker was "Chuckles Bites the Dust" (25 October 1975) on *The Mary Tyler Moore Show* (1970–1977), in which a character who'd been seen a few times got killed in a grotesque and absurd way. The clown was dressed as a giant peanut when "a rogue elephant tried to shell him."

One of the most acclaimed sitcom episodes of all time, this broke into viewers' consciousness so strongly that, from then on, many sitcoms included the deaths of guest characters, handled either seriously or wackily. *Maude* would twice pull off having a character exclaim "I'm so happy I could die!" only to promptly drop dead on the floor of Maude's living room. The death line became a punchline.

And so began the era when it became an acceptable part of the sitcom landscape even for regulars to die. Most went with quiet dignity, like Edith Bunker's passing on *Archie Bunker's Place* (1979–1983) or the paterfamilias played by John Ritter on *8 Simple Rules for Dating My Teenage Daughter* (2002–2005). A few went amid more sensational sturm and drang behind the scenes, like the car accident that killed the title character of *Valerie* (1986–1991) when Valerie Harper was fired, or the death-by-train of Charlie Sheen's character in *Two and a Half Men* (2003–2015).

We might say that sitcom deaths evolved into their final parody of meaninglessness when *South Park* (1997–) made "Oh my God! They killed Kenny!" into a catchphrase by killing the same character in almost every episode. It was only a cartoon, which is another way of saying it's only a TV show.

"Michael the Warlord" from *Good Times*
Original Air Date: 13 October 1976
By Emma Westwood

"The slum is as old as civilization. Civilization implies a race[6] [among social strata] to get ahead... They drag one another farther down. The bad environment becomes the heredity of the next generation. Then, given the crowd, you have a slum ready-made." — Jacob A. Riis, *The Battle with the Slum* (1902)

Only two episodes after the earthshaking events in the two-part *Good Times* (1974–1979) season four opener, "The Big Move" – i.e. the death of the show's patriarch, James Evans (John Amos) – "Michael the Warlord" sees the youngest of the Evans clan, Michael (Ralph Carter), getting himself into hot water. For the adolescent Michael – made even more vulnerable without a father and left with only his notoriously reckless and immature older brother, J.J. (Jimmy Walker), for male guidance – peer group influences corral him down a dangerous road, although one that is far too familiar for many black American teenagers, as history sadly confirms.

In the 20 or so years following World War II, public servants in Chicago constructed 51 high-rise public housing projects within existing black ghetto sites. Accounts suggest these public housing high-rises were no places to call home – dirty, dangerous and dilapidated – of which Cabrini-Green, the unnamed but obvious setting of *Good Times* (as imagery of the actual Cabrini-Green project appears in the opening and closing credits of the show) was an infamously high-profile example. These housing projects developed into incubators and battlegrounds for gang violence – "high-rise forts" – facilitating regular and direct contact between gang members.[7]

America's first African American primetime television family – the Evanses – were not immune to the plight of broader Black America and, in accordance with the original intent of the show, bore a responsibility to address the darker side of the Black American experience. Through an episode like "Michael the Warlord", they not only opened White America's eyes to the results of slums and ghettoization but, more importantly for this show, opened Black America's eyes to finding a way out.

By the fourth season of *Good Times*, we could argue the show had developed a high level of rapport with its predominantly black viewership. The show made a point of wearing its "blackness" on its sleeve, which means dialogue peppered with colloquialisms and "jive talking" of that era (for example, in this specific episode, Willona, played

---

6   JC Howell and JP Moore, "History of Street Gangs in the United States" (2010) 4 National Gang Center Bulletin 1 <https://www.nationalgangcenter.gov/Content/Documents/History-of-Street-Gangs.pdf>.

7   Ibid.

by Ja'net DuBois, talks about the shopping center being "packed tighter than a chitlin bucket".[8] In "Michael the Warlord", it tackles a phenomenon that, if not solely relegated to black American society, only significantly impacted on the nation's minorities and migrant populations.

Additionally, to have the character of Michael confronted with gang issues hits a timely note for the post-Martin Luther King and Black Panthers generation. Michael's late father, James, had called his youngest son "the militant midget" in response to Michael's passionate activism. While a smart kid, Michael is also an angry black man, which makes him particularly susceptible to the lure of gangs and vigilantism (but one who is very loveable and intimately connected with the show's audience).

The episode starts with a sense of urgency – Michael racing in the door, panting. We're offered a close-up of his shaking hands as they hook the security chain across the door. Inserting this close-up is an unusual choice for sitcoms of the time, given they largely played out through medium and wide shots. It creates a feeling of alarm – what is happening? We can hear it in the nervous snickers of the live studio audience that was possibly put off-guard by this seriousness in tone, having become accustomed to something far lighter as an introduction to any given episode.

In desperation, Michael hides his incriminating Junior Warlords jacket in the oven. He's aware his mother, Florida (Esther Rolle) and Willona are coming down the hallway, although they are blissfully unaware of his predicament. The security chain gives Michael a moment to compose himself before letting them in.

Then J.J. arrives wearing his beef ribs delivery boy gear in the signature "wacky entrance" we expect of his character. He talks about being rolled by a local gang, although confesses this gang "ain't nothing" compared to the Warlords that "rip the ribs out of your chest". Immediately, he positions the Warlords as a thing of danger, which heightens the gravity of our discovery of Michael's involvement.

A citizens' group of concerned parents meets at the Evans home to discuss actions for combatting the Warlords. We find out that Michael's friend, Tommy, has a fractured skull from an altercation with the gang. One of the parents says, "The schools can't do anything and the cops won't do anything". When Florida counters his opinion by stating, "Controlling those kids is up to the parents", there is sporadic clapping from the live audience. Then she adds, "We wouldn't have any gangs if parents took responsibility for their own kids", which prompts more enthusiasm in the audience's clapping. In effect, this is an interesting variation on the "breaking of the fourth wall" trope where the audience – real-life people watching the performance – are actively commenting on the teleplay through their response. In this case, they are telling us that they, representing the people of America (although we have no information about the racial or demographic composition of the audience at this particular taping), agree with Florida that people need to take control of their own children. This adds even more sting to the moment she discovers one of her own is involved with a gang.

---

8   Chitlin (or "chitterling" or "chittlin") is a form of "soul food" made from pig intestines that dates back to slavery times.

The oven ends up smoking – Michael's Junior Warlords jacket is burning; a slick metaphorical statement about the incendiary nature of the subject matter. When Michael's secret is revealed, the militant father of the citizen group warns, "Cure the fever in your own home, Mrs. Evans, before you start writing prescriptions for everyone else." But we feel for Florida because, if the Evans family wasn't struggling before, Florida is now a single mother – a tenuous circumstance that is endured by many black women. Keeping her family together and stable is no mean feat.

When asked why he's become involved with the Warlords, Michael says, "They asked Philip Smith to join the gang and he said no, so they broke his jaw. Then they asked Ernest Williams to join the gang, and he said no, so they broke his arm. Then when they asked me… [pause for dramatic effect]… they were lookin' at my neck." While his delivery of this explanation is played for laughs, Michael's situation is anything but funny. We're left with no doubt that it was the fear that made him do it:

"Ma, you're right. I only joined the gang because I was afraid."

J.J. has a heart-to-heart with Michael because he's "the man of the house now" and his confession of having gone through the same thing reveals the universality of the problem – it's something most young black men will need to negotiate. Florida laments the loss of her husband: "Oh, how I wish James was here. There'd be no way in the world Michael would be in that gang." Michael knows he needs to get out.

When Michael goes to confront the gang and Florida follows him, the camera travels outside of the Evans' apartment – a rare occurrence – and opens again on a close-up of the Warlords emptying a handbag they've stolen, revealing a measly booty of just seven cents. These kids talk about robbing from the neighborhood and make jokes about how poor the people are here. Blacks robbing from blacks – the cycle that keeps a whole race of people economically and socially oppressed.

This cycle of oppression gets echoed in Michael's encounter with the Junior Warlords. He talks about dreaming of becoming somebody, and then one of the gang speaks for the others (and a lot of other black teenagers) when he states, "We don't have those kinds of dreams because they never come true." Despite his youth, this gang member is already jaded and touting a self-fulfilling prophecy of hopelessness.

It's every son's nightmare to have their mother defend them yet, when Florida comes to save Michael with metaphorical guns blazing, we can't help but cheer her on. This would have been James' job but now, left to her own devices, Florida is the family savior and she is a force to be reckoned with. As if to emphasize the absent James, the gang wants to take her wedding ring, which sends Michael's rage and grieving into overdrive. The Junior Warlords prove no match for the all-powerful Evanses.

Michael's escape from the Warlords may be resolved a little too neatly (in the manner we've come to expect from characters inhabiting TV land) but it still offers a number of questions and answers applicable to the real world. If anything, it shows there can be hope in the face of hopelessness. And the Evanses will always stand together.

"Werewolf" from *Barney Miller*
Original Air Date: 28 October 1976
By Lee Gambin

During the seventies there was a massive wave of made-for-TV horror movies produced by major networks such as ABC and NBC, and supernatural themed television shows such as *Kolchak: The Night Stalker* (1974–1975) (which would come along after entries such as the soap opera *Dark Shadows* (1966–1971)) made a huge impression on the cultural zeitgeist of the time. Monsters were treated seriously for the most part during this decade and with the New Age movement inspiring people to look further into varied cultures, religions, belief systems and mythologies, the influence and history of vampires, ghosts and other supernatural entities sparked a keen interest in people invested in occultism and researching the traditions and folklore surrounding such spooks. Lycanthropy – the mental condition that caused humans to believe that they could turn into animals, primarily wolves – became a focal point in the *Barney Miller* episode "Werewolf", which had the boys at the Greenwich Village 12th Precinct station house deal with a loon who insists that he is a werewolf and forces the police to lock him up on the night of a full moon in order to protect the public from his bloodthirsty destructive ways.

Opening with Nick Yemana (Jack Soo) taking a call that involves UFO sightings in Central Park, the episode is a typical slow burn entry of *Barney Miller* (1975–1982) complete with its sharp writing and great characterizations of a bunch of policemen dealing with endless incidents that plague New York City. However, with Nick taking this call which involves a potential alien invasion, we get a sense that this episode may be out of the ordinary. The episode would of course air a few nights before Halloween, and in 1976 major horror movies would be released including *The Omen* and *Carrie*, so the popular genre was hot property and by this period, classic cinematic evils such as Satanism as presented in *The Omen* and telekinesis as seen in *Carrie* would be looked upon in a different light – and treated seriously and with great reverence. In many regards, "Werewolf" attempts to take lycanthropy seriously in the realm of situation comedy, and by giving it a face and voice (however hilarious and silly the antics may appear on the surface) forces the audience to look at the condition in a manner that they may never have before.

In "Werewolf", character actor Kenneth Tigar plays Stefan Koepeknie, a man who believes he's a werewolf. Tigar would play the same character again in an episode entitled "Possession" where he would think that he is inhabited by an evil spirit, and before that he would feature in an episode dealing with poltergeists, while in another he would believe that he was Jesus Christ (which would be a very different take on that same concern in the episode "Quo Vadis, Captain Chandler" from *M*A*S*H*

Kenneth Tigar guest stars as Stefan Koepeknie, a man with lycanthropic delusions in the episode "Werewolf" from Barney Miller – *an attempt to legitimize mental health concerns with a monster movie flavor.*

(1972–1983), where a wounded officer believes he is the son of God). Mental illness is something brought up often in *Barney Miller* as here is a show centered around a police division in the heart of the city that never sleeps, therefore many "fruit loops" would be running lose on the streets – some of whom would be dangerous and others not. Susan Harris's satirical *Soap* (1977–1981) would play with issues of mental illness as well as introduce aspects of the supernatural such as demonic possession, but the point of that was to highlight the extremes in which soap operas by their very nature would go. Where Harris's show parodied conventions, something like *Barney Miller* brought seldom discussed things such as lycanthropy to the fore in order to get both the laughs and the visibility.

Stefan's lycanthropy involves wild ranting, scratching, howling, barking, clawing at the prison bars and jumping around like a crazed animal, and when Barney (Hal Linden) finally snaps and yells at him: "It's a police station not a horror movie!", we understand the long standing connection made between fiction and lycanthropy. In horror movies and horror literature, lycanthropy can exist, however, in the realm of situation comedy or even non-genre specific drama, to be a werewolf is something completely out of the ordinary and bizarre, and not to be believed. However, what this episode does so nicely is present this lycanthrope with a tremendous amount of dignity in that he genuinely believes he is turning into a wolf. The B story of the episode has a nurse arriving to give the boys their annual shots (here it is to prevent pig flu) and the men react differently; some frightened and queasy at the idea of needles, others excited and aroused by the nurse herself, but what this subplot provides is an antidote to the werewolf issue in that it makes a formative commentary on the concept of fear and what aspects of life frighten or enrage someone. When Stefan explains to Barney that the full moon drives him crazy, Barney counters that with his description of accordions, that that particular instrument makes him mad.

In the same regard, when the "men in white coats" arrive to collect Stefan, one asks "What's his problem?" and is answered with "He's a werewolf" it is offered as a straight up matter of fact. Stefan pleads with Barney and laments "Doctor's don't know anything about this… you don't see much about lycanthropy anymore…" and what he is truly saying is that mental illnesses that now have been adopted by horror and the world of fiction have been rendered invisible in the eyes of progressive society. Vampires in "real life" would be people attracted to drinking blood and nothing more, and werewolves in a contemporary setting would be people with delusions of sprouting fur and physically morphing into beasts rather than men and women with a bloodlust for red raw meat and chaotic thoughts. What this episode allows is a permission to give this real life mental condition a name that is spoken out loud and summarized by Stefan's profound final words: "I'm cursed, not stupid!"

"A.K.A. the Fonz" from *Happy Days*
Original Air Date: 30 November 1976
by Aaron Graham

With fourth season episode "A.K.A. The Fonz", *Happy Days* (1974–1984) demonstrates that the series wasn't always an idealistic, rose-colored nostalgia trip through the Eisenhower era. This half-hour pushes past the superficial celebration of the then *in-vogue* decade ("Sha Na Na" and the oldies rock circuit) to confront the entrenched prejudices of the elder generation, in this case, aimed towards the breakout star of the show, Arthur Fonzarelli (Henry Winkler), and what he represents.

Spinning off of an unsold pilot entitled "Love and the Television Set" that aired on anthology series *Love, American Style* (1969–1974), *Happy Days* focused on the day-to-day foibles and misunderstandings of middle American (specifically, Milwaukee, WI) family unit the Cunninghams: teenaged Richie (Ron Howard), pre-teen Joanie (Erin Moran) and parents Howard and Marion (Tom Bosley and Marion Ross, respectively). (In seasons one and two, there was an older brother – Chuck (Gavan O'Herlihy) – who would mysteriously disappear following episode "Guess Who's Coming to Christmas", without the show deigning to reference why.) Richie's friends Ralph Malph (Don Most) and "Potsie" Weber (Anson Williams) populated the margins, mostly at local hang-out Arnold's/Al's, with most plots concerned with dating. Technically, the show would also morph early on – from a single-camera and artificial laugh-track to multi-camera and live audience recording.

But *Happy Days* really hit its stride in the second season (1974–1975), when series creator Garry Marshall allowed a wide berth for The Fonz – Winkler's leather-clad, duck-tailed bad boy with a heart of gold.

Merchandise soon followed: a 1976 "Fonzie Favorites" album put out by Juke Box International and a Ben Cooper Halloween costume, replete with a comic balloon "Aaaaay" and image of Winkler on its accompanying bib. This hot streak would continue unabated through the third and fourth seasons (when "A.K.A. The Fonz" aired), but grew a little outlandish by the seventh season. By then, the show spawned spin-off *Mork & Mindy* (1978–1982) and produced such episodes as "Chachi Sells His Soul" – a memorable jaunt that nonetheless strays away from what the series initially set out to do. By the last couple of seasons, more spin-offs occurred (*Joanie Loves Chachi* (1982–1983)), but the pretense of the show being set in the 1950s was well lacquered off.

"A.K.A. The Fonz" gets its juice from guest-star Ed Peck, as Sheriff Kirk, a taciturn officer of the law who was promoted when previously acting Sheriff Flanagan injured himself with a car jack. Sheriff Kirk is a tough cookie – an authoritative force to be reckoned with – who stops just short of violently ejecting Fonzie out of Wisconsin, based solely on the perceived notion and conjecture around town that, by appearances only, He's No Good. By episode's end, Sheriff Kirk's brought up the perceived Communist threat of the 1950s ("there was no red scare!"), while haranguing those strong enough to stand by The Fonz.

Fonzie gets to have a little fun with Sheriff Kirk, at one point brandishing what looks like a switchblade, but turns out to be a comb; Kirk is apoplectic. The moment is played semi-serious, a touch somber, as if this could be the end for Fonzie. Kirk later breaks up a Leopard's Lodge meeting, issuing citations left and right for those with backbone – Howard Cunningham's hardware store loading zone is cancelled, a dentist's permit revoked, and the entire assembly earmarked as unlawful for not brandishing a flag.

The mere image of a leather jacket sets off Sheriff Kirk (which allows for a *Spartacus*-like moment at the end, when the townspeople come to Fonzie's defense by dressing up like him – to uproarious canned laughter, even Howard).

Brian Levant contributes to the script of "A.K.A. The Fonz", a twenty-something scribe with only a couple of prior projects (most notably work on *The Jeffersons* (1975–1985)). It would take a younger writer to outline and deduce the hypocrisies of the era, the unfairness of judging a book by its cover. Jerry Paris – Jerry the Dentist on *The Dick Van Dyke Show* (1961–1966) and the man who cemented the *Police Academy* series with *Police Academy 2* (1985) and *Police Academy 3* (1986) – directs.

The network wouldn't allow a cash-cow like The Fonz to be run out of town, a.k.a. effectively written out of the series. (In fact, Winkler stayed with the series until its end, in 1984.) He's a beacon of cool in staid suburbia, a unique personality that ingratiates himself with the Cunninghams and the rest of small-town Milwaukee. He'll forever be an outsider but with a growing appreciation/fondness for the town, never judging, hoping to never be judged.

As he says in the coda of "A.K.A. The Fonz": "I love middle class families".

"The Draft Dodger" from *All in the Family*
Original Air Date: 25 December 1976
By Edward Eaton

It is unlikely that a character like Archie Bunker would survive on television in the 21st century. If he did appear in a series, he would immediately be viewed as a despicable heavy. If he actually lived in the 21st century, he would not last long in a world where everything is recorded and shared. In the 1970s, America was a different place. Archie Bunker was not seen as dangerous. He was seen as a crank. Most Americans (or, at least, most Americans who watched shows like *All in the Family* (1971–1979)) were firmly on board with civil rights and were embracing progress – even if they were not all outspoken liberal cranks like Archie's son-in-law, Mike. Most Americans, even the more liberal ones, not only knew people like Archie, they likely had relatives like him: cousins or uncles or even siblings who were not quite ready to see society change as rapidly and drastically as others wanted. Archie, like most of these people, understood that change had come; they simply did not like it and felt it was their right to grouse about the new society. Audiences could laugh at Archie for his outdated views but could not hate him, for he was a reflection of many people they knew and loved. Nor could audiences condemn him too harshly, for, let's face it, Archie Bunker is mostly harmless. He snarls and growls. However, his bark is impotent, and he has no bite. Even his targets don't take him too seriously: Mike goads him; black neighbors George and Lionel Jefferson give as good as they take; and some simply deflect his hostility with love and affection – Sammy Davis, Jr ("Sammy's Visit", season two, episode 21) and drag queen Beverly LaSalle ("Edith's Crisis of Faith", Season eight, episode 13) both react to Archie's grousing by famously kissing him. Audiences are sometimes even left to wonder how seriously Archie takes himself. However much Archie may growl, the audience, at least, knows that he is wrong. That is where "The Draft Dodger", season seven's Christmas episode, really stands out: not only is Archie not wrong, he might actually be right.

The story, which takes place on Christmas Eve, introduces us first to David Brewster, a childhood friend of Mike's from Chicago who is a fugitive from justice living in Canada (there are enough hints, in addition to the title of the episode, that he moved to Canada to avoid the draft, but only David, Mike, and Gloria know this). David is invited to stay for Christmas Eve dinner, but admonished by Mike to avoid certain subjects. Shortly thereafter, Archie's friend, Pinky Peterson arrives. Before opening the door for him, Archie asks everyone to find ways to keep the evening upbeat, especially in light of Pinky being down on holidays after the death of his son in Vietnam. During the dinner, when Archie asks his guest why he moved to Canada, David explains that he had moved there for freedom and outs himself as a draft dodger. Archie argues with David and Mike and asks Pinky to step in on his side. Pinky surprises everyone by saying that he understands David's decision to leave and that he would like to have the holiday meal with him. As the rest of the group sits down to enjoy the meal, Archie heads outside to yell at some passing carolers.

Mike and, to a lesser degree, Gloria are somewhat to blame for the outburst during the dinner. They are aware that David is a draft dodger and that Archie will object to this. Yet, they insist that David stay, not even, seemingly, caring whether or not he has plans. After all, David is from Chicago and is living in Canada. It seems odd that he would come to New York to visit just one high school friend – indeed, David does not know Mike's new address or anything about his family other than his wife's name. Presumably, David is staying with some other friend rather than in a hotel; he is, after all, a fugitive from justice, even if not a very important one. Mike does, to be fair, give David a list of topics to avoid. The list is so long, though (politics, religion, sex, books, movies, war, peace, guns, grapes, lettuce…) that one wonders if Mike wants David to provoke Archie. They have already warned David:

Gloria: David, have you met my father?
David: Not yet.
Mike: You're in for a big treat… conservatively speaking, if you know what I mean.

Gloria and Mike also give Archie vague and conflicting answers when he asks reasonable questions. When Edith lets the cat out of the bag that David lives in Canada, the audience gasps, but Archie is not suspicious. Canada might have been where draft dodgers went, but it was (and is) a major country that borders the U.S.. There could be all sorts of reasons David lives there; Archie suggests "logs or whale meat". It may be silly that he can only come up with those two possible professions for someone in Canada, but his response suggests that there is no reason for him to conclude "draft dodger". Mike knows that there are lines he cannot cross, but he might enjoy seeing someone else cross them. He even sets up an immediate conflict between Archie and David by putting David in Archie's chair, something he and Gloria (and the audience) know will antagonize his father-in-law. After all, the worst that will happen is that Archie will blow his stack. As Mike says, "He's not going to call the FBI or anything."

Mike and Gloria are not aware that Pinky is coming to dinner or that Pinky lost a son in the war. At least, after that, their attempts at avoiding the subject come across as sincere. However, they are so intent on avoiding topics that would not only be polite but even *de rigueur* that Archie of all people notices. He, himself, is so artlessly concerned about avoiding the topic of Pinky's son or the war that he does not realize that there is another forbidden topic and blunders into it.

David must take some responsibility for the ensuing conflict. When Archie realizes that David has moved to Canada from Chicago, he blurts out the question, "what the hell you got in Canada you ain't got here?" It is not, of course, a question Archie expects to be answered. Indeed, he does not wait for it to be answered, but changes the subject and starts talking about the food.

David, who knows Pinky lost a son in the war, decides to give a provocative answer: "freedom". Archie tries to laugh off the answer. He only pushes when it finally becomes obvious even to Archie that everyone keeps trying to change the subject. David does finally drop the other shoe and admit that he is a "draft dodger". Understandably, Archie is annoyed, but he is able to keep his cool for some moments. Indeed, his initial reaction is that David's presence is a danger to him and the others. They are now breaking the law, specifically, 18 U.S.C. § 1071, Concealing a Person from Arrest – AKA, harboring a fugitive. Both David and Archie realize that it is time for David to leave. It is Mike who demands that the revelation result in a political discussion on the war. "When the hell are you going to admit that the war was wrong!" he demands of Archie, to which Archie yells back, "I ain't talkin' about that war! I don't wanna talk about that rotten damn war no more! I'm talking about something else!"

The "something else" is "duty". Whereas a conservative member of the Greatest Generation like Archie might see "duty" as something given without question, an anti-establishment baby-boomer like Mike might reject any such obligation out of hand. Of course, these sorts of debates would be par for the course for *All in the Family*. The audience would know that little would be resolved. The women, batty Edith and headstrong Gloria, might try to maintain peace, but, for the most part, they side with their men. Mike, arrogantly self-righteous and Archie, cantankerously full of himself, make a lot of noise but have little bite. Mike is right when he says Archie will not call the FBI. He is wrong that he can goad Archie into a debate on the war. Archie stays on topic. He also makes a good point: people have a duty to the country. The war is not the issue, and for many people it never was. Going to war is not a personal choice – it is a policy decision. Moving to Canada to avoid the draft was a personal decision. Many people who watched the show either had made the decision to leave or had stayed and gone to their draft boards when called up (or, like Mike, had stayed in college until the draft was no longer an issue). Many had fought in the war. Others, like Archie, had fought in World War II (only thirty years before). Mike and Gloria, and later Archie, certainly expect Pinky to feel angry, even betrayed, by David's decision. The writers of the episode are taking a risk by giving Archie a stance that many of their viewers would have agreed with, even though they do try to make him sound as ridiculous as they can: "You couldn't get a decent war off the ground that way! All the young people would say no – sure they would! Cause they don't wanna get killed! And that's why we leave it to the Congress, 'cause them old quacks ain't gonna get killed!"

There is an important moment late in the episode, when Archie asks Pinky to weigh in on the discussion. Pinky agrees to speak.

> Pinky: I understand how you feel, Arch. My kid hated the war, too. But he did what he thought he had to do. And David here did what he thought he had to do. But David's alive to share Christmas dinner with us. And if Steve were here he would want to sit down with him. And that's what I want to do.
> [offering his hand to David]

Pinky: Merry Christmas, David.

David: Merry Christmas, sir.

The camera moves to a close-up, cutting to a two-shot of Pinky and David. This is not a moment for Archie and Mike. Mike has lost his right to speak on the issue by trying to hijack the conversation and force a debate on the war; Archie has yielded the floor to Pinky. Archie and Mike, who have no real dogs in this fight, might never agree on issues such as this, but the opposing sides, represented by Pinky and David, who do, can put aside their differences.

Perhaps this episode is more relevant for today's audience than many other episodes. A lot of effort has been made over the last twenty years to avoid the excesses of the anti-war movement in the U.S. in the sixties and seventies. This is especially so in the treatment of the men and women who serve. During the Vietnam War, many soldiers on returning home were humiliated and even attacked simply for serving. Moreover, even though there was no draft to avoid in the 2000s, there were a number of cases where men and women already serving in the military objected to being sent to Iraq or Afghanistan, arguing, somewhat counterintuitively, that they had not joined up expecting to have to fight. Perhaps just as important is that the episode suggests that it is possible to be civil, maybe even friendly, even when on opposite sides of polarizing issues.

Ultimately, Archie comes around somewhat. Perhaps out of a sense of duty or familial loyalty, he allows everyone to stay and eat Christmas dinner. David may have avoided the draft out of some sense of loyalty and duty to his cause. Steven went to war because that was his duty. Pinky embraces David because that is his sense of duty and of loyalty to his son. Archie is just as loyal and dutiful. As paterfamilias, he puts aside his feelings so that the others can enjoy the holiday and so that his wife can have the satisfaction of cooking and hostessing the meal. Archie says that he will process this later. Maybe he does. Maybe he does not. Perhaps he never comes around. The issue can never be fully resolved on the television show as it has yet to be resolved in the real world.

"Ed Talks to God" from *Chico and the Man*
Original Air Date: 4 March 1977
By Amanda Reyes

Ed Talks to God piece appeared on Amanda Reye's blog, Made for TV Mayhem, and it was originally published on June 24, 2011. Here's the link:
http://madefortvmayhem.blogspot.com/2011/06/chico-and-man-1974-1977.html

Chico (Freddie Prinze) was the fun loving Hispanic who charmed his way into the life of Ed Brown (Jack Albertson), an old bigoted curmudgeon who didn't like the uprise of the ethnic population in his neighborhood. A drunk and a loner, Ed crankily put up with Chico, a kid he hated to admit he liked. Well, it's not hard to like Chico, the sweet natured entrepreneur was determined to get old Ed some business into the run-down garage. The show focused on Chico and his ying/yang partnership with Ed, but there were lots of other characters filtering in and out of Ed and Chico's life, including Louie (Scatman Crothers) and Della (Della Reese), plus all the quirky folks who made a pit stop in Ed's garage. And, of course, hilarity ensued.

I always thought *Chico and the Man* (1974–1978) was created to showcase Freddie's phenomenal stand-up act, but Prinze was actually up against four other actors for the part, including Isaac Ruiz who played Mando in several episodes. The final decision came to a meeting with Jack Albertson who was then starring in a stage production of "The Sunshine Boys". The show's creator, James Komack was interested in who Albertson had the most chemistry with. And a legend was born.

There was some controversy from the Mexican-American community surrounding the casting of Prinze who was Puerto Rican. Prinze's mother said in a book she wrote about her son, called *The Freddie Prinze Story*, that he would receive threats from angry TV viewers. Prinze responded in a 1975 interview with *The Palm Beach Post* with, "The feelings are the same. Spick means the same thing in New York as it does in Los Angeles. The pain is the same." He conceded in the same interview, "I don't think it's the majority making the fuss. It's a few radicals." Eventually, the network bent and wrote in that Chico's father was Puerto Rican. Regardless of the controversy, *Chico and the Man* was an instant hit, and Prinze was what they refer to in Hollywood as an overnight success.

Many sitcoms of the seventies and eighties were far less sophisticated than what we see now. While people complain about the current state of the half-hour comedy, those unaccustomed to the stage-like productions of yesteryear are sure to detest the format. It's a shame too, because the simple sets and stories were a true showcase for the actors. Everything relied on presence and delivery and the comedy was derived from the actors' ability to grab your interest. Freddie Prinze was a natural and he hit it right out of the ballpark in the pilot, which aired on 13 September 1974 on NBC. Ed is introduced as a real cranky old bastard and it's fun to watch Prinze warm the old coot's heart. This of course would become the crux of the series, but it's apparent here why the Man isn't as keen on letting Chico go as he would like everyone to believe he is.

The series ran fairly smoothly for three seasons while Prinze was experimenting with drugs and going deeper down the rabbit hole of depression. According to his mother, Prinze was lonely and not meant for the bright lights of Hollywood, but he would reveal to a psychologist shortly before his death about his own childhood sadness and how he began experimenting with drugs at a younger age than his mom talks about. He also confesses to an earlier suicide attempt. Even now, with all I've learned about Prinze's darker side, I find it hard to believe that what I saw on screen was so different from the man himself. By all accounts, Prinze was a good guy and well loved, but he obviously didn't know how to take that love in, and all of that sadness was completely hidden on the series. Prinze actually taped his last episode just hours before his death. The episode was called "Ed Talks to God" and it aired on 4 March 1977, about five weeks after Prinze's death. This episode is especially poignant because it revolves around Ed's birthday and many comments are made about how Ed should appreciate getting to the age he has. Prinze looks especially thin and his delivery does seem to be a bit off, but of course this is all in hindsight. Knowing he was so close to the end, makes it especially difficult to watch.

For three magical seasons, Prinze brought the gift of laughter to just about everyone who ever watched an episode of *Chico and the Man*, and he shocked the country with his death. At Prinze's funeral, Jack Albertson gave the eulogy, which he ended with: "We are bound together, this family, not in a temporary chill of death, but in the everlasting warmth of his humanity and his humor. Let us not mourn his death, rather, let us celebrate his life. In the years to come, in the days and the years, this moment will have passed and we'll see Freddie again, we will hear him, we will think of our brother and we will smile again and we will laugh again, and we will be warm again."

The series tried to continue without Prinze, and 12-year-old Gabriel Melgar was brought in as a replacement. While I remember liking Melgar, who played Raul, the show was destined to bomb without Prinze. However, there were many poignant moments on the show, like when Ed busts up Chico's guitar in a fit of anger over his death. The following clips aptly capture the anger and sadness that not only Ed felt regarding the heavy loss of Chico, but also the frustration the fans endured as well. The fact that these scenes still resonate deeply proves the depth of the sense of loss we all shared when Freddie Prinze died.

"The Evans Get Involved" from *Good Times*
Original Air Dates: 21 September 1977 (Parts 1 and 2),
28 September 1977 (Part 3) and 5 October 1977 (Part 4)
By Lee Gambin

By this period of the series' run, *Good Times* (1974–1979) would have a follow up major change after the killing off of John Amos's patriarchal head in James Evans; this would be the decision leading player Esther Rolle as Florida Evans had in regards to staying on the show. The gifted actress and activist felt that the sitcom was pandering to the likes of the J.J. role, as played by spindly clown Jimmie Walker, and that his buffoonery was not at all something that appealed to Rolle. Rolle had gone on the record saying you can still have funny situations and a successful comical show without resorting to catchphrases ("Dynooooomite!") or self-mockery, of which Rolle felt Walker fell into, likening him to white fueled minstrelsy. Therefore, the character of Florida – the no-nonsense matriarch of the Evans family – would be written out for a big chunk of the show's run, and in the opening of this astoundingly unique four part VSE it is established that she will not be appearing and it also discusses the whereabouts of Florida (she has remarried and the man in question was ill and their honeymoon is also acting as a healing vacation).

With this as an aside, we get into "The Evans Get Involved" without the head of the household to take charge, instead, the sassy, sexy single neighbor Willona Woods (Ja'net DuBois) stands in as the protagonist, even reigning as top billing star in the show's opening credits. *Good Times* would have the fun loving and tough talking Willona as its lead during the time Esther Rolle/Florida Evans was on hiatus, and these episodes would be solid even with the absence of such a legendary star as Rolle. DuBois's Willona is a firecracker of a woman, dedicated to being single and stable and completely self-reliant, self-assured and self-possessed. Ultimately, Willona is another one of those wonderful decidedly single smart women of TV sitcoms that would come in the guise of legendary iconic female characters such as Mary Richards (Mary Tyler Moore) and others, and this four part saga will end with Willona possibly putting her sexually charged and free single life on hold in order to help out an abused little girl named Penny (Janet Jackson).

The scene stealing J.J. comes home and explains what happened on a local bus where he had to stand up for a little girl who was in a predicament. This girl is Penny, a precocious and white lie telling spunky urban urchin who takes a liking to J.J. simply because he showed her compassion and understanding. Penny's affection for J.J. will develop throughout these four episodes, however her dedicated love will eventually be geared towards the more substantially giving Willona, who will end up becoming a substitute mother for the dejected and put upon Penny.

Penny's endless stories are all fabricated, and this child of physical and emotional abuse seems to be making her life up which in turn allows her to hide dark secrets that are confronting and horrific. She is introduced with a Band-Aid sprawled across her forehead but counters that with a penchant for a solid Mae West impression. The introduction of Penny's single mother Linella (Chip Fields) comes with a horrific threat which has since become a cause for both kinder trauma as well as parody since. She uses a hot iron to discipline her daughter, burning her. Janet Jackson's performance here in this brief moment fearing her mother is a mesmerizing effort and something that calls for accolades as it is a confronting and sinister image, and Jackson plays it with sincerity and genuine terror. Here is a girl completely abused by a frustrated and easily agitated parent and this is something that is brought up of course throughout the four episodes in this Penny arc that has been the case before in the run of *Good Times*. A previous double episode entitled "Florida's Favorite Passenger" has a boy with a hearing issue helped out by Florida and the gang, somewhat rescued from an unsympathetic parent who eventually comes around, however, here the follow up which re-introduces Linella in "A Matter of Mothers" where she has come into money and tries to sabotage Willona in order to reclaim Penny as her child. It doesn't work out for her and her violent nature is re-exposed, reinforcing the loving warmth of Willona and the Evans family who truly have Penny looked after and whole.

With Penny being invited to the school carnival, it is established that she is being welcomed into the lives of the Evans family, and when she nurses a doll and mourns a lost childhood ("I would have loved to have been rocked to sleep") the loving Evans household get a slight understanding of Penny's alienation. Penny's love for J.J. is more about having a surrogate who showed her affection and when he moves on from helping her to tend to his date, Penny reacts violently at the same doll she nurses by slapping it and screaming out "You rotten lousy kid!" The studio audience laughs here, clearly either missing the point and the connection made between children being abused will then re-enact such behavior or just completely struck with disbelief at what they are seeing, coming "out of nowhere". But the same audience will soon feel Penny's pain when Willona and the others find that she has a burnt arm and that her back covered in bruises. Her white lies are now thrown to the sidelines and even J.J.'s priorities change from his date (a latest conquest) to caring about Penny.

From lines that sound off the black expressionism of the series whilst commenting on the issue of child abuse at the same time ("Black is beautiful but not when it's black and blue") and tackling class concerns too ("Rich parents abuse their kids too!"), the issue of ghetto life and the complexities here from the Evans as a struggling black family in the projects and Linella who is not noble like Florida, her children or neighbor Willona, makes for an interesting and captivating exploration into the human condition and what drives people to do what they do and how to right wrongs.

But of course, the spirit of Penny is bright and readily available – eager to shine and thrive – something that is remarkably empowering, that this beautiful black girl can survive and overcome the abuse and blossom into someone incredible. Her magnetic energy (brought to life by Janet Jackson's lovely performance) is embodied in the moment where she and Michael (Ralph Carter) do a Sonny and Cher impression singing "I Got You Babe". It is interesting to note that the seventies was of course the golden age of the variety television show with *The Sonny and Cher Comedy Hour* (1971-1974) being one of them. These shows including *The Carol Burnett Show* (1967-1978) and *The Muppet Show* (1976-1981) would not come without sentimental or more "serious" moments whether they be pleas for universal love or respect for the planet or a commentary on human loneliness or a musical interlude that offers an insight into the hardships of individuals. These shows could vary from Sonny and Cher singing about race relations in "Black and White" by Three Dog Night or on a Christmas special where disparate individuals congregate at a restaurant and come together to assuage their isolation, or it could come in the form of a group of woodland animals singing "What's That Sound?" as they are terrorized by human hunters or Bernadette Peters teaching Robin the Frog the importance of believing in himself with "Just One Person" on *The Muppet Show,* the musical variety show would employ efforts seen in the Very Special Episode, by breaking up the zany antics and comedy sketches with somber sobering moments of truly moving interludes.

In "The Evans Get Involved" the most moving moments come at us when there is an opportunity for – well, good times. The cast appear in lavish costumes for the school carnival but the fun turns dark when Penny is discovered waiting outside with a broken arm. She is denied such happiness and frivolity, and when she is taken into the hospital, the nurse's reaction from comical (the costumes) to posing an obstruction lends itself to being more of a barrier for Penny to break free from the oppressive abuse. There is an inspired moment where a fellow-ghetto resident in the form of a boisterous Latina woman comes in to protect Penny and stand up for her, demanding the doctor see her before her and other patients. The solidarity amongst those who are in need is made clear beyond the race barrier (and white characters will come into play also offering a helping hand).

Willona – the perpetually single lady on the make for handsome single men, introduces herself to the doctor in classic Willona fashion, however she is concerned when Penny insists on telling lies in order to excuse her mother's abusive hand. The doctor's response infuriates Willona further: "Falling down is part of growing up." When Willona stands up to him she grabs hold of his position as a health professional who has made himself a success and brings him back to the ghetto in one swift statement: "Do something about it Negro!" What this line does is pack a punch in the gut, insisting that he never forgets the state of oppressive struggle that she and this little girl are currently stuck in (and possibly stuck in forever). *Good Times* would have its fair share of racially inclined classism with wealthy black characters posing threats or obstacles for the Evans family and other impoverished blacks.

Turning a blind eye is the doctor's true "crime" here and Willona's final words about the doctor not having a heart cuts deep which will lead into Penny having to learn to tell the truth about her mother. The dramatic centerpiece of the arc here would come in the heated argument between Willona and Linella even prompting the emotionally invested studio audience to call out "You tell her Willona!" There is a conversation about Linella getting professional help, the personal struggles of Linella, Willona's forced independence ("I've been on my own for a long time") and while J.J.'s antics break the mood with humor, this is a world of women and women's issues escalating to Linella attempting to hit Penny. When she races off, running away from her daughter she mutters "She deserves something better than me" – and yes, she does.

Child abuse is a confronting topic as it is, but when presented in the situation comedy format it is even more so. "The Evans Get Involved" from Good Times *drives the message home in a direct and powerful fashion with young Janet Jackson as Penny being the victim of domestic abuse.*

"Once a Friend" from *The Jeffersons*
Original Air Date: 1 October 1977
By Sergio Mims

CBS' *The Jeffersons* (1975–1985), during its 11-season 253-episode run, gained such massive popularity that it has gone on to achieve a nearly iconic status among network sitcoms. Therefore it should not be surprising that most people don't know or have forgotten that it was originally conceived as a backdoor spin-off from another popular series.

The genesis of the show began with the mega-producer Norman Lear made the wise decision to give the occasional recurring character of George Jefferson, the more successful and black neighbor to the grumpy racist Archie Bunker in *All of the Family* (1971–1979), and give him his own show.

On *The Jeffersons*, George (memorably played by Sherman Hemsley) was seemingly the perfect candidate for his own sitcom. Obnoxious, supremely self-centered, rude, loud, and boisterous George literally strutted his way through every situation. He did not so much as enter a room, he bust through a door like a VW with his doors open announcing his presence to everyone in sight. He was a black man, who despite various obstacles and setbacks thrown in his life's path, had conquered all. His hard work and determination had given him wealth, prestige and his own slice of the American Dream complete with that "deeeeluxe apartment in the skyyyyyyy" as the show's theme song reminded us every week.

Of course most of the episodes centered around George's comeuppance, in order to be brought down a tad and taught a lesson. His close mindedness had to be opened, the balloon of his pomposity had to be popped. To that end, that was left mostly to Louise "Ouise" (Isabel Sanford), George's long suffering wife as her patience was sorely tested to breaking point every week. However, there was never any question of the deep love and affection that they had for each other – though they had to work hard to get it.

Their relationship was based on trust and understanding. And that kind of understanding came after decades of putting up with George and his own worst tendencies and behavior. But the reality was that despite all the boasting and bravado, George deep down was insecure on his throne, something that his massive ego who never let be revealed publicly.

However when it came to putting George in his place that was left to the Jefferson's maid Florence (Marla Gibbs), for George she was the ultimate status symbol that he had finally "made it" instead of the other reality of Louise and him working as a maid and a butler instead. But Florence was no Louise Beavers or Hattie McDaniel. She was not some subservient happy maid, but instead had no patience for pretentiousness and felt she had the right and freedom to say what was on her mind. No matter how much

George boasted and preened and tried to puff up his importance, it had no effect on her. She saw through his phoniness and insecurity and took every advantage to expose it to his everlasting regret. Yet, rather than firing her, he somehow knew that he needed her to keep him rooted in reality.

But when it comes to the episode "Once a Friend", George's comfortable world which he created for himself is turned upside down. There is little that Louise or Florence (who is relegated to a minor role in this episode) can do to help him. George himself has to go through shock and confusion as he struggles to understand sex roles and what defines a man and a woman and nothing seems safe or secure anymore.

In the episode, George arrives early from his business to find out that he has received a phone message earlier from someone named Edie Stokes and that she was in town and wanted to get together. This has previously aroused the suspicion of Louise who suspects that George could be "fooling around" with some other woman. He immediately realizes that Florence, who took the message, had misheard the person and that it was Eddie Stokes his old Navy buddy who he hasn't seen in nearly 20 years though that does not put Louise's mind at ease.

However when George arrives at the hotel room where his friend is staying he is confronted by a statuesque, striking woman (Veronica Redd) who George thinks is Eddie's wife or boyfriend and Eddie is hiding somewhere. However he finds no evidence of Eddie in the room and nothing but woman's clothes and underwear and thinks Eddie, who had the reputation for being a wild practical joker, has disguised himself as a woman to fool George. The surprise comes that the woman reveals that she is Eddie (and now calls herself Edie) and that she had a sex change operation a few years ago to become a woman. When he finally hears the truth George all but flies out of the room rushing Edie's spirit and hopes. Though, as anyone knows, George is not the most accepting and broad minded of people.

By the second half of the episode things become even more complicated when George tells the truth to Louise that his old Navy buddy is now transgender (a term that did not exist back then) and which, of course, she refuses to believe. Just another George's lame excuses to get him out of trouble. George tries to contact Edie to have her come to his place to explain everything, but she already checked out of her hotel room. He becomes so desperate to prove his innocence that he goes to the extreme trick to forcing a very reluctant employee of his, Leroy (Vernon Washington) to dress up as a woman and pass himself off as Edie.

Not surprisingly that plan goes disastrously wrong and it sends Louise into such anger that she announces that she is packing up and leaving George for good. But who shows up at the front door when all is lost is Edie like deus ex machina to the rescue. However it still looks hopeless when Louise refuses to believe that Edie was once Eddie. However the situation is resolved when Edie tells Louise their secret love pet names that both she and George had for each other when they were dating when he was in the Navy something that only his best friend Eddie would have known and all becomes right again in the world.

Of course being a 22 minutes sitcom episode, without commercials, it is impossible for a show to give a nuanced and searching discussion about a sexual identity. And also being the 1970's as well with American TV network Standard and Practices Department (i.e. the network censors) breathing down their necks on what can be said

The cast of The Jeffersons. *A wealthy black family living in a penthouse apartment in New York was not only groundbreaking and unique, but vitally important. One of the longest running sitcoms and also a show that dived into serious subject matter with ferocity and style.*

or heard on television, there was only so much that a show could do on that subject matter. Being transgender (or the term transexual as it was during that period) was it seen as a novelty, a freak. It was something that at that time was not truly understood or comprehended by the masses. It's treated in "Once a Friend" as a goof, a subject ripe for comedy fodder. It's an outrageous joke for George to be trapped in.

And yet the episode itself is fairly progressive in its treatment of the matter of sexual identity. The character of Edie is not a conflicted, suicidal, tortured soul as she would have been on portrayed on another show. Just the opposite, she is very content, happy and very accepting of herself. She clearly expects George to accept her the way she accepts herself. It's only until George reacts more out of his fear of the unknown than her, yet her optimism remains when she shows up unexpectedly at George's door willing to give him another chance.

But sexual identity is the subtle underlying theme in the episode. Early on when Louise tells Florence that she got Edie's name wrong saying that she mistook her voice for a man's though it is easy to distinguish a man's voice from a woman's. However that lesson is upended when Louise with her dark dusky voice is mistaken for a man's when she answers the phone.

Even more is the entire extended sequence when Leroy is forced to wear a wig and a dress in a pathetic attempt to pass himself off as Edie. Totally embarrassed and clumsy Leroy fumbles badly at first. He struggles to maintain a high falsetto voice which he continuously drops down to his real deep voice. Yet as the scene goes on he begins to slowly like playing the role of a woman and the notion of fluid sexuality begins to take ahold of him as he plays Edie.

In the end, all is forgiven and George, Louise and Edie all fall into a warm embrace after Edie pulls a real practical joke on George. All problems are resolved and all conflicts are quickly vanquished. But reality is much tougher to conquer and though *The Jeffersons* can give us a safe place where everything is reassured and content, the hard reality is that the world and society are much harder.

"Cousin Liz" from *All in the Family*
Original Air Date: 9 October 1977
By Lee Gambin

Anita Bryant was a name that sent chills down the spines of gay citizens who were just trying to live their lives and do their jobs. Bryant's anti-gay rights agenda and her joint forces with politician and conservative legislator John Briggs would introduce proposed legislation to restrict openly gay teachers from working in the public school system. Gay rights activist and San Francisco based politician Harvey Milk would fervently oppose this hate fueled proposition, and thankfully the outcome was sided with the rights of gay teachers to continue working as dedicated educators enlightening and guiding America's youth.

Outside of activists and legendary voices for the gay movement such as Harvey Milk promoting support for the rights of gay teachers was of vital importance in an episode of *All in the Family* (1971–1979) entitled "Cousin Liz", which hit a nerve with the public gay and straight alike, and influenced votes during Anita Bryant's homophobic coalition that she called "Save Our Children". What "Cousin Liz" did – outside of winning an Emmy for its sensitive and beautifully nuanced writing, as well as being one of showrunner Norman Lear's most favorite episodes – was provide a face and voice to a gay teacher who is hurting, grieving the loss of her long-time lover (the titular Liz). What is so profoundly moving about "Cousin Liz" is not only the fact that a gay character is permitted a sympathetic portrayal that is tender and heartfelt, but also the way in which our beloved Edith Bunker (Jean Stapleton) absolutely unflinchingly understands that "love is love" and that she is able to stand up to her bigoted husband Archie (Carroll O'Connor) enforcing such truth, which in turn makes the episode remarkably political. So political that when it aired on a rerun during the height of the ballot takings for the "Save Our Children" coalition, it influenced straight America into becoming allies for the gay rights movement, standing up against hate spewed out by the likes of Anita Bryant and John Briggs.

The episode would open with Archie and Edith arriving at a hotel room, so already the episode is out of the norm as it positions itself outside of the Bunker household (a rarity really). They are at this grubby hotel because they are out of town for a funeral for Edith's cousin Liz – a dead gay character whose queer ghost hovers over the episode as a tragic reminder that homosexuals die quiet deaths if their voices are not heard and their visibility is stunted or forced to reside in the shadows. Liz seems to have left a lasting impression on Archie, which once again, is a rare thing. Archie, who usually shows absolute disdain for all of Edith's relations, liked Liz and even kissed her at one stage in their younger years. This brings up the concern that Edith has about her late cousin ("It's too bad she never got married") which even allows for Archie to show a sensitive side with "She could have gotten herself a nice fella." When we learn more about Archie's kissing Liz years ago because he explains that "she didn't want to do 'anything else'" and this would possibly be the first hint of Liz being a lesbian in a very subtle manner (although, it is Archie we're talking about).

The episode then brings up an actual visible long standing regular character who had recently died in the show, Archie's pal Stretch Cunningham (James Cromwell) and his memory sparks a reminder from the episode covering his death entitled "Stretch Cunningham, Goodbye" where Stretch's Judaism becomes common knowledge, much to the shock of the anti-Semitic Archie. Having his faith and race "outed" renders Stretch as a "minority", something that doesn't sit well with Archie, until he comes to accept it and understand it, which is carried over later when he and Edith take in Stephanie Mills (Danielle Brisebois), the nine-year-old niece of Edith who is left in their care when her alcoholic father abandons her. In the episode "Stephanie's Conversion", Archie realizes that the little girl is Jewish and his love for her overshines his prejudice emphasizing Archie's growth as a human being. The parallel between Judaism and lesbianism is something that might be considered when you think about the Stretch Cunningham conversation early in "Cousin Liz" to what is to come.

Of course, Archie's interest in Liz's money and possessions is what sparks any emotion in the oaf, and seeing that Liz wasn't married and without children ignites the idea that the assets go to him. Archie's motives are clear, but the show is more concerned with a mournful figure who seems to remain invisible during Liz's wake, but is also at the center of it. This figure is Veronica (K Callan) who is first mentioned as Liz's "roommate" (a long standing coded (and closeted) word for same sex partner).

When we first meet Veronica we see a character who is feminine, serene, obviously in mourning but with an elegance and beauty shining through, therefore when she comes out to Edith, straight audiences can put aside an image of a cigar chomping dyke who looks as though she should be governing a prison ward. However, we do have a woman who is frail and depressed, which would be another long standing character trope in the realm of lesbian representation in cinema, as seen in a seminal classic such as *The Children's Hour* (1961) which would have Shirley MacLaine playing Martha Dobie, a repressed teacher in love with her heterosexual counterpart in Audrey Hepburn, who eventually kills herself after coming out. What happens here in "Cousin Liz" is not too dissimilar, except Veronica and Liz were committed lovers and one has passed away, not of suicide but of natural causes, and one remains alone. The lone lesbian figure is central to the story here, but a noble and very human one at that.

The episode taps into issues concerning where finances lie in gay relationships when one partner dies, and the silver tea set (a possible reference to the gay themed melodrama *Tea and Sympathy* (1956)) that has been in Edith's family for "a thousand years", is the point of conversation that involves Archie's greed, Edith's connection to her family and most importantly a symbol of the eternal love shared between Veronica and her dearly departed Liz. When Veronica overhears Archie's keen interest in taking the tea set seeing that it is going to be inherited to Edith, she asks to speak with Edith in order to protect what truly is hers. What follows is one of the most important moments on American television, Veronica coming out to Edith and even more importantly the transition from Edith's response. What is also very telling about the episode is the studio audience's response when they hear Veronica say "We shared everything". There is a gasp and an uncomfortable chuckle from these "regular Joes" who have come to see this live taping, and when Veronica explains to Edith that "We loved each other", the audience can be heard listening – a remarkable and chilling (in a good way) response. They are drawn in and you can feel it.

There is a long history of gay characters having to come out to straight characters on film and television and for the most part in sitcoms it is a point of comedy. This is the case here up to a certain point. Edith's initial response is a classic Edith "Ohhhhh" which would eventually become a core inspiration in the character of Marge Simpson years later – these loving and warm funny odd ducks who made strange noises when they were trying to understand something – but of course, Edith being Edith and so totally filled with love shows her admiration and dedication to Veronica and her absolute acceptance both relieves Veronica and empowers her. Edith sees Veronica as "family" and her love and relationship with Liz as one as hers with Archie – she considers the two women's union as vitally important as the marriage she has with Archie. When the episode brings Archie into the picture and Edith has to literally come out about Veronica and Liz's romantic life together, here we have one of the first moments in the series where Edith stands up to her ogre of a husband and even calls him out on his conservative handballing to God. Edith tells him that he isn't God and therefore not in a position to judge. She stands up for the right to Veronica keeping the tea set and in doing that stands up for the rights of Veronica and women like her. Hence, Edith Bunker becomes the voice of an America who stood up against the homophobic hatred fired out from the likes of Anita Bryant and John Briggs, taking a stand for gay teachers across the county to work and empower their students for decades to come. That is the power of the American sitcom, that is the power of *All in the Family* and that is the power of our beloved Edith Bunker.

Gay liberation protestors rally against Anita Bryant and her homophobic quest to ban gay teachers from teaching; a theme that would become the focus of "Cousin Liz" from All in the Family.

"Edith's 50th Birthday" from *All in the Family*
Original Air Date: 16 October 1977
By Edward Eaton

During the sixties and seventies, most sitcoms used a laugh track. When a series was exploring a particularly sensitive topic, the producers could control the types and levels of laughter. If they really wanted to, they could simply turn the laugh track off for some scenes or entire episodes. *M*A*S*H* (1972–1983), for example, quite famously did not use a laugh track when scenes took place in the operating room. There were sitcoms, though, that filmed their episodes in front of a live audience. Producers could, and did, ask audiences to react at certain times and in certain ways, but live audiences have a way of doing whatever they want whenever they want. Producers cannot control them. Perhaps this aspect, the presence of a live audience, is actually what makes "Edith's 50th Birthday" a watchable episode.

That is not to say that the episode is bad – it is simply hard to watch. No. "Hard" is not the word. "Unbearable" comes a bit closer to it. What happens is that someone tries to rape Edith. For just under eleven minutes (minus about two minutes for a scene in another location with other people), Edith is molested by her would-be rapist. The television audience is subjected to this scene: Edith Bunker – batty naive altruistic long-suffering Edith Bunker – being groped, threatened, and almost raped. For what it is worth, the rest of the two-parter (originally broadcast together), several minutes longer than the attempted-rape scene, is a brutally honest depiction of Edith refusing to come to terms with the assault. What the audience leaves the show with, though, is Edith being assaulted.

There is a story that the episode was originally intended for *One Day at a Time* (1975–1984), and the intended victim would have been Ann Romano. The producers (of both series) changed the character and the series to show that rape could happen to anyone. Edith is trusting, naive, innocent, and decidedly unsexy and non-sexual – as opposed to Ann Romano who is a very sexual character and frequently referred to as attractive. Of course, the relative attractiveness of the victim should have no effect on an audience's reaction, but this was 1977 and attitudes were somewhat different. Ann Romano is an attractive divorcee. Edith Bunker is a frumpy housewife. Gloria, Edith and Archie's daughter, had already been the victim of a sexual assault in the season three episode "Gloria the Victim." She is clearly told then, by the detective, what sort of defense the lawyers would put up: her past and her reputation would be fair game. Blaming the victim of a rape is an issue brought up in 1962's film *Cape Fear* as well as in the 1991 remake. For good or ill, a woman's reputation had an impact on how juries and audiences interpreted the events. Edith even comments on this when she refuses to go to the police to identify her attacker.

The choice of David Dukes to play Lambert, the rapist, and the way the attempted rape is pursued add to the impact of the event. Ironically, had they chosen *One Day at a Time* as the vehicle for this episode, they could not have cast David Dukes. He had played a conductor in the 1976 episode "The Maestro" with whom Ann has a one night stand. Dukes is an interesting, and somewhat bold, choice for Lambert. It was likely not an accident that Dukes somewhat resembled Ted Bundy, who was already famous and who often used his good looks and natural charm to get close to and to isolate his victims. Like Bundy, Lambert also pretends to be a police officer. To make Edith's humiliation and Lambert's crime even darker, Dukes played even the attempted rape as somewhat charming. Sure, he threatened her and Archie, but he was also relatively polite (understood: he is trying to rape her) and compliments Edith. He even undresses. Lambert makes no effort to pretend that he is not fully aware that he is trying to rape Edith, but he goes through certain motions to suggest that he wants (on a strange level) the event to be something else. Perhaps by undressing himself and her and commenting on her scent ("Lemon Pledge," Edith protests), he is setting up a consent defense should he be caught.

Director Paul Bogart, who won that year's Outstanding Directing in a Comedy Series Emmy for this episode, subjected the studio audience to the entire rape scene without taping the interstitial sequences until later. For the studio audience, then, the event was far more intense than it would have been for the television audience: there were no interruptions; they could not change the channels or, like later audiences, pause, fast forward, or rewind what they were watching. The studio audience is a participant in the scene, even if a passive one. The audience's reaction to Edith hitting Lambert with a hot birthday cake is more like something one would expect to hear at a sporting event: the members cheered wildly; they stomped their feet on the risers; they called out for Edith to run. Bogart recalls that he could not go into the next scene until the audience calmed down.

The live studio audience also, as mentioned before, makes the scene bearable to the television audience. *All in the Family* is supposed to be a comedy. However intense and personal Edith's experience is – and potentially triggering for any number of women and, yes, men in the audience – we are reminded that this is a comedy. The line, "Lemon Pledge," gets a laugh. Edith's babbling about her upcoming surprise party, a party she has to know will never happen, is funny. Lambert's nonplussed reaction to Edith's non sequiturs are an exercise in emotional and facial subtlety. Two very fine performers in a scene not only designed to make the audience uncomfortable, but also put together in a way that allows us to take a breath and remind ourselves that everything will work out. The comic bits in the scene are gallows humor at best, but the – granted, nervous – laughter is part of what makes this part of the episode bearable. A live audience reacting the way this one does, helps the television audience. Canned laughter would have sounded jarring and unnatural, ruining the effect and the scene.

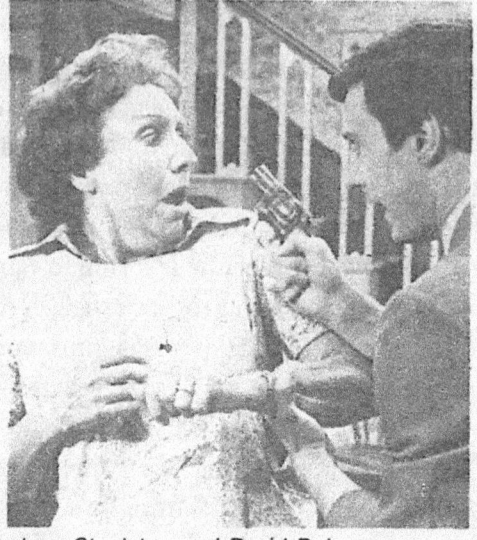

ALL IN THE FAMILY
9:00 ② ③

Jean Stapleton is superb in this one-hour episode, which probes the ordeal of a sexual assault and its aftermath.

For both its victim and her family, rape—even an attempted one—leads to a difficult decision: whether to keep silent and let the assailant go free, or whether to report the crime and live with the fear of reprisal. In this seriocomic episode, the Bunkers must overcome their differences of opinion and decide what to do.

It's Edith's 50th birthday, and while the rest of the family is preparing a party next door, a rapist tricks Edith into letting him enter the house. A desperate—sometimes comic—scene follows, as Edith stalls for time: in a few minutes the family will realize that she's late.

Edith: Jean Stapleton. Assailant: David Dukes. Archie: Carroll O'Connor. Mike: Rob Reiner. Gloria: Sally Struthers. Sybil Gooley: Jane Connell. (60 min.)

Jean Stapleton and David Dukes

After Edith goes to Mike and Gloria's house next door and informs her family what had happened, Archie and Mike investigate the house. While laughter might have been used during the attack as a means of making the scene bearable, this scene, a brilliantly executed sequence of physical comedy reminiscent of the best from Laurel and Hardy or the Three Stooges, is a welcomed relief and release. There is still another full episode and then some to go, little of which will be easy to watch. The audience needs this scene. Without it, the rest of the episode would be too much.

Following Archie and Mike's reconnaissance of the house, the police arrive and say that someone who might be Edith's attacker has been arrested. Edith refuses to go to the police station. Her reasons are similar to those Gloria used when she refused to go to the police in "Gloria the Victim" – or, rather, when Archie and Mike convinced her not to go. She is sure that she will end up being the one on trial. Of course, the effect would be much different on Edith than on Gloria. Gloria is from a different generation. Her generation is much more sexually liberated than her mother's. Even Gloria ultimately did not press charges for fear of her reputation. Imagine how Edith must feel coming from a much more sexually conservative generation (she would have been born in 1927).

Of course, Edith (unlike Gloria before her) has no real secrets from her past, but still, even being asked about her sexual life, especially by an aggressive defense attorney, would certainly humiliate her socially. For what it is worth, the look Sybil and Edith share when they see the attractive Lambert on the front porch suggests that they recognize what a physically (read "sexually") attractive man he is. Society, even as large as the 1970s and beyond, viewed women with a sexual past to have almost inherently consented. The same society would deem it unlikely that a man who could probably get most women to have sex with him willingly would rape anyone.

Jean Stapleton (that year's winner of the Outstanding Lead Actress in a Comedy Series Emmy; *All in the Family* would win for Outstanding Comedy Series) gives a powerful performance as a woman who is not only the victim of the assault but is also victimized by the experience. She refuses to leave the house for several weeks. She runs and hides whenever anyone comes to the front door. She compulsively washes and irons clothes and does household chores, making the bed several times in any given day. She is in denial and living in fear. Finally, after a confrontation with Gloria where Gloria calls Edith selfish, Edith slaps her daughter. Realizing how far this experience has driven her from whom she wants to be, she decides she must go and identify Lambert to the police.

The entire family rallies around Edith during this period. Even Archie, who does not really understand what Edith is going through, is particularly sweet and even romantic (in his own way). However, the issue is decided by Gloria and Edith. They are the women. They were each victimized. When Gloria left it up to the men, they made the decision that she would not press charges. Her attacker went free. Mike and Ar-

The controversial double episode of All in the Family *dealing with sexual assault "Edith's 50th Birthday" advertised in TV Guide with a lengthy and descriptive outlay.*

chie are delegated to supporting roles in this inner conflict. They do not understand. Archie clearly figures that since Edith was not actually raped, she should be over it by now. Gloria is the one who must confront Edith's refusal to identify her attacker, if only because this would make up for her own failure and selfishness just a few years before in season three.

When this episode is shown in syndication, it is divided into two episodes. That is, of course, one of the needs a television sitcom has to meet. There is a logical division in the story: the first part ends when Edith runs upstairs after seeing Lambert's tie; the second part begins two weeks later. However, the impact of the episode is diminished by the cut. A week, or even a day, would allow the audience members to catch their breaths, to process, to come to some conclusion as to what should happen and why. In the seventies, people would discuss television shows and special episodes at home and at work – hence the phrase "water-cooler show". With only a handful of television stations and producing networks, it was far more likely that large numbers of people would have individual episodes in common to discuss. Indeed, *All in the Family* was ranked number 4 for its 8th (1977–78) season, reaching an average of 17.8 million households. This particular episode had a viewership of 16.7 million families and was ranked 8th for the week. Given that there were approximately 57 million households in the U.S., roughly 1-in-3 or 1-in-4 households might reasonably be said to have watched this show. In comparison, forty years later, the finale for *The Big Bang Theory* (2007–2019) was watched by roughly 25 million people (in all probability, *All in the Family's* 17 million households meant more than 25 million people) – or about 1 in 12; that is, the eighth-ranked show for a week in 1977 would have had more impact and relative visibility than the top-ranked show in 2019. A lack of a break in time in the middle of "Edith's 50th th Birthday" means that the audience will not have had a chance to normalize the events. Instead of standing outside and judging, the audience is forced to remain inside and experience.

The live audience reminds us that this is a shared experience; canned laughter would have alienated the audience. The impact of an episode like "Edith's 50th Birthday" works because of the empathy. There is no time to process the events for Edith or for the audience. Had there been, the viewers would have spent a week second guessing the various actions of the characters, beating themselves up over "coulda, woulda, shoulda," responses, debating issues of interpretation, perhaps even questioning consent (Edith could run out of the house when Archie is leaving; since she does not….).

One aspect that helps to make this episode so effective is that it ties us back to "Gloria the Victim". On one level, the assault on Edith could be seen as karmic. Since the attack on Gloria went unreported, the Bunkers were complicit with the normalization of rape. By caving in because of the possibility that Gloria will be painted as a willing participant or, worse, a "bad girl", the family validates that sort of attitude and defense. Gloria also abrogates her rights and independence by allowing her husband and father to make the decision for her. The family has, collectively, helped create a society where rape is allowed to occur because the victims and their loved ones refuse to even acknowledge that it occurred. However, we also hear Edith tell a story from her youth: her date tried to force himself on her and she escaped through a judicious use of her knee; however, she always regretted not saying anything because she was worried about her reputation, even though she wondered how many other girls he had "got under the boardwalk… and how many didn't get away." An audience member new to the show will pray that Edith will somehow get away from Lambert; maybe Archie or Mike will come and somehow rescue her. Long-time fans of the show will know – perhaps without thinking about it – that Edith has the wherewithal to save herself.

Ultimately, it is not anything said to her that convinces Edith to go to the police station to identify her attacker. It is that when she slaps Gloria, she realizes what she has become and the power she is allowing Lambert to have over her. Edith, by deciding to identify and charge Lambert, reminds us that rape will not stop when men decide that it is unacceptable. Rape will stop when women decide that they cannot allow themselves to be controlled by it. It does not matter what your husband or father or child or neighbor thinks: rapists must be reported and prosecuted or they will (and, in his case, Lambert does) continue, knowing that they can assault with impunity. This realization of Edith's, and of the audience's, is what makes this a Very Special Episode indeed.

In "Edith's 50th Birthday" from All in the Family *Edith Bunker (Jean Stapleton) is sexually assaulted by a rapist posing as a police officer as played by David Dukes, who would receive hate mail for years to come from audiences not able to distinguish the actor from the man who would dare do that to their beloved Edith.*

"Archie's Bitter Pill" from *All in the Family*
Original Air Dates: 6 November 1977 (Part 1) and 13 November 1977 (Part 2)
By Michael Barrett

In 2018, the website of the U.S. Dept. of Health and Human Services (HHS) states bluntly:

> In the late 1990s, pharmaceutical companies reassured the medical community that patients would not become addicted to opioid pain relievers and healthcare providers began to prescribe them at greater rates. Increased prescription of opioid medications led to widespread misuse of both prescription and non-prescription opioids before it became clear that these medications could indeed be highly addictive. In 2017 HHS declared a public health emergency. ... Opioid overdoses accounted for more than 42,000 deaths in 2016, more than any previous year on record. An estimated 40% of opioid overdose deaths involved a prescription opioid.

What does this epidemic of addiction to pain pills have to do with a -40year-old two-parter on *All in the Family* (1971–1979)? Archie Bunker's flirtation with addiction in "Archie's Bitter Pill" isn't to pain killers, although the drug is never named. It's some kind of amphetamine that, as Archie says with typical mispronunciation, will "get you hopping like a jackrabbit with an inside hemorrood."

Here we have another example of how topical issues in sitcoms don't "date" the show nearly as much as people tend to assume. It's because the same topics are always coming around. Erin Blakemore's "A Speedy History of America›s Addiction to Amphetamine" is an excellent Smithsonian article from October 2017 (also online) covering ground from the 1930s through an epidemic in the 1960s that would be exposed by journalist Susanna McBee in 1969 as a drug "normalized during war, fueled by weight worries, and prescribed with almost reckless abandon until the 1970s."

Blakemore says that:

> McBee wrote her piece decades before the opioid epidemic that is now ravaging communities in the United States. But the rampant drug use she helped expose shares some chilling similarities with today's crisis. Like opioids, amphetamine was touted as a groundbreaking discovery, then pushed by drug companies on doctors with relentless marketing until it was considered an everyday remedy. And like opioids, amphetamine was a hard habit for the nation to kick.

In other words, Archie's mind-altering substance of choice is a valid prescription drug, although he gets it not from a doctor but from his friend Hank (Danny Dayton) and then from some connection known to his employee Manuel (A Martinez).

"Not drugs – pills!" says Hank, trying to observe a difference between the illegal substances commonly associated with the phenomenon of "drug addiction" in the public mind, and in many dramas about lowlifes and marginal figures and mixed-up teenagers, with the supposedly safe prescriptions dispensed to responsible adults by the medical establishment. In the 1970s, most TV shows about "drug addiction" covered the former, not the latter.

There were exceptions. Mary Richards on *The Mary Tyler Moore Show* (1970–1977) was probably the first main character of a sitcom who became addicted to legal prescription meds – in her case, sleeping pills. "Mary's Insomnia" (4 December 1976), in which Lou Grant (Edward Asner) helped a weeping and strung-out Mary to realize her addiction, aired only one year prior to Archie's encounter with pills.

On one hand, Mary's dilemma seems more credible in that she had a legitimate problem and no reason to mistrust her doctor. She didn't knowingly take something with the thought of doing damage to herself. Archie, however, does take the pills deliberately and with very little persuasion or reluctance. The secret to understanding his action is that he's deeply depressed and wishes to escape his current state of mind – a reason many people are tempted by things they know are bad for them. Hank and his wife may be taking the pills with no obvious ill effect, but Archie is already unbalanced.

Earlier in the season, he'd achieved his dream to becoming a business owner by buying Kelsey's Bar and renaming it Archie Bunker's Place. He'd forged his wife Edith's signature to do it, and now he's witnessed a once-thriving business turning into a ghost bar because the customers emigrated to McFeeney's new topless bar. Bill collectors are repossessing the fixtures and Archie feels like a failure. This underlying psychological basis, which the addiction only covers without addressing, is why curing Archie won't be as simple as getting him off the pills.

Each half of this two-parter has a very different tone. Both are scripted by Larry Rhine and Mel Tolkin, but part one also has script contributions from William C. Rader M.D., a psychiatrist who married series regular Sally Struthers at this time. They divorced in 1983, long before he became involved in the offshore stem-cell clinics that led to California revoking his medical license in 2014. Rader must have provided Archie's behavioral arc from manic behavior to incoherent babbling to the crash into tears and depression that ends the episode, as he sobs "I'm just a working man. That's all I'll ever be. ... I didn't mean no harm, Edith, I didn't mean no harm."

Aside from a few token gestures to verbal comedy in the opening scene (Archie answers his bar's phone with "We cater to straights"), this episode avoids comedy almost entirely. Director Paul Bogart indulges in a striking and literal "jump cut" from Archie slumping at a table to Archie landing on his porch at 3 a.m., singing various songs and suddenly deciding to paint the porch. This dark and agonized episode is highlighted by Carroll O'Connor's virtuoso enactment of a man who can barely speak in coherent sentences as his thoughts pinball through a series of far-fetched and manic ideas to his family.

These steps in his addiction function almost as a blueprint for those exhibited by gung-ho college student Alex P. Keaton (Michael J. Fox) in the *Family Ties* (1982–1989) second season episode "Speed Trap" (9 November 1983), another amphetamine journey. In a thoughtful 2010 essay for the website Tropics of Meta, "Alex P. Keaton and the Dawn of the Adderall Age", writer Alex Sayf Cummings compares that episode with a 1990 episode of *Saved by the Bell* (1989–1992) about caffeine pills, "Jessie's Song" and an episode of then-contemporary *Community* (2009–2015). He observes that these shows "tap into a latent desire for equity" and "the desire to succeed."

That certainly diagnoses Archie's problem, and part two finds his family addressing it with a new business partner while a depressed Archie vows to remain in his bed until 1997. The difference is that this part is full of genuinely funny lines and behavior throughout. There are classic Archie-ism's like "So I won't make the cover of Harper's Brassiere" and moments of insight like "Listen, Edith, it's my experience that the closer people get to me, the more they want to kill me."

The humor isn't only in the content of the dialogue but in the expressively modulated deliveries of O'Connor and Jean Stapleton, who use changes in pitch and amplitude as though singing a modern jazz duet. A priceless exchange begins with Archie railing against his disloyal ex-bartender Harry (Jason Wingreen). "He's the one that talked McFeeney into going topless", says Archie, to which Edith replies in typical wonder, "I thought just the waitresses was topless." After a perfect deadpan burn, Archie comes up with "And instead of the little pills, you want me to come talk to you."

At one point, apropos of nothing in particular yet in keeping with the series' recurring motif of nostalgia, Archie gratuitously drops the name of 1930s songstress Alice Faye, someone whom surely few of the viewers remember. That's the old Archie. The family knows he's bouncing back when he jumps up from the bed and starts arguing with everyone, allowing the show's return to its normal homeostasis of Chaos.

"Archie and the KKK" from *All in the Family*
Original Air Dates: 27 November 1977 (Part 1) and 4 December 1977 (Part 2)
By Lee Gambin

Archie Bunker (Carroll O'Connor) is strangely heroic in many ways. Yes, the man is completely bigoted with his racist and sexist slurs and his endless tirades of offensive drivel; however, he is a totem of humanitarian understanding and a measure of how we as a people can become even more compassionate than what we already like to think we are.

Through Archie's disdain and obsessive compulsion to insult via anti-black/woman/Jew/European/gay/counterculture/youth/Latino etc. rhetoric, we as the audience fall into hysterics over such ridiculous attitudes and banter, because we can feel superior to Archie's ignorance and intolerance. Through such superiority, we can safely assume that our own take on the world is far more loving, progressive and accepting than Archie's ever will be. We are allowed to laugh at Archie Bunker and his bigotry and prejudices because they are so far from our own – or are we? The magic of Norman Lear's universe, which stems from *All in the Family* (1971–1979) and carries through to other sitcoms, lies in the very heart of what is honest and what is perceived as being the tell all truth. Archie may be a hard-headed racist and sexist, he may have issues with those "Eye-talians" and "fags", but he is also a character that speaks out such vitriolic ignorance for the supposedly "voiceless" poor white working class male of a certain age who may feel the same way. George Jefferson (Sherman Hemsley) of *The Jeffersons* (1975–1985) would become a pivotal pop-cultural player in the visibility, rage and protest of angry blacks, and his racism and prejudices are seemingly just as ugly as Archie Bunker's, but warrant some kind of validity – for his people have suffered and now rightfully deserve an aggressive edge (albeit just as counter-productive as Archie's, and therefore just as funny). However, much like George Jefferson, Archie has precious moments of pure sensitivity, insight and yes, even warmth. For example, when his daughter Gloria (Susan Struthers) suffers a miscarriage in "Gloria Has A Belly Full" (16 February 1971), he tends to her, and when his wife Edith (Jean Stapleton) was paid a visit by her cousin who comes to understand that her husband is continually cheating on her in "Amelia's Divorce" (25 January 1975), the episode closes with Archie taking his wife's hand and holding it, a quiet moment of the promise of fidelity and trust. These moments are few and far between, but when they arise it is profound and memorable – Archie finally has moments of clarity and accepts that sometimes being considerate and understanding the righteous path is the way to go. In "Archie and the KKK", this is exactly what happens – the right-wing hateful institution that is the Ku

Klux Klan is no place for our Archie Bunker, even though we have come to know him (for eight seasons by this time) as a full blown bigot.

The double episode opens with Gloria, Edith and Mike (Rob Reiner) dealing with the New York 1977 blackout that occurred over two days in the middle of July which resulted in a massive wave of urban crime including looting and arson. Archie feels that most of the criminal activity to happen during the blackout was at the hands of blacks, Hispanics and other ethnic minorities, which of course enrages Mike, who of course takes the leftist stand and butts heads with the stubborn Archie. Inspired by his father-in-law, Mike takes to the power of the pen and writes a letter to the editor of a leading NYC paper expressing his outrage at the U.S. government for creating a social stigma for poor people and doing exactly the same thing in the name of free enterprise. Later, at Archie's Place, two gentlemen eavesdrop a conversation had by Archie and his pals at the bar where Archie expresses his fear of looters smashing into his beloved saloon. Approaching him with an agenda, the two men explain to Archie that "a lot of other people have the same concerns as you" and introduce themselves as proud members of the Kueens Kouncil of Krusaders (a clever masking of actually belonging to the KKK). This masking of racist intentions is a foreshadowing of the "Clean up Boulder" campaign in *Mork & Mindy* (1978–1982) which has plans to rid the city of blacks, Hispanics and other ethnicities outside of Anglo-Saxon whites in the episode "The Night They Raided Mind-ski's" (10 January 1980). Later that evening Mike gets a phone call from the KKK threatening him. Mike explains to Gloria that the caller "wanted to burn a cross on our front lawn". Gloria is terrified, but reassured by an equally scared Mike that that cannot be possible: "Well for one thing, we don't have a front lawn…" This violent threat is something that will propel the dramatic elements of this double episode, and the notion that the safety of Gloria and her infant son Joey are at risk forces Mike to question his liberalism and pro-activity in the face of societal oppression – in this case coming in the form of the mainstream media targeting impoverished groups who have to resort to stealing in order to survive. However, it must be made clear, that Mike and Gloria (much like Archie and Edith) are also poor people – poor white working class people who are trying to make ends meet – and therefore, when Mike raises his fist in the air to fight for the rights of folks living in varied projects (white, black, Hispanic et al), he is also fighting for the rights of his own family. The KKK have intruded here, cutting into social groups (white ones) that they are supposedly championing – hence, their biggest adversaries are not going to be black, Hispanic or otherwise, but fellow working class white people who are allies to the racial minorities the KKK unjustly detest.

When we finally meet the Klan, they are having a meeting discussing Mike, referring to him as a "commie", and voicing their concern about Archie being related to this "red". This sparks an attitude among the group arguing about the right for Archie to join. Outside in the "waiting room", Archie is being grilled by an elderly white male receptionist about his attitudes towards race superiority (white is of course on top) and his feelings about varied religions (Catholicism, Hinduism, Buddhism et al), to which he grunts at all of the above. Interestingly enough as a side note, Archie makes mention of Charo, the Latina guitarist, actress and singer (who would become a regular on *The Love Boat* (1977–1987)) without mentioning her race (no "Spic" jokes here). Finally, when inside the meeting room, Archie is asked by the head of the KKK what his feelings are towards his son-in-law Mike, to which Archie expresses absolute disdain. Something that we as a long standing audience are completely used to, however, what happens in the follow up episode speaks volumes about Archie's possible changing attitudes towards his baby girl's husband (and the father of his grandchild) which could pave the way for some kind of reconciliation. When Archie joins the group in hopes of changing Mike's political views, the Klan are excited and throw on their hoods, ending the first episode with Archie looking bewildered and now frightened of a group he has just become a member of – even the KKK terrifies the hardened bigot that is Archie Bunker.

The second episode opens with Archie waking up Edith to share his dumb mistake, prompting a classic turn from sublimely talented actress Jean Stapleton with her Edith to respond with "Oh…." and then upon proper realization "Ohhhhhhhhhhhhhhhh" – a trait of Edith's that would now become part of the *All in the Family* lexicon. Archie throws around the KKK's belief system and it sounds like one of his own rants ("Down with the Jews, down with the blacks, down with the Pope, down with the UN") but here he is sickened by the fact that he may have become involved with such a vile group. Upon hearing about his involvement and going to a meeting, Edith's slices of surprising profound brilliance shine: "Maybe it was the fact that you kept your mouth shut!" which advocates the necessity to voice your anger and outrage against such nasty bigotry. Archie mentions that a lot of men he knows are part of this group, which is a constant reminder of not only the fact that anyone can be a racist, but that it could be contributed to a contagious disease that hides behind the friendly veneer of locals in working class Queens, New York. It is also a superb reminder of the Warner Bros. film *Storm Warning* (1951) where Ginger Rogers comes into contact with an entire town devoted to KKK teachings including the husband of her sister (played by Doris Day who is eventually killed by the end of the picture). Archie, distressed at the fact that he has been accepted by the KKK, sets out to somehow right this wrong, and by the end of the first ten minutes of the second episode, Edith finds her husband in a state of shock and offers more profound Edith Bunker insight with "you're white as a sheet" – to which Archie can only respond with a loud burp.

Gloria and Mike realizing that Archie has been to a KKK meeting prompts the most momentous moment in this Very Special Episode double. Throughout the series, Mike and Archie of course have had many a heated argument, but this is possibly the most violently aggressive Mike has ever reacted to Archie's right-wing views. The sheer possibility that his father-in-law has joined the most hateful bigoted group since the Nazi party infuriates him and drives Gloria to break down crying. Archie spews out his rage about the young generation "spoiling the Vietnam War" which is a regressive attempt to avoid the situation at hand; being involved with the Klan, however, when his daughter and her husband catch on (after mention of the burning cross outside of their house) conversation shifts and erupts into full blown distressing arguing. "Archie's Operation" (27 October 1976) is also referred to here and this is where the climax is cemented and grounded. Gloria brings up the fact that Archie had a blood transfusion from a black woman (and incidentally was also tended to by a Puerto Rican nurse), and that if the KKK knew that, there would be absolute outrage. Prompting Archie to confront the KKK and stand up to them is the most heated moment in the show where Gloria demands that her father not talk to her and calls him a "cross burner", and when baby Joey is brought downstairs, Mike refuses to let Archie touch him or hold him. This painful response gives Archie the energy to take to the streets and grill the KKK.

When members proudly scorn: "We're gonna put the fear of God in your commie son-in-law", Archie calmly asks "Why does this club have to burn crosses?" and then mournfully mentions his grandson in passing: "He (Joey) might get the wrong idea of what the cross really means". Here, Archie the wonderful grandfather is on show for all of us to see. He truly loves and deeply cares for his family, and the idea of not being able to associate himself with his beloved grandson kills him, so he reacts in this manner, defending the right for little Joey to grow up without prejudice. After threatening the KKK with outing them (the not-so-nice residents of Queens), he proudly declares that he was saved by a black woman via a blood transfusion and that leads into shortly before fleeing the Klan's domain and tipping his hat to a God that has saved his skin on more than one occasion:

Archie: "There's a whole lot of us!"
KKK: "Us who?"
Archie: "Us blacks!"

"Barbara's Friend" from *One Day at a Time*
Original Air Dates: 29 November 1977 (Part 1) and 6 December 1977 (Part 2)
By Lance Vaughan

The sitcom *One Day at a Time* (1975–1984) has an upbeat motivational theme song that's all about plowing forward through life's many pitfalls and disappointments. In the season three, two-part episode "Barbara's Friend" we meet a young lady named Melanie Walsh (Lindsay V. Jones) who decides to reject such inspirational sentiments, take her own life and gift the series with a doozy of a dark cliffhanger. Melanie is not at all like the teens we usually see hanging out with Barbara Cooper (Valerie Bertinelli), she's exceedingly awkward and needy and follows Barbara around like an annoying albatross.

Barb's mom Ann Romano (Bonnie Franklin) good-naturedly advises her daughter to give the gawky outsider a chance but even Ann and older sister Julie (Mackenzie Phillips) find the strange girl difficult to stomach when Melanie eventually visits the apartment due to her vexatious personality.

Things come to a head when delusional Melanie develops an imaginary relationship with Barbara's current crush, Cliff Randall (Scott Colomby). Reality and fantasy collide when the trio converges at a local eatery. Cliff invites Barbara to go with him to a Grateful Dead concert, Barbara accepts and Melanie is left feeling that her best friend has stabbed her in the back. Making the uncomfortable scene even worse, Barbara drops a fragile glass giraffe that Melanie gave her and it smashes to pieces, not unlike their relationship. Later in the evening Barbara receives a phone call from Melanie who has holed up in a seedy motel. "You don't like me, nobody likes me," she says, sprawled out on a bed, pills falling from her hand as a neon sign flashes red in the background. Barbara is mortified as she puts the pieces together and turns to her mother to say, "Oh mom, help! Melanie is trying to kill herself!" The episode ends silently with only a director's credit on the screen.

The longest week of my youth started at the end of "Barbara's Friend" part one and ended at the beginning of "Barbara's Friend" part two. Sure, Melanie was an obnoxious individual with a horrid laugh but I didn't want her to die! Plus, I'm not sure I'd ever be able to look at Barbara the same way again if she ended up being inadvertently responsible for the death of a classmate. Fortunately, Melanie is found by the alerted police and rushed to the hospital in time to save her life. Before any of that happens though, we meet her abrasive parents Elizabeth and Russell Walsh who seem more worried about what neighbors might say than their daughter's well being. Melanie's mother in particular is presented as a shrill scold and it's difficult to not have new sympathy for what the young girl has been through and new understanding of her desperation for approval.

While waiting for news on Melanie's recovery Ann and Barbara have a lengthy conversation discussing the value of letting go of guilt. Besides carrying the weight of the present situation Barbara recalls childhood misdeeds like filling her Aunt's bathtub with gelatin. Ann, on the other hand, reveals she has always felt guilt that her divorce disrupted the lives of her daughters and separated them from their father. Barbara advises her mother to forgive herself and Ann points out that Barbara should take her own good advice. Meanwhile, Melanie's parents are up to their usual locking of horns. An exasperated doctor who reprimands them for their neglectful treatment of Melanie cuts their squabble short. Finally, Mr. Walsh stands up to his nagging wife and demands her to open her eyes and confront the fact that their daughter is ill and needs psychiatric help. The live studio audience is not on the side of Mrs. Walsh, as seeing her taken down a peg results in cheers.

"Barbara's Friend" parts one and two are stand out episodes of *One Day at a Time*. They take on the serious subject of teenage suicide but are gracefully able to balance it with the show's usual comedy. There's even a bit of surprisingly dark gallows humor. As Barbara struggles to keep Melanie on the phone so the police can trace the call and abort her suicide, her sister Julie who is unaware of the situation suggests that Barbara should tell Melanie to "drop dead." We are also made privy to some core information about the show's basic premise concerning Ann's complicated feelings about her divorce and its lasting impact on her children. The ultimate defining message, that social stigmas must be overcome in order for those with mental heath issues to get the help they need and deserve is impossible to argue with. Most impressively, the storyline encourages the viewer to empathize with a rather unlikable character and question the motives of a familiar and dear one.

It's safe to assume that much of what transpires will come off as a bit preachy and melodramatic for some viewers but that's part of its

The Norman Lear produced One Day at a Time *took a single mom and her daughters to the fore, struggling with life's dilemmas day by day.*

After school special sandwiched within a sitcom charm. *One Day at a Time*'s status as a sitcom ensures that by the time this hand-wringing two-parter has folded up shop, things have reset and mostly gone back to default normal. Melanie's parents are put in their rightful place and we assume that the troubled girl has much brighter days ahead. What ever her future may hold it appears it doesn't include Barbara Cooper, as Melanie is never mentioned again whilst Barbara's love interest Cliff Randall returns semi-frequently. I guess he forgave Barbara for standing him up due to Melanie's pressing mortal dilemma. Here's hoping that Melanie ended up grateful to be alive and that Barbara and Cliff kept truckin' and finally got to see the Grateful Dead.

Suicide is given the limelight in "Barbara's Friend" from the Norman Lear produced One Day at a Time *with Valerie Bertinelli.*

"The Gay Bar" from *Maude*
Original Air Date: 3 December 1977
By Andrew Mercado

In the book *Alternate Channels: The Uncensored Story of Gay and Lesbian Images on Radio and Television*, author Steven Capsuto writes that a "sitcom formula" was developed for American TV that would "remain the norm from 1971 to 1976." He goes on to describe how a series' regular character would struggle after learning that a longtime friend is gay, then after learning to accept it, the gay would never be seen again.

"On most shows, the disappearance of gay characters after one episode lets a series preach tolerance without ever having to show it. Gay libbers would be appeased, but there would be no outcry about an ongoing positive role – and not having gay regulars improved a show's marketability in post-network syndication."

The only country brave enough to introduce a regular gay character was Australia. In 1971, a new serial was being planned for the struggling 0/10 Network and when its English creator David Sale asked if he could include gays, his American producer Bill Harmon replied, "Sure, but give me homosexuality without any deviancy". Don Finlayson (played by Joe Hasham) would go on to become one of the most popular characters in *Number 96* (1972–1977) and although the hit show would have lots of "deviancy", the charming and friendly gay guy was one of its most stable characters.

Bill Harmon's use of the word "deviancy" probably referred to what was happening on TV everywhere else in the world during this period. Gay characters were either perverts, criminals or sad tragic types. Even beloved TV doctor Marcus Welby M.D. (*Father Knows Best*'s Robert Young) declared on his show that homosexuality was a "serious illness" but a curable one through "psychotherapy".

One of the first to introduce the new "sitcom formula" was *All in the Family* (1971–1979). Its fifth episode, titled "Judging Books by Covers", was about Archie Bunker (Carroll O'Connor) mistakenly thinking his son-in-law's effeminate friend was gay, only to discover that his own macho drinking buddy, former pro-football player called Steve (Philip Carey), was, as Archie had described them throughout the episode, the "fag", "pansy", "fairy" and "queer".

The use of so many derogatory terms was even sent up when Mad magazine did its parody version. "Gall in the Family" had the Edith character saying "Oh – and our 'Special Guest Shock-Word' for this week is … 'FAGGOT!'".

All in the Family struggled in those early days, and not yet the nation's top rating show, but one famous viewer who did see the gay episode became apoplectic with rage. President Richard Nixon, who preferred non-threatening fare like *The Beverly Hillbillies* (1962–1971), would later be heard in leaked recordings from the Oval Office saying, "Goddamnit, I do not think that you glorify, on public television, homosexuality. You know what happened to the Greeks? Homosexuality destroyed them. Aristotle was a homo. So was Socrates. The last six Roman emperors were fags too".

What really annoyed Nixon though was that a "good man" like Archie Bunker had been made to look like a fool. Three years later, the disgraced President was made to look slightly more foolish as he was forced to resign during the Watergate scandal. With so much sudden spare time on his hands, perhaps he may have noticed and roared further about more and more "homos" appearing on "public" television.

Despite Nixon's disapproval, *All in the Family* rocketed to number one during its second season. It introduced Edith Bunker's (Jean Stapleton) liberal cousin Maude Findlay (Beatrice Arthur) as a new foil for Archie and producer Norman Lear loved the character so much, he immediately spun her off into her own sitcom, *Maude* (1972–1978).

Determined to keep smash taboos on TV, all of his series followed the "sitcom formula" and brought on one-off gays. In 1974, "Maude's New Friend" Barry (Robert Mandan) turned out to be gay and in 1975, Archie Bunker became friends with a drag queen called Beverly LeSalle (Lori Shannon). In 1977, *The Jeffersons'* George (Sherman Hemsley) discovered his old navy buddy Eddie was now a transgender called Edie (Veronica Redd). And back on *All in the Family*, Edith discovered her cousin was a lesbian. Meanwhile, drag queen Beverly managed to return for a second episode, only to be killed off at the end, victim of a gay hate crime.

By 1977, *Maude* was in its sixth and last season and its 126th installment would feature their final "one-off" gays. In "The Gay Bar", the episode started with Maude's uptight neighbor, Dr. Arthur Harmon (Conrad Bain before *Diff'rent Strokes* (1978–1986)) moving temporarily into her house with his wife Vivian (Rue McClanahan before *The Golden Girls* (1985–1992)) while their house underwent emergency repairs. Maude was unhappy about this because Arthur's conservatism and bigoted opinions riled her up and right on cue, Arthur walked through her front door yelling "I hope you're satisfied with yourself Maude, a group of homosexual pansies have just opened a gay bar in our neighborhood!".

Part of *Maude's* success was due to her liberal viewpoints being sent up just as much as everyone else around her. *TV Guide* had originally described the character as being a "caricature of a knee-jerk liberal" and during this episode, her desire to interact with "real homosexual persons", although well-meaning, was also played for laughs. But so too was Arthur's ridiculous arguments in opposing the gar bar, particularly when he announced he was starting up a group called "Fathers Against Gays Society" with Maude's deadpan reply being, "You mean F.A.G.S.?"

With Maude insisting they must visit the gay bar to prove the world had not fallen in, it was left to her teenage grandson, Phillip (Kraig Metzinger) to deliver the episode's most devastating putdown of Arthur:

Arthur: Gay people are sick, they have some sort of disease.

Phillip: Is it a contagious disease? Is that why you want to close the bar?

Arthur: No, it's not contagious, but they shouldn't be out at a bar having a good time. They should be at home, alone, being ashamed that they're gay. Trying to get cured.

Phillip: What's the cure for being gay?

Arthur (after a pause): Bowling. These gay guys have to start doing something manly. That's what brings them around.

Phillip: I thought you didn't want 'em around?

Arthur: Phillip, I seem to be having trouble getting you to understand the dangers of this gay bar. What's wrong, I always used to be able to communicate with you.

Phillip: Oh, it's not your fault Dr. Harmon – it's just that this year in school, I'm taking a course in logic.

Arthur, Maude, and her husband Walter (Bill Macy) then went inside the gay bar, one of the first to be seen on American TV. Determined to prove that the assorted patrons were respectable, as a group of well-dressed men sat around sipping drinks, Maude introduced herself to one.

Maude: Excuse me, I don't want you to think that I am some frivolous sightseer but … are you a gay person?"

Gay Person (Craig Richard Nelson): Bingo!

Maude: Let me try to explain the situation, you see I am a liberal, but my friend Arthur here is … what's the word for a non-liberal … bigot. I want him to learn from simple human dialogue that you and your friend are just like everybody else.

Arthur: I believe very strongly that people who engage in strange sexual behavior have no place in this community.

Gay Person: I see your point, but you straight people have to live someplace.

With that, the somewhat snarky gay person (and who can blame him?) flounced away. The final kicker for Arthur came when he then ran into Mr. Duncan (Macon McCalman), his new boss at the hospital. In line for a promotion, Arthur was forced to go along with Duncan when he winked at him and said "It's alright, let's just keep this our little secret."

Arthur was then forced into an embarrassing backdown about closing the gay bar upon discovery it was situated outside city limits. Declaring to abide by the law, he and Maude (albeit briefly) hugged each other and agreed that they would each respect each other's principles.

Arthur may have been able to live with that, but *Maude* would not survive a worsening ratings slide. Despite a three-part finale revamping the show, as Maude moved to Washington to become a Democrat congresswoman, Bea Arthur quit and the show was axed.

By now, *Soap* (1977–1981) was on air and Jodie (Billy Crystal) had become American TV's first regular gay character on a hit show. As a comparison, the Australian series *Number 96* wound up just a few months before "The Gay Bar" episode of *Maude* in December 1977. TV's first ever regular gay character, Don (Joe Hasham) had remained with the show for its entire 1218 episode run, and had been just one of three characters to still be on the show after its 1972 debut.

Unlike Jodie on *Soap*, Don never did dress in drag, attempt suicide or sleep with a woman. Instead, Australia's top rating TV show had portrayed him with several long-term boyfriends whilst working as an honest and respectable lawyer. More importantly, his sexuality had never become an issue with any of the residents, not to mention its huge audience who mobbed him in public during crowds bigger than Beatlemania. In other words, Don would have been an even more "real homosexual person" for Maude to have met inside a gay bar.

"Edith's Crisis of Faith" from *All in the Family*
Original Air Date: 18 December 1977
By Lee Gambin

Airing during the holiday season and just a week before Christmas Eve, "Edith's Crisis of Faith" is a heartbreaking and acutely raw examination of personal belief systems in the face of violence against gay and transgendered people. Opening with Edith (Jean Stapleton) excited about Christmas, hanging up the mistletoe and such, we soon discover that something is even more thrilling in the eyes of the matriarch of this poor working class Queens home. Edith's good friend Beverly LaSalle (Lori Shannon), a recurring drag queen character, is set to perform at the legendary Carnegie Hall – something that she has worked towards and something that brings Edith much joy. Gloria (Sally Struthers) arrives at the house (during this season, she and husband Mike (Rob Reiner) and their infant son Joey have their own place down the street) to hear such fabulous news, and we get a wonderful sense of Beverly becoming part of the family. Playful back and forths shared between Gloria and Beverly imply that the big bawdy drag queen has made a wonderful impact on the family with Gloria calling out "Ya big bogus bimbo!" only to get the sassy Beverly bellowing back "Ya little blonde sexpot!" Here, the wonderful love the ladies of the Bunker family have for Beverly is on show, with Edith not even seeing Beverly as simply a friend, but as a blood relative – something that Beverly confides in also.

Beverly descends the Bunker staircase in full drag singing a number from the cross dressing themed hit musical *La Cages aux Folles* (a musical that actually had straight male audiences who were dragged to see it by their wives, stand up in the show's final moments and applaud loudly, cheering on the plight of gay men, drag queens and queer culture) and in classic drag "street" style lends herself to self-deprecating humor and quick wit in the face of a world outside the safety of the Bunker household that might not understand him. Edith asks if his dress maker is a "he or a she", to which Beverly replies "Yes" – a hilarious take on the blur that is gender. The friendship between Edith and Beverly is so pure and loving; Beverly makes Edith feel special and worthy, and even within their comfortable union, there are nice jibs at one another that come from a longstanding genuine friendship. Beverly does an impression of Mae West, to which Edith responds with: "Bette Davis!", sparking a funny look from the warm drag queen. A testament to Edith's love for her friend comes in the form of a scrapbook that she has made, collecting all of Beverly's reviews. "I love you Edith, to me, you're like a sister", says Beverly, and a TV friendship between a housewife in the impoverished neighborhoods of New York and a street smart drag queen is cemented forever.

Archie's (Carroll O'Connor) arrival brings in the gags strong and heavy with Beverly kissing his forehead leaving a bright pink lipstick mark and prompting wonderful facial expressions that embody confusion and disdain all at once from the super talented O'Connor. When he "tests" the fake breasts he makes mention of a certain "rubbery feeling" and the laughs come thick and fast. On top of Archie's blind sighted homophobia that is played as a joke on Archie himself, and never on Beverly whatsoever, his fear of the wave of "dirty plays and musicals" that were massively popular in the seventies steps up to the fore when he is nervous about the idea of seeing one of Beverly's shows. This advent of sexually charged theatre during the period cannot be understated when detailing the history of seventies sitcoms – musicals like *Let My People Come, Oh! Calcutta!* and *Stag Movie* embraced sexuality on stage, and of course game changers like *Hair* brought taboo subject matter onto the platform that is the mainstream American theatre. In the case of drag and gay themed plays and musicals, this would also be the case with shows such as *The Boys in the Band, Fifth of July* and *Tribute* hitting the stage. Drag queens would also become a staple in mainstream entertainment – and heterosexual audiences flocked to see such acts, including those of performer Lori Shannon who played Beverly LaSalle. Shannon would consider himself a stand-up comic in drag, and performed mostly on stage at popular night spots such as San Francisco's famed Finocchio's Club, but would be mostly known to TV audiences as Beverly LaSalle in the three episodes he would appear in, which would ultimately be the first time a drag character would be presented in a sympathetic light on American television, rather than relegated to the clown or the pervert.

Countering Shannon's camp and sass would be Carroll O'Connor's Archie who throws a fit and is angry at Edith for inviting Beverly to Christmas dinner. He even makes reference to Beverly's family "dying of shame", which in turn has Edith proudly defending her friend and making a profound and beautiful statement that will be the heart of this two-part Very Special Episode: "We are all God's children, including Beverly." Edith standing up to Archie is always a brilliant thing to see, and although it seldom happens throughout the series, when it does it is powerful television. Edith Bunker is the emotional heart of the sitcom, and her devotion to both God and her family and friends make her a character that oozes warmth and joy, even though she herself never sees anything special about who she is – as a woman who solidly believes she does not astound, she most certainly does.

Mike's entrance instantly sparks an argument (Archie's disdain for human affection, which is targeted at Mike and Gloria kissing under the mistletoe, but also an added expression of Archie just not understanding sentiment) and Beverly re-enters outside of drag, dressed in men's clothes. Archie is excited by this premise ("She looks wonderful in these pants"), even considering the fact that Beverly may be able to "turn himself around" (code for turning heterosexual). Mike and Gloria look at him with expressions of stupor and Archie turns his anger onto them, expressing the notion that perhaps it's the heterosexual liberals that are to blame for gay visibility. What follows of course is the catalyst of this double episode, where Beverly and Mike are attacked on the dark New York streets – Mike mistaken for a gay man, and Beverly persecuted for being who he is. Initial news about the attack is a "simple" mugging, however as the episode plays out, it is revealed that it was a homophobic attack on a straight man and a gay man – ultimately bringing these two men together as victims. Here the writers do something incredibly poignant, they dissect the essence of horrible homophobic violence and say "sexuality is not even a factor, even the heterosexual Mike is attacked because he is 'thought to be queer'" rendering Mike and Beverly as one and the same in the Norman Lear universe of human compassion and empathy. However, Mike survives and Beverly is killed. In hospital, Mike makes mention to Gloria that it wasn't even about money, and that it was simply a violent attack, and here we start to see the onset of an episode from *All in the Family* dealing with gay bashing. However, this would be a catalyst sidebar, as the episode truly is about Edith and her questioning her faith system – questioning the existence of God; a God who would let someone be killed on the cold frosty Winter streets just because he was "different". Upon hearing the news of Beverly's death, Edith's response is pure confusion and bewilderment that will eventually lead into disillusionment. Jean Stapleton's remarkable performance here runs a gamut of denial, anger, frustration, deep sorrow and heartache, and what is truly intelligent here is also the role Christmas has in the sphere of grief and loss.

Edith's duties at home offer an insight into her grief: serving Archie his breakfast coffee being a prime example. This is a statement clearly expressing the fact that Edith is not at all herself, and interestingly enough, when she was sexually assaulted in the episode "Edith's 50th Birthday", she threw herself into domestic duties to hide from her ordeal, whereas here in this episode, she forgets duties and rejects religion, because of overwhelming anguish. "Somebody had to kill him…" sobs Edith, held together by her daughter and husband, and when Gloria mournfully responds with "Just because he was different", her statement hits Edith like a blow in the face, and the very idea that Beverly was killed because he was gay and effeminate drives Edith into a fury against her God whom she thought accepted and loved everyone. Following her exit (supposedly en route to church), Archie voices his personal opinion on the matter, which ultimately is once again a laughable perspective: "Just be 'normal' and life can be easier". But what he is saying is absolutely profound – something that gay men have heard forever, the role of "passing", of not being themselves, and denying their mannerisms, voice, methods of communication. That the closet can keep you safe from the perils of society and that hiding will keep you alive.

The image of Edith on the porch, sitting alone, with the snow falling before her, is a quietly moody and depressing one. She angrily states "I ain't going to church", emphasizing her anger at God, and with the follow up of "I may not go to church ever!" When her faith is questioned by the jittery nervous Archie, and she is asked what going to church means to her, she angrily responds "What good does it do?" leaving both Archie and Gloria with a situation on their hands, and an audience perplexed at the normally earthy and grounded Edith Bunker, a blubbering mess confused with rage and anti-religious sentiment. This is powerful television at its best – and to use a gay bashing and gay death as a launch pad for a character like Edith Bunker to question her faith in God is a brave and honorable approach. Beverly LaSalle has died for a generation of older working class Christians to rethink their beliefs and thoroughly understand that gay people are just as important, just as valued and just as loved as their heterosexual counterparts – turning this episode into a bridge towards social (and more importantly) spiritual equality.

The second part of the double episode opens at Gloria and Mike's place, where they are playing with their infant son. Christmas is meant to be a time of merriment and joy and yet here we have Edith depressed and disengaged; something unsettling to see, especially when it comes to the usually perky and fun loving "dingbat". Archie tries to force Edith to "snap out of it" and his reasoning comes from a place of misunderstanding and horrific perspectives. He basically suggests that Beverly may have been killed earlier, and that Edith should be thankful that he got to live as long as he did. He explains that "fags kill one another anyway" and this is coming from a place of mainstream media reports that did highlight queer-centric deaths within the "gay community". Films like *Cruising* (1980) would reinforce such beliefs, that the world of gay men is dangerous, sick, perverse and contagious like a disease. And as superb as William Friedkin's thriller is, the film did spark outrage from gay activist groups in that it said what Archie Bunker (a loose representation of straight middle America) believed: that being gay is deadly.

Edith continues her anti-religious sentiment with a stern statement of "God not caring", and in turn she somehow becomes a "Grinch" of sorts, completely disinterested in the celebration of Christmas. The show once again works more magic within the realm of what makes Christmas episodes in the lexicon of the American sitcom so special, and here it tarnishes the language of Yuletide bliss and forces the audience to associate Christmas time with a period to mourn the devastating loss of queer people. There is an unspoken truth that gay people have been persecuted and killed for the sake of making heterosexual society feel comfortable; a hard hitting message that there is no place for the gay kid at the Christmas table, and therefore these outcasts should die on the street like Beverly LaSalle. What Norman Lear's universe forces its audience to do is to pay tribute to those invisible queers who have lost lives because of fear, hatred and bigotry and that sometimes it takes that "outsider" (Beverly) to make an "insider" (Edith) feel valued and appreciated.

The heterosexual Edith is drawn to the gay cross dressing Beverly because she sees joy and strength in such a character; something she admires and loves dearly. Beverly was also someone that understood Edith and loved her for who she was. This is present in the devastatingly moving sequence where Archie reveals his Christmas present for Edith (an atrocious fruit hat that does not reflect Edith at all). Later, in an attempt to keep Edith at Gloria's house in order to "celebrate Christmas", Archie collects another present addressed to her. Edith opens it and finds a lovely scarf that completely "says Edith Bunker". It is a beige earthy scarf that would well suit the working class older woman's house dresses that Edith would don. Archie even comments: "Somebody knows what you like, huh Edith?" When Edith mournfully reads the card: "Merry Christmas to my lovely friend Edith, love Beverly LaSalle" it breaks her heart (and also the hearts of some members of the studio audience too as we hear gasps and "Aww-wws") and it spirals her into a breakdown, running home – running out on her "blood relatives" and wanting to race back to her "soul sister" Beverly.

Finally, "Edith's Crisis of Faith" brings the message of faith, understanding and love home in the most unlikely manner, because it utilizes the most unlikely member of the family to offer some loving advice. Mike a.k.a. "Meathead", a devout Atheist, delivers a heartfelt speech that moves Edith and reinstates her love for a God who truly does love Beverly and truly does love "all his children". "I'm sorry I spoiled Christmas", remains Edith's sorrowful plea, and then when asked who she is angry at; she replies, "I'm mad at God." Mike consoles her and hears her out: "All I know is that Beverly was killed because of what he was, and we're all supposed to be God's children…" Following this, Mike's words of wisdom unfold and melt Edith's heart, as he explains: "Maybe we're not supposed to understand everything all at once…" and then later, in what is one of the most moving moments in the episode, he expresses his own love for his mother-in-law, "If there is a God, you are one of the most understanding people he ever made…we need you…" What Mike is also saying here is that he and the rest of the family need Edith's faith restored – that her love for God and her compassion for humankind are essential for the dysfunctional Bunkers. Edith re-enters the living room and comes back to the dinner table for Christmas lunch with her faith restored. She begins saying grace: "Dear God… E. Bunker here… I'm sorry that I can't understand everything all at once, but I am thankful for Mike and Gloria and Joey…" and eventually, "oh… and Archie!"

Transgendered representation in films of the seventies would come as varied as Doris Wishman's *Let Me Die a Woman* (1977) and *I Want What I Want* (1972) starring Anne Heywood in both the male and female counters to the character. However, television would deliver the goods also, as TV seemed to be more issues based, and could explore these topics in far more intimate and intricate spaces. *Second Serve* (1986) would be a pivotal made-for-TV movie about transgender surgeon turned professional tennis player Rene Richards, in what would be a sensitive and beautifully drawn piece about a man coming to terms with his desire to become a woman. But Beverly LaSalle would be a pioneering figure in this legacy, and her compassion, warmth, sensitivity, sass, intelligence and absolute love for performance and nurturing the long suffering Edith, will always be a vitally important crowning achievement in such representation in popular culture.

You Take The Good, You Take The Bad
1978 - 1981

"Raul Runs Away" from *Chico and the Man*
Original Air Date: 20 January 1978
By Kevin Nickelson

"When you say the name Gilligan, you know who that is. If a show is good, if it's written well, you should be able to erase the names of the characters saying the lines and still be able to know who said it. If you can't do that, the show will fail." – Sherwood Schwartz

As I'm writing this, I am reminded of the above quote that Schwartz uttered regarding *Gilligan's Island* (1964–1967). Some forty-two years later, I keep remembering the name Chico and a brilliant young Puerto Rican star on the rise named Freddie Prinze. Does it speak to the enduring popularity of both star and show? I do believe it does. *Chico and the Man* (1974–1978) is resilient, being available now on DVD and talked about to this day. Enough interest that I was asked to write about the impact of one of its episodes on both myself and, perhaps, others all these many years later.

In 1977, showrunner/creator James Komack was on a roll. He'd been having critical and ratings success with the series, such that he was able to follow it up with another hit-to-be in his co-created (with Gabriel Kaplan) project *Welcome Back, Kotter* (1975–1979). Komack was again a household name and Hollywood hit-maker. However, he was to run into an obstacle. Where he was to have a smooth run in the first three seasons that included the first of two truly stand alone episodes the show would produce, "The Manuel Who Came to Dinner", he would soon hit a big-time roadblock that would come right at the starting line of season four and play a role, in a way, with the second stand alone episode, a two-parter called "Raul Runs Away" from the midpoint of that year. After the suicide of co-star Freddie Prinze via self-inflicted gunshot, Komack and company scrambled to find a suitable replacement. Enter newcomer Gabriel Melgar, a 12-year-old talented young actor from Tijuana, Baja California, Mexico as Raul Garcia. The purpose of the Raul character was to tell the side of the obstacles faced by children of the ethnic minority working class. Ed becomes Raul's foster parent as Raul continues the work on softening Ed's soul begun by Chico.

Some really refreshing touches are added to this segment, about Raul running away back to Mexico when he comes to believe Ed only wants him around as a filler replacement for the hole left in Ed when the Chico character died rather than because he loves or feels for the kid. Those flourishes include the complete absence of a laugh track (still a rather distinct, startling tactic even in the difference-making rage of seventies television. Remember that, at that point, we were still not far removed from the canned laughter universe that was the sixties). Further, director Jack Donohue elects to take the cameras outside of the normal location at Stage 1, Studio 2 at NBC Studios in Burbank to actually film at nearby outdoor locations (standing in for the Mexican village where Raul has relatives and he journeys to) for the scenes where Ed travels to track down Raul. This allows for a more serious, subdued yet raw tone to underscore the story. It even serves to render the humor into a more casual, less obvious and forced variety.

Additionally, I appreciated the equal time devoted to both Raul's plight (the view that Raul sees while on the bus is a powerful mix of decay and cultural pride that showcases the plight of the Hispanic-American in a nutshell) and Ed's grief over the loss of Chico (it should be noted that Prinze's death was originally dealt with by having the Chico character leave Ed to work for his father. Still, the dialogue in part two of this episode clearly indicates that Chico had passed away at some point. Perhaps the original Chico is deemed dead to Ed because he left?).

The tale begins with Raul exploring Chico's van in the garage (Chico's old friend Mando gifts Raul with the van Chico lived in and Raul decides to decorate it with Chico's effects found in a closet that Ed has been reluctant to part with) and Ed becoming enraged when he hears Raul playing a Rodriguez guitar. How often in life are those who are in the grip hold of grief forced to come to terms because either the events of day-to-day life or the need to live for another person intercede in some way? Raul must also decide where he is best off living and where he is more loved. In a small way he, like Chico before him, realizes that he needs Ed as much as Ed needs him to continue growing and moving through life.

Much like the genius scientist who wins a Nobel in their early twenties and spends the remainder of life trying to recreate that glory, Komack would go on to write/produce for another eight years after *Kotter* ended its run in 1979 without ever regaining that critical acclaim he enjoyed in the mid-seventies. He had some nice fare that he ended with, a story credit for the fun retro-beach movie homage *Back to the Beach* in 1987, and as director the same year for an episode titled "King of the Building" from the critically praised *CBS Summer Playhouse* series (1987–1989). Yet a less than gloried end to a long career likely meant little for Komack. He made and left a completely distinctive imprint on the television viewing landscape, managing to squeeze in a social study lesson while we watched.

An aside on the appeal of the series being the chemistry between the series leads Jack Albertson and Freddie Prinze and any off-screen friendship between the pair. While I could find nothing that indicated the full extent of their friendship, Albertson did attend Prinze's funeral, even delivering the eulogy. Here is a portion of that especially emotional speech: "We are bound together, this family, not in a temporary chill of death, but in the everlasting warmth of his humanity and his humor. Let us not mourn his death, rather, let us celebrate his life. In the years to come, in the days and the years, this moment will have passed and we'll see Freddie again, we will hear him, we will think of our brother and we will smile again and we will laugh again, and we will be warm again." That, plus the fact Albertson did voice a tribute to Prinze over the opening credits during an episode that aired after the comic's death, should give a clear sign that the two regarded each other highly both as people and professionals.

Some may argue that it is the charisma of Prinze and the aforementioned chemistry between he and Albertson that was the thrust of the show. True, the ratings declined after Prinze's death and the show was placed on permanent hiatus in March of 1978. I remain convinced that the writing supporting the cast was an integral part of the success of the series from the start, with the actors and direction cementing it. "Raul Runs Away" proves it to a T.

"Doobie or Not Doobie" from *What's Happening!!*
Original Air Dates: 28 January 1978 (Part 1)
and 4 February 1978 (Part 2)
By Russell Dyball

In the world of mass (and social) media, celebrity is very much a superpower, amplifying one's voice and viewpoints and delivering them to the people with an impact farther reaching than anything we mere mortals can achieve. We listen to these viewpoints, and, assuming the celebrity is someone we idolize, identify with, or have some sort of affinity for, frequently adopt them as our own. This concept is the cornerstone upon which Very Special Episodes are built – we experience moral quandaries and lessons through the characters and series we admire, we learn, and hopefully imitate our idols' behavior and outlook at a given Very Special Episode's denouement, thus avoiding the first hand errors in judgment yet still emerging with the lesson learned.

But just as we have our idols, so too do the characters we idolize. Their idols often take a somewhat vague presence – a movie star poster in the background here, a timely reference to a sports hero there – but in some cases, they physically manifest themselves within the narrative of the series itself. These are the Very Special Episodes with Very Special Guest Stars, in which real life celebrities interact with fictional characters. From Nancy Reagan's famed appearance on *Diff'rent Strokes* (1978–1986) to Brandon Tartikoff's *Saved by the Bell* (1989–1993) episode, and all the others before, after, and in between, sometimes it is necessary to bring in celebrities to teach a series' characters (who are surrogates for we the audience as well as non-diegetic celebrities) so they may teach us. And this, of course, brings us to Rerun and his encounter with The Doobie Brothers.

As one of the more fondly-remembered VSEs from the generation who grew up with *What's Happening!!* (1976–1979), the plot of the two-part episode "Doobie or Not Doobie" is rather uncomplicated, even thin, compared to many of its peers. The Doobie Brothers are performing a benefit concert at Jefferson High (a few throwaway lines indicating that The Doobies – all of them – are alumni.) Raj (Ernest Thomas) and Dwayne (Haywood Nelson) have entrusted Rerun (Fred Berry) to get them all tickets, but a stop at a hamburger stand leaves him empty-handed, if not empty-stomached. A shady bootlegger, Al Dunbar (Teddy Wilson), offers Rerun three front row seats (and the pricey sum of four dollars) to Rerun in exchange for taping the concert, under the pretence that The Doobies are friends of his and totally fine with this. Rerun, desperate to see the concert and apparently clueless about the concept of bootlegging, accepts.

Later, Raj, using his position at the school paper, crashes The Doobies' rehearsal with his friends in tow to interview the band. In the course of the interview, the band takes some time to condemn the sin of bootlegging, thus explaining the serious nature of the issue for we the audience and for Rerun. Attempting to get out of this illegal activity only causes Dunbar and his henchman to threaten Rerun and his friends with violence – now they're all on the hook for the recording.

At the concert, Rerun, suspiciously wearing a long overcoat to conceal a basic, late-1970s household tape recorder (along with plenty of snacks) is obviously apprehensive, now understanding the ramifications of what he's about to do. But eventually, the sheer power of The Doobie Brothers' music causes him to forget about the crime in progress, and dances – eventually causing the tape recorder to fall from his coat to the floor, in plain view of all assembled, including the band.

Later, Rerun as explains how he, Raj, and Dwayne were forced to bootleg the show, The Doobies realize that it must be Dunbar, with whom they've had several run-ins with before, behind the scheme. They tell Rerun to go ahead and deliver the contraband tape to Dunbar as scheduled at the soda shop, and when the bootlegger tries to make his exit with the tape, he is confronted by Doobies coming out of every orifice of the joint. He and his strong arm man are terribly intimidated by the band – who, frankly don't look like they've ever been in a fight, although to be fair, there are a LOT of them. Although the tape is revealed to contain no Doobies music, but plenty of audio of Rerun eating popcorn, Dunbar is taken off to jail, while the gang and the band celebrate foiling his act of piracy as the episode ends.

The typical Very Special Episode tends to trade in issues that are, if not universal, then at least generally possible or likely. Many of us have or know someone who has dealt with, say, an eating disorder, a disease or condition, a substance problem. Most of us will not be lured into a bootlegging operation. And thus, the problem "Doobie or Not Doobie" presents is more a concern for The Doobie Brothers than it would likely be for a typical viewer. The ramifications of bootlegging, as explained by the band – "the record company doesn't make any money, we don't make any money, and the public gets a pretty bad recording", says Michael McDonald – are not necessarily the most convincing avenues to viewer buy-in on this matter, especially in the case of The Doobie Brothers, who didn't release a live album until 1983, a recording of their 1982 Farewell Tour (the band has since reformed and has continued to perform in various permutations to this day.)

Bootlegging and similar acts of piracy obviously continue, decades after "Doobie or Not Doobie." Metallica's infamous lawsuit against Napster and the file-sharing community did little to quell it, and the *Seinfeld* episode "The Little Kicks" (10 October 1996) even put a typically Seinfeldian spin on "Doobie", as Jerry is similarly coerced into bootlegging (in his case, movies) – only to find that he begins to relish his outlaw role. And of course, in any concert hall right this moment there are umpteen bootleggers, recording the show with their phones and posting the best bits, or sometimes the entire performance, to YouTube within hours after the final encore. So what's a Doobie to do?

"We thought you were our friends," a band member says as the group confronts Rerun for his transgression, though it's sincerely doubtful that they had planned to stay in touch with the *What's Happening!!* gang. They are aware of their superpower and exploit it by making sure Rerun – and the viewer – knows that this act is nothing less than a personal betrayal, a shattering of the bond between celebrity and fan. The true admonition is writ large within this single sentence: *thou hast displeased thine idols*. And so we learn to not offend our gods, not even for front row seats and four dollars. Thus endeth the lesson. Now please open your hymnals to page 37, "Takin' It to the Streets."

"Richie Almost Dies" from *Happy Days*
Original Air Date: 31 January 1978
By Stef Gemmill

In 1974, *Happy Days* (1974–1984) was launched off the back of the success of the teenage coming of age movie *American Graffiti* (1973). This film captured a unique period in history where teenagers had more choice, more control over their next steps in life from high school and were more open minded than their parents and grandparents ever were. Fueled by anthemic rock 'n' roll music, the 1950s teenager was encouraged to have fun "All Summer Long" by The Beach Boys and mock adult authority in "Yakety Yak" by The Coasters, a song directed at kids who have better things to do than household chores. The success of working in the family hardware store or lining up to fight wars in foreign countries, as their grandparents had, was seen as failure to a 1950s fun hungry teen. Each day presented life and death in popularity, in finding their way through life without leaping into marriage before the age of twenty. They questioned the status quo and the authorities of the time – government, army conscription, civil rights and, on a more familiar level, teachers, parents, the police and the decisions, right and wrong, they have made.

Gary Marshall, creator of *Happy Days*, took this teenage viewpoint and set it within a supportive family home creating a highly popular and accessible family format peppered with comedy and endearing characters. Ron Howard played gritty teenager, Steve Bolander in *American Graffiti* and delivered the movie's classic line, "You just can't stay seventeen forever" – a reflection of his teen character wanting more out of his life than what small town Modesto had to offer. He played a more innocent role in *Happy Days* as the cheerful teenager Richie Cunningham, the central character and middle child of the Cunningham family that rushes into his teenage years with a likeable impish grin and attempts to be cool. He follows his dreams like most 1950s teens – hangs with friends at local diner Al's after school, goes to the school prom, learns to drive a car, gets a girlfriend, aces his exams and is popular in his own way while still being respectful to family and his group of friends. Where *American Graffiti* was filmed out on the streets of the town Modesto, *Happy Days* is set in Midwest Milwaukee, filmed mostly in the Cunningham's living room where it gained its appeal from its focus on universal family experiences. It quickly became a favorite family television show as audiences found the challenges faced by the pre-teens and teens relatable set in a period that amplified these changing times. Certainly the first two seasons of *Happy Days* had an emphasis on more subtle themes of family and friendship dynamics reflective of the time. However, episodes featuring rebel Arthur Fonzarelli/ a.k.a. The Fonz/Fonzie (played by Henry Winkler) proved incredibly popular with audiences and so Fonzie became a star in the show. With Fonzie and Richie's dynamic now front and center, the show's themes reflected the dynamics of enduring male friendship more and more. Where many television shows of the time focused on positive relationships from a female point of view, *Happy Days* shone a light on the dynamics of the male-to-male bond in everyday life and in particular, during a man's formative teenage years. This theme is at the heart of this Very Special Episode.

The show's producers upped the stakes in *Happy Days*, introducing more and more extreme events into episodes that focused on Fonzie and Richie's dynamics, as faced in "Richie Almost Dies". Here, Richie is diving head first into adulthood – his relationship with Lori Beth (Lynda Goodfriend) has moved to a committed level and now he's after his keys to freedom by buying a motorcycle. What Richie has to contend with is two deeply caring parents, Howard and Marion Cunningham (played by Tom Bosley and Marion Ross) both not prepared to let their son take such risks. Howard refuses Richie's plea to buy a motorcycle, pointing out the dangers of such a vehicle. Richie explodes, his emotions still caught up in the world of adolescence where parental values and boundaries are challenged. His best friend, the cool rebel Fonzie, persuades Howard with a levelled argument to see things differently. For a man who lives above a friend's parent's garage, Fonzie can be incredibly worldly. Although he is essentially a "lost soul" character he has endearing qualities leading him to finding home with the welcoming Cunningham's. After convincing Howard that Richie is ready for adventure, Fonzie assures Richie's father (referred to here as Mr C.) that Richie will be safe as long as he wears a helmet.

The scene cuts to Richie on the motorcycle in the Cunningham's garage randomly kick starting the motorcycle with little success and looking like the novice rider he is wearing an unclasped helmet. Lori Beth sits on the back waiting for the roar of the engine and call to adventure. Only moments after they drive off, Lori Beth reappears at the Bronko's Auto Repairing workshop where Richie's friends Ralph Malph (Don Most), Potsie (Anson Williams), Chachi (Scott Baio) and Al (Al Molinaro) are fixing a truck. The group is alarmed by Lori Beth's distressed cries of "Help! Help!" as she runs in with streaks of oil on her pale face. She quickly summons the group to help Richie who is badly hurt after crashing the motorcycle. Richie's loyal friends rush to his aid while shaken Lori Beth stays at the workshop comforted by the young Chachi.

The first shot of Richie post-accident is alarming. The camera fixes on his still face as the unresponsive Richie lies in a hospital bed hooked up to various monitors with his arm strapped and head bandaged. His immediate family – Howard, Marion and little sister Joanie (Erin Moran) – stand nervously by his bedside, silently contemplating his condition. Their faces are wrinkled with worry as a white-coated doctor announces, "If he comes out of the coma soon and regains consciousness, he should be alright." These words provide little comfort to Richie's teary mother Marion. "If?" she questions. "Don't you mean when?" Much concern is shown by Richie's family and the doctor adds in a positive message, "It's a good thing he was wearing his helmet. It could have been worse."

This line may have been added as a message to the younger viewers in the family audience, but it also highlights Richie's struggle with his rebellious teenage dreams conflicting with his parents guiding advice to make good decisions.

The family, along with an anxious Fonzie, return to the Cunningham's house to wait out the night with hope that Richie will recover consciousness. In the Cunningham's familiar sitting room a vigil is being held with all of Richie's nearest and dearest friends and family – Ralph Malph, Potsie and Chachi sit awkwardly perched on a couch next to Joanie, Al (owner of local hangout Al's Diner) sits eating at the dining table, while Leather Tuscadero (the now legendary rock 'n' roll singer Suzi Quatro) sits toying with the keys of a fireside piano. Richie's father takes this moment to acknowledge the seriousness of the situation, however he finishes his speech stressing, "Richard is going to be alright," while Leather plays the introduction to a song on the piano and sings softly. The camera pans tear stained faces filled with worry while the hurt looking Lori Beth nurses a bandaged arm. The song continues as the scene cuts to a montage of a younger Richie's high school milestones viewed through a misty lens – a high school graduation speech, joking with a sharp dressed Fonzie at the graduation party, pillow fights with little sister Joanie and an endearing first kiss with Lori Beth. Not forgetting a spotlight on his deep friendship with his pals Potsie and Ralph Malph celebrating winning pinball at Al's diner.

Although the title of this episode points to a focus on Richie, its leading star really is bad boy Fonzie. His role in the purchase of the motorcycle is not addressed post-accident and no blame made by anyone. However, Fonzie intervened in a father and son relationship on making right and wrong choices. Through the action of selling the motorcycle the story points to some ownership by Fonzie of this life and death situation. This presents an opportunity for Fonzie to express how he feels about his adopted family, the Cunningham's, and puts a spotlight on how important his relationship is with Richie. Despite his tough guy image, its Fonzie's soft side the audience look for in each episode of *Happy Days*.

Fonzie reaches deep into his soul as he sneaks back to the hospital to sit by Richie's bedside. In this private scene he pleads to the unconscious Richie (referring to his special nickname "Red") that it's not "his time yet" and his family and friends need him, the school paper needs him, the world, and especially Fonzie, are needing a friend, a "best friend" like Richie in their lives. It's a touching moment as Fonzie apologizes for never telling Richie this before. This scene highlights Fonzie's reluctance to speak openly to Richie, on how he values their trust and enduring friendship.

Fonzie now reaches a point where he will try anything to ensure the unresponsive Richie recovers. So begins a segment often referred to by fans as "Fonzie's Prayer", where he talks up to God in his casual, cool style. Fonzie stares up to the ceiling consulting with God about how the "world is kinda going a little whacko" without Richie around and how Fonzie's always being able to "fix" things but he can't "fix this one" referring to Richie's lack of consciousness. The scene closes with the camera zooming in on Fonzie's wet cheeks as he shakes inconsolably. It's Fonzie at his emotional best.

The next day, the Cunningham family enter the hospital room to find Fonzie sleeping in a chair by Richie's bedside. It's clear to the Cunningham's that rebel Fonzie stayed close to Richie all night, not ready to let him out of his sight or worse, let him die. Both Howard and Marion wake the weary Fonzie and recommend he heads home to bed. He refuses to budge despite the mothering Marion insisting, "You go home and get some rest," kicking off a round of protest and banter which stirs Richie to consciousness. Richie, still with a bandaged head yells out, "Will you people quiet down? You're giving me a headache." For comic value, Marion tells her now recovered son to, "Quiet Richard. And don't interrupt your Father."

Fonzie and the parents hover over the top of the bandaged Richie with beaming smiles as Richie asks after Lori Beth, his selflessness shining through as he doesn't question his own condition. The doctor rushes in and confirms Richie's return to health and hungry appetite are good signs. Fonzie steps away out of shot, his eyes searching upwards for God's presence. He gives his signature one thumb up accompanied with a cool "eeeh". The audience recognizing the deal he has made God and this Very Special Episode leaves the audience with closure that Richie will recover and Fonzie will forever be his best friend.

Happy Days continues to be successfully rerun internationally, its comic self-deprecation, family appeal and relatable nostalgia still relevant now. The more recent renaissance is also championed by 21st century teenagers and in particular, tweenagers (the pre-teen eight to twelve year olds) searching for nostalgic family comedy that reflect meaningful friendships. It's portrayal of the male to male dynamic – father and son, host to customer (Al and the regulars of Al's restaurant) and especially the relationship of two unlikely male best friends, Fonzie and Richie, is as relatable today as when it was first aired over forty years ago. Even Fonzie, far removed from any bad guy on television today, continues to carry off "cool" like no other.

"What Goes Up" from *Welcome Back, Kotter*
Original Air Date: 9 February 1978
By Rachel Bellwoar

As wasn't unusual for a *Welcome Back, Kotter* (1975–1979) episode, "What Goes Up" begins and ends with Mr. Kotter telling his wife, Julie, a joke about one of his uncles. In the beginning this supports the impression that this will be like any other episode of *Welcome Back, Kotter* but by the end, the corny joke (that has no ties to the episode's storylines) doesn't land as well.

It's a wintery morning at James Buchanan High School. Snow is on the ground and we hear the studio audience clap as the camera pans to show Lawrence Hilton-Jacobs, who plays Washington, already on set. As he goes to sit on a bench, his friends arrive from the opposite direction. They're not in a fight and didn't arrive separately on purpose, but already the episode's setting Washington apart from the others.

When they discover Washington's too out of it to respond to their questions, Horshack, Epstein, and Barbarino make jokes about how sleepy he's acting. Horshack is the first to take up a note of concern in his voice and Barbarino tells Washington he has "… to take care of his body," but when he compares it to the time he had a hangnail on his finger it's clear he's still thinking in terms of Washington not getting enough sleep.

Nobody accuses Washington of taking drugs. He admits that on his own, but the way he arranges his answer sounds fishy. Instead of starting with the fact that the pills are painkillers from a basketball injury, he brings up the fact that his doctor prescribed them to him. That's his strongest argument. Bringing up the basketball game establishes a time line and, sure enough, the first comment Horshack makes is that Washington's knee injury was a week ago. The implied follow-up question: why is Washington still taking them now?

The suggestion that a doctor wouldn't give Washington pills he doesn't need is a lot more reassuring but also incomplete. Painkillers can be addictive whether they're legally prescribed or not. Twenty-two years after this episode's airing you'd have Dr. Carter on *ER* (1994–2009) develop a painkiller addiction after being prescribed them for an injury sustained on the job. This would be followed by shows like *House* (2004–2012) and *Nurse Jackie* (2009–2015), where the title characters are medical professionals with drug addictions. In all these examples you have doctors who know how easy it is to get hooked and it doesn't prevent them from becoming addicted.

Washington is a young, African American teenager going to an inner-city high school in Brooklyn. He doesn't have to look further than the boy's bathroom at James Buchanan to find a dealer who will sell him uppers to counteract the grogginess he gets from the painkillers, but this isn't how Washington's addiction started, and this is the misconception *Welcome Back, Kotter* works to bring awareness to with this episode. It's not just drugs that are brought off the streets that are dangerous. If used past the date they were prescribed or at the wrong dosage, prescribed drugs can be dangerous, too. Washington started taking the painkillers for his health. He was told to use them by a doctor. Now, when he tells the others they were prescribed, it's meant to put them in a safer category than illegal drugs but that's not a truthful depiction of painkillers.

You could argue Washington believes his line to a point, but his secretiveness, around hiding the pills in his shoe, points to him knowing this is something wrong and that he needs to hide from his friends. For their part, his friends either didn't let on to how concerned they were before or, given the time to think about it, grew more concerned, because they're soon popping their heads around the corner, Three Stooges style, and following Washington to the bathroom.

This time Washington's excuse is that the pills are vitamins his doctor prescribed – vitamins in a manila envelope, not a pill bottle. "What Goes Up" doesn't always get everything right, about how to help a friend who's dealing with addictions, but one thing that's made abundantly clear is how much the Sweathogs care about each other. They try to play it cool, making a fuss about how they were going to go to the bathroom anyway, but it's a lie. Horshack, Epstein, and Barbarino wear their hearts on their sleeves this episode, showing up whenever Washington pushes them away, and it's really beautiful to see.

It's one thing, though, to give away that they're worried about Washington. It's another to rat him out to Mr. Kotter and street rules clash with their desire to help when Mr. Kotter corners them about Washington's recent behavior. Barbarino makes a crack about Washington's shoe stash, and this acknowledgement of the truth through a joke gets Epstein talking, but the body language and blocking of these scenes imports how much these decisions aren't made lightly. Barbarino tries to avoid Mr. Kotter's eyes by staring out the window, Epstein bebops across the room to close the door, so nobody hears them, and they both look at each other to confirm that the other isn't saying isn't too much but, given that they are uncomfortable, they must believe Mr. Kotter can help, or they wouldn't be saying anything.

Their confidence may be ill-placed. In trying to approach Washington as a friend, Kotter fails in his professional duty as a teacher. Starting with engaging Washington in the men's bathroom to have a private conversation, the publicness of this location is completely ill-suited for Washington's personal business. TV magic keep the stalls unoccupied but that's unrealistic. Then, when a student drug dealer walks in and quickly flees the scene, Mr. Kotter takes no steps to report him, nor does he report Washington since Vice Principal Woodman approaches him, wanting to know what's going on. As an employee of the school he should be bound to inform somebody. The show is set in the seventies but silently standing by while drugs are being distributed on school grounds is immoral in any decade and, legally, were anything to happen to Washington, the school should be liable.

The Sweathogs, at least, are happy to keep the issue among themselves. Mr. Kotter suggests getting Washington professional help and they quickly surround his desk to discourage the idea. Mr. Kotter having their trust is no small thing. Their willingness to come and talk with him, eating lunch in his classroom so they can catch him alone, means he's doing something right, but he's also the adult in this situation and that means acting in Washington's best interests, whether the Sweathogs are on board or not. He should be taking charge and getting ahead of this situation. Instead, his slowness to act gives the Sweathogs time to enact their own plan and while ill-conceived, you can't blame them for trying.

Through all of this Horshack has refused to believe Washington is lying and has accepted his explanation that the pills are vitamins. The results are nearly disastrous. A similar, if different, situation plays out on the *Fresh Prince of Bel-Air* (1990–1996) in the 1993 episode "Just Say Yo". Overloaded between school, work, and basketball, a friend suggests Will take speed and, while he ends up not listening to him, the pills are inside his locker when Carlton goes searching for Vitamin E to assist with a pimple that's sabotaged his senior prom. Carlton overdoses and spends the prom in a hospital bed instead and Will feels horrible about it.

Carlton had no reason to suspect the pills in Will's locker were speed. Earlier Will had asked him some roundabout questions about the drug but nothing that would trigger Carlton to think that's what he was taking.

With Horshack it's different. Everyone around him is telling him that the pills are dangerous, and he deliberately takes them anyway. His faith, however misguided, propels him to demonstrate his trust in Washington and, unfortunately, the majority are right.

Worse still, nobody realizes Horshack's high right away because that's the cornerstone of their plan – pretend to be on drugs. This is the episode that includes John Travolta, as Barbarino's infamous doper imitation, which is him, walking around, arms outstretched, saying "Gimme drugs, gimme drugs" while Epstein opts for a sideways roll. While imitating addicts might not be the most appropriate source for comedy (and it's not clear where they hope to go with this plan beyond that), it does show the difference when Ron Palillo, as Horshack, and Hilton-Jacobs, act it for real.

Going from zoned out to overly hyper, Horshack runs into a desk, before getting the idea to open the window and jump the distance between classrooms. It's then that the other Sweathogs realize he's not pretending and Horshack confesses, noting he bought the "vitamins" from the same dealer as Washington (and who Mr. Kotter didn't report earlier). There's no hint of accusation in his voice. Horshack just comes out with it, but discovering that his lie could have these consequences, and that Horshack would believe him so adamantly, awakens Washington to the fact that he has a problem, and the next scene he's waiting for Mr. Kotter and suggesting they flush the pills down the toilet.

It's not a horrible ending, as Mr. Kotter makes sure to remind Washington that he was hurting himself, and that this is a decision he should make for himself, not just his friends. There's no further mention of professional help, though, and it's all too open and shut, with Washington going cold turkey, and no talk of any plan to help him withstand temptations he will encounter in the future.

Works Cited
"Welcome Back, Kotter: What Goes Up." *The Very Special Blog*, 27 Apr. 2016, <theveryspecialblog.wordpress.com/2016/04/27/welcome-back-kotter-what-goes-up>.

The cast of Welcome Back Kotter. *A sitcom that delivered the goods from the perspective of slum kids dealing with life in the ghetto while trying to breeze through school headed by a perceptive and devoted teacher.*

"The Reporter" from *Alice*
Original Air Date: 12 February 1978
By Shawn Macomber

The long-running landmark sitcom *Alice* (1976–1985) never shied away from thorny social issues. There was no sudden epiphanous, latter season discovery of a cultural conscience that only conveniently reared its head once the audience, ratings, and advertising had been secured with banal plots and ingratiating low-intensity gags. This was a show that kept its protagonists steeped in proletarian authenticity, serving up gallows humor and a gimlet eye wherever needed amidst the 1970s zeitgeist. And it was needed… basically everywhere. Hell, here in the States we had the President going on television to bemoan "a crisis of confidence… that strikes at the very heart and soul and spirit of our national will." *Speak for yourself*, the crew at Mel's seemed to tell the political class week in and week out, *we got this*. Which is to say, straight from the jump, *Alice* seized the bulls populating the seedy underbelly of industrial decline by the bloody, uncomfortably sharp horns, often armed with nothing but jagged gibes, loving sarcasm, slapstick interludes, and a hard-won realness one might dub "diner smarts."

During the first season alone our titular working class heroine (Linda Lavin) learns the perils of sex work when she's arrested on a bogus prostitution charge ("Pay the Fifty Dollars", 13 October 1976); mulls over a gun purchase to protect herself from a perverted phone stalker ("A Call to Arms", 20 October 1976); ruminates about the potential downside of outsourcing birds-and-the-bees talks to the state – embodied, deliciously, by Adam West a little less than a decade removed from his Batman years, merging Jeffrey Dahmer and Alfred Kinsey in his role as Mr. Turner ("Sex Education", 6 November 1976); grapples with suicide ("Good Night, Sweet Vera", 20 November 1976); struggles to fight the human bias toward retributive rather than restorative punishment in the face of crime ("The Failure", 29 January 1977; "The Hex", 5 February 1977); and faces down an implacable, uncompromising emissary from the Internal Revenue Service ("The Pain of No Return", 12 February 1977).

All of which makes the "The Reporter" such a remarkable departure: The sixteenth episode of the show's second season eschews the usual nitty gritty social-problem-meets-salt-of-the-earth-practical-solution in favor of a more removed, philosophical tack – think a stoic brew chased with a humanity-affirming shot of transcendentalism.

"The Reporter" opens on an abrupt, dark note: Alice is deep into reading aloud from a newspaper article on a nearby criminal trial. "The defendant, Robert Bailey, forced her at razor-point to get into her car and drive to a secluded area where he then raped her." Her voice wavers in ways that suggest this story possesses a personal dimension. "Creep!" she hisses, interjecting her own editorial line. "Twisted, disgusting creep!"

The horror is not so intimately experienced by everyone in the diner. "Do they mention I'm the guy catering the meals for the jury?" boss man Mel (Vic Tayback) for example inquires hopefully. The trial, Alice reads on in reply, had been "recessed briefly" to "replace Juror #8 who was suffering from a bad intestinal ailment." Without missing a beat fellow waitress Flo (Polly Holliday) retorts, "Yeah, Mel, they mention you," but then segues into a barb at Alice's expense. "Well, there you have it folks, the waitress report from Alice Hyatt; now here's fry cook Mel Sharples with the sports." Even sweet Vera (Beth Howland) isn't in the mood to indulge her loyal friend. "Maybe this 'creep' isn't guilty," she says airily, forcing a deflated Alice to issue a concise, plaintive query: "Don't you care?"

Truth is, they don't. At least not in the visceral way Alice does. Yes, their own struggles and fatigue have created a buffer between themselves and empathy. Yet we'd be remiss to leave contemporary culture pout of that dismissive firmament – perhaps best embodied by Mel wondering aloud, without fear of serious rebuke or consequence, whether the victim hadn't been "coming on" to her rapist. That Alice has chosen to wrestle with the metaphysical question of personal complicity in societal evil during the morning rush clearly makes her co-workers uncomfortable. The response is typical of those who take a moral stand that pricks the conscience of those who would rather not be inconvenienced: Sarcasm, derisiveness, condescension, indifference. Vera saves her righteous indignation for a customer who can't decide which salad dressing to choose; Flo is preoccupied by an upcoming date with an "unattached man" possessed of a "voice like cream cheese."

The other denizens of Mel's Diner – individually, attitudinally, philosophically – have transmogrified into a stand-in for a cold world. "Why don't you get off your high horse?" Mel roars in response after Alice asks how they can feed a jury she is sure will soon exonerate a sexual predator. "Business is business." To the surprise of precisely no one, that steed will not be getting a break. Instead the audience is about to find out not only how Alice will answer an inner voice crying out for recompense in the face of inequity, violation, and societal atomization, but also how we ourselves might answer our own compartmentalization and complicity.

Enter the highly-inebriated, chain-smoking titular journalist Gene Crowley, portrayed by veteran character actor Richard Erdman (1925–2019), whose epic *seventy-five* year career included appearances in everything from *You're in the Navy Now* (1951), *Stalag 17* (1953), and *The George Burns and Gracie Allen Show* (1950–1958) to *Beverly Hills, 90210* (1997), *Joan of Arcadia* (2004), and *Community* (2015). Vera and Flo beg off waiting on the poor scribe. "Listen," the latter says, "you show me a harmless looking drunk and I'll show you someone who's about to throw up all over your shoes." Alice, however, is in a determinedly beneficent mood.

It isn't easy.

First, Gene proves to be a straight up eccentric even by the broad standards of the *Alice* universe. When Alice dubs his pre-flight buzz "liquid Dutch courage," for example, the reporter goes off on a delightfully bizarre tangent. "Why are we always picking on the Dutch? I mean, 'Dutch courage' is artificial courage. A 'Dutch uncle' is stingy. A 'Dutch treat' is no treat at all. Even 'Dutch doors' have a tendency to swing out and hit you where you live. Why do we insist on denigrating a culture that gave us Rembrandt… and gin!"

Next, when Alice meets Gene's doe-y gaze and makes him an offer he won't refuse – "If you do have a problem, I'd be glad to help" – the reporter asks not for assistance getting off the sauce, but rather the waitress' protection from a gang of heavies that, he darkly insists, plan to murder him in Phoenix over a story he's planning to file once back in D.C. "I figured I'd stick around for a couple days and wire it in from here," he says, "but I don't write well dead."

Fair enough. Still, there are many reasons to doubt Gene's story. The man is day drunk ranting about Dutch pride for one. Then there's the hazy, detail-light nature of his "scoop" and the threat to his life. Yet Alice chooses to go all in. Why? Considering the narrative structure, it seems fairly clear her rage and despair over the rape has instilled a desperate need for positive action. That it goes unspoken only further validates it. "Don't explain your philosophy," the stoic Epictetus wrote. "Embody it." Save Gene's life and she might save – or at least salve – her soul.

Soon the pair have their joint not-so-eagle-eye on an unnamed gruff customer – Robert Costanzo of *Total Recall* (1990) / *Die Hard 2* (1990) fame – who under ordinary circumstances would be pegged as an unremarkable jerk. In this feverish moment, though, the man is clearly a high-level hired killer. Alice buttonholes Mel in the kitchen and – invoking everything from his service at the Battle of Midway to his one-time status as heavyweight champion of the Sixth Fleet(!) – seeks to break through his carefully cultivated churlishness to his well-concealed sense of justice. It works. Though cracking wise still, soon Mel is smuggling Gene out the back door, into his truck, and off to Flagstaff for a flight from a safer, less conspicuous airport.

Alice returns to the diner proper triumphant. "You're too late you know," she gloats to the hitman after slow rolling his change long enough for the drunken journalist to abscond. "He's probably out of Phoenix by now."

"Lucky him!"

We sense the jig is up, yet Alice is still running on adrenaline. "You'll never catch him," she taunts.

"Hey lady, all I want is to catch is a plane to Vegas."

Was Gene ever in real danger? Will he actually file a story that has, say, Al Pacino dreaming of gnawing the scenery in *All the Kings Men 2*? Unlikely. Sure, someone rang Mel's pay phone asking for Gene's hotel alias – Charles Foster Kane – but it could just as easily have been the front desk warning he'd be charged for leaving housekeeping with all that aluminum foil to be scraped off the windows as a threat on his life.

Was Alice buying in and stepping up meaningless? It's open to interpretation – especially once word comes in that the supposedly unwinnable rape conviction has actually been won. The ripples of Alice's leap of faith into the positivity end of the human pond, she seems to be convinced by the end of the episode, are mysterious and profound. To again connect the plot to the stoics, Marcus Aurelius once insisted that the time had come to "realize that you have something in you more powerful and miraculous than the things that affect you and make you dance like a puppet."

"Life can be so damned uphill," Flo sighs to Alice at closing.

"Especially when there's no steps," Alice agrees. Sure, she's trying to console her friend, all dressed up with nowhere to go after getting stood up by 'ol cream cheese voice. The implications, though, are clearly sprawling out into something more boundless and sublime. "Oh, Flo, every time it gets hard to climb uphill Tommy will say something terrific. Or Mel will yell at me. Or Vera saves a dying plant. Or you… you just get more beautiful all the time."

Flo suggests a beer.

"The first one is on me," Alice says. "I won my first trial today."

In more ways than one.

"Fonzie's Blindness" from *Happy Days*
Original Air Date: 26 September 1978
By Marco Antonio Santos Freitas

Happy Days (1974–1984) was born from "Love and the Happy Days/ Love and the Television Set", a 1972 independent episode of the widely popular romantic comedy anthology series *Love, American Style* (1967–1974). It came out of the brain and typewriter of Garry Marshall and was planned to be a blend of a homage and endearing, light satire of the glorious fifties. Marshall wanted to show the naiveté of that era's teenagers, make a social comment about the generation gap between the older set of family members and their kids – who were being introduced by the "perils" of rock 'n' roll – and consequently poke fun at the whole change of perception of the mores that would arrive with the explosion of the youth culture, largely disseminated by the advent of the television set in American home.

In this specific episode, wet behind his ears Richie Cunningham (played by future blockbuster helmer Ron Howard) and Warren Weber **a.k.a.** Potsie (Anson Williams) think the new TV set in the house may help them lure young women into their dorky lives.

The network head honchos didn't initially believe this slice of Americana would take off the way it ultimately did (it was even retitled, "Love and the Happy Days" when it entered syndication). George Lucas and Francis Ford Coppola – respectively at the time the director-to-be and producer-to-be of an ambitious mosaic of early sixties California life to be called *American Graffiti* (1973) – saw the episode and hired Howard. A huge worldwide critical and commercial success suddenly made the TV executives "reconsider" that obscure TV episode and the end result was that *Happy Days* premiered on 15 January 1974 to attempt to catch lightning in a bottle via the milking of the nostalgia craze for everything sixties that began after the box office millions started pouring in.

The series did catch that aforementioned electrostatic discharge and it remained an expressive force of nature in the ratings until 1984, lasting more than 250 half-hour episodes (itself also spawned many spin-offs – live-action and animated! – the most viewed being *Laverne & Shirley* (1976–1983) and *Mork & Mindy* (1978–1982)). The "device" that made *Happy Days* so memorable was not idealized from the get-go, though. To counterbalance so many "WASPy square people" in the show, a dark-haired rebellious greaser and full-time ladies' man called Arthur Herbert Fonzarelli **a.k.a.** "The Fonz" was created, initially as a supporting player, a sort of a "clutch" when the proceedings got too predictable and dull and some breaths of fresh air were needed to blow in the Cunningham family´s direction, giving it some sort of edge and a sense of danger. The motorcycle-riding Fonz would eventually become the MAIN reason audiences everywhere would tune in as women desired to be with him and men wanted to BE him (or at least to be LIKE him).

But who could personify this almost mythical stud of a man? After auditioning a few times, the powers-that-be chose Henry Winkler, a handsome 28-year-old Manhattanite, classically trained at the Yale School of Drama, of German-Jewish extraction and with a heavy New York accent. He also sported a killer smile, sex appeal in spades, a Mediterranean-look and last but not least, a very cheap price tag (he'd previously done lots of TV commercials and a "Fonzie-like" turn in the micro-budgeted East Coast-filmed gangbanger saga *The Lords of Flatbush* (1974) where he and his shiny pompadour stole many scenes from the other-then-up-and-comer in the cast, an Italian-American with dreams of becoming a screenwriter and film star, christened with the very unusual name Sylvester Stallone).

The reason why I picked "Fonzie´s Blindness" to analyze was due to the intensity of my mixed feelings when I first saw it. On one hand, these half-hours were not known for breaking any new ground as far as addressing health issues and revolving around the inner strength/power of the human spirit required for a person to overcome seemingly overwhelming obstacles (that kind of subject was usually approached by made-for-TV dramas, the type that became jokingly referred as the "disease-of-the-week" movies, sometimes full of saccharine melodrama and often awkwardly-scripted concepts – a huge sum of those inspired by facts that had made headlines in the news not too long prior to be turned into television projects – either starring promising talent on their way up or former cinematic Tinseltown starlets whose careers had seen better times and whose dream big-screen projects had stalled for a myriad of reasons). Addressing a complex subject (included in a regular half-hour episode, not a 90 minute special) like a life-changing illness or syndrome that could impair a major character that had already been established as a "healthy" person in previous episodes and who via his newfound popularity – comparable at times with the Beatlemania phenomenon – had even made execs hire personnel just to read and reply to the thousands of love letters sent by screaming fans from every corner of North America and abroad, was not a minor move.

Let's "recap" when that was made. 1978. Just three years and a few months from the fall of Saigon, the date that marked the official end of the Vietnam War, one of the bloodiest conflicts that the U.S. had ever thought of being a part of. The average hard-working American at the time wanted everything BUT to turn on their television sets just to be reminded of how frail their heroes were.

Using "hero" to describe Winkler´s role is in no way an overstatement, since he, as the series progressed, went from being a "black sheep´" to one of the most relatable beings in all of sitcom land, with his hair, clothing and mannerisms imitated by many a male (also the selling of merchandise based on the likeness of the character that was personifying Being Cool included action figures, lunchboxes, board games, t-shirts, jackets and windbreakers, pinball machines was raking in a fortune in sales). Winkler was even considered for the role of Danny Zucko in the screen adaptation of the musical *Grease*!

Richard Rosenstock (future consulting producer of the wonderful *The King of Queens* (1998–2007) and *Will & Grace* (1998–2020)) and the late Ron Leavitt (future co-creator of the gross-out smash situation comedy *Married… with Children* (1987–1997)), wrote the teleplay in question and though it showcased some of the best acting Henry Winkler has ever done his character, previously painted in broad comedic strokes, has to show his emotions without letting the larger-than-life aspects of the Fonz get in the way of believability… and still come out at the end as The Fonz.

However the whole structure of the sitcom itself is problematic for this writer, as everything is forced to be padded at its conclusion, so the beginnings of a great drama, with a character we all had grown to love, faces adversity in the shape of waking up one day and not being able to see, having to go from someone all his friends followed in his footsteps to a fallen creature who now need everyone around him to guide him through every step. By having to partially forego one of the "means to personal freedom" – symbolized by his motorcycle riding – and in the process probably even questioning his manhood); the ingredients to a superb dish are all there but (spoiler!!!) at the end, everything works out fine, as if it had all been just a bad dream.

I felt cheated but at the same time, I know it would not be right to have our sitcom idol spend the rest of the show holding a cane and I'm not daring to try to say it could have been done any other way. But again, my point is not to self-indulgently show a better route the classic show should have taken but maybe just to lay down on the table what my honest opinion was about what bothered me at the time in that particular episode… how did you feel about what occurred in the show? Food for thought, folks… enjoy your meal sans moderation.

"Block Those Kicks" from *Alice*
Original Air Date: 22 October 1978
By Shawn Macomber

Not to blow your mind while you're just trying to sit in that comfy chair, on the bus, or wherever you plant that backside when you read about seminal sitcoms taking on social issues, but there actually *is* a class component to addiction: a 2014 conducted by the University at Buffalo Institute on Addictions, for example, found that "problem gambling was twice as likely in neighborhoods with the highest levels of concentrated poverty compared to neighborhoods with the lowest poverty levels." And if you develop a problem? Well, as the research clearing house Addiction Experts notes, "It's possible to spend over $100,000 per month on inpatient rehab." And more "modest" outpatient psychotherapy options "range between $75 and $150 per hour" while residential treatments average "about $1,000 per day."

"Research shows that when a country has a healthy middle class – and low or at least moderate levels of economic inequality – addiction rates are lowest among the middle class and at least half of them (excepting tobacco) end by age 30, even without treatment," Maia Szalavitz wrote in a fascinating 2016 piece for *The Guardian*. "However, when unemployment, tenuous employment and inequality are high and the middle class shrinks, more people are at high risk. And their odds for early-life recovery decline."

Which brings us to "Block Those Kicks," an addiction-centered episode of the working class sitcom *Alice* (1976–1985) that not only explores the handicap the crew of elbow grease-dripping heroes at Mel's Diner face in curing themselves of certain habits, but also offers a vision of how acknowledging that collective disadvantage while simultaneously cultivating a sense of community and mutual aid has the potential to at least somewhat ameliorate this unfortunate state of affairs. If that sounds Pollyannish it's worth keeping in mind the entire premise of the show is that a group of individuals – diverse in personality, attitude, background, and appearance – can be tossed in an enclosed environment out of necessity yet nevertheless foster an uplifting sense of synergy and harmony. A rising tide of plates and orders raises all boats.

The episode wastes no time setting the stage. Straight off the opening title sequence the camera pans across the interior of Mel's Diner, from a booth at which its titular owner Mel Sharples (Vic Tayback) is engaged in a heated conversation (we, the audience, see this only in silent, suggestive pantomime) past Alice Hyatt (Linda Lavin) and Flo Castleberry (Polly Holliday, still six years out from her deliciously nasty turn as Ruby Deagle in *Gremlins* (1984)) bussing tables after the morning rush onto Vera Louise Gorman (Beth Howland) pausing to grab her pack of cigarettes and take a comically epic drag. "Boy, that's good!" she says through hacking coughs earning herself a trademark eye roll from Alice. Vera, it seems, has only recently returned to the vice – but she has an extraordinarily good excuse for the relapse: "I went to a Bette Davis film festival and all she did was smoke, smoke, smoke," Vera says. "I was just fine all the way through *The Letter* and *Dark Victory*. But by the time Bette and I got to *Now, Voyager* I was crazed. I jumped up, ran out into the lobby, and grabbed a cigarette from an old lady."

Alice serves up a warm-if-slightly-condescending smile. Who is she to criticize, though? She's standing there scraping the chocolate frosting off the donuts and into her mouth – a "chocoholic," as Vera notes. And Flo isn't above her co-worker's plebian urges, either. She's on her third cup of joe. "I'm a coffee freak," she says, "and it ain't easy since Mel's coffee could pass for sheep's dip."

All of this, alas, pales in comparison to Mel's conundrum. The man he's been talking to rises from the booth and the pair exchange pleasant enough goodbyes. The resolution between the two, however, takes the staff by surprise. "Hey, Mel... the guy you were just talking to is driving off in your new car!" Alice shouts pointing out the window. Mel dismisses her with a resigned wave of his chopping knife, but Flo persists: "Mel, you wouldn't let your own mother drive that car."

"I would if she wasn't such a lousy driver!"

Setting aside this bickering-old-married-couple version of the Oedipus complex, it's Flo who soon puts two and two together: Mel's breakfast date was Marty, his bookie… and the betting has not exactly been bankrupting the house. At first the boss man's self-inflicted loss is simply fodder for worker's jibes. (Alice: "Mel, if I had the kind of bad luck, I'd give up the horses!" Flo: "He can't – he's gonna need one now that he doesn't have a car.") It soon becomes clear, however, that the car is not the end of it. In fact, Mel plans to win the mom-free vehicle back and get his gambling budget back in the black with a "sure thing" bet on a horse called Pretty Baby – and he's going to put the diner up as collateral to sweeten the deal for Marty.

That insanity (temporarily) puts the guffaws on ice. "If [that horse] loses," Flo says, "I know three pretty babies who are going to be out on the street!"

Clearly something must be done. Mel, as is his wont, resists. When Alice calls him an addict, he declares he's "no sicker than the girl scraping off chocolate and leaving me with naked donuts!" He adds: "It's easy for you to talk about willpower. You're not giving up anything!"

Just like that the denizens of Mel's Diner have reached the banks of their own Rubicon. Reluctant though they may be to renounce individual vices, a common threat requires collective action. This approach, in theory, is not new. Some may recall the 1963 *Outer Limits* episode "The Architects of Fear" in which scientists seeking to thwart nuclear Armageddon fake an alien invasion in order to force the world's superpowers – and, by extension, humanity – to roll deep in the face of an existential threat from a truly "Other" foe. In 1987, U.S. President Ronald Reagan would – despite the catastrophic events of the episode – weirdly pine for something similar during a speech to the United Nations General Assembly: "Perhaps we need some outside universal threat to make us recognize this common bond. I occasionally think how quickly our differences worldwide would vanish if we were facing an alien threat from outside this world."

Global incineration of every living being certainly puts a bookie threatening to take over a workaday diner he probably doesn't actually want into perspective. Scale matters. Stakes matter. The jokes, cracked under considerably less than life-or-death circumstances, can – and do – resume.

"Alright," Flo says. "I'll go along. Mel, I'm willing to give up the thing that means the most to me."

"That's bad news for half of the guys in Phoenix!" he retorts.

Intentions are good, temptations at the diner prove too pervasive. The gang decamps to Alice's house for a thirty-six hour multifaceted detox. Still, nothing is simple, even in lockdown. For example, Alice's pre-teen son Tommy (future *Return to Horror High* (1987) / *976-Evil II* (1991) / *Ghoulies IV* (1994) actor Philip McKeon) improbably has a Vera-tempting authentic Indian peace pipe in his room. And then there's the triggering television options – *Looking for Mr. Goodbar* (1977), *Smokey and the Bandit* (1977). "Why don't we watch *Donnie and Marie*," Flo finally exclaims. "They don't do anything we'd want to give up." A Pathfinder girl knocks on the door and Alice buys all her cookies. To do otherwise, she insists, would be "unpatriotic!"

Though the reformations devolve through the long night of depravation with everyone trying to pull a fast one on everyone else. The apotheosis comes when Alice uses

The cast of Alice. *Based on the Martin Scorsese film* Alice Doesn't Live Here Anymore *(1974) starring Ellen Burstyn, the sitcom would be a much lighter adaptation following the trials and tribulations of working class diner workers.*

Tommy's tomahawk to cut the phone line to prevent a weeping Mel from calling a bet into Marty and the three women tie him up with the suddenly otherwise useless cord. The screen fades to black. When the image rematerializes, we're back in Mel's Diner. Everyone has conquered their demons. Marty hands Mel's car keys back to him… and also a cool hundred bucks to Vera. Turns out *she* bet on Pretty Baby. "I guess I switched vices," she says.

"Switching vices?" Mel says, pouring himself a nice, large cup of coffee. "That's the silliest thing I ever heard of." Flo snarks in agreement… as she stuffs a chocolate donut in her mouth and Alice lights up a cigarette. Freeze frame on the epiphanic reaction of our eponymous heroine, cue the laugh track.

Now, one analysis of this denouement is that the entire narrative has all been a 25-minute exercise in musical chairs and no one has come out ahead. A more generous take is that, having traversed the purification ordeal together, the Mel's crew have realized it isn't about eliminating vices entirely – particularly amidst the stress and strain of their socioeconomic station – but, rather, to avoid the habits most damaging to them both collectively and as individuals. In this way, Alice, Vera, Flo, and Mel act as sin-eaters for one another – not exactly selfless in their sacrifice but pretty goddamn close. This, in the context of the series, feels closer to the "truth."

If only such a pact could have been forged offstage! Alas, Beth Howland, who brought such purity and light to her portrayal of Vera – and shot a colorful cigarette ad for Salem in 1969 – died on New Year's Eve 2015 of lung cancer.

"Men Are Such Beasts" from *Taxi*
Original Air Date: 21 November 1978
By Lucas J. Gutman

In the September 22, 1975 issue of *New York* magazine, ex-cabbie and self-described "beatnik reporter" Mark Jacobson penned an article entitled "Night-Shifting for the Hip Fleet". It profiled night-shift cab drivers during the afternoon hours at the Dover Cab Company, waiting for cabs, first come, first served, as the daytime drivers returned from their shifts. They passed the time "standing around in puddles on the floor, breathing in carbon monoxide, and listen to the cab stories." The classic television show that came from this article was *Taxi* (1978–1983). It had such a pedigree of talent on the writing and production staff, that ABC guaranteed thirteen episodes without even seeing a pilot.

James Brooks, who began his career with a script for the oft-sited "worst TV show of all-time", *My Mother the Car* (1965–1966), had built a huge reputation for himself in the years he spent on the seminal *The Mary Tyler Moore Show* (1970–1977). Brooks, along with writers he had worked with on *Moore*, David Davis, Stan Daniels and Ed Weinberger, decided to step out of the MTM world and on their own. Brooks knew he wanted to make it a show about taxi drivers but had issues with the specific construct of the show. Then Jerry Belson, another MTM alum, showed Brooks the New York magazine article. Though Belson eventually dropped out of the project, thanks to him and the article, Brooks knew how to make his cabdriver-themed TV show. "The key thing about the piece was in discussion of the pirate groups of people whose occupations were working at this cab company, when their preoccupations were something else."[9]

The primary players at the Sunshine Cab Company on *Taxi* even resembled people mentioned in the article: For example, Suzanne, a 29 year-old who "…has at least three art degrees" could describe Elaine Nardo (Marilu Henner), who has big dreams and also works at an art gallery. Jacobson mentions "an actor who couldn't pay his Lee Strasburg bills". This is an apt descriptor of Bobby Wheeler (Jeff Conaway), who is always waiting for that One Big Break that will free him from this world. Also seeking the big time while he toils away in his cab is mediocre boxer Tony Banta (Tony Danza). The New York article even mentions "a former priest" and "Romanian discotheque DJ", who have at least a resemblance to Rev. Jim Ignatowski (Christopher Lloyd) and lovable foreigner Latka Gravas (Andy Kaufman). The dispatcher described in the article is not named Louie (played by Danny DeVito) but is, in fact, "Danny, who hasn't lost any weight". Even the set design evokes the article, which describes a "You are responsible for all front-end damage" sign. Multiple signs at the Sunshine Cab Company have the same tone. The only character on Taxi that doesn't seem to be a dreamer or colorful misfit is the rock of the show, Alex Reiger (Judd Hirsch). He is the one person who

---
9 Lovece, Frank and Franco, Jules. *Hailing Taxi* (Prentice Hall Press, 1988).

knows that who he is now is who he will be tomorrow and the next day: a cab driver. As Jacobson describes in the "Nigh-Shifting…" article, "The Big Fear is that…they'll put you on day shift. The Big Fear is you're becoming a cabdriver." Alex is the one character on the night shift who has already come to grips with this reality. Perhaps this is why Alex is the bond of the gang at Sunshine Cab. He was based on someone the team met on a research trip to NYC. As Brooks recalls, "…at breakfast, there was this conversation, everybody talking about what they really wanted to do, and this person says, 'Me, I'm a cabdriver'. That became the cornerstone of Judd's character."

As the episode opens, the gang's lovable naif, Tony (Tony Danza), confides to Latka (Andy Kaufman) that he's been seeing a woman for a few weeks that he wants to break up with. She's a cab driver from the Bronx named Denise. Latka engages with Tony with sympathy and wisdom using only his native tongue, which sounds Eastern European but is actually wonderfully crafted gibberish. Though Tony doesn't understand a word, he walks away enlightened. "How come I never understand a word you're saying, yet I always know what you're talking about?" In more foreign words, Latka explains why the language barrier doesn't impede their communication, which Tony completely understands. This scene was meant to set up the plot of the episode, but the interplay between Latka and Tony communicating without a shared spoken language is actually more impactful than the narrative value of the scene. It powerfully illustrates a friendship between two men who couldn't be more different. Such was the power of Andy Kaufman's acting.

Alex comes in to report that he has had an accident. While the gang is concerned about Alex's well-being, Louie wants to know what happened to the cab. Louie is outraged when he finds out that Alex hit a parked car because he swerved to avoid hitting a dog. Or as Louie artfully says, "…you had a choice between running over some mutt or into a Cordoba? A Chrysler Cordoba with Corinthian leather? Where are your values, Reiger?!" He's furious all over again to find that Alex left a note on the car even though no one witnessed the crash.

Tony meets with the gang at breakfast and asks advice on how to break up. Bobby says he should put the blame on himself and say he's not worthy of her. Tony dismisses the advice. "Nah, she'd never believe that." Elaine tell Tony to be straight forward with her about how he feels. Alex didn't have to break up with his wife because he found another man "wearing my pajamas". Upon this, Denise walks in and the gang clears out. As soon as they sit down, Denise pops a few pills that "help you stay awake" and might even help Tony "take a few pounds off". Tony rejects them saying, "You know I don't do that kinda junk." He then cuts the relationship cord quickly and Denise comments on how quick and straight he was in the break up. Then she announces she's "never gonna let you go", as she lays a sweet kiss on him.

After Louie presents a hilarious scale model recreation of Alex's accident (wherein Latka tries helpfully to use a cockroach to represent the dog), Tony returns and tells the gang that Denise did not let him go and tried to further seduce him at the restaurant.

After trying to picture the Wicked Witch of the West instead of Denise kissing on him, Tony says he still stuck to his guns and rejected her. While Louie is passing out assignments, he calls the newest driver up to the cage: Denise.

Tony returns from his shift, having only booked $19. He looks sad and exhausted. Denise comes back having booked $217, a Sunshine Cab record. In plain view, Denise pops a handful of pills. "Just a couple Bennies and a Black Beauty. You know? Uppers?" Louie worries about her until she says that's how she worked 18 hours and booked all that money. "You got any I could give to the guys", he asks. Called to the boss to discuss the accident, Alex complains about a headache. Denise tells him he needs to take two pills she claims works the same as aspirin. Within seconds, Alex has lost his headache and starts talking a million miles an hour as he heads up to the boss singing "Bye, Bye Love". Tony tells Denise the drugs are bad news and he can't be with her. To this she immediately tosses her bottle on the floor, which is rushed by several other cabbies. Throughout the episode, whenever someone questions the use of speed, it is quickly followed up by jokes that mitigate any serious concern.

Tony gives Louie an ultimatum. If he doesn't fire Denise, Tony will quit. After thinking for what seems to be under two seconds, Louie decides "It's been nice working with ya." He takes even less time in accepting Bobby's resignation is solidarity with Tony. Then Elaine, John and Latka say that they will also quit. Louie has no problem with it at all. But when all the other cabbies also say they will quit after listening to Latka's explanation (in his language), Louie finally relents. Denise is let go but she reminds Tony that he has to go home sometime. "And when you do, you're gonna find me there." Elaine tells Tony he's going to have to be mean.

Tony tries one more time to break up with Denise. She tries to sweet talk him but Tony takes a firm stance, yelling at her, "Psychologists have a term for it. What is it? Oh, yeah…you got a screw loose!", and even threatening her ("If you come around here again, I'm gonna hand you your head!"). "I love you when you're like this", responds Denise. Elaine tells Denise Tony's in love with someone else. "Yeah, who?", Denise asks. Smashing our expectations that Elaine will say she's the one, she instead points to Louie. "Louie, you're a homosexual?", says a disbelieving Denise. "I prefer to think of it as an alternative lifestyle", he growls. Tony pulls Louie close to his side. "To get rid of you, I'd marry him", declares Tony. Denise knows they're lying but leaves based on the audacity of the charade.

Alex comes down from the meeting with the boss with his motor mouth still running at top speed. As he drones on about the Pittsburgh Steelers in excruciating and needless detail, the rest of the gang peels off to go about their lives. This leaves Latka behind as Alex continues his high-speed monolog to him listening in rapt attention.

"Men Are Such Beasts" is both a Very Special Episode and an episode that rejects the notion of a typical VSE. Though the issues (stalking and drug abuse) are ripe VSE topics, *Taxi* doesn't address them in a way we are used to sitcoms doing. In this regard, the show distinguishes itself as one aimed at a sophisticated audience who does not need to be lectured to. There are two quite serious themes in play, yet both are dealt with quickly, comically, and essentially without consequence. Tony's stalker simply goes away when Tony claims (quite unbelievably) to be gay and Alex's new-found reaction to amphetamines is used exclusively for gags. Perhaps some viewers will be offended by the lack of impact that two serious issues have in this episode. I would argue that it fits well within the worldview of *Taxi*. It is a show in which true VSEs are about shifts in long-term relationships. Very Special Episodes in the Taxi universe are ones that deal with Alex and his ex-wife or Latka and his wife Simka (Carol Kane), as opposed to an obsessive new girlfriend or Alex taking a few speed pills. It is the repudiation of a typical sitcom reaction to these Very Special Episode topics that actually makes *Taxi* a Very Special Show.

The cast of Taxi. Working class and immigrant experiences all coming together to deliver the laughs and sentiment in what would be one of the most endearing of classic 70s/80s sitcoms.

"Come Back, Little Arnold" from *Welcome Back, Kotter*
Original Air Date: 24 February 1979
By Russell Dyball

Mary Johnson, we hardly knew ye – but most of what we did know, we learned from Very Special Episodes.

As played sweetly and memorably by Irene Arranga, Mary only appeared on six episodes of *Welcome Back, Kotter*'s (1975–1979) fourth and final season, but her presence was a true bright spot in the series' troubled last year. Behind-the-scenes turmoil would find Gabriel Kaplan and Marcia Strassman making infrequent appearances as Gabe and Julie Kotter, depriving the show of its strongest moral compasses. Additionally, the burgeoning superstardom of John Travolta found the charming and popular character of Vinnie Barbarino in a reduced role, limited to a series of "Special Guest Star" appearances. The halls of Buchanan High were looking a bit empty in the 1978-79 season.

The addition of Mary to the cast as a semi-regular is often overshadowed by new series regular Stephen Shortridge's Beau DeLabarre – a character often cited (unfairly) as the plainest indicator of *Kotter*'s decline. Somewhat resembling actor Ted McGinley – himself the butt of many a joke for his tendency to be a mid-series cast addition/replacement, as seen in *Happy Days* (1974–1984), *The Love Boat* (1977–1987), *Dynasty* (1981–1989), and *Married... with Children* (1987–1997) – Shortridge does a fine job with the material given to him, and it is to his credit and the writers of *Kotter* that he is a fresh and original presence in the narrative, as opposed to the Fauxbarino (or Beaubarino?) hazy memories often recall him to be. Yet in spite of this, and in spite of her limited appearances, Mary is by far the more impactful character, particularly when it came to the fourth season of *Kotter*'s most beloved remaining regular – Arnold Horshack.

Indelibly essayed by Ron Palillo, Horshack would prove to be the most clearly non-threatening of the Sweathogs, almost childlike in his innocence, as well as one of the most quotable characters on a series stuffed to bursting with catchphrases. A classically trained actor, Palillo was very much a victim of his own talent – as it is with many a breakout sitcom character, Palillo's Horshack was so perfectly executed as to make it difficult for the actor to be seen as anything else. However, with the cast (and ratings) dwindling, Palillo was given many opportunities to display his range as an actor, and perhaps most successfully within the arc presented by Arranga's Mary Johnson.

Introduced in the episode "Once Upon a Ledge" (2 October 1978), Mary is depicted as average to the point of invisibility (and the least exceptional of the three Mary Johnsons attending Buchanan.) Frustrated and distraught, Mary takes to the ledge outside the Sweathogs' classroom, with the intent to jump. All attempts to coax her back in fail until Horshack joins her out on the ledge and convinces her in his own unique fashion that there is every reason to go on living… and thus, a lasting bond was formed.

   Or so one would think, but after these dramatic events Mary Johnson was not seen or heard from until "Come Back, Little Arnold," which aired four months after "Once Upon a Ledge." Quickly re-established as a friend of Horshack's who has asked him out on a date to a party, Mary – and the potential of a romantic relationship with her – leaves an anxious Arnold consulting fellow Sweathogs Beau, Freddie (Lawrence Hilton-Jacobs), and Epstein (Robert Hegyes) on how to proceed. For his troubles, Arnold receives some rather generic advice and encouragement, interspersed with some teasing based primarily in infantilizing him ("Don't tell me – you wore out a foot in your Dr. Denton's.")

So shy as to not be able to speak to Mary in this new, romantic context, and fearful that he won't be able to sufficiently impress her on their first date, Arnold is visited by ne'er-do-well Carvelli (Charles Fleischer) and his sidekick Murray (Bob Harcum). Carvelli offers Arnold some "liquid backbone" – a bottle of whiskey that appears to have previously had a few pulls taken from it. Though Arnold initially refuses the bottle, Carvelli insists, leaving Arnold considering its medicinal purposes as the opening titles commence.

The next day at school, Mary and the Sweathogs observe that Arnold was acting odd at the party. Most specifically, there is a sense of aggression observed in him – he is said to have threatened to fight the Buchanan football team (an act which leaves the athletes afraid of the previously harmless Horshack.) This aggression is depicted for us as viewers when Arnold arrives (late) to class. Wearing an out-of-character black jacket, with a bottle of booze clearly sticking out of his pocket (a detail which none of the other characters seem to observe), an obviously inebriated Horshack threatens both Epstein and teacher Mrs. Tremaine (Della Reese), attempts to recite a dirty limerick to the class, yells at anyone who comes within three feet of him, intimidatingly tells (not asks) Mary that she will be going to the prom with him on Friday, and storms out – all within the span of less than three minutes.

As Mrs. Tremaine and the Sweathogs attempt to intervene with Arnold, his developing emotional dependence on alcohol causes a disturbing personality shift in him, threatening his friendships and his education. His decline comes to a head at prom, when Arnold arrives with a clearly unnerved and miserable Mary. As Freddie, Epstein, and Beau try once again to get through to Arnold, things quickly turn physical, with Horshack throwing a violent punch intended for Epstein, but which instead connects with Mary, sending her through a table and knocking her out cold. Arnold immediately sobers up, distraught that he may very well in fact have killed the woman he loves on prom night. When Mary comes to, as a tearful Horshack begs forgiveness, she calmly informs him that he needs to stop drinking. Horshack agrees, stating, "Who needs liquor? I got love" before he and Mary kiss, and the episode – and presumably, Arnold's drinking problem – comes to an end.

"Come Back, Little Arnold" (a play on the 1950 alcoholism-themed play by William Inge, *Come Back, Little Sheba* – who says the Sweathogs aren't well-read?) was not the first episode of *Welcome Back, Kotter* to deal with the issue of substance abuse, having been preceded by the season three episode "What Goes Up" (9 February 1978), in which Freddie develops a dependency on painkillers. Where the two episodes diverge the most strongly is a matter of support for the main character. In "What Goes Up", Freddie is confronted by Arnold, Epstein, and a still-present Barbarino, not to mention the paternal presence of Mr. Kotter himself. Additionally, Vice-Principal Mr. Woodman (John Sylvester White) is depicted as taking a very serious stance on substance use among his students. But in the case of "Come Back, Little Arnold", due to the real world events behind the scenes of *Kotter*, Horshack is far more vulnerable, with his intervention being spearheaded by Mrs. Tremaine – a character making her first of only two appearances on the show with this episode – and where she has assembled "Arnold's friends" – which does not include Mary, Gabe, Julie, or Barbarino, but does include Carvelli and Murray, who gave Arnold the alcohol in the first place. Mr. Woodman, for his part, is elsewhere – reduced to a subplot where he cluelessly believes that it is Mrs. Tremaine with the drinking problem. When Arnold comes upon this meeting, he reacts with feelings of rage and betrayal; feelings which might very well run parallel to the emotions felt on a set that so many key personnel had by this time more or less abandoned.

As is usually the case in sitcoms which deal with issues like alcoholism, Horshack's drinking is never referred to again. But what of Mary Johnson? After a benign supporting appearance in the following week's episode, "The Sweat Smell Of Success" (3 March 1979), Mary would return to her usual role as Very Special Episode Delivery System with the two-parter, "Oo-Oo, I Do" (25 May 1979), in which Arnold and Mary get married. When we last see Mary, in *Kotter*'s final episode, "The Bread Winners" (8 June 1979), she and her new husband are working happily in her uncle's mail order business, with their whole lives ahead of them. In Sitcomland, we can only assume that Arnold and Mary Horshack live happily ever after, but it might perhaps be difficult to be so optimistic for them; two high school students who have known each other for only a few months, and whose lives together have been punctuated by a suicide attempt, alcohol dependency, and a punch to the face?

Wherever the Horshacks are, let's wish them luck – they'll need it.

"Who is Gordon Sims?" from *WKRP in Cincinnati*
Original Air Date: 2 April 1979
By Michael Campochiaro

While the capture of Saigon in April of 1975 marked the end of the Vietnam War, the after effects reverberated throughout the rest of the 1970s, and beyond. Alongside the Watergate scandal, America's involvement in the war contributed to what has been referred to as the "crisis of confidence" that seemed to permeate most aspects of American life and culture in the 1970s. This crisis was reflected in interesting and nuanced ways in the realm of popular culture during those years. On television, the serious exploration of topics related to Vietnam often occurred in scripted drama series. Many of these shows featured protagonists who questioned America's involvement in Vietnam and often bristled (subtly, in most cases) against the demoralizing wasteland that was (and of course still is) the American political landscape. Many of these characters also happened to be Vietnam veterans, like Thomas Magnum (Tom Selleck) on *Magnum, P.I.* (1980–1988), or Rick Simon (Gerald McRaney) on *Simon & Simon* (1981–1989).

American sitcoms at that time, in the late 1970s, were also beginning to feature in-depth examinations of the impact of American involvement in Vietnam. In 1978, a new series featuring a spunky little radio station in Cincinnati, Ohio led the charge. Late in its debut season, in April 1979, the sitcom *WKRP in Cincinnati* (1978–1982) revealed that one of the show's regulars was not only a Vietnam veteran but also a deserter of the war, and was now living under an assumed name as a political dissident. This story, "Who is Gordon Sims?", written by Tom Chehak and directed by Rod Daniel, focused on the station's overnight disc jockey, the hilariously named and colorfully attired Venus Flytrap (Tim Reid) and combined several hot-button issues related to the war into what would become one of the series' most memorable episodes.

Before exploring "Who is Gordon Sims?" let's establish some background on *WKRP in Cincinnati*. Created by Hugh Wilson and based upon his experiences working at a Top 40 radio station in Atlanta, *WKRP* was one of the smartest and most nuanced workplace comedies on television at the time and retains that intelligence and relevance even today. As with many of the great workplace comedies of the era, *WKRP* presented the various misadventures of a ragtag crew of coworkers thrown together by circumstance, yet who wind up becoming a surrogate family for one another. It's a formula that worked beautifully in shows like *The Mary Tyler Moore Show* (1970–1977), *Taxi* (1978–1983), and *Cheers* (1982–1993), to name just a few.

The *WKRP* cast was an eclectic mix of wacky artistic types and straight-laced, suit-wearing business types. The thoughtful and intelligent Andy Travis (Gary Sandy) was the rock of the cast, acting as program director and, for all intents and purposes he was the one really steering the ship. That's because the affable but ineffectual leader Arthur

Carlson (Gordon Jump) – also known by the *WKRP* crew as "The Big Guy" – was mostly only the general manager in name only (his mother owned the station). Dr. Johnny Fever (Howard Hesseman) was the enigmatic, hilarious, cynical, and neurotic disc jockey who had previously been fired for saying "booger" live on the air in Los Angeles. Incompetent reporter Les Nessman (Richard Sanders) was completely oblivious to his incompetence and together with Mr. Carlson and Herb Tarlek formed the station's "suits" club. Herb (Frank Bonner) was the obnoxious and crass sales manager who wasn't very good at his job, probably because he spent all of his time shamelessly hitting on sexy secretary Jennifer Marlowe (Loni Anderson). The most interesting character on the show, Jennifer was a fascinating rebuke of the age-old dumb blonde trope, as the show quickly established that she was far smarter and competent at running the station than Mr. Carlson, and just about everyone else, too. Rounding out the station's group of misfits is the brainy Bailey Quarters (Jan Smithers), whose relatable introversion made her a favorite among similarly introverted fans like myself who often list her as our first television crush.

While "Who is Gordon Sims?" includes all of *WKRP*'s players, Venus, Mr. Carlson, and Andy feature most prominently. The episode opens with Herb staging an impromptu photoshoot – with Les as his photographer – for a full-page advertisement in the newspaper. They corner Johnny for a picture, which he promptly treats as a joke and strikes a cheeky pose, to the chagrin of Herb and Les. Venus arrives, Herb explains they need to take his picture, and Venus tells them in no uncertain terms not to take his picture. He even threatens Les with bodily harm. This leads Herb and Les to complain to Andy. Les even insinuates there must be some deeper, shadier reason for Venus's refusal, saying with great paranoia, "We don't even know where he lives!" Andy replies exasperatedly, "We don't know where *anybody* lives, Les!" This is one of the funnier subplots running through the episode, as Bailey and Andy discover that the station is run so loosely that they don't even have basic employee contact information on file anywhere.

Les and Herb's fear of Venus is an ongoing subplot of the series, one rooted in historical anxieties related to the Other. As a black man working in an otherwise all-white space, Venus is used to these sort of micro-aggressions, understanding that he must navigate them daily, in all facets of his life, while trying to contain his anger at having to do so. When Herb and Les persist about taking his photo, Venus barely conceals his contempt for them, and Reid plays it with raw, honest emotion. It's a powerful moment.

Soon after this uncomfortable confrontation between Herb, Les, and Venus, Andy, ever the thoughtful and compassionate program director, visits his overnight DJ in the studio and delicately approaches the subject of Venus's refusal to have his picture taken. The men share an easy rapport, thanks in large part to Sandy and Reid's genuine warmth towards each other in the scene – you believe these men respect one another and have a relationship built on that mutual respect. Venus eventually, yet cautiously and cryptically, opens up to Andy about why he won't allow his picture to be taken:

he's protecting "a friend" named Gordon Sims. He explains how Gordon is in trouble with the law and that he wants to help him, because he very much loves the man. From Reid's heartfelt but never cloying delivery of these lines, it becomes clear to Andy and to us that Gordon and Venus are indeed the same person.

Soon after, Andy and Venus enter into a heated discussion over Venus's refusal to participate in the photoshoot. At this time, Venus explains that he was a deserter of the United States Army during the Vietnam War. Tensions between the men escalate quickly, with the previous generation's Mr. Carlson, a former marine who also served during wartime (during the Korean War), becoming more and more agitated at the thought of Venus being a deserter. At one point Andy defends Venus: "It was Vietnam," a straightforward statement that encompasses all of the complexities and conflicting attitudes about this most complex and conflicted war. Mr. Carlson is offended and incensed at Venus's revelation, calling it a "cowardly thing to do." Real anger flares in Venus, who's had enough of being told what he should and shouldn't do by men like Mr. Carlson, men who rarely even try to understand him. He declares, "Mr. Carlson, look, I don't expect you to understand me, or our generation, or my color, or that war I got stuck in. But I'm a decent man. Yes, sir, I am." Venus is clearly tired of running and hiding. To his credit, Mr. Carlson calms down and responds with compassion – "Let's build off this" – offering to take Venus to the Army base and stand by him for moral support. It's an exquisite example of the electricity the best sitcoms can generate while filming in front of a live studio audience. In this case, the audience remains quiet for almost the entire scene, with only a brief, stifled chuckle on one or two occasions. Another, even more powerful, scene later in the episode will play out in front of a largely silent studio audience as well.

In the episode's third act, Reid delivers one of his finest moments in the series, a searing, devastating monologue about how and why he deserted. Explaining his story to an investigating officer of the United States Army, and with Mr. Carlson sitting next to him, Venus begins by simply and forthrightly declaring, "Well, I hated the war, so I left." Short and succinct, this statement stands as an intensely honest and powerful rebuke of war, one that we as a society usually only dance around. Prompted by the investigator to continue, Venus begins what will become the episode's signature moment: an extended, three minute monologue chronicling the horrors of war that led him to snap and run away. He describes riding in a chopper, sitting next to a mentally imbalanced fellow soldier who goes by the eerily appropriate name of "Weird Larry." The chopper, on its way to Saigon, touches down in a remote village and takes off with several Vietcong prisoners in tow. Venus recounts in chilling detail how he was sitting in the chopper, watching his fellow American soldiers question the prisoners. Eventually, someone tosses a prisoner out of the chopper – from a thousand feet in the air. Next, another prisoner is launched out of the chopper, ostensibly also for not answering the soldiers' questions. Soon enough, a now-giggling Weird Larry snaps, then steps out in the great beyond as well. Venus notes that is the moment he finally understood, emphatically declaring, "After ten months and twenty-nine days, I finally got it." Weird Larry took his way out and Venus was going to take his own way out. After landing back in the States, he "went left at the airport" and vanished. "That was the last anybody ever saw of old Gordon Sims. It was easy."

Venus is told by the investigator that charges will likely be dismissed, "given the circumstances." Mr. Carlson and Venus share a touching moment before walking out of the room. As written, the monologue is extremely powerful, but its excellence is elevated even further by Reid's extraordinary delivery of it. It's as natural and honest a performance as the moment demands, with Reid pausing for dramatic effect at just the right intervals, allowing both the audience and Mr. Carlson to fully grasp the horrors of war that he's describing. It's also worth noting that Gordon Jump's heartbreaking reaction shots deserve special mention. Apparently, Reid had been lobbying the writers for richer storylines for Venus, and once given the chance to perform one such storyline, he certainly ran with it and made it his own. It's a defining moment for the series, for the character, for Reid, and for American sitcoms that were attempting to thoughtfully and sensitively depict the effect of the Vietnam War on the American consciousness.

The colorful cast of WKRP in Cincinnati. *Bright and energetic, the sitcom would prove to be a cult favorite.*

The significance of this episode in the development of both the series and the character of Venus cannot be understated. This was the moment, eighteen episodes into season one, where the show revealed what many of us expected all along: Venus is not quite who he pretends to be at WKRP. Instead, we learn that he's built the persona, over time, as a way for him to hide in plain sight in the years since he deserted the war. This revelation adds important depth to the character, and underscores Reid's brilliant portrayal of Venus's dual personalities. As a black man, he understands that the world's default response to him is one influenced largely by distrust due to the color of his skin. He realizes that he's always going to be racially stereotyped, so by playing into these stereotypes as a jive-talking ladies' man, in essence he subverts these stereotypes and gains back a measure of control over (white) colleagues and authority figures. Thus, the episode not only offers a searing indictment on the life-altering toll that war takes on our veterans, but also explores the racist micro-aggressions facing people of color in every aspect of daily living. For all of these reasons, "Who is Gordon Sims?" will always be included prominently in any lists or rankings of the most important episodes in *WKRP*'s four-year run. And that is as it should be.

"Jack Soo, a Retrospective" from *Barney Miller*
Original Air Date: 17 May 1979
By Dean Brandum

When re-watching *Barney Miller* (1975–1982) today, the first thing that catches your eye is the aesthetic. It is that shot-on-video look that was originally popularized by producer Norman Lear for *All in the Family* (1971–1979) and was then made standard industry practice. Allowing for the use of a multi-camera setup, videotape allowed programs to be shot before a live audience, incorporating their audible reactions within the diegesis. What videotape also offered was a distinct difference to the sitcoms of the sixties. For whereas the likes of *I Dream of Jeanie* (1965–1970) and *Gilligan's Island* (1964–1967) still dazzle the screen with their primary color palette of 35mm film, the videotaped sitcoms that followed eschewed their cosmetic artificiality in favor of an immediacy and verisimilitude that approximated both the live television of an earlier era and the news bulletins that were cornerstones of each network's prime time lead-in schedules. Premiering in 1971, *All in the Family* had plenty of topical material to work with over the course of its run – Vietnam, women's liberation, civil rights, the counter-culture and Watergate. When *Barney Miller* first went to air on 23 January 1975, Nixon was four months out of the White House, the final defeated stragglers were about to leave Saigon and the country wallowed in the aftermath of a recession that would see economic growth remain stagnant for the remainder of the decade as inflation and unemployment remained high. The optimism of the late 1960s may have ended as the calendar turned to 1970, yet the state of national consciousness lingered in a holding pattern for the first few years of the decade. So much had been promised, so little delivered and when newly sworn-in President Gerald Ford announced that our long national nightmare was over, the latter half of the 1970s was the bleary-eyed hangover the nation had to suffer in return.

Screening on ABC, 170 episodes of *Barney Miller* were produced over the course of its eight seasons. Never a major hit with viewers, it still commanded a sizable core audience, ranking in the lower rungs of the Nielsen top 20 for most of its run. A sitcom set in the squad room of New York's fictional 12th police precinct, *Barney Miller* starred Hal Linden as the titular captain of the precinct, heading crew of wisecracking, idiosyncratic detectives. In the first season the group consisted of the aging and morose Phil Fish (Abe Vigoda), hot-tempered "Chano" Amanguale (Gregory Sierra), ambitious Nathan Harris (Ron Glass), naïve "Wojo" Wojciehowicz (Max Gail), philosophical Nick Yemana (Jack Soo). Also dropping by on a regular basis was Frank Luger (James Gregory), Barney's old-school superior ready to impart unwanted advice. For the first couple of seasons Barbara Barrie appeared as Barney's wife, Liz, for initially the narrative included a focus on Barney's home life. However, it did not take long for the producers to realise that the heart of the series was to be found in the squad room and Liz's appearances diminished until all that remained of her was someone Barney could be seen speaking to on the telephone. Primarily, *Barney Miller*'s principal cast was male with women featuring on as guest stars or appearing in short-story arcs. For today's viewer this may appear sexist, but it was probably an accurate depiction of such a workplace at the time and, if diversity was not found in gender then it was in the racial backgrounds of the detectives which included Hispanic, Polish, African American and Japanese.

The set up was a deceptively simple one: in each episode Barney would have to keep the squad room in order as he dealt with either some bureaucratic directives sent from up high or disruptions over which he had little control. These would often be situations that reflected the conditions of Americans at the time such as heat waves, industrial action, the dilapidated state of the workplace and homelessness. Nestled among this were the subplots which were generally balanced between involving the police cases under investigation and the personal issues of the squad's members.

Considering that New York averaged over 1600 murders over the duration of *Barney Miller*'s run, the 12th Precinct detectives rarely tackled homicides. For as much as it reflected "real life" *Barney Miller* was still a sitcom. However, time and again the writers and cast deftly dealt with dark subject matter, usually for laughs but occasionally with dramatic bite. For although most cases that found their way into the squad room were the typical tropes of New York crime drama of the period – muggers, obscene callers, religious freaks, mad bombers and sex pests – their exaggerated characterisations and situations became the fodder for wisecracks. It was when the professional distance slipped and the detectives took a personal interest in a case did the veneer crack and the humanity of each detective was allowed to be displayed. In essence though, the characters of *Barney Miller* found humor in a broken and crumbling society. Naturally there was grumbling about the job (and by extension, the city and the nation) in every episode, but with no foreseeable improvement it was best to laugh, for the alternative was too bleak to contemplate.

The core cast remained together for the first two seasons at which point Gregory Sierra left, replaced by Steve Landesberg as the droll, intellectual Arthur Dietrich. Abe Vigoda's appearances decreased during season three as the success of his character led to a short-lived spin-off series, *Fish* (1977–1978) and he left the series as a regular early in season four. Ron Carey as Officer Levitt began a recurring role in season three and was a full-time member of the cast the next season. Other than these changes the continuity of the ensemble was static but the characters were not. Over time they developed as the viewer became informed of their pasts, their aspirations, insecurities and home lives, all within the confines of the squad room set (including a visible jail cell), from which the action rarely departed. *Barney Miller* was notorious for its long taping sessions that often went into the night, which combined with the unflattering effect of videotape, left the actors generally appearing weary. Such an approach inadvertently approximated the lifestyles of over-worked city cops, for whom their fellow officers became a surrogate family. Such was the rapport between the characters on *Barney Miller* that the viewer believes the same and so well did the actors bounce lines off each other that the warmth felt was genuine – a family of cops, a family of actors.

This quality was enhanced by the series' general air of late-seventies blissed out unflappability. Indeed, the degraded, hazy aesthetic of the visuals, the funky bass of its theme and the laconic, cluttered futility of *Barney Miller* offered the impression that all involved had each inhaled a joint before the cameras rolled. That in the third season one episode ("Hash") had the characters unwittingly eating hash cookies was no surprise, nor was it that the effect was only a mild exaggeration of their otherwise stoned countenance.

After episode nine of season five Nick Yemena (Jack Soo) was not present in the cast – "He's down at the D.A.'s office for a couple of days" was the explanation. Although he remained in the opening credit sequence he continued to be absent for the next fourteen episodes. It appeared he had been written out, to be, as was the convention, mentioned a few times in passing before a replacement character was introduced and the narrative continued as if the departed had never even existed. For many viewers Nick Yemana had always been the favorite of a bunch of very likeable characters. Firstly was the novelty – Jack Soo was a Japanese-American actor and although occasional remarks are made to and by him regards his background he is playing a detective who only happens to be of Asian background. A perusal of Soo's credits reveals that race was too often a determinant in his casting, with the role as "Oriental #1" in *Thoroughly Modern Millie* (1967) being not entirely untypical of his Hollywood fortunes before *Barney Miller*. According to Hal Linden the role was originally cast (and played in the pilot) as an Italian and the actor would have received the part except that it was discovered that he had once appeared in a pornographic film (albeit in a non-sex scene). That scared the network who demanded the role be recast and the producer (and former nightclub comedian) Danny Arnold recommended his old friend and former performing partner Soo for the part. In a cast of exasperated fast talkers, Soo's Yemana spoke in a deliberately measured cadence, often stumbling over dialogue to the point where, a few years earlier, such readings would be culled for another take. But if one were to think of a slightly more sardonic Bob Newhart you may get an idea of his expert comic timing and delivery. Yemana remained the 12th Precinct's most enigmatic character with little offered of his personal life and his main shtick was as the maker of bad coffee and to offer knowing cod-Eastern philosophical homilies as a way of breaking tensions or explaining otherwise ridiculous situations.

In the final episode of the fifth season Jack Soo had the pre-credit opening scene. Here was Yemana trying to eat Asian takeaway with a single chopstick as he was on the phone, attempting to gather details of a stolen vehicle. He asks for details of the car and repeats them back to the caller, all the time as he fossicks in his drawers and across the cluttered table. Eventually he asks the caller for a moment as he needs to find a pencil, ostensibly to take down the details, but upon finding such a tool he uses it as a second chopstick to continue with his lunch. The call ends with the caller certain that his details have been taken and Nick continuing with his meal. "Oh my God, I've eaten my eraser", he exclaims as the scene ends. It was classic Yemana, but it had been seen before. This was to be a Very Special Episode clip special. Jack Soo had died of oesophageal cancer on 11 January 1979 and it was widely reported in the media and thus fans would have been aware of this development. "Jack Soo, a Retrospective" was *Barney Miller*'s attempt to deal with what was both a personal and professional tragedy for the series when it went to air on May 17 that year.

Hal Linden has stated Danny Arnold had wrestled with how *Barney Miller* would deal with Soo's death. After considering the options he told the cast, "I'm not going to trade on the death of Jack". Instead, he asked them to each write their own thoughts which they would then deliver between clips. Following the chopstick sequence we cut to the cast seated on set. Linden introduces the episode: "That was Jack Soo as Nick Yemana, a role he played in over eighty episodes of *Barney Miller* until his death this past January. I'm Hal Linden and with me is the rest of the cast of our show. What follows is a recollection of some of Jack's best moments on *Barney Miller*. Enjoy them."

After another clip the opening credits (including Soo) play. Then Linden and Landesberg pour some coffee as they speak of Nick's inability to brew a good pot (a regular go-to joke within the show). This serves to introduce a montage of Nick's lousy coffee moments. Following this, James Gregory extols Nick's humor and ability to deal with bizarre situations and people which the next montage highlights. After a brief fade to black was see Linden inspecting Yemana's name on the roster board. He turns to the camera and tells us that Jack Soo was born Goro Suzuki and, like many Japanese in America during World War II spent many years interred in detention camps. It was an indignity that was never forgotten, but rather than feel bitterness he faced the world with humor, dignity and pride. His characterization of Nick Yemana was also imbued with these qualities (here follows a segment showing instances of racial ignorance, bigotry and misunderstanding). Steve Landesberg then recollects how much the two of them would be laughing on set and that Jack was his friend and he'd miss him. Ron Carey then states that throughout the series little was revealed of Nick's private life (unlike that of the other characters). However, there were occasional glimpses, such as when, on an episode set on Christmas eve, Nick fell for a Japanese mugging victim, unaware that she was a call girl. This touching scene then plays. Max Gail then explained how that scene finished filming at 2:30am and of all the cast and crew you would not find one who had not been touched by Jack as he was just as loved off-screen as he was in front of the camera. His love of humanity was stronger than the anger he had for the terrible things people had done to him. It was this quality, thought Gail, that explained Soo's creation of Nick.

From the close-up of Gail the camera cuts to a group shot, just as they were at the beginning. Linden then explains that no one actor is indispensable to a show and that *Barney Miller* would continue. Then follows a clip of Wojo telling Nick how proud he is to work alongside him and, as thanks, has made the day's coffee. They both take a sip and realise that it tastes just as bad as Nick's. In retrospect this serves to allow a passing of the baton as the precinct's bad coffee maker. Cut back to the cast holding their cups aloft in salute, then to a freeze frame of Jack, as Nick, seated at his desk, smiling. End credits.

"Jack Soo, a Retrospective" is one of sitcom's most perfect **Very Special Episodes**. For it delicately balances and occasionally blurs the persona of actor Jack Soo and character Nick Yemana. During this episode Hal Linden alternates between "Hal Linden" and "Barney Miller", as does Steve Landesberg. Carey remains Officer Levitt and Gregory is Luger. Max Gail is himself and Ron Glass who is present but silent may be himself or Harris. The fourth wall is dismantled and rebuilt throughout the episode and at times it is not clear whether the cast are themselves or their characters.

This harks back to the earlier assertion that part of *Barney Miller*'s appeal lay in the impression that the love the characters had for each other was equal to that of the ensemble's circle of friendship. This episode is the double heartbreak of two families coming to terms with the loss of a beloved family member. Jack Soo was too fine an actor to be simply playing himself as Nick Yemana yet this episode let the audience know that the best qualities they loved in Nick were also shared by Jack. While the characters grieved and the actors grieved, the producers were well aware that the audience were grieving too. By breaking the fourth wall the actors spoke directly to the viewers as both their characters and, as themselves, sharing their sadness. That the oft-maligned videotape was used to capture this display provided the moment with the intimacy, immediacy and truth of a newscast.

By 1979 Americans had become nonchalant about being bullshitted to and would have forgiven *Barney Miller* for taking the conventional road in dealing with Jack's death – having the cast and producers share their condolences in the media and allow the fictional world of the sitcom to spin its own reality. However, as a series that dealt with the realities of the late 1970s through the prism of comedy, *Barney Miller* was not prepared to break that bond with its audience and this **Very Special Episode** only served to strengthen it.

As a tribute to a fine actor, comedian and human being, "Jack Soo, a Retrospective" is excellent. As an act of sharing the grief held by the characters, the cast, the production crew and the audience it is a masterpiece.

"Rough Housing" from *The Facts of Life*
Original Air Date: 24 August 1979
By Lee Gambin

The incredibly busy and lively pilot of this long running and much loved sitcom spin-off from *Diff'rent Strokes* (1978–1986) sets off with a bang as it ventures straight into Very Special Episode territory, dancing with the notion of sexual identity confusion and queer paranoia. Lesbianism in TV sitcoms of the seventies was as rare as hen's teeth and each example usually involved adult gay women facing the dilemmas of homophobia and rejection in the face of a cold and unwelcoming world. The incredibly moving "Cousin Liz" from *All in the Family* (1971–1979) was a benchmark moment in capturing the issue at hand with a sensitive handle, but for the most part lesbianism in comedic television was depicted as a gag either to point out male ineptness (the adage that he was such a bad lover/bad man that his woman turned queer) or presented as a cartoon butch dyke who is not to be taken seriously.

As aforementioned, adult lesbians were springing up in television during the decade but more so in TV dramas rather than episodic situation comedies and teenage girls who were gay or thought to be gay were seldom seen and rendered an invisible group entirely. However, the episode "We Love You, Miss Jessup" from the drama series *Family* (1976–1980) deals with a lesbian high school teacher who is pushed out of her career from the homophobic parent board. The teacher would befriend tomboy Buddy (Kristy McNichol) who would in turn question her own sexuality seeing that all the "signs" indicate that she might be interested in girls over boys (her love for basketball, her disinterest in pursuing the affections of the opposite sex et al). Much like Mrs. Garrett's (Charlotte Rae) advice to young tomboy Cindy (Julie Anne Haddock) in "Rough Housing" from *The Facts of Life* (1979–1988), Buddy is rest assured by her mother that she is not at all queer – yes, she is boyish, but her true feelings are heterosexual which clearly strengthens Miss Jessup's (Blair Brown) status as a woman unfairly fired from her job – of which she is excellent at. This pilot episode of *The Facts of Life* hits a similar nerve to Buddy's rethinking of her burgeoning sexuality, and offers the same assurance – lesbianism is a product of perception, and such perceptions are built from the trappings of varied stereotypical characteristics such as the love of basketball and other sports, and essentially what is learned in both TV shows is that questions of sexuality that point to queer leanings can be addressed and then quickly "cured" simply because it is the curse of the "late bloomer" in question, not a true homosexual. The trope of the late bloomer (code for someone not quite ready to relate to the opposite sex) is an oft-used character type in American television, and even in the episode "Mike's Madonna Story" from *Growing Pains* (1985–1992), Mike Seaver (Kirk Cameron) flippantly thinks he is gay because he is not quite there yet when it comes to girls, something poo-pooed quickly by his mother. However, when the subject is definite and the teenager in question is most certainly homosexual, the mood and tone of the show shifts energies and another message is driven home. Once again however, these "real" homosexual teens are seldom found in sitcoms, and find their home in television drama – for example, the gay best friend in "Rites of Friendship" from *Family* who remains isolated by the episode's end, and later come the eighties, a more devastating and bleak outcome is found for the gay kid in "Best Buddies" from *Fame* (1982–1987) who has his father downright reject him and even refer to him as a "faggot". But in the eighties (of which *The Facts of Life* would find its large appeal), the late bloomer syndrome will pop up in drama series seen with such depictions as Lance Kerwin's bookish trembling virgin whose father thinks he is gay in an episode of *Hotel* (1983–1988) – but unlike Kerwin's distressed and shy nerd, Cindy from *The Facts of Life* is offered help and it comes through the thoughtful consideration of Mrs. Garrett.

Opening with a loaded title sequence featuring all the cast members visiting from *Diff'rent Strokes* (Conrad Bain, Todd Bridges, Dana Plato and Gary Coleman), the pilot firmly establishes the lovingly warm and fun Mrs. Garrett as the den mother to a group of young girls living on campus at Eastland Private School for Girls. *The Facts of Life* would initially find its first season insanely busy with many girls featured as principle players, but by the time the second season came around, there was a major cull of characters to keep it more focused and dedicated to the development of three core teens: the fun loving journalist-in-the-making Natalie (Mindy Cohn), the eavesdropping gossip Tootie (Kim Fields) and wealthy uppity Blair (Lisa Whelchel). Streetwise hardened Jo (Nancy McKeon) would be added to the fold as a principal character come the second season, while the original group of girls would recede in importance as the series would progress – they would continue to appear, coming in and out of stories throughout the rest of the show's run, but they would essentially be dwarfed in importance to the four major players. Among such modified characters would be Cindy, a rough and tumble sports enthusiast whose streak of insecurity and sensitivity causes her to internalize attacks from the popular and showy Blair.

From her initial introduction, Cindy is different from the other girls – she wears a football jersey and her hair is tied up and concealed underneath a baseball cap, and on top of all this, her femininity is questioned straight away when she asks visiting Willis (Todd Bridges) what he's doing in an all-girl school, to which he replies "I was about to ask you the same thing!" Willis's younger brother, the wisecracking Arnold (Gary Coleman) somewhat relates to Cindy because she isn't into "all that kissing stuff", and is reassured that she is not like the other girls when she declares "I'm into sports!" before punching her baseball mitt. Arnold even describes the tomboy as "almost human" as opposed to the gooey-eyed kissy other girls, who can't resist Arnold's cherubic features (Blair being no exception). Arnold is a child, therefore girls don't interest him whatsoever, but Cindy is a teenager, and her disinterest in boys and "all that kissing stuff" is something that will alienate her and make her question her own sexuality as the show moves forward.

Never having thought of her butch nature being an issue beforehand, Cindy is forced to acknowledge her difference when Blair points it out and makes it an issue. While the girls prepare for the Harvest Festival, Cindy insists they practice for an annual tug of war competition with a rival school. She grabs hold of Blair and Blair reacts in a manner that confuses Cindy: "Would you mind not pawing me! You are strange…" Blair's use of the term "strange" is a clear reference to being called "queer" or "dyke" and this coded term is reprised moments later leaving an even more concerning impact on the troubled Cindy. While Blair mentions Greg Hockney (the off-screen hunk) and talks about how she will of course be crowned as the Eastland Harvest Queen, Cindy's self-doubt as to being "one of the girls" disturbs her. However, unlike Blair, the rest of the student body admire and love Cindy, and even champion her athletic abilities and spunk. Fellow student Sue Ann (Julie Piekarski) nominates Cindy to run against Blair for the Harvest Queen, while Molly (Molly Ringwald) proudly seconds the vote ("Cindy is the best athlete in school!") – all of this amuses Blair who remains the antagonist of the episode and who will eventually learn the errors of her ways, as it is her character who has the true lesson as delivered by the wise Mrs. Garrett.

Happy to be accepted by her peers, Cindy hugs Sue Ann and tells her that she loves her (something that doesn't phase either Sue Ann or Cindy herself) and it is met with scrutiny and taunt from the repulsed Blair. Blair moves in on Cindy and intimidates her, telling her that all of this "touching and hugging girls" and "telling girls that you love them" is strange and abnormal. Cindy is stunned by this observation and continues to protest that she never "meant it to be strange". Blair doesn't buy it and assumes boyish Cindy is gay and not to be trusted. Producer Howard Leeds – who came from the school of the Norman Lear ethos – decided early on that *The Facts of Life* would take off where *Diff'rent Strokes* would head as far as taking on various serious subject matter and placing it within a lesson-based formulaic TV sitcom. What Leeds also intended to do with the series was ensure that lessons were delivered to multiple characters, rather than staying fixed on one; and that understanding the human condition was a ripple effect, streaming out to everyone involved, rather than fixating on one sole person. One lesson taught in "Rough Housing" was a core lesson in perception and assumption, something that leads to persecution and enforces bullying and ostracizing fellow peers. In Vincente Minnelli's *Tea and Sympathy* (1956), John Kerr plays a young man who is thought to be queer and tormented by his college friends for such a thing – eventually, however, Deborah Kerr as the wife of his cold and unfeeling headmaster, finds a tenderness in him and offers to sleep with him by the end of the picture leading into a trend of films that would deal with "curing" homosexuality or possible homosexuality. In regard to girls who were "rescued" from the uncertainty of "perverse" sexuality in Golden Age cinema, one could bring up some of the roles taken by one of the most versatile actresses of a number of decades – Doris Day. Day would play two pivotal tomboys who would learn how to shed the baseball gloves and rifle and replace it with a corset and makeup in the films *On Moonlight Bay* (1951) and its sequel *By the Light of the Silvery Moon* (1953) and the Western musical classic *Calamity Jane* (1953). A woman who really only needs to learn how to be feminine, Day's progressive heroines of these three films are a precursor to young Cindy who is out of step and slow in catching up to the rest of her clique.

Defeated by her lack of self-esteem and troubled to think that she may in fact be a lesbian, Cindy turns to the advice of Mrs. Garrett and a richly written scene unfolds that jettisons the rest of the episode into play. Mrs. Garrett begins the scene "butching it up" with her fist pounding Cindy's baseball glove and this action is offered to make Cindy feel more at home. When Cindy complains that all she ever thinks about is sport, Mrs. Garrett lists some incredibly successful sportswomen to ensure Cindy doesn't feel alone. Cindy then voices her concern about not being interested in boys to which Mrs. Garrett explains that it will happen and that the "body clock" will suddenly appear – and that "part of her" will spark. Along with discussion about being confused and not understanding a solid disinterest in heterosexual pursuits, the scene involves Cindy taking off her baseball cap and unleashing long blonde hair that makes Mrs. Garrett gasp. Here, the show tips into an "ugly duckling becomes the beautiful swan" turf, but this is somehow married to the concept of unfeminine and butch girls being unappealing and unattractive to young men (and subject to ridicule to certain young women, like Blair). The final offering Mrs. Garrett has to deliver to Cindy is a response to the disturbed young girl's confusion as to why she is so affectionate to Sue Ann and the others. Mrs. Garrett firmly tells Cindy that love, compassion, tenderness, affection and all the physical attributes that showcase such feelings (hugs, kisses etc) are completely normal and welcomed. She even tells Cindy that people who can't show their emotions by expressing affection are the ones to worry about and this leads us into the Howard Leeds mandatory "true lesson learned" subplot.

As Blair shows off her stunning dress for the Harvest Festival, she is met by a clever and scheming Mrs. Garrett who insists that Blair looks so great in her new gown because she knows what men like and that she has been "around the tracks" a few times. Blair is taken aback by such remarks, but Mrs. Garrett continues to prove her point: that Blair jumped to conclusions based on appearances with Cindy, and now Mrs. Garrett does the same with Blair. Blair's lesson is learned and she apologizes to Cindy. The duo (now good friends) head off to the Harvest Festival, where Blair wins both the first place to be the queen of the festival as well as the heart of the off-camera hunk Geoff Hockney. Cindy, on the other hand, comes in second and more importantly flirted with Geoff (sharing a wink).

Cindy's supposed lesbianism is muted by "late bloomer syndrome", however the perceptions, self-reflections, questioning, shame, abuse, name calling, insensitivity and pain are very real and make this truly remarkable TV sitcom one of a kind – to open with its first ever episode tackling such subject matter is most certainly groundbreaking and a tone-setter as the show will bring up issues or race, suicide, eating disorders, rape and much more as it found its way to the hearts of teenage girls across the globe.

The pilot episode of the very topic-centric The Facts of Life *was entitled "Rough Housing", and dealt with young Cindy (Julie Anne Haddock) questioning her sexuality and being persecuted for being a tomboy.*

"Mork in Wonderland" from *Mork & Mindy*
Original Air Date: 16 September 1979
By Lee Gambin

The essence of the American situation comedy is to make its audience laugh – to provide a familiar story populated with familiar characters who will undergo certain problems or conflict in a comical manner and come out of the end of the episode either changed, learning something or solving an issue at hand all the while making the fixed and dedicated (or fleeting audience) smile. Of course, the "familiar" does not necessarily have to be grounded in realism, and a sitcom like *Mork & Mindy* (1978–1982) prided itself in being one of the most popular and successful in the realm of fantastical sitcoms well past the advent of shows such as *I Dream of Jeannie* (1965–1970) and *Mister Ed* (1958–1966) . What the show also provided was a sentimental warmth founded in its very fabric that offered a glimpse into the warm and loving hearts of its two principles: the crazy manic alien Mork (Robin Williams) and the grounded and sweet Mindy (Pam Dawber). Therefore, the science fiction embedded within the series was made all the more meaningful when the true heart of the piece was the loving depth shared by its leads. The first episode of the second season of the show was a very special one hour offering that actively comments on the importance of laughter and the power of love beyond death. Heavy topics of conversation in the kickoff for the second season of what proved to be a hit show, but ultimately had to undergo certain changes in its return to television.

"Mork in Wonderland" ends with a powerfully moving epilogue, where Mindy believes her alien friend is gone forever, but thankfully and miraculously, he returns to hold her in his arms expressing an undying love for her, making mention of never wanting to have to see her "go before he does". It is a tearful and emotionally punchy moment and this would set the mood for what would be a sitcom that went happily from zany and loony to sentimental, meaningful and deep. An actor like Robin Williams could do that beautifully – he could deliver both the necessary crazed antics as well as drop it right down and bring on the tears. The lengthy episode opens with Mork's concern about the energy crisis (something that would be on the minds of people during this period), and in a patter of a rant he makes a reference to there being more to life than *I Love Lucy*, which is an interesting aside in that it marks a comment on sitcoms of the seventies and eighties proudly displaying serious concerns outside of the pure entertainment examples of the fifties. Mork hears out Mindy, who teaches him about the ugliness of capitalism and greed as well as oil companies and corrupt politicians, and this is all a plot point that seems to disappear from obvious relevance as the show moves on, however, it sits as a backburner, to remind the audience that these grotesque attributes to the human condition can force people to become grim, unsympathetic, mean spirited and without heart.

When Mork develops signs of a cold, the caring and nurturing Mindy gives him medicine to help him, but instead the pill has an effect on him that begins to shrink him in size. Being an alien, his body cannot take the pedestrian pill, and he reacts by growing small. Mork's diminutive size emphasizes the show's fantasy elements and the camera tricks and escapades in the first half of the hour-long season opener compliment the drama of Mork shrinking into oblivion with Mindy's desperate concern and Mork's fear being the focal point. Mork even commits to a potentially last report back to Orson (Ralph James) before launching into a homage to adventure fantasy films a la the work of George Pal. Fantasy films of the fifties and sixties would clearly be an influence here, even with touches of the likes of B-movie maestro Bert I. Gordon who specialized in movies dealing with large monstrous entities taking on dwarfed people. More science fiction eschews where Mork enters another dimension and the show shifts into a politically motivated fantastical terrain. Here the alternate world is populated with multi-colored cows wearing pants hiding out alongside a community of "funnies", people who are hiding from an oppressive leader and king who has banned laughter, joy and happiness.

Mork meets mock ups of famous comedians Bob Hope, Jerry Lewis and Danny Thomas who all live on the fringes and claim to be revolutionaries rebelling against the evil king who pops up in this alternate universe as Exidor (Robert Donner) but of course as an inversion of the crazed earth bound street "prophet". Here, where these comedians live is a refuge camp for people who want to enjoy humor and laughter, and as Mork is walked through the place he sees a Steve Martin clone (complete with an "Excuuuuuuuse me"), clowns and comics. He describes it as "comedy purgatory" and is told that "the king won't let people laugh". He is taken to the head of the revolution who is Mandy (a parallel version of Mindy) and she runs the report to him that here on Mirth, the king runs a "glum party" and has outlawed humor. Mandy is serious in her mannerisms and says that she is not silly but she loves to laugh, and she has committed to the cause to fight for the right for her people to be happy. The show examines the notion that happiness and laughter are essential and it becomes the war cry for the concerned Mandy ("My people can laugh again").

Eventually Mork gets a job in the king's castle as a "Court Serious" not the conventional court jester, and he is there to deliver depressing news. He meets the king who sports a band around his arm similar to a swastika as worn by the Nazis featuring a sad face and there is once again mention of a supposed "phony energy crisis" (something that rings true to right-wing conservatives lying to the people and denying them access to what they are entitled to) and his proclamation of wanting people to be glum and miserable. When Mandy is trapped by the king, it is also learned that Mork as Court Serious had been employed as a spy, and war breaks out. In many regards the episode has a similar tone to something like the musical fantasy *Chitty Chitty Bang Bang*

(1968) where there is an oppressive outlawing of children and therefore joy plus this episode embodies incredibly chilling ideologies such as that unsettling moment in *The Sound of Music* (1965) where there is no place to celebrate a "few of my favorite things" when the Von Trapps are hiding from the Nazis. Here, on Mirth, there is no place for celebrating things that bring happiness, hiding in the dark must be accompanied by keeping quiet.

Mork and the three comedians take on the king's guards and rescue Mandy but as the war commences, Mandy is struck by a bomb and dies in Mork's arms. Her selflessness is presented in her knowing that eventually her people will be free and able to laugh again. Before she dies she says "Tell Mindy that she's really lucky", and Mork's rage makes him grow and re-enter the real world where he surprises a teary eyed Mindy who is mournfully packing up Mork's things, painfully saying goodbye. When he re-emerges and reunites, it is one of the most beautiful moments in TV history and what he says to Mindy is remarkably telling: "This may be a little selfish of me, and I know no one lives forever, but I hope I leave this life before you do, because I never want to lose you twice." The music swells and the two are reunited in love. Mork's final message to Orson reinforces togetherness and tenderness at all cost with "Love can extend beyond universes and even beyond death."

In an alternate universe, Mindy (Pam Dawber) is fronting a revolution and Mork (Robin Williams) poses as a "Court Serious", aiding in her quest. In this alternate universe, laughter and happiness has been banned, and the outcome is devastating but ultimately incredibly moving.

"The Dog Story" from *Diff'rent Strokes*
Original Air Date: 19 December 1979
By Troy Howarth

Diff'rent Strokes (1978–1986) was originally conceived under the title "45 Minutes from Harlem." As the original title suggests, the overall thesis of the show was to contrast the lifestyles of the haves versus the have-nots. The wealthy Mr. Drummond, played by *Maude* (1972–1978) veteran Conrad Bain, exists on one end of the social spectrum; at the opposite end are his adopted children Willis (Todd Bridges) and Arnold (Gary Coleman). Within the context of a generally genteel and family-friendly program, the show which became known as *Diff'rent Strokes* nevertheless managed to tackle some very heavy themes.

It has been said that the show was developed, at least in part, as a vehicle for Bain, who found himself suddenly out of work following the cancellation of *Maude* in the spring of 1978. The urbane and likable Canadian actor therefore found himself thrust for the first – and as luck would have it, the last – time when "45 Minutes from Harlem" went into production.

Good as Bain proved to be in the role of affluent and kindly Mr. Drummond, he soon found himself being upstaged by his on-screen son, Arnold, played so memorably by Gary Coleman. It was Coleman's character who really caught on with the public and his incredulous catch phrase "What you talkin' about, Willis?" soon entered into the pop culture lexicon.

The series got off to a start on 3 November 1978, and it would run for eight seasons – finally coming to an end on 7 March 1986. The first seven seasons ran on NBC, but as ratings started to sag, it made its way to ABC for what became the final season; dismal ratings ensured that it would not return for a ninth. Alas, like so many shows built around the antics of precocious children, *Diff'rent Strokes* became a victim of basic biology: the youthful characters played by Coleman, Bridges, and Dana Plato (as Drummond's biological daughter, Kimberly) couldn't stay young and fresh forever; and as anybody who has ever followed the show knows only too well, the off-screen drama surrounding the actors made it tougher and tougher for them to sell such a wholesome, family-oriented image to the public.

Nevertheless, the willingness of the show's creators to tackle weighty themes is one of the stand-out qualities of the program. It almost seems absurd in hindsight, but in the late seventies and early eighties, there was a greater willingness to get "gritty" in the context of programs such as this. These days, mainstream sitcoms tend to hew close to certain conventions; they rarely tackle anything of any real substance, and they tend to avoid delving into anything too controversial. There are exceptions, of course: the more "adult"-oriented programs will embrace the crude, the lewd, and the sexual, and they'll sometimes even delve into the murky waters of politics. But programs like *Diff'rent Strokes* were a different proposition altogether. They were pitched primarily to kids, in the hopes that their parents would also get hooked on it as well, and part of the thought process behind the show was to enlighten while also entertaining.

In much the same way that genre cinema often tackles socio-political issues in a more compelling manner than more "serious" (read: heavy-handed) fare, much the same can be said of the Very Special Episode mentality which informed shows like *Diff'rent Strokes*. Indeed, it can be argued that this was the show, above all others, which most effectively mastered this technique. The overall tone is light and frothy – instilling in the viewer a sense of ease and comfort – so that the occasional emergence of deeply unpleasant issues rooted in the real world is all the more unsettling. Some of these episodes strained harder for shock effect than others, inevitably, but by and large they were uncommonly effective at preaching a particular message while also delivering a solid half hours' worth of family-friendly entertainment.

"The Dog Story" opens with a bit of sly social satire as Kimberly proudly shows off her latest painting. She's a fan of the abstract impressionist approach, and she's made the mistake of seeking approval from Willis and her father, both of whom are firmly in the "landscape" school of art appreciation. Willis dismisses it as looking like "a bowl of spaghetti that got hit by a truck," and Mr. Drummond can't help but agree – though his paternal instincts ensure that he's still supportive of his daughter's artistic leanings while doing so. It's a throwaway scene, in a way, but it offers up a neat commentary on the struggles faced by artists. Kimberly's decision to follow her impulse and avoid the more mainstream approach of realistic painting is satisfying to her artistic sensibility, but the closed-minded response of Willis and Mr. Drummond points to the difficulties of being appreciated in a fairly conservative and conformist society. The reference to being hit by a truck also serves as a bit of foreshadowing to the action which is about to unfold. Obviously one doesn't want to make too much of it, but this little scene, like so much of what follows, is here for a reason; there was thought put into it, and it deserves to be fairly assessed as such.

From there, the narrative moves into the central theme: Arnold rushes home, proud as can be, and announces that he has just saved a stray dog from being run over in a busy street. Mr. Drummond initially scolds the boy for endangering his own life and disobeying his order to never to run out into the traffic, but he can't stay angry for long. Arnold's impulse was correct and since nobody was hurt in the process, so much the better. As the scene comes to an end, Arnold heads upstairs and begins rubbing his hand; clearly something is amiss, even if it's still unspoken.

Later that evening, Arnold lets it slip that the dog scratched his hand. Mr. Drummond looks at the mark on his hand and asks if the dog bit him. "He didn't really bite me," claims Arnold. "He just wrapped his mouth around my hand and pressed down with his teeth." Everything is played for laughs, of course, but an undercurrent of suspense is introduced as it becomes apparent that the dog bite could spell big trouble for little Arnold. Mr. Drummond takes Kimberly and Willis into his confidence and tells that that if they can't find the dog that bit him and verify whether it has received its vaccinations, Arnold will have to endure a series of 20 painful rabies injections.

Arnold, meanwhile, doesn't even have a clue what rabies is. Hence the Very Special Episode nature of the program. The very real danger posed by interacting with an unfamiliar dog is something the producers wanted their targeted audience to be aware of. In order to learn all about the disease and its effects, Arnold picks up the appropriate volume of his encyclopedia – this is pre-Google, don't forget. There's a great joke where Arnold reads what he believes to be the right entry: "Rabies... the official leader of a Jewish congregation." Willis quickly corrects him ("That's Rabbi!") and finds the appropriate entry. Not only does it sound painful, but the transmission of rabies can even cause death. It may seem absurd to think that a decent portion of the viewing audience may have been unfamiliar with such a common term, but again it pays to keep things in their proper context: the show was geared strongly towards youthful viewers, and above all this episode was designed to clue them in to the dangers in the hopes of helping them to avoid them.

The remainder of the episode focuses on the attempt to locate the dog in question – and when Willis accidentally lets it slip that if they don't find the dog, Arnold will be subjected to a series of injections, things become more complicated. Rather than endure the shots, Arnold decides to just lie and pick an arbitrary dog as the culprit. When Mr. Drummond comes back to the apartment, he brings three dog-owners with

The extremes of social message television embodied here in "The Dog Story" from Diff'rent Strokes *which discusses the valid importance of vaccinating one's dog.*

him, all of them with their furry companions in tow. One of the owners is played by the delightful James Hong – yes indeed, Lo Pan from John Carpenter's *Big Trouble in Little China* (1986) himself! – and he successfully upstages Drummond when he answers whether or not he has been vaccinated by replying, "Me, no. The dog, yes."

Arnold arbitrarily picks one of the dogs as the one that bit him and all seems to be well – and then Willis comes back with a neighbor bearing the real culprit. It turns out that she saw Arnold rescuing the dog and wanted to thank him, but he ran off before she could show her gratitude. She offers a reward, but Mr. Drummond isn't about to let Arnold off the hook for lying and volunteers to have the reward donated to the local animal shelter. Bad news for Arnold, but good news for the local strays. And a lesson learned: it never pays to lie, even if it's to save yourself from being injected 20 times. All's well that ends well, of course; there'll be no need for rabies shots, and everything is successfully and harmoniously resolved in the allotted 25 minute running time.

Ultimately "The Dog Story" may not be the hardest-hitting of the Very Special Episodes of *Diff'rent Strokes*, but it flirts with serious themes in a deft and entertaining fashion. If only the same could be said for all sitcoms.

"The Reluctant Fighter" from *Taxi*
Original Air Date: 25 December 1979
By Aaron Graham

"This changes everything – now follow me here – we all know that when a loser wants to win, naturally he loses. It's a law of the universe – Banta has proven this time and time again. But when a loser wants to lose – now pay attention, this gets real tricky – if a loser wants to lose, since he is a loser, the only way to stay a loser is to win. Ergo, Banta – the loser in question – wanting, as he does, to lose – has to win. As perverse and unnatural as this sounds: I have to bet on Banta."

So says Louie De Palma (Danny De Vito) when he learns that perennially losing middleweight Tony Banta (Tony Danza) has severe misgivings about giving it his all in a scheduled fight with Benny Foster (Armando Muniz). You see, in Banta's first press conference of his less-than-stellar boxing career, Foster wheels out the youthful Brian Sims (played by Danza's real-life son, Marc Anthony Danza). Sims is confined to a wheelchair, and as in traditional Babe Ruth fashion – "hit a homer for the young boy" – Foster has dedicated his pugilistic efforts and return to the ring to Sims. Banta is, understandably, taken aback, resigned to the possibility of throwing the fight despite it being a great opportunity for his career.

What's not explored in "The Reluctant Fighter" are the real intentions of Foster. Is it a shaky confidence ploy to take down Banta and give the aging fighter and former champion an advantage? Or, is it out of pure good will and sincerity towards the malady-laden youth? The episode doesn't delve too far into this thinking – we don't learn much about Benny, other than Elaine (Marilu Henner)'s gentle ribbing (alongside her Sunshine Cab crew) of Benny's apparent penchant for female arm-candy. ("You guys are jumping to conclusions. [The two women] could be his manager and trainer. His accountant and his lawyer. [a beat] His Tuesday and his Wednesday.")

Almost every episode of *Taxi* (1978–1983) deals with an employee of the Sunshine Cab Company attempting to escape their station in life, and "The Reluctant Fighter" is no different. Throughout the five seasons, Tony Banta is dim-witted but hard-working, never embittered. His dreams of earning a title bout or even steady career as a winner never seem curdled, despite the need to take on gainful employment as a hack in Manhattan, surely transporting the dregs of NYC nightlife (never to be warts-and-all depicted a la *Taxi Driver* (1976) on network TV, of course). It's not a glamorous existence, but *Taxi* was always more interested in the bittersweet realities and temporary hardships of day-to-day living. Yes, Tony could punch hard against Benny Foster and earn a win to help offset the career losses – but his benevolent humanity would be taking a hit.

Tony refuses, at first, to sacrifice his humanity for a chance at money and fame, but finally gives it his all, and comes out a winner. The battle at the Felt Forum (located in Madison Square Garden) is victorious for Tony. But Tony "doesn't feel like celebratin'", at least until Alex has a heart-to-heart that he should talk to the kid. Tony throws his mercy on Brian – the fight means nothing compared to the kid forgiving him.

But its towards this resolution, though, that the episode sort of cops out on the central premise: Brian Sims's personality turns out to be not unlike Addie Loggins (Tatum O'Neal) in *Paper Moon* (1973): a quick-quipping, precocious scammer who wants to know that he's pulling ahead in the deal. He smacks Tony with the ball-bearings from his wheelchair, feistily retorting (in so many words) that he "don't want a loser in his corner" after Tony suggests he could take the place of Benny. Of course, in this half-hour format, they make amends – Tony promises to visit him in the hospital and Brian can watch Tony work out at the gym. The kid grants Tony temporary mercy, and he's off the hook.

Or, at least, as Brian Sims says: "I'll stick around until ya lose one."

Most Valuable Player of the episode is Michael V. Gazzo, the gruff-voiced brute managerial type – clearly a play on Mickey from the *Rocky* films (*Rocky II* opened in the summer of 1979) – who enlists Tony with this fighting opportunity. (Never a winner, Gazzo claims Tony was sixth on his list of potential contenders against Benny.) Gazzo had recently played Harvey Keitel's fuck-up of a father in James Toback's *Fingers* (1978), with a busy seventies in film and television courtesy of his big break in *The Godfather: Part II* (1974). One last colorful note regarding "The Reluctant Fighter" and its original air date. It was due to air on October 9, 1979 – but preempted due to coverage of the US-Iran conflict. It was pushed, becoming an unintended, unexpected Christmas Day special full of heart.

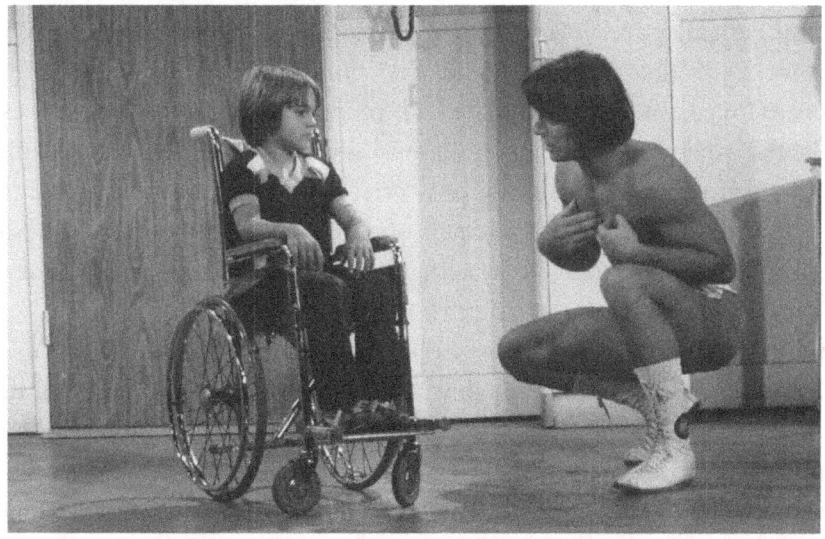

The tenderness of Tony (Tony Danza) on display in "The Reluctant Fighter" from Taxi.

"A Mommy for Mindy" from *Mork & Mindy*
Original Air Date: 3 January 1980
By Lee Gambin

On 19 September 1980, Robert Redford's landmark film *Ordinary People* opened. The picture not only shattered audiences with its power and ability to get under the skin, but it also showcased sitcom sweetheart Mary Tyler Moore's diverse acting talent, playing the cold and distant mother to Timothy Hutton, lost in perpetual grief over the death of her eldest son (Scott Doebler). Moore's character built a wall around herself, completely divorcing herself from being a loving and warm mother to the suicidal and guilt-ridden Hutton, and this complex take on grief would sometimes find itself in the world of the American sitcom. In the *Mork & Mindy* episode, "A Mommy for Mindy", the usually perky and sweet, and incredibly warm and loving Mindy (Pam Dawber), finds herself in a "cold spot" when it comes to trying to relate to her father's new wife. In many ways, Mary Tyler Moore's adorable and endearing persona on her sitcom that would be jarringly different to what she took on in the role of Beth Jarrett in *Ordinary People*, somehow acts as a foreshadowing to the beautiful Mindy, who now has to face her repressed grief – which in turn transforms her into someone that she is not comfortable being; a woman completely disengaged with a stranger who could potentially be a good friend.

Mindy gets a letter informing her that her father Fred (Conrad Janis) is coming to visit, and she also assumes that her grandmother is also coming along. Fred would be a regular character in earlier seasons, but by this point he would fill the guest spots here and there, so part of the excitement was to reteam him with Robin Williams's nutsy alien Mork and Pam Dawber's "straight man" counterpart in Mindy. Upon Fred's return, Mindy is shocked to discover that he has brought along his new wife Cathy (Shelley Fabares), introduced as someone that he had "married yesterday". Mindy doesn't know how to take the news and from this moment onward (post-jokey talk about "playing tennis on Ork") the episode examines how grief is not a fleeting thing and that many people find it hard to let go after the death of a loved one. The writers use Mindy as a vessel for people who have had loss as a lingering foreign memory that sometimes hits hard and hits home when forced to face change and moving on.

Fred makes bold statements throughout the episode such as "Think of Cathy as part of the family", which understandably Mindy finds hard to swallow. On top of this, Mindy has to explain the role of a "stepmother" to Mork, something that he finds difficult to understand. The writing also treads that fine line between progress and being insensitive, with Fred wanting to push Mindy and Cathy's relationship, but also not understanding that it has always been hard for Mindy to accept her mother's passing.

In the episode's most telling moment, Mindy prepares for bed and still has to persist in educating Mork about stepmothers as opposed to real mothers. When she goes to sleep, she dreams of being a little girl (Melissa Francis) back in her childhood home in Boulder, where her father is disheveled and under great stress, having to face the harsh reality of telling his little girl that her mother has died. He explains that her mother has been sick for a long time and that "the angels took her to heaven". Not fully understanding, little Mindy sits in her mother's chair to wait for her return from heaven and here the sad truth about death and how children react to news of a parent's death crashes into the sitcom sphere, and tugs at heartstrings. Mindy calls out that she wants her mother ("I want my mommy!"), and we come back to present Boulder, where Mindy is calling out in her sleep, waking Mork who races in to comfort her.

Part of his consoling includes Mork's naivety – he doesn't understand why Mindy isn't happy that she has an option to have a new bond with another woman who could be a mother figure. But Mindy educates him in concerns of the heart. She explains to him the role of fathers and the role of daughters and the love shared between fathers and daughters. Mork comes to a pure understanding of the complexities of love and that love can come in many forms and that it is truly possible to love more than one person. Mork's own longing for a mother becomes another factor in the show, and that is something that is summarized in the final moment of the episode where Mindy shares a hug with Cathy ("Just like a real mom").

The centerpiece of the episode has Mindy and her father in their old home, sharing a straight conversation (only tipping into joke-ville when Mork is mentioned), mostly discussing the fact that Mindy felt left in the dark with her father not ever telling her that he was getting re-married. Mindy expresses her need for some time to mourn, which in turn leads Fred to confess that he has never forgotten her mother. His confession is heartfelt and moving, as he expresses how he loved her mother so much, using repression to deal with his grief (once again, much like the pent-up Mary Tyler Moore in *Ordinary People*). As the episode comes to its third act, Mindy discovers that she needs to hear about her mother from Fred in order to cope with her personal grief, and at the same time she continually makes mention that she wishes her father to be happy (to be a husband again). But all of this wonderfully written conversation comes to a crashing halt when Cathy goes to sit in Mindy's mother's old chair. Mindy reacts in an instant: "Don't sit there!" She races out, which Mork reads it as a "signal for help".

Mork uses Orkan psychology to get into the mind of Mindy, and he gets her to talk about her mother – something that she possibly hasn't done for a long time. Eventually what emerges is that Mindy may have a fear of losing another mother. With hugging being a therapeutic method, when Mindy and Cathy finally hug and come to a treaty, all becomes right in the world and a sense of clarity and unity develops. Cathy also shuts down Fred's urgency in stressing that she and Mindy get along and also rejects being forced to be "Mindy's mother". Instead, Cathy offers friendship, which Mindy respects and accepts. With the signature ending having Mork reporting back to his authoritarian Orkan, Orson, he delves into the grand tradition of humans clinging to memories, that memories are untouchable and precious, and that sometimes these bizarre creatures known as humans can have one loving memory without giving up another.

Personal despair becomes a common trope on Mork & Mindy. *Here in "A Mommy for Mindy", Mindy (Pam Dawber) must face the fact that her widowed father has to move on.*

"The Night They Raided Mind-ski's" from *Mork & Mindy*
Original Air Date: 10 January 1980
By Lee Gambin

With a title parodying the Norman Lear produced musical *The Night They Raided Minsky's* (1968), which told the story of an Amish girl who breaks free from her strict background in order to be in the entertainment industry, this Very Special Episode of *Mork & Mindy* (1978–1982) is one of the most clear and direct message shows aimed at tacking bigotry and the ugliness of racism. Something close to the producers and writers hearts, the concept of universal love is something that *Mork & Mindy* truly values and uses throughout each season, be it understanding and compassion for animals, for children, for the poor, for the elderly, for people with disabilities and more – this sitcom about an alien who is learning about humanity through his experience and via the loving guidance of a young working class woman in Boulder, Colorado, exudes a multitude of valuable lessons and this particular VSE is noteworthy in its power to illustrate the dangers of permissive racism by being frank and open, without any hesitation.

The episode opens with young WASP Nelson Flavor (Jim Staahl) wishing to run for city council. Here is a character who is related to the good hearted, spirited and earthy lovely Mindy (Pam Dawber), but completely different in many ways. He is officious, rigid, uptight and rather conservative as opposed to Mindy's sentimental and all-hearted nature, and although Nelson is ultimately a "good guy", he is obnoxious and tricky. Sporting his "Win With Flavor" pin, Nelson is determined to win over the city and be a leading force in their political movements. Mork (Robin Williams) enters the scene in his campaign hat complete with bullhorn, and it is clear that he is "working" for Nelson, but the blonde haired, blue eyed candidate is perplexed by the fact that no one knows who he is; therefore, he needs exposure and in order to do that he needs organized groups of people to promote him. After hearing about a campaign group that is there to "clean up Boulder", Nelson assumes that they are an environmental group that is planning to tackle the city's pollution and littering issues, so he sees that as a perfect opportunity to work alongside them. He asks Mindy to meet with them for him, but she can't because she is busy, so Mork puts his hand up and agrees.

The first time we see the members of the "clean up Boulder" group, we notice them all wearing arm bands with "Pure Power" written on them. These bandages are reminiscent of the Nazis wearing their swastikas, and when we hear the leader of the group announce "We're a white bread group", we clearly understand that "cleaning up Boulder" means cleaning up the ethnic diversity that makes the city so rich in culture and beauty, and that this terrifying committee are interested in keeping everything Anglo-Saxon. Mork, of course, is innocent to racism and does not understand the undertones of the meeting, and when the members don their hoods and cloaks (akin to the KKK), Mork is thrilled because he thinks it's a costume party and asks for a Frankenstein mask. The head of the group snarls at him: "There are no Steins allowed in here!" spouting anti-Jewish sentiment, while the studio audience laughs because the joke is on poor old Mork who doesn't understand such hatred and bigotry. However, he will. And the same audience will cheer with great gusto as the episode comes into its third act with Mork avenging what happens to his friend Mindy, which is truly a shocking television spectacle.

When Mork invites the members of the group to come and visit at Mindy's apartment, the realization that the group is not at all about environmentalism comes with a heavy and clear hand. When Nelson eagerly wishes to find out how he can help with their campaign, he finds out what their first goal is: "We oughta starts with the Spics", says the leader, insisting that Latino persons in Boulder should be the first to be sent on their way – a frightening extension of what Hitler's regime essentially carried, the eradication of races that were deemed impure. This statement which crashes through the senses, sends Mindy and Nelson in a spitting frenzy, coughing up their coffee in total shock. Another committee member suggests that after the "Spics" are taken care of, they should move their attention to "The nips, gooks and Deigo breaths" – an absolute hatred and disdain for Japanese citizens, Vietnamese people and people from Italian and other Mediterranean backgrounds. Mindy is outraged, she will not stand for any more insulting garbage and she proudly declares her Polish heritage which in turn sends the racist group into a spitting frenzy themselves. Mindy kicks them out, absolutely disgusted by the racism and hatred, and because her beliefs are so strong she even snaps at Mork who insists that they're his "friends". She asks him to leave as well, seeing that he sides with them (innocently of course), and he leaves with a Polish gag "I'll pick you up a Polish sick pack… four beers!"

This Polish gag leads into the middle section of the episode which is the most interesting and complex of what this particular piece does – it dissects the essence of what is permissible and passive racism and also how the "just a joke" culture can unfortunately lead into absolute horror and abhorrence. Writers for centuries have written racially driven comedy, and in many regards, a show like *Mork & Mindy* is a perfect example of a timeless tradition of melting pot humor, as well as a very broad modern extension of turn of the century vaudeville, which was an institution and clear American art form born from the immigrant experience. Irish, Jew, Italian, Polish, black, Hispanic jokes, as well as stock characters in and outside of race (outside being such examples as the whore with the heart of gold, the loveable drunk, the sissy et al) have been part of the culture since the dawn of American theatre and performance, and therefore they move through the decades in varied constructs, and what Mindy discusses and explains to Mork is that sometimes these jokes made outside of a performative space (i.e. just in public), can be hurtful and nothing less than a slur.

Opening with Mindy and Jeannie (Gina Hecht) talking, the scene establishes the fact that Boulder is generally an inclusive and supportive town, the two women are shocked that there are hate groups in such a halcyon environment, and then when the conversation shifts to racially driven jokes, the politics of this VSE are made clear: sometimes gags can be out of context and just come across as an attack on a group that is "different". Mork bursts into the scene with a series of running race jokes – Italian, Irish, Polish, black etc, and yes, they are silly and yet funny, simply because he is coming from a long tradition of vaudeville where jokes about ethnic minorities drew people together and actually built a community.

However, here, in this context, when he spiels them out without the required "stage", they irritate Mindy, and she simply stops him in his tracks and asks: "Do you know what bigotry is?" This is a confronting moment in the episode, because we, much like the studio audience, are forced to understand the difference between the solidarity that was born from the sense of humor of many artists who built communities through their jokes (Robin Williams being one of those people, who would regularly coincide with Jewish comedians such as Billy Crystal, and black comedians like Whoopi Goldberg etc), with people who throw gags around as direct attacks on people based on race and creed simply to make themselves feel superior.

Mindy explains to Mork, "Here on earth we're all supposed to be equal", something that Mork comes to understand (and has before in an earlier episode "Hold That Mork" where he learns about sexual discrimination), and Mindy also attacks the racists by calling them out: "They're a bunch of sick, stupid creeps who can do harm!" She even drives the conversation home with her hard hitting point about the Germans "joking" about Jews, which makes Mork think and become introspective. It is an incredibly bold moment in the episode; a testament to the complexities of humor. Comedy is always going to be confronting and there to lampoon varied groups of people, but what this episode of *Mork & Mindy* does is put into a constructive reasoning, which Mindy sums up perfectly. It is not about some kind of politically correct culture where a long history and tradition of inclusive jokes built an institution (such as American vaudeville and then the American legit theatre), it is saying that some people are about universal experience and togetherness, and some are just horrendous bigots.

Mindy's educating Mork on the horrors of racism leads into the next sequence, which is super dark and chilling. Mindy and Mork return to the apartment and find it trashed. Distraught and terrified, Mindy is a shattered mess when she is forced to look upon the horrifying image of a dummy hanging by a noose from the shaft of her attic, wearing her floral hippy dress that she had worn when she met the racists, donning a "Go home Polack" sign around its neck. Frightened and held by the now reformed and "educated" Mork, Mindy feels defeated, but this only fuels Mork's absolute rage. In the final act of the episode, Mork returns to the meeting place of the racist group and announces "You want pure power, I'll show you pure power", and by using his Orkian telekinesis, destroys the headquarters, smashing it up, and burning the images of the three heads of the committee. In what is a great feat of special effects for the show, and a nice showcase of Orkian psychic powers, the moment is akin to the climactic moments in Brian De Palma's *Carrie* (1976), where the tortured teen destroys her prom and kills her tormentors – the oppressed reclaiming the night. However, much like De Palma's horror film, violence brings downfall, and the "clean up Boulder" group enter in their hoods, unleashing chains and ready to attack. But unlike *Carrie*, our heroes Mork and Mindy don't succumb to their own act of vengeance, instead, Mork sets a spell and in turn "teaches" the racists a valuable lesson. He reprograms their genes so that when they remove their hoods they are no longer Anglo-Saxon, instead they are Italian, Jewish, Irish, black, Latino, Asian, Indian and some are even orange, green and with stripes. In this terrific visual, these bigots have turned into what they fear the most: Americans. Mork summarizes this critical point with "Welcome to America!" as he and Mindy leave triumphant. Mork and Mindy for the win, bigots and racists be gone.

"Mork Learns to See" from *Mork & Mindy*
Original Air Date: 17 January 1980
By Lee Gambin

There is something remarkably moving about *Mork & Mindy* (1978–1982) – however it may be considered quite tricky as to pinpoint what exactly it is or where it comes from. Is it because the show is somewhat a celebration of personal differences and the wonders of innocence, as we see the world fresh through the eyes of Mork (Robin Williams) who is new to earth? Or is it because the heart of each story and the essence of each character is so rich in sincerity and devotion to one another? Mindy (Pam Dawber) is in essence understanding, generous, loyal and completely non-judgmental, and then countering this are the people that populate the show who aren't as compassionate as her, with the perpetually manic but also easily affected Mork sitting somewhere in the middle, who even through his insanity and wild eyed lunatic antics, is learning, and trying to make sense of it all. Ultimately, Mork is "learning to see" the world through the eyes of the people he encounters and as much as he is guided by the loving Mindy, he is also perplexed by the rest of the world that may not be completely clear in their motives. One such character is Mr. Bickley (Tom Poston) who we learn in the Very Special Episode "Mork Learns to See" has an estranged musician son – who is blind.

With the episode opening with Mork being homesick, the story quickly establishes itself as one being invested in the concept of character displacement. Mork misses his home planet of Ork, and Mindy does her best to make him feel better by offering optimistic advice with "Life can be beautiful anywhere if you just give it a chance." Here she is telling her alien friend that beauty can be found anywhere, not just on planet Ork, but also in Boulder, Colorado on a hike out in the fields. In his own special way, Mork tells her that she sees life through rose tinted glasses, and the show starts to express an interest in how people view the world. This is met with a visit from cantankerous neighbor Mr. Bickley who asks Mork and Mindy to meet up with his son Tom (Tom Sullivan) because he will be "working". Mindy claims to have never known Mr. Bickley to have a son and assumes that because he does that he mustn't be all that bad, having to be a parent and having to nurture someone else other than himself ("Bickley does have a nice side!"). Mindy's observation is an extension of her hope in humanity – even stemming from the agro and mostly cold Mr. Bickley.

When Mork and Mindy visit Tom, he is introduced reading a brail book in darkness. He is set up as a character with a great sense of humor where he throws a gag about wishing that there were a brail edition of Playboy magazine. But his humor shields secret pain, and most of that comes from his estrangement from his father, who is intentionally avoiding his son. Mr. Bickley never told Mork and Mindy that Tom was blind and as it surprises the duo, it also sets up a long series of jokes where Mork's inexperience with blind people serves as the basis. Tom explains that he is a musician and will be performing which excites Mork and Mindy, however Mr. Bickley is an obvious no-show, which seems to be a constant reoccurrence because he is someone who is guilt ridden because of his son's disability. The episode explores themes of self-shame more than anything else. It does not bring blindness into the frontier of how prejudices can hurt and destroy lives, but instead paints a picture of how parents of children with disabilities feel blame and depressive responsibility for their offspring's misfortune. Mr. Bickley's detachment from his son is a response to his sadness and when he hears himself say "Please don't send me away", it triggers a memory that sends the troubled man into a monologue that capitalizes on the backstory of Tom and how he had to be sent to a special school that helped the blind.

However, later in the episode, Tom describes his father as someone who "always seemed to have time to play with me" and sheds light on Mr. Bickley's endearing past – a time in his life where he was caring, loving and tender; something that Mindy wished to see and finally does get to experience. While Tom and his father reunite, it is Mork who begins to understand the blind musician's plight and feelings. In a montage sequence, Tom guides a blindfolded Mork through the park so the openhearted alien gets a sense of what "Tom sees". Accompanied by a Tom Sullivan number "Get High on Life", the sequence is a celebration of understanding the world from a different perspective and not from a place of disability. Lyrics in the song call out to "let your senses run" and Mork begins to understand the other senses outside of sight. He also takes into consideration the fact that Tom has been without his father for many years and is tired of being brushed off ("I think your father's the one with the handicap") and when he and Mindy finally convince Mr. Bickley to see his son perform, there is a tearful reunion set to Tom Sullivan's moving and emotionally rousing song "Beauty is in the Eyes of the Beholder".

In an episode that takes on multiple issues and delivers a number of varied lessons, "Mork Learns To See" closes with Mork's report to Orson (Ralph James) which has him explain that he had "met a man with no eyes who saw beauty everywhere…" This summarizes one of the focal points in the episode; that life is for living and that experiences – similar or displaced – can be a thing of wonderment and beauty. Mork's reports back to Orson are in many ways a Public Service Announcement without the matter-of-factness attached and instead more so an emotional reaction to theme, topic and subject matter. If you consider the tear jerk coda for "Dr. Morkenstein" where Mork cries to Orson discussing death and the repercussions of death, there is a lot going on in these nicely crafted episodes from one of the most successful of the fantastical entries in sitcoms of the seventies and eighties. "Mork Learns to See" is a pure example of how sitcoms can take a topic like blindness and drive it in varied directions with thematically complex issues to dissect.

Blind guest inclusions who come into contact with principal players provide an insight into a world that these regular fixed characters can never truly comprehend, however sympathetic and loving they are. But thankfully, some sitcoms deliver very human visually impaired characters rather than martyrs as seen in "Heather's Tutor" from *Mr. Belvedere* (1985–1990), where a young teen French tutor is still as horny and as "normal" as his able-bodied peers and in "For Your Eyes Only" from *ALF* (1986–1990), the blind woman who befriends the alien from Melmac is complicated and self-deprecating. Tom Sullivan here in this episode of *Mork & Mindy* is another richly written human being – funny and charming, not to mention incredibly talented, but also sensitive and not ashamed to get angry and frustrated.

Actor Tom Sullivan also guest starred in an episode of *M*A*S*H* (1972–1983) called "Out of Sight, Out of Mind" where Hawkeye (Alan Alda) suddenly goes temporarily blind, offering the distraught captain some solace while he recovers. The multi-talented Sullivan co-wrote the film *If You Could See What I Hear* (1982) which was an autobiographical film starring Marc Singer as Sullivan, he would become a major motivational speaker and activist and his performance in *Mork & Mindy* proves that he is a character that represents a multitude of humanity. In response to the two principals, he is everything Mindy embodies: compassion, kindness and unity and everything Mork will come to understand as decent, gentle and honorable.

Tom Sullivan guest stars in "Mork Learns to See" from Mork & Mindy, *teaching a valuable lesson in the plight of people living with visual impairments.*

"Why Did the Fireman…" from *Laverne & Shirley*
Original Air Date: 4 February 1980
By Amanda Reyes

Laverne DeFazio and Shirley Feeney were originally introduced on the wildly popular sitcom *Happy Days* (1974–1984) in the season three episode "A Date with Fonzie". As Cindy Williams said, the characters looked like they "dated the fleet," and Fonzie even politely refers to the duo as "more boisterous than I usually like." Richie thought they were edgy because Laverne drove without insurance (and beat up Shirley!). They easily stole the show with their hip swinging, easy action ways and soon got a chance to carry a series in 1976 when they were given their own spinoff.

Williams and her co-star Penny Marshall had been writing partners in the years leading up to working together as actors, and their chemistry was *off the charts*. While they lost the trampy innuendo from that *Happy Days* episode (well, Shirley did, Laverne remained a bit aggressive, but in a more innocent way), they played off each other perfectly as best buds in working class 1950s Milwaukee. Focusing on broad physical comedy and wild, cartoonish adventures, *Laverne & Shirley* (1976–1983) became an iconic series, navigating its way through the small screen landscape known as ABC Tuesdays back in the late 1970s (where they stayed for the first three seasons, and then returned in 1980 after a few months of ratings woes). If you don't remember, ABC's late seventies Tuesday night lineup was seminal. During this comedy heyday, the schedule looked a lot like this (with some variations depending on the season, mostly in the 9:30 p.m. slot):

8 p.m.: *Happy Days*
8:30 p.m.: *Laverne & Shirley*
9 p.m.: *Three's Company*
9:30 p.m.: *Taxi*

And, it was not unusual to see *Laverne & Shirley* hanging out around the top of the Nielsens, often scoring higher ratings than *Happy Days*, reaching nearly 30 million households a week! It was hijinks galore, and as the show expanded its physical humor shenanigans it grew not just in popularity but the series also nurtured a devoted fanbase (i.e. me). To its credit (and frankly to the credit of all of ABC's Tuesday night lineup during this period), the humor remains wildly relatable and laugh out loud funny.

That's not to say all of America was in love with the put upon working class duo, as noted by a really stuffy critic for the *Miami News* named Bill von Mauer. I don't mean to pick on this writer exclusively, but he obviously overlooked the components that made the show work. One of which was placing two strong women in leading roles, allowing them to exercise their enormous gift for comedy among a fairly male dominated lineup of funnymen, er, people.

von Mauer wrote that he "worried about America," and felt this show only spoke to "the male viewer with a beer can in one hand and a cigar in the other who sits in front of the tube in his undershirt. By his side is his female counterpart, the woman who still has her apron on, hasn't done her hair for a week and throws back her beer right from the can the way her husband does."

It's such a strange statement, considering how several sitcoms from the seventies dealt with the lower classes of America, and still appealed to a fairly diverse – and large – audience. And, as a non-beer guzzling pre-teen during this era, I personally felt the show spoke to females living through the second wave feminist movement. Women who felt trapped in an enduring but stifling 1950s ideology, but who were beginning to feel that they had the power to exercise their options. If they hadn't, Shirley would have married Carmine and we would not have enjoyed a long running series.

Perhaps it is also worth noting that *Laverne & Shirley* ran during the same era as the iconic female-driven detective series *Charlie's Angels* (1976–1981). Young women were growing up in a world where they believed they could be either Kelly Garrett or Laverne DeFazio – or both, if they so chose. None of which would be a bad thing.

But, even without the cultural critique, the fact still remains that *Laverne & Shirley* are oh-so relatable as flawed but good people who want the best for themselves. No amount of pratfalling is going to break them up, and like so many twenty-somethings from any era who are experiencing living as an adult for the first time, they found family with each other. And that's what keeps drawing us back to Milwaukee and, eventually to Los Angeles, where the series hit a couple of bumps, but still managed to spin gold when it could.

And, being a female fronted series, *Laverne & Shirley* was allowed to *go there* emotionally, which was an avenue that *Happy Days* didn't always have the luxury of exploring with its more male fronted cast. The series is brimming with bittersweet moments, such as the season three episode "The Debutante Ball", where Lenny finds out he's a nobleman of some-such place in Poland, so he invites Laverne to be his date at a party commemorating his family. The episode features the signature guffaws and nose-diving, but, the second Laverne goes headfirst down that walkway, all the hearts of America dropped to their knees. The pained expression of humiliation on Laverne's face is one we all recognize because we've been there. Her redemption comes from owing the mistake and facing the rich and powerful with her chin held high. She ends up unintentionally wooing a duke for her bravery. In the season two episode "Look Before You Leap", Laverne goes to a party and gets so smashed that she can't remember the events of the evening. She comes to believe she may be pregnant. Worried about what her father will think, Mr. DeFazio comes to Laverne's aid to comfort and support her, despite what the rest of the world may think of her situation and potential "bad girl" reputation.

But, perhaps the most moving Laverne-centric episode of the series entire run is season five's "Why Did the Fireman…" Laverne meets a gorgeous fireman named

Randy Carpenter (Ted Danson), and the two fall hard and fast, leaving Carmine and Shirley flustered by their intense passion. After two months pass with their feelings intensifying, Randy decides he's going to ask Laverne to be his bride. Unfortunately, right before he can pop the question, a fire breaks out, and he dies while saving a family from the burning building. Lenny and Squiggy try to break the news to Laverne but she's decided that as long as she refuses to believe he's gone, it can't be true, and he'll show up on her doorstep.

The first half of the episode plays like any episode of the series. There are plenty of genuinely funny moments, and the romance between Laverne and Randy burns bright, eliciting smiles. Months pass through this segment and the transition is smooth. It just looks like another day in Milwaukee. But Randy's death comes on as serious as a heart attack. Lenny and Squiggy have never been more sober, and the air is thick with melancholy for the rest of the episode. There are a few more jokes, but very little laughter, either canned or from a studio audience, can be heard in the last half.

Laverne's refusal to accept Randy's death makes viewing uncomfortable, because we know she'll have to come to terms with his passing and we're just not sure what that will look like. But, much like Mr. DeFazio did in "Look Before You Leap", he rushes to his daughter's side, walking her slowly towards the tragic reality of the situation. It's one of the few times the series addresses the death of Laverne's mother, and it's used here to bitterly remind the father that grief never completely goes away, *but you can move on.*

Ted Danson guest stars as the potential life partner for the eternally single Laverne in the tear-jerker "Why Did the Fireman...?" from Laverne & Shirley.

With a few exceptions, sitcoms featuring the death of a character we come to know, even if only briefly, are rare beasts indeed. It's not really fruitful ground for the structure of a lighthearted comedy, but when it's addressed in such a way, it can be a real moment of catharsis for the audience. For anyone who's ever lost a loved one, or if a certain dream perished in tragedy, we can empathize with what Laverne is going through. *And my God, it's Laverne!* A character that's never deserved such circumstances. Life is unfair even on network television. But, and it can seem difficult to understand if you haven't been there, community can be built on grief, and with thirty million viewers watching, maybe we can feel less alone, knowing someone else has been touched by the unthinkable.

It's moments like that, and which while never quite as somber in other episodes of *Laverne & Shirley*, are still affecting in the way it brings us together in TV Land, sharing something that we're often forced to push down or repress. Maybe for that moment, the same moment when, at the end of the episode, Laverne is able to move on, we feel we can too. And like Laverne, we may fall over a couple of more times, but there's no stopping us.

"In Concert" from *WKRP in Cincinnati*
Original Air Date: 11 February 1980
By Steven T. Boltz

"As God is my witness, I thought turkeys could fly."

Mention *WKRP in Cincinnati* (1978–1982) to anyone with even a passing familiarity, and this is most likely the line that gets thrown back at you. From the episode "Turkeys Away", where Station Manager Arthur Carlson (Gordon Jump), feeling left out of the actual managing of the station, sets up a super-secret Thanksgiving Day promotion, "the greatest promotion idea of all time," entrusting the details only to Sales Manager Herb Tarlek (Frank Bonner), and leaving everyone else at the station in the dark.

Carlson's promotion consists of nothing more than tossing live turkeys out of a helicopter from 2000 feet in the air. WKRP news anchor Les Nessman (Richard Sanders) covers the event from the ground in explicit detail ("They're hitting the ground like sacks of wet cement!") as the horror escalates, recalling Herbert Morrison's coverage of the Hindenburg disaster.

In the episode's tag, Carlson and Tarlek return to the station, errant turkey feathers in their hair and clothes. Beaten and quite honestly bewildered, the line above, Carlson's only defense.

"Turkeys Away" is *WKRP* at its comedic best, second only (maybe) to "Fish Story". Which is a shame, really, considering it's the seventh episode of the first season. Not a great place to peak for a series that would run for another 83 episodes over the next four years.

But comedy wasn't *WKRP*'s only strength. For every "Turkeys Away" or "Fish Story" ("I'm a giant carp, Andy!"), there's a "Les on a Ledge" (Nessman climbs out a window of the WKRP building and threatens to jump after an athlete accuses him of being gay) or "A Family Affair" (Program Director Andy Travis (Gary Sandy) overcompensates to prove he's not racist after getting angry at night time DJ Venus Flytrap (Tim Reid) for going out with his sister). There are times when it seems that *WKRP in Cincinnati* sees itself as more of a drama with *comedic flair*. And sometimes it loses itself in the drama altogether, as in the second season episode "In Concert".

On December 3, 1979, The Who's world tour brought them to Cincinnati to play at Riverfront Coliseum. Almost 20,000 tickets were sold for the event, and over three-quarters of those were for festival seating, or general admission. Meaning, over 15,000 people were vying for seats on a first-come-first-served basis.

Thousands of people packed themselves up to the entrance and, when the doors were finally opened on the west side of the Coliseum, rushed the gates, crushing people in the front few rows. Eleven people died of "compressive asphyxia" and 23 others were injured.

Hugh Wilson, producer and co-creator of *WKRP in Cincinnati*, rejected the premise of an episode based around the tragedy, but relented when writers pointed out that a show about rock 'n' roll that was set in Cincinnati couldn't *not* address the incident.

The first half of the episode is standard sitcom fare, and classic *WKRP*, opening with DJ Dr. Johnny Fever (Howard Hesseman) giving away tickets to the "big concert" that night. To win, callers must complete the sentence "Disco is _____" correctly (or at least to Dr. Fever's satisfaction), and after answers like *fun* and *heaven*, a caller suggests that disco is, in fact, Hell, and wins the tickets. This segues into Johnny's desperate search to find a date for the show, culminating in his going with Mr. Carlson himself. Carlson, having been directed by his wife to take their son, has so stressed himself out over going to a rock concert (which he insists on calling an orchestra) that he's made himself ill. WKRP's legendary receptionist, Jennifer Marlowe (Loni Anderson), has him wear a "European Aqua-Pack" over his face to help alleviate some of the stress, and this leads to several comedic exchanges, including Carlson actually forgetting he's wearing the mask as he and Johnny leave for the show. Johnny calls the "disco bondage headgear" to his attention and Carlson removes it, saying, "Alright, how's that?" Johnny looks him up and down apprising Carlson's business attire, overcoat, and Trilby hat, and says, "Great. Just great. Now it looks like I'm going to see The Who in the company of a narc." At 13 minutes, 39 seconds, this is the first mention of the band.

This would have been a hugely effective reveal when the show first aired in February of 1980, a mere 11 weeks after the disaster. After multiple mentions of "the big concert" and "the show" by various characters, naming The Who in relation to a concert in Cincinnati would have been like dropping a bomb.

The show returns from commercial break and, in somewhat of a jarring transition, it's the next day, after the concert. Contrasting the pre-concert excitement with the post-concert despondence, while skipping the concert altogether, is a bold narrative move. But it was the correct one. The compassionate one.

We find most of the cast sitting around dejectedly in the bullpen, while Johnny paces, agitated, around the room. "I don't know, man, I just can't believe it," he says. "I mean, eleven kids lose their lives. For what?" Which is when Herb pipes up.

Herb: What do you expect at these things?
Venus: What the hell does that mean, man? You ever been to a concert?
Herb: No, sir. But you're going to get this when you got a lot of teenagers
crowded together and worked up by a lot of loud rock music.

This is victim-blaming, pure and simple, but the fact that it's coming from Herb, he of the obnoxiously-patterned suits and personality to match, he of the white leather belt-and-shoe combo, it seems less harsh than it might coming from Mr. Carlson, for example. Herb is sometimes abrasive, but by this point in the series (nearly halfway through its 90 episode run), we know his personality and why he is the way he is. We may not forgive his flippant attitude toward the death of eleven young people, but we can understand it.

But then Les points out that this happened before the concert even started, taking any weight – if there was any to begin with – out of Herb's argument.

Mr. Carlson enters, cheerful and robust, having no idea what transpired the night before. He had a great time at the concert. This, too, is tragic, because Carlson is not a fan of rock 'n' roll, but sees the economic advantages it has over the "supermarket music" WKRP used to play. This could be a turning point for him, and it's marred by tragedy as Andy and the team break the news. This further exposition is as important to Mr. Carlson as it is to the viewer. If anyone at the time missed the bombshell reveal that "the big concert" was The Who's 1979 Cincinnati show, the audiences of ten, twenty, thirty, and now forty years later would've had no hope.

> Les: It happened before the concert started, Mr. Carlson. There was this large crowd outside the Coliseum. They'd been waiting there for hours and hours. It was very cold.
> Johnny: Somebody inside decided to open some doors…
> Andy: There was *some* reserved seating…
> Venus: Mostly general admission. It's what they call 'Festival Seating'.
> Johnny: It's what they call a stampede.
> Les: And that's what happened.

It's clear by this point that Festival Seating, and not the concert-goers or the band, is being targeted. Andy mentions a show in Atlanta where the same thing happened, luckily with no loss of lives. "It's that damn general admission seating," Venus says.

Carlson, sick to his stomach, leaves the bullpen, followed by Jennifer. Les mentions a candlelight vigil being held that evening and suggests they all go. Johnny says they should meet at Snookie's, their local bar, where he, Venus, and Herb are headed for drinks, and the scene ends in a lovely exchange between Les and fellow reporter Bailey Quarters (Jan Smithers), who hasn't said a word since the scene started. Les reminds her that they're newsmen ("I mean, uh, 'newspersons.'"), and that they've got a very important story to cover. Bailey, sad, angry, and confused, says she doesn't think she can handle this story. And Les, who was adamantly against Bailey joining the news team in the first place, tells her that he needs her. "You were at the concert, and I wasn't." He suggests they work together. "It'll be just like Holmes and Watson. No, or um… No, I mean, uh, Woodward and Bernsteen… Bernstein… Bernstein and, uh, Barbara Walters!" This generates the first laugh in five minutes. Amazing, in a medium where "a laugh every thirty seconds" is the rule. He helps her on with her coat, and they hug. Another huge moment for these characters.

The episode ends with Venus playing a gentle jazz number (Bill Evans' "Remembering the Rain") as Mr. Carlson enters the booth. Carlson feels guilty; his station promoted the event, he was there. And what hurts him most is that there's nothing that can be done about it. Venus says what's important is that they see that it doesn't happen again. Carlson says there's been some talk about setting up a commission to investigate what happened. "It's not going to be just talk, this town's going to do it. This is a good town, Venus. We're responsible people here."

In fact, on December 27, 1979, the city of Cincinnati imposed a ban on general admission seating. With a few minor exceptions (including a Bruce Springsteen concert in 2002), the ban held for 25 years. It was repealed in 2004 in an effort to attract more big name acts to the area. This move was met with some criticism despite the city mandating "nine square feet per person" at the venue, and the number of tickets sold for each show adjusted accordingly.

"In Concert" remains one of the most memorable episodes of *WKRP* (if not for the reasons one usually remembers a sitcom). Though controversial, it is one of several groundbreaking episodes of a show that, while a comedy first and foremost, was always willing to go beyond mere entertainment.

"Dieting" from *The Facts of Life*
Original Air Date: 21 March 1980
By Lee Gambin

Anorexia and bulimia are quite clearly obvious major issues concerning teenage girls – the need to stay thin and beautiful in a world that praises and worships such heavenly bodies is something that the Very Special Episode phenomenon has examined, most notably in episodes such as "Shape Up" from *Full House* (1987–1995). However, here in "Dieting" from *The Facts of Life* (1979–1988), it is the concern of the unhealthy crash diet trend that is the focal point of conversation and the reasoning behind why one of the girls from Eastland falls victim to such a trap. Yes, the images of gorgeous models play a factor, but more importantly here, young Sue Ann (Julie Piekarski) wants to be the object of desire for a teenage boy (who she never has met or even gets to meet) who is from a world where the body beautiful is the norm.

Eating disorders were still relatively new to cultural understanding during this period of the early eighties, however, with superstar artists such as Karen Carpenter giving a face and voice to such diseases, the image and the effects of starving oneself became a subject explored on various talk shows and current affair programs to come. Karen Carpenter's eating disorder brought such matters into the limelight, as much as Rock Hudson's AIDS diagnosis did for that dreaded immune deficiency disease, and the factors that lead to eating disorders and crash diets – peer pressure, self-worth, self-loathing, body issues, body-dysmorphia and so forth – became a story launch pad for dramatic works to spring off, including the situation comedies that felt the need to address it in times of "serious" undertakings. With the world of the fashion industry being so intertwined with the world of television, there was (and still most certainly is) a stress on being thin and perfect for young talent, and it has to be said that legendary and hilarious social commentator and comedienne Joan Rivers – whose job was to be funny as well as confronting as the anarchic woman she was – would dub *The Facts of Life* as "The Fats of Life", commenting on some of the cast members fluctuating weight loss then gain. The show would have this critical assessment throughout its stay on network TV, and Mindy Cohn's Natalie would be a sturdy important example of the importance and necessity of "larger girl" visibility on TV. Here was a big girl whose weight is seldom an issue throughout the show – she is also notably the girl who seems to get the attention from the "hot guys" and also is the one girl to finally lose her virginity in a series that seemed to have a moral high ground concerning sex. However, in this episode in question, Natalie has a speech that assertively states that big girls have it hard and it is profound, moving and even revolutionary. Funnily enough it comes as a response to the one token male in the school's hierarchy (the headmaster Mr. Bradley (John Lawlor)) who pleads with the girls that "having some meat on your bones is a good thing". Mr. Bradley's anti-diet and pro-body image ideals are actually countered by a big girl who voices her anger and frustrations (for what would be, fundamentally, the only ever time). The issue of weight among the core four girls is never an issue throughout the show, and although the vivacious Blair (Lisa Whelchel) may cop some weight gags from her eternal rival/best friend Jo (Nancy McKeon), there is primarily invaluable support and solidarity among the friends at Eastland.

Opening with Nancy (Felice Schachter) trying to get her jeans on in order to appeal to her off-screen boyfriend Roger, the girl whose episode this is, Sue Ann – a working class girl from Kansas – comes into the common room eating cake. Blair has set her up with a date, a boy from society, who, much like Blair, is wealthy and supposedly sophisticated. Sue Ann being from a farming background (much like the den mother Mrs. Garrett (Charlotte Rae)) is nervous and unsure, but Blair assures her the date will go well. However, there is one thing: Blair comments on Sue Ann's weight, insisting that she lose some pounds. Although the head strong Sue Ann gives it back ("bacon butt!"), she is convinced that she needs to lose weight and when Blair repeats a common mantra dictated by fashion magazines with "Thin is in", Sue Ann is determined to starve herself. Other girls voice their opinions: Molly (Molly Ringwald) is defiant and protests: "No magazine is gonna tell me how to look!", while Mrs. Garrett weighs herself and is shocked that she has put on some pounds. She too decides to go on a diet, and her own personal happiness is in question as is Sue Ann's as the episode progresses.

Enter sexy delivery guy Steve (Greg Bradford), a muscular and handsome hands-on "piece of meat", referred to by Mrs. Garrett as "merchandise" who becomes a pinnacle plot point in the episode. Here, this Steve person is absolutely objectified and preyed upon by the girls which flips the idea of beauty as a feminine thing on its head. Natalie shows major interest and he flirts back, pointing out the factor that weight should not be an issue and that boys who are sensitive should be perceptive to all types of girls – thin, tall, short and yes, plump like the charming and sweet Natalie.

But this is an aside to the core dilemma at hand. Upon the first mention of a crash diet comes Mrs. Garrett's warning of the danger of losing weight too fast, but it fuels Sue Ann's determination to lose weight ("I'm going on a starvation diet, and I'm gonna lose ten pounds in one week, even if it kills me!"). Molly's advice stirs a cheer from the studio audience ("You're crazy! Starving yourself for some stupid guy you haven't even met!") and this kind of feminist agenda cements a purpose in a show that is run by girls and complicated by varying degrees of belief systems by all kinds of girls. The Molly character would eventually be dismissed which is a shame, as the brassy kid would be artistically inclined, political and anti-establishment. As much as it was a shame that she would be cut, it is interesting to note that actress Molly Ringwald who gave her life would go onto become a major teen star of the eighties dealing with the pressures of teen girls in mall culture for years to come; crying out a complex feminist agenda and representing multiple factors in suburban teen girl terrain.

Sue Ann lies about eating to Mrs. Garrett – a telling sign of someone living with an eating disorder, and then she faints at the dinner table, which now sets the episode into a discussion piece about self-worth and self-esteem among girls in response to how they feel about what they look like. Mr Bradley's anger about Sue Ann starving herself is one means of getting the point across; here is a man who says that women and girls should be happy with their bodies, but also has no idea about the complexities involved in body image and body positivity and negativity. He also wishes to be hard with Sue Ann, wanting to scold her for being so nonchalant about her health, however Mrs. Garrett protects the fragile girl and dismisses Mr. Bradley's outrage, opting for a better approach. With Sue Ann rejecting food, the vain and self-centered Blair begins to feel a sense of regret for egging on Sue Ann's dieting, and now endlessly tries to help her – once again, Blair has learnt a vitally important lesson by the twenty minute mark of the episode. However, it is of course Mrs. Garrett who will come to the rescue, entering Sue Ann's room in her "new dress" that she showcased earlier in the piece. However, it is learned that the actual new dress was a size 12 and that Mrs. Garrett had to lose a bit of weight before she could fit in it. This dress she has on in this scene is her old size 14 variant and she struts into Sue Ann's room with confidence and elegance. Proudly Mrs. Garrett declares that she is happy to wear the size 14 for now and that when she is ready she will get herself on a sensible diet and work her way to the new size 12. Here, Mrs. Garrett is expressing her absolute belief in healthy living and keeping fit and strong – after all the woman is a dietician – however, she warns Sue Ann (and the rest of the teenage girl population out there in sitcom audience land) about the dangers of crash diets and self-forced starvation. Mrs. Garrett is all about eating healthy, working out, sticking to a steady intake of food, but she is not at all a fan of girls feeling bad about what they look like. A sublime positive role model for girls everywhere, this den mother with a heart of gold, sings out to Sue Ann "You're a beautiful girl" giving the sensitive Kansas blonde beauty a new edge and sparkling self-confidence; here in *The Facts of Life*, feeling beautiful about oneself is important, but it comes from love, loyalty, honor and above all, lasting friendship.

"The First Store" from *The Jeffersons*
Original Air Date: 6 April 1980
By Kevin Nickelson

I may have the unfettered bias of an old couch potato but I refused to waver from my long-held belief that television can (and still does, though to a lesser extent) teach us if we allow it. And I do not, specifically, refer to just the documentaries and news programs we grew up on in weekly doses back in the day or can now be seen 24 hours a day on whichever niche cable or satellite network. I am referring to the fictional variety of programming. To be factual, I must admit that learning curves haven't always been the priority of many a TV writer or showrunner. Afterall, number one on the list of to-dos for those striving for paydays and a modicum of success in the small screen industry really does have to be being entertaining enough and have a certain level of ratings to warrant second episodes let alone second seasons. Yet I am one of the few who thinks a certain level of creative daring is still lacking among the talent behind the scenes today.

Certainly it shows up in hour dramas of the legal and crime show variety. For those devotees of the situation comedy (such as myself), the fare imbued with social more themes is still rather scarce to come by. Oh sure, there are shows that deal with issues of relationships, personality clashes etc. However, where is the study of larger scale humanity issues hidden behind razor-sharp barbs of wit? In the sixties and seventies, the urge to dissect the human condition while making folks laugh seemed much more prevalent among the young, up-and-coming writers in TV backrooms. Gene Roddenberry and Gene L. Coon of *Star Trek* lore, Rod Serling and *The Twilight Zone*, Larry Gelbart of *M*A*S*H* fame, Noam Pitlik and James Komack to name but a few. Perhaps towering above even those pioneers is a guy who has made a lengthy career mixing biting bon mot wit with a rather acid-etched view of society. Notably the area of racial bigotry. From New Haven, Connecticut and the son of Russian immigrants of Jewish faith, Norman Milton Lear would not seem, at first glance, a guy who'd lead the charge of illuminating racial strife through television. Yet, his resume of societal more challenging would have no peer even in its early beginnings. *All in the Family* (1971–1979), *Maude* (1972–1978) and *Sanford and Son* (1972–1977) were already under his belt when he began work on what may be his most potent study of seething race hostility underneath the surface of the upper class, *The Jeffersons* (1975–1985).

The main characters of husband and wife George and Louise Jefferson and their son Lionel started out as semi-recurring roles of neighbors of Archie and Edith Bunker on *All in the Family*. Becoming popular enough with fans, Lear decided to spin the trio off into their own series in 1975. The show would enjoy a lengthy eleven season run as it explored George and company living in Manhattan's Upper West Side swank environment as George became owner of a highly successful chain of dry cleaning shops and dealing with the issue of race in the heart of the wealthy elite. Maybe I gravitated toward this show because it showed me an example of where bigotry is most common and, indeed, thrives: under the surface of genteel civility.

Lear had the inspiration to create George as controlled rage against oppression just underneath a well-dressed businessman exterior and drop him neck deep into the mire. As played by the inimitable Sherman Hemsley, George usually dealt with the risible attitudes regarding skin color with quick wit and brief vitriol spurts and dusted himself off and moved on. However, there was one episode which stood out above all others, delivering one of the few true gut punches that staggered George's resolve and allowed his full hate against institutionalized bigotry to spew out like lava from a highly active volcano. "The First Store" came late in season six and tells the story, via flashback, of the trials and tribulations of how Jefferson got his first store. It flashes back to 1968 where, in one package, he deals with the racist undertones exuded by a banker he is trying to get a loan from and his own feelings regarding son Lionel's militant beliefs. The trigger, though, is that while this is going on Dr. Martin Luther King Jr's assassination is being played out on radio and television. Gone are George's shields holding down his venom. Exploding, he tosses furniture and gives the audience a peek into the sadness, loathing and anger that he and all oppressed cultures feel. A display that many in society do not wish to see but everyone needs to in full frontal raw variety. Unless we can see the damaging results that systemic holding down of cultures causes, the mental and physical degradations, the divide between cultures will never hope to be closed.

It is well-known that the origin of the Jeffersons' first store was quite different here from the depiction in the *All in the Family* 1971 episode "Archie's Aching Back". In the latter, written by Stanley Ralph Ross, it is revealed that George received an insurance settlement from a motor vehicle accident and used it to open his first store. The episode premiered three years after Dr. King's assassination. Though a pungent, very funny episode in its own right, I gather that Lear altered the events for a more explosive, impactful dissertation on race. If you look at Lear's resume, it very much appears that that aspect of the human condition was especially pertinent to the writer. In researching his background, I discovered just how activistic his personal life was. Lear founded advocacy group People for the American Way in 1981. Among the group's ideals is the promotion of Secularism, and opposing the interjection of religion in politics.

The multi-talented Ross (a songwriter and author who began his career in advertising) offers up a very layered story for episodic TV. He seems most interested in the subtext of Lionel's growing militant mentality clashing with George. In fact, it seems more that the son's leanings and approach are rubbing off on the father the longer the story goes. George tries to stick to Dr. King's preaching of non-violence but is tested every time he hears the news updates about the assassination or the bank loan officer's derisive comments like referring to the neighborhood where George wants to open the store at as filled with "animals". It is when the latter happens that George finally has his fill and throws the man out. Ross lays it out with George and Lionel as opposite views destined to come to a middle ground. Louise is the voice of common sense. A necessary contrivance to bring the polar extremes together. Almost the arbitrator finding the common ground.

When it comes to making you laugh and think at once about life and breaking cultural divides, Norman Lear is one for the elite class. Though I also think that, if there were no barriers, he'd be just that much happier.

"Dope" from *The Facts of Life*
Original Air Date: 11 June 1980
By Lee Gambin

Smoking marijuana would become a staple go-to for the Afterschool Specials that frequently aired on television during the eighties. Specials such as the ABC produced *Stoned* (1980) starring Scott Baio (made during his stint as Chachi from *Happy Days* (1974–1984)) would introduce youngsters to the perils of pot addiction. However, cannabis use would become part of the youth culture during the late seventies and into the next decade as a strange hang over from the flower power movement of the late sixties – which would be an all-encompassing counterculture that swept an entire generation who would eventually wind up being the parents of the preteens that would be watching such PSA-driven eighties offerings. Therefore, it would be a drug completely understood and for many urbane "progressive adults" somehow accepted in the culture. But when it came to the sitcom *The Facts of Life* (1979–1988) which would drive home a sturdy moralistic message of being true to oneself and navigating the hardships of life with a clear head that ultimately makes good and decent decisions, marijuana would not be an affectation of the cultured, but instead a waste of time and a choice for those living in a dead-end state of mind. In the episode "Dope", this is exactly what is explored – marijuana usage distinguishes the experienced and supposedly "worldly" from the juvenile and inexperienced, but essentially, the joke is on those with such socially cultured pretentions and those who become aware of the "dangers" of pot may be symbolically "virginal" but ultimately good and destined for a fulfilling life.

The basic plot summary here is that naïve and sweet Sue Ann (Julie Piekarski) longs to be included in Blair's (Lisa Whelchel) elitist club that is dominated by senior girls who live on the other side of Eastland. Blair is a rich kid and popular and Sue Ann is everything completely opposite. She is also not a senior and a self-described "square", who is at the prestigious school because she has a scholarship. The most alienating of all her character attributes is the fact that she is a girl from Kansas, a working class kid who longs to be accepted. The stakes are high for young Sue Ann, and eventually she will be too. The character would be one of the many who would ultimately be culled from the series come the second season as the show would fix its point of action around Blair, Tootie (Kim Fields), Natalie and the soon to be introduced Jo (Nancy McKeon). And although Sue Ann would pop up from time to time as an additional character, she would soon become a TV sitcom casualty alongside fellow students Nancy (Felice Schachter) and Molly (Molly Ringwald). Also, by this point in the first series, Tootie would be established as an eavesdropper which would generate plot points or land her or the others in trouble, and here in "Dope" this is something that does both.

Tootie is the youngest of the gang, however, she is also incredibly savvy and smart for her age. However, when her gullible side surfaces it does so as an entry point for her tripping over her words and falling into a deep heap. When she enters the world of Tumpy (Hillary Horan) and Emily (Helen Hunt), two senior girls who are guest characters, she is put amidst older more "worldly" young ladies who like to smoke pot and see self-perceived benefits from drug use. Initially, Tootie refers to Tumpy's room as "snob city" and the difference between the worlds of these senior pot smoking girls and Tootie and her clan made up of Natalie, Molly, Nancy and co. are set in stone. However, the desire to feel older and be treated in a more mature manner exists and forces Tootie to understand the "secret door knock" that will grant her entry into such a world, and also Sue Ann attempts at becoming "one of the gang". Interestingly enough, in a later episode entitled "Pretty Babies", Tootie grabs the attention of a fashion photographer who sees Tootie as the "new face of the eighties" and as much as the world of modelling excites Tootie who is tired of being seen as "just a kid", the episode takes a serious dark turn when she is forced to take up down dressing and appearing nude in various shoots, which sparks outrage from housemother and devoted caretaker to her girls Mrs. Garrett (Charlotte Rae) who even refers to what the photographer's intentions are as "child pornography". The series would take up the issue at hand of girls desperate to grow up, but ultimately not ready to handle what that means. In "Dope", this is the case at hand.

When it is learned that the more "experienced" Nancy was not accepted in the group, we get the impression that Tumpy and her friends are keen on more vulnerable additions – to turn into mind-numbed stoners. Blair's joint, hidden in a lipstick canister, shocks Sue Ann but she is told that this is something that she is going to have to get used to if she wants to be part of such an elitist subsector of Eastland. When Sue Ann and Blair enter Tumpy's room, they find her and her pals stoned and the use of bongs and other smoking devices come into the fore, all up on show for preteen centric television. A series derived from the Norman Lear canon, *The Facts of Life* would never shy away from the hard truths about being a teenager, and in showing young girls smoking pot is something that hits the message home, rather than having it be implied.

On Tootie's arrival at Tumpy's room she remarks "so this is how the other half lives" and when she hears Tumpy explain that bongs are simply jars for jellybeans, the sweet kid believes her. Blair also defends Tootie and protects her, like a big sister, and angrily snaps at Tumpy who offers the youngster a puff on a joint. Blair protests "She's too young for that!" and in that swiftness of keeping Tootie away from drugs, we get a strong point of focus on heartier friendships – Blair and Tootie are good pals, but are Blair and Sue Ann? Also cultural impressions are made in snide ways: Tumpy wants to sell her stereo at a low cost because she needs the cash, but Blair makes a point that it was a very expensive gift from her parents. Here an old adage of rich kids always seeming to be without cash is referred to, and also that "doing it well" kids seem to fall victim to drug dependency during this period of television, making the narcotic war a middle class one. However, smoking pot is made to look stupid here in "Dope". Tumpy's struggle with words as she tries to unravel the positive aspects from smoking pot are funny and also bleak – where is the glamor or sophistication in drugging? But while Blair's fear of smoking grass is evident, Sue Ann's desire to fit in (and also believing that it will help her with her essay on "Moby Dick") take hold and she puffs away. In turn, her use of words (in this case, in essay form) becomes an extension of the earlier gag where Tumpy getting sentences all muddled up. Mrs. Garret reads out Sue Ann's essay:

"Moby Dick was a white whale

With a big tail

Captain Ahab was a sea captain with one good leg

And one good leg."

It goes on and gets worse ending with Sue Ann writing that Moby Dick was not really a whale but a desert which prompts Mrs. Garrett to ask "What have you been smokin'?" But the jokes come to a crashing close when Tootie and Natalie arrive from a local record shop with bongs. Tootie explains that although she and Natalie and the others can't belong to Tumpy's elitist group, they can still have the things they own, like bongs – still believing that they are used to hold jellybeans. Here, Mrs. Garrett gives them the low down on the use of bongs and eventually Tumpy and her cohorts are expelled.

By the end of the episode, Blair comes to the understanding that social cliques are not as important as genuine friends (of whom Sue Ann is one) and when she rejects the notion of getting stoned she gazes into a mirror and proudly proclaims "I'm gonna stick to being high on me" – her vanity being endearing and the butt of many jokes to come throughout the series. Sue Ann also defends Blair by pretending that the lipstick hiding place was hers, and a friendship between a green Kansas girl and a rich kid from the most well-to-do part of New York is established. Meanwhile, Mrs. Garrett is angry: "I'm furious that these bright young girls are messing up their lives with dope!" However, in classic sitcom fashion, those doing such things are gone, and the core gang remain, happy, healthy and doing OK. Lessons are learned over sharing jellybeans as the credits begin to unfold and the classic TV theme song bounces in. The love the girls have for one another is evident as they crowd around Mrs. Garrett, their protector, defender and a goddess of good honest living.

"Archie Alone" from *Archie Bunker's Place*
Original Air Date: 2 November 1980
By Andrew Mercado

When popular actors decide to leave a long-running TV series, especially ones about close-knit families, scriptwriters are left with a dilemma – do they send their characters away temporarily (often stretching credibility), or is it more realistic to kill them off? Taking the latter path is very final, and only *Dallas* (1978–1991) has dared staging a "resurrection", by deeming an entire season, when Bobby Ewing (Patrick Duffy) had been killed, as being "just a dream" from his wife Pam (Victoria Principal).

Too many characters exit other shows by leaving to "look after a sick relative" but in the case of *The Waltons* (1971–1981), having seven children of her own prohibited Olivia Walton (Michael Learned) from ever doing such a thing. So instead, the beloved mother was diagnosed with tuberculosis and sent away to a sanitarium – and dutifully replaced in the crowded household by her cousin Rose (Peggy Rea). Not killing Olivia off proved to be very fortuitous for the future because several years later, after the series had ended, Olivia was able to return for several reunion telemovies (*Mother's Day on Walton's Mountain* (1982), *A Walton Thanksgiving Reunion* (1993), *A Walton Wedding* (1995) and *A Walton Easter* (1997)). Olivia Walton left *The Waltons* in 1979 and later that same year, the wheels were set in motion for an even more legendary TV mom to depart the canvas, as actress Jean Stapleton took a step back from the phenomenon that was *All in the Family* (1971–1979). Edith Bunker was the quiet backbone of the show but with a new decade approaching, it was morphing into a new beast, and the unthinkable was about to happen.

All in the Family was based on the hit British sitcom *Till Death Us Do Part* (1965–1975) which had inspired two movie spin-offs (*Till Death Us Do Part* in 1968 and *The Alf Garnett Saga* in 1972) and also spawned numerous remakes all over the world. Brazil, Germany and The Netherlands all did their own versions and Australia had two, *The Last of the Australians* (1975–1976) and *Kingswood Country* (1980–1984). But it would be the American adaptation that would outshine them all. *All in the Family*, after a shaky first season, became the number one show on TV for five years and won 22 Emmy Awards (out of 56 nominations). It was also extremely influential for revolutionizing American sitcoms, because it dealt with taboo issues and uncomfortable realism in among the laughs.

Legendary producer Norman Lear thought *Till Death Us Do Part* was "all hate and testiness" but nevertheless he saw the potential for a Stateside version and cast Carroll O'Connor and Jean Stapleton as the leads. ABC ordered two pilots, in 1968 and 1969, insisting that the rest of the cast wasn't quite right, but the truth was the network "didn't quite have the guts" to put the show on. By 1971, however, CBS felt braver because they wanted a "more urban" image. This led to what is infamously called their "rural purge" as the network cancelled still-popular shows like *Petticoat Junction* (1963–1970), *Green Acres* (1965–1971), *The Beverly Hillbillies* (1962–1971) and *Hee Haw* (1969–1997). Johnny Speight had created *Till Death Us Do Part* to challenge views about racism and Norman Lear was out to do the same with *All in the Family*, not to mention other thorny things like homosexuality, feminism and the Vietnam war. When it finally got to air, *The Los Angeles Times* described it as providing a "mirror of the worst part of ourselves, and occasionally the best part" but *The New York Times* was less impressed, writing "what is lacking is taste".

Till Death Us Do Part's Alf Garnett (Warren Mitchell) had turned into an equally bigoted, conservative, working class loudmouth called Archie Bunker (Carroll O'Connor) and his bitter wife, the "silly old moo" Else (Dandy Nichols), became the more genial "dingbat" Edith (Jean Stapleton). British sitcoms generally aired just six episodes per season, and although *Till Death Us Do Part* ran for over a decade, it amassed just 54 episodes. The output was vastly different for *All in the Family* though, which, together with its continuation series *Archie Bunker's Place* (1979–1983), amassed 302 episodes over 13 years.

Even when it was axed, the show still commanded a massive audience, which led to Bill Cosby saying that "Archie Bunker is like a junkie shooting up in front of 40 million people weekly". Meanwhile, Lucille Ball remarked, "Look, I get as big a kick out of it as anyone but it's – well, it's kind of dangerous for kids." Nothing could stop its popularity though, and by its third season, an "Archie Bunker for President" campaign had been launched as a laugh, with one slogan being "I'm a Dingbat for Bunker". By its fourth season though, the actress playing the "dingbat" began promising that Edith would be "taking more of a stand against Archie this year." Over the years, the comment was repeated again and again. Jean Stapleton based Edith on a favorite aunt of hers, and the character's nasally voice came about because she "had to do something to get laughs". During *All in the Family*'s long run, Edith Bunker went through menopause, lost her faith in religion, discovered a lesbian relative and got herself a job (despite Archie's objections). "When she punctures Archie's hot air it's not with a wisecrack," Stapleton said, "she does it out of honest, naïve intuition. To unmask all those prejudices and be able to laugh at them is a great healer." Her honesty was apparent even when Edith was nearly raped on her 50th birthday. "You smell nice", the would-be-rapist said, to which Edith replied, "That's not me, that's Lemon Pledge." The episode got the actress a standing ovation from the studio audience.

By 1979 though, after nine seasons and three Emmy Awards for Best Actress in a Comedy, Jean Stapleton felt that "they had done everything that they could" with Edith, and her appearances on the show became sporadic as Stapleton departed to concentrate on theatre work. CBS were unhappy with this arrangement and kept agitating to make Archie a widower so that new relationships could be explored. Norman Lear couldn't bear to kill Edith off, so he rang Jean Stapleton for advice. "Norman, you do realize she is only fiction?" she asked and after a long pause, during which Stapleton wondered if she had "hurt this dear man I love so much," he replied, "To me she isn't". The Bunkers had already seen off his feminist daughter Gloria (Sally Struthers) and "meathead" son-in-law Mike (Rob Reiner) to live in California and the loss of Edith meant that there would be no more family in *All in the Family*. Episode 205, which turned out to be the last show in its current format, aired in April 1979, and showed Edith collapsing on the stairs. This led to Archie discovering that his wife was hiding from him that she had been diagnosed with phlebitis and he cradled her in his arms, telling Edith he loved her. Ever since, many fans have confused this episode as being Edith's swansong.

But the old girl still had a bit of life left in her and a few months later, the show returned as *Archie Bunker's Place*, a re-invention which had begun two years earlier when Archie bought into a neighborhood bar. Edith had only appeared in four episodes of *All in the Family*'s final season, and she would only be in five episodes of *Archie Bunker's Place*. Her last appearance was in December 1979, as Edith prepared food for "The Shabbat Dinner". That episode ended with her happily singing along with their Jewish friends, as Archie gritted his teeth at having to wear a Kippah on his head. Edith seemed healthy enough, but when the show returned for a new season in November 1980, it started with a very special one-hour episode titled "Archie Alone".

The episode opens with Archie (Carroll O'Connor) waking up, not in his marital bedroom, but downstairs on the couch. He wanders upstairs to get Stephanie (Danielle Brisebois) out of bed, the 11-year-old daughter of Edith's step-cousin, who had moved into the Bunker household after being abandoned by her father. Over breakfast, Stephanie refuses Archie's offer of going to the circus on the weekend, telling him she would rather go to the "cemetery". Archie clams up and changes the subject, and in the next scene, it's left to Archie's friend Barney (Allan Melville, who also played Sam the butcher in *The Brady Bunch*) to confirm to the audience that Edith has died in her sleep from a stroke a few weeks beforehand.

After Stephanie is caught wagging class, a teacher tells Archie she is concerned about whether or not the young girl has been allowed to grieve properly. She suggests that Stephanie be allowed to go through Edith's belongings and take something that is meaningful to her. Archie, still in denial, palms off cleaning out Edith's wardrobe to his bar/restaurant cook Veronica (Anne Meara) and his neighbor Polly (Janet MacLachlan). He then tricks his business partner Murray (Martin Balsam) into having a chat with Steph, but he is not prepared for Murray to tell him that the problem is with Archie, not his young niece. After the bedroom has been cleaned out, Archie ventures in to look at the empty wardrobe and drawers, but he comes undone when he finds one of his wife's pink slippers under the bed. "It wasn't s'posed to be like this, y'know, I was s'posed to be the first one to go", he says. "I know I always used to kid ya about you going first, you know I never meant none of that. And that morning when ya was layin' there, I was shakin' you and yellin' at you to go down and fix my breakfast.

I didn't know. Ya had no right to leave me that way, Edith, without givin' me just one more chance to say I love you." Hearing him break down, Stephanie rushes into the bedroom. Archie has finally had his breakthrough and after agreeing to take her to the cemetery, and put carnations on Edith's grave, he then announces he will move back into their marital bed, which has been stripped of its sheets. The episode ends with Archie wisecracking about Edith's relatives, describing them as "brutes from New Jersey".

Archie Bunker was still able to make an ignorant or politically incorrect joke, but he had mellowed considerably from the gruff bigot first seen over a decade beforehand. He now even had a gay bartender and Jewish business partner, and in the very next episode, Archie would hire his neighbor's sister called Ellen (Barbara Meek), thereby sharing his home with a black housekeeper.

Off-screen, Norman Lear donated half a million dollars to the National Organization for Women and the National Women's Political Caucus as part of a memorial fund in the name of the character he thought of as a real person. *The New York Times* also felt the same way, publishing a full obituary for Edith Bunker, "a woman distinguished by her remarkably keen sense of the human equation in the broad social issues of her time." Meanwhile, *The Washington Post* wrote "Edith, Edith, Edith – how could you ever up and die on us?"

Carroll O'Connor later wrote that he "always thought that the Edith that Jean Stapleton created was more interesting than Archie because Edith was a character that changed with widening experience. Many people wrote me, or told me face to face, that the later shows sorely missed Jean. They were right. I, too, wished that she had stayed on. I wanted to make the show more hers than mine." O'Connor doesn't give himself enough credit for changing Archie too, because in the later years, he even stopped referring to his wife as a "dingbat". Well, at least in public anyway. And despite his sadness that he didn't say it more often, at least Archie had told Edith that he loved her, most memorably in the last episode of *All in the Family*. That was more than Alf Garnett (Warren Mitchell) ever managed to say about Else (Dandy Nichols) on the British original. Ironically, *Till Death Us Do Part* also phased out the long-suffering wife, not because Dandy Nichols wanted a break but out of necessity as she struggled with illness. Therefore, in its final season, Else left the show by moving to Australia to "look after a sick relative". When ratings dropped without her, the show was axed and in the last episode in 1975, Alf got a telegram from Else asking for a divorce. Sadly for Else, but luckily for fans, she never went through with it, because the unhappy couple returned to a new network (ITV) six years later where it was now known as *Till Death*, due to the BBC owning the original title. Alf and Else had moved from the East End of London to the seaside town of Eastbourne, but their reboot flopped and only lasted six episodes. In 1985, the Garnetts returned again, this time back at the BBC with a more successful continuation called *In Sickness and in Health* (1985–1992). Dandy Nichols needed a wheelchair because of her rheumatoid arthritis, so Else got one too, leaving

Alf to reluctantly push her around. Unlike Archie Bunker, however, Alf Garnett had not softened at all towards his wife and the couple still came across as if they could barely tolerate each other. Alf still drank to excess and Else still scoffed chocolates and sweets at every opportunity, although her chain smoking seemed to have eased off.

In February 1986, after making just six episodes and a Christmas special, Dandy Nichols died aged 78. *In Sickness and in Health* returned for a second season that September and its first episode opened with family and friends arriving home from Else's funeral. Alf seemed genuinely bereft as he came through the door, but as soon as he drank the first of many whiskeys, the truth about his sadness came out, given his first rant was about not having enough money to get by without Else's pension. At the end of the episode, after he woke up alone from a drunken stupor, he looked at her empty wheelchair and muttered "silly old moo" one last time. *In Sickness and in Health* continued until 1992 and wound up with a total of 47 episodes. *Archie Bunker's Place* ran for 97 episodes and finished in 1983. Both shows took advantage of their lead character being a widower, with Alf and Archie dating various women, but neither wound up getting married again.

When *Archie Bunker's Place* ended, *TV Guide* celebrated the historic run of *All in the Family* by devoting 14 pages to "So Long Arch". *The New Yorker*'s Broadway drama critic, Brendan Gill, described Carroll O'Connor's "round, boyish face and candid blue, bright blue eyes that led us immediately to discount the worst of what Archie Bunker said. Looking so winsome, he couldn't be as disagreeable as he pretended." When it came to Edith, "Jean Stapleton was similarly capable of conveying to us that there was more to her than met the eye and ear; it was plain that, whatever the script might imply, she was neither a dingbat nor a doormat."

Jean Stapleton died in 2013 and was eulogized by Lynette Rice in Entertainment Weekly, who wrote that "in the hands of the beloved actress, she became one of the most fully human characters in television history. In the process, the character also humanized Archie, and gave America a vantage point from which to consider him. Archie may have been close-minded and foul-mouthed, but Stapleton's Edith was openhearted and forgiving – a naïve, bird-like woman in a lumpy housedress who was always closer to the heart of the matter than anyone else on the show." R.I.P. Edith Bunker and Jean Stapleton (and also Else Garnett and Dandy Nichols).

"Mork in Never-Never Land" from *Mork & Mindy*
Original Air Date: 20 November 1980
By Lee Gambin

Milos Forman's *One Flew Over the Cuckoo's Nest* (1975) would not only be a landmark of seventies cinema, be critically acclaimed, win the Best Picture Academy Award and cement actor Jack Nicholson as one of the most important stars of the decade, but it would also help humanize the long standing stigmatized mentally ill. With its rich tapestry of characters desperate to find one iota of charity and compassion and stuck in the oppressive cold bleak world of a totalitarian institution, the film would gradually inspire multiple artistic offerings (including homages found in the format of the American situation comedy) in regards to commenting on the systematic dehumanization of the diagnosed (and misdiagnosed) psychologically disturbed.

It could be argued that this is most certainly the case here in "Mork in Never-Never Land", an episode that devotes itself to two core serious topics: mental illness and the lack of compassion for those struggling with identity, as well as the power of belief. As Mork, Robin Williams, the master comedian and impressionist, apes Jack Nicholson at one point, quoting from Milos Forman's adaptation of Ken Kesey's groundbreaking novel with "We took a vote and we want to see the damn World Series" which comes from the rousing sequence where Nicholson's character McMurphy and his fellow inmates attempt to overthrow the towering menace that is Nurse Ratched (Louise Fletcher). But this throwaway gag is not delivered in vain – yes, it is a pop cultural reference point, but it is also a profound summary of what this Very Special Episode examines: the concept of perceived reality and distinguishing a trusted truth from necessary escapism.

Guest starring as an inmate of a mental institution is character actor David Spielberg who believes that he is in fact Peter Pan. Much like the Very Special Episode from *Night Court* (1984–1992) dealing with an elderly man's mournful belief that he is in fact Santa Claus in "Santa Goes Downtown" and later in 1991, the episode of *The Simpsons* "Star Raving Dad" where a mental patient believes he is pop superstar Michael Jackson, "Mork in Never-Never Land" scrutinizes delusion and offers a more complicated examination of the hidden factors behind personal belief and the triumph of the human spirit.

Opening with Mindy (Pam Dawber) eagerly awaiting her results for a scholarship for journalism grad school, the episode seems to shy away from Mork's madcap alien habits and mannerisms. Besides imitating a dog and going out to "fetch" Mindy's mail, Mork seems to remain almost human in this episode, mostly to lend room for Peter Pan's quirky eccentricities. Of course, the premise of *Mork & Mindy* (1978–1982) is that people (and aliens) can learn from one another if there is enough level of understanding, respect and unity, and for the most part either Mork or Mindy learn something by the end of each episode – and here there is no exception, however, Mindy will learn that her inner child and the freedom to let go of personal struggle and worry is something to value and treasure and most importantly, exercise.

When buxom bombshell Glenda Faye (Crissy Wilzak Comstock) pays Mindy a visit, it is established that Mindy is incredibly stressed about not getting accepted into grad school, while Mork (who enjoys the simple things in life) is excited to receive a letter from his pen pal, Peter. Heading out to Happy Valley Hospital (the name of Boulder's one-stop mental asylum), Mork enters a room populated by an assortment of unconventional oddities who seem completely normal and respectable in the eyes of the ultimate outsider alien. *Mork & Mindy* would of course enlist as a series regular the character of Exidor (Robert Donner), a homeless man plagued by mental illness who would win over audiences and become nearly as popular a character as Mork himself, but here in "Mork in Never-Never Land", this one off visit to the world of psychological disturbance is a somewhat maudlin and yet sobering tear jerker.

In a series like *Mork & Mindy*, childlike wonderment and innocence certainly must be allowed to breathe the same air as the trappings of responsibility; in other words, Mork running around like a dog fetching the mail needs to be valued and treated with the same amount of importance as Mindy's determination to get into grad school. However, the brilliance in *Mork & Mindy* is the hard hitting truth of the matter – that the world is not as simple as a magical balancing act shared between silliness and sturdiness, that it is in fact a place of disenchantment and loss, and the only way to cope with this sobering reality is that you must have that Peter Pan edge. It is interesting to note that the opening titles for the first season would feature in its montage an image of Mork standing up on a football goal post, with Mindy on the ground beckoning him to "come back to earth" and by the third season (which would be the season this particular episode in discussion featured), both Mork and Mindy would be at either end of the goal post, embodying the balancing act of zany wackiness and stability and reason.

Mork struggles to understand why people are so down, and he is told by Peter Pan that "They're unhappy because they grew up" (moments before he actually comes out as the "real life" Peter Pan to which Mork completely accepts). "I'm the real Peter Pan!" he proudly states, and Mork replies "What's not to believe?" While Mork learns about the inner child, and the importance of imagination and fearless dedication to being eternally young, Peter is overjoyed and cries out "Somebody believes in me!" and that is the heart of the episode – the fact that people on the fringes of society (including the institutionalized) can feel validated if someone has faith in them. In 1977, singer and actress Bernadette Peters would appear on *The Muppet Show* (1976–1981) and sing to Kermit the Frog's nephew Robin a song from the musical *Snoopy* entitled "Just One Person". Joined by fellow Muppets such as Fozzie, Rowlf and Gonzo, Bernadette Peters lets Robin know that "if just one person believes in you… then maybe even you can believe in you too…" This sentiment would be a recurring mantra in seventies and early eighties popular culture and in this Very Special Episode, it would sit at the heart of the piece.

Adding to this genuinely moving expression is the fact that Mork feels overwhelming sadness when a nurse explains that the inmates cannot leave Happy Valley. "This is where he belongs" she says, "You have to understand Mork, they have to be locked in at night, for safety." The dire situation at hand here goes beyond Mork wanting Peter Pan to help Mindy find her inner child and not be lost in a swelter of stress, but it also pains the alien to know that people have to be locked up and trapped in their own misery because of a cold unfeeling world. Peter explains "I'd like to help Mindy, but I can't" while Mindy laments that "Life on earth isn't always fair" – two incredibly well constructed counterpoints of unintentionally poignant character development and storytelling.

Peter's long history of distrust in the outside world and his apprehension about dealing with adults who have "stopped believing" lead him to have crushing anxiety to leave the institution. When Mork attempts to break him out of Happy Valley, he is distressed and not sure. But Mork insists that he "rescues" Mindy from her sadness, and with some persuasion, Peter retrieves his famous green hat and assumes position (and status) as the "real life" Peter Pan. When Mork introduces Peter to Mindy she is at first reluctant to even have him at her place, and she struggles with even mentioning the words "asylum" and "mental institution" (politeness that can also be interpreted as a response to society not being comfortable with mental health concerns), and she also makes a double loaded statement that guarantees her belief in the alien Mork but a disbelief in Peter being the "real" Peter Pan.

Much like the "boy who refused to grow up", Peter insists that Mindy crow like a rooster (something that he taught the Lost Boys and Wendy and her brothers in the fairy tale) but Mindy refuses. When she finally gets the call from the university with news that she didn't get the scholarship, Mork and Peter egg her on to crow (to embrace the inner child and shed the shackles of seriousness for a moment of happiness). She attempts to crow over the phone to the dean, but it doesn't sound right – it doesn't have the "edge" necessary. Peter finally tells her, "Mindy why don't you enjoy what you have, instead of worrying what you haven't?" instantly inspiring her to crow – a loud, proud cock-a-doodle-doo, and in that she learns to believe in her inner child that doesn't need to worry and doesn't need to feel trapped by the pressures of success and self-worth.

By the end of the episode, the openhearted Mindy crosses over to Peter and tells him that she believes in him (that second person who does – harkening back to Bernadette Peter's advice to the young frog Robin) and although Happy Valley wardens come to collect him (a reinforcement of reality crashing in), Peter pops up outside Mindy's window, magically flying. Amazed at this feat, Mindy puts two and two together and figures it must have been the work of Mork (a gifted alien of telekinetic ability), however, the dialogue that closes the episode embodies the mysteries of faith and the fairy tale wonder of believing:

Mindy: Did you help him do that?
Mork: Do you really want to know?
Mindy: No.
Mork: Me either.

David Spielberg plays a mental patient who believes he is Peter Pan in "Mork in Never-Never Land" from Mork & Mindy. *Mork (Robin Williams) celebrates the whimsical fantasy world, and the blurring of reality and believing in something magical makes life worth living.*

"Fathers of the Bride" from *Taxi*
Original Air Date: 3 December 1980
By Michael Campochiaro

I came screaming into the world smack in the middle of the grooviest decade in history: the 1970s. Looking back now, it's obvious that my – and many in my generation's – formative years in the late 1970s and into the 1980s were dramatically shaped by what I like to consider the Golden Age of the American sitcom. During those years, shows like *All in the Family* (1971–1979), *The Mary Tyler Moore Show* (1970–1977), *Good Times* (1974–1979), *Bosom Buddies* (1980–1982), and *WKRP in Cincinnati* (1978–1982), to name just a few, elevated the half hour situational comedy by seamlessly melding uproarious humor with the sort of thoughtful introspection that became a hallmark of American television during that era. These shows were able to inject topical, serious elements into their episodes while never sacrificing comedy. The balance was just right and made for truly affecting viewing.

One such sitcom that excelled at striking this perfect balance of comedy and drama was *Taxi*. Created by James L. Brooks, Stan Daniels, David Davis and Ed. Weinberger, the series aired on ABC from September 12, 1978 to May 6, 1982, and then on NBC from September 30, 1982 to June 15, 1983. Earning eighteen Emmy Awards, including three for Outstanding Comedy Series, *Taxi* is in many ways one of the absolute sitcom gold standards of its era. Documenting the everyday lives of a group of cab drivers in New York City, *Taxi* is also one of the finest workplace comedies ever made. The characters were an eclectic, lovable mix, played by a company of actors who shared an undeniable chemistry together. Several of the cast members were native New Yorkers, which only enhanced the show's authentic New York vibe (even though it was, of course, filmed on Stage 23 at Paramount Studios in Los Angeles).

Judd Hirsch headed the ensemble as cantankerous cabbie lifer Alex Reiger. Marilu Henner played the smart, sensitive redheaded bombshell Elaine Nardo, a divorced mother of two whose day job is at an art museum. Jeff Conaway and Tony Danza starred as struggling actor Bobby Wheeler and struggling boxer Tony Banta, respectively. 1960s hippie burnout, the Reverend Jim "Iggy" Ignatowski, was brought to life hilariously by Christopher Lloyd, while eccentric performance artist Andy Kaufman played the eccentric mechanic Latka Gravas. Danny DeVito rounded out the cast as the de facto den mother of this mangy assemblage of misfits and outsiders, as Louie De Palma, the crude head dispatcher at the cab company.

Even the name of the show's fictional workplace – the Sunshine Cab Company – winked and nodded at its premise, as these characters were anything but "sunshiny", and instead were cynical, sarcastic, at times hopeless but always fighting to persevere through life's trials and tribulations. That is what ultimately makes *Taxi* such an inspiring sitcom.

For five seasons we saw our own life struggles reflected back at us through these characters. Watching them navigate the often-disappointing aspects of adulthood was consistently uplifting. The series explored topics including relationship troubles, parenthood challenges, dealing with loss and grief, feelings of insecurity, and that constant nagging fear of never quite reaching one's potential, plus many more. These characters rarely came out on top, but they still found reasons for hope, and reasons to continue to face whatever obstacles life threw in their paths.

In terms of the era's Very Special Episode phenomenon, *Taxi* was as equipped to produce thought-provoking episodes of this nature as any show on television at the time. Interestingly, the season one episode titled "Men Are Such Beasts" (21 November 1978), directed by James Burrows and written by Ed. Weinberger and Stan Daniels, contained an obvious Very Special Episode subplot that here is mostly used as a springboard for comedy. Tony becomes the object of unwanted affection from a spurned lover named Denise (Gail Edwards), who becomes increasingly fanatical about never letting Tony go, even going so far as to take a job at the Sunshine Cab Company just to be closer to him. What follows is a series of comedic moments based on Denise's continued advancements and Tony's inability to firmly put an end to the relationship. The manic Denise quickly establishes an all-time one-day record for fares at the company, and we soon learn where she's getting all of her energy: she's popping amphetamines like they're candy. The show's portrayal of Denise isn't the most nuanced; she falls squarely into the time-worn "crazy ex-girlfriend" zone. She even gives Alex a few of her pills – without disclosing what they really are – and what follows is definitely played for laughs, as Alex bounds around the garage brimming with energy, singing and almost walking on air he's so high. Thus the episode contained themes often explored in Very Special Episodes – drugs and breakups – but it was a season three Very Special Episode where everything gelled just right.

While "Fathers of the Bride", directed by James Burrows and written by Barry Kemp, features the regular cast in the first act, it quickly segues into being an Alex-centric episode, with Elaine tagging along and receiving some wonderful character flourishes. Alex discovers that his ex-wife Phyllis (Louise Lasser) has made sure he is not invited to their daughter's upcoming New York wedding, unbeknownst to their daughter Cathy (Talia Balsam), who is currently living in Brazil. The pain this causes Alex is palpable, thanks in large part to Judd Hirsch's expertly realized performance. From an initial brush off, to shouting with contempt for his ex-wife, to looking absolutely defeated, all within minutes, Hirsch makes Alex's distress readily apparent and achingly real. Phyllis left Alex when Cathy was only two, taking their daughter with her, so much of Alex's pain is fraught with feelings of being an absentee father all these years. Thankfully, Elaine is there to encourage him to find a way into the wedding, while declaring that if he's going then he'd better take her with him because she wants to be there to support her friend (also, the series was occasionally flirting with the notion of Alex and Elaine becoming a permanent item). This leads to some spectacularly funny comedic moments for Lloyd (Elaine tries to convince Alex maybe the invitation just got lost in the mail "Rio De Janeiro to here. Do you know how far that is?" Jim chimes in: "Six thousand eight hundred and forty-two miles."), and for DeVito ("Reel her in, Reiger! Reel her in!").

After the first commercial break, we cut to the wedding reception at a posh New York location (Cathy is marrying a foreign diplomat's son, after all), and thus begins the heart of the episode. Elaine works her feminine wiles to sneak them into the reception, and she's both sultry and hilarious while doing so. Henner truly shines here, as the scene calls for her natural allure and pitch-perfect comedic skills. Soon enough, Alex spots Phyllis, who immediately tries to hide behind a stranger's leg. Alex and Phyllis's ensuing conversation is fraught with the accumulated animosity they've each built up over the years, and manifests in one sharp put-down after another. Phyllis takes some snarky digs at Alex's blue collar profession, leading Alex to hit her where it hurts most, by cruelly insulting the mother of the bride's weight gain: "You haven't lost a daughter, you've *gained a ton.*" This is particularly hurtful for Phyllis, because embarrassment over her weight gain is one of the main reasons she wanted to avoid seeing Alex again.

After Cathy tells Alex of Phyllis's extreme sensitivity to her weight, she adds, almost rhetorically, "But you wouldn't say anything about her weight, would you?" to which Alex quickly replies, "No, no, no, I wouldn't," while the studio audience breaks out in laughter. Soon after, while dancing and talking about his predicament with Elaine, Alex realizes he must apologize. Phyllis may have engineered his exclusion from the invite list to their only child's wedding, but there's also an important history between them – and a child – which at the very least deserves a level of respect. He then asks to cut in between Phyllis and her current husband, who are dancing, and after protestations from Phyllis her husband relents to Alex's request. Thus the two former lovers are reunited on the dance floor, dancing close together and beginning the arduous work of repairing their damaged relationship.

Alex suggests they continue their conversation in the dingy back room packed full of supplies and dry sinks, to which Phyllis sarcastically notes upon entering the room, "Gee, looks just like our first apartment. What a nice touch." This scene is where an already excellent episode elevates into an all-time classic, as Hirsch and Lasser are allowed to carry the entire emotional weight of the episode, between the two of them. It's as if we've segued into a two-person stage play, and we're thrilling to the marvelous abilities of two world-class actors operating at the tops of their games, playing off one another magnificently. As Alex and Phyllis begin to break down the walls they've built between themselves, we are treated to subtle yet extraordinary moments. Slowly but surely they allow their defenses to crumble, and before long they're sharing smiles and laughter. After Alex notes how good they once were together, Phyllis replies, "Yeah, we always knew how to push each other's buttons, didn't we? But now I don't know whether I can push anybody's buttons anymore or anybody can push my buttons." It's a remarkable moment thanks to Lasser's excellence, as she shows us how happy those memories with Alex make Phyllis feel, yet they also serve as a reminder that those days are long gone and she's not sure she'll ever be able recapture those feelings again, with anyone. This leads to one of Hirsch's great line readings in the episode, as Alex quickly responds, "Well, listen, if they ever get up a search party…" and smiles affectionately at Phyllis. She's moved by his expression of love and solidarity and breaks out into a lovely and entirely genuine smile, "Oh, Alex you are so sweet." It's a gentle, heartfelt moment, with perfect direction that allows for space and quiet between the actors' words, letting Lasser's and Hirsch's wonderfully expressive faces tell some of the story.

Those quiet reaction shots offer powerful reminders throughout the scene that these two characters were once madly in love. When Lasser looks at Hirsch, in that moment we see decades of complex and contradictory emotions Phyllis feels for Alex. In scenes where Alex is framed in the foreground and Phyllis in the background, Lasser reacts to Hirsch's line readings with a natural ease that's a joy to behold. A sly smirk transitions into an honest smile, subtly conveying just how much Phyllis will always love Alex, even if that love will never be what it was in the early years of their marriage. Hirsch masterfully matches Lasser's honesty in these moments, and together the two craft an organic relationship that transcends acting; we believe these two have had a long, tumultuous relationship. They have the power to hurt one another so deeply precisely because, despite divorce and distance, their love will never be fully extinguished.

All of this culminates in a lovely – and very funny – final embrace between Alex and Phyllis. What begins as a goodbye hug quickly turns amorous, with Alex giggling as Phyllis nuzzles his neck and eventually throws her left leg around him, resulting in a cute moment of physical comedy as Cathy enters the room. Alex steps back quickly, but then immediately reaches back and taps down Phyllis's leg, as she'd hilariously left it hanging in the air even after Alex broke the embrace. Cathy expresses how seeing her parents together is the best gift she could've received, to which Alex deadpans, "Yeah, well, five minutes later, you would've had a better gift, " and he and Phyllis share a quick laugh as the studio audience boisterously roars with laughter of their own. Cathy says that a hug between her parents would really make her happy. Alex and Phyllis hesitate for a moment before embracing, "For the kid." Within seconds they comically resume their previous, amorous, leg-locked embrace before cracking up. Hirsch and Lasser, once again, imbue Alex and Phyllis's relationship with an honest realism that makes us forget that we're watching two actors performing. Their performances together feel sincere and true.

Lasser would reprise the role of Phyllis once more, in *Taxi*'s fifth and final season, in the episode "Get Me Through the Holidays" (16 December 1982), directed by Michael Zinberg and written by Ken Estin and Sam Simon. While not as strong an episode as "Fathers of the Bride," it does add subtle texture and depth to Alex and Phyllis's long, complicated relationship. Phyllis, beset by the Christmas holiday season blues, arrives at Alex's apartment door on Christmas Eve. She begs Alex to let her hang out with him for the night so she can avoid being alone once more on Christmas Eve. Eventually, after much hemming and hawing, Alex agrees and the two wind up attending a party at Latka and Simka's (Carol Kane) apartment. Later, while Alex drives Phyllis home for the night, the two share a tender, heartfelt moment, as Alex eventually relents to Phyllis's request for an early New Year Eve's kiss. It's a perfect final moment between these characters, reminding us once more of the unbreakable bond they'll always share.

With Alex and Phyllis, the cast and crew of *Taxi* created something truly special in the annals of television sitcoms: an honest portrayal of a complicated adult relationship. They did such an incredible job, in fact, that even a young child like myself could grasp much of the intricacies of Phyllis and Alex's relationship. I can still remember watching "Fathers of the Bride" in reruns, just a few years after it originally aired (syndicated reruns throughout the 1980s were how I watched all five season of *Taxi*, over and over again) and feeling the emotional heft of the episode's content, even though I was far too young to have any understanding of complex adult relationships. So there I was, just a naïve elementary school-aged boy, watching Alex and Phyllis attempt to break down the walls adults construct around themselves for reasons that they can barely remember after the passage of so many years and so much water under the bridge. In their scenes, though, I recognized that whatever had transpired between these characters was influencing every single moment they spent together in the episode. To watch them fight against those self-imposed restrictions in order to find some tentative connection once again – and to remind each other of why they once fell in love – was and still remains one of the most memorable and inspiring sitcom moments I've ever witnessed.

After a bit of a fumbling attempt at a Very Special Episode in season one, with "Fathers of the Bride" the cast and crew of *Taxi* crafted a stellar example of what makes the show so special in the pantheon of great American sitcoms. The episode serves as an important reminder that adult concerns can be handled with thoughtful introspection and *still* be extremely funny. *Taxi*, like other great popular culture productions, reflects our own realities back at us, while being funny, thought-provoking, and also providing much-needed comfort. Ultimately, this is what makes *Taxi* so enduring – at its core it's a show about this thing called life, this human condition we all strive to understand. Even if I had not yet traveled that journey into and through adulthood like the characters on *Taxi*, that humanity at the center of everything in the show still resonated and will continue to resonate with audiences of any age. That's also why the story of Alex and Phyllis, and their messy, complicated, conflicted love, will live on in all of us, forever.

"Elaine's Strange Triangle" from *Taxi*
Original Air Date: 10 December 1980
By Shawn Macomber

At first, it seems like man-na from Heaven: The gang's all at Mario's, struggling to cheer up Elaine Nardo (Marilu Henner) despondent at the nonexistent state of her love life in the wake of a breakup. Then a well-mannered man in a dapper suit approaches her and Tony Banta (Tony Danza) at the bar. He's brandishing a mug of beer that shows he can get down with the proles, sure, but also an assured gait that no doubt would've pegged him as an aspiring "Master of the Universe" in Tom Wolfe's *Bonfire of the Vanities*. "Excuse me, are you together?" he asks. Tony – endearingly slow on the uptake, per usual – answers in the affirmative before catching himself, correcting the "just friends," record, and dragging the man back over to the cabbie table for some unsubtle group matchmaking. "She's a cab driver, but she also works in an art gallery," Bobby Wheeler (Jeff Conaway) enthuses to their new French impressionism-loving, self described "amateur art buff" pal. The gambit works. *Voila*, one Mr. Kirk Bradshaw (John David Carson), investment analyst, has got the digits. How you like them apples!

Flash forward ten days. The gang is now chilling at dispatch. Elaine's at the coffee dispensing machine, swinging her hip, humming a gay tune, and giving off a glow that registers all the brighter among the soot and oil-shellacked surroundings. Tony takes a victory lap for his skills as the attending love doctor. Alas, it is short-lived: A few minutes after Louie sends Elaine out on a run, Kirk pops in. Once Louie is done crassly busting the dandy's balls – "How far'd you get?" the dispatcher says to a blanching Kirk, demanding a little "guy talk" and to know whether he'd "hit a home run" – Tony excitedly steps in to bask in more praise. Kirk isn't feeling it. In fact, he'd come to talk to Elaine about an issue he'd had "ever since I met her." He adds, "I just can't seem to be able to."

Tony, concerned, encourages Kirk to open up to him – and gets far more in the way of "guy talk" than for which he bargained: "I honestly never meant to get involved with Elaine. You remember the night I came up to you at the bar and said, 'Are you two together?' Well, she wasn't the one I was after, Tony."

"Oh, no?" Tony says over the laugh track.

Kirk affixes a smoldering stare upon him. "No."

Now, watching Tony struggle to keep his cool, we may at this point be tempted to write off "Elaine's Strange Triangle" as a time capsule from a less enlightened, less sexually liberated era. After all, we're talking about an episode that aired a mere seven years after the American Psychiatric Association at long last issued a resolution declaring "by itself, homosexuality does not meet the criteria for being a psychiatric disorder" and removed it from the Diagnostic and Statistical Manual of Mental Disorders

(DSM). (The vote, incidentally, of 5,854 to 3,810 illustrates how many psychiatrists nevertheless remained inhospitable to the autonomy of individuals determining their own sexual preferences.) Further, according to Gallup no fewer than 43 percent of Americans in 1980 believed gay and lesbian "relations" should be *outlawed*. Two years later more than half surveyed (51 percent) answer the question, "Do you feel that homosexuality should be considered an acceptable alternative lifestyle or not?" with a straight up, "No."

It wasn't exactly the pre-Stonewall days of outright state terror, violence, and oppression, but we were still thirteen years out from the "… not that there's anything wrong with that" *Seinfeld* episode and a quarter century ahead of Obergefell v. Hodges – the United States Supreme Court case legalizing same-sex marriage – and it shows.

What's amazing about "Elaine's Strange Triangle" is it only remains a time capsule for the first half – roughly from the freaked out look on Tony's face when Kirk confesses his ardor through the moment when we find out Tony is broke because he paid off Louie to keep his secret after the dispatcher coaxed it out of him with *faux* empathy and concern. (Classic Louie-locks-himself-in-caged-office-to-avoid-physical-violence scene here.)

The second half, however, ditches the of-its-time line-towing and serves more like a premonition or harbinger of a better, freer future.

This shift encompasses two encounters Tony has while ruminating over whether to tell Elaine about Kirk's predilection, each nudging the old school dude's dude toward the ultimate conclusion that his conundrum is really, truly no cause for despair.

The first is with Latka Gravas (Andy Kaufman), who offers to help him with his "blues." Tony at first demurs, but then asks if Latka has any experience with bisexuals.

"Of course, they are very popular in my country," he replies. "Almost everybody have them and one of our favorite sports is racing them. And when we are not using them we have special racks where we chain them up at night."

"Latka, I'm not talking about bicycles. I'm talking about bisexuals!"

"So am I. Listen, I hope that you feel better, okay. Goodbye."

It's an absurdist take that nevertheless suggests little else is warranted.

Next, Tony buttonholes the show's heart and soul anchor Alex Reiger (Judd Hirsch), begging him for help with "the worst problem of my whole life." Though he briefly attempts to back off from his designated group problem-solver role – "'Alex, I've got the worst problem of my life' is right up there with 'Alex, is that thing on your neck getting any bigger,'" he grouses. "I don't want to hear it!" – Alex winds up hearing him out.

"No. You must've misinterpreted what he meant."

"Well, he said my simplicity was engaging and that we'd be wonderful together."

Reluctantly, Alex agrees to accompany Tony to set Kirk straight (so to speak).

"I don't understand," he says. "Why can't you do this yourself?"

"I can't be alone with him. I'm the one he spends tortured nights dreaming about."

"He said that?"

"No, I'm just assuming."

Suffice it to say, when Alex later finds Kirk at a genial and swinging gay bar, he is about as far from "tortured" as it is possible to be. In fact, the man is so accommodating he kindly wraps up the drama and plot in a pat and tidy package.

"Look, Kirk, I have a really terrible, difficult thing to talk to you about…"

Kirk offers up a wan smile. "Alex, I think I can guess what you're trying to tell me. But I've already told Elaine that I'm bisexual."

Alex instinctively seizes up and tries to shush him then catches himself. "Oh, it's okay here."

"Anyway, we're still friends and we had a fine talk. By the way, I understand that Tony's not interested and that's okay, too."

"Wow," Alex says, relieved. "I thought this was going to be difficult but instead it's a snap. Can we have a couple beers?"

Sure. Kirk's treat, even. Before they can knock one back, though, a bear of a man saunters up to ask Alex to dance. He resists, going so far as to drag hold the chair to his ass as he'd led onto the floor. Alex *wants* to hold back. He's *desperate* to hold back. He wants, in truth, to remain "the other" – to use a phrase that is well on its way to hackneyed status, if nevertheless appropriate here – in an establishment full of those who have been "other-ized." But the outcasts will not let him cast himself out. Instead, they overcome him with confidence, with *joie de vivre*, with acceptance. Resistance, it turns out, is futile. By the time Tony arrives Alex is up on the bar doing a modified *Saturday Night Fever* routine and having the time of his life. There is no discomfort, no division.

By 2020 "woke" standards is it progressive enough for contemporary culture cops? Hell, *no*. What is? I'm sure the hamminess of some of the extras in the final sequence is unacceptable to those without a sense of history, perspective, or humor. The truth is, however, in the context of that time – and considering the stats cited above – it's difficult to call the episode anything save a bold and visionary public service. According to research by PRRI, today 70 percent of Americans have "a close friend or family member who is gay or lesbian." When "Elaine's Strange Triangle" aired that number was in the low twenties.

Why does that matter?

"[R]esearch dating to the 1950s has consistently shown that social contact with members of particular communities eases prejudice and distrust," Daniel Cox of the American Enterprise Institute wrote at the FiveThirtyEight blog. "Social contact has been shown to reduce racial animus, religious prejudice and, more recently, antipathy toward gay and lesbian people. One reason negative stereotypes and discomfort with homosexuality endured so long was that relatively few people formed close relationships with those who were openly gay."

Taxi (1978–1983) chose to beam a humanizing, real portrait of fundamentally ostracized and persecuted people into the homes of a populace that was then – but would not remain – largely indifferent or outright hostile to their plight. We should be grateful to it as well as to Carson, who portrayed Kirk with nuance as well as swagger and sadly died in 2009 at age 57 of lymphoma.

Tony (Tony Danza) begins to realize that the beau (John David Carson) who has been courting Elaine (Marilu Henner) is also romantically interested in him in "Elaine's Strange Triangle" from Taxi. *Bisexuality would be seldom discussed in TV sitcoms, as homosexuality would be the more commonly placed "other than straight" orientation.*

"Who Am I?" from *The Facts of Life*
Original Air Date: 17 December 1980
By Lee Gambin

Actress Kim Fields – who played the role of Tootie – would join her fellow cast members at the TV Land Awards when *The Facts of Life* (1979–1988) would be entered into the television hall of fame and make a profound and moving statement. She would make mention that she always felt as an equal; an implication that her heritage and race was not at all ever an issue being a black actress among her white co-stars. Tootie would be the sole black girl in the central group of girls at Eastland in the hit sitcom, and when her race was brought up as a topic of conversation, it was because a fellow black character questioned her unity with white friends.

In the Very Special Episode "Who Am I?", black visibility and the importance of friendship that knows no color is a major focal point that is addressed in a very intelligent and matter of fact manner. It paints a picture of the vital need for black kids to be proud, but also highlights that genuine love among people is what severs the color divide. White kids and black kids are pals in *The Facts of Life*, and that is one of the core components of what makes this series so wonderful in the canon of discussion of inclusion and diversity without diversity being an obvious (and embarrassing) prerequisite.

Tootie's instant attraction to Fred (Erik Moses), the boy who tends to the candy machine, is made clear by her overt statements whilst ogling the teen. Fred is not only cocksure and proud, but he is a militant black – an extension of the always socially aware Michael Evans (Ralph Carter) from *Good Times* (1974–1979) (who even infuriated his parents with his Malcom X inspired brilliance) and even from the cantankerous George Jefferson (Sherman Hemsley) from *The Jeffersons* (1975–1985) (who was the black racist in sitcom history, the Afro-American variant of Archie Bunker (Carroll O'Connor), except wealthy and living in luxury). When Fred gets talking with Tootie, he starts to question her friendship with the rest of the girls, and his reference to "an ivory tower" and "real sisters" being "black sisters" sparks anger in Tootie at first – however, eventually, Tootie will start questioning her place in her social group. Fred makes bold statements scrutinizing Tootie's love for making Blair (Lisa Whelchel) a dress for the school dance, such as "Just like our people wanted to pick cotton", and his lack of seeing individualism and only seeing the color divide prompts Tootie to declare in great defense of her friendships with "we're like a family". Fred ultimately has an issue with white people and holds a bold resistance in trusting them, he even shows disdain for the loveable Mrs. Garrett (Charlotte Rae) in his expression when the ex-farm gal reminisces about her forties style dance entitled "The Jersey Bounce" – her poor white background and the hillbilly experience given a moment of clarity. And it is the ever-loving Mrs. Garrett who always supports and protects her girls. She is genuinely impressed with Tootie's flair and talent for fashion design, reinstating that she is most certainly the best friend to these girls; something that transcended the series itself as at the same TV Land Awards ceremony aforementioned, Kim Fields would make a clear point that Charlotte Rae was the absolute heart of the sitcom. Blair's admiration for Tootie's dancing talents also comes up, as Tootie is a star on the floor with her partner Carl (David Coburn), a Jewish boy (who "has rhythm"). However, none of this impresses Fred, who insists Tootie be exclusively friends with fellow black kids.

Tootie's attempts at making new friends doesn't turn out well. The three black girls she invites to hang with share no common interest with her and this confuses her even more. Thankfully, Mrs. Garrett's beautiful words of wisdom come into play and the crafty writing expresses a sensitive view point from a nurturing but white woman assisting the needs of a perplexed and angst-ridden black teen girl. Mrs. Garrett says "the black experience isn't my experience", which is a sublime reasoning and a valid point; what she is saying here is that the world is not easy and that life is not the same for one to another, however, the value of friendship should override any issue concerning place or integrity of spirit. She says "the answer is inside yourself and when you hear it, you'll know what to do", and Tootie eventually does know what to do: she wins the dance with Carl, reinstates her loving unity with Blair and the others, and also remains friends with Fred. When Mrs. Garrett explains that she is not the "black experience" so she has no point of reference to comment about Tootie's disposition, she is giving a selfless take on advice while making it known that she is most certainly a dear friend to Tootie – something that lives outside the realm of simply being her headmistress.

But the episode allows for Tootie to be frustrated at the lack of her embracing a black heritage – so before she learns that friendship is more important than race division, she explores black history by using her artistic talents to bring it to her attention. Blair's dress turns out to be an African design, something that the vain and uppity Blair embraces and is proud to wear. When Tootie begins to question her position among her white friends, she starts to doubt her place. This feeling is completely unwarranted as Mrs. Garrett points out "You always seemed so happy here", however Tootie's angry cry is that she is terrified of never knowing who she is, in that racial recognition may be important and writers Linda Marsh and Margie Peters ensure that it is important for many people, it's just that Tootie is on her own road of self-discovery and what she learns in the end is that the "sisterhood" she shares with the rest of the gang knows no racial heritage because it isn't an issue. *The Facts of Life* presents a color blind world, where white kids and black kids are equals, however, when race becomes an issue – either brought up from a bigoted white person or an expression of black visibility that makes note of exactly that – characters can be rendered divided. But it is in the closing moments of the episode where the union of Tootie and Carl dancing together summarizes the togetherness aspect of such a show: their dancing representative of color blind glory, which even evokes Fred to cheer on.

The Facts of Life is a perfect example of inclusionary television without harping on about the concern and making it completely organic and also sweet. In this series, the chubby funny girl can be best friends with the vain and well-to-do blonde beauty, and the wiseass tomboy can be best buddies with the sassy privileged black girl and so forth. Black and white friendships in television is a trope that has stemmed from the likes of Jack Benny and Eddie "Rochester" Anderson. One of the most lasting and most pure black and white friendships in TV sitcom history would be shared between Edith Bunker (Jean Stapleton) of *All in the Family* (1971–1979) and Louise Jefferson (Isabel Sanford) from *The Jeffersons*. There is a remarkably touching moment in the pilot for The Jeffersons from *All in the Family* entitled "The Jeffersons Move On Up" where Edith gives a heartfelt goodbye to her friend – "Louise…. did I ever tell you that I love you?" This touching moment in television showed the entire world that the compassion, loyalty and dedication shared between people who truly love one another is completely without a question of color whatsoever. As Louise leaves Edith for a life of wealth and privilege, we see the white working class woman left in the shambles of a disheveled home while her black counterpart gets to celebrate "movin' on up" to a "deluxe apartment in the sky". *The Facts of Life* would be spearheaded by *All in the Family* and *The Jeffersons* creator Norman Lear, and what Lear does is bring these topics to the fore and not only details the ugliness of prejudice, but also highlights the beauty in interracial love and togetherness. "Who Am I?" is a proud episode that delivers the essence of finding oneself and yet seeing that search as an obsolete take on, simply because what matters is the individual and the personal quest for happiness – something Tootie finds with a little help from her friends.

"Cousin Geri" from *The Facts of Life*
Original Air Date: 24 December 1980
By Lee Gambin

Actress, comedienne and writer Geri Jewell grew up like many youngsters, escaping into the world of television. However, for Jewell this means to escape was to find refuge in secret worlds that would shield her from the prejudice she'd face from people who thought of her having cerebral palsy as something to mock or pity. Jewell would stay strong and defiant and grow into one of the most inspirational artists of her generation, finally getting to star on a sitcom – a medium she loved so much as a youngster. In her debut episode of *The Facts of Life* (1979–1988) named after her character "Cousin Geri", Jewell would introduce the world to a self-possessed, confident young woman with a disability who would use comedy and a vibrant sense of humor to tackle people's prejudice or even discomfort when in the company of people living with varied physical disabilities. With Jewell playing the cousin of the self-involved but gorgeous Blair (Lisa Whelchel), the episode tackles issues as varied as ignorance and the right to ask questions.

On top of the world, winning the fine arts festival prize, Blair's vanity and self-obsession is interestingly a façade built from a tremendous amount of self-doubt and fragility and in this episode we see her vulnerabilities and also her pure ability to see her cousin as an equal, Blair doesn't seem to "see" the disability. When she hears news of cousin Geri visiting there is a stillness in the air, Blair is not at all comfortable and it is learned that she has never mentioned her before to the other girls nor to house mother Mrs. Garrett (Charlotte Rae). A question arises when we first meet cousin Geri – is Blair embarrassed of her because she has cerebral palsy? This lingering question sits to the fore as we have come to know how superficial and shallow Blair could be, however, we also know that deep down hidden inside is a girl who has a tremendous amount of warmth and decency. This is something that is on show as this particular episode develops.

Characters with disabilities on long running shows are seldom main players, with the exception of legendary actors such as Chris Burke who played Corky, a young man with Down syndrome in the series *Life Goes On* (1989–1993), however they would pop up as one-off guest stars often to point out the importance of disability rights or to teach able-bodied persons about the plight of such individuals. Geri would become a semi-regular, appearing on follow up episodes which would develop her character including her having a romance with a handsome beau, and Geri Jewell's real life friendship with Lisa Whelchel is a wonderful aside in chronicling the legacy of *The Facts of Life*. Jewell and Whelchel would both be struggling young actresses and move in together, living as housemates and developing a loving sisterly friendship, that truly comes across in the final moments of "Cousin Geri".

Tootie's (Kim Fields) eavesdropping (a character trait of the youngest of the gang) lends an ear so to speak into gaining an insight into Blair's distress over the news of Geri coming to visit. She is overheard talking to her mother on the telephone and one line sticks out: "Did you tell Mrs. Garrett *about* Geri?" There is something *about* Geri that is clearly a concern – and upon Geri's entrance it remains unclear until Mrs. Garrett approaches her asking "You must be her (Blair's) cousin Geri?" The shaky walking and disorientation in the muscles of her neck have Geri liken having cerebral palsy to being drunk, which is something that showcases her ability to turn her disability into a point of humor – it is her disability and therefore hers to own and treat it how she wishes, and being a comedienne, she has it as a springboard for well-developed jokes that actually empower her.

The girls response to someone with cerebral palsy is honest and delicately performed, and they are put as ease in seconds when Geri proclaims "Don't worry I'm not drunk, I have cerebral palsy", exposing a t-shirt that reinforces the joke. Tootie is the first to laugh at Geri's self-deprecating humor, and Natalie (Mindy Cohn) nudges her and warns her to be careful about what she laughs at. Here the episode takes on a major topic – the role of jokes and humor in the face of something that is serious and could be considered an affliction to pity. A delicate subject of course, but handled here with dignity and power from Geri Jewell. Blair's reunion with Geri is just as controversial, because of course it seems that Blair is embarrassed of her cousin, but as the show moves forward we see that she is actually jealous of Geri; that Geri gets a lot of attention from the family and is a success which infuriates Blair who wants to be the center of attention. Therefore, as selfish as Blair seems, she is also the character here who doesn't seem to acknowledge Geri's disability as something as a negative.

When the girls ask questions about cerebral palsy, they are careful and cautious, but Geri once again puts them at eases with a statement that would become a war cry for people living with disabilities: "Questions don't hurt, ignorance does."

When Blair actively avoids Geri, it pisses off Jo (Nancy McKeon) the most and she angrily confronts Blair with Blair not fighting back, a rarity in their relationship. This is because Blair doesn't wish to admit the real reason behind her avoidance of Geri, so she sits there and takes the abuse from Jo. It takes the ever-loving Mrs. Garrett wanting Blair to hang out with Geri to prompt Blair's confessional – explaining the real reason as to why she is upset about Geri's presence. This churns out Mrs. Garrett's realization: "You're not embarrassed of Geri, you're jealous of her." Blair sees Geri as competition and admires her ("Geri is out there winning battles") and she sees Geri's achievements as noble and vitally important whereas she sees her own achievements (like winning the fine arts fair award) as trivial. Blair is a complex character – a girl who is seemingly selfish and vain, and yet not at all. Underneath it all, she is someone who is not at all certain of her own abilities and qualifications, she wins awards and excels in varied undertakings, but in the grand scheme of it all, she sees them as meaningless compared to the strength, talent and resilience of her cousin.

By the end of the episode at the arts award dinner, Geri is a smash hit with her stand-up show, and eventually Blair – who has come around since having words with the forever wise Mrs. Garrett – joins her on stage and the duo perform "Tea For Two" complete with a jokey vaudeville-style shtick. When we hear "hit it partner", we understand that this is a union completely born from love and solidarity, there is a sisterhood that knows no ability or disability, and it stems from a deep mutual respect that has been around since the two were little girls. Blair turns to her cousin and says "I think you're terrific", with Geri replying "I love you, Blair". Mrs. Garrett collects the girls into her arms, kisses them and the entire gang of Eastland High join a chorus singing the praises of sisterhood and unity, something that comes from a place of togetherness and unity.

Actress, comedienne and activist Geri Jewell makes her debut in "Cousin Geri" from The Facts of Life, *an episode that would deliver a plea for respect toward people living with disabilities in "Questions don't hurt, ignorance does."*

"Shoplifting" from *The Facts of Life*
Original Air Date: 31 December 1980
By Lee Gambin

Airing on New Year's Eve in 1980, *The Facts of Life* (1979–1988) episode "Shoplifting" would be a staple in the realm of TV sitcoms, dramas and PSAs dealing with teens who think that stealing is not a "serious crime". In "The Big Heist" from *Diff'rent Strokes* (26 November 1981), "Christmas Shoplifting" from *Punky Brewster* (15 December 1985), "The Thief" from *Mr. Belvedere* (26 September 1986) and so forth, it was a safe bet that hammering home the issue of light fingered kids and teens would be an easily conveyed message for youngsters glued in front of their TV sets ready to watch the latest antics of their favorite sitcom characters.

With the impending birthday of Mrs. Garrett (Charlotte Rae) who is incidentally feeling great about her appearance and how she feels ("I am older, and that's OK!"), the girls of Eastland want to surprise their headmistress with lovely gifts. The prissy but loveable Blair (Lisa Whelchel) refuses to chip in for a present and instead opts for getting her own gift (an expensive Gucci handbag), while Jo (Nancy McKeown) devises a plan to bring together whatever cash Tootie (Kim Fields) and Natalie (Mindy Cohn) have between them in order to get Mrs. Garrett a "pretty nice" gift. Blair and Jo's rivalry is of course a centerpiece for the show; it is one of the hearts the show runs by. The constant digs at one another are reflective of one girl being wealthy and from a life of privilege and the other being a poor kid from the street and from a broken home, and here, there is more of it and based upon the value of gifts.

The temptation of stealing items from hoity stores like Harrisons (featured here) is a trope in sitcoms and other teen-centric television, as for the most part the teens don't have the cash and are met with snide, rude and arrogant shop clerks always ready to judge. Jo selects a rather loud Hawaiian blouse that Mrs. Garrett might like but the price is way too high, so Jo – being from the street and also already angry by the tone of the shop clerk – introduces the other girls to the world of shoplifting. When they protest, Jo says "A big store like this is not gonna miss one blouse." The sentiment here is that big chains and so forth are mass marketed institutions that don't suffer at the hands of measly teen five finger discounts. Jokes come by such as Natalie's paranoia "If we get caught, we'll be accessories!", with Tootie replying "How can we be accessories when we're in sports wear?" and the show keeps the issue at hand relatively lighthearted. The mood for this episode only really shifts when it comes to the point of Jo addressing the feeling of not being alone anymore; in that now this tomboy with a hard edge suddenly feels at home and just wanted to do something nice for the person who made her feel that. Therefore, the intention behind the shoplifting is relatively speaking an admirable thing, however, a fact of life that is driven home here is that stealing is absolutely wrong.

When Jo, Tootie and Natalie bring in their gift for Mrs. Garrett, Blair asks about the Harrisons box and Jo is quick with an answer. Her hardened life has prepared her for these kind of sticky situations, however she cannot fool Mrs. Garrett for too long. When the fun loving house den mother finds that the blouse is roomy on her (harking back to her self-worth and the joy she feels for losing weight), it inevitably sends her back to Harrisons to exchange the gift and the episode tips into a farce where she is deemed the thief. All of the snappy set up gags have Mrs. Garrett thought of as being the culprit. The store detective interrogates her with sly implications that Mrs. Garrett confuses as a come on ("Are you trying to pick me up?") and here we get to see Charlotte Rae's exquisite handling of comedic timing, reactions and breathy delivery of lines on display with great fun and gusto. Upon returning to the school, Mrs. Garrett gets the girls to confess to shoplifting and she teaches them a lesson about the importance of gifts being from the heart and not as a status symbol (like Blair's Gucci offering). Mrs. Garrett lays out examples of her simple loves – flowers, seashells, a simple note – and where she teaches Jo that stealing is wrong, we get a sense of Jo's sentiment being misguided, but also how it comes from a place of how she feels. The character of Jo would be a late addition to *The Facts of Life*, as she would be included in season two, and interestingly enough, added after the famous season one girl-cull. Therefore, when progress is being made – that this stoic and self-righteous tough can soften and get closer to the gang and most importantly Mrs. Garrett – it is a positive thing, even though it is expressed by criminal means.

"Shoplifting" from The Facts of Life *lays down the law in regard to one of the most popular "pastimes" of eighties teens cruising the shopping malls.*

"Breaking Point" from *The Facts of Life*
Original Air Date: 28 January 1981
By Lee Gambin

Suicide would become a big cultural conversation among the youth in the early eighties; in many ways, the issue would develop into one solely "owned" by teenagers in an era that was oft described as a period of excess and societal comfort, but also documented as a period of severe alienation and disenfranchisement. In eighties America, teens did not have a war to fight against as their parents did during the hippy movement of the sixties, nor did they have civil rights issues at hand as the teens of earlier decades faced – here in this landscape of shopping malls and MTV, teenagers felt the new enemy was peer pressure and parental figures who just did not understand them, and this was reflected in the films, TV, music and theatre of the time – some of which dealt head on with teen suicide. On top of such a grim scrutiny of one of society's biggest taboos was the examination of various methods of "opting out" with drug induced suicide being a major contributor to the universal dialogue. This episode of *The Facts of Life* (1979-1988), "Breaking Point", is one such case study – a teenage girl who is pressured to do well and also alien to her estranged parents (who are also about to divorce) takes pills to "see herself out"; keeping true reasons a complete secret, adding to the mystery of it all for the surviving girls at Eastland who just cannot figure it out.

With the episode opening with glamorous but uppity Blair (Lisa Whelchel) nominated for class president, the show provides a running commentary on competition and drive. This running for such a pivotal role at the school is important for Blair, and her being the most popular girl at Eastland, it is a given that she will win it. However, young Cynthia (Denise Halma), an "in and out" character, never before seen in an episode on a sitcom that had a hefty amount of characters running the hallowed halls of Eastland, is about to give Blair a run for her money – eventually winning the coveted role.

As housemistress Mrs. Garrett (Charlotte Rae) brings in the ballots, we learn that Cynthia knows fluent French whereas Blair pretentiously only knows a tiny bit – reinstating the fact that although Blair may consider herself worldly and sophisticated, there are other girls who surpass her. But the common grounds the girls share is profound and is not overstated, but thoughtfully established. It is understood that Cynthia is the daughter of a diplomat – a father who is distant and always absent – and this systematically links she and Blair, in that both are from wealthy backgrounds (referred to by working class Jo (Nancy McKeon) as "two Royals Royce's") with Blair also having an estranged relationship with her own wealthy mother as seen in an early episode "Like Mother, Like Daughter" (31 August 1979). For these two girls, wealth and class has pushed them out of their family's lives – there is no place for Blair or Cynthia in a world their parents have become oppressed by; therefore, the struggles of the "poor little rich kid" rings true in these two characters who are up against each other but also sculpted out of such similar clay.

Leading into the final act that deals with suicide, the episode has some surprising elements that foreshadow the darkness with a light approach. At one point, Jo suggests that Blair lose the election in an honorable fashion much like the suicidal samurai in the martial arts classic *Shogun* (1980), miming the self-mutilation of a sword entering the body and hitting all the vital organs. But this is not an attempt to make fun of the heavy subject matter that will eventually be addressed, it is an extension of Jo's means to understand death. Jo, unlike Blair and the soon to be dead Cynthia, is hardened and street wise, however, death and loss is something she cannot face at ease. So instead, this tough talking teen puts up the front of humor to confront such morbid realism. On top of such interesting side pieces that pepper the episode, Blair's plans to "revolutionize" Eastland by changing the school anthem is yet again a prime external example of her superficiality that will eventually (by the time the episode comes to a close) diminish and make way for a higher learning. This would be a common trope for the character of Blair, who will start at one point and end at another far more clearly and obviously than her counterparts. When Blair loses the election to Cynthia, there is a lot of time spent on her being a sore loser, but the next sequence which has the girls cleaning up the kitchen, brings everything home and sets up the final act of the episode which will examine the dire after effects of suicide. However, Blair's face-front angst over not winning class president becomes a sluggish (but important) B story that treats teen depression in a light comedic approach, but subversively says something about deep rooted issues that teens have which can lead to suicide. Mrs. Garrett offers wise advice: "Blair, it's not healthy to keep your emotions all bottled up", which right now is funny, but acts as a precursor to later words of wisdom that can save lives.

Back to the scene at hand, Cynthia enters the kitchen bouncing happily and is met by the other girls greeting her wholeheartedly. She makes mention of her father but wants to change the subject quickly and taking a shine to Tootie (Kim Fields), she hands over a medallion that she says symbolizes friendship and hospitality. Tootie's gratitude and admiration of Cynthia leads into Mrs. Garrett bringing over a newspaper where there is a report that Cynthia's father is off to Germany for business. Blair is thrilled by this (if Cynthia leaves, she will be president instead), but Cynthia explains that her father doesn't want her to come along and that it is important for his daughter to stay in one place and have friends and "be a teenager". There is an indication that Cynthia is "growing up way too fast" and not permitted to enjoy life as an adolescent.

Following up from this subliminal "discussion" on growing up too fast and the disallowance of the teen years, Tootie breaks into the scene hollering about Cynthia being unconscious and finding pills by her limp body. Mrs. Garrett takes charge – she tells Natalie (Mindy Cohn) to get the headmaster, Blair to call the ambulance and lets everyone know that she is going to see Cynthia. Later, Mrs. Garrett has the girls making fudge because it is learned that when Cynthia wakes up from being unconscious she will be hungry. During this sequence, Jo lets in on her own suicide story, about her New York friend Gloria who threw herself off a building. Interestingly enough the eighties hit song "Gloria" from artist Laura Branigan which would become a dynamic smash in 1982 (the year after this episode aired) would be a song about a young woman struggling with mental illness, social anxiety and depression and there are some reports that the song was about a real life woman who had killed herself because of such emotional anguish.

"Suicides among young people happen every day" says Mrs. Garrett, and Jo's tough exterior begins to soften just as Blair's self-importance starts to simmer. The news of Cynthia's death via a phone call from the hospital devastates Mrs. Garrett and the girls, and it especially affects Tootie whose friendship is represented by the pendant she was given. The closing sequence of the episode is the most telling and also a package deal of public service announcements dressed up as a finely written piece of television drama with tiny moments of comedic ease in there just to ensure that yes, we still are watching a situation comedy. While the girls pack up Cynthia's bedroom, there is talk about the reasons behind Cynthia's suicide, and more importantly moments of regret from some of the girls. Blair looks at some of Cynthia's clothes and mentions that the girl had style which fires up Jo who remarks "You should have told her!" Here the idea that people being there for others while they're alive is hammered home and Jo's realist attitude is a driving force throughout the scene. As much as the girl has softened throughout the course of the episode, she still pushes the hard truth: her response to suicide is "Dying is brutal!" – a clear indication that the girl has dealt with this kind of situation before. Another fascinating element to the episode marks commentary on what other TV shows and films of the time dealt with, the idea of supposedly having the perfect life not being perfect whatsoever and that seemingly cheery, happy, comfortable and "normal" youngsters can harbor deep dark desires to kill themselves. In many teen suicide case studies it has been found that teens who have to be moved around often and have no sense of "home" have a high risk of killing themselves, and this is also the case for teen girls under a lot of pressure to succeed especially when in direct competition with other girls of varied social classes, and on top of that young people who have strained relations with their parents and feeling guilt from impending or current divorce status. All of these attributes make up Cynthia's dilemma – and although it is not clear as to why she did it, it doesn't matter; the concern is that it can be anyone, as the loving and perpetually nurturing Mrs. Garrett explains. Her warm words of advice echo through the tube universally as she cries out in a desperate plea for adults to stop and listen and understand their teenagers and for teens themselves to know that yes "life is always changing" but "when you feel that you're at the end of your rope, tie a knot and hang on!" Mrs. Garrett wants teens to survive and live and thrive and be the best they can, and most importantly to know that they are loved and cherished – as she teaches Natalie, Blair, Jo and Tootie the facts of life, we too, as her secondary wardens, learn to heed her advice and welcome her knowledge. That this earth-mother that actress

Charlotte Rae embodies, is a woman from a poor farming community who is now in charge of a generation of girls who will grow into wonderful women, and that we too can take from that and understand what it truly means to be human.

Tootie being the youngest and most affected is taken under Mrs. Garrett's wing. She understands how it hurts her most when the normally upbeat and spunky kid asks "How could she do that to herself? And not even say goodbye!" Mrs. Garrett suggests that the pendant was a way of saying goodbye and this resonates with Tootie eventually, after her anger leads to forgiveness and bewilderment dissolves into understanding. Mrs. Garrett jumps in and out of personal insight and dives into broad lessons when she talks about the signals that could prevent teen suicide and the importance of telling friends and family. She lets the girls know that she understands the pressures of being a teen and explains that "it's ok to feel confused and frightened and insecure…", to which Blair responds with the aforementioned higher learning, where her new idea for the school is to create a life line phone number that troubled teens can call in order to reach out and get support.

The closing moments of this super somber Very Special Episode has the now quietly confused but forgiving Tootie collect the pendant and put it on – a symbol of eternal friendship with an understanding that suicide is not an answer but something that can be forgiven for those who just hurt too much with no way out, while the final shot features Mrs. Garrett turning off the lights in Cynthia's room, mournfully letting go and yet just as quietly confused as her young pupil Tootie. Strangely this moment is similar to the last scene in the three part final episode of *Cheers* "One for the Road" (20 May 1993) where Sam Malone (Ted Danson) closes the bar for good when he sells it to move out to California. In both episodes, the end of an era is marked with a dramatic sign off: in

Teen suicide becomes a topic of conversation at Eastland in "Breaking Point" from The Facts of Life.

Cheers (1982–1993), it establishes Sam's new life and the death of an old world that we have come to love ("where everybody knows your name") and for "Breaking Point" in *The Facts of Life* (an early episode in the long running sitcom) it marks a sense of more dark terrain to come – as the show will be a heavy duty deliverer of the VSE phenomenon.

"Mork Meets Robin Williams" from *Mork & Mindy*
Original Air Date: 19 February 1981
By Lee Gambin

On 11 August 2014, superstar comedian and actor Robin Williams committed suicide at his home in Paradise Cay, California at the age of sixty three. An artist who continually struggled with drug and alcohol dependency (going in and out of rehabilitation centers throughout the years) as well as someone who wrestled with mental illness and depression, Williams would shoot to stardom from working the stand-up comedy circuit before landing a guest role as erratic and nutsy alien Mork from Ork on the *Happy Days* episode "My Favorite Orkan" (a play on the classic sixties sitcom *My Favorite Martian* (1963–1966)). This would ultimately act as a backdoor pilot for the character who would soon receive his own sitcom *Mork & Mindy* (1978–1982) – a successful and beloved show that ran on the coattails of Williams's impressive improvisational skills and masterful handling of broad physical comedy. Of course the series would also counter Williams's irreverent insanity and playfulness with sturdy situation comedy writing that would be anchored primarily by the lovely and talented Pam Dawber as the titular Mindy McConnell – a compassionate and understanding young woman who teaches Mork what it "means to be human".

With a magnetic chemistry set in place, Williams and Dawber would bounce off one another in a sitcom devoted to understanding American culture and institutions through the eyes of the ultimate outsider – a thematic arc that would resurface in sitcoms such as *Small Wonder* (1985–1989) and *Perfect Strangers* (1986–1993). This lesson learning would lend a lot of opportunity for many moving and heart wrenching maudlin moments throughout *Mork & Mindy*'s run – and with Robin Williams being a comic who most definitely enjoyed (and was very good at) tipping into the realm of heartbreak and watery eyed dramatics, *Mork & Mindy* would quite often shift its focus from highly energized frantic gag-a-minute craziness to solemn, introspective, quiet snippets of delicate sentimentality.

However, referring back to the preface of this piece in addressing the suicide of Robin Williams, one episode sticks out like a sore thumb in its eerie foreshadowing of future events to come. Amidst the shock of Williams's death, global conversation would spark scrutinizing the concerns born from the role of celebrity and the perils that come with living in the limelight – thirty three years before this Hollywood legend ended it all, an episode of *Mork & Mindy* would detail the frailty of stardom and the desperate agony of never being allowed to have one moment alone. "Mork Meets Robin Williams" is a chilling example of life imitating art and brings the topic of public responsibility to the foreground with the very reasonable highly articulated notion that "sometimes stars need some time out" as the formative backbone to the core issue at hand.

The episode opens with a keen focus on Mindy's newfound career as a local reporter which is a detail that is essential not only for the plot of the episode, but something that feeds her character as a young working class girl finally achieving aspects of success that she has worked hard for. Mindy is on the telephone to her boss with the intention of getting an interview with "a famous comedian" and her drive and ambition propels the story forward. When Robin Williams enters the scene as Mork, he gets a massive applause from the studio audience, and coming into shot ready to interact with his co-star Dawber, we understand his appeal and popularity outside the trappings of the sitcom itself. Even to the naked virginal *Mork & Mindy* eye, the common belief here would be that this frizzy haired, impish and hyperactive joker is a massive star, loved by millions.

With bouncy back and forths delivered from straight (wo)man Dawber and crazed clown Williams, such as:

MINDY: Don't forget to hold in your stomach!

MORK: Don't forget to hold in your thighs!

The episode throws itself into semi-meta material where Mork is "introduced" to the idea and religion of celebrity via the existence of a comedian that is incredibly successful. When Mindy tells him that she will hopefully be interviewing Robin Williams, Mork responds with "Who?" He also makes fun of his name and explains to Mindy that "Robin" means something vulgar back on his home planet of Ork. When he whispers the Orkian meaning of "Robin" in Mindy's ear, she pulls an offended face, exclaiming "Oh that's disgusting!"

The concept of celebrity as something meaningless to an alien being who can only hear profanity is a profound statement here in this episode of *Mork & Mindy*, in that the finely tuned balance between darting to and fro from performer and artistry to conceptual reflexive knowledge and personal analysis is a mesmerizing and complicated nuanced examination of not only character and vocation, but the self-worth of a baggy pants clown.

Mork is perplexed as to why Mindy is so desperate to interview this Robin Williams person, so she explains: "A lot of people on earth are real interested in what celebrities have to say". Mindy also tells Mork that she thinks he looks a lot like Robin Williams (a physical linkage is established) but Mork insists on criticizing the comic – he mocks the record cover sporting Williams's face etc – and in doing this, Mork trivializes the seemingly important role of Robin Williams in the world of entertainment. What is happening here is more than surface laugh inducing gags with a meta-edge, instead, we have the mask of the character of Mork permitted a moment on mass commercial television to comment on his "real life" counterpart – and in many regards, the real tragedy here is that the "mask" has a concerning disdain and flippant disrespect for the tortured clown behind Mork. This aspect of "character" commenting on and passing judgment on "performer" can be a confronting dichotomy, and the intricate and delicate equilibrium between reality and fantasy and comfort and disorder is a controversial insight into mental and emotional stability. Magically, what could be unnerving in an off-putting sense is manipulated beautifully by the incredibly emotionally aware Robin Williams both as Mork and later in the episode, as himself. Williams has a sturdy control on his emotional availability and much like performers such as Danny Kaye and Gene Wilder before him, he could turn on the flamboyance and the comedy, but just as easily bring his audience to tears with a simple gesture or expression.

"Mork Meets Robin Williams" taps into the cult of celebrity and examines the influence of fandom over grounded earthy friendship. The mere presence of this popular comic starts to infiltrate and influence personal connections throughout the episode. When Mindy finds out that Robin Williams had visited Da Vinci's (a restaurant her friends, siblings Jeannie (Gina Hecht) and Remo (Jay Thomas) own), her friendship with them is tested because they had forgotten to let her know. And with the rumor that Robin Williams would return to Da Vinci's, the usually subdued Boulder Italian eatery is buzzing with excitement, loaded with people ready to catch a glimpse of their favorite comedy star. WASP friend/foil Nelson (Jim Staahl) even insults Mindy by calling her "Some kind of groupie!" This all culminates when Mork enters Da Vinci's, and people (believing him to be Robin Williams) crowd him and swamp him, chasing him out of the restaurant and onto the streets. Technically, this is a strange scene and somewhat cinematic in its depiction of mass crowds chasing after Mork/Robin Williams. It aesthetically lives outside of the television studio format and with that comes a sense of pseudo-realism in its depiction of actual fans getting a piece of this damaged comedian.

The frenzy of celebrity chasing also leads to the normally honest and good Mindy lying as she pretends to be leading media figure Barbara Walters in order to land an interview, while Mindy's boss comes to represent the everyday Joe who seems to be trapped by the perils of overbearing responsibility. He drinks to handle stress and this is a correlative thematic nerve that connects substance abuse to handling high demands – the difference here is that he is to suffer in silence, while even a star's personal vices are up for the world to see.

With the public thinking that Mork is Robin Williams (he returns to Mindy's house with his clothes ripped to shreds and in a state of panic), the dark side of never getting a moment's peace come crashing into the heart of the piece, delivering the fear it instils in the usually happy go lucky Mork. With Mindy as his emotional anchor, Mork tries to understand fandom and the hazards that come with show business and stardom, and although during the early moments of the episode these themes are given a comic injection, things suddenly turn rather grim and meditative as the show progresses. This second wave begins when Mork and Mindy are mobbed outside the stage door – once again, fans waiting to meet Robin Williams mistake the alien as the famous comedian – and they are rushed inside by a concerned security guard. Here again, this sequence looks vividly different from the studio audience set-up, it reads in filmic terms and breathes with a celluloid pulse: the mobbing of Mork/Robin Williams is possibly a real account of fandom. When Mork and Mindy are allowed in Robin Williams's dressing room, the show turns dark and morphs into *sitcom therapy* with Mork undermining the role of stars, while his meta-counter Robin Williams gets a huge applause from the studio audience (a bizarre bookend to Mork's first appearance on the episode).

With use of the Hayley Mills/*The Parent Trap* (1961) gag to keep Robin Williams and Mork in the same shot (and the use of some not-so-convincing stand in performers), the sequence unravels with Robin Williams granting Mindy her interview. During the course of the chit chat, Mindy is saddened by Williams's loss of identity, struggle with personal space, addiction to his work, inability to "switch off" and his endless servitude to his public. She coins a weighty sentiment with: "The comedian who can't say no." Robin Williams's desperation for people to like him (stemming from childhood) is discussed and thoughtfully plotted under the microscopic lens, and this tortured and tragic alienated clown is given a moment of counsel and deeply philosophical introspection. Mindy suggests "If you learnt to say 'no' you'll have more time for yourself", and following this without a moment's pause is Robin Williams's response: "Maybe that's the last thing I want." This quiet and deeply somber confessionary summarizes the artist who just cannot disconnect from their work and if they are forced to "deal with themselves" they would implode. The hit therapy musical *A Chorus Line* (originally performed in 1975) would be influential in sitcoms such as *Mork & Mindy* (the episode "Reflections and Regrets" would use the format of personal exorcism as its fundamental root), and in that Pulitzer Prize winning success story about dancers auditioning for a new Broadway show, one of them confesses: "Give me lines to read, just don't get me to talk. I can't do that." In "Mork Meets Robin Williams" this is exactly the same sentiment – that performers purely on earth to entertain are there for their audience, and seldom there for themselves.

When Mork attempts to break the seriousness of the episode ("You're breaking her perky little heart"), Mindy sacrifices her burgeoning career as a journalist and wishes to give Robin Williams space. She refuses to interview him and wishes to allow him a sense of personal freedom. Williams however grants her something even better – an on-camera interview before leaving to tour (once again, the artist who doesn't stop). In this seldom discussed Very Special Episode, the frightening aspects of stardom are simmered when Robin Williams talks about the characters that he created as a child that could speak for him and do things for him; the mask he created (Mork from *Mork & Mindy* being just another one) to cope. As Mindy and Mork follow Robin Williams out to watch him perform, they remark "hear that applause!" and Mork turns around to take one more look at the dressing room and mouths a triumphant "Yeah!" – when fame brings so many people so much joy, somehow the loneliness, isolation, addiction, questioning of self-worth and denial of privacy seems all worthwhile (but with a heavy price).

When Mork reports back to his leader Orson (voiced by Ralph James) from Ork, he discusses the personal sacrifices celebrities endure in order to serve the public and their art. Orson remains confused by the notion of humans taking issue in being success stories ("Isn't being famous a good thing?"), but Mork teaches his godly superior that fame can be personally damaging and also fatal. He lists stars that died in their prime; whether from drug overdoses such as Elvis Presley, Marilyn Monroe, Janis Joplin, Jimi Hendrix and Lenny Bruce or by suicide such as comic legend Freddie Prinze and finally John Lennon, who was killed by deranged Beatles fan Mark David Chapman only less than two months before the episode aired. The incredibly somber coda to the show, with a teary eyed Mork/Robin Williams talking about stars from film, music and comedy who had died is a creepy forewarning and revelation into his own personal demise.

The not-so-perfect life of a celebrity is examined in "Mork Meets Robin Williams" from Mork & Mindy – *this would have Robin Williams himself meet his alien counterpart and make a profound statement on the stresses and anxieties facing those in the limelight.*

"Reflections and Regrets" from *Mork & Mindy*
Original Air Date: 14 May 1981
By Lee Gambin

Producer and show runner Gary Marshall was no stranger to sentiment in his situation comedies. Marshall had delivered some wonderful tender moments in classics such as *Happy Days* (1974–1984) and its multiple spin-offs such as *Laverne & Shirley* (1976–1983) and then later with short lived but cult favorites like *Joanie Loves Chachi* (1982–1983), but here in *Mork & Mindy* (1978–1982) there was a lot of room for such sweetness and elegance within the comedy and this was primarily due to actor Robin Williams's uncanny ability to drop it right down and deliver the softness, heartfelt warmth and sincere affection to his loveable usually manic alien from Ork. Somber episodes of *Mork & Mindy* were a prominent fixture, and most notably a lot dealt with Mork (the outsider) teaching the "regular folk" (human beings from earth) valuable lessons, and here in "Reflections and Regrets" – a rarity in that this is an episode that does not end with Mork reporting back to Orson – Mork teaches Mindy a valuable lesson in the memory of her mother, that she is a much loved beautiful young woman and that regrets are something you can use and become empowered by.

The episode takes place on Mr. Bickley's (Tom Poston) 50th birthday which sparks conversations about regrets among the party guests. Mr. Bickley opens the discussion with a comical take on not ever telling his son (a blind man who would make a magnificent impression in the Very Special Episode "Mork Learns to See") the facts of life ("I bet he's with some girl, wondering what to do…"), which in turn prompts the loving Mindy to suggest that Mr. Bickley not be so hard on himself and makes mention that everyone has regrets regardless of their age. Ultimately, by the end of the episode, Mr. Bickley comes to understand that age has most certainly nothing to do with having lifelong regrets, and decides that he will start "living again", and optimistically looks forward to the "next fifty years" with a brand new outlook on life.

The lovely Glenda Faye (Crissy Wilzak) makes the suggestion for everyone to discuss their regrets in life and what unfolds is somewhat a "therapy play", which was a major trend happening in the theatre, spawning primarily from the hit groundbreaking Pulitzer Award winning musical *A Chorus Line*, which focused on a group of dancers auditioning for a new show who had to reveal their personal pains, demons, darkness and so forth in order to win the heart of their hardened and somewhat unfeeling (and unseen) director. Characters expressing their deepest regrets would be something that mostly belonged on the theatrical stage, so for Gary Marshall and his team to reposition this onto the television set was revolutionary and remarkably interesting. This group therapy would play out like an excursion into the deep recesses of each character's psyches, and of course some stories are comical, but some are tragic and heavy – but all of them showcase a truth about each character. Although this runs its course in sitcom time (less than thirty minutes), we still get a feel for the characters and their dilemmas and personal desires.

Jeannie's (Gina Hecht) self-worth is scrutinized and dissected when she talks about having a brief romance with a wonderful man whose only problem was that he was married, while Nelson's (Jim Staahl) dream girl of his teen years lends itself to being less of an important anecdote. Nelson, a character not normally allowed such tender moments, has his recalling a young girl who "could have been the one" leave a public bus, sidelined to make way for Robin Williams' mimicry of the young girl he is describing. Here, Williams the master mime, steals the limelight and even prompts some of the cast members to laugh in hysterics while trying to stick to the script and hold momentum. One of the most touching stories is directly inspired by *A Chorus Line* in that it is all about dance. Glenda Faye expresses her love for dancing (ballet, jazz, contemporary et al) and sees dance as an expression of freedom as well as an art form, but then loses all interest and all desire for the craft when her man – who shared her love for dancing – died tragically. But the spark in her still exists ("It's not right to close off part of you is it?") and Mork comes to the rescue, proving the aforementioned point that Robin Williams can jump from comic (reinterpreting Nelson's story) to dramatic (saving Glenda Faye from her loneliness and reigniting her love for dance). The influence of *A Chorus Line* is undeniable – here the dance number between Glenda Faye and Mork (which inspires overhead camera work – something seldom seen in TV sitcoms) is an extension of many of the therapy numbers that shape that Michael Bennett musical about those who "put themselves on the line".

After Remo's (Jay Thomas) comic relief moment, which in itself does make a broad if silly comment on women objectifying men during the seventies where the male body as a place of admiration would become prevalent in the arts, Mindy's father Fred (Conrad Janis) shares a dark Korean War story, which rattles everyone and brings the mood way down. The grim nature of the story is something that the writers just know how to handle and actor Janis delivers it with serious conviction and truth. The shooting down of the bayonet wielding soldier is an old as time story in regards to war recollection and post-traumatic stress disorder driven anecdotes, but here in an American sitcom that is not say *M*A*S*H* (1972–1983) it is heavy and deep, and profoundly important. When Fred somberly mutters "Mindy, I killed a man", the air in the room grows heavy, and while Nelson defends with "He was the enemy, Uncle Fred", Fred cuts that sentiment down with "When he's three feet away he's another human being." Life is precious and war is a travesty, and *Mork & Mindy* remind us of this, in one very fast but super valuable exchange between uncle and nephew.

Jeannie summarizes the point of these kind of shows or plays or musicals, in that in this darkness and sharing of grim stories, characters can feel closer to everyone – hence why these kind of stories are regarded as "therapy" or "therapeutic". This is interrupted by the maniacal Exidor (Robert Donner) who, while serves big loud comedy, is a character that represents a take on mental illness and homelessness. He storms in, carries on, becomes a "breather" of sorts and then leaves in a flurry, only to reinforce the fact that Mindy has been holding off from telling her main regret to the group.

When she is finally on her own with Mork, Mindy confesses that she wishes her mother was alive to meet Mork. When asked what her regret is, she states "That my mother had to die before she got a chance to meet you" which is soon followed by the sensitive and nurturing Mindy that Mork is the most important thing in her life. "My mom would have liked you Mork, I just know it" she tells the teary eyes alien, who then reprises what he had offered Nelson earlier, however here, the jokes simmer and truth is put into place. Mork mimes a meeting with Mindy's mother, and he lovingly tells the imagined maternal figure that love is something that is told through action – that him wanting to share everything with Mindy, to spend every day with Mindy and to care for her for all time is a true testament to what love truly is. This breaks Mindy's heart as she watches with wide eyed wonderment, and when the door miraculously closes behind the "imagined mom", Mindy asks "Mork, was my mother really here?" – child-like innocence is reawakened (a major player in the writing of this show) and magic re-inforces the ability to trust and love. Mork delivers a kiss from Mindy's mother, and in this thoroughly moving finale, he says "I love you Mindy", to which she replies, "I love you too, Mork." A loving capsule of the heart of the show, and a testament to the beauty of American sitcoms doing so much more than making you laugh or think, here, as seen in this Very Special Episode, the role of such a medium can make you feel too.

"Louie Goes Too Far" from *Taxi*
Original Air Date: 17 December 1981
By Helen Paschalis

The problem with "Louie Goes Too Far" is that the episode doesn't go far enough. To be fair, how deeply can the topic of sexual harassment in the workplace be explored in a 22-minute situation comedy show from 1981? When the essence of a teleplay is the humorous interaction between its weekly protagonists, a subject as loaded and, unfortunately, as current and prevalent as sexual harassment can only be touched upon. And when it was presented in 1970s and 1980s television comedies, it was primarily used as a comedic device. Running gags that revolved around this theme prevailed throughout a series; audiences anticipated laughs based on the lecherous behaviors of recurring characters.

In this episode of *Taxi* (1978–1983) (season four, episode 10), writer Danny Kallis exposes yet another despicable trait in Danny DeVito's Louie De Palma, dispatcher at the Sunshine Cab Company, though he ultimately goes unpunished for his actions. His amorality, selfishness and inability to become a better person is apparently what audiences loved about his character, even inspiring *TV Guide* in 1999 to place De Palma at the Number 1 spot on its list of the 50 greatest TV characters of all time. DeVito played the award-winning part to slimy perfection. Louie is "a broken toilet of a man" as Alex (Judd Hirsch) describes him in the episode. But all is forgiven and sexual harassment instead becomes an act of no consequence by the closing credits.

Louie is discovered spying on Elaine, his gorgeous and ballsy employee (played beautifully by Marilu Henner), through a peephole in the company's bathroom as she changes for a date with a new man she has met. Elaine and her male co-workers, Alex and Tony (Tony Danza), are suitably outraged. Elaine takes immediate action, hiring lawyer Andrea Stewart (Noni White) from the National Organization for Women to investigate, essentially getting Louie fired. The problem is she goes from being purposefully driven by her conviction that Louie will never change, to tearful forgiveness as Louie shares his personal story of feeling "violated" at the end of the episode when, on her insistence, he attempts to understand her feelings.

In the final act of the story he intrudes on her date with her new man at her apartment, begging her to ask management for his job back by withdrawing her allegations. Elaine refuses, repeatedly telling him she knows he will never understand how he violated her privacy. Unable to endure more of his pathetic pleadings, she eventually implores him to think of a time when he felt violated. She speaks of one's right to privacy and challenges Louie to empathize with her, forcing him out of his comfort zone. He struggles to relate, finally sharing his experiences of having to shop in the boys' department of clothing stores to find the outfit he needs to fit his diminutive stature. He movingly quotes the hurtful words of a mother in the store who observes, "You're lucky. At least you won't outgrow it in six months." Like Elaine, we feel sorry for Louie as he remembers the pain he felt in that moment, but his is not an example of "violation" or having one's privacy ripped away. He feels humiliated and injured by the experience, but it can't be compared to being sexually harassed. However, Elaine softens at his admission because she is a compassionate person and this is why we love her. She forgives him after he shares his memories, forgetting her earlier declaration of Louie as a "filthy, lecherous monster who does not deserve our sympathy." His hand cupping her bottom as they embrace in the final scene and her surrendering smile betrays her previous reactions and Louie, again, is off the hook, leaving audiences assured of his return to the dispatcher cage in episodes to come.

In light of today's #MeToo and Time's Up movements, this resolution doesn't bode too well, though it is consistent with many sitcom episodes from the same era. The most a male perpetrator of sexual harassment will suffer is a severe verbal reprimanding by his accuser. *M*A*S*H* (1972–1983) featured regular sexual innuendoes directed at Major Margaret "Hot Lips" Houlihan (Loretta Swit) by Hawkeye (Alan Alda) and Trapper John (Wayne Rogers). Loni Anderson's receptionist Jennifer Marlowe in *WKRP in Cincinnati* (1978–1982) was regularly harassed by the radio station's vain sales manager Herb Tarlek (Frank Bonner) and though she was the antithesis of the stereotypical dumb blonde and clearly the most potent character at her workplace, a stern dressing-down is the worst her harasser ever copped.

Conversely, in *The Mary Tyler Moore Show* (1970–1977), Betty White's Sue Ann Nivens is the predator whose unwanted advances on men, particularly Lou Grant, are played strictly for laughs. In "Adult Education" from *The Golden Girls* (1985–1992) (season one, episode 20), Blanche's tutor proposes a passing grade for her if she agrees to sleep with him. In "Feelings" (season six, episode 6), Rose is molested by her dentist while undergoing a procedure. A similar storyline played out in *Seinfeld* (1989–1998) as late as 1995 when Jerry experiences the same in "The Jimmy" (season six, episode 19).

Ironically, such outcomes in these sitcoms of the day, in that perpetrators of sexual harassment usually get away with it, are reflective of what continues to exist in societies all over the world. Sexual harassment was mainly treated as a joke in situation comedies probably up until the late 1990s, well after American lawyer and academic Anita Hill accused U.S. Supreme Court nominee Clarence Thomas, her supervisor at the United States Department of Education and the Equal Employment Opportunity Commission, of sexual harassment. This historic case shone a light on many issues facing victims, though Thomas's position in the Supreme Court was assured. In 2017, ABC News and *The Washington Post* conducted a survey that concluded 54% of American women proclaimed to have suffered "unwanted and inappropriate" sexual conduct with 95% of those polled stating that this behavior usually goes unpunished.

Despite the backlash and criticism that the #MeToo movement has incurred, one of its admirable prime objectives is to empower individuals through solidarity against sexual intimidation, misconduct, assault and abuse. Women, and men, are encouraged to speak out without fear of recrimination against those who have violated them. Social media has revealed the magnitude of the issue and consequences have been great for Hollywood power players like Harvey Weinstein and Bill Cosby. When voices rise up against the abuse and justice prevails, the story ends differently and change is imminent.

It follows that, while momentarily victorious in having management believe her allegations and take decisive action in firing Louie, Elaine ultimately does herself a grave disservice in accepting Louie's story as evidence of him understanding what she felt. This is the man who addresses the Director of the National Organization for Women as "Toots" earlier in the episode and who suggests "a spanking" as penance for his behavior towards Elaine, and the audience laughs. Even Alex, who briefly pities Louie as he starts to leave with his things after being fired, quickly comes to his senses and says a definitive "Goodbye!" to the louse as he exits the garage. If only Elaine had been as steadfast in her resolve. As Louie tells Alex in season five's "Crime and Punishment" (episode 6): "Let's face it, Reiger, crime pays. You know people go around thinking if they do something bad, then something bad has gotta happen to them. Well, I am living proof that's not true."

"Reunion" from *Bosom Buddies*
Original Air Date: 22 October 1981
By Russell Dyball

For many a straight male character in television and movies, enlightenment comes in an unfamiliar dress. The common comedic trope of drag in contemporary comedy is all about learning to be better men through ostensibly experiencing life as a woman via disguising oneself as one. The juxtaposition of a male in typically female clothing for comedic purposes has been seen in everything from Shakespeare (*A Midsummer Night's Dream*) to Best Picture nominees (*Tootsie* (1982)) to ... less acclaimed entertainments (*Sorority Boys* (2002) and *White Chicks* (2004), to name but two.) An interesting exception might be made for the character of Jerry/Daphne in Billy Wilder's classic *Some Like It Hot* (1959); as played by Jack Lemmon, one could argue that the lesson for Jerry appears to be not how to be a better man, but rather a better woman. In *Bosom Buddies* (1980–1982), which clearly takes its inspiration from Wilder's film suggests another exception in this time of comedy: learning to be a better man not by exploring one's feminine side, but their masculine.

Bosom Buddies is best remembered today as the series that helped launch Tom Hanks into the stratosphere, but here we shall focus on the character played by Peter Scolari, Henry Desmond. Henry is structured very much like Lemmon's Jerry character – ostensibly in place as a sidekick character (Henry to Hanks' role of Kip Wilson, and Jerry to Tony Curtis' Joe), and also exhibiting a similar pattern of questionable morals. In the premiere episode of the series, when Kip and Henry (in their alter-egos of Buffy and Hildegarde) find themselves lodged for the first time at the all-women Susan B. Anthony Hotel, they meet the impossibly stunning (and Marilyn Monroe-like) Sonny (not to be confused – too much, anyway – with Monroes' role of "Sugar" in *Some Like it Hot*), played by Donna Dixon. Henry's first impulse is to suggest to Kip that they get Sonny drunk. Comparing this moment with a scene in *Some Like It Hot*, where Jerry attempts to take advantage of his female appearance with Sugar in the sleeping car of a train by – you guessed it – getting her drunk, we see a clear, if perhaps a little disturbing, commonality between these two men who may look and act like women (well, sort of), but are representative of men's lower impulses. And yet, on *Bosom Buddies* Henry generally reads as a nice guy. But clearly, he has some learning to do.

In the first season episode "Macho Man" (whose title itself is a call back to the premiere episode, where the Village People song is used ironically in a scene where Kip and Henry, in their Buffy and Hildegarde wigs, are shaving and working out in their room at the Susan B. Anthony), Henry laments that women don't seem to take him as anything other than a friend of brother figure, rather than an object of desire. In a move akin to Peter Brady's "pork chops and applesauce" phase in the

Brady Bunch episode "The Personality Kid" (22 October 1971), Henry explores different personas designed to make himself more appealing. First employing a disco-inspired look complete with multiple medallions, an open black shirt, and extremely tight pants, he enjoys some success as "Hank", then immediately ups the ante with another Travolta-inspired personality, adopting the then-resurgent Western look ("Urban Cowpie", Kip remarks, underlining the Travolta homage.) Taking his friends to show off the new, manly version of himself in a country/western bar complete with mechanical bull, Henry's attempts at exhibiting masculinity only read as sad and desperate, leading to him picking a fight – twice! – with a man nearly twice his size, getting a punch to the face and a black eye for his trouble. The disastrous night culminates in Henry's insulting treatment of friend and co-worker Amy (the tragically underappreciated Wendie Jo Sperber), who has openly harbored a crush on Henry. Looking for someone to dance with but having no takers, Henry says "Well, I guess it's Amy", thereby attempting to take advantage of her known feelings for him in a pathetic last ditch attempt to escape the evening feeling like a "man." Rightfully, Amy, Kip, and the others walk out on "Hank", leaving him to consider his own failings not as a man, but as a friend.

The next day at work, a humbled Henry (no longer adopting a persona) pleads for Amy's forgiveness, eventually breaking down and crying. Now doubly ashamed of his behavior and his weakness, Amy sagely remarks, "It's the most masculine thing you've done all week." When Henry questions this, Amy observes, "You're a gentleman. Broken down, that means *gentle man*. That's what you are, Henry." Finally getting it, Henry abandons his attempts at becoming "Hank" and learns to just be himself. All is well.

Except as it turns out, there's more work to be done in season two. Though *Bosom Buddies* largely abandoned the men in drag high concept of the series with the season two premiere episode "The Truth and Other Lies" (8 October 1981), in which Buffy and Hildegarde's true identities are revealed to the regular cast of characters, the exploration of Henry's manhood continues in "Reunion", in which Kip and Henry attend their five year high school reunion, conveniently held at the Susan B. Anthony. Faced with his classmates from "Edgar Allen Poe High" (apparently a different Poe than the famed writer, judging by the spelling), Henry flashes back to his school days, where it turns out that he wasn't necessarily all that good in his treatment of women then. As told to Amy, Henry's senior year was marked by the expected hijinks with Kip, and the regret of his treatment of a classmate of Sheila (Nanci Kendall), a pretty and vivacious woman who happens to be deaf. On patrol at school in his capacity of hall monitor (indicating a desire to hold power over others – and in context of the story, a signifier of Henry as a literal gatekeeper when it comes to the Sheila character), Henry is asked by Sheila to be her date for the prom. Henry, clearly lying, turns her down, explaining that he has to attend his grandparents' fiftieth anniversary. Sheila, embarrassed by her failed attempt to ask him out, is clearly crushed, but Henry has a hard time even looking her in the eye. Back in the present, Sheila appears at the reunion, and Henry, still ashamed of himself, almost immediately abandons her again, retreating to his room. Amy follows him, leading to a continuation of the flashback, in which Henry is at the prom with his date, is confronted by Sheila, who, unable to find a date, is being escorted by her father. "That's Henry, daddy. The boy I told you about," Sheila says, clearly hurt by this betrayal. Even in this moment, Henry is unable to look Sheila in the eye, eventually walking out on her – and ostensibly his prom date – crushing the sweet Sheila's heart all over again.

Back in the present, Henry, apparently goaded by Amy off-screen, returns to the reunion and faces Sheila, apologizing for what he did to her in high school. His explanation for his bad behavior: "I thought other kids would make fun of us ... of me", the last two words hastily thrown in, almost thrown away by Scolari as an actor – encapsulates the difficult admission of his poor behavior and his shame beautifully. Sheila, for her part, has moved past this painful moment which still haunts Henry. "Stop hurting yourself for something a boy named Henry did," Sheila tells him. "Boys do dumb things. *Now you're a man.*"

Henry, as a way of further reconciliation, then observes that he owes Sheila a dance. The two hit the floor, and it's a sweetly sincere moment. The music soon stops, and the only sound is the thumping of a record at the end of its groove. However, Henry and Sheila continue to slow dance. As the record thumping continues, Henry and Sheila's dancing embrace tightens. While the other assembled guests look on, Amy asks her dance partner to continue dancing, with Kip and Sonny joining in. The three couples dance to the thumping sound as the episode ends and the audience applauds.

Bosom Buddies, in spite of its silly initial premise and hip humor, always had a great sense of heart to it. "Reunion" remains one of its powerful and elegantly executed instances of that heart. Within it, and in context of what we have seen before, we ultimately see Henry's journey of self-discovery finding a natural conclusion, through the steps of learning who he is, and who he isn't, and then, most importantly, owning up to and subsequently forgiving himself for who he used to be.

"Fear Strikes Back" from *The Facts of Life*
Original Air Date: 4 November 1981
By Mike "McBeardo" McPadden

Season two of *The Facts of Life* (1979–1988) began with a silent Gotterdammerung striking Eastland School, the all-girls boarding academy in Peekskill, New York that served as the series' (initial) setting. Gone were four of the show's original seven lead student characters (including, famously, Molly Ringwald as Molly) and in stormed Bronx biker scholarship winner Joanna "Jo" Polniaczek (Nancy McKeon). Producers found the original septet ensemble unwieldy, particularly as one of seven adolescents had to face a highlighted crisis each week. The volume simply proved too daunting to keep track of who was who.

The solution of season two, then, was to focus on a core four – i.e., the aforementioned white ethnic gearhead Jo, old money W.A.S.P snob Blair Warner (Lisa Whelchel), plus-size Jewish jokester Natalie Green (Mindy Cohn) and spunky African American roller-skater Tootie Ramsey (Kim Fields).

Early on, *Facts* trafficked in routine teen troubles such as sneaking out after curfew, experimenting with alcohol, and shoplifting. Heavy-duty trauma typically got relegated to classmates we had never seen before, nor would we again – e.g., one-and-doners on the order of Denise Halma as suicidal Cynthia ("Breaking Point") and Heather Kerr in the role of single mom Alison ("A Baby in the House").

One noteworthy aspect of "Fear Strikes Back," then, is that a tremendously serious incident befalls no less an essential quartet member than our beloved, boisterously funny Natalie.

Specifically, a stranger sexually assaults Natalie while she's on the way home from a campus party, and the show confronts the issue head-on, both figuratively and (sort of) literally.

Halloween fever has hit Eastland as the episode opens. The theme of this year's school costume party is Hollywood stars. First prize is four tickets to see Bruce Springsteen at Madison Square Garden. The phrase "Springsteen tickets" recurs repeatedly, as does the term "hormones" – a supremely popular word in the initial seasons of *Facts*.

We see Natalie brandishing a Charlie Chaplin mustache straightaway, as she sews together her Little Tramp gear. Blair announces she's going as Jane Fonda because "she's liberated" and, besides, "someone else is already going as Bo Derek." Jo protests because her plan is to dress up as Peter Fonda in his *Easy Rider* get up, which is not a huge stretch for her, wardrobe-wise. Tootie glams it up as *Mahogany*-era Diana Ross.

Mrs. Edna Garrett (Charlotte Rae), Eastland's dietician and house mother of the four leads, enters the common area. She's clearly rattled as she informs the girls that

Mrs. King, the headmaster's secretary, was attacked while walking to her car. Stunned, but not flinching, Mrs. Garrett says, "She was raped."

The frank language choices made by *Facts* here and elsewhere in the series writers is bracing. No matter how commonplace it was to speak to children in adult terms back in the seventies (which, culturally, stretches all the way to the end of 1982), it's remarkably refreshing to experience it when viewed in the bubble-wrapped anti-reality of 2020.

As the party looms, Mrs. Garrett specifies how many "precautions" the school is taking as it goes forward, from electric gates to closed-circuit TV cameras to hypersensitive alarms. "I slammed the refrigerator door this morning, and so many bells started ringing," Mrs. G jokes, "I thought I'd won the Secret Square!"

Jo, very much in the spirit of *Easy Rider* (1969), voices her libertarian streak by countering, "I know all about these 'precautions.' They may lock a few people out, but mostly they lock people in."

The next scene starts in the common area after the party. Somebody dressed as Sophia Loren won the Springsteen tickets. Blair and Jo bicker. Tootie laments to Mrs. Garrett, "Just imagine 14 Diana Rosses in the same room – and two of them were white!"

While midnight snacks are being prepared, Natalie stumbles in. She is dirty, disheveled, and in shock. Through tears, she says, "I was coming home, and I knew it was late, so I was hurrying. I wasn't far, Mrs. Garrett. I was almost home. A man grabbed me, and I tried to scream, but he covered my mouth. He pushed me down, and he was holding me down, and all of a sudden, I heard people's voices. He must have heard them, too, because he just got up and then ran away. Mrs. Garrett, if those people hadn't passed by… Mrs. Garrett, I was almost home."

Canned studio applause. Break for commercial.

Several days later, the girls mention that Natalie is still bedridden and melancholy. They sympathize, especially since, as Blair says, "We all bear the burden of being attractive and feminine." Then she sneers in Jo's direction, "Well, *almost* all of us."

Mrs. G explains that the sexual assault has nothing to do with attractiveness and that the exertion of power is the issue and that Natalie is suffering after realizing how vulnerable she is. Jo snarls, "I'd be angry!" Mrs. G says that Natalie is angry, "Angry on the inside."

With her signature sensitivity, Blair proclaims, "Enough with this depressing rape talk already!" and whips out four passes to see Bruce Springsteen that night.

Natalie, she perks up for a second when she gets the news. Then she announces she's not going and that, in fact, she's not going to go outside again.

Mrs. Garrett requests a little private time with Natalie. She goes through the books by Natalie's bedside and picks up *Walden* by Henry David Thoreau. Natalie longs for a Walden of her own, a private utopia she'd never have to leave. Mrs. G says that Walden always reminded her of Appleton, Wisconsin, her hometown – but that even she left when she realized life was about experiencing more than just Appleton, Wisconsin.

"Fear is fear, it has to be overcome," Mrs. G counsels. "Natalie, you don't really want to hide behind a locked door all your life."

Natalie not's buying that *or* Mrs. G's proposal that they attend a women's self-defense seminar being held on campus. She will, however, cover the class in keeping with her duties as a reporter for the Eastland newspaper.

Now we get to the self-defense seminar. The Olivia Newton John/"Let's Get Physical"-era workout fashions are *awesome*. Stylish innovations to the standard Eastland blue-and-gold gym uniforms abound. Plush headbands are everywhere.

Inspired by the NBC miniseries *Shogun* (1980), Blair sports a kimono. Inspired most likely by Charles Bronson, Jo wears prison-yard gray sweatpants and a sleeveless gray t-shirt.

At the center of it all is a curly-maned hunk of martial arts machismo in a maroon velour tracksuit billed only as "Self-Defense Instructor." He's played by Louis Welch, a charismatic heap of handsome with a remarkable run-up filmography that includes the automotive *Jaws/Exorcist* hybrid *The Car* (1977), the post-*Grease* TV movie *Frankie and Annette: The Second Time Around* (1978), and the flop 1980 CBS spin-off series *Beyond Westworld*.

The Self-Defense Instructor – SDI, for short – barks it out bluntly to the assembled lasses: "Half of you will be the victim of a violent crime at some point in your life… but you don't have to, if you don't go around like victims."

After hearing about a rape that happened on campus, Natalie (Mindy Cohn) is sexually assaulted on her way back to her dorm, causing profound PTSD in "Fear Strikes Back" from The Facts of Life.

In short order, the SDI demonstrates how both Blair's casualness and Jo's cockiness makes them easy targets, specifically by flipping them down on to the floor mat in a flash. Advising the subjects to use a free hand to "go for the groin," he insists they forget about worrying whether it's "ladylike," because "You're not going to be dealing with Prince Charles out there!"

The SDI next asks a seated observer if he can see her purse. He dumps the handbag's contents onto the mat and goes through the items, pantomiming how each can be used to thwart an attacker – keys, a pencil, a hairbrush, even a lollipop. "Hold it like this," he says, "and it becomes a dangerous weapon."

From the side, Natalie observes and half-smiles. She tells Mrs. Garrett that the SDI just helped her realize she could have used the cane from her Charlie Chaplin costume as a defense item… but she was afraid.

Mrs. Garrett responds, "Everybody's afraid. These are crazy, crazy times. Don't let your fear paralyze you. Use it – to make you alert, aware, and smart."

With a wink, then, Mrs. G enters the lineup of students on the mat. Natalie joins her. The SDI mounts a pose, the girls mimic him, and he moves to strike forward, declaring, "All together now – hi-YAH!"

Everybody "hi-YAH's." Lesson learned. Eastland School grows stronger. We do, too.

"First Day Blues" from *Diff'rent Strokes*
Original Air Date: 5 November 1981
By Lee Gambin

Todd Bridges as Willis Jackson grew up in front of TV audiences throughout the entire series of *Diff'rent Strokes* (1978–1986). Not only was this young actor in the limelight as a child/preteen/teen sensation, but he would also provide a voice and visible reference point for various aspects of such development for the young demographic tuning into the sitcom. Although a lot of the show's focus was on younger brother – the cherubic, cheeky Arnold (Gary Coleman) – Willis's lengthy arc from childhood to late teens leant more room for issues to be raised and tackled. During season four of the series, Willis would not only tackle social concerns such as racism as seen in episodes like "Health Club" (17 December 1981), he would also experience relationship woes with on and off again girlfriend Charlene (Janet Jackson). The episode before "First Day Blues" ("Growing Up") is all about Willis wanting to lose his virginity; with father Philip Drummond (Conrad Bain) offering much needed advice (ultimately explaining that there is no rush), and ending with a coda that has Willis answering Arnold's now legendary catch phrase "Whatchu talkin' 'bout Willis?" with "I'm talking about growing up!" Willis comes to understand the complexities of growing up, and here in this episode dealing with marijuana, he learns the hard way and comes out of the episode stronger and aware of peer pressure and the ugliness of subtle bullying. Willis's dilemma with making friends at a new school are at the heart of this VSE's major concern, and this acts as a launching pad for the issue that will be the additive that makes this an episode dealing with a social ill – teen usage of marijuana.

The precocious Tootie (Kim Fields) from *The Facts of Life* (1979–1988) guest stars and offers alternative advice for Willis to break the ice and make new friends, while Mr. Drummond explains that "people's favorite subject is talking about themselves." Mr. Drummond asserts the fact that human beings, by their very nature, are self-involved and self-serving, and Willis takes this on board and attempts to use this in order to reach out to seniors at his new school. Willis's old friend from junior high Julio (Joe De Cenzo) is no help, as he expresses his need to break out of old friendships and re-establish himself at a new school. Later, it is learned that Julio knows the ins and outs of the cost of marijuana, but refers to himself as "Mr. Clean" (shaking the remains of Spanish Harlem), while the two seniors who taunt Willis about being the adopted son of a wealthy man, force Willis to source pot for a proposed party. The first mention of "grass" jets the episode into a drug-centric one and with Willis trying to act cool about such an issue, he comments that there are "Narcs all over the place…"; a finely written moment of both Willis trying to deflect and also riding the wave of knowing the lingo of urban culture – a world that he genuinely comes from outside of being adopted by a wealthy penthouse living business man.

The bullies trusting Willis to get marijuana is a test more than anything, and when we see Willis smoking the pot it is an indication to his curiosity and lives outside the peer pressure angle the show baits. Interestingly enough – along with the relative *The Facts of Life* episode "Dope" from the series' first season – these takes on marijuana and youth seem slightly displaced in the larger spectrum of the drug culture of the late seventies and shifting into the excesses of the Reagan-era eighties. During this time, the advent of cocaine and hard narcotics would become the focal point for many TV shows including the child-centric *Punky Brewster* (1984–1988), rather than the now sanitized pot which would become part and parcel within the mainstream culture and smoked socially, normalized as much as drinking.

Willis also falls victim to the perils of drugs being linked to being in debt, and he approaches sister Kimberly (Dana Plato) and Tootie for a loan – already money becomes an issue in regards to drug costs. Tootie comes across his marijuana en route to feeding Abraham, Arnold's goldfish. Both she and Kimberly are shocked, and later when Mr. Drummond discovers a stoned Willis, great jokes get thrown about the place including references to "flying high" and the school's football field not being made of turf but of "grass". But because this is a VSE, the laughs have to make way for a social message, and Mr. Drummond's love for his children eases him into a stern and hearty motioning of parental discipline. He is angry that Willis is stoned, but he is more disappointed that he would stoop so low just to impress would-be friends. Along with Kimberly and Tootie's beautiful friendship that is on show for a number of inter-running episodes of both *Diff'rent Strokes* and *The Facts of Life*, their care for Willis is massively evident as well. Kimberly even defends her brother, and even admits to smoking pot on one occasion because of peer pressure. Within this revelation, Mr. Drummond comes to understand that marijuana is evidently available because it is "all over the place", and something that kids get into early. Because of its accessibility, Mr. Drummond is defeated and when he makes the loud statements of the Very Special Episode nice and clear, the show stands still for a moment allowing the PSA message to be delivered within the construct of the narrative; forcing it to become a quick departure from the jokes. Mr. Drummond's anger and disappointment is questioned however, when Willis brings up the subject of drinking and that he has seen his father and his friends drink many times, however, this argument is severed when Mr. Drummond explains that alcohol "happens to be legal" while pot most certainly is not. His final words of advice to his son follow up with: "If friendship with them depends on marijuana, you better start looking for new friends" and this reasserts Willis's disdain in what he has done. Not only does he feel sick from smoking pot, he is annoyed at himself for letting the senior bullies pressure him into sourcing the drugs.

The final sequence is a proud presentation of Willis's strength where he happily tells the bullies that his father flushed the pot down the toilet. Willis's triumph comes with:

"You're the one who's lost, brother!" after being told that he has lucked out in making new friends. Willis has grown and developed and become someone his father can be proud of, and his disdain in what he has done (providing drugs for older kids who are dead-end youths, stuck in a "loss") is proof that he is a young man with a great self-judge of character. Attracted to such brightness and decency is a young classmate who represents the golden hope at the end of the episode – an episode about fitting in more than about pot smoking. He approaches Willis and makes mention of knowing Willis by reputation in the sports arena, and by the end of the episode, a friendship is made.

Everybody's Got A Special Kind Of Story
1982 – 1985

"Legacy" from *The Facts of Life*
Original Air Date: 6 January 1982
By Mike "McBeardo" McPadden

The Facts of Life (1979–1988) episode "Legacy" delivers quite the shock to snooty rich girl Blair Warner (Lisa Whelchel) and, by extension, to fans of the show in the middle of season three.

For Blair, it's the discovery that her beloved, recently deceased maternal grandfather, Judge Carlton Blair (after whom she was named) lived as a hardcore segregationist and dedicated member of the Ku Klux Klan.

For viewers, it's the prospect that Blair – who so bombastically oozes Mayflower-borne, north-eastern old money – has at least one major family root rising up from the Deep South.

A little context is called for here. At the dawn of the 1980s, the KKK had unfortunately barged yet again into the national consciousness.

In 1979, sheet-head Klansmen and American Nazi Party numbskulls opened fire on Che-shirted Communist Workers Party pistol-packers at a North Carolina "Death to the Klan" rally. All that lethal LARPing led to five dead and eleven wounded in what has since come to be known as the "Greensboro Massacre."

Apparently emboldened by the Greensboro idiocy, KKK Imperial Wizard Bill Wilkinson publicly announced his support of Ronald Reagan in the upcoming 1980 presidential election. Governor Reagan, even more publicly, rejected Wilkinson's supposedly wizardly endorsement.

True horror came to a head, then, in 1981, when Klan members fatally beat and hanged 19-year-old African American student Michael Donald in Mobile, Alabama. That tragedy stands, to date, as the last legally recorded lynching in the United States.

So consider all that going into "Legacy," which aired very early in 1982. If the Ku Klux Klan wouldn't realistically be stomping about The Facts of Life's suburban New York setting, then Facts would find a way to work the long, evil arm of the Klan into its weekly campus crises.

"Legacy" opens in the Eastland School's dining room/common area, where dietitian and perpetual font of matriarchal wisdom Mrs. Edna Garrett (Charlotte Rae) is prepping a meal plan. Roughneck greaser student Jo Polniaczek (Nancy McKeon) enters, followed by dork-fro'd delivery boy Roy (Loren Lester), who's carrying a box of bread. Jo states emphatically, "No, Roy I will not go out with ya tonight! Absolutely not, no way, negative, no!" Smarmily, Roy beams back, "I gotcha. You want to think about it!"

Loren Lester, who plays Roy, is a character actor who specialized in gross but not entirely unlikable creeps. He's best known as Principal Togar's goon hall monitor Fritz

Hansel in Rock 'n' Roll High School (1979). In the role of Roy, Lester returned sporadically to annoy Jo throughout five seasons of Facts.

Talk turns to an upcoming fundraiser to supply books for a new library presently being erected at Eastland. Roy suggests Jo should sell kisses. Mrs. Garrett dispatches Roy back to the bakery from whence he came.

The new building is being financed with $500,000 willed to the school by the late Judge Carlton Blair, grandfather of Blair Warner. It's a fact she won't stop boasting about, even as she enters the scene with headmaster Mr. Parker (Roger Perry). Most importantly, she brags, the installation will be officially called "The Blair Library."

After Mr. Parker steps into the kitchen for a slice of Mrs. Garrett's supposedly famous apple pie (in future episodes, it would become her famous apple strudel, which Mrs. G always pronounces hyper-Teutonically as "schrtoo-dell"), Natalie happens in, looking out of sorts.

When Jo asks what's up, Natalie says that in researching Judge Carlton for the student newspaper, she's discovered information that will make Blair "want to hang herself from her family tree."

Upstairs in the core foursome's bedroom, Blair glowingly flips through her grandfather's photo album. Jo and Tootie lay nearby, mildly annoyed. Natalie enters and cautiously puts a halt to Blair's gush-fest, saying she's got some news about the judge.

First, Natalie says, Carlton Blair worked really hard as a judge and was a decorated World War I veteran. Then she carefully drops the boom, telling Blair, "In the sixties, your grandfather was involved in civil rights."

"Civil rights!" Blair enunciates. "Is there no end to the man's dedication?"

"Well, yes," Natalie says. "Actually, he was more involved in denying civil rights. He closed down the schools in his county to keep them from being integrated."

Flabbergasted, Blair insists that the research is off base, but Natalie presents her with a clipped-out newspaper obituary that reveals the truth.

Blair reads aloud, "Judge Blair was a staunch defender of state's rights, and an opponent of …." Her eyes bulge, she tosses the clipping, and runs out of the room.

Jo picks up the paper, and continues, "… an opponent of desegregation. It was discovered after his death that he was a longtime financial supporter and member of the Ku Klux Klan."

No applause break, fade to commercial.

Coming back, we hear talk of how Blaire is flagellating herself and attempting to make amends with the world by washing Jo's motorcycle tires and taking on the grimiest of campus chores. Tootie adds, "And I keep finding credit cards under my pillow!"

When Blair returns, she announces that such doings are her duty, stating, "If he was prejudiced, then I might be prejudiced… I'm a snob. I've forgotten about the little people. I'm caviar and cashmere; teach me about pretzels and polyester! Teach me to be common, Jo! Bring me down to your level!"

It's a funny forerunner of the classic Britpop ditty "Common People" by Pulp.

Just then, Roy barrels back on the scene waving two tickets to that night's local "Bowl-O-Rama," which he describes as, "All night bowling, free shoe rental, and pork rinds!" Despite Jo's protests, Blair jumps at the chance to go, stating, "Penance! Penance!"

Cut later to inside the under construction Blair Library. Mrs. Garrett and Mr. Parker stroll in, whereupon Blair, who's been waiting for them, announces that she's cancelling the library. She says, "Carlton Blair stood for everything I despise. I'm ashamed to have his name. I feel like I'm a part of something horrible, and there's nothing else I can do about it!"

In a quiet panic, Mr. Parker urges Mrs. Garrett, "Please talk to her. Even as we speak, the cement is hardening."

Time for Mrs. G to shine. She says, "Blair, the things your grandfather did, he did. You can't take the blame for his mistakes any more than you can take the credit for the good things he did…. Your grandfather was good to you. He read you bedtime stories, took you fishing, and always had time for you. "

"Yeah," Blair snaps back, "and it couldn't have been easy for him, squeezing me in between sheet fittings!"

"Is that the only way you want to remember him?," Mrs. G asks.

"I don't want to remember him at all," Blair says. "But I do remember him. I can still see him sitting on the edge of my bed, holding my head all night long when I had the chicken pox."

"Then hang on to that," Mrs. G says. "Blair, even though someone disappoints you – deeply disappoints you – well, that doesn't mean you have to stop loving them."

"Even a man like that?" Blair wonders.

"Yes," Mrs. G assures her. "Blair, you can't change the way he was, but you can give him a chance now to do something good. You know, from a man who spent a lifetime promoting ignorance, maybe a library is a fitting gift."

Still, Blair says she is taking her name off the library. Mrs. Garrett responds by encouraging a little benign vandalism. She points out a wet patch of cement and hands Blair a nearby yardstick. With a smile, Blair draws the initials "B.W." into the building's foundation.

Just as both Blair and Mrs. G allow this lesson in acceptance to settle deep into the moment, Roy comes bounding in, bedecked in his Brunswick Lanes best and bellows, "Hey, Blair! Ready to go to Bowl-O-Rama?"

Presumably, then, Blair gets to live, at least for one night, like common people and do what common people do.

Blair (Lisa Whelchel) discovers a shocking secret about her beloved late grandfather in "Legacy" from The Facts of Life. *She learns that he was a member of the Ku Klux Klan which makes her re-evaluate her past relationship with him.*

"Runaway" from *The Facts of Life*
Original Air Date: 24 February 1982
By Mike "McBeardo" McPadden

"Runaway" addresses an issue I found of severe importance as a youngster growing up in New York City throughout the 1970s and 1980s: the underage sex trade in Times Square.

Years ago, I penned an autobiographical confection titled "All I Ever Wanted Was the Glamorous Life of a Child Pornography Star." It detailed my preteen preoccupation with the prevalent media presences of pimps, chickenhawks, kiddie porn, and a so-called Minnesota Strip lined with pubescent sex pros fresh off the bus from the Midwest.

In a less torch-and-pitchforky cultural moment, I may reprint that essay, but the gist is that all such exciting action lay (pun absolutely intended) a mere half-hour subway ride away from boring, provincial, sewage-for-brains Brooklyn where I was stuck, and all I wanted was out of there and into that!

Please bear in mind: I was very much a child and I was a child very unhealthily fixated on adult pornography in any form I could glimpse it (shoplifted magazines, tabloid ads for X-rated films, torn-out pages from a swingers' newsletter weirdly taped to a wall inside a Roy Roger's men's room).

Somewhere around age eight, then, I concluded that "child pornography" must have been the equivalent of the grown-up version – just with kids. By that I mean I believed the "industry" had name stars, fancy movie sets, glamorous premieres, etc., and I clutched on to this article of faith for quite a while.

Even as I inched toward teendom, the "Tres jolie, Coco" scene from *Fame* (1980) and the Dana Hill-Richard Masur TV movie *Fallen Angel* (1981) didn't really disabuse me of this notion. Instead, those moments torpedoed my self-esteem to new nadirs, because as a lumpy, oily, bespectacled, peri-pubescent mess, I knew I wouldn't warrant attention from kid porn biz movers and shakers.

So by 13, when I watched the "Runaway" episode of *The Facts of Life* (1979–1988), I no longer automatically rooted for groomers and traffickers as I had back in, say, the third grade. Plus, with age came a smidge of wisdom regarding the real world. I started to understand that the child sex trade was actually quite the tragic opposite of the hedonistic "Disneyland done RIGHT" wonderland I'd been envisioning (again: I earlier applied the descriptor "unhealthy" to this mental snapshot, so let's invoke that again).

As a result, "Runaway" pulled me in tight from moment one and delivered hard all the way to its minimal-punches-pulled payoff.

Snooty upper crust blonde Blair Warner (Lisa Whelchel), hard-knocks Bronx biker Jo Polniaczek (Nancy McKeon), and post-Bat Mitzvah zaftig wise-cracker Natalie

Green (Mindy Cohn) announce they're heading from the Peekskill HQ of Eastland boarding school into Manhattan to catch a Broadway matinee.

Tootie Ramsey (Kim Fields), their normally peppy African American bestie, is left moping in the kitchen of dietician/matriarch Mrs. Edna Garrett (Charlotte Rae).

At issue is that Tootie is a year or two younger that the other girls and her parents have decreed that she's not ready yet to traverse the city sans chaperone.

Naturally, Tootie slips out and hops a Metro North train express into the core of the deeply rotten early eighties Big Apple.

We cut to a midtown diner. Blair, Jo, and Natalie stumble in. They're upset that the show they'd been planning to see sold out at the last minute. Jo is positively apoplectic that the reason is because Blair forced them on a detour through Bloomingdale's. Ms. Warner, of course, is beamingly loaded up with bags and boxes.

Near our heroines sits a gaggle of girls about their age, done up more elegantly than provocatively, but noticeably different than our trio. A sharp-dressed man we'll come to learn is named Mike occupies a payphone in a corner.

In a fine bit of casting, Darrell Fetty plays Mike. He debuted as "Tough Kid" in a 1974 episode of the high school drama *Room 222* (1969–1974) titled "The Noon Goon" and, more recently, had appeared as "Hoagy" in the sucking-sand pseudo-slasher *Blood Beach* (1980).

The Eastland gals make note of Mike and wonder what's up. Jo, eased back in her unbuttoned Navy pea coat, doesn't even look over as she bluntly tells them, "He's a pimp. And those girls work for him."

Natalie gasps, "You mean they're hookers?!" It's jarring now to hear such matter-of-fact language on what's collectively remembered as so squeaky clean a sitcom. Such were the times, though, and such were the strengths of this particular sitcom.

Again, not bothering to glance over, the entirely unfazed Jo lays out the whole scenario. She explains that the guy on the phone is setting up an appointment, he's going to select one of the girls, he's going to give her a scrap of paper, and send her on her way to… work. It all plays out exactly as Jo calls it.

Blair's flesh crawls. Natalie's curiosity is piqued, but she's equally frightened. Jo simply declares it's time to go.

Moments after they depart, of course, Tootie rushes inside the diner, distressed. She lost her wallet and doesn't know what to do. Kristy, one of the teenage call girls, welcomes Tootie, asks her to sit down, and offers to buy her lunch.

Tammy Lauren, who plays Kristy, was quite the familiar TV face back then. In 1979 alone, Tammy was cast as the lead kid in three big-time swing-and-miss sitcom flops – *Angie* (1979–1980), which had momentarily been a hit and then fizzled fast; *Out of the Blue* (1979), an angel-themed spinoff of both *Happy Days* (1974–1984) and *Mork & Mindy* (1978–1982); and *Who's Watching the Kids* (1978) with Scott Baio, Caren Kaye, and James Belushi.

Kristy and Tootie hit it off and become fast friends. When Tootie asks where she goes to school, Kristy says, "I'm done with school. I work now. I'm an actress and a model."

From there, Kristy rattles off about her fun, independent, no-hassles life in the big city and even suggests Tootie move in with her. That's when Mike the pimp approaches.

Back at Eastland, the school's resident Asian student, Miko (Lauren Tom), lets slip to Mrs. Garrett that Tootie snuck off into the city. Mrs. G hilariously blows her stack and hightails it down to the theater district, picking up Blair, Jo, and Natalie along the way.

While the searchers scour Broadway for Tootie, they're mistaken as scalpers by an outer-borough ethnic couple played by Belle Ellig, a reliable "Jewish mother" actress of the era, and Larry Gelman, a classic schmendrick in dozens of films and TV shows from the sixties to today. If you're reading this, you likely best know Gelman as The White Rabbit in the X-rated *Alice in Wonderland* (1976).

After Mrs. Garrett makes it clear they're not scalping, the disappointed missus supplies a nice rundown of recent Broadway hits, as she laments, "We missed Elizabeth Taylor, we missed *Nicholas Nickleby*, and now we can go over to 41st Street and miss Lena Horne!"

In 1981, Taylor debuted on Broadway in *The Little Foxes* opposite Maureen Stapleton. *The Life and Adventures of Nicholas Nickleby* was an eight-and-a-half-hour Dickens adaptation that played out over two nights to colossal acclaim and success. *Lena Horne: The Lady and Her Music* had been the toast of the Great White Way in 1982.

Back in the diner, waitress Bernice (Linda Darlow) overhears Tootie accept Kristy and Mike's invitation to leave with them.

After Tootie's marvel to herself about how her new friends are such nice people, Bernice leans close and interjects, "Those two nice people are going to take you to a nice apartment, give you a nice warm drink, and you're gonna wake up three days later. Do you want to be for sale – like Kristy?"

At last, Tootie gets it (even when I still didn't quite!).

Finally, Mrs. G and the other Eastlanders make it into the diner and whisk Tootie away. On the way out, Tootie looks over her shoulder through the front window and sees Kristy standing amid the other call girls, looking lost. The episode ends there. It's a heavy moment, well executed.

The following fall, I started attending high school in Manhattan and hanging around by myself in Times Square. I saw pimps and I saw prostitutes and they looked a lot more like Ralph Bakshi cartoons than *Facts'* Mike and Kristy, and they'd do things like snort cocaine off coffee shop counters and get into violent altercations while also somehow being physically affectionate.

Even given that reality versus the network-cleansed sitcom version, if I had I been in Tootie's position at the time, I'd have been in serious, serious trouble – despite the straight-talking of brassy waitress Bernice.

Tammy Lauren plays a teenage prostitute in "Runaway" from The Facts of Life. *She befriends Tootie (Kim Fields) while Tootie and the gang venture out to New York.*

"Crime Story" from *Diff'rent Strokes*
Original Air Dates: 11 March 1982 (Part 1) and 18 March 1982 (Part 2)
By Troy Howarth

For many years mischaracterized as "kids just being kids" school bullying is far from a safe rite of passage; if anything, it can leave lasting scars (emotional, psychological, and physical) and destroy young lives before they even have a chance to really get started. These days, with the prominence of social media and the way in which that technology can make such horrific behavior even easier to inflict on others, it's a topic that carries more resonance than ever. What was once deemed "mere horseplay" is now rightly recognized as a major social problem – especially when so many young people, broken by their experiences dealing with bullies, have been prone to self-harm and even suicide as a means of escaping from the pain.

As such, it's not entirely surprising that *Diff'rent Strokes* (1978–1986) elected to cover bullying as one of their Very Special Episodes – they even went so far as to award it the two-part treatment, as they had done with their pedophilia-themed "The Bicycle Man" episode. While nothing in the run of the show can compete with "The Bicycle Man" in terms of sheer creep factor, "Crime Story," also known as "Crime in the Schools," manages to touch on some pretty serious themes and concerns as well.

Part one kicks off innocently enough as Arnold (Gary Coleman) and his best friend Dudley (Shavar Ross, who went on to play Reggie in *Friday the 13th Part V: A New Beginning* (1985)) decide to "blind trade" their lunches. It turns out they're both stuck with peanut butter and jelly sandwiches, so they decide to leave things as they are. Things take a darker turn when a pair of high school-age kids, Eddie (Shannon Presby) and Roberto (Sal Lopez), show up and start intimidating the two boys. Arnold tries acting tough, but when it becomes apparent that he is no match for the two bullies, he quickly backs down. Eddie and Roberto make it clear: not only will they take their lunches every day moving forward, but they also expect to be paid, as well. If they tell anybody about what's going on, they're in for a beating.

The dynamics between the bullies and the bullied is played pretty light. However, anybody who ever experienced the trauma of being bullied will surely have a strong emotional reaction to scenes such as this. The overall approach is far from "gritty," it's true, but in addressing this topic, the idea is to prepare the kids in the audience to face the possibility of running into this in their own lives – and to hopefully be better prepared to avoid some of the problems encountered by Arnold and Dudley.

The performances by Shannon Presby and Sal Lopez definitely add to the overall impact of the episode. It helps that they're both credibly menacing figures. They also seem to legitimately enjoy playing such vile characters, thus making the two bullies even more enjoyably loathsome. Of the two, Lopez definitely has enjoyed a more prolific career in front of the camera: he would go on to play one of the grunts in Stanley Kubrick's *Full Metal Jacket* (1987) and he has remained active on the big and small screens in everything from episodes of *King of the Hill* (1997–2010) and *ER* (1994–2009) to *Batman v Superman: Dawn of Justice* (2016). Presby's film career dried up around 1985, at which point he switched career paths. As of 2009, he was elected Deputy District Attorney for the county of Los Angeles; one wonders whether anybody he ever had in the hot seat recognized him as one of the bullies who menaced Arnold and Dudley.

Worried that the bullies mean business, Arnold tries to keep the information about what's happened from his family. He finally trips up and admits the terrible truth to his older brother Willis (Todd Bridges), who decides to step up to the plate and stand up to the bullies himself. Arnold sensibly realizes that Willis is out-muscled and decides to tell their foster father, Mr. Drummond (Conrad Bain), what is going on. Mr. Drummond makes the mistake of thinking that going through the proper channels is the solution: he notifies the principal of what is going on and is convinced that will be the end of it.

The next day, Arnold and Dudley are targeted once more. And now the bullies are even more vicious, having been "tattled on" by Mr. Drummond. The two boys come up with the only solution they can think of: they'll start skipping school, thus removing themselves from harm's way. When word gets back to the Drummond house that Arnold has been playing hooky, Willis decides to go against their father's wishes and promises Arnold to handle the matter personally.

Running through *Diff'rent Strokes* is a strong theme of familial love. It's one of the things that makes the show so very charming and affecting. The bond between Arnold and Willis unshakable, even if the inevitable annoyance of the big brother/little brother relationship occasionally rears its head. Though far from imposing, Willis puts himself on the line to protect Arnold from the bullies – and it doesn't end well.

Part one ends on a cliffhanger, as Mr. Drummond receives a phone call from Arnold; he's in the hospital with Willis, who has suffered some undisclosed injuries requiring stitches. Clearly the show isn't afraid of toying with darker subject matter, but leaving things on a note of ambiguity, with the fate of one of its young leads in question, was still a pretty audacious move.

Part two resolves that ambiguity in short order, as we learn that Willis has suffered some bruised ribs, a sprained hand, and a head injury requiring five stitches; not exactly life-altering, but still pretty vicious for a schoolyard confrontation.

The police, represented by Detective Simpson (Brad Turnbull, reprising his role from the episodes "Almost American" and the second half of "The Bicycle Man"), try to get Mr. Drummond to allow Arnold to wear a wire to catch the bullies in the act – a strong tactic on the face of it, but considering the damage they inflicted on poor Willis, it seems fair in context. Mr. Drummond is reluctant to use Arnold as a pawn in their game, however, and he refuses to sign the necessary paperwork. Drummond's desire to protect Arnold is understandable, but he is missing sight of the bigger picture; in allowing the bullies to continue, he is endangering the welfare of many other children. He will eventually come to that realization, but in the meantime his stubbornness nearly results in more violence.

With Willis recuperating from his injuries and his stepfather refusing to allow him to step forward and be a hero, Arnold decides to "go rogue" and record his interactions with the bullies via a concealed tape recorder. The scene of him trying to entrap them while "subtly" thrusting his chest forward, hoping to capture incriminating comments on tape, is played for broad comedy. There's a suspenseful undercurrent, however, in that we've already seen that these two bullies are capable of real violence. Had the filmmakers pulled their punches by not allowing Willis to suffer for his hubris, the climax may not have carried so much weight. Eventually the bullies get wise to what's going on, but Arnold is able to break free and run home without getting caught.

The finale sees Drummond coming to the realization that not allowing Arnold to assist in stopping the bullies is hypocritical on his part – just in time for Arnold to rush in and reveal that he's already gone and done it without his approval. That's a fairly common *Diff'rent Strokes* trope, really, as the harried foster father is forced to undergo a series of exasperating conflicting emotions while trying to exert control over his kids. Willis sums it up best when he says, "We're from the streets and he's from

Sal Lopez, as a local thug, terrorizes Arnold and Dudley in this special two part episode "Crime Story" from Diff'rent Strokes, *which tackles bullying in the schoolyard.*

Park Avenue." Conrad Bain is at his best when playing these moments of exasperation which ultimately yield to warmth as his unconditional love for the kids comes to the foreground.

Arnold's bravery is rewarded when Detective Simpson congratulates him on the tape and says that it's just what is needed to get those kids off the streets – though what will happen to them is inevitably left a bit … tenuous. Simpson offers to make Arnold an honorary detective – and with typical humility, he replies that "honorary mayor" will suffice.

"Me and Mr. T" from *Silver Spoons*
Original Air Date: 16 October 1982
By Nathaniel Thompson

During his presidential campaign in 1980, Ronald Reagan introduced sweeping changes to the national U.S. economy highlighted by policies that would reduce the number of tax brackets and benefit Wall Street immeasurably. The ensuing eight years would see the rise of yuppies and financial indulgence on a worldwide scale, with pop culture responding accordingly through celebrations of wealth including the ascendance of night-time soap operas like *Dallas* (1978–1991) and *Dynasty* (1981–1989).

Enter *Silver Spoons* in the fall of 1982. While 1980s American sitcoms tend to focus on blue collar or middle class families, *Silver Spoons* (1982–1987) shifts the focus to upper crust society as experienced by an overgrown man-child millionaire and trust fund brat, Edward Stratton III (Joel Higgins), and his son, Ricky (Ricky Schroder), whose existence he becomes aware of years after separating from his wife. In marked contrast to comic strip antecedents like *Richie Rich* and *Little Orphan Annie*, the show doesn't position the child at its center as a scrappy dispenser of wisdom; rather the father and son take turns teaching each other life lessons, with interference often run in the form of secretary and eventual love interest Kate Summers (Erin Gray). That format also means the show lent itself to the VSE format quite readily from the outset, with even the second episode, "Boys Will Be Boys," introducing the troubled home life of Ricky's manipulative friend and former military school roommate, Derek (Jason Bateman), which would eventually lead to discussions of discipline, infidelity and divorce. The show entered full-fledged VSE territory with its fourth episode, "Me and Mr. T," an examination of school bullying through the prism of wealth and celebrity.

The economic and familial tension at the heart of the show is present in the opening moments as Edward tries to slip a hundred-dollar bill for milk money to Ricky, who insists on going to public school so he can be just like other kids. Edward is irrationally overjoyed when Ricky returns home intact from his first day, at least until he notices his boy sporting a nasty black eye. The reason for the beating? The other kids saw Ricky being dropped off in a limousine. "Let me handle this by myself," pleads Ricky about Edward's attempt to move him to private school to get away from the bully, Ox (played by John P. Navin Jr., who would headline his own sitcom a year later in *Jennifer Slept Here* (1983–1984)). Kate proves just as clumsy at addressing Ricky's problem by offering a rape whistle, but that's nothing compared to Edward's ultimate solution: hiring Mr. T as Ricky's personal bodyguard at school.

Mr. T's intimidating presence provokes anxiety among Ricky's teacher and fellow students, with Ricky himself balking, "These are supposed to be my carefree years!"

The arrangement provokes conflict between Edward, who tries to pull rank as Mr. T's boss, and Ricky, who wants to fend for himself and refuses to hand over his milk money on his own. Ultimately Edward physically confronts Mr. T over the proper treatment of Ricky's predicament, which triggers a revelation that Ricky himself should be allowed to face off against someone bigger without the amenities his wealth can provide. Back at school, a dual transformation takes effect as Ricky tries to rally his classmates to stand up to Ox, while the bully himself adorns gold chains to appear even more imposing. "You'll just have to beat me up the rest of the school year," Ricky rationalizes before he defends himself by punching Ox down to the ground. His example serves as a rallying cry for the rest of the class, an imposing wall of resistance against Ox – who's shamed with the talismanic utterance of his real name, Hobart.

At the end of the episode, Ricky's assimilation with his peers appears to be complete. However, there's an uneasy flicker beneath the closing shots as we see Ricky being hailed as a newly arrived savior by a group of children of other ethnicities and social classes; it isn't too far a leap to make from this finale to the far more infamous reception to the ending of *Indiana Jones and the Temple of Doom* in 1984, with its hero freeing hundreds of enslaved children from bondage after their entire village of relatives seemed to take no aggressive steps at all to save them.

Designed to appeal to younger viewers, *Silver Spoons* in its earliest days already featured a barrage of visual hooks including a miniature train running through the house, a bank of arcade games in the foyer, and Ricky's bedroom decked out like a young boy's dream playground. The show famously began life as an attempt to translate the Oscar-winning comedy *Arthur* (1981) to the small screen, but when the rights to the antics of the alcoholic millionaire proved unavailable, the concept was tweaked with that can't-miss tactic of the situation comedy: a cute kid. And kids at the time didn't come much cuter than Schroder, who made an auspicious debut in Franco Zeffirelli's 1979 tearjerker *The Champ* before moving on to Disney's *The Last Flight of Noah's Ark* (1980), *The Earthling* (1980), and a high-profile 1980 made-for-TV version of *Little Lord Fauntleroy*. That last credit is most likely responsible for his casting in *Silver Spoons*, which draws liberally from the playful wealth signifiers of Francis Veber's 1976 French comedy *Le Jouet* and its controversial 1982 remake, Richard Donner's *The Toy*.

As far as wish fulfilment goes in the mid-1980s, it's difficult to top the chance to meet one of the biggest icons for young boys: Mr. T. Born in Chicago as Lawrence Tureaud, the bling-heavy, Mohawked actor had launched from obscurity to instant fame in May of 1982 with his flamboyant role as Clubber Lang in *Rocky III*, which launched his catchphrase, "I pity the fool"; the film was also preceded by one month in theaters by the less successful *Penitentiary II*. Soon Mr. T mania was spreading, and in this episode Edward even explicitly calls out the Mandinka tribe inspiration for Mr. T's signature Mohawk.

The casting of Mr. T also provides a unique counterpoint to the narrative thrust of the episode, with the guest star's flamboyant use of heavy layer of gold chains standing in stark contrast to Ricky's struggle to suppress any outward signs of his well-off existence from his peers. Mr. T has been very forthright since the beginning about the meanings behind his hairstyle and accessories, with the chains holding particular significance. As he told *The Harvard Crimson*, "When my ancestors came from Africa, they were shackled by our neck, our wrists and our ankles in steel chains. I've turned those steel chains into gold to symbolize the fact that I'm still a slave, only my price tag is higher."

This particular episode also stands at a junction between two significant 1980s films about high school bullying, coming on the heels of the 1980 sleeper favorite *My Bodyguard* about a wall-of Manhattanite, Chris Makepeace, who hires a misunderstood but imposing outcast Adam Baldwin to protect him from bully Matt Dillon and his minions. Both stories come to similar conclusions, that a kid has to resort to physical violence to assert himself and put bullies in their place ("You broke my nose!"), though *My Bodyguard* marinates in a richly felt New York City atmosphere far removed from the more upstate, suburban New York setting of *Silver Spoons*. The other key film here is *The Karate Kid*, another key title from 1984, which flips the formula by moving the setting to Southern California and positioning the persecuted schoolboy (Ralph Macchio in this case) as a lower-class transplant singled out for attack by a gang of rich Aryan preppies from the local Cobra Kai dojo. Here wisdom is dispensed not from Mr. T but Mr. Miyagi (Pat Morita), the apartment complex handyman who turns out to be a

Mr. T guest stars on "Me and Mr. T" from Silver Spoons, *helping the lead Ricky Schroder deal with school bullies.*

karate teaching maestro. Again, our young protagonist learns to discover his identity through physical combat, albeit in a more public, competitive setting and a far more overt act of self-defense.

Both this episode and its larger pop culture counterparts ultimately depict a world of predators and prey, where even a simple gag like Kate brandishing that rape whistle carries an unspoken level of meaning about how those who don't have a dog-eat-dog spirit have to use their wits to find a way to survive. (Or to paraphrase one of the most famous films about bullying, *Song of the South* (1946), sometimes you have to use your head instead of your feet.) That also means determining the right moment to apply physical force in each case, an inevitable conclusion that ran throughout the 1980s with its apotheosis ultimately reached in George McFly's time-altering, yuppie-birthing slug to face against Biff in *Back to the Future* (1985). Even at a very young age, Ricky and his 1980s counterparts will always have to adapt to a world wrestling with the temptations of immense wealth, the need for self-preservation, and the demands of honoring one's own moral code.

"The Peacemaker" from *Diff'rent Strokes*
Original Air Date: 30 October 1982
By Troy Howarth

Aired just in time for Halloween of 1982, in the early stages of the fifth season of *Diff'rent Strokes* (1978–1986), "The Peacemaker" addresses a topic that's still very much in the ether: gun control. It also touches on a theme already covered in the previous season's "Crime Story," as well: namely, school bullying. That's a good amount of thematic material to sift through in the space of 25 family-friendly minutes – but writer Don Segall manages to make it all come together in a cohesive fashion. Segall – not to be confused with the great gritty action filmmaker Don Siegel – was a veteran journeyman who had contributed scripts to such TV shows as *M*A*S*H* (1972–1983), *Good Times* (1974–1979), and *The Jeffersons* (1975–1985), but "The Peacemaker" would remain his sole credit for *Diff'rent Strokes*.

In a move typical of the structure of the show, the episode starts off with a sketch in miniature which sets the stage for what is to follow. The Drummond family housekeeper, Pearl (Mary Jo Catlett), is on the phone arguing with a man over an item he had previously agreed to buy from her. Now that the man is reneging on the deal, she's hopping mad – and in her distress, she's ignoring her duties as the family (im)patiently waits for their breakfast. Deciding it best to defuse the situation, Mr. Drummond (Conrad Bain) takes over for Pearl on the phone and smoothly negotiates a compromise. His ability to wheel and deal makes a profound impression on Willis (Todd Bridges), who is anxious to develop similar skills himself. Willis may come from the streets, where such disagreements are typically resolved in a more aggressive fashion, but now that he is comfortably part of the upper crust of New York society, he sees the value in handling things with greater finesse.

Pearl, incidentally, was the third and last of the Drummond housekeepers, following in the footsteps of Charlotte Rae's Mrs. Garrett, who appeared in the first two seasons before being promoted to her own show, *The Facts of Life* (1979–1988), and Nedra Volz as the more grandmotherly Adelaide Brubaker, who was in residence through seasons three and four. Different fans have different opinions on the quality of the Drummond family help, but the overall fan favorite definitely seems to be Charlotte Rae – which should come as a surprise to no one. Catlett's portrayal of the well-intended but occasionally acerbic Pearl was definitely a valuable addition to the series, which would begin to struggle maintaining its favor with the public as the child actors started to hit the really awkward part of their teenage years.

Drummond's biological daughter, Kimberly (Dana Plato), seems poised to play a larger role than usual early on – but she is soon sidelined from the majority of the action. Even so, it's she who first ends up nearly being compromised when a slick operator at school named Marko (Arye Gross) tries to sell her some stolen jewelry. She's more than a little sheltered and naïve, but fortunately her street-wise foster brother Willis knows the score. The contrast between the haves and the have-nots is laid bare here, as Kimberly nearly agrees to purchase some stolen goods, only to be rescued from potential humiliation by Willis.

The character of Marko provides Arye Gross with his first screen acting role, and he makes the best of it. The character is a bit of a sleaze, but Gross imbues it with easy charm; he would go on to enjoy much success as a character actor, notably playing Adam Green on *Ellen* (1994–1998) and appearing in everything from Steven Spielberg's *Minority Report* (2002) to episodes of *CSI* (2000–2015).

Things soon taken an even darker turn when Willis decides to interject himself into a conflict involving a bully named "Crazy" Larry (Andrew Clay). Looking to follow in his foster father's footsteps, Willis naively decides to play mediator by offering to find a peaceful solution to the problem at hand. Larry has commandeered another student's locker and is anxious to keep its contents hidden. Rather than stand by and allow the two boys to get into an epic scrape, Willis promises to think on it and find a compromise that should satisfy both parties.

The character of "Crazy" Larry was popular enough to warrant bringing Andrew Clay back for another episode – "My Fair Larry" from later in the fifth season – and it provides an ideal showcase for the up-and-coming comic actor. He had yet to establish his moniker as Andrew Dice Clay, of course, but much of the swaggering mannerisms and tropes are very much in evidence in his portrayal of Larry. Within a few short years, he would become one of the major comic figures of the late eighties and early nineties, but for now he was lucky to get a chance to steal a few scenes from the *Diff'rent Strokes* regulars.

Willis' good intentions do not go unpunished: the next day, the locker is revealed to have been broken into and its contents stolen – and Larry is convinced that Willis is to blame. He isn't the culprit, of course, but that doesn't deter Larry from threatening to brain him if his items aren't returned in short order. Marko offers to help Willis by selling him a handgun for his protection. Willis is afraid of owning a gun, but Marko sells him on its practicality.

Up until this point, Gary Coleman's character of Arnold – the one that really caught on with the public – has been somewhat sidelined. That changes when he discovers what Willis has done. "If Dad knew you had a gun, he'd shoot you!" It's interesting that, of the two boys, it's the younger, more impulsive, and more "precocious" Arnold who realizes just how dangerous and stupid this all is. He's terrified at the prospect of having a loaded weapon in the house, and none of Willis' attempts to placate his nerves do much to calm him down.

That night, with Mr. Drummond away on business and Pearl away visiting her mother, the three siblings are left on their own. In the middle of the night, Willis and Arnold hear somebody rustling around downstairs. Convinced that it is Larry com ing to do him harm, Willis arms himself with his gun and heads down to investigate. It turns out to be Mr. Drummond, who has arrived back earlier than expected from his trip. When he sees Willis armed with a gun, he's understandably perturbed. "What the *hell* are you doing with a gun?!" The inclusion of some brief "salty" language is not typical of *Diff'rent Strokes*, but given the seriousness of the situation, it certainly fits the mood. He proceeds to read Willis the riot act and the young man comes to realize how reckless and foolish he was being – and how easily this whole thing could have ended in irreparable tragedy. "A gun doesn't solve any problems," he tells Willis, "all it does is create more." Lesson learned.

The next day, Drummond escorts Willis to school, hoping to tell the principal about what has been going on. They're interrupted by Larry, whose macho act does little to impress Mr. Drummond. "What's he going to do?," he asks Willis, "Stab me with one of his sideburns?" Seeing the unflappable Bain staring down the hotheaded Clay is undoubtedly one of the episode's greatest joys.

It is finally revealed that the culprit responsible for ripping off Larry in the first place was Marko – and Larry goes to settle the score with him, leaving Willis free to enjoy peace once more. Just what happens to Marko is never revealed; we never see him again, even if Larry would show up again in just a few more weeks.

As for Willis, his determination to follow in his father's footsteps by becoming a master negotiator may be a positive impulse, but now it is tempered with a better sense of reality: sometimes it really does pay to pick your battles. But above all else, Willis learns an even more important lesson: tact and diplomacy inevitably trump violence. In exposing the young viewers to such lessons, the show manages once more to perform a valuable service – all in the guise of a sedate and good-natured half hour of sitcom goodness, to boot.

On that level, the Very Special Episode format was particularly well-suited to the tropes of *Diff'rent Strokes*; arguably no other series utilized the concept with greater insight or sincerity, thus ensuring that their many forays into such terrain remain as accessible and indeed valuable today as they were when they first aired so many years ago.

"The Perils of Punky" from *Punky Brewster*
Original Air Date: 20 October 1985
By Edward Eaton

The creators of the television show *Punky Brewster* (1984–1988) were never shy about putting the eponymous character through the wringer. In the very first episode, "Punky Finds a Home: Part 1", Punky is left by her father, abandoned in a Chicago mall by her mother, and forced by necessity to squat in an abandoned apartment. That sort of life would be tough for anyone of any age – Punky is eight. Over four seasons, Punky and company deal with cheating, drug addiction, medical emergencies, a near suffocation death, car accidents, repeated threats of being sent to an orphanage, a serial killer, and even the Challenger explosion. Indeed, Gary Portnoy's lyrics to the opening theme, "Maybe the world is blind/or just a little unkind", serve as foreshadowing for episodes that might, thematically at least, come across as grim. The second season two-parter, "The Perils of Punky", stands out as a special episode in a series made up of special episodes not only because of the emotional impact on the main character but also because of aesthetic decisions by the episodes' writer and director. The episodes force Punky, and her young at-home audience, to face up to issues of duty, death, loss, and abandonment; they are also downright terrifying at times.

The story starts off simply enough: Punky, Cherie, Margaux, Allen, and Brandon (the dog) go on a camping trip with Punky's foster father, Henry, and Cherie's mother, Betty. The children and the dog go off into the woods to find firewood and get lost. They decide to wait for Henry and Betty to find them by going into a dark cave. They are approached by four members of the Waxahatchie Indian Tribe who tell Punky and the others that an evil spirit has awakened and is threatening to destroy the forest and the lake. Punky, the champion foretold by prophecy and the incarnation of an Indian Princess, and her friends are the only ones who can conquer said spirit. The kids accept the challenge and head deeper into the cave. They are confronted by a number of obstacles, including moving stone walls, cave-ins, a seemingly bottomless crevasse, and a vicious giant spider. After overcoming the obstacles, Punky is stripped of her friends and faced with her worst fears. Punky rises to the occasion, vanquishing the evil spirit by using her innate goodness and optimism to combat the fear and despair that are the spirit's weapons.

The first episode is fairly tame. The children do get lost in the woods, but it is warm, and the shadows show that it is still fairly early in the day. Moreover, the children are not scared, and the adults, while concerned enough to look for their charges, do not seem unduly worried. It is only at the end of this episode that the visual aspects experience a tonal shift when they are followed by rats, a multitude of watching eyes. Not only is that a sudden and drastic change from the atmosphere of the episode up to this point, but the show's audiences were not left with an upbeat ending or a funny comment or situation but rather with a cliffhanger every bit as effective as those that could be seen in Hollywood serials (The shared title of the episodes harkens back to the silent-movie era, *Perils of Pauline* (1914), as well as to the cartoon series, *The Perils of Penelope Pitstop* (1969–1970)). It is not hard to imagine young viewers being terrified by the closing shot, even knowing that the next episode was immediately following.

Right away, in part two, Punky and friends run into Mr. Pieces, played by the ubiquitously and unforgettably unknown Vincent Schiavelli, whose still-working arms and legs have been placed in various parts of the chamber. Although the scene is played for laughs:

Margeaux: Arms and legs can't move by themselves. Heads can't talk without a body. You aren't real.
Mr. Pieces: Yes, I am. Pull yourself together.
Margeaux: Look who's talking.
("The Perils of Punky: Part 2" 03:58-04:08)

The image of a man who has been dismembered but whose limbs still function is certainly creepy, to say the least.

A few minutes later, they are attacked by the giant spider, which Punky must kill before it eats her friends. Moments after Punky hacks at it with a magic tomahawk, the giant spider dies in a show of otherworldly pyrotechnics. Then, her friends are taken, one by one, until she is left with only Brandon – and he is stripped of his flesh and blood and turned into a walking skeleton. Brandon as a skeleton may be a little hokey, but the visitations by her doomed friends are graphic and effective. Allen, as a fusion of boy and rock with razor-sharp fangs (15:09) is shocking, and the close-ups of Margeaux's face (15:22 and later) could remind an adult viewer of shots of Regan from *The Exorcist* (1973).

During the final confrontation between Punky and the evil spirit, the writer tries to lighten the mood:

Spirit: You must die. The only question is: how?
Punky: Old Age?
("The Perils of Punky: Part 2," 19:07-30)

Instead of serving as comic relief, the moment diminishes the scene, falling into what has become the tired cliché of the hero facing certain doom with a witty quip. However, the Spirit's demise, as it is stripped of its corporeality and banished back to its prison in the living rock, pulls us back, with the Spirit's rage and pain, into the very high stakes game Punky is playing.

Of course, at no point in time would an adult, or even an older child, feel that any of the characters are in any real danger – it is *Punky Brewster*, after all – but a younger child, the target audience for this show, might. The images are strong, graphic, and effective. Some of the shots – the first shot of the spider, Allen in the rock, and zombie Margeaux, for example – are chilling. Punky Brewster is a brightly colorful character who is perennially upbeat and sweet; the show generally reinforces this idea visually. These two episodes are a major break from the norm – indeed, from the norm of most of the relatively vanilla sitcoms of the period. The producers of these two episodes are happy to scare the bejesus out of a mostly preteen audience. Considering the age of most of the viewers, these episodes might well have been those kids' first experience with the horror genre. In all likelihood, these episodes are also responsible for any number of nightmares.

The episodes are not just visually significant for the series. They also raise some provocative and disturbing themes that Punky must deal with. There is a certain casualness to part one which is almost as if the producers are trying to lull the audience into a false sense of security before the disturbing elements in part two.

As said earlier, Punky Brewster's life has had some rather grim moments. However, so far, she has never been completely alone. If Brandon has not been there to comfort and protect her, someone always has: Henry, another of the several adults in her life, or more of her friends. The Evil Spirit effectively strips away all of Punky's potential support. She is even more alone than she was when her mother abandoned her. Then, she is forced to watch her guardian talk about how much he is going to enjoy life without a bothersome and expensive child (16:10-17:06). An adult, or even an older child, might realize that this scene is a vision created by an Evil Spirit that plays on its victims' fears. For a child Punky's age, the exchange is believable and hardly unexpected. Punky has to know that Henry is not a young man. When he meets Punky, he is sixty. While Punky might bring all sorts of joy to his life, she can not make him younger. Statistically, he should already have died: the life expectancy for a man born in 1924 was 58. Still alive in 1985, he would likely have about fifteen years left. Instead of looking forward to retirement and ten years or so living in Florida, Henry has to face the probability that if he is going to give Punky any real start, he will be working until she is 22 or 23 and out of college – when he will be 73. The very issue of Henry's ability, financially and physically, to take care of Punky as he approaches old age is a significant part of season two's five-part story, "Changes", which sees Punky ultimately adopted by Henry.

Faced with the loss of all those who support and love her, and the pressure of knowing only she can save them, Punky almost surrenders to the fear and despair. However, with a little help from Princess Moon (played by Punky – or rather, Soleil Moon Frye – herself), Punky learns that she has the courage, optimism, and willingness to stand fast in the face of hopelessness that are some of the reasons her friends love her in the first place.

The producers of these episodes apparently realized that they were pushing boundaries, not only emotionally but visually as well. They made some attempts at tempering the impact of the events. For example: they chose Moon to portray the Indian Princess; the name of the Evil Spirit is "Owa Tagu Syam", and, just in case the young audience did not get the joke, Punky comments on it; they also end the quest to defeat the spirit with a return of the whole gang to the campfire, where Punky finishes the "ghost story" she has told about the adventure. If, indeed, the whole affair was just a story within a story, then Punky's fears of abandonment really are bubbling just below the surface. The producers pull a twist by having Princess Moon materialize in the cavern once everyone has left. In a world where Santa Claus might well exist (see season one's two-parter, "Yes, Punky, There is a Santa Claus"), a magic Indian Princess might well exist, which would certainly then allow for the possibility of an evil spirit, even if its name is Owa

Soleil Moon Frye as Punky Brewster *(here with trusty dog pal Brandon) would give a voice and hope to poor kids of urban settings facing a cold harsh world.*

Tagu Syam. If Owa Tagu Syam exists, then it is a powerful spirit that can force someone to face some pretty dark and damaging fears. If Punky is just telling a story, then the events in her life and her inability to believe in a world where she is able to maintain healthy relationships with her family and friends because they will leave and/or reject her suggest that there is a lot of damage that needs professional care... not a quick hug.

A modern pre- or early-teen would likely have a much more sophisticated palette for entertainment, having likely watched *Harry Potter* or Peter Jackson films. An audience member in the mid-eighties would probably have been affected by the disturbing, and surprisingly effective, graphic visuals in the two episodes. To make matters worse, they would have seen the reappearance of Princess Moon as confirmation that the adventure indeed happened – at least in the world of Punky Brewster. The idea that young audiences believe what they see on television or in films might be hotly debated, but many people who grew up reading the *Harry Potter* books were distraught when they did not receive their invitation to Hogwarts. They might have understood, on an intellectual level, that Hogwarts was fictitious; their emotional acceptance was another thing altogether. The children who watched "The Perils of Punky" went to bed that night aware that Owa Tagu Syam might be real and preyed on fear. They also went to bed that night thinking about being left alone, without family or friends.

"The Perils of Punky" is a Very Special Episode, but it is also unusual in how it is special. Special episodes often address a specific issue or situation where a resolution is reached that puts everything in perspective. When young characters (or audience members) are involved, adults who are part of the story are able to address the issues and help the characters reach some sort of resolution. Often, real-world parents are asked to speak with their children about the issues. "The Perils of Punky" is surprisingly irresponsible in that there is no real closure. The friends tell Punky, "Great story!", and off they go. The adults do little more than say, "Thank God, you're safe!" and off they go – indeed, they leave Punky behind for a few moments. The final appearance of Princess Moon suggests it really did happen. As we learned from the Indian Chief in part one, the prison Owa Tagu Syam is kept in is only temporary: he will return someday and terrify other children.

"Give Your Uncle Arthur a Kiss" from *Family Ties*
Original Air Date: 10 November 1982
By Edward Eaton

> What are we going to do with Uncle Arthur?
> A blinking stallion, is Uncle Arthur.
> When he goes a-strolling in the park,
> Watch your step, girls, especially after dark.
> Any old skirt's a flirt to Uncle Arthur,
> He's over eighty, but how he can run!
> "Give us a kiss, my dear," he'd say,
> And tickle you up the boom-di-ay,
> And say it was just an 'armless bit of fun.
> > "What are we going to do with Uncle Arthur?"
> > (Music: Alexander Faris; Lyrics: Alfred Shaughnessy)

It simply cannot be an accident that the title of (and the guest character) of this episode use the name "Uncle Arthur". Gary David Goldberg had been in the business too long not to have heard of *Upstairs, Downstairs* (1971–1975). Moreover, Steven Keaton works at a Public Broadcasting Station, whence *Upstairs, Downstairs* would likely have been broadcast. Goldberg must have thought it would be a neat little Easter Egg to name a character after the subject of a raunchy music-hall number from a prestigious British serial.

The episode concerns a family friend, the eponymous "Uncle Arthur", making a pass at Mallory. Mallory approaches Alex, who at first laughs off the incident then, realizing that it is serious, recommends his sister talk to their mother. Elyse initially confronts Arthur publicly. Then she and Steven talk with the man. Arthur apologizes to Mallory.

"Give Your Uncle Arthur a Kiss" rather neatly parallels "The Summer of '82" (season one, episode 4). The two episodes expose something of the series' naivete and its double standard.

"The Summer of '82" explores Alex losing his virginity to an older woman. Therein lie some of the differences between the episodes. Alex is 17, over the age of consent in Ohio (16). Stephanie, the older woman, is a 21-year-old college student. Alex is, eventually, a willing, though awkward, participant. Mallory is 15, and Arthur is a contemporary of her parents. She is certainly not a willing participant.

Perhaps it was the attitude of people in the early eighties: no one seems concerned with Alex's encounter with a college student; Arthur is handled with little more than some serious finger wagging. Perhaps it was the writers trying to reflect the parents' former free-living hippy openness to anything. Of course, throughout the series, one never really gets the idea that Steven and Elyse did anything more rebellious than wear some beads and maybe walk around barefoot. They certainly never "turned on, tuned in," and/or "dropped out"; they were married in 1964 and had Alex in 1965; Mallory came in 1967; they were certainly too "establishment" to participate in the Summer of Love. Arthur does try to explain away his two passes at Mallory. He explains that after his divorce he has been going through a lot; he is not really sure why he did what he did; he has a big problem – one, Steven says, Arthur should see a professional for. That, it appears, would be that. He is even left alone, giving him an opportunity to apologize to Mallory, who accepts it and is now okay. From a 21st century perspective, the Keatons, or at least the show's producers, are rather jejune. At least no one accuses Arthur of being a pedophile (had his victim been Jennifer, then maybe). However, scolding Arthur then leaving him alone to speak with Mallory might strike someone as dangerous. It does, though, let us know that the Keatons accept Arthur's apology and excuse. We know that Arthur regretted the kiss – that shows on his face within seconds. His approach is awkward and shows no evidence of being contrived or practiced. He does nothing to "groom" Mallory, the way a predator might. When he tries to deny it, he does so in a blustering kind of way which in no way resembles the kind of smoothly aggressive compulsive lying a predator or addict might use, and he admits to his mistake very quickly. The Keatons are concerned that their daughter might be hurt, but they show no indication that they fear she might be scarred. Arthur needs professional help; Mallory does not. Of course, that could reflect their concern over any stigma that going to a mental health professional might have brought with it in 1982.

The audience might agree that the Arthur situation was an unfortunate occurrence, but that does not excuse us from ignoring the Alex-Stephanie case. We can brush off Arthur's transgression. He is going through a lot, so it might be an anomaly. "Nothing" really happened other than a kiss and a pat on the rear. Mallory is fifteen and may not have wanted the attention, but she did not actually say "no", and once she walked away, Arthur did not pursue her; this is 1982 and no one had ever heard of affirmative consent. This is not an attempt at diminishing the situation but more of trying to understand how people in the early 1980s might have understood it – Arthur was wrong, but there were levels of wrong in the 1980s that many people in the 2020s simply would not understand. Alex is as much a victim as is Mallory. This is what many people in the eighties, as well as today, also will not understand. That is because there is a double standard when it comes to men.

In *Family Guy's* 2010 episode "Peter-assment" (season eight, episode 14), Lois laughs off Peter's complaint that his boss, Angela, is sexually harassing him, telling Peter that men like that sort of attention and he should enjoy it. In the 2006 *South Park* episode "Miss Teacher Bangs a Boy" (season 10, episode 10), when Kyle goes to the police to report that Ike is being molested by his teacher, the police are immediately concerned.

Yates:	Oh my God! This is terrible! Ya-you did the right thing telling the police. Now, who is the teacher? What's his name?
Kyle:	Well, it isn't a guy teacher. It's a woman.
Officer 2:	Oh, but, but she's ugly, right?
Kyle:	Well no, not really. It's the Kindergarten teacher, Miss Stevenson.
Yates:	The blonde?
Kyle:	Yeah.
Officer 1:	Some young boy is having sex with Miss Stevenson?
Kyle:	Yes.
Officer 1:	Nice!
Yates:	Nice!

Of course, these two shows are satires, but they serve to remind us that attitudes have not changed all that much since the 1980s.

People might say that the Alex situation is completely different. Is it? Alex is legal, to be sure. However, he is a minor, and Stephanie is an experienced adult who knows what she wants and does what it takes to bed her target: she compliments him, repeatedly tells him how different he is from other boys his age, how mature he is, how he is someone she can really talk to – even more than young men her own age; she takes him to a talk that she just happens to have tickets to, she plies him with alcohol, stops him from leaving the couple of times he tries, tells him how special he is, then takes him to bed. How is that not grooming? The next day, when an infatuated Alex goes to see her, Stephanie has another lover in her apartment and has no real interest in seeing Alex again. She got what she wanted. Alex has been the victim of a predator and one whose methods appear to have been well-practiced.

Therein lies the double standard. Mallory has been the victim of what everyone in the show seems to agree was an unfortunate occurrence involving a troubled man. Yet even before Steven and Elyse are aware of the facts, Elyse has publicly humiliated Arthur (possibly ruining his career) and Steven has threatened to kill him. Alex has been groomed and used (even possibly raped – Stephanie gave a minor alcohol to help relax him before she made her move) and then cast aside without any consideration for his feelings. His parents mock him. Finally, Steven has a man-to-man talk that is supposed to resolve everything.

The song from *Upstairs, Downstairs* is appropriate for each episode. A potential sexual predator is not taken seriously. In the case of Stephanie: she is an attractive young woman, and Alex is a guy – consent is understood to be automatic. In the case of Arthur, no harm no foul, and he promises to get his act together. Stephanie, no doubt, will continue using local stores and other places filled with high-school boys as her own personal hunting grounds. Arthur might be going through problems but telling him to get some help and walking away does little to solve the issue. Indeed, quite the opposite, the older Keatons' reaction enables it: if the worst that will happen to him is he is yelled at, then why not try it again with someone else?

"Give Your Uncle Arthur a Kiss" is a sweet episode. It helps to establish that Mallory is growing, which will affect her relationships with her parents ("You used to tell me everything," Steven laments. "I'm older now," Mallory says. "It's not as easy."). This was early enough in the series that they had not committed to making Mallory the family ditz. The maturity of her reaction to what must have been frightening encounters suggests that the writers might have been considering a different direction for her character. Being only the sixth episode of the series, this is fairly early to delve into Very Special Episodes. Little has really been established and the audience is hardly invested in the characters yet. However, this episode, especially when coupled with "The Summer of '82", serves as an affective "proto-Very Special Episode" and sets the stage for future episodes that will explore the characters deeply and go in directions that are somewhat off-the-beaten-sitcom track.

David Spielberg plays a "friend of the family" Arthur who sexually harasses the unsuspecting Mallory (Justine Bateman) in the confronting "Give Your Uncle Arthur a Kiss" from Family Ties.

"The Chiefs Gay Evening" from *Gimme a Break!*
Original Air Date: 13 November 1982
By Lee Gambin

A trope utilized quite often in American television drama series as well as situation comedies when dealing with the issue of homosexuality is the concept of "the gay guy could be anybody" – the possibility of the "average Joe" "batting for the other team". Whilst effeminate sissy characters would pop up here and there on TV, for the most part, the queer guest star of the week was usually a masculine, innocuous "real man" who shocks the heterosexual lead or regular into understanding that gay people can come in all shapes and sizes, and may in fact be one of the football-loving, beer guzzling boys rather than a limp wristed lisping theatre loving queen. When you look at dramatic series such as *Family* (1976–1980), the gay male episode entitled "Rites of Friendship" has a childhood friend of mainstay Willie Lawrence (Gary Frank) being forced out of the closet after getting in trouble at a gay bar, where his future becomes uncertain and riddled with problems. Like all good queers, he disappears from the series and therefore from the lives of his straight counterparts. In an interesting take however, the excellent *Family* poses a question upon its straight teen lead Willie, who questions his own sexuality for a moment, even making an entire sequence aim its focus on male to male crushes.

In the hard hitting episode "Best Buddies" from *Fame* (1982–1987), Ivan Kane plays a gay teen who comes out to series regular Danny (Carlo Imperato) who struggles with accepting this fact – especially when his best pal is incredibly "straight acting" (whatever that means). What makes this episode so gritty and tough is the fact that the gay teen's father (in a terrific performance from Richard Bright) is unapologetically anti-gay, and even calls his own son a "faggot". Kane plays the personal struggles of this gay teen with such gusto and power that it makes for incredibly truthful and densely heartbreaking television viewing. By the end of the episode, Danny and his friend find a common ground by not discussing sexuality anymore, but enjoying a common love for Bruce Lee martial arts films. If the sexuality of these young men is ignored, then perhaps the straight world can feel more comfortable – sadly, for the most part, invisibility becomes an essential weapon and defense mechanism for both the gay and straight character alike.

When it came to comedy, the straight dude who is actually gay motif popped up in a number of shows such as the groundbreaking "Judging Books by Covers" from *All in the Family* (1971–1979) and is then resurrected years later in "The Chief's Gay Evening" from the Nell Carter vehicle *Gimme a Break!* (1981–1987). In this episode, Chief Carl Kanisky (Dolph Sweet) is on a stakeout at a laundrette, in attempt to catch a mugger who is targeting little old ladies. The first instance we get a sense of gender-bending and sexuality blurring is where Carl shows housekeeper Nell (Nell Carter) an outfit that one of his men will be wearing completely comprised of flowing dress, handbag and wig. The officer in question who has to go undercover as a woman is Baxter (Frank Bonner), a dim-witted goof whose sexuality is assumed heterosexual therefore when he wears the dress and heels it is treated as a joke – after all, everybody laughs at the straight guy in the dress, because to take on feminine qualities is to "step down" in power and to lose all sense of masculinity, submitting to the mockery that the patriarchy associates with femininity and "what it means" to be a woman.

The other policeman on the case is the older and more hardened Jerry (Eugene Roche) who is completely unassuming, tough, loaded with machismo and is completely at ease with his associate Baxter having to get in drag in order to bust this violent mugger. His casual take on this is an indication that this is a man who is comfortable with any situation at hand – even the misunderstanding that Nell and Carl are married or live-in lovers (one black, one white) doesn't faze him as it does his younger counterpart.

At the stakeout Carl and Jerry reminisce about their years together as policemen, and even discuss their former wives (Carl's of course has passed away and Jerry went through a painful divorce), before they are interrupted by Baxter in full drag. With jokes involving groping and gender politics, the show shifts into a confessional that is written with a biting intelligence and even frustrated anger. Carl's statement about transvestism (calling them "sickos") leads into a fag joke, where he goes through the entire gag mimicking a "pansy" and "camping it up" with utter disdain and repulsion directed at gay men on mass. Jerry sits there and listens to the anecdote involving a sissy queen and his dog, completely unimpressed. Instead of taking the joke in his stride, Jerry stands up to Carl and spews out an onslaught of Polish jokes – one after the other. Carl being Polish is taken aback by these gags and finally admits that he doesn't find them funny because he is a Polack, prompting Jerry to explain that he doesn't like gay jokes because he is gay, which in turn makes the studio audience verbally react, vocalizing both surprise and slight disgust.

The character of Jerry had appeared in a few episodes prior to this one and was established as a seemingly heterosexual male – with an ex-wife. But here, his character has moved forward and learned to accept his homosexuality and is not up for taking jabs from the likes of Carl. Jerry would appear in one more episode, before completely disappearing, but here his sexuality is worn proudly like a badge of honor – similarly like the one he would wear as an excellent police officer.

Carl doesn't want to believe that his partner and good friend is gay and tries to distract himself by the packed lunch his daughter has provided. When he finally snaps and asks, "How can *you* be gay?" it is a testament to what was afore discussed – the questionable notion of "real men" being fags. Carl struggles to understand how this can be, and Jerry argues that he has always been gay and that his marriage was a mistake, he also expresses his belief that gay men can make excellent cops. The rationale of the homophobic Carl is that gay men can't be policemen, and the blurring of sexuality and gender roles and vocations that require action associated with masculine energy is examined. What Carl fears is not so much gay men or even gay sex, but issues concerned with the fragility of masculinity. His lengthy monologue about his gay English teacher and his stoic manly Uncle Joey is a poignant touch to the well-constructed script.

Carl opens this soliloquy with "Being gay can lead to a lot of trouble", which is something that many queer people have heard for decades – ultimately, "trouble" meaning oppressive loneliness and even suicide. Carl tells a story about wartime and his father having to leave his wife and kids with "Uncle Joey". Joey, a bricklayer who is described by Carl as an "iron fisted type" took them in and remained a male role model for Carl. However, as a young boy Carl was shy and introverted and also suffered from a torturous speech impediment which made him the target of bullies. His English teacher took a shining to Carl and worked with him until the stutter disappeared. The two would become good friends. Carl continues the story and explains that one evening Uncle Joey came home telling him and his mother and siblings that the English teacher was busted at a gay bar and outed as "the pervert he was". The faculty and everyone thought he had left the school soon after, however, it was learned that he drove his car into a tree and killed himself. The prenotion that gay men are suicidal or that being gay leads to self-harm is something that sat with Carl for many years, and during this somber moment in the episode, which acts as a great counter to the angry cry from Jerry who wishes for acceptance and understanding, we get a sense that Carl understood what his Uncle Joey didn't: that gay men can be heroes. However, when Jerry confronts Carl with this possibility, Carl falls into an angry defense and sings the praises of his uncle. He holds Uncle Joey's stoicism in high regard and seems proud of anti-emotional connections that should never even factor in when concerning men, even in the face of impending death ("we didn't hug, we didn't kiss, he just closed his eyes and went"). Carl's "masculine love" for his Uncle Joey supports the episode's interest in the complexities of masculinity, and he denying the heroism of his teacher aids the concept of what makes a man a man.

By the closing moments of the episode, solo Jerry heads out to arrest the mugger and over the bugged speaker we hear gun fire and later learn that he is gunned down. Landing in hospital (and yes, "going to be ok"), Jerry is rendered the sacrificial gay, an interesting peer of the "magical Negro" that Nell Carter represents throughout the entire series. When Carl finally admits "That Jerry is one hell of a guy", we come to the understanding that this tough talking masculine Polack copper is slowly going to be accepting of his pal's sexuality; and this is something that we had seen hints of in previous shows that decided to not choose an easy route of total acceptance, but bring the gay experience to a fore that made it like every other experience be it the women's plight, the black or Latino struggle, the rights of the elderly and so forth: it made it complicated, unique to the individual and ultimately very human.

"The Bicycle Man" from *Diff'rent Strokes*
Original Air Dates: 5 February 1983 (Part 1) and 12 February 1983 (Part 2)
By Andrew Rausch
With Very Special insight from actor Shavar Ross

Diff'rent Strokes (1978–1986) produced an exorbitant number of Very Special Episodes during its eight-year run, most of them ending with Mr. Drummond (Conrad Bain) delivering a heavy-handed morality lesson. But none is more memorable than the disturbing two-part episode "The Bicycle Man." The episode has become somewhat infamous since it first aired, and it's telling that when actor Gordon Jump, who plays the titular character, died in 2003, almost as many publications noted him having appeared in this episode as they did *WKRP in Cincinnati* (1978–1982), on which he was a central character for four seasons.

Much of the episode's notoriety comes from its willingness to explore the particularly dark theme of pedophilia, which would seem at odds with a laugh track family sitcom. It should be noted that actor Todd Bridges, who played Arnold's brother Willis on the show, tried to opt out of appearing in the episode due to his own victimization at the hands of a sexual predator. (He didn't tell anyone his reasons for not wanting to appear in the episode until 2017 when he appeared on an episode of *Dr. Oz.*)

"The Bicycle Man" begins with an introduction by actor Conrad Bain explaining that this will be a two-part episode dealing with a "sensitive and important subject." The proceedings are quite ominous, with Bain never giving so much as a single hint as to what that subject might be. He encourages families to watch the episode together and then discuss the issue it details. And then the joyfully upbeat theme song begins to play and the differing tones of the episode are already jarringly at odds with one another before it has even begun.

Once the credit sequence concludes, we find Mr. Drummond, Arnold (Gary Coleman), Willis, and Kimberly (Dana Plato) returning rental bikes to "the Bicycle Man's" shop. The jovial joking and juggling Bicycle Man – real name Mr. Horton – attempts to persuade Mr. Drummond to purchase new bikes for his kids rather than repeatedly paying rental fees. Mr. Drummond has no interest, saying something that foreshadows the events to come: "There are a lot of strange people out there and I don't like the thought of [Arnold] riding alone in the park." Arnold, with some help from Mr. Horton, begs for a bike of his own. At this point Willis says something that will prove to be even more relevant: "As far as crazy people go, they're everywhere." Finally Mr. Drummond relents and agrees to buy Arnold a bike for his upcoming birthday.

Having assisted him in convincing his adoptive stepfather to buy him a bike, Mr. Horton strikes up a friendship with Arnold. At this point everything still seems completely innocent and there is no indication that Mr. Horton has any ill intent. Now that he has Arnold on his side, he convinces the young boy to hand out advertising fliers and persuade his schoolmates to visit the bike shop. For Arnold's work Mr. Horton says he will pay him with a handlebar radio for his new bike. Arnold jumps at this opportunity and then enlists his pal Dudley (Shavar Ross) to assist him in this endeavor.

Just before Arnold shows up at the bicycle shop, we see Mr. Horton leading another young boy (alone) out from his back room apartment, telling him to keep their activities (which so far only seem to include the adult plying the child with candy) a secret from his parents. After Mr. Horton ushers the boy out of the shop, Arnold arrives. Mr. Horton thanks Arnold for handing out the fliers and leads him into the backroom apartment, offering him ice cream. Arnold notes that the apartment is filled with toys and games of all kinds – things that could easily entice young children into his lair. "You sure understand kids," says Arnold. All of this should be a red flag for the audience, but it's done in such a way that it goes largely unnoticed at this point. During Arnold's visit, Mr. Horton works out a deal with the boy, telling him he can secretly come to the shop any time before his birthday and ride his new bicycle. Again, he encourages Arnold to lie to his adoptive father, telling him to keep their meetings a secret. "I really like you," says Mr. Horton, putting his arm around the boy. He tells him the two of them are going to "have a lot of fun together." There is a slight change in tone, and for the first time the audience is given reason to believe that Mr. Horton's motives might be less than pure.

The next time Arnold visits Mr. Horton's shop, he brings Dudley along. Mr. Horton skillfully plants a pornographic magazine in a stack of comic books – clearly something he has done many times before. He tells the young boys he is baking some pizza for them. While he is cooking, Mr. Horton encourages them to look at the comics, which inevitably leads the boys to discover the porno mag. It's at this point that Mr. Horton's intentions are clearly spelled out for the first time. He tells the two boys not to be embarrassed looking at the naked women in the magazine. He tells them the naked body is beautiful, leading into his next saying, "You can have an awful lot of fun with your clothes off." This statement intentionally segues into the adult man showing the boys photographs of himself naked, frolicking with naked boys. He then gives them glasses of wine, all the while reminding them not to tell anyone about any of this. He then convinces them to pose for photographs.

As one would expect, this entire scene is uncomfortable. However, it's not only uncomfortable to watch for the reasons the show's producers have intended. The accompanying laugh track unwittingly adds to the unease. As writer Genevieve Koski explains in a 2013 *AV/TV Club* article: "Throughout the episode, including when Arnold and Dudley are staring goggle-eyed at nude photographs being proffered to them by a middle-aged man, the hysterical laughter of children is audible in the studio audience (laugh track?). Now, granted, the idea of an audience of *any* demographical makeup (real or digitally induced) laughing at that moment is discomfiting, but hearing the bubbly, innocent laughter of children in the mix heightens it even further, taking it almost to the realm of the surreal."

Here the first episode concludes.

The second episode opens once again with Arnold and a shirtless Dudley posing for photographs and playing Tarzan. Mr. Horton suggests that this game would be even better if Dudley had a lion to wrestle with. Not surprisingly, Mr. Horton, who encourages the boys to call him "Curly," suggests that he himself be the lion. Soon the shirtless Dudley is riding on Curly's back. A particularly creepy moment leading up to this finds a shirtless Dudley standing suggestively behind Curly, now on all fours, briefly causing the audience to fear some sort of sodomization may be about to occur. Thankfully, it does not.

Curly gives the boys more wine, encouraging them to drink freely. Throughout all of this, the characters continue to deliver the show's typically unfunny jokes, which are then met with canned laughter. All of this seems at odds with the subject matter being depicted here. One gets the idea the show's producers weren't sure how best to handle this material, giving way to this awkward, uneven approach. While this may come as little surprise considering this is an otherwise silly sitcom, the heaviness of the situations and subject matter presented might have been more effectively portrayed without the daffy jokes and accompanying laugh track.

Soon Curly is encouraging the boys to pretend his bed is a trampoline, and Arnold and the shirtless Dudley are jumping on it wildly. At this point a bell in the front of the bicycle shop rings, indicating there is a customer outside the apartment. Curly looks out the peep hole and sees that the customer is in fact Arnold's father, Mr. Drummond. He asks the boys to keep their voices down, and he goes out to assist him.

Of course Mr. Drummond has no idea what's going down in the next room. He jokes around with Curly and pays off Arnold's bike. As this is happening, the audience wants desperately for him to somehow figure out what Curly is up to and then save the day, but that isn't realistic. So instead, he sort of loiters around for a few minutes, making jokes, despite Curly doing his best to make him leave. When Curly returns to the backroom, he finds that Arnold and Dudley, who figured out Mr. Drummond was there, have now slipped out the back.

Later when Arnold arrives at the Chateau de Drummond, Willis and Kimberly smell booze on his breath. Being the smart kid he is, Arnold concocts a story, saying that Dudley's father gave the boys a taste of alcohol to celebrate the birth of some hamsters. After being forced to swear on his *E.T.* alarm clock, Arnold convinces his siblings that he won't drink again and they decide not to tell. A few moments later, Mr. Drummond arrives and attempts to hug Arnold. Fearing that his adoptive father will also smell the booze on his breath, Arnold declines.

The following day, Arnold and Dudley return to Curly's shop. Arnold admits that he doesn't feel right about sneaking around behind his father's back. To this Curly says, "We're not sneaking around. We're just trying to keep me out of trouble for giving you all these treats after school." He then redirects Arnold by offering him cartoons and Boston Cream Pie. However, Arnold's trepidation returns when he realizes that something is amiss with the cartoon Curly is screening for them. It's called "Murphy the Mouse" and is an animated X-rated sex movie. This is enough for Arnold, who decides to leave.

Undaunted by this and recognizing an opportunity in Arnold's departure, Curly says, "We can have more fun without him."

The show then takes us back to the Drummond's apartment, leaving poor Dudley alone (without even the audience) with the middle-aged pedophile Curly. Someone knocks on the door. When Mr. Drummond answers it, he finds that it's Ted Ramsey, Dudley's father. Ted expresses concern about the boys' drinking alcohol. The audience and Mr. Drummond learn together that Dudley was caught with the alcohol scent on him and then lied to his father, saying it was Mr. Drummond who gave him the alcohol. Now realizing that there's more to this story, Willis and Kimberly tell Mr. Drummond about Arnold's similar story. This leads to a conversation with Arnold in which the boy confesses to sneaking around with Curly. After he has told Mr. Drummond and Ted Ramsey about the things Curly has been doing, the concerned adults call the police.

Soon they, along with police detectives, pay a visit to the bike shop. They find Dudley shirtless and drugged. The frightened boy comes clean and tells them Curly has touched him inappropriately.

Later, after Curly has been whisked away to jail where he will perhaps receive the same kind of attention he gave Dudley, the Drummond family and one of the police detectives have a conversation back at the Drummonds' apartment. The cop gives a heavy-handed speech about parents often blaming their child for being the victims of predators, and explains to Mr. Drummond (and the audience) the appropriate ways to deal with such situations. He also explains misconceptions about sexual predators. "In a strange way they actually love children," he says. "Most of them would never intentionally harm a child."

Mr. Drummond basically concludes both the episode and the lesson by saying, "If more kids knew the facts, less of these things would happen."

The show's writers and producers' collective heart was in the right place when they crafted "The Bicycle Man." However, the episode's execution was one of the most wrongheaded hours in the history of television. Many audience members – a lot of them children – found the episode so jarring that no one who has ever seen the episode ever forgets having done so. It's also for this reason that it's one of the most famous (and infamous) sitcom episodes ever produced.

After watching the episode, one must wonder if its storyline inadvertently served as a "how to" lesson for any would-be sexual predators watching the show. The reason for this is because "Curly" Horton slowly and carefully constructs and enacts a detailed step-by-step scheme to circumvent the boys' reasoning and get them to let their guards down. And it works. Sure, it might be argued that a would-be sexual predator could conceivably be dissuaded from engaging in such activities after seeing Curly arrested at the end of the episode, but that seems unlikely for the same reason that crime films of the 1930s (like the original *Scarface* (1932)) didn't dissuade anyone by ending with the bad guy being arrested after having shown him getting away with literal murder throughout the rest of the film's running time. (And, not for nothing, it should be noted that Curly's insistence that it's okay for the boys to drink wine because "Jesus drank wine" is almost word-for-word what Michael Jackson reportedly told his alleged molestation victims.)

> **SHAVAR ROSS:** At the time I started working on "The Bicycle Man" for *Diff'rent Strokes*, I may have been about thirteen or fourteen, and at the time this kind of episode wasn't thought of or known as a Very Special Episode, it was more or less just another show and just another episode to shoot. The only thing that made it incredibly different from other episodes was the fact that it wasn't filmed in front of a live studio audience. We were all very much used to taping in front of an audience, with people laughing and feeding off that energy. So for this episode, the producers laid an audio track afterwards with the canned laughter, so it was strange to see that occur. For me personally, I never saw "The Bicycle Man" as a Very Special Episode until many years later, in fact five years ago I just became aware of its cult status and that was because people contacted me and asked me about it. So I looked it up on Wikipedia and other sources, [and] this episode is most definitely considered one of these Very Special Episodes, but at the time of making it I wasn't aware of its importance.
>
> The show came through two of the core writers on the show Robert Jayson and A. Dudley Johnson Jr. – and as a side note, that's how I got my name Dudley on the show, I was named after the writer – who had a huge writing staff, but I would assume it came from those two. I remember there was a lot of talk at the time in the media about child molestation claims and there was also the Atlanta child murders which happened in the late 1970s, so they specifically may have not been that influential but there was definite buzz around the spotlighting of child molestation at the time. I was living in Georgia for several years before coming out to California and just after I had left there were reports of this black man killing lots of black children, and I remember that I had left right before that happened.
>
> We didn't have a table reading, we just found out that we had Gordon Jump as our guest star and he was terrific. We went straight into it and it was only afterwards when I started to slowly realize how important this episode was. We won several awards for it, and I remember travelling to different schools talking about it with other children, letting them know that if something was going on in their

lives that was similar to what happened to me in the episode that it was okay to tell the authorities and not be afraid or ashamed.

At the time, there was nothing that really came up that would make Gary Coleman and I sit down and discuss the issue raised in the episode. I was already well into my character, I was familiar with being on the set. I had already done many episodes prior to this one, the only thing that was very different was the fact that it wasn't filmed in front of a live studio audience and that was very eerie for me. Years later I would go onto YouTube and see the episode and read the comments and there were a lot of people complaining about the laugh track! That's when I realized I really had to sit down and re-watch the episode and see how inappropriate the placing of some of the laugh track was! At that time in television they tried to mix serious issues with comedy – there was a sense of "Hey people! This is still a funny show, even though we're talking serious issues here!" and so the laugh tracks would have to be placed at the right moments. If there wasn't any laugh track then the show would turn into a straight up drama show. I enjoy doing both drama and comedy equally.

It was fun for me to take off my shirt and show off, because as a young person back then I would do one hundred push ups a night, so I was into physical health and reading Black Belt Magazine, and I was into karate, so to actually do that at that time, all that flexing and such, in my mind it was the case of "Hey, I'm gonna show people my muscles". I remember that Gary had a line in the episode where he comments on my muscles and says something like "They ain't nothin' to brag about", so it was fun to have that all as a focus. It all came across very genuine to me, because I always thought there was a great deal of chemistry between Gary and I and Gary and Todd Bridges. Gary was such a great actor and I learned a lot from him. A lot of that stuff during "The Bicycle Man" was fine, you have to be a professional and you tend to black out a lot of things. Now, something happened to me a year after this episode, this terrible situation actually happened to me personally in real life. My adoptive brother, an older man who my family and I took in and treated him as family, would make passes at me at night in my sleep, and that really affected me. But learning from the TV show I spoke up and I told my parents. The show helped me realize that I should never be afraid to speak out on these kinds of issues.

Gordon Jump was a wonderful actor and I wish that he was alive for you to talk to. He was fun to work with, and I never remember feeling uneasy about the scenes with him. He always made Gary and I feel comfortable. I think I was more of a professional at the time, so you don't have too much time to take everything in, you only have five working days to shoot and then you move on to the next episode or the next TV show or whatever. I was already in professional mode at the time.

At that age I wasn't affected by child molestation, until afterwards. So at that time I never understood the impact or importance, until later, when I saw that the episode would lead me to go and speak to children at schools. Schools would call me in and get me to talk to students about child molestation and talk about the issues, relating it back to the episode.

Le Tari who played my father was incredible. That scene at the end of the episode with him was very intense. I remember shooting it and he being very, very nervous and I couldn't figure out why he was so stressed by it. He took it very seriously and he played it very straight and was very tortured by it. I think for the adults, that episode was incredibly difficult, whereas for us kids it seemed all fine. I also remember, that even as a young kid, Le Tari would take me to these amazing parties, and I mean real eye-opening parties where there were a lot of women, scantily clad, gorgeous, gorgeous women, who would walk around and entertain if you know what I mean. I would be in another room by myself with my coloring books waiting for Le to finish up! My dad would go with him and we would all end up getting home at around five in the morning!

Possibly the most recognized and celebrated Very Special Episode in the history of the phenomenon would be the double hitter "The Bicycle Man" from Diff'rent Strokes. *It would introduce children to the dangers of predators in the guise of Gordon Jump's grotesque portrayal of the slimy Mr. Horton.*

"Goodbye, Farewell and Amen" from M*A*S*H
Original Air Date: 28 February 1983
By Samm Deighan

With more than 105 million viewers, the *M*A*S*H* (1972–1983) season finale episode – "Goodbye, Farewell and Amen", episode 16 of season 11 – is one of the most watched in American television history and it remains the most watched finale of any series. This is an incredible feat considering that the episode is two hours long, longer than many feature films, speaking to the series' continued boldness and innovation. While more recent television finales sometimes result in feature films, such as sci-fi show *Firefly* (2002–2003) and its film *Serenity* (2005), which was produced after the series was abruptly cancelled, *M*A*S*H*'s grandiose conclusion seems like the appropriate farewell to one of the most beloved shows in American television.

The finale is not necessarily an upbeat conclusion to the series but emphasizes a lot of its main themes: namely that the major characters are forever changed by their exposure to war. Many of them are leaving Korea to go home, but the conclusion is clear that you can never really go home again. The breakdown of series protagonist Hawkeye is the culmination of this idea; witnessing a woman kill her own baby (to prevent its cries from alerting North Korean soldiers) is too much, even with all that he has seen. The revelation of his haunting, disturbing memory is proof that the series hadn't lost it power. Creator Larry Gelbart said, "We wanted to say that war was futile and to represent it as a failure on everybody's part that people had to kill each other to make a point."[10]

More than just a finale, the episode questions what it might be like for characters to finally return home and say goodbye to their colleagues after more than a decade of wanting to leave South Korea and the war behind. Directed by star Alan Alda – who had a hand in writing the episode with a much larger number of writers than the typical *M*A*S*H* episode – Hawkeye doesn't overwhelm the narrative, but his story becomes one of several that weave together with the last days of the Korean War. Of course, there are the expected emotional goodbyes between characters that audiences grew close to and fell in love with for 11 years, the hospital throws a party, and peace is negotiated. Perhaps this could have been done in a drawn out farewell season, but it certainly couldn't have been accomplished in one 25-minute episode. Part of what made *M*A*S*H* so groundbreaking was the way in which it pushed television boundaries and broke convention: not only with the exploration of taboo social themes and its critique of war, but in its very narrative approach.

The series finale is no exception: while it pushed convention by asking audiences to sit down for a two-hour episode – effectively a long made-for-television film it

---

10 Todd Gitlin, *Inside Prime Time*. Pantheon Books, 1983. 189.

also questioned ideas of home, personal loyalty, trauma, and transformation. Alda's Hawkeye is finally not able to rely on his trademark humor and sarcasm; he is (however temporarily) broken by witnessing death and violence. By including this storyline, "Goodbye, Farewell and Amen" is brilliantly able to confront the issue of war trauma before the character has even left the war. The character who has effectively become the show's backbone is shown to be helpless, with his own mind turned against him by the horror he witnessed. In one of the most devastating scenes, he realizes that his own memory is incorrect and to spare himself, he unconsciously selected a false memory that buried the truth of what really occurred. In a sense, the episode has a positive overall message, because Hawkeye is able to overcome his trauma. He returns to camp to practice medicine about halfway through the episode.

Two other storylines that are unexpected but also uplifting depict the relationships between American *M*A*S*H* personnel and Korean or Chinese people. In a warmly comedic subplot, the prickly Major Winchester (David Ogden Stiers) reveals his human side by ultimately bonding with a band of Chinese soldiers who surrendered themselves to the camp. They are revealed to be musicians and, to Winchester's surprise, work with him to form a ragtag orchestra. When they are later evacuated from the camp in a prison exchange and killed in an ambush, he smashes his beloved Mozart record in a rage. Another such storyline follows Corporal Klinger (Jamie Farr), who is always outspoken about his love for his hometown and his excitement about returning to his family in Ohio (and the local hotdogs). Klinger's ongoing comedic turn throughout the show was focused on the fact that he was so determined to return home, he was

Behind the scenes on the legendary final instalment of the much loved series M*A*S*H.

willing to get a psychiatric discharge in order to do so, often wearing dresses or engaging in other behavior meant to be outrageous or eccentric. But in this episode, Klinger attempts to help a Korean woman, Soon-Lee Han (Rosalind Chao), find her missing family. In this course of this, he falls in love with her and decides to stay behind in Korea– confronting the nationalistic notion that America is the only place a character like Klinger could call home.

M*A*S*H also confronted masculine stereotypes in a variety of ways throughout the show's run, however subtly, and much of that occurs in this episode through Hawkeye's behavior. He is shown sobbing at one point, when the true horror of what really happened returns to him, but the outpouring of emotion is portrayed as positive and healthy; Hawkeye isn't shown as weak but rather the trauma he is experiencing seems inevitable, with the male characters around him depicted as sensitive and supportive. The emotional farewell between Hawkeye and B.J. Hunnicutt is another such example. Though B.J. initially leaves camp without saying goodbye to Hawkeye – because of timing – he is eventually forced to return. In their final moments together, B.J. tells Hawkeye that he'll miss him and says, "I can't imagine what this place would've been like if I hadn't found you here." They hug and Hawkeye takes off in a helicopter to find that B.J. has left him a "note": "GOODBYE" is written out on the ground in stones.

"The Reporter" from *Diff'rent Strokes*
Original Air Date: 19 March 1983
By Russell Dyball

Ah, youth – the formative years, the era of lessons learned, and mixed messages. Where our authority figures ask us to "do as I say, not as I do", and – most paradoxically – where we are asked to both Grow Up and Act Our Age. Every generation experiences this in some form or another, of course. In my youth in the late 1970s and early 1980s, the mixed messages revolved primarily (as they so often do) around sex and drugs. The fears of teen pregnancy and the AIDS epidemic, countered by steamy music videos from gloriously sexual artists from Madonna to Prince, as well as a slew of youth-oriented films about utterly relatable kids who, like many of us, just wanted to get laid.

Meanwhile, we were warned about the dangers of illicit substances from Monday through Friday in school, whispered in the halls about the untimely deaths of the victims of drugs such as John Belushi or Len Bias – only to kick off our weekend sneaking a couple of our parents' wine coolers, watching *Scarface* (1983) on late-night cable (or a few years later, *Miami Vice* (1984–1989) with the whole family!), and grooving to songs like Laid Back's "White Horse" or Melle Mel's "White Lines (Don't Do It)." Sure, these entertainments were and are explicit and direct in their directives to avoid the temptation of drugs. But how could something so cool, so stylish, or so danceable be all *that* bad? What's a kid supposed to do?

Efforts were made in the entertainment and political community to take a stand – a public stand, anyway – about drugs; frequently, this would be in the form of various Public Service Announcements, most of which could essentially be summarized in a segment from monologuist Eric Bogosian's 1990 play *Sex, Drugs, Rock & Roll*: "I've done a lot of drugs. I had a lot of adventures on drugs. Some of my music has been inspired by drugs. In fact, I think it's safe to say that I've had some of the best times of my life on drugs… That doesn't mean you have to do them." Ultimately, the only weapon left to combat the implied hipness of drugs was one of the least hip people of the eighties: First Lady of the United States Nancy Reagan – and that brings us to *Diff'rent Strokes* (1978–1986).

In "The Reporter," Arnold Jackson (Gary Coleman) is looking to win a journalism contest held by New York's (fictional) newspaper, the *Tribune*, but he's coming up empty as far as finding something to write about, and it's causing him to lose sleep, passing out into his textbook in class on the deadline day for the contest. Arnold's friend Robbie (Steven Mond) offers Arnold a bit of a pick me up in the form of a pill. Dudley and Arnold are understandably skittish of any drug, due in part, perhaps, to their experience with The Bicycle Man a few episodes earlier, who had plied them with wine. Smelling a scoop, Arnold asks Robbie to set him up with his connection, who turns out to be a fellow student, Sidney (David Mendenhall) but whom Arnold immediately refers to as "Scarface" (apparently, little Arnold stayed up perusing late-night cable himself.) Inspired, Arnold dashes off his entry into the contest, an article entitled "My School Is Lousy With Drugs."

Having turned in what he considers to be a sure-fire winner, Arnold receives some bad news when the school principal, Mr. Langford (J. Jay Saunders) informs him that his article will not be entered into the contest, as it must be a complete fabrication. Langford has naively assumed that his campus couldn't possibly be experiencing an infestation of drugs. Unwilling to give up his sources, an undaunted Arnold submits his story directly to the *Tribune,* which results in Langford's censorship of Arnold making the front page.

Disturbed by Arnold's findings (though seemingly not the censorship), Mrs. Reagan arrives unannounced at the Drummond household (not wanting to make a fuss about her arrival, she arrives with only two Secret Service agents in tow.) After a brief phone call with "Ronnie", allowing Mrs. Reagan some light comedy, the First Lady joins Arnold at school to defuse the situation with Mr. Langford and to address Arnold's classroom. Talking with the students, she quickly learns that several students have in fact been offered drugs, and at least four of them in a classroom of about twenty have experimented with drugs. Mr. Langford's eyes have been opened, and Arnold has been vindicated.

Originally when the producers of *Diff'rent Strokes* reached out to Mrs. Reagan, they had merely hoped for her to contribute to the episode only in a sequence to be recorded separately from the episode, appearing in her office at the White House, offering her support to Arnold via the phone. To her credit, Mrs. Reagan chose not to take the subject that clearly meant a lot to her and simply phone it in, instead offering to appear on set, believing that it would be far more impactful for the series' young audience. Frequently publicized as her first acting role in 25 years (an inaccuracy; while it had been 25 years since her last film role, Mrs. Reagan (then Nancy Davis) appeared in guest roles on television as late as 1962), the First Lady was paid union scale for her appearance, which she donated to the National Foundation Of Parents for Drug-Free Youth. It was reported that Mrs. Reagan was excited to take part, and most of her scenes, totaling about five minutes' worth of screen time, were completed in a single take. At the time, her appearance on the show was something for the headlines – only Betty Ford, with her cameo on *The Mary Tyler Moore Show* in 1976, had preceded Mrs. Reagan in the "First Ladies Appear On A Sitcom" subgenre, though Speaker Of The House Tip O'Neill had beat Mrs. Reagan by a few weeks with his cameo on the *Cheers* episode "No Contest", which aired on 17 February 1983.

Ratings for "The Reporter" received a big boost from the norm, jumping from *Diff'rent Strokes*' average audience of 26.3 million viewers to 32.5 million. According to Mrs. Reagan's press secretary, the White House switchboard lines were jammed immediately after the broadcast, with no negative feedback received.

But the question is: did any of this amount to anything? Most evidence indicates that Mrs. Reagan's efforts, particularly with the "Just Say No" campaign popularized by her, didn't have a particularly notable impact on the drug problem. Certainly, her appearance didn't deter series co-stars Todd Bridges and Dana Plato from the very real challenges addiction carries. In part, the messaging must take most of the blame – like many campaigns aimed at young people, Mrs. Reagan's anti-drug messaging was often based on less-than-solid information and fear-mongering. When Robbie raises the question to her about "soft" drugs such as marijuana, Mrs. Reagan relates a likely-apocryphal tale about a young man so burned out on pot that he brutally beat his sister when she refuses to steal money for him that he can buy more – a story that frankly sounds like a deleted scene from *Reefer Madness* (1936) (a movie, it must be said, nearly fifty years out of date at the time of "The Reporter"), or a more family friendly version of the classic urban legend "The Baby Roast", in which in some tellings

First Lady Nancy Reagan visits the set of Diff'rent Strokes *during the Very Special Episode "The Reporter", there to promote the "Just Say No" campaign. TV sitcoms that once angered conservative leaders were now being used as vehicles to carry out social causes such as Reagan's anti-drug crusade across America.*

involves a babysitter who, high on LSD or marijuana, accidentally mistakes her infant charge with a turkey, and ends up cooking the sleeping child. (Another variation on this story appears in the undeniably sincere but perpetually out of step with the times 1960s incarnation of *Dragnet* in that series' episode "The Big High", in which a pair of stoner parents get so high, they forget they left their baby in the bathtub to drown.)

And as always, the ultimate message in "The Reporter" is mixed, as are most lessons when presented as binary, black and white morality. "All drugs are dumb", Mrs. Reagan informs the children in "The Reporter", a series who counted among its sponsors Unisom, a sleeping pill like, with any drug, "hard" or "soft", "good" or "bad", carries a risk for a psychological dependency – a dependency that, if you believe Mrs. Reagan's daughter Nancy Davis (and there is reason to believe and also to not), the First Lady herself suffered from.

I ask again: What's a kid supposed to do?

"What Price Glory?" from *The Facts of Life*
Original Air Date: 19 October 1983
By Shawn Macomber

Though "What Price Glory?" initially carries the vibe and lilt of a leisurely swim around the shallow end of the topical theme pool, the episode soon takes a darker, considerably more profound turn, revealing that the stakes are much, much higher than we'd perhaps presumed.

First the setup: Jeff Williams (Todd Hallowell) – young, suave, black – wanders into Edna's Edibles, the gourmet food shop Mrs. Garrett (Charlotte Rae) opened after quitting Eastland a few episodes back and now staffs with her former wards. And with the predictable exception of loveable curmudgeon Jo Polniaczek (Nancy McKeon), none of the ladies maintain their chill.

"Haven't I seen that man on a box of Wheaties?" Mrs. G asks.

"Jeff Williams is the star quarterback at Bates," Natalie Green (Mindy Cohn) tells her longtime overseer. "Every football college in the country is after him."

"And so am I," Dorothy "Tootie" Ramsey (Kim Fields) – also young and black, if not suave – replies, commandeering a baguette and some cheese to make the already feted boy who Mrs. G will shortly refer to as a "very nice young hunk"(!) a free sandwich.

In the real world laying it on as thick as a clearly beguiled Tootie does here – "You'd make a hero out of any sandwich you ate," she somewhat perplexingly coos – and the pair's glaringly divergent high school caste system positions would be about as conducive to hormonally-charged young love as an anvil would be to keeping a lifeboat afloat. This, however, is the Very Special Episode universe. Accordingly, Jeff falls hard, not only somewhat arrogantly inviting Tootie to be his guest at the victory party for a game that he has not yet played, but follows the public outing with the promise of a more intimate date – "a real romantic double feature – *Jaws* one and *Jaws 2*." (Okay, so maybe now *I'm* swooning, too...)

Alas, in the second act of this relationship the Adonis betrays a hitherto well-hidden flaw: His suddenly not-so-fawning girlfriend transforming before his very eyes from "heroic" sandwich maker to a supervisor demanding he help do Edna's Edibles inventory *gratis* – ah, how soon the bloom is off the rose! – Jeff proves unable to differentiate between the "horseradish" and "peppercorn" mustards. Tootie, increasingly furious, finally blurts out, "What's the matter with you? Can't you read?" The pregnant pause tells us all we need to know, even if Jeff quickly regains his swagger. "Hey reading's not my thing, okay?" he says. "I'm into football. Coach says I shouldn't get distracted." When Tootie protests, Jeff shuts her down: "I don't walk into places through the exit. I don't sit in wet paint. I've never ended up in the ladies room. Huh! I can read enough." Cue the laugh track. Still, an uneasiness – among both characters and audience – remains.

Like Tootie, you may wonder how one ascends to the senior class of a presumably elite private school without the ability to read. "People think I'm special," Jeff explains. "They want to do things for me. It's not cheating! It's helping. Look, I take my own tests. I get copies of them and my friends look up the answers. But I memorize them. Just like I do with my playbook." "And nobody knows about it?" "If they do they haven't said anything to me."

We now arrive at a crossroads. Much like Aphrodite cradling Adonis after the wild boar gores him, Tootie feels compelled to accept the disaster and simply hope her tears eventually bloom into flowers – that something beautiful will come of her comprising herself. Which is to say, rather than rat out this lovely boy so manifestly out of her league, she joins the crowd and helps him cheat on a test as well. When Tootie confesses her sins at the makeshift Edna's Edibles confessional, Mrs. G takes off her teenage boy ogling hat and puts on her disappointed adult bonnet. "I'm sorry but that really steams me," she warbles. "These so-called friends aren't helping him at all. They're cheating him out of his future!" In fact, Jeff has avoided most of the future-decimating aspects of illiteracy. According to statistics compiled by the web-based volunteering portal DoSomething.org, "[Two-thirds] of students who cannot read proficiently by the end of fourth grade will end up in jail or on welfare. Over 70% of America's inmates cannot read above a fourth grade level." Further: "Students who don't read proficiently by the third grade are four times likelier to drop out of school… and 90% of high school dropouts are on welfare."

His method of success may not exactly be kosher, but – *pace* Mrs. G – hate the playa not the game: Jeff is about to graduate from high school. His prospects for earning that cash money appear sky high. The legions of minions he's delegated his literacy to are a clear indication of leadership skills and X-factor charisma. Never mind a ladies room, unlike so many others in his situation this guy never wanders into a jail cell. In a striking confrontation, however, Tootie makes a stirring philosophic case against utilitarianism and in favor of a devotion to honor that transcends time, death, and the benefits of a stint as Big Man on Campus:

"I know how important football is to you but what happens if…" she begins.

"Yeah, yeah, yeah," Jeff replies. "I know, I know. What happens if I get injured? What happens if I don't make the pros?"

"No! What happens if you do get everything you want? So you're rich and you're a star and you've got a babe on each arm and you're idolized by millions of kids…"

"Yeah," Jeff replies dreamily, unaware that Tootie has not actually stuck the knife in yet.

"All you'll really be is an illiterate jock. Don't you have any pride?"

"Tootie, you're getting out of line!"

"Good! I don't understand you. It used to be our people had to work in the fields and if they wanted to learn to read they did it in secret. Now an education is your right and where are you? Still out on the field!"

This invocation of slavery is brutal – and also appropriate. The journey to a literate society is *not* one Americans took together. In 1870, five years after end of the Civil War, the National Assessment of Adult Literacy notes, 11.5 percent of white were illiterate while nearly *eighty* percent of their black counterparts handicap. In fact, blacks would not lower their collective rate to 11.5 percent until 1940 when the native-born white rate had been brought down to 1.1 percent. By 1979 – the closest year to the airing of "What Price Glory?" for which statistics were available – black illiteracy sat at 1.6 percent. Low, sure, but still lagging when compared to the miniscule white rate of .4 percent.

Material and social success by the standards of the 1980s isn't enough, Tootie avers. Not if you fail to keep faith with the predecessors who suffered centuries of oppression and violence in order to ensure she and Jeff could be born, never mind thrive.

This would be stirring, heavy stuff in a political debate, never mind on a sitcom. Indeed, the secondary plot of Blair's cousin Geri (Geri Jewell, television's first prominently-hired actress with cerebral palsy) fretting over whether her next stand-up comedy set will be opening for a rock 'n' roll band or legendary comedian Robert Klein is completely subsumed by the drama. You've really got to give it up to writer Alan Spencer – who went onto create the wild eighties action-comedy series *Sledge Hammer!* (1986–1988) – and director Asaad Kelada (*Family Ties*; *Who's the Boss?*) for not shying away from that history or its implications.

That said, though Jeff Williams returns in another eight episodes spread over the next five years, Tootie is not transformed into some sort of reverse white knight. There's no multi-season arc of Tootie and Jeff skipping *Jaws* screenings to get themselves hooked on phonics in the back room of Edna's Edibles. Aside from a brief appearance in the January 1984 episode "Crossing the Line," the next time we get a glimpse of Jeff's life is in the season six episode "My Boyfriend's Back" (24 October 1984) which sees him return from Penn State rhapsodizing about the wonders of college life and openly musing about whether he's outgrown Tootie – leaving us to presume that whatever books he's been burning through, he sure as hell hasn't yet picked up one on *gratitude!*

Another few years on Jeff pops in for a cameo in the season eight episode "Cupid's Revenge" (14 February 1987). He's now scuttled football in favor of marine biology. It's played a little maudlin. In truth, however, the relationship brought belated honor and vindication to those who once toiled in fields and were forced to hide their understanding of words like a sin. Rejoice, don't cry.

"Speed Trap" from *Family Ties*
Original Air Date: 9 November 1983
By Lee Gambin

Alex P. Keaton (Michael J. Fox) would be a rarity on television screens in 1980s America. Conservative and yet sensitive, a Republican but also socially aware, an over-achiever but not without his hang-ups and insecurities; Alex would become a formidable counterpart to his teen boy peers in the world of situation comedy of the Reagan-era. For example, as opposed to the frazzled Kevin Owens (Rob Stone) from *Mr. Belvedere* (1985–1990), Alex was confident and cocksure, and in relation to comparing these two young men, high school is a place that birth most of their personal dilemmas – Kevin (along with his sister Heather (Tracy Welles)) is an underachiever, tormented by his lack of good grades, whereas Alex is driven and zealous in studies, decidedly active in his achievements and proud of his status as the "top of the grade". In "Speed Trap" however, Alex starts to feel the strain in his constant drive to succeed and when he gets the sense that he is drowning in impending deadlines, endless study and near-approaching exams he takes to the most sought after drug of choice in the history of eighties American sitcoms – amphetamines.

Speed and diet pills got a hold of Archie Bunker (Carroll O'Connor) in *All in the Family* (1971–1979), who wanted to keep up with his new duties as a bar manager and were a temptation for young Heather from *Mr. Belvedere* to lose weight, however, the drug was primarily used by characters to stay on top of their studies in order to excel in their work. In the same episode Heather is tempted to take speed to control her weight, her mother Marsha (Ilene Graff) gets hooked in an attempt to stay on track of her legal studies, while Jesse (Elizabeth Berkley) in *Saved by the Bell* (1989–1992) binges on caffeine pills to stay awake to take in homework. Alex P. Keaton falls into the same trap, in the cleverly titled "Speed Trap" which is a nice analogy of relating speeding cars being caught by authorities with young teens getting pepped up on amphetamines in order to take on the lonely road of study.

The promo for the episode features the voice over making mention of Alex P. Keaton being a character completely on top of it all, when he suggests that "Alex of all people needs help". Here, in this tiny sound bite, it is made clear that this episode is going to be a show that features Alex "out of the ordinary" and "not himself" – something that will be a core focus throughout the piece. In many regards, the episode reads like a possession-themed horror film, where Alex morphs into someone completely different. As well as making comment on Alex's change in personality and that he "needs help", the voice over in the episode's promo TV spot uses the phrase "Just Say No", which was of course the war cry from First Lady Nancy Reagan's anti-drug campaign which she began with a trip in 1980 Daytop, New York teaching children the dangerous effects of drugs. Alex P. Keaton – a character completely pro-Reagan and the Reagan administration – is clearly not a person immune to such liabilities such as addiction, and it is interesting to note that he becomes a character in the grip of such a social disease, making the episode even more enlightened in its commentary on both conservatism, the moral right-wing upheld by Reaganism and the hypocrisy of political belief systems.

The episode opens with Alex having missed dinner because of studying for midterms, reinstating the fact that Alex is of course an overachiever. His sister Mallory (Justine Bateman) has a totally different approach and attitude towards school (she is more arts orientated and lives outside of the academic world). But this drives Alex to ensure that his plight at the moment is very different to Mallory's, him being a senior and all; which make his studies all the more vitally important. When left alone in the kitchen (the first out of two pivotal moments of the episode set in this space), Alex asks Mallory for a favor. She asks

"Do you want me to write one of your term papers for you?" which in turn gets a "This is no time for jokes, Mallory" from Alex. The line is loaded: "no time for jokes" – an absolute summary of the tone of the Very Special Episode phenomenon. It is also a segue for Alex to ask Mallory about her friend Effie's diet pills. Effie is an off-camera character with a weight problem who has a prescription to take the drugs, and unlike other characters subject to addiction in the VSE verse, Alex knows exactly what the pills do. Mallory also make a commentary that is a social message, she expresses that they are illegal for anyone to take them outside of Effie who has a prescription. A backstory comes ringing in where it is learned that Mallory had tried the drug before and that Alex had scolded her about them – his conservatism in play.

Alex's dilemma as to taking the pills or not in a terrific sequence where talented actor Michael J. Fox gets to showcase his great handle on the performance of soliloquy – performing on his own and having an internal dialogue expressed out loud ending with him talking to his bedside photograph of President Jimmy Carter – a physical extension of his right-wing leanings. In the following scene, a game of Monopoly excites the speeding Alex with capitalism enticing him. Alex's ranting cuts through a friendly family game of Monopoly and although the scene is hilarious it is also disturbing because the young son is affected by amphetamines and his breakdown is inevitable. His obsession with rules ("This is a sin against capitalism") causes him to leave the game where he jumps into expressing a seemingly bizarre desire to clean the kitchen floors (washing and cleaning being a commonly depicted effect of speed in television) whilst it is also learned in the follow up scene, that he has even cleaned out the neighbor's garage.

"What has gotten into Alex this week?" asks kid sister Jennifer (Tina Yothers) and here we look at what was aforementioned – the analogous reading of teen boys under some kind of supernatural threat – becoming alien and different. However, while eighties horror movies such as *An American Werewolf in London* (1981) and *Amityville II: The Possession* (1982) featured young men alienated from their families and succumbing to dark forces (be it lycanthropy or demonic possession), dramatic works of the same period also dealt with teen boys driven to dark places: *Ordinary People* (1980), *Endless Love* (1981), *The Boys Next Door* (1985) et al. None of these films featured young men addicted to drugs, however, Alex P. Keaton's emotional divorce from his familial unit because of drugs mirrors these works and there is most certainly a cultural zeitgeist at play.

Alex now in the throes of speed addiction startles his parents but his interaction with Mallory in the kitchen (the second pivotal sequence in the kitchen with these two) is a telling point of his character transition. It starts off funny with mention of Alex refurnishing Jennifer's dollhouse building extensions because he feels the dolls were a little cramped, then the scene ends with Mallory telling him never to talk to her again – his aggression is out of hand and going through her handbag pushes her to this. He even threatens his sister if she tells their parents: "You're not exactly innocent here."

Alex becomes a full blown addict, and in the near-end of the episode he is seen in his bedroom painting his walls, overjoyed by the thrill by getting questions right (the famous wheel across the bedroom floor on his office chair which would become a fixture in the montage credit sequence). The paining of the walls somehow reflects the mania and mental disturbance of Scott Jacoby as the titular *Bad Ronald* (1974), a made-for-TV horror movie, where a young disturbed boy paints an entire civilization on the inside walls of his deceased mother's home.

Dad Steven (Michael Gross) enters the room asking "How many hours have you slept this week?", and conversation about amphetamines unfolds with Steven knowing that he is on speed ("Alex, don't lie to me"). Steven also speaks from experience (knowing about the drug because of taking it when he was in school) but from this history is informed enough to make judgments and also comment on the legit "softness" of Alex, for Alex is not Steven, a hardened hippie from a troubled family household (a distant father etc) but instead a boy from a comfortable and loving home, with parents who are endlessly there, sensitive and knowing. Steven expresses his love with "I'm your father and I see you taking a risk with something you know nothing about." Alex tosses out the rest of the pills and collapses in his bed, sleeping the drug away.

The next morning is of course the day of his exam which he has slept through leading to his breakdown where Michael J. Fox once again gets to shine as a multifaceted actor who can throw himself into a great physical performance. Alex's major turning point is his apology to Mallory and when the two are left alone (ending with a hug which also becomes a fixture in the montage that makes up the opening credits), there is talk that truly reflects themes and tones of a horror film. Alex says "It was like it wasn't even me" and that it was "very scary, Mallory". Akin to possession, Alex P. Keaton's dance with speed turned a likeable Republican youth (as hilariously unlikely that could be) into a frenzied demon. "Speed Trap" would be a soft peddle compared to other made-for-TV fare such as the devastating film *The Death of Richie* (1977) starring Robby Benson as a drug addled teen whose father (Ben Gazzara) is forced to kill him to "free him from such suffering". In *Family Ties*, Steven is just as sympathetic and soft spoken as Gazzara's parental figure in the made-for-TV film based on a real life case, however, the nature of the American sitcom paints a picture of easy understanding and listening prevailing and taking care of business – insert kind words instead of resorting to violence.

The seemingly most popular drug of the Very Special Episode phenomenon would be amphetamines or diet pills, and here in "Speed Trap" from Family Ties, *Alex (Michael J. Fox) falls victim to the crashing repercussions.*

"The Van Drummonds" from *Diff'rent Strokes*
Original Air Date: 19 November 1983
By Lee Gambin

Sometimes the Very Special Episode formula can fall into a place of straight up bizarreness and possible outcries from networks reaching for ratings and to provoke conversation – especially after the episode in question airs. Therefore, once audiences saw what they saw (and could not believe their eyes) there could be possible conversations sparked by executives and producers to bring more of the unusual same to TV sets across the nation. One such episode of unique weirdness is "The Van Drummonds" from *Diff'rent Strokes* (1978–1986), which had actors Conrad Bain and Dana Plato portray Dutch relatives and of swapped genders. Using the classic Hayley Mills *The Parent Trap* (1961) split screen trick to have actors playing dual roles appear on screen at the same time, "The Van Drummonds" is a high concept episode that would come out post-the advent of revisionist and satirical series such as the inventive *Soap* (1977–1981) and *Mary Hartman, Mary Hartman* (1976–1977), where deconstructing conventions was fashionable and necessary to a savvy audience who were beginning to get smart to the inherited formulaic sitcom traditions. Oddball episodes from TV sitcoms varied throughout the years where moments of surrealism peppered the usually standard set up, and here, where actors firmly established as sometimes legendary pop-cultural fixtures got to portray someone else, the results can be either welcomed and inventive or just plain strange. When you consider the history of this phenomenon there are excellent and successful examples such as Elizabeth Montgomery playing Samantha's conniving cousin Serena on *Bewitched* (1964–1972), Barbara Eden getting to be sneaky as Jeannie's sister on *I Dream of Jeannie* (1965–1970) and Carolyn Jones taking on the blonde harp playing Ophelia, who would be both Morticia's cousin and Gomez's (John Astin) first wife on *The Addams Family* (1964–1966). There would also be innovative moments later that dissected the concept of "performance" as seen in the episode "Mork Meets Robin Williams" from *Mork & Mindy* (1978–1982), however here, the call for such dualism is a strange, baffling one. However the episode is remarkably entertaining and showcases the varied talents of both Conrad Bain and Dana Plato.

When there is a long distance phone call from Holland hitting the Drummond household, there is news that European cousins Anna (Conrad Bain) and her son Hans (Dana Plato) are coming to visit. Hans is a fourteen-year-old boy who is struggling to find a sense of independence from his oppressive mother who treats him like a prison warden complete with a heavy hand of abusive discipline. Hence, the episode does a dual act in presenting a Very Special set up with having established cast members take on a dual role (and having them cross dress be the clincher) and also addressing themes of discipline and teen rebellion.

Whilst normalcy and togetherness keeps the Drummond household afloat (Kimberly (Dana Plato) teaching Willis (Todd Bridges) and Arnold (Gary Coleman) Dutch and Mr. Drummond (Conrad Bain) on his health kick), the entrance of Anna and Hans startles the audience and as we begin to see the excellent Conrad Bain and his

When the Very Special Episode does more than one thing: provides social commentary on a "serious concern" such as stealing, while also delivering a gimmick here in the guise of actors Conrad Bain and Dana Plato playing gender reversed counterparts to their regular Philip and Kimberly Drummond in "The Van Drummonds" from Diff'rent Strokes.

performance of Anna and Dana Plato and her performance of Hans, we start to ease into the weird nature of the episode. Hearing the studio audience (or fabricated studio audience) respond to Hans as played by Dana Plato as he/she first appears is an interesting telling sign of how people react to something outside of their comfort zone, however, as we get into the piece, this eerie element beings to grow on us. The creepiness of the episode and the way in which Kimberly and Arnold's reaction to how the relatives look are an extension to our own disbelief at what we're seeing play the audience like a fiddle and this cross dressing and dual role issue opens up as a state of shock, but then gradually recedes as we become invested in plot.

The transvestism of the piece seems to have a connective tissue to Europe and gender bending, when you consider films such as *Cabaret* (1972) which was set in Berlin making its mark a decade earlier. And in terms of cinematic landscapes, Hans's interest in American film (quoting Jimmy Cagney etc) is an outcry of someone who has learned the way of the USA via film and film language, which is yet another layer in the episode's cultural experimentation with adopting alternative visions of oneself. Hans is not allowed to watch films as his mother is not a fan, therefore this concept of being from a strict and rigid background marries into the notion of repression leading to forms of expression that may not necessarily be admirable. Anna punishes Hans and therefore Hans reacts aggressively and sneakily to the point where Arnold describes him as a "backstabber". Arnold and Willis have a somewhat permissive lifestyle – Mr. Drummond is kind to them and his disciplinary style differs from Anna, and at the end of the episode, where Hans's misdemeanors are outed this is firmly stated. Mr. Drummond will lay down the law, but do it with kindness and fairness, and all the while he thinks that it is Willis and Arnold who are responsible for the bad behavior caused by Hans, he punishes the boys with a steady firm style. The naughty behavior from Hans includes dropping water balloons from the balcony, trying to sneak in a drink of wine and stealing money from Mr. Drummond. These shifty dealings always seem to end with Hans passing the blame over to Willis and Arnold, who will have to face the strict but endlessly loving disciplinary take from their adopted dad.

However, Anna has no concept of how to treat her son Hans in the same light, and instead cheerfully expresses her trust in physical abuse – the episode seems to paint the issue of child abuse in a light manner, without the seriousness brought up from episodes such as "Conduct Unbecoming" from *Major Dad* (1989–1993) and so forth. As far as the episode is concerned, that is a sidebar compared to the presentation of the piece where characters share visual space in cross gender visage, and this is something that ties in thematically with plot and purpose, but can truly be overshadowed by the sheer "shock value".

"A Keaton Christmas Carol" from *Family Ties*
Original Air Date: 14 December 1983
By Michael Varrati

In the television landscape, it's an unquestionable fact that if a program has a long enough life, it will invariably have a Christmas episode. As certain as death or taxes, the Christmas episode is not only a matter of art reflecting cultural tradition, it's quite simply just good business. At a time of year when all forms of commerce are geared toward seasonal imagery for sales, it should come as little surprise that networks would want to get in on the action.

While this particular perspective of the holiday's more commercial aspects may seem shrewd, it's a consideration that plays particularly well when applied to the sitcom *Family Ties* (1982–1989) and its much beloved second season holiday special, "A Keaton Christmas Carol."

As implied by the episode's title, the zeitgeist defining suburban sitcom treads into some Dickensian territory to execute the week's story, but the themes presented actually speak to the series as a whole.

For those not hip to the Keaton cause, the general conceit of *Family Ties* centers around a pair of Berkley grads turned suburban parents (Michael Gross and Meredith Baxter Birney) trying their best to raise their three kids, one of whom happens to be a budding young Republican (Michael J. Fox) who is frequently at odds with the family's liberal ways. The show and the Keaton family, for all extents and purposes, put a face to a cultural inversion that was happening in the eighties. In the decades previous, the rise of counterculture causes saw that the generational narrative was focused on the idea of youth breaking free of the more traditional views of the generations before. With the arrival of the eighties, the hippies were finally grown up and forced to answer the question: What if the reverse occurred and the liberal mindset had to raise a conservative generation?

Family Ties tackles this notion head on, and with the show landing squarely during the midst of the rise of the Reagan era of American politics, also immediately puts a comedic face to very real struggles occurring in homes across the country.

As one can imagine, the number of topics the show was able to tackle on a week to week basis had no end, as the rapidly morphing decade of excess provided ample material to drop at the Keaton's door. Concurrently, the show's jovial culture war allowed it to be prime real estate for the occasional Very Special Episode and as it turns out, Christmas is a great time to stop and reassess one's values.

Naturally, the eighties had no short supply of TV Christmas specials, with almost every major sitcom taking a swing at festive delights. Most were light-hearted and within the good-natured spirit of the season, while others like the *Golden Girls* (1985–

1992) episode "Have Yourself a Very Little Christmas" (16 December 1989) concerning issues of homelessness, or the *ALF* (1986–1990) episode "ALF's Special Christmas" (14 December 1987) which saw everyone's favorite alien spending the holiday with a terminally ill child utilizing the time of year to remind us to count our blessings and think of those in need.

Relying on the fact that most audiences look to holiday programming for escapism during an otherwise occasionally stressful or financially draining time, "A Keaton Christmas Carol" attempts to find a happy medium between the good tidings and message material. Unfortunately, the episode also struggles with this mission statement due to the very confines of the show's overarching narrative.

As previously implied, the show relies heavily upon the audience's knowledge of Charles Dickens' *A Christmas Carol*, here reframed for the half hour format and presented with much more of a wink. The episode opens on Christmas Eve, with the family setting up final decorations. Young Jennifer (Tina Yothers) is doing her best to overcome a cough that she's gotten from a seasonal cold, while Mallory (Justine Bateman) does her cool teen best to help her parents finish up the yule preparation. In the midst of everything, Alex (Fox) returns home and immediately begins chastising his family for their over reliance on sentiment and holiday cheer. It's revealed that Alex has not only forgotten (or perhaps willfully ignored) to get holiday gifts for the rest of the family, but has also neglected to get Jennifer the cough syrup he was supposed to pick up for her while out. It's not exactly presented as very dire, and is mostly played for laughs, but is certainly meant to showcase a certain level of selfishness that Alex is operating under.

With his family unable to convince him to get in the holiday spirit, Alex heads to bed, making it known for one last time he wants no part in what he perceives to be the crass commercialism of Christmas.

With his outsider grump status firmly locked into place, Alex is set-up to be the Scrooge archetype for the episode and it doesn't take too long for the story to kick into holiday haunting gear.

As Alex settles into bed, he's visited by a ghost (who looks conspicuously quite a bit like Jennifer), who takes him on a journey to see his past. We learn that Alex wasn't always such a Christmas naysayer, but that he still was way more into Richard Nixon than Santa. Later, the Ghost of Christmas Future (a.k.a. an ethereal version of Mallory) shows up to give Alex a glimpse into his fat cat, Fortune 500 future. One can only assume the episode's writers skipped Christmas Present due to the truncated timeline, though the bucking of convention does seem jarring, considering the episode's cheeky intent on following the Dickensian structure.

The future the Ghost/Mallory shows to Alex is one of an aged, impoverished Keaton family who are struggling to get by. Only future Alex, albeit sans hair, is thriving. What's more, it is revealed that Alex's greed and avarice is partially responsible for condemning his parents and sisters to their sad fate. The Alex of the present day is mortified by this revelation, and refuses to believe that his world view could lead to such despair. However, as tends to be the journey of any Ebenezer or Grinch, Alex's heart grows three sizes and he realizes he must amend the error of his ways and fully embrace Christmas, and by proxy, his family, to set things right.

By showing Alex the darker path his family's future could take, this particular episode of *Family Ties* is attempting to utilize the "Christmas Carol" pastiche to give the audience a teachable moment about the importance of family and the evils of greed. Unfortunately, it's also because of the show's tenants that, unlike other Very Special Episodes, it doesn't necessarily completely work as intended.

As is expected, Alex returns from his dream journey with the ghosts a renewed man (well, teen) and vows to set things right. He manages to pull together an assortment of gifts for his family, albeit paltry ones (he is, after all, still a cheapskate) and the Keatons share a moment of eye-twinkling family togetherness, proving that blood is thicker than water and that Christmas can save us all.

End credits.

Except, the issue here is that any longstanding fan of *Family Ties* knows that Alex hasn't really changed. For Alex to have actually evolved would have altered the fundamental DNA of the show itself. Although the episode's writers quite cleverly use the Scrooge parable to directly attack the conservative tenants they believe lead to wealth disparity and division of family (particularly prescient now in Trump's America), they do so a little *too* jovially. Alex's misdeeds, although certainly heinous, are still presented mostly for laughs, and the family's tumultuous future feels more like playful pantomime than hard hitting drama.

Of course, this could exactly be the point. When we tune into sitcoms, we don't necessarily expect them to take a deep, gritty look at the hard-hitting issues of the day. But, for a Very Special Episode with a built-in message, this one does ultimately seem relatively light.

That being said, there's plenty to love about *Family Ties*' festive take on this old holiday chestnut. Looking at the Scrooge archetype through the lens of Reagan-era politics is particularly revealing about where the writers and creative team were concerned the country was heading. More so, from the more frivolous angle, it's nice to see the cast cut loose and get to embody aspects of their characters they normally wouldn't. Meredith Baxter Birney and Michael Gross seem to relish the opportunity to play future, wackier versions of themselves, and Tina Yothers and Justine Bateman get a moment to live a full-blown Stevie Nicks fantasy in their ghost costume pieces.

Ultimately, the show's mixture of heart and message encapsulate what holiday specials are all about. The goal of any Christmas movie, show, or special is to present an idealized version of the holiday that is removed from its very real world stresses, or, to show people overcoming those trials and coming together with love and warmth. "A Keaton Christmas Carol" doesn't fully dissuade the audience from believing that Alex has truly changed, but we can at least buy the idea that he's put aside his more problematic aspects for the time being to celebrate with the ones he loves. For families whose own holiday gatherings may seem fraught with division, maybe seeing that momentary unity represented by their favorite TV clan is enough to get them through another season.

… and that, ultimately, is the reason for the season. At least, that's what TV tells us.

Christmas time is a point of family togetherness and lessons learned, and this is no exception here in "A Keaton Christmas" from Family Ties. *However, a Dickensian element is in play here, where Alex (Michael J. Fox) is visited by the ghosts of Christmas past and future (in the guise of his sisters) and is forced to see what "could be".*

"Santa Goes Downtown" from *Night Court*
Original Air Date: 11 January 1984
By Jessie Lilley

To present as a situation comedy and tackle myth, mental illness and pathos in the second episode, you have to be confident. Reinhold Weege was nothing, if not confident. Not only was *Night Court* (1984–1992) his creation, this and several other episodes were written by him. In "Santa Goes Downtown", the legendary actor and acting coach Jeff Corey plays John Stevens, an escaped mental patient, also known as Santa Claus. Or is it the other way around? Booked into the local precinct on a charge of trespassing, Santa was winding down from the Christmas rush and apparently had a bit too much eggnog. He fell among some local derelicts and they were all sleeping in a department store doorway when the local constabulary made their appearance. Of course, the denizens of the night court have their flip commentary to start off the episode, and Selma Diamond has the best throwaway of the evening:

Santa: "Hi! I'm Santa Claus."
Selma: "I'm the Easter Bunny. We'll have lunch."

Having endured this sort of ridicule in the past, Santa takes all this with a grain of salt, while dropping little bombs about the regulars that only an intimate could know. All of this is, of course, explained away with the typical rationalizations adults regularly hand out to convince themselves that none of this is true. Such bravado tends to keep things on an even keel. Having dispensed with the possibility that this might actually be the legendary Jolly Old Elf, the next case is called.

Enter Eddie: the young, hard, angry and desperate for love bad boy, with his girlfriend in tow. These two have been arrested for shoplifting. Refusing to give their real names, the kids are sent over to their seats to await their fate and Eddie immediately starts to harass Santa. Michael J. Fox as Eddie is his usual extraordinary self, easily filling up the screen in a one on one with Corey (which is not easy to do). He is completely believable in the role and helps to sell the concept to the viewer. Eddie so completely wants to believe, but childhood is gone for him and he rationalizes with the best of them. It's up to Santa to reignite the magic of the Yule log in all these hearts of stone. There is only one possible way to regain control of the situation.

He collapses in the court room. Cut to Chambers, where a doctor is pronouncing Santa well enough for now, and just needing a bit of rest which is all one can do with this kind of heart trouble. Santa thanks him and asks if he was happy with the new putter he got for Christmas. The doctor affirms and blinks and backs slowly out the door while Harry (Harry Anderson) declares that as a doctor, of course he would receive a golf club for Christmas!

Harry, having again rationalized himself out of believing, accepts the report on the identification of the two street kids and Santa convinces him that he can help get the kids to go back home. Willing to try, Harry sends for the two runaways and hands the unopened file to Santa, just as his keeper shows up with paperwork to prove legal guardianship. It seems Santa, a.k.a. John Stevens, disappears every year just before Christmas. The sanatorium manages to find him every year by February, and lock him back up. Every. Year. So, the establishment "knows" that John Stevens is not Santa. The night court staff "know" he is not Santa and the runaways absolutely "know" that he is not Santa. The only one who knows that John Stevens *is* Santa, is John Stevens. And he tries to explain this to Harry while suggesting that the Judge would be a good candidate to take on the magic, now that John's mortal time is coming to an end.

But before this can be further explored, Bull and the lawyers arrive with Eddie and girlfriend Mary. Eddie having previously confided that he didn't mean the old man any harm, is willing to hear him in Chambers. But when Santa states that Eddie's family really does care about him, he blows it off with hopeless aggression and demands a lawyer. Harry's heart breaks for the lonely boy and wraps him in a bear hug that Eddie finally can't resist and he breaks down. Santa, having supplied the true names and addresses of the children earlier, smiles and the kids are taken away, presumably to be returned to their respective families. Still not believing – but truly wanting to do so – the lawyers ask how Santa knew that information. He tells them Harry gave him the report. Harry smiles and opens the report and finds the names and addresses of two young people he's never met. He looks at Santa and Santa just smiles.

As his keeper takes him away, Santa reminds Harry of his offer and the door quietly closes on the magic. Digesting this session in Chambers, the night court staff discuss

Mental health issues are addressed in "Santa Goes Downtown" on Night Court.

the possibilities, when a scratching is heard at the door. Harry tells whomever it is to come in. When they don't he goes to open it and finds a reindeer strolling the hallway. Weege was no fool. This episode set the tone of the show, with Harry, the magic-loving judge who answered the phone, being one of the most beloved television characters of the decade. His desire to believe in all things good is set in stone during this, the second offering of a remarkable television show. Judge Harold T. Stone represented compassion, desire, humor and above all – the inability to grow old within his heart. Childhood was reignited in Harry during "Santa Goes Downtown". That combined with his natural empathy and hard-won wisdom, made him a fair and respected jurist whose rulings, while sometimes questioned, nonetheless stood at the end of the day. And the citizenry over which he presided, not to mention the viewing audience, are forever the better for it.

"Where There's Smoke" from *Diff'rent Strokes*
Original Air Date: 14 January 1984
By Troy Howarth

One of the great pitfalls of navigating the roadmap of adolescence is peer pressure. The desire to conform in order to fit in is a strong impulse, especially in the formative years of junior high school and beyond. It's during this crucial phase that many kids fall into bad habits with long-lasting consequences. Not surprisingly, this is a theme which runs throughout *Diff'rent Strokes* (1978–1986) – and nowhere is it more obvious, and poignant, than in the twelfth episode of the show's sixth season.

"Where There's Smoke" opens with Arnold (Gary Coleman) rushing back to his upscale town house apartment, where he finds siblings Willis (Todd Bridges) and Kimberly (Dana Plato) and the family maid Pearl (Mary Jo Catlett) watching an old murder mystery on TV. Arnold is anxious to tell them about some problems he is having at school, but they're too engrossed in the movie to care. The scene ends with an obvious but not ineffective gag as Arnold, desperate for his family's undivided attention, switches off the set just as the identity of the murderer is about to be revealed.

As a side note, it's touching in hindsight to see Dana Plato in one of her sporadic season six appearances, especially given the theme of the episode. Plato incurred the displeasure of the producers thanks to some well-publicized issues with substance abuse; when she found out that she was pregnant (she gave birth to a son in July of 1984), she tried to persuade the producers into making her pregnancy part of the show, but they decided to fire her and explain that her character was off studying in Paris instead. She would continue to make sporadic appearances in the show's final two seasons, but for all intents and purposes, season six was the end of the line for her and her most significant role. She still appears bright-eyed and enthusiastic here, but later appearances would find her looking a bit worse for wear; tragically, she succumbed to a drug overdose in 1999, at the age of 34.

Arnold's inability to fit in with his peers at junior high school is an all-too-common dilemma, of course, and his boundlessly sympathetic foster father Mr. Drummond (Conrad Bain) proposes a reasonable if unrealistic solution: if you want to fit in, just invite the kids over for a party and win them over! To help Arnold fit in even better, he even gets the boy a nice new sweater in the school's colors; clearly his idea of how young people relate to each other is a little… out of touch.

Arnold does his best to follow Drummond's advice and he brings several classmates back to the apartment, along with his good friend Dudley (Shavar Ross). Arnold's attempts at playing the ultimate ingratiating host prove to be anything but ingratiating. The boys are eager to watch porno on the Drummonds' state-of-the-art VCR, but Arnold hasn't reached a point where that's of much interest to him – and when they pull out some cigarettes, he is positively aghast. He's even more shocked when Dudley produces his own pack of smokes – pilfered, as he later explains, from his father. Pearl ends up busting up the party, leaving Arnold with egg on his face.

At this stage, Arnold isn't particularly interested in going to extremes in order to fit in. Mr. Drummond has already preached to him about the dangers of smoking and he doesn't have the rebellious streak of some of his classmates. Dudley, however, talks him into giving smoking a try. In the episode's most amusing sequence, the two boys share a cigarette in Arnold's bedroom – Arnold's attempts at mimicking old school cool and sophistication by way of some bad Humphrey Bogart impressions generates chuckles, while the spectacle of the two boys inhaling cigarette smoke (even if Arnold needs to be reminded to exhale!) reminds one of how different things were in the 1980s; it's hard to imagine such a scene being staged with children these days. Of course, the whole thing ends in a fiasco as Arnold inadvertently sets his new sweater on fire.

It's a typical part of the *Diff'rent Strokes* formula, of course – and said formula is also evident in so many other sitcoms of the era, as well – but the ensuing action revolves around Arnold's attempts to avoid getting into trouble with Mr. Drummond as he conceals the smoking as well as the damage to the sweater. Poor Pearl elects to get herself into hot water by claiming to have been smoking, while Arnold and Dudley feverishly conspire to find a way to keep the damage to the sweater away from Mr. Drummond. At one point Arnold tries tucking the sweater into his pants and stooping over, but as he correctly observes that only ends up making him look like Groucho Marx. Dudley suggests that Arnold just try keeping his hand on his hip, where he can at least keep the offending burn covered up. Always quick with a comeback, Arnold objects to the idea, saying "people will talk!"

Inevitably, all of his efforts go for naught, and when Mr. Drummond notices something fishy going on, he presses for answers until Arnold finally collapses and admits to his wrong-doing. It's interesting that, no matter how "heavy" *Diff'rent Strokes* occasionally got in its subject matter – and it certainly wasn't afraid to touch on some very dark themes – it always managed to do with a lightness of touch. That light tone sometimes may make it appear as if it was frivolous in its attempt to address serious themes, but that would be an unfair knee-jerk reaction. Far from being shallow or insensitive to the complexities of reality, the show deserves a lot of credit for dabbling in such thematic material; in exposing the children in the audience to the life lessons of these Very Special Episodes, it arguably carried more weight than a stern lecture from real-world authority figures, whether it be parents, educators, or whatever.

The most striking part of the episode is a double whammy reserved for the final few minutes. Dudley has already admitted to copying his smoking habits from his father, so when the latter (Le Tari, of *The Onion Field* (1979) and *Amazon Women on the Moon* (1987) (his final role)) admits that an upcoming "knee surgery" is actually to remove one of his lungs, it carries a particularly strong impact. There's no attempt at diluting the grim reality of the situation with facile humor, and the episode ends on an uncharacteristically poignant note as the father leaves the apartment... and lights up another cigarette. The message is clear: even with the devastation done to the man's body, the addiction is too powerful to overcome; he'll continue smoking, even as his body continues to deteriorate.

Of course, no program could have done much to have curbed the epidemic with teenage smoking – especially with the all-important aspect of peer pressure and the desire to achieve acceptance being so thoroughly hard-wired into our collective psyches. That said, it's interesting, and perhaps ever-so-slightly heartening, that these days the move towards vaping provides a potentially safer alternative from the dangers of smoking. The desire to appear "cool" and "sophisticated" by adopting such habits is still very much in place, but despite the protestations of the tobacco industry that the nicotine content of vaping is an insidious problem in itself – one must also consider the source and how this move has affected them where it hurts: namely in their sales. Whether it will ever be possible to have a truly "smoke free" society remains to be seen, but as more young people move away from smoking cigarettes in search of healthier alternatives, there is room for cautious optimism. "Where There's Smoke," however, remains a lasting time capsule of a period where the pressure to fit in by adopting such adult vices was all too common; its lightness of touch makes it readily accessible as entertainment, but it also delivers where it counts, making it one of the most potent of the Very Special Episodes of this quintessentially eighties program.

"Say Uncle" from *Family Ties*
Original Air Date: 26 January 1984
By Lee Gambin

Two time Academy Award winning actor Tom Hanks had made a name for himself for television audiences playing the cross dressing Kip Wilson in the short lived sitcom *Bosom Buddies* (1980–1982) – a show inspired by the Billy Wilder comic masterpiece *Some Like It Hot* (1959). Before this cult series hit the small screen, Hanks had appeared in the Edgar Lansbury produced slasher classic *He Knows You're Alone* (1980) which allowed Hanks to play in the realm of dark territory, which is something that would resurface come 1984 where he unsettled sitcom enthusiasts with his portrayal of Elyse Keaton's (Meredith Baxter Birney) tragic, desperate and booze addled brother Ned Donnelly in the *Family Ties* (1982–1989) Very Special Episode "Say Uncle".

From the earliest mention of Ned's impending arrival, Elyse talks about her brother being unpredictable and impulsive, while her son Alex (Michael J. Fox) lauds Ned's success in the business world and has a deep rooted admiration for his ruthless ambition. However, Ned is instantly established as "damaged goods", and somebody who has jeopardized his position as a young tycoon-to-be in the opportunistic and overtly driven cutthroat eighties. It is learned that Ned had embezzled four and a half thousand dollars from his previous job and is haunted by this fact, rendering him a failure in his own eyes and possibly driving him to the bottle.

If *Family Ties* is a sitcom where capitalism, industry and enterprise factor in as a core social/narrative backbone (embodied by the likeable conservatism of its star character, Alex P. Keaton), then the repercussions of self-sabotage (Ned's self-destruction) inject this attribute with solid drama, allowing for some disturbing but incredibly well constructed tension and spectacle.

Elyse's considerate and sensitive husband Steven (Michael Gross) has set up an interview at his public TV station WKS for Ned, making it possible for this former "screw up" to re-enter the world as a functional and, more importantly, honest man. On the surface, this kindly gesture and vocational opportunity is appreciated by the charming but highly erratic Ned – who goes through the motions in order to get to the job interview – however, in an utterly repugnant display of disrespect for Steven (and the Keatons as a family unit), Ned blows the interview by being incredibly drunk and by behaving in a ludicrous (if comical) fashion. Enraged by this drunken tomfoolery, Steven feels betrayed and Elyse is eventually forced to address Ned's alcoholism.

Writers Gary David Goldberg and Ruth Bennett weave successful visual gags into the episode early on, not only to serve the comic elements of the show, but also to establish Ned's problem. The first drinking joke has Ned retrieving a six pack of beer from the fridge only to snap one can off, offering it to Steven and then taking the remaining five. The intelligence here is that Goldberg and Bennett set up the social issue and very personal concern as a throwaway joke – something that doesn't necessarily have to be taken seriously. By presenting Ned's booze problem as something funny at first glance, there is an organic commentary made on how the characters (primarily Elyse) view his drinking: as a non-issue until it's too late.

Eventually, Elyse catches on and notes: "Going pretty heavy on that stuff aren't you Ned?" Here, Meredith Baxter Birney's quiet concern ushers in the first moment of seriousness in the episode, and the gradual tone of the show shifts – drifting from Jennifer's (Tina Yothers) newfound interest in playing the clarinet (badly) and settling into the dark terrain of a broken man battling with personal demons and the seductive lure of liquor. Ned Donnelly is a man terrified by the trappings of responsibility, and when his devoted sister insists that he gets "settled" (translating to obtaining job stability), the episode does a lot more than present a problematic situation at hand; instead it morphs into an intimate character study. This is a perfectly realized testament to the elegance of *Family Ties* – here is a sitcom that most certainly examines social ills and topical subject matter, but does so without treating such concerns as standalone issues. Instead, Goldberg and Bennett carefully integrate grueling subject matter within the fabric of character driven narrative. In other words, Ned's drinking is part of the teleplay patchwork, rather than being a situation comedy "sore thumb".

Ned's defeatist attitude is summarized by "Who's gonna hire me now?" – a hangover from his embezzlement – and meshing with that is his bipolar persona, something that leaps from a charismatic playfulness to a trembling mess. Tom Hanks does an incredible job at throwing himself from joyous, silly and hypnotically hyperactive clown who charms his way through a scene all the way through to having a great finely tuned handle on those dark recesses of the distraught human condition. The image of Ned drinking and sitting in the dark alone in the Keaton kitchen is a nightmarish vision of events to come, and the focal point is materialized there – the central confrontation with Alex, who once looked up to his uncle.

Ned's desperation to find alcohol in the house cements the notion of drinking being a "terrifying" problem that disturbs the family unit. It's as if Ned's addiction is a malevolent entity that upsets the warmth and camaraderie within the Keaton household. Interestingly enough, the Keatons who are liberal thinkers and ex-hippies, are still adverse to alcoholism in their structured setup that includes their three children, careers and upholding of quasi-traditionalist American suburban domesticity. When Alex witnesses Ned's addiction getting out of hand, escalating to the point where he downs a bottle of vanilla extract (spewing out a comical throwaway with "Don't drive and bake!") the lightness within the darkness of a sitcom's handling of alcoholism shines through, but never smothers fans out of the intensity of both the subject matter and the performances.

When Ned turns malicious, bitter and frightening, Tom Hanks's performance epitomizes a young man consumed by alienation, loneliness and fear. The scariness of the situation is even more heightened because we sense Alex's fragility and nervousness. This usually cocky and self-possessed young republican, is now a terrified boy, trapped in his own kitchen with a manic addict. Michael J. Fox's diminutive presence and frenzied jitters perfectly counter the irrational and unreasonable schizoid performance from Hanks, and it is equally disturbing as it is captivating to watch. Ned snaps at Alex, getting angry when he is called "a drunk", but from that defensiveness comes an insight into the emptiness of Ned's life and his overwhelming sadness. Ned spits out hateful venom, calling Alex a "pious conservative" and it is in a moment like this where Michael J. Fox's right-wing money-loving preppy is permitted some pathos and understanding. For a TV sitcom to establish this iconic character as someone with traits that are not traditionally appealing, redeemable or even righteous is a brave offering, however, when he is pitted against a guest star with problems (Tom Hanks as an alcoholic uncle) then he is allowed to garner sympathy – something that will eventually grow with the character as the series would develop.

Determined to help Ned, who was once an idol of his, Alex pleads with his mother: "Uncle Ned has a drinking problem and you gotta do something about it!" Although Elyse questions Ned's drinking early in the piece, she remains skeptical of it being an intense problem ("He was always a drinker in school, but he will be able to handle it") but in time she accepts it and addresses it. Their conversation makes for gripping television – a somber and quiet moment, built from familial anxieties, regret, bitterness and anguish. It is a reflective back and forth, as opposed to the frantic mania of Ned's interview at the TV network. Character actor Ben Piazza guest stars as network head Mr. Wertz who sits in shock and is thoroughly not entertained by Ned's goofiness and madness. As it is comical to bear witness to as Tom Hanks goes full throttle with his physical comedy prowess, it is also completely cringe worthy to sit through because it is a stressful watch. Essentially, what we the audience (as well as Steven and Mr. Wertz) are witnessing is a man's breakdown totally exaggerated and made all the more outlandish because of alcoholism. Returning home, Steven tells Elyse "He made a fool out of me and Mr. Wertz" and then goes on to explain that what he sees in Ned is "a sick self-destructive individual". Disgusted by their moral judgment, Ned strikes back claiming that "You Keatons will always be around to hold the family banner high" – but his hostility is completely unwarranted and only exposes his pathetic depression, anger, unresolved angst and childish resentment.

Something innovative that this VSE does is present alcoholism as a disease (Steven tells Ned that he "has a disease and needs help"). This is something that would gradually be the case when the issue was to be discussed in years to come, but in 1984, a drinking problem was usually a systematic problem bought upon by social conditions (i.e. stress, work load, personal pressures, marital issues, peer pressure et al). However, thanks to television sitcoms such as the responsible and always forward-thinking *Family Ties*, alcoholism would be classified as much of a serious legitimate disease as anorexia or schizophrenia. While long time addicts such as major celebrities like Liza

Minnelli would bring alcoholism and drug addiction into the limelight and boldly declare these as genuine ailments and chronic diseases in the nineties, Tom Hanks's Ned Donnelly would be one of the first television characters to have his drinking be something more than just an elongated mistake.

The climactic moments of the VSE are powerful and monumental, starting with Alex championing Ned's successful past. The fact that he has kept a number of newspaper clippings that report Ned's professional accomplishments and following this loving moment with Alex's genuine declaration of his love: "Whenever I think I can't achieve something, I look at those." However, the situation gets heavy and the fed up Ned throws a punch at Alex, knocking him to the ground. Shocked by the blow, Alex retreats to the couch, flinching when his regretful fallen down mess of an uncle reaches out to him. Coddled by his angry parents, Alex nurses his face, while Ned sobs incessantly, moaning "I hit Alex…" Fuming with rage, Steven shouts out an ultimatum "Either you get help or you get the hell out of my house!" The tension, sorrow and unsettling silences make for an astonishing VSE, and the remarkable performances from the talented cast give this thirty-minute saga a gravity that is rich with emotional turmoil and torture. The final image of Ned picking up the telephone and admitting his problem to AA is a quintessential moment of television VSEs – the reluctant wreck finally opening up to the idea of salvation. This would be a staple for VSEs to come, as well as a benchmark in comparison to those that had come before it, where a miserable mess finally gets their act together (or at least attempts to). Of course, the magic of the TV sitcom is that even in this dark, somber and yes, sobering moments, the writing and delivery of a stab of light has to find its way through the darkness, and here it does with Ned casually noting that he will meet women at AA who have the same interests as he does. This is the power of the VSE – it paints a portrait of oppressive all-consuming darkness, but offers shards of necessary light that never offset, but always bring us back home.

"The Hitchhikers" from *Diff'rent Strokes*
Original Air Dates: 28 January 1984 (Part 1) and 4 February 1984 (Part 2)
By Lee Gambin

With this double episode opening with actor Conrad Bain addressing the audience with a public service announcement explaining that the theme and content of what "you're about to see" might be confronting and terrifying to children, devoted *Diff'rent Strokes* fans would be reminded of the other time this was the case with Bain doing the same thing for the infamous "The Bicycle Man" two-parter. A PSA sets up the serious tone and does something more than inform and warn, it paints the picture in a creepy and unsettling manner, something that the situation comedy is not at all normally known for. "Some of the scenes may be disturbing for young children" is something that would be associated with other ventures, not a TV sitcom, especially one that is so child-centric. "The Hitchhikers" is just as harrowing as "The Bicycle Man", and possibly even more so in that Kimberly Drummond (Dana Plato) is dealt with in a very aggressive manner, as is her younger brother Arnold (Gary Coleman) and the threat of rape and death is a continual jab whereas in "The Bicycle Man", actor Gordon Jump as the child molester keeps the mood light for the most part with Arnold and pal Dudley (Shavar Ross) being clueless in what is happening, whilst Kimberly and Arnold here are wise to the horrific actions of freelance artist and would-be rapist/murderer Bill (Woody Eney).

It is a harsh New York Winter, and it is Philip Drummond's (Conrad Bain) birthday and his partner Maggie McKinney (Dixie Carter) is preparing a surprise party for him. Kimberly and Arnold decide to go out into the city to buy their father a present and after doing so (with Arnold also buying himself a rocket ship with the money they have on them) they find themselves penniless – on the street without a dime. They decide that the doorman at their building will pay for a taxi fare, but they also struggle to get a cab. The underlying issue of blacks not being able to get a cab somehow creeps into the model here with Arnold being in need (something that will pop up later in a more dire scenario), however for Kimberly, who is white, she struggles too. Arnold cheekily tells Kimberly that he reeks of money whereas she looks poor and this reversal in what is usually presented as black means you're poor and white normally doesn't is a testament to the change in America and what this sitcom represents. And this class issue will become a source of attack from the predatory Bill. With no luck at catching a cab, Kimberly and Arnold hitchhike, taking a ride with a seemingly friendly stranger Bill and although it is established that they have been told never to take rides from strangers, they do so. This episode emphasizes the dangers in the act of hitchhiking, everything else that comes with it acts as the repercussions of such a decision. Bill builds trust with the youngsters at first by noticing Arnold's new toy rocket and he suggests that they come over and watch some spacecraft tapes. It turns out Bill is a freelance artist who works for NASA, which is something that instantly appeals to space buff Arnold.

Upon arriving at Bill's place, Kimberly innocently compliments Bill's artwork and his apartment, and Arnold races into a separate bedroom to watch the NASA videos. While Arnold and Kimberly are charmed by Bill and his work, there is a disarming moment where the first image that lends itself to being that of a threat comes to the fore and it is Bill locking Arnold in the separate room to watch the video of the rocket launch, with his intentions set on sexually assaulting Kimberly. The same year as this episode airing, the made-for-TV movie *The Burning Bed* aired in October showcasing Farrah Fawcett's excellent acting chops as a fed up battered wife who is raped by her husband and finally lets him have it by setting him alight on their bed. This confronting and violent telemovie would inspire women to discuss their own sexual assault stories, and critics would be wowed by Fawcett's power as an actress which was something possibly unsung in the realm of a series such as *Charlie's Angels* (1976–1981) of which she was prominently known. Here we have a similar asset in the excellent performance from Dana Plato, who audiences have seen grow up on this sitcom. In "The Hitchhikers" Plato delivers a nuanced, fragile performance that is not only believable but heartbreaking – there is something so delicate and sorrowful in her struggle to escape the vile rapist, and something more is going on in the performance when you consider the tragic outcome for the talented and lovely Plato, that she herself would fall victim to the coldness of the world, and be so abused by manipulative people who would use her and a system that failed her.

Bill suggests that he will do a sketch of Kimberly for a "present for her father", and in comes the first compliments on her looks as well as making her sit closer to him. Bill's inappropriate comments are an insight into his psyche, and he makes mention of commonly used tropes from lonely mentally unhinged men who use their isolation as an excuse to be grotesque. He talks about being rejected and laments that people don't have time for one another – but all of this paints a picture of not only a possibility that human loneliness can create such ugliness, but also what he does in his gas lighting and excuses for bad behavior. When Kimberly tries to break free from the increasingly intense situation, he commands "Sit down" and the show is now in dark terrain. Woody Eney's performance is genuinely terrifying, he plays up a thoroughly menacing, sickly demented creep and as the violence comes into play we can be reminded of the treatment of sexual violence in American sitcoms being seldom seen, which in essence makes them harder to watch; especially when the potential victim is a character we have come to know and love. Of course, "Edith's 50th Birthday" from *All in the Family* (1971–1979) is a pinnacle moment and there the much loved Edith Bunker (Jean Stapleton) was attacked, but here a young teen who we have seen grow into her teen years on screen is the victim. Interestingly enough both shows feature a lead character's birthday celebration interrupted by sexual assault.

Arnold calling out to be let out of the room and Kimberly calling back to him is a heartfelt moment that emphasizes not only their mutual struggle but the love shared between brother and sister. Bill's threats are there to not only scare the audience, but infuriate them. When he uses Kimberly's previous compliments against her and when she cries out to her brother, we are left to feel as helpless as these kids we know so well and care so deeply for. We get a glimpse of hope when Kimberly tries to smash Bill's head with a heavy art piece and we get a sense of sacrifice when we see that Kimberly is far more terrified of what will happen to Arnold. She is desperate that he doesn't threaten Arnold's safety and she is more than happy to have her life sacrificed for the safety of her brother. This is a lovely take on race reversal in that for many years black folk would sacrifice their own personal happiness for the sake of their white peers, but here, in 1984 the white girl would risk her own life to save her black brother's. By the end of the first episode, Bill ties up Arnold and gags him, a shocking image of a young boy forced to be silent, and this is especially confronting when it is a white man doing it to a young black child. This is a loaded image, and in relation to 2020's horrific actions against black man George Floyd by police officials, this eighties sitcom marks an introspective retroactive response: that white oppressors have silenced black voices for way too long. Bill threatens Arnold with "If you love your sister and you don't wanna see her hurt then you'll shut up!" These vile actions from this terrifying man are countered by a pre-gagged Arnold still cracking jokes, however the threat of death silences both our young hero and the episode prompting the mandatory silence as the pre-end credits roll.

The second episode in this VSE once again opens with a PSA from Conrad Bain addressing the audience, with mention again about the dangers of hitchhiking and how it may upset young children watching. Following this is a recap ("Last week on *Diff'rent Strokes*") and we open with Arnold gagged and tied up, with a focus on Kimberly potentially being raped and killed. Bill has kept her locked inside his closet while he dealt with Arnold and when he opens the door attempting to have his way with her, he calls his abusive kidnapping a "date", wanting to keep her. Kimberly's response is very mature and not at all from the lips of a teenage girl who would romanticize love at first sight ("You can't just suddenly feel affection for someone you've never met before"). This reflects the changing nature of teen girls in American sitcoms, from boy-crazy fifties bobby-soxers fawning over teen heartthrobs, through to Marcia (Maureen McCormick) and Jan Brady (Eve Plumb) from *The Brady Bunch* (1969–1974) having alternate ideas on what love and romance will entail, right through to more complicated and then again more vulnerable teen girls like Mallory Keaton (Justine Bateman) from *Family Ties* (1982–1989) who would have her trust betrayed in the sexual abuse episode "Give Your Uncle Arthur a Kiss".

While Philip starts to worry about Kimberly and Arnold, the savvy Arnold escapes and manages to get out on the streets desperate to have someone help him rescue Kimberly. Of course, people are apathetic and not helpful, while the fact that Arnold is a black child running the dark streets of New York hinders the situation in that racism is prevalent and there is an assumption that he is a "ghetto kid" after a "hand out". No one knows of Arnold's class status (he is the son of an incredibly wealthy man) and he is even offered money from a stranger thinking he is begging for spare change. The class issue is also made as an aside commentary when Bill asks where Kimberly lives, and when she says she and Arnold live in a penthouse apartment he makes mention of "looking down on the world", something that both Kimberly and Arnold never would imagine doing. Assumptions are another evil here in this episode.

With the landlady's insight into Bill, although played out for laughs, is telling about rapists and child molesters (men who keep to themselves and remain secretive) and the final sequence in Bill's dark room (the most secret of places) is a place of sexual trauma for Kimberly. Just in time Kimberly is rescued by her father and police, and a reminder of Gloria (Sally Struthers) insisting her mother press charges on the sexual assailant in "Edith's 50th Birthday" in order to empower other women is brought up here with Kimberly terrified of facing the ordeal ("I wish I could put this whole thing out of my mind") with the thoughtful Maggie sharing advice about not facing the trauma. This moment is grounded to a cemented realism and general advisory when the episode ends with a straight up PSA insisting audiences inform police or medical centers if they know of any sexual assault that has occurred or is recurring.

"A Hunting We Will Go" from *Silver Spoons*
Original Air Date: 18 February 1984
By Nathaniel Thompson

At 8:53 p.m. on Saturday, February 18, 1984, an entire generation of children was shocked into silence by what happened on NBC. The upbeat sitcom *Silver Spoons* (1982–1987) hadn't shied away from occasionally touching on serious subject matter, but nothing could have prepared regular viewers for what happened when newly reunited father and son Ricky Stratton (Ricky Schroder) and Edward Stratton III (Joel Higgins) wound up taking an afternoon hunting trip with Ricky's "Grandpa," a.k.a. Edward Stratton II. The eldest Stratton was played for the sixth time in the series by John Houseman, the Julliard drama head, original Mercury Theatre co-founder, and Oscar winner for *The Paper Chase* (1973), which inspired a TV series starring Houseman during the same period this episode aired. Possessing one of the most distinctive voices in pop culture, Houseman had also stepped in to provide an indelible campfire prologue in John Carpenter's *The Fog* (1980) and had a charming role in the cable TV favorite, *My Bodyguard* (1980). However, his casting in *Silver Spoons* was most logical given Houseman's spokesman status for brokerage firm Smith Barney (later absorbed into Morgan Stanley) with the oft-quoted catchphrase, "They make money the old-fashioned way; they *earn* it." With Houseman's presence, this episode seemed poised to be a reassuring bonding experience between three generations of Stratton men. What actually ended up happening was something quite different.

Silver Spoons tends to be more cohesive about working its central theme into the entire episode than the average sitcom, and this one doubles down from the very beginning as we see the Stratton household inexplicably decorated as an out-of-control jungle filled with foam trees. "It's a work of art," explains Edward to his father about the dramatic change in environment. From there we segue to the revelation that the eldest Stratton has just made a mint by purchasing a fast food chain known as Mel's Mostly Meats, "a pioneer in the burgeoning business of pseudo-food." From there it's a string of references to unsettling engineered food like Partly Potatoes, It Could Be Fish Sandwiches, Close to Chicken, and Possibly Pastrami, all indicators of human domination over wildlife and natural food sources including living animals. Hints of death even extend to throwaway lines of dialogue in the scene like Ricky's "If I lie, may I fry." As it turns out, the visit is really about Grandpa's annual hunting trip and his offer to bring Ricky along. "I've wanted to go hunting ever since I read *Last of the Mohicans*," Ricky gushes, setting up the harsh collision between fiction and reality soon to come. Edward's immediate concern clearly comes from a place of personal experience: "I'm afraid of what the experience might do to your emotional health. It's one thing to say the phrase 'bag a deer.' It's another whole thing to actually sight down a rifle and actually shoot one." The first act closes not with a laugh but with the disquieting image of Ricky raising his arms to mimic a rifle and making a firing sound just off center of the camera, stopping in a silent freeze frame.

The rest of the episode takes place entirely in a forest on Mount St. Stratton, Grandpa's personal thousand-acre property, where the personalities of the three Strattons are laid out more clearly with Grandpa telling Ricky a joke about a shrink seeing a man who thinks he's a dog (man vs. animal rearing its head again), whipping out a wind-up woodpecker for a sight gag on his forehead, and just stopping Ricky from firing at his own father when he shows up unexpectedly to keep an eye on them. The trio soon sit down on a fallen tree and enjoy a bagful of Mel's Mostly Meats in unison, a harmony that reaches its purest form when they share compliments about the beauty of the land and Edward's parenting abilities. All that soon changes with the arrival of a young passing deer, and Grandpa quickly advises Ricky, "Aim for the heart. Squeeze the trigger." What follows is perhaps the most brutal moment in sitcom history as Ricky fires, the deer collapses, and we see it bleeding and dying on the ground as it looks up at the young boy's face. A distraught Ricky can't finish the job as he tearfully aims the rifle over the suffering creature, leaving Grandpa to finish it off with one loud, final shot. "Did you see his eyes?" Ricky sobs. "I never thought hunting would be like this."

At the end of the episode, we never leave the woods and get back to the Stratton home; instead we're left with a voiceover disclaimer from Schroder: "The deer used in this episode was not harmed in any way." This may not be in the territory of genuine animal slaughter a la *Cannibal Holocaust* (1980) or *Apocalypse Now* (1979), but the realistic depiction of the deer's demise at least makes this the 1980s equivalent of *Bambi* (1942) with its traumatic depiction of the reality of hunting. The commingled debates about gun control and hunting rights had already been heated for decades by the time the decade rolled around, including the passage of the Gun Control Act of 1968 following several high-profile assassinations. Those wounds still hadn't healed when John Lennon was assassinated in 1980, followed by an attempt on the life of President Ronald Reagan in 1981, which led to a years-long discussion culminating in 1993's Brady Handgun Violence Prevention Act. The ownership and use of sporting guns has remained sacrosanct in the American consciousness for centuries with children regularly taught how to hunt either for sport or food in many areas of the country, with fictional cartoon characters like Elmer Fudd closely associated in their minds without focusing on the consequences of pulling the trigger.

However, this episode penned by series co-developer David W. Duclon (also a key player behind *Family Ties* (1982–1989), *Laverne & Shirley* (1976–1983), and *The Jeffersons* (1975–1985)) manages to subvert expectations at every turn. Far from a clear anti-hunting polemic, it instead raises that early question of whether Ricky is psychologically capable of hunting (he isn't) and implies that Edward, obviously not a fan of the practice, suffered ramifications himself in the past during outings with his father. Television comedies almost always relied on stock tension between different generations of parents (a tactic that later reached the level of sublime perfection on *Gilmore Girls* (2000–2007)), but *Silver Spoons* adamantly refuses to take that route either. The two Edwards may have their differences of opinion but always express respect for each other, a behavior that Ricky comes to appreciate at the close of this particular tale when his grandfather praises him for reacting naturally and being true to himself. Whether Ricky ever goes hunting again (which seems unlikely), his willingness to try and his refusal to cover up his horror at what he's done is enough to earn a commendation from the two earlier generations with him.

Given the deeply ingrained nature of hunting in the American consciousness right next to cars, fireworks, and rock music, it should come as no surprise that few films or TV shows have taken much of a stance one way or another since *Bambi*, still the work of pop culture most responsible for sharping public opinion on the subject. There have been a few outliers, most notably Harvey Hart's tragically underseen *Shoot* (1976) with Cliff Robertson or its use as a metaphor in *The Deer Hunter* (1978), but for the most part hunting has been used as a neutral backdrop for survival tales like *Hunter's Blood* (1986). That a popular, prime-time American sitcom in 1984 would tackle the subject so directly seemed shocking then and feels utterly alien now. There would be future VSEs to come on *Silver Spoons* (with another major one to come just a little over a month later), but never again did the show stray so far outside its comfort zone and its core setting to upend viewers' ideas of what a sitcom could actually accomplish. All on a weekend night right after dinner, no less.

The episode also marks a rite of passage of sorts for Ricky the character and the actor, laying the ground for a televised Bildungsroman as it draws a harsh dividing line between the sweet kid who came from a rich but deeply broken family and the young man learning the value of family and the price of taking a life of any kind. From here the show becomes an expedition to adulthood with stops along the way including the joys of dating, trendy clothes, and Whitney Houston, but for many viewers, there will always be a feeling of limbo at the end of this episode. Just as that freeze frame in Act One preserves Ricky in the act of playing hunter at thin air, the episode's closing moments leave us with the three Strattons at their closest and most vulnerable, frozen in time in the woods with blood left in their tracks.

"Spare the Rod" from *Silver Spoons*
Original Air Date: 24 March 1984
By Nathaniel Thompson

After taking the VSE to harrowing new heights with "A Hunting We Will Go," *Silver Spoons* (1982–1987) had ably demonstrated that the gloves were coming in its second season. Beneath the façade of an upbeat series about a wealthy father and son teaching each other life lessons against a backdrop of toy trains and video games, viewers had come to realize that tuning in on Saturday night at 8:30 could deliver a shocking grenade at any moment. In fact, it was only four episodes later that the program delivered its next figurative smack in the face with "Spare the Rod," a sober examination of how to deal with child abuse when you're witnessing it either as an adult or a youngster.

Everything starts innocently enough as, per common practice by now, the theme of the show is discreetly woven into the opening comedy scenario. Edward Stratton III has by now established his romantic relationship with Kate and presents her with a gift-wrapped box for her birthday containing an antique porcelain floral design. "But my birthday is next week," Kate responds. "I knew that!" Edward responds, passing his flub off as a pre-birthday present. Already we're shown how lies can weave into the happiest of domestic relationships even for the best intentions, and it's complicated even further when Ricky shows up after a basketball game with his heretofore unseen buddy, Toby (Meeno Peluce). Immediately Toby starts spinning a yarn to explain his sprained arm in a sling due to climbing up and falling from a tree while saving a stray cat named – wait for it – Brian Setzer. "I'm a walking disaster area," Toby says of his regular injuries, but any savvy viewer can already guess what's in store. As counterpoint, Edward orders Ricky to stop dribbling his basketball in the house – only for the ball to smash Kate's present. An angry Edward aggressively grabs his son by the arms and threatens, "I oughta take it out of your hide" as punishment. Instead he ends up demanding an apology to Kate, who fibs to conceal her lack of attachment to the gift in the first place. The secrets and lies mount as the themes of disobedience, consequences, and denial reach an early crescendo when Toby forces Ricky to swear to never reveal his big secret: "When my dad gets mad, he gets physical. But he does it for my own good. I'm a real screw-up."

Of course, Ricky has to break his oath when Toby shows up again sporting dark bruises all over his face and makes up a story about walking along a picket fence and hitting the sidewalk. The abuse pattern is spelled out as Toby explains he was beaten for tracking mud all over the new family carpet, but his dad bought him a present to compensate. Edward decides it's time to have a man-to-man chat with the abuser (played by *Lou Grant*'s Allen Williams), who turns out to be another upper class businessman with the most normal veneer imaginable. The violence manifests against Edward as well when he angrily smashes a drink out of his hand, but Edward uses his own experience with the basketball to teach a lesson about how to deal with anger issues. That in turn triggers a revelation that Tony's dad was in turn the product of an abusive father, creating a cycle that Edward feels can only be broken by going to a therapy group, Parents Anonymous. "I'm not going to a place full of freaks and weirdos" is the immediate response, to which Edward counters that no parent is perfect. It's either that or calling the police and sending Toby to a foster family because, in an incredibly grim moment, Edward explains he'd recently seen an identical scenario that led to the battering parent on trial for murder.

Child health and welfare was a hot topic in late seventies and early eighties pop culture, and made-for-TV movies really had the market cornered with fare like *Mary Jane Harper Cried Last Night* (1977), *When She Was Bad...* (1979), *Please Don't Hit Me, Mom* (1981), *Fallen Angel* (1981), *The Best Little Girl in the World* (1981), and the most infamous of them all, *Something about Amelia* (1984). That last film is the most relevant here as it focuses a particular strain of child abuse that had never been touched on before on network television: forced incest. In this case the victim is teenager Roxana Zal, who's so afraid of what may happen to her younger siblings that she reveals her father (Ted Danson) has been forcing himself on her for years. The film ends on a note that clearly informed "Spare the Rod" with Zal, Danson, and mom Glenn Close deciding to stick it out and go through treatment rather than splitting up the family. The family first attitude at the time made any other kind of resolution impossible, especially for a film already dancing on the edge of a very sharp razor, though today it feels shocking and against the cultural grain for that solution to be considered even remotely acceptable. *Amelia* aired on January 9, 1984, a little over two months before "Spare the Rod," and its presence can be felt all over the episode even if the story involves violent abuse instead of sexual and is portrayed from the perspective of outsiders. When Toby and his dad agree to work through this mess together at the end, at least it comes with the caveat that they'll need to split up for a little while as the therapy takes its course. The episode ends on a downbeat note (in dead silence) as Edward escorts father and son to their first meeting with Kate and Ricky looking on. We're still all too aware that things might not turn out so perfectly in the future.

In addition to made-for-TV films, the topic of child abuse wasn't exactly alien to network television shows and had already been explored in such episodes as "The Crying Child" (*Starsky and Hutch* (1975–1979)), "Child of Pain" (*Little House on the Prairie* (1974–1983)), "A Child in Need" (*The Incredible Hulk* (1977–1982)), and "A Good Smack in the Mouth" (*Quincy M.E.* (1976–1983)). However, seeing it treated so bluntly on a sitcom was jolting in 1984 with the laugh track subsiding dramatically once Toby starts walking around with hellish bruises all over his face. Adding to the shock value is the fact that the victim is Peluce, a guest star fixture on dozens of television series (including *Diff'rent Strokes* (1978–1986) and *Happy Days* (1974–1984)) who had previously appeared alongside *Silver Spoons* star Joel Higgins on the single-season 1981 series, *Best of the West,* as father and son no less. Anyone familiar with their prior collaboration had to feel a bit uneasy watching Edward struggle with how to save his one-time TV child from being repeatedly beaten by his current father, a situation that had no previous parallel in sitcom history. Though he never had a regular hit series (*Voyagers!* (1982–1983) probably came closest), Peluce was a very familiar face to TV-watching kids at the time, and seeing him battered for half an hour led to a lot of intense discussions with parents once the episode aired. Furthermore, with the floodgates now open, other series were free to tread into these waters as well, most notably on *Family Ties* (1982–1989) ("You've Got a Friend") and *Mr. Belvedere* (1985–1990) ("The Counselor").

On top of these factors, the news at the time was increasingly full of stories about abused and even murdered children, with the infamous McMartin preschool trial (alleging serial abuse at a Manhattan Beach preschool in California) starting its first day in court only two days before this episode aired. The trial hadn't yet reached the full-tilt hysteria that would tie it to wildly ill-conceived Satanic panic movement of the era, but the timing of its opening salvo is too eerie to ignore. Child welfare had been a mounting concern since the murder of Adam Walsh in 1981, with his father spearheading a long-running campaign to prevent such a horrible fate for other children.

It's fascinating to note that throughout the decade, the child safety movement was mostly male-driven with both its crusaders and monsters; while the newspapers were filled with stories of abusive mothers or other female relatives as well, that aspect was too uncomfortable for casual entertainment to grapple with on a primetime stage. Significantly, Kate is largely relegated to the background in this episode as well after the first few minutes and mostly stands on the sidelines. In this particular scenario, not only are mother figures entirely absence but any kind of maternal instinct is suppressed as well. The men cause it, and the men try to resolve it. In real life that would never fly, but in the world of eighties sitcoms, it took baby steps to bring public awareness to the horrors that could be unfolding right next door to even the most seemingly innocent, affluent, or harmonious of families.

"Good News, Bad News" from *Happy Days*
Original Air Date: 19 July 1984
By Craig Martin

Very Special Episodes in series comedy from yesteryear provided a significant community service that brought public attention to important social issues that may have been hidden, misunderstood or stigmatized. In season 11 of long-running hit sitcom *Happy Days* (1974–1984), a Very Special Episode titled "Good News, Bad News" addresses social stigmas associated with diabetes and seeks to normalize the disease while increasing empathy and understanding of its impact on those living with the condition. The episode follows Fonzie's (Henry Winkler) younger cousin, Milwaukee teenage heartthrob, mechanic and musician Chachi Arcola (Scott Baio) who is diagnosed with diabetes and thinks of it as a death sentence. Chachi is so overwhelmed by the diagnosis that he reacts by instantly surrendering to the disease and quite literally withdrawing from life.

Before discussing the episode in detail, it is useful to begin with a number of key points about diabetes, which over the last few decades has become an increasingly prominent disease. Diabetes is a chronic condition caused by the body's inability to produce insulin that delivers glucose to cells. Insufficient insulin can lead to serious health complications, such as increased risk of heart disease and a weakened immune system that compromises the body's inability to heal even small cuts and infections. It occurs in two main forms: type 1 and type 2. Type 1 diabetes is an incurable lifetime condition sometimes referred to as juvenile diabetes as it commonly develops during late childhood or adolescence. Typically the immune system will attack and destroy the beta cells in the pancreas that produce insulin. Once these cells are gone, the body is no longer able to create its own insulin, which must thereafter be introduced into the bloodstream from an external source. While linked to genes and hormonal changes in the body, the causes of type 1 diabetes remain unknown. While there is still much unknown about type 2 diabetes, research confirms that its causes involve a combination of genetics, excess weight gain, poor diet and insufficient physical activity. Whereas type 1 diabetes is permanent and incurable, if managed carefully the impact of type 2 diabetes can be significantly lessened, or the condition even reversed. Although not specified in the *Happy Days* episode, Chachi is obviously diagnosed with type 1 diabetes, a condition he must live with for the rest of his life.

In 2015 the American Centre for Disease Control released figures indicating that over 100 million Americans are either prediabetic (at serious risk of developing type 2 diabetes) or living with diabetes, averaging one in four people and elevating the disease to the category of epidemic. The American Diabetes Association confirms that in the United States alone the disease is responsible for more deaths per year than breast cancer and AIDS combined, and that diabetes almost doubles the risk of heart attack if not properly managed. Management of diabetes in today's world has become complicated by the growing reliance on pre-packaged and highly processed foods that often contain hidden sugars. A large proportion of healthcare professionals and the wider community tend to think that diabetes is not a stigmatized condition, yet people living with the disease often report feeling embarrassment, failure, guilt, shame and even self-blame for their condition. There also exists a general perception that diabetes represents some kind of character defect or is indicative of an individual who does not take responsibility for his or her own personal health and wellbeing. Diabetics also report feeling vulnerable about how their condition is perceived socially or in work contexts and can become highly self-conscious when refusing unhealthy foods offered to them in social settings, or when they must administer an insulin shot in public. It is these feelings of shame and stigmatization about diabetes that the "Good News, Bad News" episode of *Happy Days* is particularly interested in addressing. The episode does this by normalizing diabetes and even demonstrating that the condition has the capacity to make the diabetic a more reliable, conscientious and effective person than many of his (or her) peers.

The eleventh season of *Happy Days* was also the final season of the highly successful sitcom, which ran between January 1974 and September 1984. The final season sought to tie up the narratives of its characters, ending with a one hour double episode titled "Passengers" in which Fonzie becomes the legal adoptive father of an orphaned boy named Danny (Danny Ponce) while Joanie (Erin Moran) and Chachi's on-again-off-again relationship concludes with a wedding in which Richie (Ron Howard) and Lori Beth (Lynda Goodfriend) make a last minute appearance in time for the vows. The episode ends with a final heartfelt toast by Howard (Tom Bosley) in which he directly addresses the camera and raises a glass to the loyal television audience in what is a moving farewell. As the series finale, "Passengers" was the last episode screened at the usual Tuesday night timeslot, marking an official end to the series on 8 May 1984. However, ABC later screened a further five episodes that had been produced for season eleven but were excluded from the official season line up. These "burned off" episodes were screened during the summer months on Thursday nights, potentially confusing audiences that had followed the series and seen the "Passengers" finale. No doubt some viewers may have wondered why Chachi and Joanie were suddenly not married, or why Danny was not with Fonzie. One of these burned off episodes was "Good News, Bad News", which became the second last episode of *Happy Days* to be screened in its first run by ABC before the series was sold for syndication. The final episode, "Fonzie's Spots", sees Fonzie, Chachi and Roger (Ted McGinley) agree to be recruited by Howard to his exclusive fraternity, the Leopard Lodge, in order to safeguard his position as Grand Poobah of the society.

Written by William Bickley and Michael Warren and helmed by longtime series director Jerry Paris, "Good News, Bad News" opens with high energy as Marion (Marion

Ross) dances on the coffee table in the Cunningham family room, wearing polishing socks to buff the tabletop to a high gloss. Phil Williams' "Rock 'n' Roll Cavalcade" plays on the radio as she twists, glides and slides. As she sits on the couch to take off the polishing socks, an announcement comes on the radio that causes her to suddenly leap to her feet and frantically call Howard and Joanie downstairs. The radio DJ has announced that the next track he will be playing is by "Milwaukee's own Chachi Arcano" and Marion rushes to the radio to take it upstairs but in her excitement she drops and breaks it.

The song played on the radio supposedly sung by Chachi is not actually Scott Baio but the work of British pop outfit Racey performing their song "Some Girls". Recorded and released by Racey in 1979, the tune was penned by prolific songwriting duo Nicky Chinn and Mike Chapman and became a number 2 hit single in the UK. Chinn and Chapman had initially written the song for American new wave band Blondie but instead gave it to Racey on the strength of the chart success they'd had with an earlier number written by the duo called "Lay Your Love on Me". While "Some Girls" went to number one in twelve countries, including Australia, New Zealand and South Africa, it did not chart in the U.S. and was unknown to American audiences, making its retro rock style ideal for the purposes of the *Happy Days* episode. It seems ironic that a song that did not break into the American music charts in 1979 is finally heard by U.S. audiences five years later in the context of being a song that has broken into the charts, albeit fictitiously. An intriguing parallel exists with another Chapman and Chinn song written for Racey titled "Kitty" and recorded by the band in 1979. While unknown in the United States, "Kitty" was re-recorded in 1981 by Toni Basil, who changed the song title and lyric to "Mickey", which went on to take top position on the Billboard Top 100 in December 1982.

As Howard and Joanie come downstairs to investigate the commotion, Marion blurts out that Chachi is on the radio but that the radio is broken. Animated by the thrilling news, Howard suggests they go out and listen to the song on the car radio. The trio rush through the kitchen and step outside, providing one of the few moments in sitcom history when the entire cast exits the set during filming, leaving the camera with nothing to shoot besides an empty set. In this moment of emptiness the soundtrack becomes the sole storytelling device as a screech of tires is heard followed by a loud crash and protestations from Howard yelling at Chachi.

Howard storms back into the house flanked by Marion and Joanie with Chachi apologizing profusely about the fender bender but unable to contain his excitement about his song playing on the radio. Howard quickly forgets about the crash as the foursome decide to go next door to listen to the neighbor's radio. They make to leave when Fonzie appears on cue and repairs the Cunningham's radio with his trademark magic touch, just in time to hear the DJ back announce Chachi's track. As Marion and Joanie squeal with excitement Chachi declares, "That's it everybody, I'm on my way! Next stop gold record and then pretty soon you'll be going to the movies and watching my life story". Howard dryly retorts, "When they make the story of your life, how will they get our cars apart?" and Chachi returns to earth, again apologizing for the bungle and explaining that he's been having trouble with his brakes. When Fonzie points out that Chachi was meant to fix the brakes yesterday, Chachi tells him that he's been feeling fatigued and took a nap instead. Fonzie and Chachi go out to inspect the crash damage as well as work on Chachi's brakes. On their way out Chachi tells the Cunninghams that he will take them out for dinner that evening to celebrate his good news.

That night at Al's Diner, Howard, Marion and Joanie sit at a booth looking over the menu when Chachi struts through the diner's double doors dressed in a bejeweled white jump suit and Howard quips that he looks like Liberace's milk man. Chachi tells the Cunninghams that he has been invited to tour with the Beach Boys and actress Marion Ross exclaims, "Oh, Scott. I'm so proud of you". Realizing her gaffe, Marion instantly turns to Tom Bosley and asks, "Aren't you proud of him, Howard?" Bosley doesn't miss a beat, retorting, "I'm proud of him Marion, I'm proud. Now can we order?" The seasoned cast charges ahead, glossing over the mistake so effortlessly that for the most part it goes unnoticed.

Bursting in with big promotional plans for Chachi, Fonzie brings in a life-size photographed cardboard cutout of his younger cousin and explains how the diner's jukebox is programed to only play his record. Fonzie arranges to accompany Chachi to the tour rehearsal scheduled later in the week and noticing how Chachi has been helping himself to glass after glass of water remarks, "You're drinking more water than a fish on fire." Without calling attention to Chachi's condition, the narrative has been subtly introducing symptoms of diabetes, first with his fatigue and now his unquenchable thirst.

The time for the rehearsal arrives and Chachi is sitting alone in the diner dejectedly throwing vinyl copies of his single into a cardboard box. Fonzie enters agitated and angrily demands to know why Chachi was not ready to meet him for the rehearsal. Chachi tells Fonzie that he quit the tour, explaining that a doctor that gave him a physical examination for insurance purposes diagnosed him with diabetes. Bemused, Fonzie replies, "You don't have diabetes. You're my cousin. You're strong. You're an athlete. You're young. You don't," but Chachi insists, "I got it. That's why I'm thirsty all the time and losing weight." Fonzie's attempts to convince Chachi that he's not diabetic become increasingly desperate until Chachi barks at him, "Why can't you face it Fonz? We're not all like you. Most of us are mortal. We get sick." Resigned to his fate, Chachi walks out, but not before explaining to Fonzie, "Don't you understand? I'm a man without a future. I got no reason to go on tour, or to make records, or fall in love." Alone in the diner and overwhelmed by the prospect of losing his beloved cousin, Fonzie looks heavenward, raises his fist and screams, "Don't you do this to me!"

Later at Al's Diner, Joanie finds Chachi at a table surrounded by books and seemingly on his way to finding a positive path to living with diabetes. She quickly discovers that the books he is consulting are all concerned with morbidity: *Dealing with Death*, *Death and Dignity*, *Death of a Salesman*, and *Death: The Ultimate Diet*. Chachi tells

Joanie that the books are helping him to accept his imminent demise and motivating him to take life threatening risks, such as a skydiving session he has organized for that afternoon. When Joanie attempts to reason with Chachi, he explains, "Once you know you're on the Titanic and you realize all the lifeboats are gone, you might as well join the band, right?"

Desperate to help Chachi, Fonzie is at the Cunningham residence where he seeks the advice of Howard and Marion's Yale-educated nephew Roger who teaches at Jefferson High School. Roger tells Fonzie that people with diabetes must watch their diet, exercise regularly, and take their insulin. He assures a somewhat surprised Fonzie that if diabetics do these three simple things they can lead long, happy, healthy normal lives like everyone else. When Fonzie quizzes Roger as to why Chachi is acting as though diabetes is a death sentence, Roger explains that the change in lifestyle can be daunting. At that moment Joanie rushes in to let Fonzie know about Chachi's skydiving caper in the hopes that he can talk some sense into his cousin. As Fonzie leaves, he quips, "If that boy breaks his leg, he better not come running to me."

Outfitted with a parachute, Chachi has chartered a plane and is having second thoughts about jumping. Glancing at the earth below, he nervously asks, "Aren't you a little high?" Omar assures him he hasn't had a drink in days, and that they need to be high up so that Chachi's chute has sufficient time to open. Losing his footing, Chachi falls out of the plane leaving Omar to chide himself about not getting paid up front. Although the chute opens Chachi gets stuck in a tree, leaving him dangling a few meters from the ground where Fonzie sits on a rock waiting for him. Fonzie shares the good news about managing diabetes but Chachi explains that he is young and irresponsible. "If I forget to take one little shot," he mistakenly says, "I'm history". Fonzie reframes Chachi's situation, suggesting that while diabetes is a drag, it might also be the best thing that has happened to him as it will force him to take responsibility for himself. He promises to buy a new watch with an alarm to remind Chachi to take his insulin, and Chachi finally reveals his true feelings, admitting to Fonzie that he is scared. "Scared is okay," Fonzie replies. "You know what's not okay? To feel ashamed because you got diabetes. That's not allowed."

Back at Al's Diner, everyone is waiting to welcome Chachi home from the tour. Marion presents him with a scrapbook containing all the tour dates and although he is not named in them, Chachi tells her that the crowd's positive response to his performances has convinced him he has what it takes to succeed. "You know," he boasts, "I was the only guy on tour who made every rehearsal, every bus, ever plane." Looking at his new watch, he tells Fonzie that he remembered to take all his insulin. Fonzie expresses his pride in Chachi and Joanie begs him to play a song. Chachi swaggers over to the jukebox and delivers the final line of the episode. It's a sly wisecrack about the song and the truth of its source: "Fasten your seatbelts," he warns, "cause I'm gonna play this song like I never played it before in my life." As he slips a coin into the jukebox the strains of Racey's "Some Girls" take the episode to the end credits.

"Good News, Bad News" contains important narrative arcs for both Fonzie and Chachi. Fonzie's journey from denial to panic and fear reflects a response to diabetes that comes from a place of ignorance, where a lack of information elicits a highly negative reaction. For a moment, Fonzie joins Chachi in viewing diabetes as a death sentence. However, after Fonzie seeks more information about diabetes from Roger, his newfound knowledge empowers him to support Chachi and see the disease not as some frightening aberrant affliction but a condition that, managed properly, will not adversely impact his cousin's quality of life. Chachi's emotional arc in the episode shifts powerfully from elation about his song landing in the charts, where he dreams of a shining road of possibilities ahead of him that even includes a biopic, to nothing but a dark impending death and suicidal ideation. With Fonzie's support Chachi confronts his fear of change that diabetes means for him and finally recaptures his zest for living. Furthermore, he finds that his new regimen has made him more organized and dependable, prompting him to apply a newfound maturity in his life that will help make his dreams a reality.

It is disappointing that this entertaining Very Special Episode of *Happy Days* was omitted from ABC's ratings season line-up for the series and was instead relegated to the network's less popular summer program. The message contained in "Good News, Bad News" about the stigmatization of diabetes is important, discussing as it does the shame and fear that young people diagnosed with diabetes can experience. The episode is also crucial for showing how Chachi's diagnosis gives him the courage and motivation to turn his life around and pull himself together, thereby preparing the way for his eventual proposal and marriage to Joanie in the series finale.

"Landlady" from *Kate & Allie*
Original Air Date: 15 October 1984
By Lee Gambin

Originally, the CBS network that produced the sitcom *Kate & Allie* (1984–1989) wanted to ensure that the two leads went their separate ways at the end of each episode to their own personal bedroom in order to ensure audiences that these women were heterosexual and that there was no lesbianism whatsoever. Critics came to the conclusion that this stated order of direction became the seed for one of the most progressive and intelligent episodes ever written in the realm of queer representation in television, "Landlady" – an episode that dissects not only sexuality and the plight of gay people to be accepted and respected, but it also scrutinizes the role of passing, honesty, the structure of the "new American family" and puts straight characters in the shoes of gay ones, in order to get an understand of "what it feels like to have to hide".

The basic premise of *Kate & Allie* is two single mothers who decide to move in together and raise their kids while struggling with money and being besieged with the problems every working class woman has to face in the big city. These ladies come from a great long line of the working class gal trying to make ends meet in television from those depicts in *It's a Living* (1980–1989) to *Laverne & Shirley* (1976–1983). Kate (Susan Saint James) found the place and has her best pal Allie (Jane Curtin) move in and the two support one another as best they can while juggling jobs, parenting and occasional boyfriends. In this episode, the land lady Janet (Gloria Cromwell) arrives explaining that Allie is an additional renter and therefore the rent must be upped. She tells them that the apartment is a one family home, and therefore this will see an increase in rent, unless of course Kate and Allie are living as lovers. Janet would be completely fine with keeping the rent as it is if these women were a couple ("Gay liberation being what it is!") which is initially a concept not even taken seriously by Kate or Allie. However, after seeing a new possible residence which is a shambles that looks as though multiple murders have taken place there, the ladies decide that they will pretend to be a gay couple in order to keep the rent as it is. Allie initially protests against the idea ("I know I haven't done that much with my heterosexuality lately, but I'm not giving it up!") but comes around and what we see are two straight women having to pass as a lesbian couple.

Eventually, Kate and Allie will have to come out as heterosexual after they take painstaking efforts to build the façade of being gay, which is something that queer people have had to do for centuries: therefore, the role of "passing" is an essential element here in this sharp and intuitive episode. When Janet herself comes out as gay, introducing her lover Miriam (Chevi Colton), the show delivers more of a farcical set up that could be a sitcom extension to *La Cage aux Folles* (1978). The audience's reaction to Janet introducing Miriam, is a combination of shock and then hilarity – it is confusing as it kind of suggests that they are nervously laughing about the fact that this very straight laced old woman could possibly be a lesbian, however these laughs are about the situation that Kate and Allie have gotten themselves into; they don't have to fool a straight woman, they have to fool an out and proud lesbian and her lover. Kate and Allie's lie is an acute representation of years of gay people having to cover up their sexuality and some great scenarios eschew including a moment where Kate's boyfriend Gary (Gary Beach) calls and is referred to as a romantic interest but is quickly dismissed and rendered "just a friend", so it is like a reverse outing.

Something more important about this Very Special Episode is its treatment of the gay couple. Janet and Miriam are wonderful examples of loving lesbians in their senior years and not at all what audiences had been used to previously in representations of lesbians on television. For the most part, a lot of lesbian side characters that would pop up in reference to a male character being romantically involved with them in the past only to point out their inadequacies as men, which would go on right through to something like *Friends* (1994–2004) where the neurotic nerdy Ross (David Schwimmer) had an ex-wife who was "now a lesbian" because he wasn't "male enough", and a semi-running gag in *Seinfeld* (1989–1998) related to George (Jason Alexander). When lesbians turned up as fully fleshed out interesting and sympathetic characters they were usually tragic figures such as Liz in "Cousin Liz" from *All in the Family* (1971–1979), however, here, Janet and Miriam are happy, healthy and functional women. What makes them even more human is the fact that they have a different reaction when they discover Kate and Allie have been pretending to be gay in order to avoid having to pay more rent. Janet is enraged, and takes it as a personal and political attack, that these straight women have used heterosexual privilege to somehow trivialize the plight and struggles of gay women, however Miriam understands their decision to play up the façade of homosexuality. When Kate and Allie are finally outed as straight, there is a brilliant conversation had and it truly has nothing to do with sexuality at all, but all about the concept of family and the complexity of what makes up a family. Janet is just as guilty as Kate and Allie in that she showed no empathy towards these two struggling single mothers trying to survive a world that is just as cold and unfeeling to struggling mothers as it might be to gay senior citizens – her main concern was ensuring that more rent was paid. Kate and Allie plead with Janet, they explain that "A family is anybody who wants to share their lives together" and that them being two single straight mothers with kids living together is just as valid as people living in monogamous relationships, they also admit that they "now understand" lesbian couples.

Another element in this episode that makes profound commentary on the role of passing and homosexuality depicted in American situation comedy is the fact that Allie makes reference to another hit show whose basic premise was built upon the central character pretending to be gay, where she says "I refuse to live *Three's Company*!" Here she is mentioning a television series which has the running gag of a straight man as played by John Ritter posing to be gay in order to "get away with living with two hot women". Ritter would throw himself into the role with great comic gusto and deliver some hilarity, however, when he would camp it up to exaggerate "what it means to be a gay man" (which is code for what it means to be mincing, effeminate and also lascivious in a swishy sleazy manner), gay activists and lobbyists would take offence to the portrayal as not only a done to death stereotype but also a bit of a dig at an oppressed people who have for centuries had to accommodate and hide in order to make the straight world feel more comfortable. In essence, as fun as *Three's Company* (1976–1984) could be, this episode of *Kate & Allie* somehow cures that running joke and brings it home and delivers an interesting and important statement: that gay people have been forced to hide forever, and now when straight people are put in that situation, possible redemption may be made.

Two divorced single moms trying to make it work in Kate & Allie *as played by Susan Saint James and Jane Curtin. Balancing relationships with men, jobs, children, Kate and Allie would represent an era of women struggling to make ends meet in a world lacking opportunity.*

"It Only Hurts When I'm Gay" from *Brothers*
Original Air Date: 25 October 1984
By Lee Gambin

Years before *Will & Grace* (1998–2020) came out and revolutionized queer themed television, Showtime, a network that never shied away from supposedly controversial subject matter, delivered a seldom discussed situation comedy that featured a gay character as its principal, and had him navigate a world that for the most part posed crucial conflict. In its early seasons, *Brothers* (1984–1989) was fundamentally about a masculine gay man who comes out late in life and is forced to face a whole lot of misunderstanding, abuse, isolation as well as higher learning while his heterosexual siblings have to work through their own homophobia in order to see their younger brother as the "Cliffie" they always loved. While Billy Crystal's Jodie from *Soap* (1977–1981) was part of the fabric of a sitcom dominated by heterosexual plots, *Brothers* – which ran for five years and impressed critics with its rich writing and complex methods of dealing with social topics – gave a sturdy and dominant voice in the character of Cliff Waters (Paul Regina), a sports journalism major who comes out as gay on the day of his wedding. His brothers, Lou (Brandon Maggart), an uncouth and rough construction foreman and Joe (Robert Walden), a retired footballer who now owns a sports bar called The Point After, are initially shocked and disheartened by their younger brother's homosexuality, and as the series moved forward, subject matter centered on the misconceptions, diverse issues gay people of the mid to late eighties had to face and the endless hushed to overt homophobia were examined in an intelligent and incredibly thoughtful manner. *Brothers* presented fag jokes as well as empowered sissies, it expressed character complexity and social politics that did not paint a clean cut and dry picture of how people are – in this series, gay men and straight men had one major core point of similarity – they were both men.

The series would have a number of episodes that would tackle issues that would be deemed Very Special Episodes, however, because this show would easily fit into the wave of television sitcoms such as *Cheers* (1982–1993) and then later *Roseanne* (1988–2018) that would merge character arcs, drama and outstanding comedic writing, it would tap into a dramedy status that would bring audiences to tears through the laughter, after all, this show would be focused on a group of mostly single working class people (including Robin Riker as sassy waitress Kelly and Hallie Todd as Joe's daughter Penny) all working life out together (but fundamentally, on their own). However, there are a number of episodes that would be revolutionary in that they would take a subject that would normally be left for a dramatic series or a police procedural. Gay bashing would be the focal point of "It Only Hurts When I'm Gay" (a beautiful take on the Neil Simon play and subsequent film adaptation *Only When I Laugh* (1981)) and what the episode does is not only express an interest in how homophobic police authorities can be so callous in regards to such a matter, as well as the horrors of being beaten to a pulp by men who have such a deep rooted hatred of sexuality outside of heteronormative, but it also paints an interesting picture of the character so remarkably bigoted in the show and gives him a moment of reflection and sincere compassion. Lou is a hard as nails Archie Bunker-type, and upon meeting a shy and lonely older gay man in this episode, he comes to understand that the "gay world" is more diverse than what he initially thought of it to be.

The episode opens with Cliff expressing his need to go out and meet men. In an attempt to find sexual encounters, he tells his brothers that there is a cruising place in the park near the local amusement park. Donald (Philip Charles MacKenzie), Cliff's effeminate and proudly swishy friend and confidant, enters the scene after Cliff re-enters a follow up sequence where he sports a mighty nasty shiner. Donald, an empowering character and a terrific throwback to the "sissy faggot" characters of Hollywood's pre-code era but made overtly homosexual and unapologetically flamboyant and verbose, serves as not only a "funny fag" but also as the guiding light of absolute truth and enlightenment. Donald is the character throughout the series that helps the gay Cliff not hate himself, teaches Joe and Lou all about compassion and builds Kelly's confidence in being a decidedly single woman who doesn't have to feel lonely. Cliff's shiner prompts hiding ("it's nothing, I got into a fight") and the episode reinforces the ideology that for centuries gay people have had to remain silent and invisible in order not to upset the heterosexual world. The interaction between straight people who are allies (Kelly and Penny) and straight people who are nervous about homosexuality (Joe and Lou) is what serves a lot of the comedy in *Brothers,* but when the subject is gay bashing and with the likeable Cliff being the one getting the beating, the less sympathetic characters act up and decide to become make-shift vigilantes, fighting back. What is especially telling about this sequence is when a statement is made that homophobes are not homosexual (Joe explaining to the simple minded Lou what "homophobia" means), and this is met with the incredibly insightful Donald remarking "Don't be so sure". Here, the sentiment is made clear and an acute commentary on the history of gay bashing is dissected. Studies during the mid-eighties reported that closeted gay men made up a large quota of those committing gay bashings. Violence against gay people in public spaces (such as parks, city streets, suburban landscapes et al) increased during the advent of the AIDS epidemic, and it would be noted that a lot of these violent acts were perpetrated by self-loathing gay men who felt that men who were out and proud could jeopardize their closeted and secretive rendezvous that lived in the shadow of the fear of contracting the dreaded disease.

Homophobia also lives in the police's response to Cliff after he called them to report his attack. "You got what you deserved, faggot" is a striking statement that lingers as the scene closes. The fade to black to commercial break is grim and leaves a bad taste in the audience's mouth. It also shuts up any queer jokes as made by the incorrigible

Lou. While the series dealt with gay issues and the complexities of relations shared between gay men and the straight world – as well as gay men navigating a world they are oppressed within – the show would feature a few episodes that would stand out as major social commentators including one dealing with a sports star coming out as both gay and HIV+, the strained relationships gay men have with their fathers as well as the fear of being lonely and not permitted to be loved. Here in "It Only Hurts When I'm Gay" the idea of straight men "coming to the rescue" is a basis of the rules of masculinity – in that it seems that what the writers are saying here that even in a world solely understood by gay men (a world of being crucified simply because your sexuality angers people) needs to be "saved" by the supposedly righteous fighting tactics of hetero counterparts. Joe and Lou wish to trap the assailant, and joined by Donald (the gay man who can give these hopeless straight men an "in" to the cruising world) they set out to avenge Cliff.

A lot of the gags come from the notion of what heterosexual men think gay men do. When Lou spots two men in flannel shirts walking through the park holding hands, he says "They ain't gay, they were dressed like construction workers!" The perception of the blur between masculinity and homosexuality is at play here, and in Lou's eyes "real men" are tough like labor workers and "faggots" are effete like Donald. This ideology remains as Lou attempts to lure men in order to chase up the gay bashers, but he does learn something else, as aforementioned. Upon meeting the older gentleman who is shy and walking through the park hoping to meet someone kind and affectionate ("I'm just an old fashioned guy looking for a nice relationship") and not solely for a meaningless sexual encounter, Lou's perception of gay men changes. He even asks the elderly gent if he could be appealing to him, which has the sweet old man reply "I'm lonely but not crisis center lonely". His joke then sadly leads into self-pity, but honesty: "Not many guys find me appealing". Here, the self-loathing, the sadness, the isolation and the endless rejection as components of many gay men's lives comes to the fore, and Lou's attitude is altered. In this episode – which is fundamentally about the horrors of gay bashing – issues of ageism and alienation within a "gay community" is equally scrutinized.

Lou's interaction with the police officer who is posing as a man cruising for sex leads him, Joe and Donald to being arrested for loitering and proposing sex in public places. The jail cell sequence is a microcosm of gender politics with one of the thugs who had beaten Cliff being scared off by Donald's well-poised threat that echoes generations of strong, street smart sissy gay men who can fight for themselves and stand up to oppressive bullies. When this moment happens it is a counter to what Joe and Lou intended – the idea of straight men being able to defend their "fag brother". Here, the pansy Donald is the heroic figure, terrifying a homophobe and sending him to the corner of the cell. With the narrative inclusion of police being completely unhelpful and the head gay basher being a police chief's son who "learnt homophobia", the episode comes to a close with Cliff announcing his pride in his brothers for defending him and standing up to him but also defiant about having to hide and remain closeted. He also discussed the fact that hate is intergenerational and when people start to accept and be compassionate for everyone, then the future may look promising. When asked if they will still continue to cruise that particular beat, Donald responds: "I'm not being scared off" and this fearless warrior with his limp wrists and lisp continues to fight and defend his rights as a man living in a world that remains a constant enemy. However, it is Lou's final statement which shines an insight into his newfound learning about the diversity of gay people (in that homosexuals are just as varied as heterosexuals) that cements this episode as a special one. Lou tells his brother and his brother's best pal that if they ever come across the elderly gent he met in the park not to dismiss him simply because he isn't young or good looking. Lou says, "Don't be put off by appearances – he's a nice fella". This is a testament to diversity; that a man like the straight and rough 'n tumble Lou has more in common with the older gay man cruising the park looking for love and not just sex than youthful Cliff would have with him even though he's also homosexual. Donald's smile over Lou's sentiment is loving and the idea of gay men not being superficial is the counter argument to them not having to accept the fact that they should be rejected, hated or beaten.

"Baby of the Family" from *Gimme a Break!*
Original Air Date: 8 December 1984
By Lee Gambin

Nell Carter was a force of nature, both as an actress and singer, but also as someone who faced a multitude of struggle. Without going into a lengthy history of Carter – the woman and the artist – there is a lot of what the sitcom *Gimme a Break!* (1981–1987) gave her that bounced off her personal labors and fed into what she stood for and what shaped her. *Gimme a Break!* would reintroduce the archetype of the sassy mammy, a black stock character heavily used in cinema of the thirties and forties, and bring her into an eighties context for audiences eager to see how Carter would take on the role of a caretaker to a white household marked with an absentee mother. Considering the stunning performances from actresses such as Hattie McDaniel and Louise Beavers who embodied the classic role of the mammy, upon reaching the complicated eighties the purpose of such a character would be remodeled and repurposed but still possessing the major attributes that made the figure a culturally significant and multi-dimensional one: she was a woman who was strong, forthright, independent minded and always with a stern mindset as to what was correct and what was wrong.

Nell's (Nell Carter) love for youngster Joey (Joey Lawrence) and her love for teenage Samantha (Lara Jill Miller) is infinite and without question, however, the episode "Baby of the Family" forces the audience to consider the possibility of black oppression even in a supposedly enlightened period and within the construct of a series that always had its white children love and respect their black housekeeper without any issue of race being something that made a negative impact. The addition of Joey Lawrence, a child star who made a huge impression on an episode of *The Tonight Show Starring Johnny Carson* (1962–1992), would fall into what the American sitcom lexicon would have us consider as the "Cousin Oliver Syndrome" – established by *The Brady Bunch* (1969–1974), where a series that was proving to have ratings concern would introduce a young cute kid to the fold to mix it up and deliver something new and fresh. Sometimes this worked, other times it did not – and here, in "Baby of the Family", the meta-concern of having a cute kid brought in to take center stage is somehow discussed in a fascinating and complicated way. Samantha clearly was the youngest before the addition of Joey, and throughout the episode she laments that she is not the "baby" anymore (the way an older sibling may find the affections going to the youngest problematic). Actress Lara Jill Miller would go on the record to say that the addition of Joey Lawrence wasn't something she was too fond of, and this was clearly because of the quality of the show possibly going downhill, however Lawrence's talents proved to be a hit with audiences and in this particular episode, his take on Al Jolson come into play – albeit to shock.

The episode unfolds with Samantha wanting to go on a camping trip with boys which of course sparks protest from Nell. Nell's protection of Samantha is palpable and super real, and the angry teen defends her right to the trip with "Stop treating me like a baby!" (a sentiment that will highlight a hypocrisy as the episode moves forward). Joey, who is going to perform for Nell's church congregation, comes off as competition to Samantha, and Nell mothers him with cushy warmth. When Samantha hollers at the boy, Nell barks at her: "Don't yell at this child!" Samantha's responds: "Why are you always on his side?!" Samantha's anger grows and becomes destructive, while Nell tries to keep the household in shape and in working order.

Enter Nell's best friend and sometimes friendly rival Adelaide "Addy" Wilson (Telma Hopkins) who discusses the handsome reverend who is going to be in attendance at the church sermon. This subplot is vitally important as it is there to point out that *Gimme a Break!* is a brilliantly conceived TV sitcom that generates the notion that Nell is more than a one dimensional domestic. Here we get to understand that there is a wonderfully rich and rewarding black world that exists outside of being a housekeeper to a white family. In many ways, this is similar to the white Lana Turner coming to understand that the black Juanita Moore has an entire world outside of their own relationship in the second version of the heartbreaker *Imitation of Life* (1959). Also, Nell Carter's incredible singing talent is showcased in this episode when she knocks out a magnificent number at the church congregation that sends chills down the spines of anyone who understands remarkable vocal ability. Also inside the family household, Nell runs the roost – she is in charge – and being part of the lineage and elongated history of mammies in film, she is a perfectly realized addition to what truly is an empowering model; yes these characters were in servitude roles, but they were almost always dynamic, captivating, richly constructed and with a lot to say.

Joey's addiction to Johnny Carson (more meta details) influences Samantha's snitching on him, and the grouchy teen does everything she can to get the boy into trouble because she is not allowed to go camping. Nell has her own issues with Joey, who is supposed to be rehearsing his number for the church sermon coming up. Joey's take on vaudeville is peppered throughout the show, and more throwbacks to a bygone era are established and propel the episode forward. But these sidebars are easily missed as the plot thickens – and at the heart of the plot here, the rivalry between a teenager wanting independence yet being jealous of a younger "sibling" and the stoic sass of a housekeeper is what matters. "You raise a child and you give them love and what do you get in return? Hate!" A powerful statement in this episode which eventuates into something heavy and politically grim. Nell's maternal role being questioned is matched by Joey doing an impression of Michael Jackson's "Thriller" (white kids' admiration of black artists) and the writing dances with race and the arts as it progresses.

When Grandpa Stanley (John Hoyt) shares his love of vaudeville legend Al Jolson with Joey, the precocious boy learns the American Songbook classic "Toot Toot Tootsic", and he is set to perform the number for Nell's church service. Nell's attempts to talk to Samantha and smooth over their fight over the camping issue is interrupted by Joey's singing and in turn Samantha's anger turns into something more malicious. When she hears Joey's insecurities about his impending performance and when he says "I wish I could do it like Al Jolson!", Samantha has an idea – something nasty to get back at Nell. Samantha gets Joey into blackface (a costuming device used by the likes of Al Jolson) as an attack on Nell, and something to shock her congregation.

With the aforementioned handsome reverend in attendance, Joey's performance rattles the service, and the stunned and silent reaction of the black folk while Joey parades around donning the concerning minstrel attire is deafening. The ghoulishness of blackface (and especially on a child) is unsettling but not without its complications. Al Jolson was an artist who ushered in the rights of black performers and was a massive champion of black artists, however, in an eighties sensibility, the idea of performing a minstrel show without any understanding on how it could enrage or upset people of color is remarkably shocking and possibly disrespectful. The history of blackface, much like Nell Carter's life and career, does not need to be examined or discussed here in this essay, however, it is a complex artistic form that is vitally important when exploring the history of American theatre and entertainment. Samantha's intentions were ugly, Joey's performance came from not knowing any better, and the reaction from Nell and her congregation is a genuinely appropriate one.

While Nell doesn't see race – she doesn't see "white", much like the good-hearted white people in television history who don't see "black" – she does take massive offence to what Joey has done here. When she scolds him: "Don't you realize you were making fun of black people?", the poor tyke says that he wanted to do it like Al Jolson, and that Al Jolson was black. Nell informs him that he wasn't (Jolson, a white Jewish entertainer) and it leads to her racing home after discovering that it was Samantha's idea to get him into blackface all along. Nell's fury and the confrontation in the kitchen is the heart of the episode, and when Samantha obnoxiously remarks "Didn't all your church friends love little cute Joey?", we see her pain come through a mask of bratty behavior. "You are being a baby!" yells Nell, and Samantha cries "I'm not your baby anymore!" The jealousy and spite all coming to the fore, and the fear of losing Nell to the smaller and younger Joey expressed and outed. But this is an aside to the first issue at hand, Nell's rage at the blackface performance. The episode cuts deep with Nell spitting out: "I never thought that I would live to see the day when you would use the word 'nigger.'" Much like the audience, Samantha is shocked. "Nell, that's horrible! I would never say that!" This girl who never once saw race is repulsed by the idea of being labelled a racist. She is disgusted by the very thought. But Nell educates her: "That's what you did by putting Joey in blackface".

When Nell says "I never loved you because you were the baby, I loved you because you were Samantha", we all begin to understand the heart of this sitcom. What this line is actually saying is that race does not matter and that love is for everyone. Here, we accept and honor the beautiful fact that feisty black women who run households can love angst-ridden white teenage girls and that the same teenage girl can find solace in loving a hyperactive musically inclined youngster who also happens to be white. Samantha also comes out of this empowered, thanks to Nell. She learns that it is enough to be Samantha – not the "baby of the house" – but a young lady who is devoted to her loving Nell, the magician who works wonders in the household she governs.

Interestingly enough, blackface had been used to out racism and to bring unity. In the *Diff'rent Strokes* (1978–1986) episode "Skin Deep or True Blue", Kimberly (Dana Plato) comes to understand that her latest boyfriend is a racist, which inspires the bright teen to don blackface to make a point. Her triumphant rejection of this bigoted kid empowers the young lady who loves her black brothers and never sees color whatsoever. Earlier examples of blackface used to point out racism and to make an attempt to overcome bigotry and prejudice can be seen in the episode "Sisters At Heart" from *Bewitched* (1964–1972), which has Samantha (Elizabeth Montgomery) fight horrible viewpoints on black people with her magic by turning herself and others, including husband Darrin (Dick Sargent) black for a moment in an expression of racial solidarity with hopes of changing a racist's politics.

A TV Guide ad for "Baby of the Family" which delves into the problematic nature of blackface on Gimme a Break!.

"Jill's Decision" from *Charles in Charge*
Original Air Date: 23 January 1985
By Lee Gambin
With Very Special insight from actress Julie Cobb

The whole premise behind *Charles in Charge* (1984–1990) is based on working parents needing that extra help around the house with domestic duties as well as helping in the rearing of their children. Within this construct was the incessant reminder that these working parents were continually – and for the most part, unapologetically – far too busy to take on the vacuuming, dusting or reading little Johnny and Susie a bedtime story. The eighties television sitcom exploited this wave of story structure giving the movies of the time that dealt with similar concerns a run for their money. Motion pictures such as *Mr. Mom* (1983) featured working mothers leaving their households and domestic duties in order to pursue their careers, while husbands were left wrestling with the washing machine or struggling to keep children in line, while films like *Baby Boom* (1987) fixed their focus on ambitious and driven professional women who had to find the balance between vocation and motherhood. For the most part, these films would employ what could be construed as sexist overtones, but the gender politics examined in such comedy outings gave a responsive voice to the questions left behind by second wave feminism of the seventies, and a difference in opinion come the Me-Generation pull of the eighties.

A television show like *Charles in Charge* is an inversion of *Mr. Mom* and its peers, because here long-standing TV and movie star Scott Baio provides hope as Charles, the college student who takes on the role of care taker to a family that needs that extra hand. In the softly peddled Very Special Episode "Jill's Decision", Charles has to balance being confidant, friend and teacher to young Lila (April Lerman), Douglas (Jonathan Ward) and Jason (Michael Pearlman), while tending to household duties as well as courting a new girlfriend. All of this hangs on the fine line that matriarch of the house Jill (Julie Cobb) dances between being a working writer – who has just gotten a promotion that demands more of her time and focus – and being an active and "dutiful" mother.

> **JULIE COBB:** Back then I had just become a mother, my daughter was born in 1983 in September and we did the pilot in early 1984, so I was juggling those things – being a mom and having a career. I auditioned for the show like I auditioned for everything back then, but I was also very excited to be a mother so I was not too eager to go out of town to work, and I wasn't too keen on working on single camera one hour drama shows where you would have to work all day and into the evening. So, with *Charles in Charge* which was a situation comedy and

using the four camera technique would mean we would rehearse for four days a week and then tape on a Friday night. The Friday nights could get very late however, because long after the studio audience had left, we would do reshoots. So I was able to go to work at Universal Pictures which was very close to where I was living, and I had a nice big dressing room and I had a playpen in my dressing room, so by the time we did the pilot and the show was picked up by CBS, I would come to work with my baby, with Rosemary, and everybody knew her, and I would bring my housekeeper who was much more than that to us, she was like another grandmother. Anyway, they would all come along to work and every time I wasn't needed, I would go to them and play with Rosemary which really characterized the rest of my career quite frankly. I wanted to be with Rosemary. And this episode really resonates with me because of how personal it was to me. *Charles in Charge* was a blast – we would go to work and laugh all day. It was a lot of fun.

The opening of the episode features Charles polishing the floors; instantly establishing him as a young man comfortable with taking on traditional "women's jobs" – which is essentially a concoction founded by the lore of situation comedy: the endless slew of TV moms cooking and cleaning throughout history such as June Cleaver from *Leave it to Beaver* (1957–1963), Harriet Nelson on *The Adventures of Ozzie and Harriet* (1952–1966) and so forth. Adding to this, when his girl crazy best friend Buddy (Willie Aames) enters the scene, Charles lists the endless tasks he has to do also stating that he has to make time to win the heart of his latest lady friend Michelle Harris (Michelle Nicastro), who is lauded as an ideal potential long term partner and not just a fleeting fling. Besides all of this, Charles has to help out the kids – Douglas's problem with dancing, Jason's issues with his school play and Lila's newfound interest in softball. The episode hammers a not-so-subtle message here, which all comes down to Jill's role as a mother: that all of these issues Charles is forced to deal with, would possibly be non-issues if Jill was around to tend to her own children's needs.

Outside of eighties sensibilities, "Jill's Decision" sings the same tune as many "Women's Pictures" from the thirties and forties, where incredibly gifted and ambitious (and sometimes successful) women would have to make life altering, life affirming but sometimes devastating sacrifices in order to keep husbands and children happy. These films would star the likes of Joan Crawford, Claudette Colbert, Bette Davis, Olivia de Havilland, Katharine Hepburn and many more – actresses that kept studios afloat and with great vigor did things their way. However, the difference between these films from this period such as *Imitation of Life* (1934), *Jezebel* (1938) and *A Stolen Life* (1946) and eighties corporate world/domestic domain comedies was that the early Hollywood masterworks were intricate in plot and character and painted with dramatic flair and a complex, powerful glamor, while films such as *Baby Boom* reflected a disdain and discredit to what seventies second wave feminism opened doors to. The concept of being both a dedicated mother and corporate professional seemed foreign to many filmmakers taking on the subject in the format of comedy cinema.

> **JULIE COBB:** The truth is I probably didn't want more acting jobs. I was a good actress and I was very fortunate to get some excellent roles and some great jobs, but I wasn't that ambitious. Another thing that I wish I felt differently about in retrospect is that James Widdoes who played my husband on the show went on to direct and I also went on to be a director in the theatre and made a short film that I wrote and directed, but in those days I never really went on about my career or thought about my career. For me to say if I wish my character had more to do on *Charles in Charge*, I don't know if I could say yes to that, I had a wonderful time on the show and more so a wonderful time with Rosemary, my daughter. I got to have a career in spite of my lack of ambition, and I'm the person I am today and not at all chomping at the bit to have more to do. I know that James Widdoes had a very healthy appetite to do more.

Charles in Charge gives the matriarch of the household a freelance job as a writer, however when Jill is promoted to a full time position as the arts and fashion editor, the stress of it all gets to her and puts a strain on her own connection to her children. From her first appearance in the episode, she tears herself away from her work and races downstairs where she declares "I wanted an excuse to come and see everybody!" Bubbly and vivacious character actress Julie Cobb throws herself into the role of a woman who feels growing guilt, and the performance is honest and valid. Cobb, who had become a pop-cultural icon with her performance of Bonnie Sawyer in Tobe Hooper's epic TV miniseries adaptation of prolific horror author Stephen King's *Salem's Lot* (1979), is a versatile and buoyant actress, and here in *Charles in Charge*, she does more than play the woman of the house who comes in and out happy to let her live-in ward take control of the situation. She is actively interested in her household, just as much as she is with her off-screen work. When she expresses her desire to spend more time with her family, we understand her dilemma; however, the show tips her promotion down the gurgler and turns her career into the unseen "monster" of the piece.

> **JULIE COBB:** My feelings on working mothers has changed since the time I shot the show. "Jill's Decision" mirrored my career at the time – being a new mother, not wanting to go out of town to work, the idea of not doing more demanding and possibly more fulfilling work because it would have taken me away from being a mother. But now, looking back at that episode I wish that the writers on *Charles in Charge* could have resolved the issue where Jill could have done both – had the promotion and been a mom. I don't know how, but it could have worked somehow. I mean she took the old fashioned decision, they set her up in a modern world with these conquests and choices and challenges, but at the end of the day,

at the end of the show, she falls back into type, shall we say? She makes a sacrifice. I wish she could have had it all. My father Lee J. Cobb left a big impression on me. When I was a child and I wanted to be an actress and also have a family, he said to me "No. You can't have both. If you have an acting career, you can't have a family, you can't have both." So as a child we absorb what our parents tell us, but I went ahead and tried to do both but frankly I did both not really believing that I could do both. Today, there are a lot of great actresses who do both and are also excellent mothers, they just work it out and do both. But in 1984 it was a very different time and it was right on that cusp of transition. We never followed Jill or Stan to work. I think it was cool that they made Jill a writer instead of say a part time substitute teacher or something. But her writing career was never developed. Her job was more so just a tag.

Adding insult to all this, Charles is forced into having to take Douglas and Jason with him on his date with Michelle, while Jill desperately insists on having a moment away from writing. When she puts her foot down to taking on more work with her editor in chief, she says yes to three propositions from her children, which paves the way for her to playing with the boys. A clumsy attempt at showcasing Jill's detachment from her sons comes with her playing with their toy tank and bleating out a "Beep beep" which instantly disturbs young Douglas and Jason. Interrupting this awkward moment comes a phone call where it's learned that a fellow writer has the flu and is unable to cover the mayor's daughter's marriage. "It comes with the job" says the defeatist Jill, and being the head of the department, she is obligated to work and cover the story. Jill remains flustered by juggling between being active in her children's lives and her career and her conversation with Jason (set to maudlin music that ushers in and highlights the "serious moment") in regards to his play sits at the heart of the piece – the message here being that mothers should always have their children's best interest at heart, and that everything else (including a supposedly important writing gig) can wait. The scene ends with Jill accepting the fact that her job detracts from her time with her family ("I know this promotion takes up more of my time") and her promising to work on the play with Jason. Jill's career affecting Charles's own life (most notably, his romantic life) is also a major factor here, and with the kids being needy, Jill is basically pushed back into the role of freelance writer and full time mother.

JULIE COBB: I remember distinctly the scene where I was playing with the trucks with the boys and going "Vroom! Vroom!" and that was clearly there to point out my estrangement from the kids. This kind of thing would then of course force Jill to go back and do a part time role in the workplace and make more time for the family. I don't think the show was meant to be some kind of educational piece, but I do know for a fact that it was co-produced by an educational department head. Michael Jacobs, who created the show, remained with the show for the first season. He had a

Julie Cobb (with co-star James Widdoes) as Jill Pembroke from Charles in Charge *represents another version of the quintessential 80s TV mom; careerist and independent but also devoted to her children and husband. Cobb and the cast of characters that made up her family would sadly be replaced by the second season of the show.*

deal with producer Jane Rosenthal who ran a Scholastic company that was geared towards kids, but I don't think she had any creative input for the show. It was definitely on prime time here in the USA and was never aimed at young viewers.

When Michelle makes a point of missing the noise of a busy household (sometimes that she is not privy to now being a college girl), Jill relates and decides that she doesn't want to keep her promotion. Jill's sacrifice for her children is this VSE's answer (understandable to personal circumstance, socially sexist or whatever), and this is something that builds what truly is a subtle but important thematically driven account.

JULIE COBB: It wasn't innate for me to play a mother before having children. I had made a career out of playing the ingénue or the young girl or the sexy single girl, so playing a mother wasn't an easy task for me. I remember April Haney who played my daughter Lila who was fourteen years old at the time and I was like "How can I be her mother? She's a teenager! It doesn't feel right." So it took a while for me to get a handle on that and make it feel right. Creatively it took me a while to get my head around the fact that I was playing a woman who had a fourteen year old daughter! Eventually I became incredibly maternal to them all, and we were very much like a family, so when the show ended that is why it was even more painful for me than anyone else. I lost touch with them and that was that. Scott Baio was easy to work with and he was very professional. He was managed by his father and his mother was always on the set. She was a very sweet Italian woman named Rose, and she and her husband were ever present. I felt that Scott was a little bit under the thumb of his father. Scott was like an overgrown teenager. He and Willie Aames were really like their characters. We all loved each other, there was a lot of warmth and fun and laughter on that set, and Scott and Willie were all part of that. I never heard of Willie Aames's addiction problems at the time, he was completely professional. Michael Pearlman could not get through a line without cracking up! He would deliver his joke and you would always see a grin, ready to break out into laughter! He was so sweet and adorable. We would always laugh at that and leave it. I mean Jerry Seinfeld does the same thing! He can't keep a straight face. You know Meg Ryan played an almost girlfriend of Scott's and I got Matthew Perry his first television job, I was friends with his mother and father and I knew this part was coming up, and I knew they were moving down from Canada and I suggested him and he got the role. Meg and Matthew of course would go on to be major stars. The studio audience were very enthusiastic. They came from everywhere and were big fans. I do remember one time I had the flu and I was off-camera and about to enter the scene, and I almost passed out trying to not cough. Live television is very challenging, I mean there are a lot of start/stops unlike theatre where you would just keep going, but you don't want to be the one that causes the stop. When the audience would go home, we would be there until 2 a.m. or 3 a.m. tidying off the scenes.

"The Uh-Oh Feeling" from *Webster*
Original Air Date: 25 January 1985
By Matthew Krause

When *Webster* premiered on ABC in September 1983, it was hard *not* to draw comparisons to NBC's *Diff'rent Strokes* (1978–1986). Both shows were about a white family given charge over black child/children, but ABC, perhaps anticipating criticism, took pains to differentiate *Webster* from its network rival. While Mr. Drummond (Conrad Bain), the adoptive parent of *Diff'rent Strokes*, is a widower, *Webster*'s titular figure is given *two* guardians – recently married George and Katherine Papadopolis (Alex Karras and Susan Clark). Arnold and Willis (Gary Coleman and Todd Bridges), the two black children of *Diff'rent Strokes*, are underclass boys from Harlem whose deceased mother worked for Mr. Drummond; young Webster comes from an upper-middle-class background, the son of a former pro-football player and product of a two-parent home (Webster ends up with the Papadopolises when his parents die in a car accident and godfather George is given guardianship). Both shows draw much of their humor from their pint-size black stars, but while Arnold Drummond on *Diff'rent Strokes* is sassy and streetwise (Gary Coleman honed his style through guest appearances on *Good Times* (1974–1979), *The Jeffersons* (1975–1985) and *Hello, Larry* (1979–1980)), Emmanuel Lewis's Webster stole our hearts with his quirky voice, unbridled optimism, and infectious laugh. Promos for *Webster* promised laughter and life lessons, and Nielson homes responded, sustaining the series for six seasons.

Despite the similarities, *Webster* quickly became its own animal. Emmanuel Lewis, twelve years old but playing a child of five, was charismatic and charming, with the comedic timing of a seasoned pro (TV audiences were already familiar with his commercials for Burger King, Campbell's Soup, Life cereal, and Welch's grape juice). Alex Karras and Susan Clark, who played Webster's guardians, had been married for three years at the start of show, and their natural chemistry as a married couple shines in even the spottiest of dialogue (the two actors had worked together previously as gold medalist/pro golfer Babe Didrikson and her husband George Zaharias in the 1975 biopic *Babe*). The show's writers gave *Webster* a lighter touch than that of *Diff'rent Strokes*, at times almost too light. Early episodes dealt with innocuous family crises – Webster lies about his birthday to get a party at school; Webster makes the school football team despite his diminutive size because his father played pro; Webster arranges a "real" wedding for George and Katherine, who eloped in episode one, so they won't fight, and so on. The issue of Webster's race wasn't really addressed until mid-season when Katherine's sociologist friend Ellen (Freddye Chapman) states that Webster belongs with black parents (a premise similar to the *Diff'rent Strokes* episode "The Social Worker" premiering five years earlier).

Webster found more dramatic legs late in the first season, introducing Ben Vereen as Webster's Uncle Phil and ending season one with a custody battle cliffhanger. After resolving custody, the series took its first step toward more maturity with "Knock, Knock," in which Webster witnesses George and Katherine having an intimate moment and tries to recreate it with his best friend Charlene. The suggestion of childhood sexual experimentation was vague to say the least, but "Knock Knock" did set the stage for "The Uh-Oh Feeling," a Very Special Episode airing three months later just after the series' winter hiatus.

While sexual abuse of children has been present throughout history, widespread public awareness in the United States did not occur until the 1970s. When the Child Abuse Prevention and Treatment Act was enacted in 1974, legal action against sexual abusers became more prevalent, resulting in a dramatic increase in the number of documented sex abuse cases. Nonetheless, many cases still went unreported, compelling activists and advocates to create the National Abuse Coalition in 1979 with the intent of pressuring Congress to create more sexual abuse laws. In the early 1980's, research indicated that as much as 63% of adult women had been molested as minors, bringing child sex abuse to the forefront. Counselors and social workers looked for creative ways to reach children, giving them tools they could use to avoid and report sexual predators.

The subject of child sexual abuse remained a somewhat taboo subject for television until the ABC TV movie *Something About Amelia* premiered in January 1984, in which nice guy Ted Danson (whom audiences had fallen in love with on NBC's *Cheers* (1982–1993)) portrays a respectable and likable family man who is secretly having sex with his fourteen-year-old daughter (Roxana Zal, in an Emmy-winning performance). One year later, ABC would follow up on *Something About Amelia*'s themes with the *Webster* episode "The Uh-Oh Feeling," in which Webster witnesses a popular substitute teacher making inappropriate advances toward his best friend Beth (Alison Sweeney).

"The Uh-Oh Feeling" opens with an establishing shot of Webster's school, while the voice of Mr. Todson, Webster's substitute math tutor, drones over the soundtrack. Mr. Todson tells the children to do their homework before dismissing them for the day. Cut to the hallway as children leave the classroom, and Webster tells Beth how much he likes this new tutor even though other kids warn him: "Uh-oh, you got Mr. Todson." As for Mr. Todson himself, it is interesting that his face is never seen throughout the episode. He remains a disembodied voice, in many ways adding to the horror of his actions (the actor who supplies the voice is not even listed in the credits). As Webster expresses his enthusiasm for the new tutor, Mr. Todson voice calls out from the classroom, asking Beth to come in and speak with him alone.

"Wow, he must really like you!" Webster exclaims, a hint of jealousy in his voice.

Beth, however, does not want to reenter the classroom, stating that she just saw Mr. Todson alone the previous day. "I don't think I like the way he likes me," she says.

What follows are an unusually tense 60 seconds for an otherwise ingenuous show like *Webster*. After Beth goes into the classroom, the voice of Mr. Todson states that Webster needs to wait outside the building ("I'll speak to him tomorrow; today is *our* day"). Webster is excited that he will get his own day with the tutor, and he eagerly agrees. He turns to go outside but realizes he has Beth's books. He opens the classroom door to return them... and discovers the true nature of Mr. Todson. The camera locks on Webster's confused face as he witnesses the sexual assault of Beth. Mr. Todson's voice is heard asking for a "big hug" and Beth's voice asks him to "stop tickling me *there*." Mr. Todson reminds her that she let him tickle her yesterday, adding that they are friends and "you can tickle me too." Beth begs to go home, and Todson's voice becomes menacing: "But I don't want you to go home."

Webster springs into action and saves the day, shouting that George and Katherine are outside waiting. Beth escapes, but not before Mr. Todson tells her that their encounter should be "our little secret," adding that if she should tell her parents, "they're not going to like you anymore." In the hallway, Beth is visibly shaken. She asks Webster to promise he won't tell anyone. After some modest objection, Webster agrees.

Viewers catch their collective breath when the show cuts away to the Papadopolis kitchen. George is preparing dinner, singing a song about his cooking prowess. Katherine walks in just as George makes a blunder and teases him with a verse of her own. It is a much-needed return to the show's comedic form. This is the first time in the episode that a laugh track is used. Dinner is served. At the table, Katherine asks Webster what he thinks of his new math tutor, Mr. Todson. Before Webster can answer, George interjects, assuring Katherine that "substitute tutors are a snap," then tells a story about a science tutor he used to torment when he was in school. Katherine's annoyance is played for laughs, but it also establishes an important parental dynamic: as more information is revealed, Katherine will respond appropriately, George not so much, until the gravity of the situation brings them together.

The scenes leading up to the first commercial break is peppered with humor, but a growing sense of unease permeates them. When Webster wakes George and Katherine up in the night pretending to be sick, the viewer squirms, hoping the two adults will notice that something is not quite right. The next morning, Webster rebounds, appearing perhaps *too* chipper as he skips out the door to catch the bus ("Us kids *love* to ride on the school bus," he says when Katherine offers to drive him to school). Katherine is unsettled by the shift in Webster's behavior, but George remains the fool, dropping Yogi Berra one-liners to escalate his oblivion ("Kids. They're just like children").

Just before commercial, the show takes a hard turn back into drama. George and Katherine discover that Webster did not go to the bus and is hiding upstairs in his closet. "I don't want to go to school today," he whimpers. "Please don't make me." After commercial, we rejoin the scene *in medias res*; the viewer is spared a recap of the horror Webster witnessed. Webster punctuates the tale of Beth's sexual assault by expressing his own fears. "Tomorrow is *my* turn," he says, recalling the promise of a meeting with Mr. Todson, "and today is tomorrow."

Once again, George and Katherine contrast in terms of reaction. Katherine is the wise nurturer, George the reckless warrior. George's instinct is to rush to the school, confront Mr. Todson and "make patio furniture out of him," a sentiment with which most parents can identify. Katherine provides the voice of reason, suggesting they find a more healing course of action. George is resistant, and his wry sarcasm comes out. "How 'bout if I wrote him a letter," he growls, "saying, 'Dear Mr. Todson, please don't molest our children. It ruins their day.'" The sarcastic wit is just what we want and expect from George, but the absence of a laugh track alerts us that this is no longer the place for it. Instead, George and Katherine contact Beth's mother, Amanda (Meredith MacRae), who at first cannot believe what she is hearing. When Katherine suggests they report the incident, Amanda refuses, fearing humiliation. In the end, however, she will come around, and "The Uh-Oh Feeling" will morph from Very Special Episode to Public Service Announcement.

Katherine lists for Amanda (and for the viewer) the signs a parent should look for if they suspect their child is being abused, according to the Center for Child Abuse – nightmares. loss of appetite, withdrawal from family life. The action then moves back to Webster's school, where child specialist Jan Morgan (Miriam Flynn) instructs Webster, the other children, and their parents about the difference between good touching and bad touching. Good touches turn to bad touches, Jan explains, when the child

Child molestation as the topic in "The Uh-Oh Feeling" from Webster.

experiences "that uh-oh feeling," a sense that something isn't right. With a gentle voice and nurturing smile (Miriam Flynn is captivating in this small role), Jan emboldens the children, informing them that they have power, and that power is the word "no". The focus then falls on Webster and his reconnection with Beth, who forgives him for breaking his promise not to tell. Webster holds Beth's hand, she smiles at her mother and says, "This is a good touch". The episode ends with a title card displaying the number for National Child Abuse Hotline.

For all its well-meaning sentiment, "That Uh-Oh Feeling" is still one of *Webster*'s more awkward episodes. Certain dramatic beats are not earned, and George's comic relief (at times he comes off as almost stupid) is not well-placed. Nonetheless, what the show gets right still resonates, and the balance of the first act (which plays almost like a horror movie) and the last (which offers hope and engages the audience) more than makes up for its flaws. Writers Madeline and Steven Sunshine, and show creator Stu Silver, make a valiant effort of balancing a disturbing subject with the lighter expectations of *Webster*'s audience. It's not perfect TV, but its courageous, and it does its part to open the door for much more challenging discussions about a very real and difficult issue.

"Cheers to Arnold" from *Diff'rent Strokes*
Original Air Date: 16 February 1985
By Lee Gambin

In 1980, Scott Baio and Lance Kerwin, two teen icons of TV movies and more, starred in a sport-centric made for television drama all about teen alcoholism, *The Boy Who Drank Too Much*, while five years earlier *Exorcist* sweetheart Linda Blair starred in the Richard Donner cult favorite *Sarah T. – Portrait of a Teenage Alcoholic* (1975). In 1984, a children's book entitled "The Elephant in the Room" from Jill M. Hastings and Marion H. Typpo was released to help kids learn about alcohol dependency in their families – primarily their parents, however, texts for children about *children* drinking were seldom seen, it seemed to be TV's job to do the teaching. "Cheers to Arnold" from *Diff'rent Strokes* (1978–1986) does exactly this and keeps it at the perspective of children. When the episode features the influence of the adult characters (primarily Philip Drummond (Conrad Bain)), it is only used in order to represent a voice of authority and also one that can be cross checked and questioned. One of the most interesting factors in "Cheers to Arnold" is the point made where Mr. Drummond is asked what the difference is between him having night caps or cocktails with friends and Arnold (Gary Coleman) and his buddies taking to some scotch or vodka. Mr. Drummond explains that there is a major difference in adults knowing how to handle booze appropriately and that being of a certain age entitles you to such decision making – Arnold, however, remains somewhat confused by that sentiment, but moves forward and ultimately helps his friend Ricky (Bobby Jacoby) to a road of sobriety.

Two years earlier, "A Growing Problem" dealt with alcoholism in the teen realm and also First Lady Nancy Reagan would make an appearance on *Diff'rent Strokes* to push her Just Say No campaign; using actor Gary Coleman as an instrument to gear kids away from the dangers of drugs and alcohol, which she would also do with Soleil Moon Frye who of course was the titular iconic Punky Brewster. These conservatives such as Reagan who once despised these liberal sitcoms for their inclusive ethos and their essentially left leanings, were now taking on the medium and using it as a platform to influence votes and "help" America. However, these sitcoms would take on these issues at hand – such as underage drinking – and provide a far more sensitive route that understood that pain and social dilemmas facing the vulnerable and misguided young. "Cheers to Arnold" paints this picture, as Ricky does come across as someone feeling hopeless, alienated and disliked. In one scene, he explains to the popular Arnold that he feels alone and not regarded as anything but a loser, he even laments that his teacher now has lost interest in him as a student, but Arnold pushes positive reinforcement and explains that it is Ricky's abuse of alcohol that is driving people away.

In an episode that has Arnold involved in a miscommunication that renders him suspect of being addicted to alcohol, the relentless repetition of Philip Drummond exasperated by the very notion of children drinking and "boozing up" becomes a heavy handed point made that steers itself in the direction of an ethos that pertains to the idea that good kids (Arnold) with good parents (Mr. Drummond) won't become addicts, however lost kids (Ricky) who seem to have absentee parents (we never meet Ricky's folks, nor do we really get a glimpse into his family life) can fall victim to such horrors. *Diff'rent Strokes* and its spin-off *The Facts of Life* (1979–1988) would boast a massive amount of Very Special Episodes, and a fair few would deal with addiction of varied kinds – when Mr. Drummond's girlfriend Maggie (Dixie Carter) makes mention that "at least it's not drugs", her agitated and angry partner responds with "alcohol *is* a drug!", reinstating the fact that it is still a case of children ruining their lives, wrecking their health and becoming addicts. In many regards, VSEs that detail drug abuse are treated with a far heavier hand, which reinforces Maggie's sentiment (narcotics are a trickier subject matter to tackle and therefore overcome), however Mr. Drummond's facts laid out about booze becoming so easily accessible in high schools and so forth, brings the nonchalance of everyday drinking to the fore. The reasoning behind the conversation Arnold has with his father is essential – why is casual drinking (at sports games, events et al) okay? There is no reasonable answer here; it is just how it is. So the episode leaves this open-ended question unanswered which is a very brave thing to do – and also, possibly the only option the writers had.

What makes the episode so effective is the sensitivity and affection it has for the guest starring kid, Ricky. With a lovely performance from the young actor (a relation to Scott Jacoby who would win an Emmy for his portrayal of a young boy whose father is coming to terms with his homosexuality in the made-for-TV classic *That Certain Summer* (1972)), there is something incredibly tender and nurturing in the delivery of the show's message – and, as aforementioned, so much more warm and sincere than the calculated Nancy Reagan push to "keep kids off drugs" campaign, that seemed to come from a selfish route. When Ricky breaks down and cries in the school bathroom, Arnold consoles him and offers to help him out. Not only does he lead him into taking alcohol prevention classes with his parents, but in the closing moments of the episode he gets him involved with the school paper and the promise of meeting new friends and having fun. The final image of the episode has Ricky surrounded by good friends, strolling off to have lunch together and reinforcing a loving message of unity among kids, who sometimes need a little help from their friends.

"Scenario" from *Benson*
Original Air Date: 22 February 1985
By Paul Freitag-Fey

The early eighties were a prime time for Cold War nuclear paranoia, and popular culture was certainly not shy about addressing the fears of nations in the midst of a potential nuclear winter. As had the Cold War era of the sixties produced works of literature as *On the Beach* (1957), *Red Alert* (1958) and *Fail-Safe* (1962) (all memorably the inspirations for major motion pictures), the eighties brought the potential horrors of nuclear destruction to every medium available, be it literature, film (*Mad Max* (1979) and its infinite rip-offs, *One Night Stand* (1984), *When the Wind Blows* (1986) and *Miracle Mile* (1988) or television.

The latter proved to be a mixed bag, as while the medium produced numerous one-off films centered directly around nuclear war (*Special Bulletin* (1983), the theatrically released *Testament* (1983), *Countdown to Looking Glass* (1984), the BBC's *Threads* (1984) and, most notably, *The Day After* (1983), which remains the highest-rated television film in history[11]), few television *shows* outside of news-related programs tackled the hot-button issue.

One of the few exceptions was "Scenario," the twentieth episode of the sixth season of ABC's *Benson* (1979–1986), which aired on a cold Friday in February 1985, well over a year after *Special Bulletin* and *The Day After* had broken the barriers for network television nuclear paranoia. It was, in fact, ABC's success with *The Day After* that prompted the network to approve the episode, a storyline that writers Rob Dames and Bob Fraser had attempted to pitch for several seasons but had found the network too skittish to approve.

> **ROB DAMES:** At the time they were just beginning to work on *The Day After* and they were terrified that no one would watch the film. So they certainly didn't want another program about nuclear war. We came back year after year with the idea, and they kept turning it down. Finally, when *The Day After* came on and was a huge success, they lost their main argument.[12]

Benson, a spin-off from *Soap* (1977–1981), followed one-time butler Benson DuBois (played by Robert Guillaume) to the household of Governor Eugene Gatling (James Noble) first as Head of Household Affairs and then, as the seasons progressed, up the ranks to Lt. Governor. It would seem, from its political premise, a natural show

---

11 TV By the Numbers, "Top 100 Rated TV Shows Of All Time", 21 March 2009.
12 Stephen Farber, "'Benson' Takes on the Subject of Nuclear War", *The New York Times*, 18 February 1985, <www.nytimes.com/1985/02/18/arts/benson-takes-on-the-subject-of-nuclear-war.html>

for which to address controversial issues of the era. However, *Benson* was a relatively conflict-free zone, choosing to avoid political confrontations (it's never even quite clear to what party the governor belongs or over which state he presides) in lieu of standard domestic conflicts a majority of the time. Sure, there were occasional issues mentioned in passing, but most of the conflict was found to be the result of one specific person or event rather than a larger, overarching system in need of examination. True to most sitcoms of the era, the problems were resolved at the end of 30 minutes or, at worst, at the end of the second part of a two parter.

Tackling nuclear war, then, was punching a bit above *Benson*'s weight, but Dames and Fraser managed to come up with a situation that both respected the characters that audiences had spent six (or, in the case of Benson, eight) years with and still presented a compelling discussion of the effects of a nuclear war. It's a tricky line to tread, but "Scenario" certainly had ambitious goals for a show that followed the family-centered *Webster* (1986–1989) and *Mr. Belvedere* (1985–1990) at the time. (While *Benson* did have one teenage character, the governor's daughter Katie played by Missy Gold, she was rarely the focus of the storylines, a trend very counter to the sitcoms of the era.)

As a sitcom can obviously not end in a nuclear attack that kills all of the characters (unless it's *Sledge Hammer!* (1986–1988)), *Benson* sets up a premise that forces the characters, and by design, the audience, to confront the idea of a nuclear holocaust without actively experiencing it. As a test of nuclear preparedness by the National Guard, the Governor and his staff take refuge in a bomb shelter as a two-day simulation of what would occur in the event of an attack. As a result, the characters aren't taken off guard by the situation, knowing full well that they're going to be confronted with the horrors of nuclear war as an abstract, but being in a simulated version of the situation that they can't control (news from the "outside world" being represented only by a computer readout) will force them to confront it as an actual event, one where they will need to examine their own motivations and tactics for survival.

The simulation premise is necessary for the sake of the continued existence of the characters, but it's also what makes "Scenario" a more effective examination of nuclear war than *The Day After* or *Special Bulletin*. These are characters that audiences have known for years, and just as they're forced to use a simulation of horrific events to take a look at their own authentic reactions to them, the audience is doing the same through their eyes. The made-for-television movies, with their one-shot characters who we're aware didn't exist before and won't exist after the two hour time-block, can be dismissed with a "it couldn't really happen here" shrug, while realistic characters who will still be around next week, even those in a sitcom, would need to keep considering their own humanity even after the credits for this episode roll. "Nuclear war" is an abstract, but "contemplation of nuclear war" is a concept it's all too easy for audiences to identify with.

The episode begins on a standard note, with Benson prepping for the simulation and poking fun at Chief of Staff Clayton (Rene Auberjonois). Even early on, among his ribbing, he emphasizes the seriousness of the situation, stating "This exercise may not seem important to you, but if it ever really happened, it'd be damned important to the people in this state that we know how to handle it."

As the group gathers in the fallout shelter where the remainder of the episode takes place, Benson's Administrative Assistant Kraus (Inga Swenson) instructs everyone involved to pick a number, allowing the National Guard's computerized simulation to choose a random person for whom events will occur. ("I've already got mine, I'm a five," states Kraus, to which Benson responds, "Only if you wear makeup.") After some confusion in regards to the map, the exercise begins, as the computer alerts them to the three stages involved, the details of which are chosen from one of 4,200 different potential scenarios of indeterminate length.

The first stage, "Warning of Nuclear Attack" begins, with Clayton arriving just in time for the doors too close. The governor sounds a warning siren and must make the decision to order people into shelters or to evacuate the populated areas. The reality of the minimal information to go on soon becomes clear as the targets themselves are unknown, and the Governor decides to evacuate, using toy cars to simulate evacuee movement.

Suddenly the second stage, the attack itself, begins, and the warheads are expected to touch down in fifteen minutes – no time for the evacuation to be completed, nor for the evacuees to return to shelter. Katie, among the group in order to do a report for school she titles "Waiting for the Bombs to Drop," asks her father about those trapped in cars, but the Governor brushes her off in order to do what he can for those that are still alive.

This is about the time when the laugh track for the episode starts to take more and more of a prolonged hiatus, the references to "toasted buns" and being cooked "medium rare" starting to no longer trigger laughs but instead reflect the grim realities of the situation. The laughs that come border on gallows humor – the Governor takes too long in explaining the necessities of shelters to give residents enough time to get to them, chef Rose (Billie Bird) takes her job measuring radiation too seriously, the canned food is a decade older than Katie.

The situation continues, with the bombs hitting the ground and an undisclosed number dead, the cities destroyed noted by atomic blast tokens on the map. A radiation leak causes Clayton to die, which he refuses to acknowledge until he gets a "DEAD" sign placed over his chest. His body is used as a barrier for the leak. The surviving population is cut off from any food supply. Katie is designated in need of medical attention – which can't be reached.

Benson's lack of taking the scenario with utter sincerity due to realizing the hopelessness of an actual nuclear attack prompts a discussion of a survivable nuclear attack. The Governor has faith in government research that states that a portion of the population will survive if there's a plan in place. Benson, however, dismisses this by pointing out that life after the attack may not even be worth living, and the government is basically just trying to placate us by telling us what to do to survive so they can justify keeping up the arms race.

The final scene of the episode features a discussion in which Benson promotes the idea of total nuclear disarmament by all countries, with no conclusion as to how that can be achieved, only hoping for the humanity and morality to eventually achieve it. It's the closest thing to hope that the episode offers, but the note that if there were to be a nuclear attack, humanity is doomed and no amount of preparation will change that, stays. The episode ends with everyone deciding to end the simulation and go outside, Benson disconnecting the computer on the way out and the camera closing in on the atomic blast tokens on the map.

"If you asked me, this kind of thing is never going to happen," Rose offers in the final segment. When prompted to explain why, she simply replies, "it makes me feel better." It's an attitude that many sitcom watchers no doubt shared, but the "Scenario" episode of Benson makes them confront it, and makes them aware of what would be going on in the world of those in charge during such a situation. Like the sequences in *Threads* depicting the slow disintegration of a local government bureau during an attack, only with characters that we're familiar with and invested in, *Benson* forces us to acknowledge not only the long-term death associated with nuclear war, but that those in positions in charge of our lives are just as helpless as we are.

"A Special Friend" from *Diff'rent Strokes*
Original Air Date: 4 May 1986
By Lee Gambin

Dressed as a pseudo-Charlie Chaplin tramp and entertaining New Yorkers in Central Park, Karen (Lori Lethin) is a bright, bubbly, vivacious young woman, who performs her comedy and magic show with her heart firmly sewn to her sleeve in the *Diff'rent Strokes* (1978–1986) Very Special Episode, "A Special Friend". Street performers in the Big Apple would be a staple fixture and would be presented in film and television as a prominent addition to the fabric of many a seventies and eighties outing. To be a street performer calls for a lot of freedom of expression but it also requires the rhino-skin of hardened theatricals who could be vulnerable to the taunts and disdain of the public. There is also something miraculously childlike in many regards to these people and from this, sometimes, these minstrels and mimes would be associated with characters who suffered from mental illness in the television realm. In *Sybil* (1976), Brad Davis plays a singing clown who becomes a glimmer of hope for the titular character as played by Sally Field in that he offers her some tenderness and solace as she combats multiple personality disorder which stems from emotional and physical abuse she copped from her mother, and in an episode of *Hotel* (1983–1988) entitled "Confrontations", Parker Stevenson plays a mime who attracts the attention of a mentally challenged young woman. However, in this *Diff'rent Strokes* episode, it is the performer herself who is affected – not by mental illness, whatsoever, but by the seldom discussed (as far as television during the period) neurological disorder epilepsy. This episode directly confronts issues concerning discrimination faced by people living with it and also seeks to enlighten others and offer a sensitive helping hand, expressing that people with epilepsy who are prone to have seizures are not to be feared.

Arnold (Gary Coleman) and Sam (Danny Cooksey) have befriended Karen and even help her with her act. She is so kind to the boys that she even takes them to the movies (even seeing Disney's *Pinocchio* (1940) multiple times in order to please Sam and feed his obsession with the classic). When she is first discussed at home, their father Philip is concerned because she is older (she is twenty three) and a street performer (which also has a stigma). He brings up the issue of Karen's friendship getting in the way of Arnold dating and Sam playing soccer with his friends. When the disappointed boys have to let Karen know that they can't hang out with her anymore, she has an epileptic seizure and it terrifies them. The image of Karen taking to the ground convulsing with a nearby police officer and a pedestrian tending to her burns in the young minds of Arnold and Sam who decide that it be best that they don't see her again. In turn, their own prejudices emerge as a result of ignorance and fear. When Philip finds out about Karen's epilepsy, he educates the boys and explains that there is nothing to be frightened about and that epilepsy is a neurological disorder. Sam remains terrified and says he doesn't want to be around it, describing the seizure as "creepy", while Arnold begins to "see the light".

When Philip goes to see Karen she is upset that the boys "don't come around much anymore" and begins to open up about her struggles with the disorder. She admits the sad truth that a lot of epileptics are discriminated against, mocked, ignored and left to feel lesser than people who don't have the condition. She cries "the whole world thinks that I'm a freak because of my epilepsy" and delivers some backstory where she tried to live a normal life (a.k.a. a life that did not involve dressing as Chaplin and collecting money from strangers) and wanted to be a kindergarten teacher. There was never any intention to work the streets. She also tells Philip that she had a seizure in front of her work placement class and was told to not come back because it would upset the children. The episode therefore tackles the issues concerning employers being discriminatory and not offering jobs to people living with epilepsy. Karen lays out the facts: she takes medication, but that does not always work. When she explains that this recent incident was her first seizure for multiple months, she laments that "the only thing that they're [Arnold and Sam] going to remember about me is that seizure." Philip listens to her and takes her into full consideration and changes his tune about the boys seeing her. He insists they rekindle their friendship in order to understand people living with such a condition.

In a great sequence that really relies on the VSE model of making a joke out of something that is most certainly not to be mocked, Philip asks Pearl (Mary Jo Catlett) the housekeeper if she would like to talk to Arnold and Sam. Hesitant, the usually vivacious domestic says no and continues with her duties; she seems uncomfortable. Arnold and Sam begin to make jokes about Karen's seizure, crass and crude and insensitive. The jokes finally grate on Pearl's nerves and she angrily tells them off. She then comes out as someone who has epilepsy and then tells the boys she loves so dearly that her own initial career choices were jeopardized because of discrimination. It is learned that she trained to be a legal secretary but wound up a housekeeper (a job she now loves) because there "aren't enough giving people in the world like Philip Drummond". To have a character who has lived with the boys for so long admit to having epilepsy is a profound statement in that this is someone who had seizures but is lucky enough to have them controlled with medication, but also part of the family and not to be feared. The episode pushes that message, not only teaching children that neurological disorders like epilepsy are not scary, but that friendship and family is something that should be embraced without question and that love should be unconditional. It is interesting to note that the B story of the episode has Kimberly (Dana Plato) return from her modelling stint in Paris where she is seen lovingly roughhousing with her brothers on the sofa, grabbing them and kissing them saying "it's so nice to be back!" Here, in that simple moment, the show celebrates love and paints it as a genuine and true aspect in the Drummond household – where white girls and black boys are best pals and race is never an issue. This comes as an extension in "A Special Friend" that explains that children and people with epilepsy and other conditions that cannot be helped should understand one another and waddle off together through Central Park like Charlie Chaplin, happy and without fear, ignorance or judgment. Another important aspect to this episode is the fact that Arnold even helps Karen grow as a young woman. He insists that she also combat her fear (a la Sam killing off his own of Karen's seizures) and not be scared of getting back into the workforce ("You'll never know if you never try") and this inspires Karen to move forward, shedding the Chaplin moustache and ready to start afresh.

"Street Smarts" from *Diff'rent Strokes*
Original Air Date: 23 March 1985
By Adrianne Traylor

By the time it had reached its seventh season, the NBC sitcom *Diff'rent Strokes* (1978–1986) had changed considerably from its original incarnation. The story of two rebellious yet vulnerable African American boys from Harlem sent to live with their mother's wealthy employer after her death, the show found early traction from the amusing attempts of Arnold (Gary Coleman) and Willis (Todd Bridges) Jackson to acclimate to their new Manhattan penthouse home and foster father, Park Avenue executive Philip Drummond (Conrad Bain) and foster sister, Kimberly (Dana Plato).

But by this point in the show's run, the Drummond family had experienced several cast changes and absences. They were now on their third housekeeper, and daughter Kimberly was off studying in Paris. Dana Plato's off-camera pregnancy and public struggles with drug use had led producers to write her out of storylines and limit her appearances beginning mid-way through season five. Widower Mr. Drummond re-married, adding TV aerobics instructor Maggie (Dixie Carter) and her son Sam (Danny Cooksey) to the household.

But the biggest changes were seen in the show's central duo, Arnold and Willis. The two formerly distrustful, smart-mouthed kids had become fully absorbed into the family, calling Mr. Drummond "Dad", having their needs tended by a housekeeper, and occasionally enjoying rides to school in a limo. As early as season three the show had addressed the idea that Willis and Arnold were losing touch with their racial and cultural roots, but by this stage of the show, the transformation of Harlem street kids into privileged Park Avenue teens was fairly complete. Which is partly what makes the season seven episode "Street Smarts" a fascinating cultural artefact, not just of the Very Special Episode trope, but of the evolution of the show and its central characters.

"Street Smarts" opens light-heartedly enough, with Arnold presenting a school paper and then sniping as usual with his classroom frenemy Lisa. As class is about to be dismissed, the teacher cautions the students to be careful on their way home, as recent muggings have been reported in the area near the school.

In the very next scene, Arnold is shown walking through a "park" that is clearly a stage set, when a man shown only from behind and standing what appears to be some distance away hisses, "Hey, kid. Come here." Arnold immediately begins cowering in fear, rather unconvincingly it must be said. The "mugging" is not actually shown, but Arnold soon arrives home with an empty wallet and a ripped jacket, which he unsuccessfully tries to hide from Willis and Sam. He confesses what happened, but immediately downplays it, claiming the mugger only got away with a few dollars and begging Willis not to tell their father, so as not to worry him. Willis reluctantly agrees, believing Arnold when he insists that he is unhurt, either physically or emotionally.

The passage of time is awkwardly handled in this episode; the next scene appears to be the very next morning, but it transpires that a few days have passed since the mugging. As the family gathers for breakfast, Arnold is in a great mood: it's Friday, meaning no homework and getting to stay up late to watch horror movies! But his cheerful mood is quickly dampened when Willis tells him that his best friend Dudley has called to advise that he got a ride, and therefore can't walk to school with Arnold. Arnold looks concerned, then brightly suggests that Mr. Drummond give him a ride to school in his limo. Unfortunately, Mr. Drummond has a meeting with his accountant and is going in the opposite direction. Arnold's face crumples slightly, and while he casually claims that it's no big deal for him to walk to school alone, he suddenly loses his appetite and pushes his oatmeal away. He tells Mr. Drummond that he suddenly doesn't feel well and takes his father up on the suggestion to stay home from school.

When Arnold heads upstairs back to bed, Willis worries aloud that he may be coming down with the flu. Sam blithely remarks that Arnold is just tired from staying up all night. Under questioning from Mr. Drummond and Willis, he admits that when he wakes at night, he's seen Arnold sitting at his desk in the dark. He then offers a starker revelation; opening the binder Arnold has left behind on the table, he shows Mr. Drummond and Willis, to their shock, a kitchen knife Arnold has secreted in his pencil bag.

After a commercial break, it is clear the secret has come out, and Mr. Drummond is highly upset with Willis for not telling him about the mugging. Willis himself seems both strangely passive about Arnold's experience and disconnected from his brother's feelings, a marked contrast from their relationship in earlier seasons. After Willis sheepishly apologizes, Mr. Drummond calls Arnold downstairs and confronts him with the truth. Arnold deflects, claiming he was carrying the knife to loan to a friend at school. When Mr. Drummond reminds him of the danger he faced and insists that Arnold must have been truly frightened to feel he needed to carry a knife for protection, Arnold digresses again with jokes and airily asserts that he had practically forgotten about the attack. He agrees when Mr. Drummond observes that he suddenly seems to be feeling better and offers to drop him off at school, noting that even if he's late for his appointment, Arnold comes first. Mr. Drummond tells Arnold that he's available when Arnold is ready to talk, an offer Arnold waves away dismissively, insisting that he's fine.

While Arnold runs upstairs to get his jacket for school, Mr. Drummond and Willis discuss the situation. Both agree that Arnold is far more disturbed than he is letting on, and Mr. Drummond tells Willis he plans to consult with a child psychologist he knows, stating that he will send Arnold to see him if he feels it necessary.
This is a rather surprising turn for a light eighties family sitcom. Although the word

"trauma" is not used, the show is clearly addressing Arnold's problem as just that: an unprocessed traumatic event that will emerge in some way if left unaddressed.

After speaking with the psychologist, Mr. Drummond then tells Willis that his friend agrees that Arnold is avoiding dealing with his feelings about the mugging. Willis then touches on another important aspect of victimization: feelings of powerlessness. He suggests that Arnold might feel like a wimp, as he did when he was bullied. Mr. Drummond notes that in order to help Arnold, he must understand that the mugger was a bad person responsible for his own actions, and that Arnold has nothing to be ashamed of. But in order to grasp this, Arnold must confront what happened and deal with his own feelings. And the child psychologist has offered Mr. Drummond a suggestion to help prompt Arnold to do just that.

The next day in Arnold's class, the students are having an undoubtedly riveting lesson in the concept of Manifest Destiny when suddenly, a man runs into the classroom, snatches Arnold's classmate Lisa's purse from her desk, and runs out of the room. As the students react in shock and surprise, their teacher calms them down, then gestures to the classroom door to welcome… Mr. Drummond. When Arnold asks what he's doing there and if he saw what just occurred, Mr. Drummond informs the class that the man they just saw is a police officer, and his actions were intended to get their attention, so that he could speak to them about "street safety."

Arnold's friend Dudley is confused, asking why they would need such a demonstration, while a fellow student is bemused, uttering the laughably ironic line, "Yeah, we live in New York. We're already street smart." This line, uttered about a group of clearly upper middle class and relatively sheltered kids, is all the more fascinating considering the evolution of Arnold and Willis as characters. The young, fast-talking and wary Arnold Jackson *was* street smart, from necessity and circumstance. The later Arnold, now officially adopted by Mr. Drummond, has become quite a different child, as this episode perhaps unintentionally makes evident.

What follows is a sitcom-predictable lesson in the unreliability of eyewitnesses and the importance of alertness and awareness. None of the kids can correctly identify what the "purse-snatcher" was wearing, and when Sgt. Coletta re-enters the room, he borrows Lisa again to demonstrate how, while "walking down the street," her purse is easily snatched again because she is distracted by instead of attentive to her surroundings.

Sgt. Coletta corrals Arnold as the next volunteer, and at first the young man is in his element, strutting across the classroom "like John Travolta" to project confidence on the street. But when the police officer brings up Arnold's mugging in front of the class, and Dudley asks why Arnold didn't mention it, once again Arnold blows it off, insisting it was no big deal. Sgt. Coletta asks him if he got a look at his attacker, and Arnold says it was only for a few seconds, and that most importantly, he didn't "look like a mugger." Sgt. Coletta notes that there is no stereotypical description of a mugger and offers tips for evading an attacker, including changing direction and zigzagging to throw the assailant off. But when Arnold asks what happens if you follow all of the police suggestions and someone still pursues you, the episode comes to the crux of the matter.

Sgt. Coletta asks the class what you should do if someone grabs you and puts a knife to your throat while grabbing Arnold to demonstrate, with what appears to be a real knife. When the students shout that they would fight back, the officer points out, with Arnold as model, how dangerous it would be to do that with a weapon close to your neck. But while the sergeant is talking, insisting that Arnold did the right thing by not fighting, the camera moves in close-up on Arnold's face, wide-eyed and stark with fear. As Sgt. Coletta relaxes his grip, Arnold tears away, yelling to get the knife away from him, that the mugger did the same thing to him. Arnold finally voices his terror and fear, shouting how scared he was and that he thought the mugger was going to kill him. As he runs into Mr. Drummond's arms for comfort, the camera pans to show his classmates' realization of how frightening Arnold's ordeal truly was. Sgt. Coletta apologizes to Arnold, but reassures him that he did the right thing "… because you're still here." As Mr. Drummond embraces Arnold, he tells him he's glad he's finally expressed his feelings, and now they can go somewhere for a talk. The episode ends quietly, with Mr. Drummond gently leading Arnold out of the classroom.

The ending of "Street Smarts" features a "Story by Gary Coleman" closing credit. Coleman was approximately seventeen at the time the episode aired, although because of his diminutive size, Arnold as a character was middle school-aged. While it's not clear if a specific incident prompted the episode, many contemporaneous shows were addressing the issue of street crime, "stranger danger" and safety strategies for young people. "Street Smarts" is a surprisingly somewhat different beast, making primary the aftermath and emotional impact of being a crime victim on a child, although the treatment is necessarily didactic and rather facile, given the limitations of the primetime family sitcom. Though there was no ongoing arc in subsequent episodes of Arnold dealing with his experience, the show's attempt to even briefly address the psychological impact of a traumatic event and the emotional risks of attempting to repress and compartmentalize such an incident was quite progressive for the time, making this a truly *diff'rent* Very Special Episode.

"Fenster Hall" from *Punky Brewster*
Original Air Date: 31 March 1985
By Clem Bastow

When it comes to television industrial practice, there are pilots, and there are back-door pilots. A traditional pilot is produced as a standalone episode, often created on "spec", to sell a series to a network. A backdoor pilot, as the name suggests, is an altogether sneakier affair. Though they may resemble "break-out" or "stand-alone" episodes, they're less about pushing the formal boundaries of a show (such as *Buffy the Vampire Slayer*'s "Once More, with Feeling" musical episode), and are instead specifically designed to test the waters and see if regular viewers might be intrigued by the notion of spending more time with a particular character.

In the case of *Punky Brewster*, a show that quickly established itself as a heartwarming entertainment never afraid to engage with hard-hitting social commentary, it was no surprise that its backdoor pilot – "Fenster Hall" – would also be a Very Special Episode unto itself. What was perhaps more surprising was the extent to which the episode would delve into especially dark thematic territory, even for a show about an abandoned child navigating the foster system.

By the mid-1980s, crime rates in America were well on their way to the peak they would hit in 1990, and "Fenster Hall" taps into the collective tension surrounding what many perceived as an unravelling of societal mores. The FBI reported a 5% increase in crime (with a 4% spike in violent crime including rape and murder) in 1985 and released a study that revealed that American citizens lost nearly $2.9 billion in cash and property due to burglary in 1984 alone.

Chicago, Punky's home city, was no exception. The Chicago Police Department's 1985 Statistical Summary leads with the P.D's focus on the ills of family violence, missing children, and gang problems, all of which are concerns echoed in "Fenster Hall".

Punky fans were already familiar with the eponymous shelter for orphans and abandoned children, so it seemed logical that show creator David W. Duclon would feel audiences might be open to meeting a new brace of Fenster Hall characters. Directed by Art Dielhenn and written by Rick Hawkins, Liz Sage, and Duclon, the season one finale "Fenster Hall" was a one-hour special (later split into two shorter episodes for syndication) that aired on March 31, 1985.

In an upbeat promo circulated ahead of the episode's airing, NBC's friendly male voice-over asks, "Will Punky's power give this little crook a big surprise?" The "little crook" was T.C. Finestra (Billy Lombardo), who breaks into Punky's bedroom through the window to steal her beloved jewelry box.

It's an ominous beginning: T.C peers into Punky's cheerful room, his red balaclava standing out starkly against the now familiar streetscape beyond the apartment.

Sneaking in, he grabs Punky's jewelry box, and is about to head through into the rest of the apartment when he's busted by Punky and Brandon. He shoots out of the window, and Punky – her trademark cry of "I've got Punky power!" sounding a little less confident than usual – commands Brandon to call the police.

(In a brief but memorable example of animal trainer Glen Garner's exceptional work – he had also worked on *Cujo* (1983) and *White Dog* (1982), and would later train the eponymous *Beethoven* (1992) – Brandon rushes into the lounge room and picks up the receiver as though he's about to dial 9-1-1.)

When T.C. flees, however, "Fenster Hall" moves away from the cozy surrounds of Punky and Henry's apartment building and into altogether darker territory. It transpires that T.C. is not just a cheeky thief, but an orphan in the employ of dastardly criminal Blade (James Le Gros, no stranger to a ne'er do well role), who has raised T.C. to steal and has the boy trapped in a web of emotional blackmail.

Though these introductory scenes are laced with familiar *Punky* humor – when Blade upbraids T.C. for letting "a 76-year-old lady outrun you", T.C. exclaims by way of exclamation, "She was wearing Adidas!" – the dynamic that Le Gros brings to the episode is darkly tense. After all, we assume, given his name, that that's his flick-knife jammed into the wall; the knife becomes the episode's "Chekhov's gun". Hand-held camera work, seemingly from Punky's point of view, gives the scene an added grittiness.

Punky, who has followed T.C. to Blade's hideout, watches from just outside as the career criminal discovers that the jewelry box T.C. has stolen contains nothing but "two pencils and a Hello Kitty eraser" – and Punky's wind-up chicky toy. After Blade leaves, she bursts in (wearing T.C.'s discarded balaclava) and confronts him… only to discover a sad and lonely boy, who she is quick to invite home for dinner (in one of the episode's sweetest jokes, when T.C. asks if Henry would mind if he came to dinner, she exclaims, "Henry loves street kids!").

Before long, and despite Punky's pleading to "keep him", Henry advises the kids that T.C. would be better off going to Fenster Hall. T.C. responds sourly; Blade has told him "those joints […] are just junior jails". But we know what Punky does, which is that despite the foster system's myriad failings, Fenster Hall is a better place to be than in Blade's dungeon.

There, we meet a new gaggle of Fenster kids: aspiring middleweight boxer Lester "Sugar" Thompson (Martin Davis), sweet, tiny Dash (Benji Gregory), flamboyant intellectual Lyle (Gabriel Damon), and Conan (B.J. Barie), who is big for his age (according to Lyle, he's "always hungry"). We also meet Mike Fulton (T. K. Carter), the chief boys' counsellor at Fenster Hall. Once a Fenster resident himself, Mike's mix of street smarts and a caring nature endear him to the boys under his watch.

En route to meet with his boss, Rita J. Sanchez (Rosanna DeSoto), an impromptu uprocking session in the hallway with some other Fenster boys tells us all we need to know about this character: Mike is young and cool enough to kick it with his youthful charges, but has earned their respect as someone who has first-hand understanding of their circumstances.

It was the producers' intention that Mike would be the star of the possible *Fenster Hall* spinoff, and it's easy to see why: when Carter arrives in the scene, the episode takes a jump into another stratosphere. Carter – who'd made a name for himself playing nervy, idiosyncratic characters like the chef Nauls in John Carpenter's *The Thing* (1982) – brings an effervescent energy to Fenster Hall.

It's also an impressive casting choice: given the broader focus on crime and gang activity in Chicago in the mid-1980s, it would have been easy to make Blade and T.C. African American characters, and Mike a white savior. By subverting the audience's expectations, "Fenster Hall" quietly but assuredly pushes the boundaries of TV comedy.

Mike eventually wins T.C.'s respect after a tour-de-force series of impressions, during which characters including "Michael Jackson" and "Mr. T" assist in interrogating the tight-lipped street kid, who eventually grudgingly cracks up. But it's not long after T.C. is introduced to his new roommates that he makes a break for it, and escapes through the window. "What do you think we ought to do??" Dash exclaims; "Celebrate," Sugar responds.

T.C. returns to Blade's dank hideout, only to be summarily sent back to Fenster Hall: the crim commands T.C. to return in order to steal the proceeds of an upcoming charity auction Mike and Rita are organizing. Once again, the flick-knife appears, as Blade violently cuts up an apple, foreshadowing the emotional (and possibly physical) trauma that awaits. T.C. returns to Fenster in time for Mike's "Gripe Night", a weekly forum for the boys to share their thoughts.

It's here that Mike encourages T.C. to open up and tell the boys what he's thinking – "Why the Mr. Tough Guy act?" – by revealing that he's been "here since I was seven-years-old". Realizing he's among equals, T.C. shares his truth: his mother died in childbirth, and his father blamed young T.C. for "killing" her. Lombardo delivers his tale of woe in a steely speech that eventually dissolves into tears. It's a powerful moment, reminiscent of Will Smith's "How come he don't want me?" monologue from *The Fresh Prince of Bel-Air* (1990–1996) episode "Papa's Got a Brand New Excuse".

But T.C. can only remain vulnerable for so long. Rebuffing Mike's offer of a hug by returning to his tough facade, T.C. watches as the boys leave the room one by one, until only little Dash remains. "Good night, T.C.," he says, giving the older boy his toy robot, "I'm glad you're here. I've always wanted a big brother." Dash gives T.C. a hug and a kiss and then exits, leaving T.C. alone to reveal what we know to be true: he, too, is happy to be at Fenster Hall.

The bucolic mood doesn't last long, however, as Blade sneaks through the window late at night to bully T.C. into robbing the auction cashbox; we can tell, from T.C.'s sighs, that he's realized it's a bad idea.

The auction rolls around and Punky's extended chosen family arrive; to Punky's horror there's even a love connection, complete with heart-swelling sound effect, between Sugar and Cherie. In a gesture of his growing connection to Fenster Hall, T.C. has made a wooden birdhouse for the auction. A bidding war breaks out between Henry and Betty, before Henry is victorious with a top bid of $175. The birdhouse sale sets the tone for an upbeat montage (to a *Punky*-fied tune that's an echo of Herbie Hancock's "Rockit") as the auction goes from strength to strength – the viewer torn between excitement for the Fenster kids and concern as to whether the rapidly filling cashbox will prove too much for T.C. to resist.

Our fears are realized when T.C. waits for Mike to be distracted by a colleague, and sneaks over to the cashbox. Mike catches him making a break for the exit, and T.C. pulls the guilt card: "Don't you trust me?" he asks, explaining that he was just taking the money to Mike's office. Mike replies that, yes, he trusts him, but it's clear to anyone that Mike is testing T.C.'s resolve.

Alone in his room, and counting the money, T.C. falters but it's too late: Blade appears at the window and once again violates the sanctity of Fenster Hall. The sleazy crim tries to intimidate T.C. into returning "home" (and once again to a life of crime), but the young boy takes a stand.

"You haven't helped me, Blade!" T.C. exclaims. "You make me do things that make me feel bad about myself." He goes on to explain that living at Fenster Hall has taught him what true help and care is: that the people at Fenster "make me feel good about myself". It's a poetic echo of T.C.'s vulnerable, angry monologue in the Gripe Night sharing circle – only now, this at-risk boy has become a young man who is prepared to stand up for what he believes in.

Blade, naturally, doesn't want a bar of it, and is about to drag T.C. from the room when Mike appears. Finally, the flick-knife tease is paid off and, with it, our worst fears confirmed: Blade engages Mike in combat. "If you take the money, I won't hassle you," Mike says, "But if you try and take T.C., you're gonna have to kill me." Blade takes the cowardly option, and flees with the cashbox, wounding Mike in the process.

T.C.'s tough facade melts in the face of Mike's bravery and commitment to T.C.'s wellbeing, and when his new roommates rush back in, they're met with the news that not only did T.C. survive a kidnapping attempt... he also took the money from the cashbox before Blade fled. T.C., Mike and the Fenster Hall boys celebrate in a shower of dollar bills.

A sweet coda back at Henry's apartment finds Punky in an upbeat mood: the police caught Blade. "He got so mad when he found out the cashbox was empty," Punky exclaims, "that he threw it down and broke his toe!" Thrilled with this turn of events, Henry agrees for Punky to invite T.C. and Mike for dinner, only for Punky to open the door and reveal the entire Fenster Hall crew has arrived, bellowing en masse, "Hi, Henry! What's for dinner?"

Ultimately, NBC declined to commission *Fenster Hall* as an official spin-off by the 1985–1986 upfronts. (Carter appealed enough to viewers that he would go on to introduce Mike as Punky's fourth grade teacher the following season, maintaining the character's "social crusader" status.)

Perhaps the "Fenster Hall" special was, ultimately, too hard-edged a concept even for viewers who had come to appreciate *Punky Brewster*'s affectionate navigation of the often-bleak realities of orphanhood, homelessness and the foster system. Had "Fenster Hall" evolved into a series, its harder-edged – but soft-hearted – approach to tough issues of social justice, along with its diverse cast of characters, may well have marked it as a trailblazer (indeed, it's the sort of material that would be well at home in contemporary network television or even "prestige" cable or SVOD programming). Instead, "Fenster Hall" remains a curious outlier in the annals of backdoor pilots: out of time in its day, but ahead of its time in retrospect.

"For Every Man, There's Two Women" from
Too Close for Comfort
Original Air Date: 20 July 1985
By Amanda Reyes
With Very Special insight from actor Jim J. Bullock

Like many urban legends, this infamous *Too Close for Comfort* episode featuring Monroe's rape is similar to the stories of the alligator in the sewer or having a kidney stolen. It's one of those whispered things where you know someone who knows someone who knows someone who saw it. The fifth season episode of *Too Close for Comfort* (1980–1987) titled "For Every Man, There's Two Women" should really be called "For Every Man, There's One Woman and a Huge Guy in Drag", but we'll get to that. From what little I was able to garner about this episode, Ted Knight refused to do the episode during the fourth season, because he probably felt there was no place for it in such a lightweight sitcom (he was right), but he must have been coerced into it because it was finally shot and aired in July of 1985, during the fifth year of the show. When *Too Close for Comfort* finished its original run and went into syndication, this controversial episode was dropped from its package and the world continued on as though Monroe (Jim J. Bullock) had never experienced any true acts of violence. As the years passed, and the internet became a great tool for connecting the hazy dots of childhood, the "Monroe rape" episode began to catch some attention. I came to know about it through the excellent site The Retroist <https://retroist.com>, and I became almost as obsessed with seeing it as the person running that site did. My timing was a bit better though because I had much less of a wait. The greatest TV station in the world, Antenna TV had been airing *Too Close for Comfort* and I began to monitor the episodes more closely. Lo and behold, they actually re-ran it last week!

> **JIM J. BULLOCK:** We would do a table read on the Monday with all the actors and then we would start rehearsing and tape the show on Friday. When you do a table read it can either go two ways, either you read through and you just know that it's wonderful ... and the script is great and the show will be funny, but then other times you would get a script and it would just bomb at the table read – so it was always hard to tell. I do remember, this one getting a lot of laughs at the table reading, but looking back at it I am thinking that writers will laugh at their own stuff to make it funnier than what it actually is. Of course not all writers are like that, but writers like these particular ones working on this show laughed extra boisterously. Now the script was not that funny, but they thought it was hilarious and did all that extreme carry on and laughing to make sure that we knew that what they wrote was funny – which it wasn't. I wish I was more insightful back

> then, but at the time I was in the cycle and along for the ride. Ted Knight, on the other hand, was very concerned about the subject matter. I was uncomfortable because they had these two fat women, these very heavy set women, in there and I felt they were being made fun of also. I have some big friends and I remember back then being a bit turned off by that fact, that cheap shot at big women. Everything that that episode was riding on was offensive. It was supposed to be a noble show, but it was just awful and kept getting deeper and deeper in the shithole.

If I had not been prepared for what I was about to see, I'm not sure how I would have reacted. The canned laughter at the male rape jokes was disturbingly reminiscent of that crazy Rodney Dangerfield segment of *Natural Born Killers* (1994) and I felt like I was watching a sick parody of the show (it should be noted the R word is never used). Monroe reveals to everyone that he was abducted by two women and blindfolded in the back of a van while the "big one" sat on him. They took him back to their place and had their way with him all night. The joke about breaking his beeper elicits a round of applause from the laugh track machine. The females acted completely out of character, tossing about insulting remarks about rape and in general, stereotyping men and sex while giving Monroe not one iota of sympathy. Jackie (Deborah Van Valkenburgh) finally admits that she just simply doesn't know how to react, which may be the most honest moment of the show (and probably was the exact feeling the actress had when she read the script). The women on the show seem frustrated and disgustingly nonchalant about the whole ordeal. They mostly disappear after the first half and after a much-needed commercial break, this becomes Monroe and Henry's show as they head off to confront Monroe's attackers. Henry (Ted Knight) comes off a lot better, but he bounces around from being thoughtful and concerned to acting bothered because Monroe interrupted Henry and Muriel (Nancy Dussault) during a tryst. Apparently dealing with a rape victim all day must make you all hot and stuff. Once they get to the women's apartment, the audience is treated to an extremely overweight woman aggressively forcing herself on Henry and a giant man in drag. The first woman is credited simply as Charlene and the drag queen has no credit at all, making the whole affair even more disturbed. Does this gargantuan man still walk the streets and could I possibly be hanging out in a bar one night and overhear, "Yeah, I played one of Monroe's rapists." It's enough to make me never leave the house again!

> **JIM J. BULLOCK:** Ted Knight called the writers down and they had a big talk about how terrible the script was and how it was not funny. I felt sorry for the two women cast as the fat rapists, and I just personally thought it was painfully unfunny and for us actors, well, we can only be as funny as the material is. Sure, I could make goofy faces throughout it, but that can only be funny for a fleeting moment. Ted called a meeting and he exploded. The writers had all come down and these

rewrites were happening all week long, so it was never calm. It was a very tense week, there was a lot of stuff happening and a lot of pink and blue and yellow pages! Ted was never happy with it. We ended up doing it, but it was done because we had to, and no one enjoyed working on that episode. I don't even know how ABC passed it! I mean Standard Practices missed the ball there; it was completely inappropriate. I really don't know how the episode happened and how this script got shot in the first place. It did air and then ABC pulled it, there was talk from audiences complaining and just mentioning that it was the worst episode ever. The network pulled it and after that it never aired in syndication. It was offensive on so many levels. I didn't make a stand, it wasn't my place to do that, but Ted threatened to walk out on the job, it was very much like Ted to do that. I mean, not quit his job, but walk off and give the orders of "You call me when you've fixed it!"

This infamous episode aired just months after the made-for-TV movie *The Rape of Richard Beck* which is a Golden Globe nominated film starring Richard Crenna as a gruff cop who is assaulted by an even gruffer assailant. If I wasn't going to laugh at Mr. Beck's horrifying encounter, why did the crew behind this *Too Close for Comfort* think anyone would be chuckling at Monroe's unfortunate evening of violence? Seriously, guys. 1985 was all kinds of awesome, but this is really reaching into neon-dripping madness! When I think about male rape in pop culture (I know, why should I be thinking about that?!?), I recall stuff like *Oz* (1997–2003) and *Deliverance* (1972)… you know… stuff that isn't funny.

JIM J. BULLOCK: I don't know what the true intention was for the episode, but I can guarantee their intentions were not to bring male rape into the social consciousness. There was no intention to shine a light on it. What they thought was funny was the fact that they had this androgynous goofy character with Monroe, played by me, who was always presented as a character who you were never sure of his sexuality – "was he gay?" "was he straight?" "Oh I know! Let's get him raped by two fat women in a bathtub of jello!" – there was a lot of pot smoking and drinking done by these writers, for sure, I don't think they sat down and went into it with the thought of "You know what? Let's write a serious episode about male rape." Because it wasn't done seriously. I remember at one point in the episode, Ted says to me "What these women did to you was not right", so the way we approached it as actors came from a humanitarian point of view, especially Ted. The writers were just piling on the fat jokes and whatever else they were taking stabs at. The show definitely took a dip at that point. I do remember working with the actresses who played the overweight rapists, but I couldn't point them out now if I were to see them in person. I wouldn't remember their faces. But I remember being incredibly uncomfortable, however, I never knew or asked if it was uncomfortable for them. I do remember them wanting to make it funny. And they were doing the best they could do, but it was not fucking funny. Standards and Practices were so strict about everything at that time, so I have no idea how this episode was passed. I even had a problem with the issue being called "rape", I felt that it was more of a case of Monroe being taken advantage of. And that is much more palatable and that could be funny. But Monroe being raped, well I don't think that's funny. There is a scene where Ted comes up to me and talks to me and I tell him what happened and we have this moment. Ted gave it dignity; the dignity it could have. He managed to muster up some dignity for such a terrible script. There was a short film made called "Was Monroe Raped?" I was kind of oblivious about this episode until the filmmaker came along and reached out to me and showed me. In that film there are some short clips from the episode, it's all very vague. There are some images of me in there, all mopey and being "Oh no…" So much of Monroe is tied to my personal life and where I was. I am a gay man, but I was not comfortable with who I was during the time of *Too Close for Comfort*. I was fighting it, I was not out to my family, but I wanted peace within my own life, and finally accepted who I was. But I was having major struggles. I was having religious struggles, personal struggles with how I was bought up and dealing with this other side of me. So it was a hard time. But now, looking back on the show, I think "Oh my God, how awesome would it have been if they had let me play Monroe as gay!" I mean I could do "straight" roles, but these "straight" roles were kind of the character where someone would say to a woman "Oh you better watch your husband in ten years coz he's gonna be with men!" But at the time, I didn't have that strength of belief in myself to approach that. The producers came up to me one day and said "Look, you have all this fan mail and people want to know if you're gay or straight". They told me that they didn't want my character gay. Originally when I first auditioned I thought they didn't like me because I came across as "too gay" and that was correct. But I met with Arne Sultan and Earl Barret and had a lovely conversation with them, and then left and then the network called them up three months later to see me again, and they told them that I was "too gay"! But then I got to read again and I had this character Monroe written up and he was a character that worked, and I was nervous as shit and what happens when I get nervous is that I stutter and I'm totally awkward and so that's what Monroe became. He was this sort of good looking, awkward, weird androgynous character who you never knew if he was gay or straight. Here he was hanging out with these two hot girls all the time, but he never tried anything with them… so, when they did call me in and told me that they want the character to be straight, I did tell them "I know I can't be who I am, but I also can't change Monroe midstream, he can't go from being awkward and weird to super macho and butch". I told them that Monroe was established and audiences like this character, but I told them to give me a storyline where I did have some sexual interest. They did that, and gave me two – one was with a transsexual woman and the other one was with Selma Diamond, who was like ninety! So finally I said, "Okay, give Monroe a girlfriend and make it believable", so they gave me Lisa Antille. If there was going to be a *Too Close for Comfort* thirty years later, I would certainly love Monroe to be gay and out and not living with a wife and two kids, but being a proud open gay man. I would have liked to have evolved. If the show had continued, I would have liked Monroe to evolve as I had evolved as a person. Bless him, but Ted would tell me "Take it down a couple of notches" when I got "too gay". Ted would say that, but only once or twice would the director come up and say "Not so flamboyant, let's do it again". I was never tortured on that set at all. They loved me and they loved what I did. But they were afraid of people being gay. They were scared of what people thought. But I was like "Oh man, if you trust it, if you let my character be gay you would be a huge success, it would shoot the show through the roof!" I've never had to do love scenes. I am very self-conscious and I don't think love scenes would come easy for me, straight or gay. And certainly at that time, when I had the onscreen girlfriend it was coming to an end, and Ted was so sick by then and they had changed the name of the show to *The Ted Knight Show*, and it was all very different, I mean the lead girls had left… the whole show changed and no one cared anymore. I loved played Monroe because it was something that came very easily and naturally for me, I was never out of my skin with that character. Now, as an actor I have changed, I could never go back and do that innocent wide-eyed character again. I have evolved and changed, but I never want to play Gilligan from *Gilligan's Island* (1964–1967) all my life, if you know what I mean – I didn't get to play Monroe all my life, thankfully, because I evolved. However, financially, I would have loved to have played Monroe all my life! But as an artist it is something that I never would have wanted. I don't think they ever intended the episode to be dark. It could have worked if it went to dark places, rather than being awkward. "Awkward" is a perfect description for that entire week dealing with that episode. This episode was in season five, so it was very late, and I don't think there was any more talk about Very Special Episodes. There was a change of writers during this period and a new producer came on board. Ted was spearheading that. He always wanted a quality product. He wanted it to be as good as *The Mary Tyler Moore Show* (1970–1977), but it didn't have the writing behind it that made it a stand out. There is a great series on CNN at the moment called *Decades* and it chronicles the great movies and music and TV from various decades such as the seventies and eighties and nineties, and *Too Close for Comfort* is always left out. In the eighties there was Metro Media Television and when ABC cancelled *Too Close for Comfort*, they picked it up and the other TV show they had was *Fame* (1982–1987). They were the two shows that were picked up and had new episodes produced for syndicated television which had never been done before. In this CNN show they talk about *The Joan Rivers Show* (1989–1993) and *The Alan Thicke Show* (1980–1982) which were from Metro Media as well, but never once did they mention *Too Close for Comfort* or *Fame* for that matter. So *Too Close for Comfort* is most definitely an overlooked show. *Fame* [was] spawned from a very dark, gritty film from 1980 which I love, and the show was definitely not the movie, but it still tapped into dark territory there, but it could because it wasn't a sitcom, it was a dramatic show. *Too Close for Comfort* was a sitcom and it was too hard for the writers to deliver serious topics embedded within the show, and so what we're left with is this stupid episode about male rape. The show was supposed to be funny and of course have those touching moments, but those touching moments should never overshadow the comedy. This was a sitcom. You

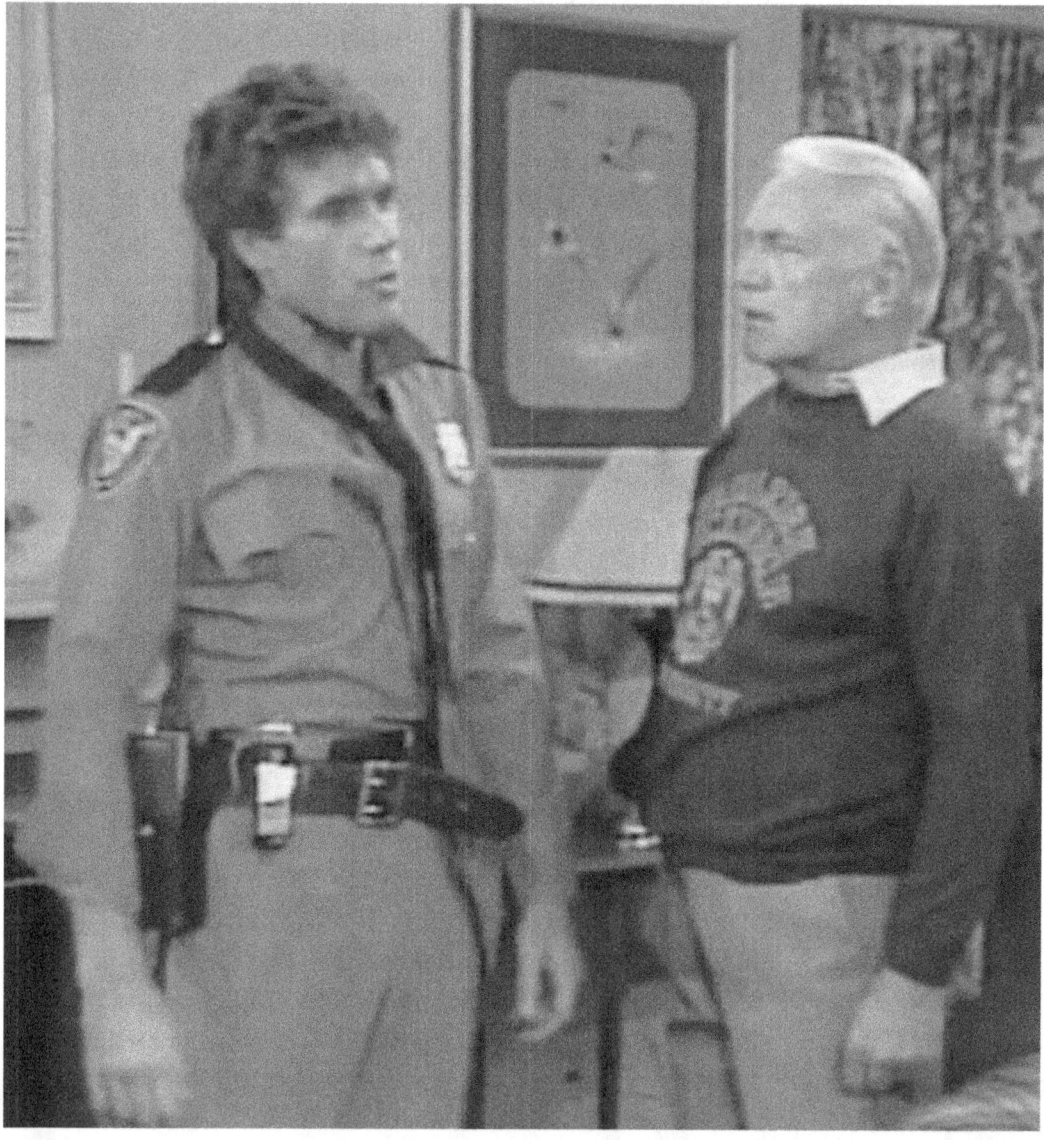

Male rape as a taboo conversation point in the infamous episode "For Every Man, There's Two Women" from Too Close for Comfort.

know Ted and I wanted it to be funny, because we were funny! I had never done drama or anything heavy at that time, and I shied away from that kind of acting. Ted had done a great episode of *The Twilight Zone* ["The Lonely", 13 November 1959]. Ted was a wonderful actor and he could have had a career in dramatic roles, but I don't think he ever wanted that. He just wanted comedy and that was great. We all knew that *Too Close for Comfort* wasn't ever going to be *Hill Street Blues* (1981–1987) or anything, we knew it was a sitcom, and that was fine. If it weren't for Ted I don't know if I would have gotten that job. Ted saw the comedy gold between he and I. He couldn't belittle his wife or daughters all the time, he needed that person to pick on, and I was perfect for that. Monroe was a perfect foil for Ted Knight. Ted saw that immediately and he pushed for me to be part of the show. He was always encouraging and always gave me advice, and some of it wasn't the best. He suggested that I stop doing stand-up – I had gotten the job by doing stand-up – instead of telling me to cultivate it because like all sitcoms, they all end, and at least I'd have that to fall back on. I remember he insisted I buy a house and then we were cancelled the next year. So his advice wasn't always great, but it didn't matter, I loved him dearly.

Now that this demented episode has recently re-aired – for the first time in years – some beautiful soul took the time to upload it onto YouTube! Those of you who caught Monroe's rape during the original run can now relive the nightmare while us newbies can create new, lurid memories of our own. Sweet dreams!

"Sam's Missing" from *Diff'rent Strokes*
Original Air Date: 27 September 1985
By Craig Martin

Stranger danger became the focus of a very special two-part episode of *Diff'rent Strokes* (1978–1986) penned by series writers Bob Brunner and Ken Hecht with additional contributions by Richard Gurman. Titled "Sam's Missing", the double episode kicked off the eighth and final season of the series by sacrificing its usual hilarity to deliver a serious message on the topic of child kidnapping. Few fears chill parents' blood more than the threat of strangers abducting their children and in this Very Special Episode the subject is approached with particular grimness. Absent are the regular jokes and laughter that even in the sitcom's other Very Special Episodes dealing with serious issues is nevertheless still present. Although the kidnapping of children by strangers is uncommon, the prospect of child abduction is so nightmarish that when it does occur, histrionic media coverage reinforces the fallacy that predators and kidnappers are ubiquitous, lurking in every shadow and around every corner.

Despite the fact that contemporary western society has grown statistically more secure over time, a prevailing perception insists that our own childhoods were somehow much safer than those of the next generation. Such perceptions are nothing new as social commentators have been making apocalyptic claims about the disintegration of western society and the perils facing our children for centuries. Most of us can attest to hearing such sentiments expressed by earlier generations. During the post-Civil War period as America was transformed by mass immigration and urbanisation, New York writer Augustus Kinsley Gardner articulated a sentiment in 1872 all too familiar in our own time: "Locks, and bars, and bolts are needed for our dwellings, our families also require watching, and our young sons, and delicate daughters must be guarded". Mourning the passing of the world of his childhood, Gardner's remarks reveal an underlying resentment and fear of change. But they also typify a common antagonism directed by the powerful against the powerless during times of upheaval when the underclass is blamed for a perceived breakdown of social cohesion. For the privileged elite, this imagined "Other" is perceived as some form of bogeyman out to get him and his household. Film critic Robin Wood tells us that fear of "the Other" and the demonization of difference is a conservative ideology propagated by the ruling classes to maintain social control. Stranger danger is a foundational articulation of the fear of Otherness upon which further prejudices can be built. It is a concept so fundamentally simple that even children can effortlessly grasp its meaning.

Diff'rent Strokes dedicates several Very Special Episodes linked to the issue of stranger danger covered elsewhere in this book, however "Sam's Missing" provides its most overt presentation in what is one of the most mirthlessly dramatic episodes in the series.

Affirming familial bonds irrespective of age, class, race or kinship, *Diff'rent Strokes* is founded on "blended family" and "rags-to-riches" tropes, following orphaned brothers Arnold (Gary Coleman) and Willis Jackson (Todd Bridges) as they adapt to life with their adoptive father, widowed Manhattan millionaire Philip Drummond (Conrad Bain) and his teenage daughter Kimberly (Dana Plato). In season six the blended family expands to include Philip's new wife, Texan divorcee and TV aerobics instructor Maggie McKinney (Dixie Carter) and her seven-year-old son Sam (Danny Cooksey). With the sitcom's younger cast members growing older and losing their childish appeal, the introduction of Cooksey's character allowed the series to reinstate the idiosyncratic childhood naivety and frankness that had been a crucial hallmark in earlier seasons. Playing Sam's mother, Dixie Carter continued in the role of Maggie until the end of season seven when NBC cancelled the sitcom in response to flagging ratings. Mary Ann Mobley (who had played Arnold's elementary school teacher in the series two episode, "Teacher's Pet") replaced Carter in the role of Maggie when ABC picked up the sitcom for what became its eighth and final season.

"Sam's Missing" opens on the Drummond household as we've never seen it before. Tarpaulins cover the balustrade while tea chests and tools are scattered around the living room, suggesting the family is moving house. It is quickly revealed however that the disarray is due to Maggie's penthouse renovations. Being the first episode produced at ABC, Maggie's makeover suggests a symbolic overhaul by the series' producers, keen to give the sagging sitcom a facelift to herald its arrival at its new home network. As the old furniture is removed – artefacts from NBC – Arnold records the event for posterity with his flash camera, insisting the family assemble on the sofa for a final snapshot before it is hauled away. The significance of the sofa in the family sitcom cannot be overstated. Traditionally the family room is typically the most used domestic space in the sitcom, being the arena within which its characters most often congregate, and the sofa is the most consistently prominent furniture item in this communal space. Whereas in most real life homes the sofa is commonly placed against a wall or window, in the world of the sitcom, it is invariably positioned in the middle of the room, at the epicentre of the action. An iconic signifier of communality, the sofa symbolises intimacy and togetherness, which for Arnold's family photograph is precisely how the Drummonds are represented, pressed in together to create an idyllic portrait of an American family.

Juxtaposed to the Drummonds image of the happy family is the despondent suburban living room at the Brown residence where May Brown (Ronne Troup), a pale mousey woman, is perched forlornly at one end of the family sofa silently repairing a garment with needle and thread. Still mourning the death of her youngest son Tommy who, we learn, died in a "terrible accident", May has withdrawn into herself while her husband Donald (Royce D. Applegate) and surviving son Bobby (Donald Thompson) vainly attempt to reach out to her. In desperation, Donald suggests that the family might open its doors to a homeless boy. Seeing a vague smile briefly flash in May's eyes at this suggestion, Donald resolves to find a child on the streets and bring him home to live with them.

Back at the Drummond's apartment, Arnold's photography project comes to a standstill when he runs out of developer. Pestered by Sam's requests to be his assistant, Arnold sends him to the store to buy more developer ... and a packet of potato crisps. At the grocery store, Sam is preoccupied with finding the freshest packet of crisps when Donald approaches, holding a packet of dog biscuits. Donald asks Sam for his help to find his dog Rocky – an obvious fabrication – but Sam tells him he is not supposed to talk to strangers. Persisting, Donald finally says, "Little fella, I know we shouldn't be talking at all, but do you suppose maybe you could be a Good Samaritan? Help me find little Rocky? You know, a Good Samaritan? Like it says in the Bible?" The various forms of cajoling that Donald uses on Sam purposefully demonstrate to younger viewers how an adult stranger might seek to manipulate and deceive a child. Swayed by Donald's Good Samaritan reasoning, Sam agrees to help find the dog and they exit together.

The parable of the Good Samaritan describes three sanctimonious religious leaders who ignore a man attacked by thieves and left to die while a lowly Samaritan, despised by the religious leaders, stops to aid the wounded stranger. While the parable is chiefly about hypocrisy, the Samaritan character is commonly read as the more important figure, being a model of compassion and charity to be emulated. Donald's evocation of the parable is fiendish because he uses its fundamental principle of humanitarianism to manipulate and deceive. Although his reason for kidnapping Sam is driven by a misguided desperation to heal his own family, Donald's actions render him monstrous, intensified by a malevolent threat he later makes to guarantee Sam's cooperation:

Donald: You remember what I told you I'd do if you tried to run away, or if you talked to anybody, huh? Remember that? I'll kill your parents, Sam.

Sam: No you wouldn't.

Donald: No? I kidnapped you, didn't I?

To viewers, Donald's threat is obviously fictive, but it is delivered with terrible menace and successfully deceives a child too frightened and inexperienced to know any different. A common fear among children connected to their sense of security and attachment is the death of a parent. Donald's threat to kill Sam's parents exploits this simple childhood nightmare in the most appalling way. However, Donald's deception is not limited to Sam. When he introduces Sam to May and Bobby, he tells them that he found the boy living in a cardboard box, subsisting on restaurant scraps. Most disturbingly, Donald carefully controls Sam's interactions with May and Bobby, standing at his side and forcefully clutching his neck like a ventriloquist controlling his dummy.

Searching for Sam, Philip and Arnold trace his steps to the grocery store where the sales clerk shocks them with the chilling news that Sam left the store in the company of a man she presumed to be his father. Philip immediately calls the police and later at the apartment Detective Harris (Michael Durrell) and Officer Fernandez (Daniel Martinez) arrive to find everyone on edge, especially Maggie whose traumatized state mirrors that of May. The Very Special Episodes of Diff'rent Strokes typically offer important information to audiences about focal issues. In the case of kidnappings, the detective tells the Drummonds a vital fact that, in some ways, challenges the sweeping claims of stranger danger: though there are numerous famous cases of child kidnappings by strangers (Amber Hagerman, Adam Walsh, Charley Ross, Jaycee Dugard and Charles Lindbergh Jr.) more often than not, parents or other family members are responsible for the majority of child kidnappings. Part one of this Very Special Episode ends with the detectives offering their assurances that they will find Sam. Heading for the door, the men stop in their tracks at the pitiable sound of a mother's desperate cry: "Please, find my son". Where most episodes conclude with applause from the live studio audience, part one of "Sam's Missing" ends with ominous silence.

Written solely by Gurman who penned three other episodes of Diff'rent Strokes, part two of "Sam's Missing" begins with the Drummonds gathered around their television set, soberly watching the news as the anchor introduces Philip who is appearing on television to offer a reward for Sam's safe return. Following Philip's emotional plea, the newscaster invites Sergeant Aaron Williams of the Los Angeles County Sheriff's Department to discuss stranger danger. Playing himself, Williams is an accomplished magician and ventriloquist who developed a successful stage act in the 1960s, opening for big name performers like Jerry Lewis and Sammy Davis, Jr. He became a regular guest on television talk shows and had a returning role on NBC sitcom The Smothers Brothers Show (1965–1966). He later joined the Sheriff's Department where his unique skills were put to use delivering the anti-drug message, "say nope to dope and ugh to drugs", to schoolchildren with the help of his moustached dummy, Freddie. On Diff'rent Strokes, Williams and Freddie offer advice to children on how they can take precautions and keep themselves safe in public, and what to do if an unfamiliar adult approaches them.

In response to his reward offer, Philip receives a call from a man who agrees to return Sam for a price and names the time and place for the exchange. At the rendezvous undercover police apprehend the man, who knows nothing about Sam and is little more than a conman. When Philip returns with the bad news, Maggie's hopes are dashed and she has a breakdown. Her fragility is further tested when housekeeper Pearl (Mary Jo Catlett) serves pancakes to the family at the newly delivered dining table and absent-mindedly sets a place for Sam. The brief moment of comfort offered by the meal is instantly dashed as Sam's empty chair reminds the family of his absence and Pearl, unable to hide her own grief, flees to the kitchen. The impact of Sam's abduction on the Drummond household confirms the assertion made by Ernie Allen, former president of America's National Center for Missing & Exploited Children, who notes that for the families of kidnapped children there exists "a kind of suspended animation … [that] hovers over everything they do; it's part of their lives every minute."

At the Brown's house, Sam is dressed in Tommy's old clothes and May has transformed from the earlier grief-stricken woman into a mother excitedly fussing over the newest addition to her family, believing him to be homeless and without a family of his own. Alone with Donald, Sam asks his kidnapper when he can return to his own family and is met by snarls insisting he will never see his own family again. Reading the newspaper, Donald notices a headline concerning the reward for Sam's return and tears the story out so that May and Bobby never see it. Sam later finds the discarded article in the trash and shows it to Bobby. Disillusioned by his father, Bobby becomes sullen, echoing May's earlier withdrawn behaviour.

Having memorized his home phone number (advice provided by Sergeant Williams), Sam sneaks into the lounge room alone where he calls home and briefly speaks with Arnold, giving him the area code and phone number inscribed on the Brown's telephone. With this information the police locate the Brown's suburban address and stage a dramatic raid on the house. Sam runs into Philip's arms as the police handcuff Donald and begin reading him his rights. Disoriented and afraid, May is arrested as an accomplice while Donald insists she had nothing to do with the kidnapping. Sam steps in and assures the arresting officers that she is innocent and knew nothing of the kidnapping. In the episode's denouement Sam returns to the penthouse and is smothered with hugs.

"Sam's Missing" is certainly an arresting Very Special Episode, but while it presents a compelling drama, its message is undermined by a lack of clarity and purpose. Where, for instance, the Very Special Episode in season five, "The Bicycle Man", is uncomfortably matter-of-fact in its informative representation of the grooming tactics commonly employed by child sexual predators, "Sam's Missing" lacks such lucid candour. Its atypical representation of child kidnapping is highly contrived and does little to depict the unthinkable reality of what actually happens to most children abducted by strangers (unlike the Very Special Episode "The Hitchhikers" (28 January 1984 and 4 February 1984) in season six where Arnold is bound and gagged while Kimberly is victimised by a serial rapist, played with unhinged menace by Woody Eney). Where other Very Special Episodes on *Diff'rent Strokes* confront social issues that urgently require open and honest public discourse (alcoholism, bulimia, drug addiction, epilepsy, **pedophilia**, and so on), the issue of stranger danger presented in "Sam's Missing" is already front-of-mind for most parents of young children. What's more, it is a topic often addressed in children's television so that young viewers are taught to be cognizant of the risks of consorting with adults unknown to them. With the exception of the very well written sequence at the grocery store when Donald manages to trick Sam into going with him, the episode fails to accurately represent the reality of child abductions. As Detective Harris points out, most child abductions happen within families and are very rarely perpetrated by outsiders.

Bona fide abductions are a terrifying prospect, and while "Sam's Missing" attempts to drive this message home, the episode shies away from putting Sam in any real danger, and instead contrives a situation that is awful and sad but, in this writer's opinion, mostly for the unfortunate Brown family. Ironically, for children watching the episode who live in situations where neglect or abuse are a daily reality (which is shamefully far more pervasive than the real threat of stranger danger), the Brown household makes a great fuss over Sam and might actually represent an appealing option to the child viewer whose home life is ugly and untenable. Furthermore, in relaying its message of stranger danger, "Sam's Missing" incidentally touches on other arguably more pressing social issues, such as youth street homelessness, surviving the death of a child and, related to this, issues of grief and depression, but the episode never gives these topics the serious attention they deserve.

Further weakening the effectiveness of the episode is the two-dimensionality of the Brown family where Donald, May and Bobby are presented as little more than a collective McGuffin providing the narrative with the rationale for Sam's abduction. Applegate's Jekyll and Hyde performance as Donald rivals that of serial rapist Bill (Eney) in "The Hitchhikers", but tests credibility as he swings between the role of caring husband and father who sincerely strives to heal his family, and the menacing monster that deceives and betrays the ones he loves, ultimately making their lives much worse. While we are expected to (and do) empathize with Maggie Drummond's grief, which ends

Royce D. Applegate plays a kidnapper trying to reconstruct a family haunted by loss in "Sam's Missing" from Diff'rent Strokes. *His victim is Sam McKinney (Danny Cooksey) a character who would be added to the fold come the latter seasons of the series in order to give the show a "cutesy facelift".*

with Sam's rescue, May's debilitating trauma surrounding the death of her own son is permanent, yet this plot point is tritely reduced to a dramatic device providing Donald with motivation to commit his crime. When Sam is recovered the episode unceremoniously abandons the Browns after they have served their narrative purpose and never addresses the trauma that haunts this family. While the episode ends happily for the Drummonds, we can assume that the future is not so bright for May and Bobby who must, in addition to Tommy's violent death, deal with the shock and shame of Donald's abominable actions and subsequent arrest, yet this issue is never addressed and there is certainly never any sympathy directed towards them.

Despite moments of intense and well-acted drama, ultimately "Sam's Missing" is a flawed Very Special Episode that is so fixated on the topic of stranger danger that it misses the opportunity to deal with some other very real, complex and far more prevalent social issues. As with the many enduring myths surrounding stranger danger (aided by the high profile that abductions receive in the media) and the ubiquitous threats from unknown Others, "Sam's Missing" ultimately perpetuates the xenophobic fear of Others, opting for the simpler route of demonizing a traumatised working class family rather than exploring the realities of child kidnapping, or dealing with grief and loss.

"Bully for Arnold" from *Diff'rent Strokes*
Original Air Date: 10 October 1986
By David Michael Brown

No parent wants to hear the word "bully". Whether their child is the perpetrator or the recipient, the mental and physical torment for all involved is distressing and in some cases life-changing. For the victim, in particular, the personality of the child can be intrinsically altered. Forced into situations from which they see no escape, their behavior is often unrecognizable. And for many the act of telling anyone about the horrendous situation, whether a teacher, a parent or figure of authority, is a huge decision to make. In their mind the repercussions do not bear thinking about. This kind of moral dilemma formed the crux of many a soap opera storyline and *Diff'rent Strokes* (1978–1986) is no different.

The much-loved long-running sitcom starred then relative newcomer Gary Coleman and Todd Bridges (Loomis from the Abe Vigoda starring comedy *Fish* (1977–1978)) as Arnold and Willis Jackson, two African American boys from the poor side of Harlem who are taken in by a rich white Park Avenue businessman and widower named Philip Drummond (Conrad Bain, who starred as Dr. Arthur Harmon in *Maude* between 1972 and 1978) after the boy's mother, who was under Drummond's employ, passed away. Living in a new affluent neighborhood brought a whole set of problems. In the eighties two black kids hanging out in such a salubrious part of town would have turned heads and the pointed, and occasionally casual, racism became a constant challenge for the Jacksons. They also had to deal with having a new sister in the shape of Dana Plato playing Kimberly Drummond and a new young brother Sam (Danny Cooksey) when Mr. Drummond married recently divorced television aerobics instructor Margaret "Maggie" McKinney (Dixie Carter of *Desperate Housewives* fame). As the series progressed everyone in the Drummond household was learning to deal with each other and the outside world's opinion of this multi-cultural family unit.

At the show's peak, *Diff'rent Strokes* was a world conquering phenomenon attracting star cameos from the likes of the then First Lady Nancy Reagan pushing her "Just Say No" to drugs agenda, David Hasselhoff and his *Knight Rider* car K.I.T.T. and a young Janet Jackson taking an early acting role as Willis's girlfriend Charlene DuPrey. But this was Coleman's show, thrusting the then ten year old actor into the global spotlight but there was far more to *Diff'rent Strokes* than Coleman's cute-as-a-button schtick, incessant mugging to camera and that catch phrase, "Whatchu talkin' bout Willis?".

The culture clash comedy had plenty to say about the great class divide. So much so that *Diff'rent Strokes* pre-empted Will Smith's equally popular and similarly themed star making turn in *The Fresh Prince of Bel-Air* (1990–1996). *Diff'rent Strokes* was such a blatant influence on that show that Arnold and Mr. Drummond both had a walk-on cameo in the series finale, "I, Done".

One of the first shows to fully embrace the idea of a Very Special Episode, *Diff'rent Strokes* won the ratings war by covering such serious topics as drug abuse, alcoholism, bulimia, child abuse, the perils of hitchhiking and in the case of the later season eight episode "Bully for Arnold", the effects of bullying. Not that this is Arnold's first dalliance with a pugilistic schoolmate. He has constantly had to use his wits, and his brother's brawn, to save face but this episode is the first time he "danced with the devil". Over the first seven seasons of the show the school bully has been a constant worry for the two brothers. The unseen character of The Gooch, a supposedly mean-spirited, hulking but not very bright bully at Arnold's school was been constantly name checked. He first "appeared" in the first season episode "The Fight" but we never see him. Now, however, bullying is given a face. And it's the face of the future Oscar winning star of *The King of Scotland* (2006), Forest Whitaker. Whitaker, playing the ominous bully Herman, had just been seen in a small role in Harold Becker's wrestling drama *Vision Quest* (1985), also starring Matthew Modine, and had a small part alongside Lee Majors in an episode of *The Fall Guy* (1981–1986). Even at this stage of his career, at the tender age of 24, you get a glimpse into the immense talent we will see flourish over the years. Whitaker gives the initially thuggish Herman a surprising depth of character proving the old adage; never judge a book by its cover.

One message that the writers of *Diff'rent Strokes* have ensured is the constant presence of a caring parental figure. In Philip Drummond, played with warmth and grace by Bain, the boys have a benefactor who listens when they talk. And Arnold talks a lot. Constantly using his brother and adoptive father as a sounding board. As adults such a simple decision as whether you should get involved with the school bully is an easy one but for a high school kid, worried about the violent consequences, there seems to be only one answer. When Herman announces he wants to have a meeting, Arnold is terrified but stands his ground, despite the advice of his brother Willis, and he welcomes Herman into his home. The central conceit to test Arnold's conscience not once but twice as he finds himself dealing with the unwanted house guest. Should he run or should he stand his ground? ("Nothing scares this guy, he takes vacations in Beirut!") Against the formidable bulk of Herman, he flounders and fumbles his way through the conversation, desperately trying to talk his way out of a beating until he realizes that there is an ulterior, and far less sinister, motive to the visitation.

The school bully asks Arnold to look after his girlfriend Ramona (Beverly Brown) while he's away from school for a week, entertain her and make sure that no other guys even cast an eye on her, let alone talk to her. And Arnold does the job only too well. Yes, she doesn't look at other guys but she does start looking at Arnold in a different way. It's an initially unlikely scenario. The diminutive Arnold and Ramona make an odd couple. But when you realize that Herman has been stifling and restricting his partner, you understand why she would fall for the cheeky wisecracks, innocence and generosity of her new "bodyguard." Even the fact that Arnold is happy for Romana to order anything she desires from the menu including the juicy Atomic burger whereas Herman tells her to watch what she eats, to look after her figure. Arnold lets her choose the booth next to the jukebox, Herman picks his favorite table. Herman's restrictive nature may come from a place of love but in trying to survive his week as a bodyguard, Arnold is just acting as himself. Using the trademark "Jackson" sense of humor to survive the week he inadvertently woos the young lady and she proclaims her love for him. His response is a delight. At once beguiled but terrified. Both at the prospect of a relationship with an older woman and with the more likely beating he would receive from Herman if the illicit relationship blossomed. ("If Herman found out about us, we'd be going to prom in a hearse!")

The expected final confrontation between Arnold and an understandably perplexed and infuriated Herman does not go down as you would expect. Using his smarts and guile, Arnold talks his way out of a beating. Just. We discover Herman does it all for love. He only wants the best for Romana and has been away for a week looking at new schools where he can start over again, without the stigma of the school bully hanging over him. From an early age, Herman's hulking size has ensured he is constantly misunderstood and he has fed that stereotype and his schoolmate's fears. He decided to give the kids what they expect. ("They wanted a big dumb thug, so that's what I gave them. And now I'm trying to change that.") Being the school bully is easier than trying to fit in. Arnold latches onto Herman's Achilles heel and goes into verbal overdrive in his typically self-depreciating style which persuades both Herman and Ramona that they should give each other another chance. And by playing matchmaker he manipulates the situation in his favor, narrowly escaping physical violence.

That's why the show succeeded for as long as it did. The handling of delicate and often controversial subjects with humor and poise, delivered with a snappy one liner or an inevitable catchphrase, ensured that *Diff'rent Strokes* worked beyond the confines of the sitcom, like all the best sitcoms did. And with Gary Coleman on a charm offensive that way exceeded his acting talent, his instant likability ensured that when *Diff'rent Strokes* tackled bullying and thrust Arnold into the arms of an older woman, the show handled the subject matter with the respect it deserved. Now that is what we are talking about Willis!

"Just Say No" from *Punky Brewster*
Original Air Date: 27 October 1985
By J.R. Taylor
With Very Special insight from actress Cherie Johnson

NBC President Brandon Tartikoff knew how to cash in on child actors. He quickly took notice that Gary Coleman was the network's only reliable star when Tartikoff joined NBC in 1981. He soon took over the entertainment division, and commissioned a new show based on a little girl with the same name as his childhood crush. Staffers didn't need to be told that Tartikoff – who'd die young in 1997 at 48 years old – wanted a big push for *Punky Brewster* (1984–1988).

Punky wasn't just a simple revisiting of a sitcom trope, though. The character was a lot more like Little Orphan Annie than some suburban moppet. We never found out what became of the mother that abandoned her, but being taken in by cranky-but-lovable photographer Henry Warnimont didn't keep Punky stuck in her Chicago apartment complex. There would be multi-part episodes where Punky would be adopted by a cruel rich lady, run across a gang of thieving kids, and even battle evil spirits in a cave.

Pretty much every episode also crammed in a literal teaching moment for kids. There were also multiple VSEs, of course, covering subjects including cheating, bullying, and the 1986 explosion of the Space Shuttle Challenger. And that was all before the show was canceled by NBC and went syndicated for two more seasons.

Plenty of those special episodes would – in VSE tradition – introduce characters who'd come and go. "Just Say No" is something special, though. You can already tell because it's named after Nancy Reagan's anti-drug crusade of the eighties. The powerful campaign would also corral in kiddie stars like Mr. T and La Toya Jackson. (The First Lady herself stopped by for a "Just Say No"-themed episode of *Diff'rent Strokes* (1978–1986.)

"Just Say No" is also notable for a script that utilizes the treehouse that Punky managed to build in the back of her apartment complex earlier in the second season. It's no coincidence that nine-year-old Punky and her best friend Cherie (played by Cherie Johnson) are playing there when some slightly older girls come parading in with their best Madonna Wannabe clothing.

Punky recognizes clique leader Emily from her school, which is helpful. Otherwise, you'd fer shure think that these gals had all wandered over from Los Angeles. Emily likes Punky's cool name, and introduces her pals as fellow members of "The Chicklets" – adding that they're a "very cool and exclusive club [who] hang out at the mall after school and mostly just stick together and do stuff."

Emily also helpfully advises that "being in the right club is, like, everything… especially when you get to the sixth grade." That's right before Emily points out the local architecture: "Is that treehouse unbelievable, or what?" Turns out the whole school is talking about the treehouse. In fact, this prime real estate gets Punky and Cherie an invitation to become Chicklets.

"We'll have your initiation at tomorrow's meeting," says Emily, "in our new club-house!"

Cherie's sassy grandmother Betty stops by later to retrieve her child at Henry's place. ("Get yer butt out here before I blister it!") When the girls come out of Punky's bedroom, both adults are shocked to see the kids dressed up in their own Wannabe garb.

Henry is so upset that he doesn't even get a laugh track when he asks: "Why are you two dressed like the Cat Women from Mars?" After learning that their young charges are "Chicklets now," Betty wisely asks: "Why would sixth graders want to hang out with you?"

Henry and Betty both get the point when Punky explains: "We're so cool, they're letting us use their treehouse for their meetings." The adults try to lay down the law and forbid them from being Doublemints or Chicklets or whatever. They reconsider after the girls do some pleading – "but," adds Betty, "I want you girls dressing like Punky and Cherie. *Not* pint-sized Pointer Sisters."

The next day's initiation involves drinking raw eggs mixed with ketchup, mustard, and horseradish. ("Could you hold the mayo?" asks Punky) Then they have to take the pledge: "I, state your name, [yes they use the "state your name" gag] promise my most precious promise to maintain my cool at all times, to pray every night that Michael J. Fox doesn't get taller, and to hang with the Chicklets through good times and bad."

"Now," intones Emily, "let's really have some fun" – as she breaks out a little tin full of suburban nightmares. There are perfectly rolled joints, plenty of pills, and some ominous smaller containers. (The hypodermic needle probably didn't get past the censors.) "I think we ought to let the newest Chicklets get first choice," says Emily as the screen darkens for a commercial break.

The show returns with Punky and Cherie looking properly shocked and uncertain. "Are those drugs?" asks Punky.

"Just some grass," Emily explains, "a few uppers, and a little nose candy." After clarifying that the latter is slang for the cocaine that she gets from her older brother, she adds: "It makes you feel happy and relaxed."

We'd like to know what kind of suppliers Emily's brother knew back in the eighties. Anyway, Punky insists that she's already feeling that way, with Cherie adding: "Real happy! Real relaxed!"

Kate – the only other Chicklet given real dialogue – has some sympathy for the troubled new recruits. "They're just kids," she tells Emily. "They don't have to do it if they don't want to."

"Yes, they do," responds Emily, upset at Punky and Cherie being out to "spoil their fun," before adding: "If you don't want to have good times with us, then maybe you shouldn't be Chicklets!" (In Emily's defense, that treehouse really does look like a psychedelic shack.)

Emily's still outraged and heads off with the older gals to "party at my place and leave these little girls alone." But first, Punky and Cherie are told they'll get one more chance the next day to party like a true Chicklet.

Punky goes to her school at Fenster Hall and talks to savvy school teacher Mike Fulton, played by T.K. Carter. (He was originally introduced for a *Fenster Hall* spinoff show as part of Tartikoff's grand vision, but ended up hanging out with the main cast.) Mike's struggling to spell "arithmetic," and Punky helps out by showing him how to remember difficult words with a mnemonic. That's typical. *Punky Brewster* was serious about cramming in all kinds of important and educational moments.

Then she tells Mike that she has a serious problem, while also giving parents at home a hint about how to deal with their kids. "I've got this problem I need to talk over with someone older and wiser," Punky explains, "but all the old wise people I know get mad at me for getting myself into this mess."

"Why don't you forget that I'm your teacher," he suggests, "and just think of me as Mike Fulton, your friend… I won't get mad, and anything that you tell me will remain our secret. Now what's this all about?"

"Drugs," says Punky – and quickly notes that Mike's very concerned: "Are those mad wrinkles on your head?"

"No," Mike assures her. "I'm just aging fast."

Punky tells the whole story, and Mike is quick to explain that she's dealing with a classic kiddie problem: "Peer pressure is the feeling of wanting to fit in, to be like your friends – but sometimes that feeling can be so strong that it makes it hard for us to resist doing something that we know isn't right."

"That's it," says Punky. "I have peer pressure up to my eyeballs!"

Mike then tells a story from his own wayward youth: "I started hanging out with a group of guys that I thought were real cool, until I found out that their idea of cool was riding around in fast cars."

"That doesn't sound so bad," says Punky.

"It is when the car belongs to someone else!"

But, Mike continues: "I found myself a new group of friends to hang out with. Guys who really knew what was cool. Staying in school, throwing a little basketball, listening to James Brown!"

That last one inspires a James Brown impersonation with full instrumentation of "I Feel Good." The moment feels like a hallucination, which is nicely defused when Punky asks: "Who's James Brown?"

That leaves Mike feeling like he's aging even faster. He still tells Punky that he's sure she'll do the right thing. He also gives Punky a brochure that has "some information about another club for children all across the country." We'll be getting back to that.

But first, we return to the treehouse as Emily offers up a joint. Punky and Cherie, however, boldly say no. (Even if they're just saying "no," it seems dramatic – probably because of a synth-heavy soundtrack playing a Morricone tribute.) A disgusted Emily declares: "What wimps!"

"We're not wimps," counters Punky. "Wimps do what anybody tells them to do."

"She's got a point," says Kate, which encourages Punky to declare: "We're going to start a club that makes us feel good about ourselves!"

"What's the club called?" asks Kate.

"It's called the 'Just Say No' Club, and Mike Fulton says he'll be our sponsor."

"Wow," says Kate, "he's so cool!" She then gets applause from the audience by telling a protesting Emily to "shut up" before asking Punky: "How do I join?"

"It's easy, Kate. All you have to do is just say no!"

That cuts to a montage where Mike is seen helping Punky get her club going to a fine and funky tune that declares "Don't have to be part of a crowd/Just be who you are and stand up proud." But things get alarming as the entire cast – except for any Chicklets – is seen marching out to the treehouse while carrying protest signs and wearing matching "Just Say No" shirts. It briefly seems as if everybody's gotten together to give that bitch Emily an epic beatdown.

Don't be concerned, though. We're simply watching one of the most Very Special Episodes of all time. As noted, "Just Say No" isn't a mere morality lesson. The episode title was backed up by a national movement. The show begins to wrap up with T.K. Carter's narration about how "on April 26, 1985, simultaneous marches were held in cities all across the country, where thousands of children took the opportunity to 'Just Say No' to drugs."

There's video documentation, as well. The sitcom cuts to actual footage of a marching crowd, as Carter continues: "Cherie Johnson led a rally in Oakland, California, and Soleil Moon Frye led this march in Atlanta, Georgia. Won't you join us and just say no?"

The video suggests that it'd be pretty stupid not to go along with the crowd. That's a lot of people taking to the streets and watching Soleil practicing karate moves. (Martial arts seem to be an official alternative to doing drugs.) This footage takes up a good three minutes of the show, ending with a slightly disturbing stretch of regular folks chanting "Just say no!"

History's been kind to this episode, though. Soleil and Cherie didn't end up as any kind of Hollywood drug casualties. T.K. Carter's the sole weak link with some DUI busts back in the early nineties. Usually, in the words of Punky, that kind of thing wouldn't sound so bad. *The Los Angeles Times*, however, reported at the time that one of the arrests had included "investigation of car theft." You have to admit that's oddly specific.

CHERIE JOHNSON: Soleil travelled for four years promoting the Just Say No campaign. She would travel all around the United States. I would be in Georgia and she would be trekking it around the U.S.. Every weekend for four years, we lead rallies around the country. It was phenomenal. I think as a child I didn't really understand how important the show was and how important its message of Just Say No was. I knew we were popular, because there were thousands and thousands of people on those rallies with us in the frontline. But fame was never discussed at my house. My reality in this situation was the fact that we travelled and made hundreds of friends and made that decision together that we would never take drugs or drink and never ruin our lives with that kind of lifestyle. It is such a lasting message. I have carried that with me for all those years. People would stop me now and say "Hey I was at that Just Say No rally that you lead and I have never taken drugs because of it!" I get that all the time. All these people's lives have been touched, and they are drug and alcohol free because of these rallies that came about because of *Punky Brewster*. I grew up in a very wealthy neighborhood and cocaine was the drug of choice. I had a conversation with my principal at the time in high school and mentioned that I had done *Punky Brewster* and that he needed to bring in a kind of D.A.R.E. program into the school of a Just Say No campaign, just like we did in *Punky Brewster*. He said that drugs weren't a problem at our school because we were a private wealthy school. I was like "Are you kidding me? These little girls here are doing drugs" I never understood how they had the personal money to buy cocaine, because all I got given to me was twenty dollars which would go to gas for my car and lunch, so I never had any extra money. So it always struck me as to how they could even afford this! People think that drugs are strictly an urban problem, but it's not, it can also totally affect white, rich neighborhoods. Years later, a very well respected high profile actress who I will not name, was handing out what I thought were breath mints around set. And I was like "Oh yes please! I'll have a couple" and she was like "No, no, no, not for you" and I was like "Why? What, my breath don't stink?" and everyone on set laughed at me. Some time later I found out that those breath mints were drugs, and they were all taking them, but "little Miss Punky Brewster" was not allowed to have any, because they were protecting me. And that was because of doing a show like *Punky Brewster*. It made me out to be a good kid, and I'm thankful. I would have put that thing in my mouth and freaked out!

Punky and Cherie are so much like the real life Soleil and Cherie. I met Soleil in our audition, she was a quiet, little sweet girl sitting there reading her script and from just seeing her, waiting to see the producers, I knew I was going to know her forever. Then we read and got the job. Being on the show, our characters mirrored who we are and the love that we had for each other which continues today. We have grown up together and all of our personal progress has been shared – we were kids together, we got boobs together, we got our first period together and

Actress Cherie Johnson starred as a character named after her own namesake, the spunky spirited best pal to the titular Punky Brewster. *Johnson would be a pivotal player in the role of "kid power" and children's rights which was something that the sitcom would be culturally invested in.*

now we're both mommies together! Basically, when children are working together they are either going to hate each other or love each other and we are family, we really love each other. A lot of Punky and Cherie on-screen is what happened off-screen. We had a wonderful wardrobe person who would ask us what we liked to wear. He really wanted us to make sure that we were comfortable. He would say

"You are what you wear". I hated pink, because I grew up with boys and he would make sure that Cherie always wore green or blue. He would let us pick our own accessories, and in the Just Say No episode, Cherie and Punky get to dress up in "grown up" gear with make-up and everything, so we just went to town there! Back then, in the eighties, little girls tended to want to grow up fast, clearly now, everyone wants to go back and remain in youth as long as they can, but in the time of *Punky Brewster* there was a sense of wanting to grow up fast. The little girls who play the in-crowd were older than us and were actually part of a cool clique that Soleil and I knew. We went to camp together and they were totally those kind of girls. Of course they were never into drugs and would never dream of pressuring us into doing drugs, but they were very much like the girls you see on that episode. They also really enjoyed playing their cool selves on TV and they also got to play out their roles in a real nasty and mean way, which is great for an actor because everybody loves to play the villain. I would love to play the bad girl one day! I have never been allowed to do that because I am still "that cute little girl from *Punky Brewster*" and how boring is that?! Playing Cherie is a double edged sword, because the people growing up watching *Punky Brewster* are now producers and directors and writers, so it's hard for me to get work because they don't want to see little Cherie do drugs or get raped or be sexy because "that will hurt people's feelings!" I can't even be cast as a mother! I'm like "I am a mom!" and so sometimes it's hard for people to accept that child actors grow up. Corey Feldman and I grew up together and he got a lot of backlash recently about his dance performance, but I knew that he loved Michael Jackson and that was a tribute to him, and he got to live his dream – he got to do it, so I am proud of him for that! I was like "Go Corey!" I love him and I don't care what people think about him, and I get to reflect on my own work and I see stuff that I have done that audiences don't "approve" of such as this film I did where I had a threesome on film with two women. I am getting to work and living my dream, so people need to stop attacking and understand that we're doing what we love as actors.

Contributing writers (my Very Special team):

Rachal Aza has been a fan of U.S. sitcoms since she can remember. Her youth was fondly spent with *ALF*, *The Golden Girls* and numerous others. A keen reader of TV and film history, Rachal and a friend have begun a bi-monthly classic films podcast called "When Movies Were Good." The podcast can be found on YouTube and Vimeo.

Michael Barrett is a Texas-based film writer who never outgrew the influence of two mighty planets in the sitcom heavens: Norman Lear and MTM Productions. He continues to be obsessed with shows from TV's earlier decades and has written for PopMatters.com about such items as *The Goldbergs*, *M Squad*, *Johnny Staccato*, *Perry Mason*, *Search*, *Medical Center*, *Way Out* and *Harry O*.

Lisa Rae Bartolomei is a composer, sound designer and writer from Melbourne, Australia. As a child of the eighties, sitcoms were essential viewing, a surrogate family of the small screen, other worlds that taught us about our own and how to be kind, laugh and love one another.

Clem Bastow is a screenwriting researcher and award-winning cultural critic from Melbourne, Australia. Her work appears in *The Saturday Paper* and *The Guardian*, and her books include *ReFocus: The Films Of Elaine May* (Edinburgh University Press, 2019), *Hell Hath No Fury Like Her: The Making of Christine* (BearManor Media, 2019) and *Investigating Stranger Things: Upside Down In The World Of Mainstream Cult Entertainment* (Palgrave MacMillan, 2021). She holds a Master of Screenwriting from VCA/University Of Melbourne, and is currently undertaking a PhD in Hollywood action genre at RMIT.

Matt Baume is the co-creator of the comedy podcast and live show *Queens of Adventure*, featuring drag queens playing Dungeons & Dragons, as well as the queer interview show *The Sewers of Paris*, the YouTube pop culture series *Culture Cruise*, and the LGBTQ news shows *Weekly Debrief* and *Marriage News Watch*. His book, *Defining Marriage,* chronicles the personal stories of people who fought for marriage equality over the last forty years.

Rachel Bellwoar is a writer for the websites, Comicon, Flickering Myth, *Diabolique Magazine*, and others. If she could have one superpower it would be the ability to twitch her nose like Samantha Stephens.

Film historian/filmmaker/video essayist **Howard S. Berger** is the perpetrator of innumerable Blu-ray audio commentaries and is the co-director of the satiric cult horror film *Original Sins* (1995) and the music doc *A Life in the Death of Joe Meek* (2013). Unimpressed with modern film criticism, he is also the co-creator of "Destructible Man", an alternative method of studying cinema and its complex, interweaving and metaphorical intricacies via a film's dummy-deaths.

Marcelline Block's publications include *Le Grain de la voix dans le monde anglophone et francophone* (2019); *An Anthology of French and Francophone Singers from A to Z: Singin' in French* (2018); the first English translation of *Propaganda Documentaries in France, 1940–1944* by Jean-Pierre Bertin-Maghit (2016); *French Cinema and the Great War: Remembrance and Representation* (2016); *French Cinema in Close-up: La vie d'un acteur pour moi* (2015; named a Best Reference Book of 2015 by *Library Journal*); *Fan Phenomena: Marilyn Monroe (2014); World Film Locations: Boston (2014); World Film Locations: Prague (2013); World Film Locations: Marseilles (2013) and its French version, Filmer Marseille (2013), which she co-translated into French; World Film Locations: Las Vegas (2011); World Film Locations: Paris* (2011; translated into Korean, 2014), and *Situating the Feminist Gaze and Spectatorship in Postwar Cinema* (2009). Her writing appears in *Afterall, Art Decades, The Big Picture Magazine, Cahiers Tristan Corbière, Cineaste, The Guardian, The Harvard French Review, Periodical, Soledad,* and *Women in French Studies,* and is translated into Chinese, French, Italian, Korean, and Russian.

Every job **Steven T. Boltz** ever dreamed of having as a kid was inspired by a sitcom – Disc Jockey (*WKRP in Cincinnati*), Detective (*Barney Miller*), Teacher (*Welcome Back, Kotter*) – but he would come to realize that they weren't as much fun without a studio audience. Instead, he chose a job where an audience would be a distraction, and he now writes articles, plays, and movies.

Rebecca Booth has a master's degree in Film Studies from the University of Southampton. Formerly the Managing Editor of *Diabolique*, she has a forthcoming book on *The Devil Rides Out* (Liverpool University Press) and co-edited House of Leaves' *Scared Sacred: Idolatry, Religion and Worship in the Horror Film*. In addition to contributing essays to printed collections, most recently *Lost Girls: The Phantasmagorical Cinema of Jean Rollin*, she has been published on several popular culture websites such as *Den of Geek, Scream* and *Wicked Horror*.

Sam Bowron works in the Australian film and television industry. His passion for its cultural and historical significance has driven his focus toward the field of audio visual restoration and preservation, ensuring future access to original materials both analogue and digital.

Peter M. Bracke is one of the world's foremost authorities on the contemporary genre film. He is the author of the award-winning book and documentary *Crystal Lake Memories: The Complete History of Friday the 13th* and has produced numerous documentaries about the genre. He has written for *Entertainment Weekly*, *Empire*, *Premiere*, and other publications, and is currently co-host of the podcast *The Commentary Under the Stairs*. A graduate of the USC School of Cinematic Arts, he currently lives in Los Angeles.

Dean Brandum gained his PhD in 2016 for an alternative study of box office taking in the 1960s. He is now an independent researcher with a particular interest in film distribution and exhibition history.

Nat Brehmer is an author, screenwriter and film journalist who has written for Bloody Disgusting, Dread Central, *Diabolique Magazine*, Wicked Horror and other outlets, as well as the upcoming *The Complete History of Puppet Master*. He currently lives in Florida.

David Michael Brown is a British ex-pat living in Sydney, Australia. Working as a freelance writer he has contributed to *Rolling Stone*, *GQ*, *Filmink*, *The Big Issue*, SBS Movies and *Empire Magazine Australia*, where he worked as Senior Editor for almost eight years. He is presently writing a book on the film soundtracks of German electronic music pioneers Tangerine Dream.

Michael Campochiaro is a writer whose obsession with Michelle Pfeiffer is legendary. He was raised on American sitcoms like *Taxi*, *WKRP in Cincinnati*, *Bosom Buddies*, and so many others that influenced and shaped his tastes in pop culture.

Dennis Capicik has been a fan of classic American sitcoms since he first watched reruns of *Sanford and Son*, *Good Times* and *All in the Family* with his parents as an impressionable tyke. Dennis considers the *All in the Family* episode "Cousin's Maude's Visit" to be one of *the funniest* episodes ever made, and he has always been amused by Maude's quick-witted sass and steadfast cheekiness!

Lesley Chow is an Australian writer on music and film who has appeared on film festival juries including Venice, Berlin and Toronto. Her first book, *You're History: The 12 Strangest Women in Pop Music*, will be published by Repeater in 2021.

Sally Christie is a writer, critic and educator from Melbourne, Australia. She has written for numerous publications with her research interests focus on nineties erotic thrillers, censorship and the occult in cinema and pop culture in education. Sally currently co-hosts Primal Screen, a film criticism program and podcast on Triple R FM. Sally is a proud member of Melbourne based film collective, Cinemaniacs.

Martyn Conterio is a writer from England. To date, he has published two books, studies of Mario Bava's *Black Sunday* and George Miller's *Mad Max*, and has contributed to several others. *Saved by the Bell* and *Blossom* were particular weekly favorites, growing up.

Patrick Cooper is the author of *'Aren't You Gonna Die Someday?' Elaine May's Mikey and Nicky: An Examination, Reflection, and Making Of*. He co-wrote the film *Sex Madness Revealed*, released by Kino Lorber in 2018. His short fiction has appeared in several online and print publications, including ThugLit, Dime ShowReview, Shotgun Honey, and Akashic Books.

Tim Creevey is a hobby writer and servant of the public from Melbourne, Australia. From his teenage years working for a suburban video store, he's spent his entire life absorbing idealist, euphoric, confident performances of life from television and will continue to forever advocate for the underdog, the geek, the freak and peculiar characters, just like him, to win.

Samm Deighan is Associate Editor of *Diabolique Magazine* and co-host of the Daughters of Darkness and Evil Eye podcasts. She's the editor of *Lost Girls: The Phantasmagorical Cinema of Jean Rollin* and author of a monograph on Fritz Lang's *M* (1931).

Russell Dyball is a film and television historian and Blu-ray producer from Eugene, Oregon where he is highly involved in the local theatre scene. He considers it a tremendous honor to have contributed to this book, particularly due to the fact that he never learned to read.

Christopher Eaton is the recipient of a Poetry Award (1st Place) from the Agency for Overseas Bulgarians. A volunteer teacher at Sv. Sv. Kiril and Methodii School in Boston and Cape Cod, he studies at Noble and Greenough.

Edward Eaton received his Ph.D. in Theatre History and Literature and has taught Theatre and English at a number of colleges in the Boston area and internationally. He has written articles on films for several book series and published young adult books, verse novellas, and plays. He is also the host of the popular YouTube series, "Haiku Reviews with Dr. Ted" and "Lessons with Dr. Ted".

Paul Freitag-Fey is a Chicago-based writer who has been writing about offbeat movies and television for 20 years or so. His work has also appeared in *Are You In The*

House Alone? A TV Movie Compendium 1964-1999 as well as regularly on the Daily Grindhouse website.

Marco Freitas is a movie critic, historian, researcher and, basically, film addict who studied at Columbia and UCLA and collaborated with Portuguese-language books on Soul Cinema, the sixties TV series *Lost In Space*; the making of *The Planet of the Apes* and *Casablanca*; and Brazilian erotic Cinema. A perfect day for him has the sprightliness of *Mediterraneo*, the intensity of Pialat´s *Police* and the sexiness of Jim McBride's *Breathless*. To Marco, a better world would consist of most politicians, with all their might, reading more often, delving into Buster Keaton´s filmography and/or just going ahead and kicking the nether regions of each other´s bodies.

Stef Gemmill's writing career kicked off reviewing live gigs and albums, later swapping the mosh pit for kids, toys and tantrums and is the author of children's books *A Home For Luna*, *In My Dreams* and *Toy Mountain*. Stef dreams of writing a *Happy Days* picture book where Fonzie's dog Spunky is kidnapped by a Hollywood agent and the old gang must reunite to rescue him from the evil animal acting factory.

Aaron Graham is a writer and Production Manager (full Director's Guild of Canada member) based in Winnipeg, Manitoba Canada. He's written for a number of diverse film publications in the past, including *Senses of Cinema* and *Screem Magazine*. More of his writing can be found at ArmoredCarRobbery.com.

Author and screenwriter **Lucas J. Gutman** adores old TV, exploitation films, and his family. He supplements his children's education with *Mad Magazine*, Turner Classic Movies, and tales of 70s-style child-rearing (a.k.a. "Look how good I turned out!").

Lindsay Hallam is a Senior Lecturer in Film at the University of East London and is author of the books *Screening the Marquis de Sade: Pleasure, Pain and the Transgressive Body in Film*, and the Devil's Advocates edition on *Twin Peaks: Fire Walk With Me*.

Chris Hallock is a screenwriter and film programmer in the Boston area. He has contributed to *VideoScope Magazine*, *The Boston Globe*, *Paracinema*, *Shadowland*, *ChiZine*, and Planet Fury. He serves as a programmer for the Boston Underground Film Festival and the Massachusetts Independent Film Festival and is a former Co-Director of Programming for Etheria. He is currently writing a book on the horror genre for Midnight Marquee Press. His other passions are cats, drumming, and fiercely independent art.

John Harrison is a freelance writer, author and film historian based in Melbourne, Australia. As a kid growing up in the seventies, Harrison's life dream was often to stowaway on a ship bound for America so he could live with The Brady Bunch. Ultimately, he settled for the even more impractical life of a writer. Harrison's most recent book, *Wildcat!*, was published by Bear Manor Media in December 2019 and is an examination of the film and television career of former child evangelist Marjoe Gortner.

Troy Howarth is a Rondo-nominated writer specializing in European Cult Cinema. In addition to authoring such books as *The Haunted World of Mario Bava*; *Splintered Visions: Lucio Fulci and His Films*; *Human Beasts: The Films of Paul Naschy*, and the *So Deadly, So Perverse* trilogy, he has recorded audio commentaries for nearly 100 films in wide array of genres.

Travis Johnson is an award-winning film critic, cultural commentator, and broadcaster whose work has appeared in too many publications to list.

Olivia Jones grew up watching American television sitcoms and is grateful that shows such as *A Different World* were not afraid to tackle taboo subjects and challenge mindsets in attempts to raise awareness, create understanding, and contribute to a more equitable world.

Matthew Wayne Krause is a writer, musician, philosopher, *peregrino*, and part-time superhero on Tuesdays and Thursdays (according to his grandson, an aspiring comic book artist). He is a DIY *ronin* author of seven books, five fiction, two nonfiction. He is the recipient of the Walt Disney/ABC Screenwriting Fellowship, and his first novel, *Pitch*, won first place in the 2012 Balboa Press Fiction Writing Contest. His favorite sound is a laugh track, and Darren Stevens is his spirit animal.

Jim Laczkowski founded the Now Playing Network as well as Voices + Visions, two websites that host a number of creative endeavors featuring musicians, filmmakers, writers and podcasters. Jim sporadically hosts the Voices + Visions podcast as well as Director's Club the latter of which will be celebrating 10 years in 2021. He was also a freelance film critic for Magill's Cinema Annual, previous talk show guest on WGN Radio and a contributor to a number of podcasts. His day job involves collection development as a future librarian currently employed at the Harold Washington Library in downtown Chicago. He loves cats, hats, coffee and recording music.

Susan Leighton has written for many entertainment sites. She is a huge fan of sitcoms and lives her life like an episode of *The Love Boat*.

Jessie Lilley knows that with Harry Stone, there would be no justice in this world. She lives in Santa Cruz, CA with four cats and a husband.

Shawn Macomber is a writer, editor, and noted pug wrangler in the Greater New York City area (a.k.a. Jersey). His fiction, essays, and reporting span five continents and hundreds of appearances in the pages of a diverse array of publications including *Fangoria*, *Decibel*, *Rue Morgue*, *Maxim*, *The Wall Street Journal*, *Reason*, the *Los Angeles Times*, the two volume heavy metal horror anthology *The Healing Monsters* (which he co-edited), and the Grey Matter Press anthology *Savage Beasts*. He believes Rob Lowe is the King of Christmas.

Craig Martin recently completed his doctorate at the University of Melbourne focusing on representations of monster children in American cinema from the early silent era to 1960. As well as writing for various scholarly journals and contributing chapters to such collections as *Children in the Films of Alfred Hitchcock* and *Misfit Children*, Craig also serves on the board of *Red Feather Journal*. His favorite sitcoms growing up were *Growing Pains*, *Happy Days*, *The Good Life* and *Mind Your Language*.

Ian McAnally has been in the arts industry for over 15 years and worked for some of Australia's leading arts organisations including the Sydney Opera House, Melbourne Theatre Company and Opera Australia. He helped to launch the Funnnybone500 short film festival in Sydney and worked on the 2019 Virtual Reality season for the Melbourne International Film Festival. He is currently engaged with multiple projects for Arts House, Melbourne's home for contemporary performance.

Mike "McBeardo" McPadden is the author of *Teen Movie Hell: A Crucible of Coming-of-Age Comedies From Animal House to Zapped!* (Bazillion Points, 2019) and *Heavy Metal Movies: Guitar Barbarians, Mutant Bimbos, and Cult Zombies Amok in the 666 Most Ear- and Eye-Ripping Big Scream Films Ever!* (BP, 2014). He also co-hosts the podcasts Crackpot Cinema with Aaron Lee and Busted Guts with Kat Ellinger. He watches, talks, and writes stuff in Chicago.

Andrew Mercado is a TV and film historian who specializes in Australian content and gay-themed productions. He was the first openly gay man on Australian TV when he appeared on music network Channel [V] before then becoming the first VJ on its sister channel Max.

Sergio Mims is a film critic and journalist and is the host and producer of the weekly Bad Mutha' Film Show WHPK-FM (88.5PM Chicago), he is also a screenwriter and appears every week on the Movie Madness podcast on the Now Playing Network. He is the co-founder and co-programmer of the annual Black Harvest Film Festival in

Chicago which is one of the largest black film festivals in the world. A former member of the Director's Guild of America as an assistant director both in Chicago and Los Angeles, Mims is also a member of the Chicago Film Critics Association and is a commentator for Blu-ray and DVDs for Vinegar Syndrome, Kino Lorber and Arrow Films.

Nell Musolf has clearer memories of television sitcoms than of her own life and still hopes some day she'll have either Millie Helper or Rhoda Morgenstern as a next-door neighbor. Nell has written two cozy mysteries (*Catered to Death* and *Black and White and Dead All Over*) under her pen name, Marlo Hollinger, and blogs very sporadically at her Blog Opera, "Schuyler Square: A Daily Maybe Drama" as well as at her other blog, "Blah Blah Blah Blog." Nell is not sure of many things other than God is good and television makes life more interesting.

Alexandra Heller-Nicholas is a film critic and author who has written books on *Suspiria* (2015), *Ms. 45* (2017) and *The Hitcher* (2018), as well as *Rape-Revenge Films* (2011), *Found Footage Horror Films* (2014) and her 2019 Bram Stoker Award nominated *Masks in Horror Cinema: Eyes Without Faces*. Alexandra is a programmer at Fantastic Fest in Texas, a board member of the Miskatonic Institute of Horror Studies, and an Adjunct Professor at Deakin University.

Kevin Nickelson is a writer, reviewer, interviewer and the author of the upcoming *Keeping His Head: The Films of David Warner*.

A fan of explosive action films and Turkish cinema, **Hande Noyan** is currently working on a book about Turkish rip offs from the 1970s and 1980s. Hande's worked and organised the Darwin Pride Festival film nights, worked as an educator and counsellor for LGBTQI youth and adults in health prevention and management for HIV and Hepatitis. Hande is also a film maker and photographer working for Melbourne's Cinemaniacs film collective.

From her childhood crush on Peter Brady to her lifelong love of *The Golden Girls*, **Helen Paschalis** has been enjoying American sitcoms pretty much her entire life. An instructional writer by profession, Helen wrote film reviews for several years for a work-related periodical she founded simply "to stay sane". Recalling the impact of landmark episodes of *All in the Family* and *Maude* even as a youngster in the socially-conscious 1970s, Helen's world view was shaped by the extraordinary writing of those gifted creators. Like television's *Rhoda*, the "first thing" she remembers "liking that liked me back was food." Helen lives in north-central Victoria with her equally pop culture-obsessed husband and cats.

Sophie Perillo is an interdisciplinary performance artist, musician and writer. She has devised independent and collaborative performance works for Artist Run Initiatives, major galleries and festivals. She has performed in Melbourne bands The Ancients, PSA and Hi God People. Her writing and research is centred in gender theory, performativity and theatricality.

Andrew J. Rausch is the author of many books on popular culture. Some of his favorite things include turkeys falling from the sky on *WKRP in Cincinnati*, watching *M*A*S*H* reruns ad-nauseam, and getting emotional every time he watches the "Damn! Damn! Damn!" episode of *Good Times*.

Amanda Reyes is a film historian, academic and writer from Austin, Texas. She is the editor and co-author of *Are You in the House Alone? A TV Movie Compendium: 1964-1999* (Headpress, 2017). Her writing has appeared in several publications, and she's lectured at academic conferences and guested on panels at international film festivals in such places as England, Scotland, Australia, Germany, and stateside. She's contributed commentary tracks for the Blu Ray releases of *Pray for the Wildcats* (Kino Lorber, 2020), *Don't Be Afraid of the Dark* (Warner Archives, 2019) and *Last House on the Left* (Arrow, 2018), among others. She was the curator and co-presenter of the Alamo Drafthouse's Made for Television Mystery Movie series, which ran quarterly as part of Terror Tuesday, and has hosted screenings at the Austin Film Society. She also has a podcast called Made for TV Mayhem that explores the uncharted world of the telefilm.

Adam Richards is the co-creator, co-writer and co-star of ABC TV narrative comedy series *Outland*, produced by Princess Pictures. He is also the producer and presenter on the podcasts *Adam Richard Has a Theory*, and the wildly irreverent *Talking Poofy presents The Poofcast*. For ten years Adam served as The Fabulous Adam Richard broadcasting celebrity gossip on several Southern Cross Austereo stations around Australia, most notably the high rating Matt and Jo Show on Melbourne's Fox FM. Adam has appeared on *Celebrity Splash* and *Celebrity Dog School*, been a team captain on the rebooted *Spicks and Specks*, and a regular guest on the *Doctor Who* aftershow, *Whovians*. He has written for *The Weekly with Charlie Pickering* as well as the game shows *All Star Squares*, *The Chase Australia*, and *Think Tank*. He is currently a senior writer on the Gold Logie winning ABC TV game show *Hard Quiz*.

Stuart Richard lectures in Screen Studies at the University of South Australia. His first monograph The Queer Film Festival: Politics and Popcorn is published as part of the Palgrave Macmillan's "Framing Festivals" series. He has previously worked with both the Melbourne Queer Film Festival and the San Francisco Frameline International LGBTQ Film Festival. He has a very healthy obsession with *The Golden Girls*.

Kelly Robinson is a Bram Stoker Award-nominated writer and researcher with an interest in silent films, horror, and popular culture. She is a recipient of the Horror Writers Association's Rocky Wood Memorial Scholarship for non-fiction writing and is the host and founder of Knoxferatu, an annual silent horror film event in Knoxville, Tennessee.

With degrees in journalism, physics, and law, **David Siegel** is a freelance cynic and aspiring bon vivant whose reference frame was shaped by Swedish cinema of the fifties and American sitcoms of the sixties. He currently resides in a state of apprehension.

Michael A. Smith began writing film criticism while still in high school. His reviews have appeared in newspapers and he has shared his opinions on both NPR radio and ABC television, as well as on his own website, Media Mikes.com, which he co-founded in 2010. He is the co-author of *Jaws 2: The Making of the Hollywood Sequel* and most recently contributed to, and helped launch, the 45th Anniversary edition of Edith Blake's *On Location: On Martha's Vineyard – The Making of the Movie 'Jaws'*. Smith and his wife reside in Lee's Summit, Missouri.

Michelle J. Smith is a senior lecturer at Monash University, where she researches children's literature and culture. More than three decades after the *Punky Brewster* episode, she is still wary of discarded refrigerators.

Growing up, **Bianca Stapleton** wanted to be just like D.J. Tanner. Instead of following her idol into veterinary science, Bianca gained a degree in journalism and became a professional writer. It is with this journalistic objectivity, she now realizes that spunky Stephanie Tanner was the true hero of the piece.

J.R. Taylor is a proud staffer at the *National Enquirer*, and has also written regularly for lesser publications such as *Entertainment Weekly* and New York's *Daily News*.

Nathaniel Thompson is the author of five books, has been involved in over 150 audio commentaries, is a regular contributing writer for Turner Classic Movies and the Academy of Motion Pictures Arts and Sciences, and can be seen in several documentaries about filmmaking. His life role model is still Rhoda Morgenstern.

Adrianne Traylor grew up watching far too much television, which hasn't paid any bills but makes her the ideal pick for your trivia night team. A native Texan transplanted to NYC, she loves Broadway but misses Tex Mex, barbecue and peach cobbler. Her New York stage reviews have been published on Theater Jones, a website devoted to the performing arts in North Texas, and her film analysis in the UK-based magazine *Multitude of Movies*.

This tome features **Joshua Turk's** first ever piece for a printed publication. Making it extra "very special".

Lance Vaughan is the co-creator of the website Kindertrauma, which focuses on exploring and archiving the films, books, TV shows, and media that scared us as children. He has been interviewed by *The New York Times* and *The Los Angeles Times* and has previously contributed to *Butcher Knives & Body Counts: Essays on the Formula, Frights and Fun of the Slasher Film*; *Are You in the House Alone?: A TV Movie compendium* and *If I Only Had A Brain: Scarecrows in Film and Television*.

Michael Varrati is the screenwriter and filmmaker behind a number of critically-acclaimed horror films, as well as an array of holiday TV movies such as *A Christmas Reunion* **and** *A Christmas in Vermont*. He's a frequent pop culture commentator and currently serves as the creator and host of *Dead for Filth*, a streaming radio program all about the intersection of queer identity and the horror genre.

Emma Westwood is an author and broadcaster on cinema who has written a compendium book on Monster Movies, a monograph on David Cronenberg's *The Fly*, and co-written a monograph on John Frankenheimer's *Seconds*. She is also preparing a book of essays on James Whale's 1935 classic, *Bride of Frankenstein*. Emma thinks *Get Smart* is a very special television series and would have written about it for this book, except it never got serious.

Nadine Whitney grew up in a small country town with little to do but watch loads of sitcoms and skip school to watch *Donahue*. Even when she got older she skipped a lot of more important things to watch sitcoms and *Donahue*. Now she gets to skip doing important things to watch sitcoms and write about them for your pleasure. She does mourn the fact that *Donahue* is no longer.

Jake Wilson is a Melbourne writer who reviews films for *The Age* and *The Sydney Morning Herald*. He is the author of the 2015 monograph *Mad Dog* Morgan and recently contributed a chapter to the collection *Refocus: The Films of Elaine May*.

A Very Special thank you to Adam Dallas, Antony Botheras, Justine Ryan, Anthony Biancofiore, Jarret Gahan and Monster Fest, Cinemaniacs, Cris Wilson, Kat Ellinger and the team at Diabolique, Ilene Graff, Cherie Johnson, Adrienne Barbeau, Richard Vaczy, Barbara Gallagher, Julie Cobb, Shavar Ross, Jim J. Bullock, Troy Fromin, Michael Horton, Jay Moriarty, Nancy Allen, John Sobanski, Darren Cotzabuyucas, Jay Fosgitt, Ben Ohmart, Robbie Adkins, my family who sometimes watched these shows with me when I was a kid – my mom Grace and sisters Gracie and Lisa – and to my best pal Buddy, who is the best TV watching companion there is – and everyone else who supported me along the way, thank you.

Lee Gambin is an author and film historian who has written several books on cinema including Massacred by Mother Nature: Exploring the Natural Horror Film, We Can Be Who We Are: Movie Musicals of the 1970s, Nope, Nothing Wrong Here: The Making of Cujo, Hell Hath No Fury Like Her: The Making of Christine and The Howling: Studies in the Horror Film which was nominated for a Bram Stoker Award for best non-fiction text. He has recorded numerous audio commentaries for blurays for companies such as Kino Lorber, Arrow Video, Eureka Entertainment and Shout Factory and is the editor on Tonight on a Very Special Epsiode: A History of When Sitcoms Sometimes Got Serious.

STAY TUNED NEXT TIME FOR THE EXCITING CONCLUSION OF....

TONIGHT, ON A VERY SPECIAL EPISODE WHEN TV SITCOMS SOMETIMES GOT SERIOUS

www.ingramcontent.com/pod-product-compliance
Lightning Source LLC
Chambersburg PA
CBHW081822230426
43668CB00017B/2348